Dedication

For my family.

For each and every person – named and unnamed, known and unknown – who contributed to the benefit and advancement of the National Art Museum.

In memory of Raymund van Niekerk.

Acknowledgements

I AM INDEBTED TO Robin Stuart-Clark for believing in this book and for allowing it to evolve and grow.

To my editor, Sean O'Toole, I owe an enormous debt. He engaged critically with the text every step of the way for nearly two years – he questioned, polished and refined, and he was instrumental in shaping the book.

My gratitude goes to Albie Sachs for making time to add his erudite and astute insights.

I am grateful to Rooksana Omar, CEO of Iziko Museums of South Africa, for the support I received in so many ways, and to the following individuals: Bongani Ndhlovu, Shameem Adams, Wendy Black, Baheya Hardy, Lailah Hisham, Andrea Lewis, Sepadi Moruthane, Nigel Pamplin and Hamish Robertson. Shaheeda Dante, Carol Kaufmann, Hayden Proud and Angela Zehnder spent many hours assisting me in my research. To Joe Dolby, ever my sounding board, a big thank you.

The Iziko SANG Library and the Libraries of the University of Cape Town were crucial in facilitating my research.

What would this book be without the art works? My heartfelt thanks go to the artists and their galleries, as well as the trusts, foundations and institutions for giving their permissions. Their preparedness to waive copyright fees and accept copies of the book instead, constitutes a huge contribution. Seeking permission allowed me to connect and reconnect with artists, a process that was in itself inspiring and affirming.

This publication would be wanting without the voices of the individuals who responded to my requests for their personal views and experiences at SANG – thank you so much.

My gratitude goes to the financial assistance received from the University of Cape Town, the Cape Tercentenary Foundation and Strauss & Co.

I wish to acknowledge my daughter Catherine, on whose interest, insights and critical eye I can always depend.

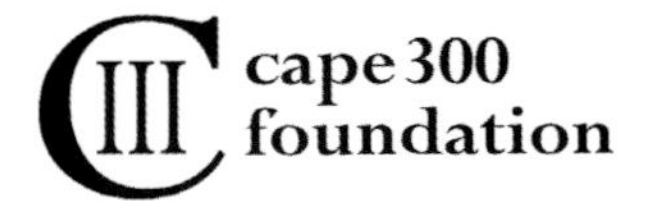

Contents

Foreword by Albie Sachs

A GRACIOUS 1930s classical building that stands in a serene landscape of ponds, fountains, tree-lined avenues and other stately buildings. Welcome to the South African National Gallery (SANG), now referred to as the Iziko SANG. I expected the story of its development from the last quarter of the nineteenth century to the first quarter of the twenty-first to be equally calm and serene. I imagined that the tale of the evolution of our country's national art collection would be couched in respectful, even reverential, language with occasional polite hints of problems along the way. I was wrong, totally wrong. In a complete inversion of my expectations, this candid, forceful and meticulously researched account by Marilyn Martin, who was director of SANG from 1990 to 2001, and until 2008 director of art collections for Iziko Museums, tells the story of an institution subject to almost non-stop turbulence, punctuated with occasional moments of serenity.

My first visit to the National Gallery was calm enough. I was an innocent nine-year-old schoolboy at South African College (SACS) Junior School, which was then situated nearby at the top of the Company's Garden. The only woman teacher at our very masculinist, boys-only school took our class on a surprise excursion to the Gallery. At first we were jubilant ... anything to get away from class. Then came the agony – being obliged to look at boring landscapes when, right behind us, Table Mountain towered majestically. Then suddenly we were jubilant again: one of my classmates whispered that three rooms away there was a painting of a woman without any clothes on, yes, she was stark naked! Giggling quietly, we were determined to compel our teacher to move in that direction. But to our total astonishment, she herself led us there, and what's more, pointed her finger to the thigh, telling us to look at the beautiful brushstrokes. Thank you, anonymous teacher, little did you know that you would be preparing me for two later shocks in life.

The first was one of amazement at discovering that a director of SANG had refused to hang pictures of what he called disrobed women in his gallery, and even greater amazement at learning that he had gone on to declare that Hitler was right to suppress degenerate art. The other shock was one of joy at learning that another taboo-breaking woman, Marilyn Martin, unafraid to confront prudery and conformism, had taken over at the Gallery's helm.

Marilyn in fact became director in 1990 – the same year that I returned to South Africa from decades in exile. Apartheid was still in force, but there were great expectations of change. From the start she faced problems. I remember her crying copious tears of frustration. She was being hammered mercilessly by influential sections of the art establishment for committing what they regarded as the highest form of treason – she was challenging the hegemonic position of Anton Rupert, the self-made Afrikaner millionaire. Rupert had been funding the prize given for the best works at the Cape Town

Triennial. Marilyn had asked why the National Gallery should devote considerable resources towards the realisation of the competition when it got no direct financial benefit from it.

The response in the Afrikaans newspaper *Die Burger* was predictable, and painfully sexist. The headline declared 'Kunsmuseum se onderrok het uitdagende kleur' (Art Museum's petticoat has a provocative colour), and the article went on to say that 'the petticoat was beginning to wave like a flag'. A doughty defender of her core values, always very professional in manner, Marilyn was not going to be bullied by the powers that were. She held out and got sufficient support from the SANG board and Friends to win that battle. But the price was high – a corps of influential opponents waiting for her to slip up. And the more she succeeded in later projects, the more toes she trampled on – the greater the number of critics. It was not failure that led to the animosity, but success.

During her more than eighteen years at the national art museum Marilyn did an enormous amount to initiate change and develop a team of highly professional and imaginative curators. Everything they did was stylish, well thought through and correct. Is it possible to be too correct, too refined? I have a theory that great leaders of art institutions require three special qualities. The first is a thorough understanding of the inner rhythms and nuances of the particular art form involved. The second is an ability to see the big picture in the tiny detail and the tiny detail in the big picture. And the third is to be a little mad. The reader can make up his or her own mind from the way that Marilyn has written this extraordinarily rich book as to which of these qualities she possessed. But whatever conclusion they come to, no-one can doubt that she provided formidable aesthetic and organisational mooring to a highly significant institution at a time of exceptional change.

Marilyn tells us that she has written this book in three different capacities. It is clear that she has done prodigious research as a highly qualified art historian, citing from masses of documentary evidence. Secondly, she has written as an influential participant-observer drawing on her own intense experiences as the museum's director; and thirdly, as the occasionally involved and still embedded witness. I would detect two other Marilynesque personae. One is the young Afrikaans-speaking girl who had been on a float in a rural town in the Cape to celebrate the arrival of Jan van Riebeeck on 6 April 1652, and who had grown up to become a staunch critic of racism and patriarchy. And finally, there is Marilyn the Modernist. Modernism captured her as, I should mention, it captured me. In its day it was revolutionary, iconoclastic and visionary. It developed our ways of seeing in a most profound and enduring way.

The most prominent and persistent theme of the book is in fact the challenge presented to new leadership at SANG to break away from representing the artistic imaginations and output only of white producers and consumers of art. This theme starts with a moving account of the work of the young Gerard Sekoto exhibiting with the New Group in Cape Town before he went into exile in Paris, and the SANG board declining to purchase his paintings in 1944. Later it proceeds with the first exhibitions of San rock art and Rorke's Drift tapestries in the 1960s, and later still with the first exhibition of beadwork from the Eastern Cape. The first major show of West and Central African art came from France, lending French respectability for showing African art in Africa!

This was followed by a phase of brilliant new energy coming from the art produced in the late-apartheid period, such as Jane Alexander's famous *Butcher Boys* (1985–86) sculpture, which confronted the perverse cruelty of apartheid head on. It ends with Dean Hutton's installation *Fuckwhitepeople* (2016), shown as part of an exhibition called *The Art of Disruption*, which provoked a storm of controversy and ended up with a court ruling in favour of freedom of expression.

Yet there was a problem. Although black artists were represented in increasing numbers, there were still challenges to what was declared to be: white artists appropriating and representing black pain. We are told, however, that everything that rises must fall. Does that mean that everything that Falls must rise? I hope so. One of the main challenges made by the Fallist movement was that whites were not only curating black pain, but were curating black curators who were seeking to curate black pain. I believe that institutions like SANG are indeed robust and resilient enough to contain and benefit from the disruptive energies that emanated from the Fallist movement. One of SANG's main achievements has in fact been the training of highly qualified black curators to work in and take over the management of other public and private collections in the country.

Which brings me to consider the major challenges facing SANG today. From its very inception, the art museum has faced extreme shortages of governmental funding. At the time when the collection was founded, its main support came from wealthy Randlords who had made their fortunes by means of ruthless and cutthroat competition to control the diamond and gold mines. One way of acquiring respectability for themselves and their wives was through buying up and donating expensive artwork to the Gallery. In one case, the benefactor made no secret of the fact that he was hoping to get a title from the British Crown as a result of his donation.

How things have changed! Today, the billionaires no longer seek to buy titles; they buy whole art galleries. Cape Town now has the Zeitz Museum of Contemporary Art Africa and the Norval Foundation. Private funding and fund-raising enable these museums to put on spectacular exhibitions, which the National Gallery could never seek to match. What then would the future of SANG be?

Our national gallery has one great asset which the private museums could never equal: its patrimony. This is an extraordinarily rich collection of artwork produced in South Africa in the twentieth century and the first part of this century. These works possess enormous educational value. SANG must continue to conserve this great repository of South African art and consistently add to its stock. Let other museums do what they are good at, which is to provide entertainment, provocation and spectacle. Let SANG quietly grow its audiences, train its personnel, provide new exhibitions, liaise with public galleries throughout the world, and maintain our continuing debates about the multiple meanings of life in South Africa.

There is a second great role that SANG could play, and that is to provide other public bodies with fine South Africa artwork. I recall the time when SANG loaned eight works by Gerard Sekoto to the Constitutional Court Art Collection. It was wonderful to see them in our building and to watch members of the public looking at them. For reasons that were never made clear to me they were subsequently retrieved, and now they sadly join the rest of Sekoto's Paris period collection in what I would call their new internal exile, banished to the basement of SANG. But there is every reason to hope that they can be released from their obscurity, and as part of the national patrimony, find their way to other public buildings, as shrines of art.

Let me end where I began, with the serene building in the Company's Garden that has become the scene of non-stop vendettas and calumny. The reader might wonder why public art should evoke such intense emotions. Henry Kissinger once famously said that academic debates could be so furious and so enduring because the stakes were so insignificant. Perhaps there is some parallel with the art museum world. This book shows that in fact most of the disputes and vendettas that reverberated over the decades at SANG were not about the deep and really serious issues that beset it. Rather, they related to personalities and cliques: the more trivial the issue, the more passionate and lasting the dispute. Only on occasion was the soul of the art museum – perceived as a mirror of South African society – at stake.

Kudos to Marilyn Martin, then, for rising above the intensity of these divisions, even of those that rankle to this day. Marilyn the art historian takes over and provides different sides to the argument. She distinguishes clearly between presenting evidence and offering her own opinions. At the very least it is a wonderful compendium of what happened and when over a century and a half at the National Gallery. At its best it offers thoughtful commentaries on profound aesthetic controversies. The personalities are there, the provocations, the vituperation, the moments of glory and the times of despair.

Meticulously researched and carefully written, this book is more than just a rich repository of information about an important public institution with high intentions. It is the pained life story of an organic body that was dedicated to idealistic pursuits and yet found itself bedevilled by egotism, materialism and official indifference. In making a striking and substantial contribution to the history of the South African National Gallery, Marilyn Martin presents a rich story, with perhaps more agony than ecstasy, of our constantly evolving South African aesthetic imagination.

Albie Sachs

Cape Town

May 2019

Introduction

Between the idea
And reality
Between the motion
And the act
Falls the shadow.
T. S. ELIOT[1]

BETWEEN DREAMS AND REALITIES is a history of the South African National Gallery (SANG), the country's pre-eminent art museum. The book's narrative begins in 1871, when Thomas Butterworth Bayley bequeathed forty-five paintings and money for the establishment of a public art gallery in Cape Town, and ends in 2017, a time of extraordinary changes in South Africa's art and museum sectors signalled by the opening of new privately-funded "public" art museums. Things changed in 2018 while the manuscript was being edited and revised, and significant occurrences during that year are recorded and analysed.

A history of an institution such as SANG is necessarily a public history. A key ambition of this book is to consider the aspirations and role of civil society in creating and maintaining a national art institution for the common good; concurrently, it also examines long-standing government disinterest in and neglect of this collective project. The history is told chronologically with chapters ordered to reflect the tenures of SANG's successive directors, myself included. Some chapters are organised to reflect the historical circumstances, for example the constitutional and social watershed years 1910, 1948, 1976 and 1990.

This book centrally deals with the difficulties that confronted SANG's directors in acquiring a collection worthy of a national institution, and to fill historical and even contemporary gaps in the absence of adequate funds. In this regard, the book draws attention to an obvious contradiction: while located on the African continent, throughout its long history the gallery has remained ambivalent about collecting and displaying historical and modern African art. This is an unresolved issue, notwithstanding South Africa's renewed role on the continent since 1994. *Between Dreams and Realities* also details the political agendas and strained relationships resulting in tensions that, at times, led to vendettas against directors from inside and outside the institution.

During the writing of this book leitmotifs connecting past and present, as well as history and contemporary challenges, emerged and affirmed the rightness of drawing from T. S. Eliot's 1925 poem *The Hollow Men* for the book's title. However, the realities described in this book are not singularly negative and cloaked in shadow. *Between Dreams and Realities* also tells the story of excellent cooperation and support, at many different levels and in many ways, and of boards of trustees, directors and staff together overcoming the realities of budget cuts, government interference and severe space constraints. Many dreams were realised at SANG, and at the best of times outcomes exceeded planning, vision and expectations.

No book can provide a complete history of such a long period of time; all the same, I trust that *Between Dreams and Realities* will contribute to the fields of museum and cultural studies, art history and the visual arts, and that it will open up the discourse and revive interest in our public art museums in general and in the national art museum in particular. By its very nature much of this book is inward looking: it parses the nitty gritty of a public institution; unavoidably, the narrative dwells on procedural matters. This does not, however, exclude its value to readers other than specialists, for they may enjoy discovering what goes on behind the scenes, in the chambers and archives inaccessible to the public.

Between Dreams and Realities is in the first place constructed on primary and secondary research. Added to this are many years of personal experience: representing the South African Association of Arts as its national president on the board of trustees in 1989; working in the institution as its director for eighteen years (1990–2008); and serving as a council member of Iziko Museums of South Africa (2010–13). But one cannot tell a story as complex as this from one perspective. This book embraces many voices. I often quote these voices at length – drawing from writings and lectures, from archives and libraries, as well as from wide-ranging personal correspondence – largely because I want them to speak directly to the reader. I am deeply indebted to the many individuals who took time to respond to my requests and to answer my questions. I hope that the authenticity of their voices will challenge minds and move hearts.

Raymund van Niekerk, my predecessor at SANG, also recognised the vital contribution that various people have made to this public institution. In a speech delivered in the early 1980s, Van Niekerk stated:

> All those who have worked and work here have sought through their devotion to the growth of the collections and the animation of the gallery to provide a stimulus to the cultural life of Cape Town and the country as a whole, to encourage an understanding of the art of our time, to present the works of South African artists and provide a picture of the significant achievements in the art of our country past and present. In short, to try and make of the institution, which bears a name which does demand a degree of identification whether for pride or for shame, something of dignity and something vital.[2]

While the four chapters on my directorship are extensive, I have attempted not to neglect the individuals or governing bodies that worked tirelessly for the advancement of art and the national art museum. In his speech, which was very much about the history of SANG, Van Niekerk described the process of going through old files and newspaper clippings, sharing the achievements and frustrations of his predecessors and sympathising with "their more harassed moments". He concluded that retelling this history "should be undertaken by a more impartial observer".

I cannot pretend to be that impartial observer. The reader may detect a mix of narrative styles in my writing, and the agency of three distinctive personalities: the art historian researching and interpreting the gallery's early history; the museum director and protagonist implicated in leading SANG; and the distant, occasionally involved but still embedded observer keen to uncover and share information. Facing and crossing the shadows formed part of the process and writing. I trust that my dedication, empathy and passion for the gallery and its history are tempered by the demands and rigours of dispassion required of an art historian.

Over the years many misconceptions and factual errors have crept into the official record of the national gallery. This book is an opportunity to set the record straight. In defence of SANG as an idea, I criticise those who have abdicated their responsibility to this national institution. To this end I reveal facts and uncomfortable truths that are not in the public domain. I attempt to capture and share a history, and reclaim legacies which are either no longer remembered or have been conveniently ignored. At the time of writing, South Africa's national gallery (and I include here the people who built it over nearly 150 years) runs the risk of being divested of its formidable achievements, often in the face of daunting obstacles and adversity. With public art museums in the state they currently are and the attendant shift to private initiatives, it is easy to lose sight of the fact that SANG has a magnificent collection and that it is there for the benefit of all.

The role and meaning of the national gallery is inseparable from the social, political and art contexts that frame it. SANG is perceived as a mirror of South African society, a site for cultural activism that cannot and should not strive to achieve ideological neutrality or, worse still, political correctness. This history therefore frequently makes reference to the larger political circumstances and profound changes that occurred in South Africa between 1871 and 2017.

A cautionary: given that this is a history of a public institution, the reader will shortly encounter a profusion of acronyms for the state and private bodies somehow involved in the life of the institution. Indeed, the name of the national art museum itself is a matter of some perplexity. First known as the "Art Gallery", in 1910 it became known as the "South African Art Gallery" only to change to "The South African National Gallery" in 1931, until it acquired the prefix Iziko in 2001. I have chosen in this book to honour the moniker that endured for seventy years. The terms "art gallery" and "art museum" are used interchangeably in this book, sometimes with the adjective "national" prefixed; just as often I use the acronym "SANG".

A word of clarification on SANG's different appellations in English and Afrikaans, which sometimes create confusion, is pertinent. Act No. 23 of 1931 provided for the constitution of certain state-aided institutions that included "The South African National Gallery". The authorities followed the example of public art museums in Britain, for example the National Gallery, the Tate Gallery and the National Portrait Gallery in London. It was originally translated into Afrikaans as "Suid-Afrikaanse Kunsgalery" (South African Art Gallery), but the following year government notice was given of the proposed change to either "Nasionale Kunsmuseum van Suid-Afrika" (National Art Museum of South Africa) or "Suid-Afrikaanse Nasionale Kunsmuseum" (South African National Museum of Art); the latter prevailed.[3]

In 1961 the renowned Afrikaans poet and academicv W. E. G. Louw, then a member of the board of trustees, put forward a motion that the English name be changed to South African National Museum of Art. For him this would bring "a closer allegiance" between the languages and would "more readily provide for the inclusion of other forms of art, such as the Davis Collection of pottery, which was wrongly housed in the South African Museum". Trustee C. S. Corder disagreed with this far-sighted proposal, arguing that "gallery" was closely associated with the history of SANG, and proposed South African National Gallery and Museum of Art instead.[4] The board was in favour and the idea was submitted to the secretary for education, arts and science, J. J. P. Op't Hof, who provided a detailed opinion – in which he cited various dictionaries in English, Afrikaans and Dutch – in May 1962. He concluded that using both "gallery" and "museum" was a tautology. Unlike the English examples mentioned above, in Dutch the word "galerij" was not applied to museums, for example the Rijksmuseum and Gemeentemuseum, and this was also the case in Afrikaans; "galery" would be incorrect and an Anglicism.[5] The board accepted the secretary's opinion and the status quo remained.[6] In 1990 the Xhosa name "IGalari Yobuzwe Yomzantsi Afrika" was added.

Whatever the national art museum is called, the reality is that it started out as a British colonial project, and that it now finds itself in a democratic South Africa. Efforts to retool the institution and embrace the artistic, cultural and political language of the times run parallel with attempts to move away from the European model on which it is based. The extent to which this has succeeded or failed constitutes the grain of this history.

PLATE 1: Herbert Meyerowitz, *Liberman Memorial Door*, c. 1929-1934, Burma teak, presented by the Hyman Liberman Estate.

1

From colonialism to apartheid – the role of civil society and the battle for a building

1871 – 1948

SET AGAINST A BACKDROP of political and social strife, this chapter recounts the beginnings of the national art museum. It identifies the key players behind the formation of the South African Fine Arts Association, which organised exhibitions, started a collection and acquired a building. The spectre of government neglect and indifference, a major theme of this book, first asserts itself in 1895 in the form of the South African Art Gallery Act, by way of which the fledgling collection becomes the property of the Cape colonial government. The long-anticipated opening of the art gallery in 1930 is overshadowed by an exhibition that includes works for sale, a betrayal of the principles of an official, state-aided art museum. In the absence of a full-time director, John Wheatley and Edward Roworth from the Michaelis School of Fine Art step in and assist. In the 1940s Roworth embarks on a scandalous selling spree of works in the permanent collection, which leads to his resignation. This chapter also covers Max Michaelis' gift of seventeenth-century Dutch and Flemish works and the establishment of the Michaelis Collection.

An art collection and gallery for public benefit – 'an important and indispensable aid in the education and refinement of the masses of the people'.

ABRAHAM DE SMIDT[1]

The beginnings – a publicly owned collection on permanent display

IN EUROPE THE OPENING of many royal, aristocratic and church collections to public access, which began in the seventeenth century, as well as gifts to art academies, associations, universities and government bodies, were often motivated by the egalitarianism that led to the English Revolution (1640–60) and the later French Revolution (1789–95). These benevolent actions frequently went hand in hand with expressions of national identity, aspirations and pride.[2] The genesis of the colonial collection at the Cape colony was vastly different and can be more appropriately likened to museums initiated by philanthropists. In this regard England took the lead with the Ashmolean Museum at Oxford University, founded in 1683, to house the cabinet of curiosities that Elias Ashmole gave the university in 1677. Although the Cape Colony lagged far behind Europe in the appreciation of the arts, there were individuals – some recent settlers, other locals with experience abroad – who believed that they could emulate European culture and bring about change in a distant colony. They were the colonial elites, but also collectors, artists and art lovers.

By the middle of the eighteenth century, Cape Town was an important outpost for the trading Dutch empire. The German immigrant Joachim Nikolaus von Dessin came to the Cape as a soldier in the service of the Vereenigde Oostindische Compagnie (VOC, the Dutch East India Company), but he was soon promoted to junior merchant and he became the secretary of the Orphan Chamber (1737–57). His wife and only child died before him and the Masters of the Orphan Chamber selected thirty-two paintings from the seventy-four in his estate upon his death in 1761.[3] The works, together with approximately 4,500 books and manuscripts, which in 1820 became the nucleus of the South African Public Library, were left to the Dutch Reformed Church in Adderley Street, which is still extant. They were housed with the library on the first floor in the adjacent Sexton's House.[4] The ethnological and natural history items went to the South African Museum (SAM), where they were accommodated in a new building from 1897, while there were many accounts of indifference to and neglect of the paintings. This was par for the course in a colony where science and natural history were regarded as far more important than the arts.[5] In 1860 the *Cape Argus* complained that the Cape "is a country that may give an artist breath but cannot give him bread," and again in 1869 that "art of all kinds is but poorly appreciated and supported".[6]

In 1814 the Cape finally became a British colonial possession and by the end of the nineteenth century Cape Town was the capital of a key colony in the British Empire.[7] It was the seat of parliament and it was also known as "The Mother City". Artists, teachers, surveyors, topographers, naturalists and scientists arrived from all over Europe, but by far the greatest number came from Britain. An art exhibition was held in Cape Town in 1816, but many years would go by before, in 1851, art lovers formed the Cape Fine Arts Society and took a decision to organise regular exhibitions, to award prizes and to secure a permanent building for such exhibitions. The exhibitions that followed in 1851, 1852, 1858 and 1866 typically comprised work by local artists and European art on loan from private and the Von Dessin public collection, but by 1871 no premises had been acquired.

FIGURE 1: Portrait of Abraham de Smidt (1829-1909).

R. R. Langham-Carter credits Thomas Butterworth Bayley – a patron of the arts, public figure, leading silviculturist and horse and cattle breeder – for realising the prospect of a "publicly owned collection on permanent display in its own building" and consequently as the originator of the South African National Gallery permanent collection.[8] This would, however, not have happened without the vision of Bayley's friend and advisor on the purchase of pictures, Abraham de Smidt (Fig. 1). I tend to agree with Dr. W. H. Ross, who wrote in the *Cape Times* (6 June 1910) that De Smidt:

> ... was the prime mover and pivot in starting the Art Gallery. He and I were the first trustees, but De Smidt, who was on intimate terms with old Tom Bayley and with F. R. Lee – the distinguished English landscape painter – succeeded in interesting these two powerful personalities in his views, thereby drawing in others.[9]

South African-born De Smidt was one of the few Cape art connoisseurs of his day. Aside from being a gifted painter, collector and founder of the South African Drawing Club in 1888, he was also the government surveyor-general. De Smidt's many trips abroad included visits to museums.[10] His art teacher was Thomas Bowler, who lived and taught at the Cape from 1834–68, and they shared a great admiration for Joseph Mallord William Turner. Colonial topographic order and a quiet romanticism came together in De Smidt's paintings.

De Smidt took the lead in promoting the need for a public art gallery with an article, "An Art Gallery for South Africa", in the *Cape Monthly Magazine* (April 1871). In an extravagant display of knowledge and erudition, he set out what the ideals of such an institution could be and how to achieve it. His article provides fascinating insights into the kind of art that was valued at that time, as well as a view into colonial society and its unquestioned social and racial hierarchies.[11] De Smidt proposed the establishment of an art society that would organise exhibitions, build a collection and focus on the formation of a "Colonial Art Gallery". He envisaged a room in the Library for display, meetings and lectures, and, in time, extending the southern wing of the building eastwards. It would house works of art and, considering the high cost of original sculptures, plaster casts of ancient Greek and Roman sculptures, as well as work by modern classical sculptors. All along he informed the reader about the advances made in another colony, in Melbourne, Australia. Interestingly, at this early date, De Smidt included photographs in a room with watercolour drawings, chromo-lithographs and engravings; oil paintings would be exhibited separately.

He described the roles and power of the art critic and connoisseur, and he was scathing about the *soi-disant* (so-called) critic, who used his "stock-in-trade of terms, a well-appointed battery of technical missiles fresh from the armoury of his Art vocabulary" to make in the "eyes of an undiscerning public quite a creditable show of artistic lore, by which mediocre works are trumped up as master-pieces, and the mature productions of experienced artists – approved as such by consummate judges in Europe – are flippantly noticed, or charitably damned with the faintest of praises".

What would the purpose of De Smidt's colonial art gallery be and who would it serve? For him the visual arts spoke universally and more directly than any other form of communication. He had seen a writer moved to tears by Sassoferrato's *Mater Dolorosa,*[12] and "even in the wilds of Kafirland the deeply hidden emotions of the soul would be stirred by beholding such a picture". In South Africa "more light has been cast on the habits and character of the Bushmen and their own rude drawings in caves and on rocks in various localities, than by all the books that have been written about these people".

De Smidt's plan included lectures, admission of students to copy works, a school of design and instruction in art history. Driven by the conviction that art was a powerful, beneficial tool for education, he outlined his vision: exposure to art would enhance the lives of the "higher classes" who already enjoyed access to art and literature, while ameliorating their pursuit of material wealth at the expense of the mind; it would educate and refine the public at large. Rich and poor would be likewise enraptured and ennobled by contact with fine paintings and sculpture, suitably arranged.

Moreover, there was a strong social and moral purpose. Cape Town had seen a constant influx of people from 1652 and by the 1870s a complex and hybrid society had developed. Recognising that he was treading delicate ground, De Smidt ventured to suggest that the art gallery should be open to the public on Sunday afternoons, as many people toiled six days a week and required recreation. A large part of the population did not attend places of worship: "The alternative is not between the church or chapel and the museum or picture gallery, but between the place of worship and the public-houses and pocket-Edens of Newlands." The works of art would exercise their beneficial effects and keep people away from "the canteen and other haunts of debasement and debauch".

There was an urgent need to act decisively. For Bayley, who had suffered ill health since he was a young man, time was running out and at a meeting of like-minded individuals, held on 21 April 1871, the Cape Fine Arts Society became the South African Fine Arts Association (SAFAA).[13] Both Bayley and De Smidt were elected to the committee, Sir Henry Barkly, then governor of the Cape Colony, was the first president and Sir Richard Southey the first chairperson. The new association produced a *Book of Rules* with the object of promoting "Fine Art in the Cape Colony" by forming a permanent art galley and art library; holding occasional art exhibitions; establishing "Art Unions" that would provide facilities for the disposal of works of art; and offering prizes. The twenty-two rules proposed at the first general meeting in August 1871 included an important stipulation: "All Works of Art presented to the Association on Trust, or for Exhibition, to be submitted to a Special Committee to decide upon whether they shall be accepted or declined." One hundred and twenty "gentlemen" became members.[14]

As in the past, the exhibitions – held in various venues – would consist of work by professional and amateur artists, and loans from private individuals. Although there is no reference to female members in 1871, the exhibitions included women. Local artists were stigmatised as "colonial" and therefore regarded as inferior to the foreigners. Reviewers were suitably cautious. A reviewer for the *Cape Argus* ("The Local Work", 21 December 1871) noted: "The task is a very delicate one, since in a small community where there are only one or two professional artists and as many amateurs, criticism is a little invidious, or at all events, runs the risk of not being kindly received." The paucity of local artists is exaggerated, for the exhibition included fourteen "colonial" men and nine women. Among them were Thomas Baines, Bowler (deceased), De Smidt and the highly regarded teachers Wilhelm Hermann and William McGill.[15] The situation changed as education and the association grew and developed, and by 1879 local participants numbered thirty-eight, twenty of whom were women and among the prize-winners.

Bayley died on 29 December 1871. He bequeathed forty-five paintings to SAFAA and left £500 towards the cost of a gallery, provided that a further sum of not less than £1,500 were raised from other sources. Heedful of the twenty-one years of inaction that he had experienced, Bayley stipulated that a building be acquired for a permanent collection within eighteen months of his death.

The first home for the collection was Groote Schuur, which belonged to De Smidt, the interim trustee of the paintings. In 1873, SAFAA honoured Bayley's will, raised money and acquired a building for the sum of £1,600 at 30 and 32 Nieuwstraat (later on 38 Queen Victoria Street) in a former school aptly named "Tot Nut van 't Algemeen" (For the Benefit of the Community). De Smidt and W. H. Ross had inspected the premises and found them to be adaptable to the purposes of the association, the former observing: "It is not exposed to the South-East dust, it has large halls and rooms which may at once be fitted up for galleries, and it is in the immediate neighbourhood of the Public Library, Museum, Botanic Garden, and the site of the proposed new Houses of Parliament".[16]

There were ample spaces for the permanent collection, temporary exhibitions, art classes and offices. Activities commenced straight away, although Sir Henry Barkly only formally opened the gallery two years later. By 1877 the collection comprised forty-six oil paintings, thirteen watercolours and fourteen engravings. It was given a boost in 1883 with the addition of fourteen of the best works from the Von Dessin Collection, with more following in the next decade, as well as paintings from the collection of the Library.

A significant characteristic of the SANG's history is the emphasis, from its inception, on education. Katherine Goodnow, academic at Bergen University and writer on museum practice, maintains:

> … art galleries especially have a history of starting off as signs of one's civilised status, either as a collector/donor/patron or as a viewer who can appreciate 'the finer things of life'. The move into being more of a public institution with aim of 'education' typically comes later in the day.[17]

The civilised and civilising ambitions are indeed characteristic of the benefactors of the Cape colony in general and the art gallery in particular, but the foundation of the Von Dessin and SAFAA collections, as well as De Smidt's references to education in his 1871 article, went hand in hand with the desire to educate. In 1881, *The Cape Monthly Magazine* described the building as:

> ... the home of the Educational Museum as well as the Art Gallery, and two of its halls have been fitted up for the use of Art students. A competent Art teacher has been engaged by the Superintendent-General of Education, and has his classes in the Art Gallery ... The combination of the three – Art Gallery, Educational Museum, and Art Classes – has now placed the [South African Fine Arts Association] in its proper position as one of the great educating powers of the country.[18]

De Smidt followed Bayley's example by devoting a great deal of his energy and talents to the Cape colony, even after he retired to England with his family in 1890. He was elected an honorary member of SAFAA in 1894 and two years later he became their representative in England, assisting with the purchase of paintings. In her biography of De Smidt, Marjorie Bull describes his reluctance to be the sole judge.[19] To spend the £450 available for purchases in 1897, De Smidt enlisted the advice of Havelock Ellis, an English physician, writer, progressive intellectual and social reformer who studied human sexuality, and who displayed a "disinterested" knowledge of art. Correspondence reveals that this arrangement did not work. Ellis was passionate about Old Masters and the paintings by the Pre-Raphaelites, and the two could not see eye to eye.

De Smidt was distrustful of the quality of works displayed at the Royal Academy exhibitions and infuriated by the "slapdash school of artists and critics," as well as the "affectation" of the "Impressionistic" school. He had at any rate been advised by his friend and SAFAA secretary, J. A. Fairbairn, not to buy "pronounced nudes" and De Smidt agreed that "we should for some time at least, be careful not to be in advance of the times and of the feelings of many persons in respect of undraped figures ... What you have to do is to hit the popular taste, as far as you can, without sacrifices of Art principles, and the requirements of a training School for Artists."

De Smidt made his final purchases in 1900, assisted by Thomas Armstrong of the South Kensington Museum. Secretary Sydney Cowper was not impressed with the selection and he advised his successor, John Fairbairn, that a hunting scene had arrived damaged and that "there is a shocking tragedy by Douglas Adams ... that might well be disposed of by Art Union – it is not fit to hang in a decent Art Gallery. We might perhaps keep the print, but the picture, or rather "pot-boiler" must go".[20] De Smidt was undoubtedly a main player in the early history of the national gallery, but his innate conservativism and propensity for "true transcripts of Nature" had a negative impact on the nature and quality of the art acquired for the incipient collection.[21]

The vexed question of high customs duty on imported works of art, which surfaces again and again in *Dreams and Realities*, was addressed by De Smidt and J. A. Fairbairn in a meeting with Sir Gordon Sprigg in London in 1890. They "urged that as paper for newspapers, books, specimens illustrative of natural history and photographs were admitted free, there was equally sufficient reason for placing works of art on the free list".[22] It is not clear whether he succeeded, nor whether the cost of customs duty affected purchases in any way.

De Smidt's own collection was on loan to SAFAA and it was displayed in the gallery in a joint exhibition with the South African Drawing Club in 1890.[23] By all accounts, his presence was sorely missed at the Cape.

A significant gift and a "fatal date"

IN HIS CONTRIBUTION to the centenary booklet of the *South African National Gallery 1871-1971*, former professor and then director of the SANG, Matthys Bokhorst, divided the first hundred years of the institution into three periods:

> The first 25 years of brave attempts but constant removals; the following 35 years vegetating in a dead end, behind the South African Museum; and finally the past 40 years at new, beautifully situated premises, at first more than adequate, then constantly expanded, but finally bursting out of their precincts.[24]

Exhibitions were organised, the collection grew and by 1895, when the South African Art Gallery Act was promulgated, it comprised well over 100 works. The statute came into force the next year, the institution was incorporated, the collection was declared the property of the Cape colonial government and a board of trustees was established. It sounds encouraging, but in reality the spectre of government neglect and indifference, coupled with the exploitation of the governing body for its own ends, reared its head – this apathy continues to dog the national art collection. Bokhorst called 1 September 1895 "the fatal date" and summed up what had actually happened:

FIGURE 2: A corner of the South African Art Gallery in the South African Museum, 1910; photographer T. D. Ravenscroft.

The Government wanted the site of the Gallery to build an "Art School and Training College for the Education Department". They bought the premises [for £6,000], paid off the bond, and kept the remainder of the proceeds "to be devoted to the purposes of this act". These purposes were "the provision of a suitable place ... for the reception and custody of the said collection, and any works of art hereafter acquired, etc." In fact, they left the collection for another two years in the now derelict building, then took it to the Public Library in 1897, and in 1900 moved it again, now to two rooms and a well-staircase in an annexe behind the new South African Museum where only a portion of the collection could be shown to the public. The fact that, under the Act, the Cape Government could appoint three of the five Trustees, as against two, representing the previous owners – the S.A. Fine Arts Association – explains why the Board of Trustees, although it had to be "consulted" put up such a poor fight against the banishment order of the year 1900, which would strangle its activities for the next thirty years (Fig. 2).[25]

Already faced with severe space constraints, the Alfred Beit bequest of some forty plaster casts of antique statuary that arrived in 1908, was not enthusiastically received – government refused to provide temporary storage space, and the nude figures were a source of concern for the moral well-being of the public; they were in fact kept in the SAM annexe, behind a locked door.[26] Many years later, in 1947, SAFAA's submission to a government enquiry offered a graphic description of the appalling conditions to which the collection was subjected:

Here, and up the staircase, were crowded together a portion of the collection, with pictures of all sorts indiscriminately mixed up with plaster casts. Only a few of the exhibits could be seen properly, whilst many others had to be packed away behind the scenes in grim darkness. Surely no other city in the British empire of the importance of Cape Town could have been so neglected in the manner of an Art Gallery! [27]

In every available *Report* [28] – presented first to the parliament of the Cape of Good Hope, and from 1910 to the new Union of South Africa parliament – the trustees of the Art Gallery bemoaned governmental neglect and unwillingness to act on the agreement entered into with SAFAA on 25 October 1896, namely the erection of a suitable building for a permanent gallery and for exhibition purposes. Moreover, by 1905 SAM trustees needed the space and wanted the art collection moved. After 1910 the first name change occurs, from the Art Gallery to the South African Art Gallery, affirming its national aspirations.

The 1912 *Report* details the history of SAFAA and the collection, and tells the sorry tale of futile approaches to successive governments to honour the 1896 undertaking.[29] In spite of its relegation to two rooms and a stairwell, the trustees did their utmost to activate the spaces: Sunday openings were supported by the city and the public, with 81,567 visitors recorded in 1912.[30] This compares favourably with the numbers in the centenary year (1971), 91,846,[31] and even more so in 2017 – 43,253.[32]

In the meantime, a major art collection was about to enter the country. German-born financier and mining magnate Max Michaelis offered a collection of seventeenth-century Dutch and Flemish works, specially acquired from Irish art dealer, collector and gallery director Sir Hugh Lane, to the Union government. Art historian and dealer Michael Stevenson describes it as "the most substantial benefaction of art to South Africa by a Randlord", but qualifies his statement by noting, "Michaelis's motives for this gift were more closely related to his plutocratic aspirations than a desire to give South Africans the opportunity to see old master paintings".[33] Like his fellow Randlords, Michaelis wanted a title and Lady Florence Phillips, an art patron married to mining magnate and politician Sir Lionel Phillips, became his guide in achieving this by suggesting various initiatives, including housing it in Pretoria.[34] A significant act was required and her friend, the statesman Jan Christian Smuts, suggested that a collection of Netherlandish paintings would "recall to the Dutch population of the Dominion the glories of their past civilisation in the days when they first colonised South Africa, and, by the representation of the art in which the Dutch and English first met in spirit, symbolic of a new Union".[35] This was easier said than done.

On 31 May 1910 the Act of Union brought together four separate British colonies (Cape, Natal, Transvaal and Orange River). The intention was to unify the colonies, but the Union of South Africa was born in the tense political climate that followed the South African War (1899–1902) and the annexation of the Afrikaner Boer republics, the South African Republic (Transvaal) and the Orange Free State in 1902. An alliance between Afrikaners and British was loaded, on the side of the vanquished, with the fear of British Imperialism, liberalism and capitalism, and haunted by memories of loss of land, life and the concentration camps. There were also bitter divisions among Afrikaners.

There was, however, one unifying factor: the preservation of white privilege, and the power this entailed over the black majority, which would manifest itself in acquisition and exhibition policies at the national art museum over many decades under the rubric of "Founder Nations" – by 1935 the chairperson of the board of trustees, J. J. Smith, would describe South Africa as "a nation composed of two peoples [the British and Dutch] famous in the realms of art" (*Cape Argus*, 17 July 1935).[36] Black South Africans had fought on both sides of the war and died in the camps. Prior to 1910 some people of colour at the Cape had the vote, but rather than extending it after Union, all black South Africans were denied the franchise.[37] An increasing number of educated black people were emerging from the mission education system and the University of Fort Hare (UFH), a key institution of higher education founded in 1916. African nationalism was on the rise.

In terms of the Act of Union, nationhood was a socio-legal concept predominantly reserved for "two races", meaning whites only; this provided the impetus for the founding of the South African Native National Congress, later known as the African National Congress (ANC) in 1912. The conservative white Afrikaner National Party (NP) came into being two years later. The NP gained power in 1924 in coalition with the Labour Party and in 1930 the government of J. B. M. Hertzog granted voting rights to white women, but worked tirelessly to have Coloured people, who were still on the common voters' role in the Cape Province, stripped of their rights, leading to a constitutional crisis in the 1950s.[38]

The Michaelis gift was the presumed but contested peacemaker between English and Afrikaans speakers (Dutch was no longer spoken at the Cape).[39] However, the collection itself was already fraught with controversy before its arrival in South Africa, specifically in relation to its quality, authenticity and attribution. Where should it be housed? In 1912 the government approached the gallery trustees to take charge of and temporarily house the collection. They accepted responsibility, but clearly it could not be accommodated at SAM, so rooms in the City Hall were loaned for the purpose.

The government also re-opened the question of suitable premises for the South African Art Gallery collection. Various options were suggested: The Castle of Good Hope, the Old Supreme Court Building, the Koopmans de Wet home, the Old Town House and the Good Hope Hall. After careful consideration, the trustees agreed that none of these buildings would meet the requirements of "a modern Art Gallery", and that none could be altered without destroying architectural features that should be preserved. They proposed that a new building be erected on the present Government House kitchen-garden and emphasised that "the presentation of this magnificent Collection of Dutch Masters necessitates *immediate action*"; they were confident that a new building would be proceeded with at once.[40]

It was not to be, and once again – as had been the case with the formation of SAFAA and the foundation of the collection – public opinion, supported by the local press, compelled the trustees to address the untenable situation. A deputation consulted with Smuts, who was then minister of the Interior, in February 1912; they reminded him of government's obligation in the matter. Smuts understood and suggested Government House as a possibility. The trustees accepted the offer and approved the preliminary plans for the alterations. However, the offer was subject to the erection of a new Government House, for which money still had to be found.[41]

Recognising that this could take years, on 18 September 1912, SAFAA's committee convened a "meeting of Art and Kindred Societies" in the Old Town House. A number of diverse organisations – including the South African Society of Artists (SASA),[42] South African Drawing Club, Institute of Architects, National Society, Photographic Society and the Mountain Club – formed a Standing Committee, comprising two representatives of each society, which would meet regularly and fight for a building. It was unanimously resolved:

> That this Meeting is of the opinion that the pictures and other works of Art in Cape Town, at present held in trust by Government, are so inadequately housed as to be almost entirely useless for the purposes for which they have been purchased, and that it is in consequence highly desirable in the best interest of Art in the Union that there should be no delay in the provision of suitable accommodation for them.[43]

There were more twists in the Michaelis bequest. The trustees were serious about their custodianship of what was regarded as an exceptional gift for a British colony, one that could form the nucleus of old master works for the gallery. They hoped that they would occupy a refurbished and extended Government House and that a wing would be reserved for the collection, "probably separated from the modern wing by a Hall of Statuary, containing reproductions of the finest examples of Greek and Roman Art." [44] But Sir Lionel Phillips, acting on behalf of Michaelis, wanted a separate building for the collection. Lady

FIGURE 3: The Old Town House, Greenmarket Square, with Ye Old Thatched Tavern on the left, Cape Town c.1911; collection Western Cape Archives and Records Service, E9358.

Phillips regarded the Old Town House (OTH), completed in 1761, as the ideal space and she succeeded in obtaining it from the Mayor of Cape Town.[45] However, for the trustees the building and location were unsuitable – it was situated among business premises, a tavern, a printing office and a seed store, all presenting fire hazards, and they expressed their concern for the safety of the Michaelis gift in a letter to government (Fig. 3). At the same time they had become aware that some members of the public opposed the alterations to Government House.

In their Report of 1913, they concluded:

> Therefore your Trustees, who are a voluntary Board appointed as Custodians of certain Government property, feeling acutely the position in which they have been placed by successive Governments, make this urgent appeal to the present Government to acknowledge its responsibility, which is of a national character, and strongly urge it to proceed at once with the Art Gallery, including a separate wing for the Michaelis Collection.[46]

Much correspondence followed, and with it a growing acrimony. It is clear from all the correspondence that the art gallery trustees were official custodians of the collection, to the point that their advice was sought regarding the authenticity of a painting by Rembrandt included in the gift.[47] Although there was no professional art expertise residing in the board at that time,[48] the trustees were powerful and influential men, who behaved impeccably in this regard: they repeatedly enquired about the provision that would be made for the upkeep of the collection and in the end accepted the OTH as the home of the collection, undertaking "to carry out, not only the terms of the Deed of Gift, but the spirit of the wishes of the donor".[49] When asked to assist in the hanging of the pictures, they declined, for they did not wish to

FIGURE 4: The Old Town House, the Frans Hals Room with the panelling dating to Joseph Solomon's 1913-14 conversion.

interfere with the architect appointed by the Phillips family, Joseph Solomon, who had particular ideas about the installation. He wanted "to retain the old work as far as possible and let the building take the form ... of the Mauritshuis at The Hague instead of giving it a cold formal experience of a gallery".[50] Art and architectural historian Hans Fransen challenged this approach:

> Solomon undoubtedly saw a number of things in Holland which influenced his design, but his interpretation of a seventeenth-century Dutch guild-hall and kitchen can now be seen as a highly personal fantasy, showing traces here and there of what may have influenced him. In the process, he retained practically none of whatever original features were left in the original interior.[51]

Nevertheless, Solomon, a protégé of Herbert Baker, crafted a fine interior that reflects late nineteenth-century eclecticism and the tenets of the Arts and Crafts Movement (Fig. 4). In his 1942 appreciation of the Michaelis Collection, Lord Harlech, trustee of the National Gallery and British Museum and president of the National Museum of Wales, noted that the pictures were displayed in a beautiful eighteenth-century building: "In fact, nowhere in the world, except in the Mauritzhuis [sic] at The Hague, can Dutch Old Masters be seen by the public in a more appropriate setting."[52]

The trustees were surprised to learn – unofficially – that a separate board had been appointed for the Michaelis Collection (MC). This had been gazetted in June 1916, without reference to the gallery trustees and in the ensuing correspondence it appears that their respect for Solomon's work was interpreted as indifference. Aspersions were cast on the trustees and they came to the conclusion that the information on which the government had acted "must have had some other source than any word or deed of the Trustees".[53] One can only speculate about who that powerful source might have been. The trustees were prepared to let the matter rest, particularly in light of the condition that the "collection should be properly housed in Cape Town in a building to be approved by, and to be permanently appropriated for this purpose in such a manner as shall be satisfactory to Mr. Michaelis or his representatives in South Africa", that this should happen within three years and that it always had to be known as the Max Michaelis Gift. Access was to be free, except on days reserved for students, when a small entrance fee would be charged.[54]

Stevenson draws attention to the issues of patronage and official responsibility for museums.[55] There was neither an endowment for the collection, nor provision for realising its educational potential as Cape Town's only public art gallery. The first keeper of the collection, Pauline Mary Thomas (until 1921), did not take any initiative, nor did the trustees, including Lady Phillips. A catalogue was published, but the opportunity for students to copy paintings was only mentioned in minutes of trustees' meetings in 1925 and lectures in 1932. The government, which converted the building at a cost of about £11,000, did not see its way clear to further supporting the museum. Two influential artists succeeded each other as keepers of the collection – Florence Zerffi (1921–27) and Ruth Prowse (1928–56).[56] They devoted their lives to art, not only as prolific and excellent painters of portraits, landscapes and cityscapes, but as art teachers and active members of the Society of Artists and the New Group (1937–53).[57] In terms of the history of South African art and its museums, it is significant that the custodianship of the collection was entrusted to women in what was a male-dominated profession elsewhere in the world. The inclusion of women artists in art history books from the beginning also sets South African art history somewhat apart.[58]

Beset by problems related to the collection, and ostracised as a German in London, Michaelis acquired the Montebello estate in Newlands and moved to Cape Town with his wife in 1919. Michaelis had hoped to gain a peerage, but it never materialised. It was only after he acted on Lady Phillips' proposal to endow a school of art at the University of Cape Town (UCT), now the Michaelis School of Fine Art (Michaelis School), that a knighthood was finally bestowed.

The museum, with its art collection and furniture, for which Michaelis paid, was autonomous. The conditions attached to the gift required the Cape Town City Council (CTCC) to ensure the building remain in place:

> That the Council consent to the Old Town House being vested in the Government for the purpose of the display of the Michaelis Collection, subject to the condition that should at any future time the Collection be removed from the building and the premises cease to be used for the purpose of an Art Gallery or Museum of Antiquities, the building shall revert to the Council.[59]

These conditions would prevail when an opportunity for it to be integrated into the national gallery collection presented itself in 1953. A deputation of the City of Cape Town general purposes committee approached the trustees with a view of offering the Michaelis Collection to them. Their ambition was for the city to take over the premises to house its collection of antiques, as well as to create a reading room and library. The proposal was accepted, but poorly handled by both the board and SANG's director, John Paris. Ignoring the conditions of Michaelis' bequest and the trustees of the collection, as well as the fact that the deputation only represented a committee and not the CTCC, a sub-committee was formed to investigate the offer and to report, while representation was made to government for an opinion.[60]

Many meetings and discussions resulted in a "minority report", with one member, H. Buisman, communicating his opposition to the idea directly to the minister of the interior without reference to the chairperson. There was a bitter split in the board, to which Paris was not immune. Ruth Prowse, who was keeper of the Michaelis Collection at the time and an observer on the sub-committee, regarded the very consideration of the proposal as harmful to the gallery: "The minority report covered the attitude that should have been taken up by the Director, he failed to advise the Board that the National Gallery was the Mother Gallery. Nation-wide opposition killed the proposal."[61]

An amalgamation of the two art institutions was again raised in joint meetings of the boards in 1962, at the time of the Booysen Commission of Enquiry, discussed in chapter two, but the commission recommended against it.[62] The Michaelis Collection would remain autonomous until 2001 when it became part of the new national museum structure in Cape Town.[63]

A new building

IN APRIL 1914, gallery trustees were informed that a new building would be erected on Stal Plein, so named because it housed the Government House stables, a decision with which they concurred. However, city councillors protested against the decision and resolved that, if the site were vested in them for use as an open space, park or garden, they would offer another site in return. Much correspondence in the press and many meetings with the city authorities, ratepayers and "various art and kindred societies" followed. It was finally agreed that the gallery building would be erected in the Good Hope Gardens and parliament voted £20,000 as a first instalment. Richard Stuttaford, son of the founder of Stuttafords department store, member of the CTCC, parliamentarian and minister with different portfolios in the Smuts cabinet, was enthused by the developments and offered £1,000 for the purchase of a picture.[64]

This was a telling example of the role that civil society, combined with political will and advocacy, could play, but unfortunately the outbreak of World War I in August 1914 meant that much construction work was suspended. Two years later, a plan was received from the Public Works Department (PWD), which the trustees approved. Tenders were due in February 1917.[65] Trustees reported that excavations for the foundations were nearing completion by the end of the same year.[66] However, more disappointment was to follow.

World War I ended on 11 November 1918, but somehow the government could not give any assurance that they would proceed with the building.

> The Trustees regret extremely the attitude which the Government has taken up in the matter. Ever since 1896 – 22 years ago – when the Government took over the collection of pictures from the South African Fine Arts Association on the understanding that a suitable building would be provided for housing the same, the Trustees have annually approached the Government on the subject and have pressed for the carrying out of the scheme. On more than one occasion amounts have been placed upon the Estimates but up to date all that has materialised is the laying down of the foundations. Everything has been done that the Trustees could do to obtain the attention which was their due and every Government has done nothing save promise consideration at a future date! The Trustees regret they have no further hopeful course open to them than to continue their representations, and trust that the Municipal Authorities and the Provincial Public will take sufficient interest in the matter to bring pressure to bear and thus assist the Trustees in their efforts to obtain an Art Gallery worthy of the Mother City.[67]

SAFAA only took up the matter again in 1921. Three years later a delegation to Thomas Boydell, minister of Public Works and Posts, managed to secure £33,500 for the new art gallery. Boydell's secretary for public works, Oscar W. Staten, was put in charge, a site identified and a team of architects selected: J. S. Cleland and F. W. Mullins of the DPW in Pretoria, and Franklin Kay Kendall from Cape Town, with Herbert Baker as adviser chiefly for the lay-out of the gardens in front of the building.[68] The CTCC contributed £6,000, to which the Union government added a like amount, and the Liberman Estate presented £10,000 to commemorate Hyman Liberman, the first Jewish mayor of Cape Town (1904–07). The Liberman Hall was designated for the exclusive display of South African art.

In 1934 the Liberman Estate presented the magnificent memorial doorway, carved in Burmese teak by sculptor Herbert Vladimir Meyerowitz, which fronts the hall. The doorframes depict the history of the Jews: *Hebrew Migrations from many lands* on the left and right jambs, and *Arrival in the Land of Peace and Prosperity* on the lintel; the whole is surmounted by an elaborate over-panel titled *Rebecca at the well*. The subjects on the doors place the history of the Jews in the context of Africa and the Cape: *African girl* and *Malay boy carrying grapes* on the left hand door; *African warrior* and *Malay boy carrying fish*, all portrayed in individual panels (Plate 1).[69]

Boydell's role was crucial and was later affirmed by the chairperson of the board, Cecil Sibbett, when the trustees were offered a portrait of Boydell. He pointed out that it was "entirely due to him that the Gallery was eventually built. For years successive governments had been urged to build the Gallery, but nothing was accomplished until Mr. Boydell became Minister of Public Works".[70] There was a great deal of correspondence in the local press regarding the design in 1926, the year in which UCT took over the Cape School of Architecture and incorporated it with the Michaelis School under British artist and educator John Wheatley, a professor at the Michaelis School. Lady Phillips entered the fray, calling for a national style in architecture.

Writing in 1988, SANG's then director Raymund van Niekerk maintained that the history surrounding the design of the building has never been sorted out, and that the extent of Kendall's role is in doubt as there was strife between him and public works.[71] As president of SAFAA and a gallery trustee for twenty years, Kendall was a major player in Cape Town society, but it is evident from his entry in *The Arts in South Africa* (1933–34), that he did not design the building, as it was not listed among his projects.[72] British-born Cleland, who was chief architect at public works (1920–32), was clearly in charge and interviewed in the press. He explained that the foundations for the building had been laid six or seven years before, that tenders would be called in January 1927. He further described the design as follows:

> The structure will be very simply treated. It is designed to harmonise with the environment and while in a general architectural sense it will be of a distinctive character, the predominant note will be according to the Cape Dutch style … The building is to be executed in brick and concrete with some stone dressing. Careful attention has been paid to the lighting arrangements for the Galleries, which have been planned on the most up-to-date lines.[73]

Cleland's description of the style is puzzling; apart from some detailing, there is nothing Cape Dutch about the gallery. His role as chief architect of the building is confirmed in an article that appeared in *The South African Builder* in February 1938.[74] The article provides valuable details of the materials, construction, plan and architectural details.

Bokhorst regarded the building as "exceptionally modern" for its time, "with its windowless walls and top-lighting throughout".[75] Considering the advances in international architectural design by 1930 this was something of a contradiction, as the gallery was stylistically backward looking in its eclecticism. The 1930s was a period of great interest in international modernism in this country. The epicentre of this interest was the Department of Architecture at the University of the Witwatersrand (Wits) in Johannesburg, where architects Gordon McIntosh, Norman Hanson and Rex Martienssen – influenced by European modernists like Le Corbusier, Walter Gropius and Mies van der Rohe – initiated an anti-historicist, progressive architecture.[76]

This interest reached a peak in 1937, with members of Architectural Students' Society organising a conference and exhibition under the title *Abstract Art*. The exhibition drew on works held in private collections, as well as copies and reproductions. While the focus was on abstraction in painting, photography and architecture, the examples shown and discussed were really late-Cubist works by Georges Braque, Juan Gris and Fernand Léger, amongst others, as well as Purist paintings by Le Corbusier and Amadée Ozenfant and two abstract paintings by Wassily Kandinsky. The Russian Constructivists, Suprematist Kasimir Malevich and artists and architects associated with De Stijl did not feature. Be that as it may, these were extraordinary initiatives at a time when the revolutionary art forms that had emerged in Europe were of little or no interest to most South African universities, art museums and critics. These institutions were comfortable in their parochialism, a situation that would endure into the 1960s.

Out of tune as the design may have been with contemporary architectural directions, the building is a fine remainder and reminder of architecture as symbol, and the appropriateness of a predominantly classical vocabulary for art museums that would last well into the twentieth century in South Africa.

FIGURE 5: South African National Gallery exterior, c. 1930; collection National Library of South Africa.

It is also a manifestation of Baker's pervasive influence long after he left the country.[77] Kendall, who joined Baker and Francis Masey in partnership upon his arrival in Cape Town in 1896, was regarded as the successor to Baker's practice and style in the Cape. This kind of "traditionalist" architecture was diametrically opposed to the "heroic modernism" of the Wits group and other forms of modernity prevalent during the 1930s.[78] The "Baker School" was characterised by an eclectic borrowing of classical and other styles, an Arts and Crafts attention to detail, and traditional use of material to suit circumstances and ambitions. Cleland was evidently also influenced by Baker.

FIGURE 6: Eva Meyerowitz, plaster bas-relief over the SANG main entrance, 1939.

While the divergences in South African architecture at this time were profound, the gallery building is an excellent example of the congruences - the overlaps, shifts and affinities - that were possible (Fig. 5). That the building has stood the test of time architecturally is due to its superb exterior proportions and details, and the interior spaces that vary in size and (before the closure of some rooms for storage) provided for perfect circulation. The gallery faces Government Avenue and the Delville Wood Memorial that had recently been erected. The foundations are of Paarl granite, all external walls are of cavity construction to protect against damp and the cornices and roof are of Italian tiles. The impressive classical portico, defined by Doric columns, is flanked by symmetrical walls and crowned with urns. While the white-walled façade appears austere at first glance, it is carefully articulated with setbacks, columns and niches of different sizes. Blinds protect the windows against the sun, and the influence of the Arts and Crafts movement is evident in the domestic scale of the wings.

Eva Meyerowitz, an artist and scholar of West African art, executed the plaster bas-relief over the main entrance in 1939 (Fig. 6). According to Van Niekerk, Cleland and the PWD jointly commissioned this work:

> What an architect of considerable refinement of taste [Kendall] thought of that action is mercifully not on record. The two bored and anatomically unfortunate nudes, who contemplate an armless companion between them seem disinclined to move towards creative action. That may well have been indicative of the state of the visual arts at the time of making.[79]

Nonetheless, the artwork is characteristic of the flattened, stylised Art Deco-inspired rendering of the figure in relief sculpture at the time. It accentuates the entrance and symmetry of the façade and is an example of the integration of sculptural decoration with architecture that was an important aspect of design – it would virtually disappear after the 1940s. Relief sculpture is integral to the gallery's exterior and interior architectural scheme. Access to the portico is gained via steps with copper railings and a teak doorway, with Dutch fanlight and central lantern, opens onto the foyer. The door is surrounded by elaborately carved stonework in rose-coloured Ladybrand stone, with Adam and Eve presented on opposite sides in the Garden of Eden, each being threatened by a snake. Meyerowitz's carved panel depicting two semi-naked female figures on either side of the tree of life surmounts the whole.

FIGURE 7: John and Grace Wheatley, the F. K. Wiener memorial murals, c. 1930, distemper on canvas.

The back of the building, facing St Johns Street, is completely closed off and a small garden is home to British sculptor Abraham Broadbent's bronze *Atlas*, presented to South Africa by A. O. Edwards in 1936. Alan Crump and Van Niekerk credit Broadbent's son, Eric, with the sculpture and point out that there are two more casts on the cupolas of the towers of the Union Buildings in Pretoria.[80] These are by Broadbent senior, and it is likely that Herbert Baker, architect of the Union Buildings (1909–13), recommended another cast for Cape Town.

In 1930 the gallery was composed of six galleries: one centre, four ends, the Liberman Room, as well as the "miniature room" – the oval space connecting two end galleries. The foyer opened into a grand exhibition space with a top-lit barrel-vaulted ceiling terminated by semi-circular panels, which were decorated by Wheatley and his wife, Grace. Executed in distemper on canvas, the Wheatleys created an Arcadian scheme populated with figures and the flora and fauna of South Africa; the ceiling was embellished with animals and floral strips (Fig. 7). Businessman F. K. Wiener offered the paintings in memory of his wife. All the galleries had hidden artificial lighting behind the cornices and recessed picture rails. The east and west galleries have double-barrel ceilings with a central colonnade. The rolling teak doors between the spaces slide into cavity walls and all the floors are in teak parquetry laid out in a herringbone pattern. In addition to the Liberman doors, Herbert Meyerowitz was responsible for the carved relief panels above the doors in every gallery.[81]

The exhibition rooms are anchored by a light-filled classical atrium with a solid and imposing colonnade, deep-set surrounding spaces and niches carried out in red *klompje* bricks. It is paved in Ladybrand stone with a red Warmbaths sandstone border and fountain in the centre. It provides an ideal space for the display of sculpture and for receptions.

Betraying the principles of a national art museum

THE GOVERNOR-GENERAL, the Earl of Athlone, accompanied by Princess Alice, opened the building on 3 November 1930, this despite it being incomplete as planned. The long-awaited and momentous occasion was unfortunately overshadowed by the inaugural exhibition. It comprised gifts, loan collections, works loaned by artists, and some from the permanent collection, but large areas were devoted to paintings imported by a British dealer Murray Fuller, which were offered for sale. The exhibition rightly caused an uproar and public scandal throughout the country. The launch exhibition's approach was totally opposed to everything that art museums stood for, and furthermore was a slap in the face of the numerous individuals and organisations that had fought, over a long period of time, for its realisation.

The exhibition catalogue reveals that the hundreds of works on display were set out predominantly according to medium and single-loan collections (for example, the Michaelis collection and prints provided by Howard Pim were grouped together) in rooms of different colours – grey, red and green – rather than following any curatorial or thematic principles. The Alfred de Pass presentations, the first of which had entered the collection in 1927, and other gifts were mixed with works provided by Fuller and local artists, as well as gallery purchases. Contrary to Hyman Liberman's wishes, the gallery carrying his name contained some works by South African artists, but was largely occupied by the Fuller collection. The long-awaited national art museum must have resembled a nineteenth-century Paris Salon at its worst.[82]

SASA published a pamphlet in English and Afrikaans, the English title of which speaks for itself: *A Protest on Behalf of the Artists of South Africa against the Slighting and Belittling Attitude of the Authorities on the Occasion of the Inauguration of the South African (National) Gallery on the Third of November, 1930.*[83] The pamphlet detailed all the correspondence surrounding earlier requests for the omission of South African artists to be addressed, as well as analyses of letters that appeared in the *Cape Times* and *Die Burger.* It further accused Wheatley, the chairperson of the board, of incompetence. There was a great deal of obfuscation on the part of the board members and not one of them was willing to admit that the Fuller collection was installed with their sanction; Sir Thomas Muir told SASA that he had heard about the Fuller pictures via the press. SASA concluded: "... the Management of the South African Art Gallery has displayed such ineptitude at its very first trial that few people, and certainly no South African Artist, can feel the slightest confidence in its future".[84]

Much good and adverse press coverage ensued, revealing the high level of public interest in the institution. While praising De Pass' gift, one writer described the English pictures as "examples of modern work – not the last word in modernity, but the work of well-established British artists, such as Clausen, Orpen, Sickert and John," and stated that Fuller was asked to bring them and that he was furnished with a list of the artists. Many British artists had cooperated as a gesture of good will to the new gallery.[85] Wheatley's complicity in the selling exhibition is confirmed in another article. It mentions that Fuller, at the invitation of Wheatley, had brought two hundred pictures, valued at £30,000, for the show. As a result of lack of sales, Fuller abandoned the idea of taking the collection to Johannesburg.[86]

Fuller expressed his disappointment and explained his position in a letter to the press: he had arranged similar exhibitions in other parts of the British Empire, the pictures were provided by the artists themselves and as a result the prices were reasonable. W. L. Dawson responded:

> While Mr. Fuller deserves sympathy, he must not lose sight of the fact that South Africa is suffering from a depression and that there is not the money to-day [sic] to buy paintings from oversea [sic] artists with which to equip our new art gallery. But most important of all, there are our own South African painters to consider, some of whom ... would very much welcome the sale of their works.[88]

A year after the opening, the trustees responded positively to a proposal by the Suid-Afrikaanse Akademie vir Wetenskap en Kuns (South African Academy for Science and Art), represented by Senator F. S. Malan and Dr. F. V. Engelenberg, to establish a National Portrait Gallery.[89] It would combine South African portraits already in the collection with those in the Houses of Parliament. Afrikaner nationalism, to which the promotion of the Afrikaans language and culture was integral, was on the rise and the influence of both government and J. J. Smith, a professor of Afrikaans at the University of Stellenbosch (US), was felt. Wheatley, a successful portraitist who held a powerful position, was naturally also in favour of such a move.

The idea was potentially fraught with problems, not the least being the establishment of a separate entity while the original architectural scheme for the gallery was still unfinished. The issue of a portrait gallery lapsed until after World War II when there was reference in the *Annual Report* to the piece of land adjoining the museum that had been allocated for extensions. The trustees undertook to take steps towards the erection of a portrait gallery.[90] The reply from government was in the negative, and trustees were informed: "as there were far more important buildings to be erected in all parts of the Union, no indication could be given when it would be possible to include this building in the Government's programme of works".[91] For once pressing national priorities and government indifference would prove to be in the best interest of the institution.

Four years after its official opening, the gallery building still required completion and to this end the board successfully approached the government. Adjacent properties had to be purchased, not only for this purpose, but also for "future extensions".[92] Clearly the board was anticipating growth and the concomitant need for expansion. Four additional galleries and a director's house were handed over before the end of 1939.[93]

A national museum without a full-time professional director

ACT NO. 23 OF 1931 provided for the constitution of certain state-aided institutions that included the "The South African National Gallery". It was to be governed by a board of trustees comprising nine members: four appointed by the minister; two representatives of SAFAA, which had succeeded the founding Cape Fine Arts Society; one representative from UCT and US respectively; and a representative of CTCC. Later augmented by the addition of the University of the Western Cape (UWC) and the Friends of the Gallery (FONG), this body served SANG for many decades – for better or for worse at times. For all that, government interests would, in decades to come, be mitigated by the presence of SAFAA and some high-profile academics who brought intellectual capacity, scholarship and expertise to meetings.

Even after the incorporation, the gallery did not have a full-time director. Instead, there was one non-professional custodian and a secretary-keeper, P. Thatcher, who served until 1940. There was no regular purchase grant and acquisitions were completely dependent on the insight of the trustees and their advisors abroad. Their lack of interest in South African art was particularly glaring: after 1895 not a single presentation or acquisition of local art occurred for twenty years. It was a continuation of the early collections and a manifestation of prevailing colonial attitudes. Bokhorst estimated that among the seventy-four works that Von Dessin owned and the thirty-two that were bequeathed to the Dutch Reformed Church, not one was by a South African artist. Bayley, encouraged by De Smidt, acquired three Cape scenes by the German artist W. H. Hermann, who had immigrated to the Cape in 1869 and he supported the artist, cartoonist and publisher William H. Schröder. The CFAS exhibitions comprised art from abroad and work by local artists and art students. Once again it was De Smidt who took the lead, both as regards SAFAA's acquisitions and the nature of the exhibitions held in the gallery.

Increasingly the absence of a museum professional came under fire, both from the public and the press. This untenable situation, which thwarted the efficient and expert running of the institution, was partially rectified with the appointment of Wheatley and Edward Roworth, artists who held professorial titles at UCT's Michaelis School, as honorary part-time directors. However, their involvement presented new challenges. There were obvious conflicts of professional and personal interests: both were artists who, as teachers and public functionaries, contributed to shaping opinion, as well as to the on-going blurring of the difference between a commercial concern and a national art museum. Both Wheatley (curator, 1925–35; board chairperson, 1927–35; director, 1935–36) and Roworth (board member, 1930–38; acting director 1939–41; director 1941–48), would, however, become enormously influential through their involvement with the gallery. Bokhorst politely describes them as "well-known artists" and "competent teachers, but by no means trained museum men". He adds: "Old photographs of exhibitions held in the period bear this out, if only by the rather clumsy display."[94] By the mid-1940s the board requested a grant-in-aid to appoint a director, but this was not forthcoming.[95]

Roworth was a bastion of intransigent artistic attitudes and, at the height of his power, a virtual dictator of taste. He both stoked controversy and criticism, as well as engendered the same in kind. As early as 1910 he attacked the "mass of inferior paintings" in the collection "which could with advantage be removed from the walls and consigned to oblivion".[96] Once he had established himself, nothing could stop him. Three years after taking over the directorship of the Michaelis School from Wheatley, Roworth boasted of his ambition to create a national school and movement "for freedom, truth and beauty," and how the teaching offered was "free from the alien and disintegrating influences" of modernism. In his inflammatory vilification of all modern art, particularly in France, he used descriptions like "poisoned art", "beauty sabotaged", "obscene half-wits", "mountebanks and madmen" and "mental anarchy". France was occupied by the Nazis and as far as Roworth was concerned, the country was "ripe for national downfall" because the French were chiefly responsible for the decadent art forms and unable to "cleanse their art and their country".[97] Among his actions, he took down works by the pioneering Jewish expressionist painter Wolf Kibel.[98]

The avalanche of criticism and support that followed, as well as Roworth's lengthy response informing the public of the depth of his knowledge of "Modernismus" – and his concomitant ability to judge – was summed up in the *Cape Times* (27 September 1940). The article records the shock and dismay of artists like Cecil Higgs, François Krige, Lippy Lipshitz and other members of the New Group, a vanguard association of artists founded in 1938. In his letter to the *Cape Times* (26 September 1940) Harry Trevor referred to the "pathetic illogicality of his verbal attack on Paris," adding:

> I would like to point out that there is one country that has had the "moral courage (?) to cleanse their art and their country," and that is Germany. We have no knowledge of any significant art developed under the dictatorship of Hitler, but obviously the aim of German artists in Germany today is the idealisation and glorification of Germany and all she stands for.

In his reply to Roworth, titled "Nazism in Art The World's Debt of gratitude to the "Modernists" in France" (*Cape Argus*, 27 September 1940), artist Neville Lewis outlined the history of modernism in France and again linked Roworth's speech to Hitler's views on art. "And what has happened to art in Germany since? The few good artists (and architects must be included) that she possessed have fled from the country, and the rest do what the Nazis order them to do. Is this the sort of thing Professor Roworth would do for South Africa?"

A "critic" worried that students at the Michaelis School were subjected to Roworth's "bumptious intolerance" and hoped that some of the more gifted students would have "the courage to ignore the prejudices of their mentor and go, artistically, where inspiration drives them" (*Cape Argus*, 26 September 1940). W. H. Gravett suggested in the *Cape Times* (27 September 1940), that members of the public view the exhibition of Roworth's "artistic attempts" and those of his associates at Ashbey's Galleries in order to assess the "revolution" he was preaching. In the same newspaper, a correspondent identified only as Hazlitt urged a visit to the SASA exhibition "where a number of Prof. Roworth's star pupils are exhibiting the most anaemic and technically incompetent imitations of Turner, Etty and Wheatley".

In his fulminations against modernism and his pro-Hitler stance, Roworth was enthusiastically supported by the reactionary art critic Bernard Lewis, who also served as a trustee. One of Lewis' most notorious articles was entitled "Exhibition in the Avenue What Would Hitler Do?" It was a tirade against the "modern" painters represented on *The Third Annual Exhibition of Contemporary South African Art* at SANG. He quoted from a speech made by Hitler at Nuremberg on 1 September 1933, and praised Hitler's "wise words" and condemnation of Cubism, Dadaism, Expressionism and "the cult of primitiveness generally". Hitler labelled this art as "degenerate" – *entartete Kunst* – and regarded the exponents as a danger to society. Lewis wrote:

> Insanity or insincerity – that is the alternative Herr Hitler puts before his people, when animadverting against modern art. Well, I ask myself, is he wrong? No, I think Hitler is right, and that this alternative – insanity or insincerity? – continually arises when one examines this so-called modern art. [99]

Roworth's reactionary viewpoint endured and was endorsed by the board chairperson, Cecil Sibbett, who wrote and circulated a pamphlet denouncing modern art among members of parliament.[100] The art critic of the *Cape Argus* (25 September 1947) questioned what he perceived as Sibbett's personal prejudice in art being conflated with an official attitude emanating from the board. Sibbett's retort as board chairperson appeared in the *Cape Argus* (29 September 1947) and was titled "Against the 'Cult of the Ugly'". On the one hand it was another tirade against the evils of modernism; on the other it promoted the Bailey Bequest, a recent gift to the art museum:

> Visit art galleries and see what the Great Masters of art have done, and thus cultivate your taste. In the National Gallery in Cape Town, there will soon be the Bailey collection. It contains some of the most beautiful pictures ever painted, as well as a huge collection of delightful sporting prints. The collection will probably make it the finest south of the Equator.

In 1948, towards the end of Roworth's directorship, artist Jean Welz denounced the Michaelis School and the "so-called National Gallery" as British Victorian institutions (*Cape Times*, 25 June 1948). Welz was quoted as saying:

> Please do not misunderstand me – I think that the British culture is a very high one and that it contributes a huge amount of human thinking knowledge to South Africa and the South Africans, but I do think that the time has arrived when our own art should be independent and forceful.

Welz refuted the allegation that modernists distorted art, when in fact they worked with meaningful, holy and mysterious symbols that are not readily understood. He blamed the United Party (UP) government for the disinterest in art and hoped – mistakenly so – that matters would improve under the newly-elected National Party, in particular the interior ministry of Dr. T. E. Dönges.

Writing in 1971, Bokhorst referred to Wheatley's and Roworth's roles in the history of SANG:

> Both were ... practising artists of the old style with a conservative personal taste in matters pertaining to art. The result was that the modern art of South Africa in the period from 1930 to 1948 was neglected as regards purchases. Of the leading artists of the period, like Maggie Laubser, Irma Stern, Lippy Lipshitz, Hugo Naudé and [J. H.] Pierneef, only one work of each during almost twenty years, was bought, while of [John] Dronsfield, Cecil Higgs, Kibel, [Strat] Caldecott, [Walter] Battiss and the Everard family nothing was obtained. As excuse it can of course be brought forward that the purchasing funds were extremely limited in those years, but then again we notice that in the year 1943 alone no less than eleven sculptures by Mitford-Barberton were bought.[101]

This was the context in which four paintings by Gerard Sekoto arrived before the board on 15 December 1944. Sekoto was well on his way to gaining a reputation as a pioneering modernist painter. After winning second prize in the May Esther Bedford Art Competition, organised by Fort Hare University College in 1938, he gave up teaching and moved to Sophiatown in Johannesburg to establish himself as a full-time artist. Sekoto met artists Judith Gluckman and Alexis Preller, participated in exhibitions and had work accepted for the annual exhibition of the South African Art Academy in 1939. The following year the Johannesburg Art Gallery (JAG) bought his painting *Yellow houses: A street in Sophiatown* (1940). Living in District Six in Cape Town from 1942 to 1945, Sekoto met members of the New Group and exhibited with them. Bernard Lewis may well have seen Sekoto's work at his show with sculptor Louis Maurice in 1944, which prompted him to write to Roworth:

> There is something Big about this native's work and I would like to ask him to let a couple of the oils be sent up to our Board Meeting, Friday, for you & all of us to see, as I think the Gallery aught to possess one of Sekoto's early work [sic]. I think he is a forerunner of real native modern art. Nos 20, 28 & 32 (especially 32) are most impressive.[102]

Lewis' enthusiasm and efforts were in vain, as none of the paintings – *The Swimmer* (thirty guineas), *Mother and Daughter* (forty guineas), *The Evening* (twenty-five guineas) and *The Green Plant* (fifty guineas) – were purchased; no reasons were given in the minutes. How utterly disappointing this must have been for Sekoto.

There was no regular purchase grant, but works of art were bought locally and abroad. The minutes of the meeting of 15 December 1944 confirm that there was at least £400 in the special purchase grant and that British painter William Maxwell Reekie, who bought art works from Manchester on behalf of the board, would be paid £300 owed to him for out of pocket expenses, as well as 5% on the price of pictures. [103]

On a positive note, under the directorship of Wheatley and Roworth, fifty-nine paintings previously on loan from Lady Michaelis – architectural drawings by Baker and Solomon and costume designs by Melvin Simmers – were acquired. The acquisition reveals the catholic approach taken to building the collection.[104] More temporary exhibitions, for example presentations to SANG and memorial exhibitions of South African artists, were organised and the need for labels and catalogues identified. Remarkably, an exhibition of South African prehistoric art – including a large number of rock art tracings – was arranged in collaboration with the South African Archaeological Society and the South African Association of Arts (SAAA) in 1946. A checklist of the holdings was started.

Trustees of the Carnegie Trust supported educational activities and their donations of colour reproductions, combined with "lantern slides" from the Michaelis School, meant that in the financial year 1938–39 some 2,000 pupils from sixty schools in the city and suburbs could visit SANG and benefit from instruction. Art was sent to various schools and associations in Windhoek, Morreesburg, Somerset East and the East London Museum.[105] However, there was no education officer at SANG. It would take six years before the education programme – still supported by the Carnegie Trust with collections of photographs and reproductions – benefitted from the Cape School Board's decision to appoint an "itinerant art teacher". [106]

Much was changing for the better, but financially the institution remained in dire straits. The grant-in-aid from government was £2,950, and CTCC provided £500 in the 1941–42 financial year. The lack of financial support was duly noted in that year's *Annual Report*:

> There can surely be no *National* Gallery in the world so niggardly provided with funds by the State! That the Gallery is a distinct addition to the amenities of Cape Town may be deduced from its large number of visitors, which during the year averaged three hundred a day, a fact which might be expected to elicit a more generous treatment from the City.[107]

A scandalous chapter in the history of the Gallery

THE RICHNESS of the foreign collections is largely due to the generosity of the early patrons of the arts who donated or bequeathed important collections to SANG, and its history is inextricably linked to their gifts and loans. During the period 1930 to 1950 there were significant presentations from Alfred de Pass, Sir Abe Bailey, Lady Michaelis, Sir Edmund and Lady Davis, and Henry van den Bergh.[108] The institution also benefited from British donor agencies like the Contemporary Art Society and the National Art Collections Fund.[109] The Abe Bailey Bequest comprises portraiture and one of the world's largest collections of nineteenth-century British sporting and hunting pictures, including fine paintings by George Stubbs, Alfred Munnings, Henry Alken and J. F. Herring.[110] As will be discussed below and in subsequent chapters, this sub-collection within the bequest was controversial from the start – it is extensive, uneven in quality and in some quarters it was, and still is, deemed inappropriate for the national art museum.

The story of long-term loans to SANG started in 1948 with the Lycett Green Collection, which remained for six years. There was, however, still a dearth of works by South African artists (immigrant as well as locally born) in the collection. Alfred de Pass took the lead by adding examples of European as well as South African art over a period of twenty-five years (1927–49).[111]

Entrance to SANG was free, and, according to the *Annual Reports*, the combined impact of the additional galleries and World War II saw a dramatic increase in the number of visitors, many of them foreign servicemen passing through Cape Town. In 1934–35 the visitor numbers were 86,337, growing to 100,751 in 1940–41, reaching a peak of 131,708 in 1942–43, after which numbers would fluctuate – they were never below 120,000 during the war years. A visit to the gallery was potentially hazardous:

> As the problem of safeguarding the gallery, should there be an air-raid in Cape Town, had arisen, the trustees instructed the acting director to take measures for the protection of the building from incendiary bombs and the pictures, visitors, and staff from high explosive bombs. Containers for sand and long-handled scoops have been placed on all the roofs and in the interior of the building. Ladders have been provided for scaling the roofs. A shelter trench has been constructed in the garden of the gallery which will afford protection for about fifty people. First-aid equipment has also been provided for the staff when dealing with incendiary bombs.[112]

Two years later valuable works were removed to a "place of safety"; three galleries were closed and used by students of the Michaelis School for the duration of the war.[113]

Fortunately these precautions were not needed, but nothing could protect the permanent collection from Roworth and the board – the body appointed to safeguard it, in perpetuity, for the South African nation. Art historian Jillian Carman states:

> Between 1944 and 1947, the South African art archive suffered a series of incidents that would be amusing had they not been so tragically pathetic. Because of monumental ineptness – the bombastic arrogance of one individual and a lack of oversight from his board of trustees, no doubt due to preoccupation with the effects of the Second World War – South Africa lost some of its first publicly owned paintings and, in the process, an irreplaceable visual archive.[114]

Bokhorst summarised the loss in 1971:

> Unfortunately, not only many minor works and doubtful attributions to masters thus left the Gallery, but also a large number of works of real historic or artistic value, amongst them some twenty from the nucleus bequeathed by T. B. C. Bayley, which cannot be traced any more to present ownership.[115]

Of Von Dessin's collection – the first to be displayed for the benefit of the community – only a few remained, and some forty paintings by South African artists were sacrificed, including one by Gregoire Boonzaier, a board member from 1946, seemingly without his knowledge.[116]

At the June 1944 board meeting Roworth referred to clause five in article twenty-three of the 1931 statute that governed SANG and advised the trustees that they could sell any work of art:

> ... provided it had not been transferred or bequeathed to the Board subject to a prohibition of alienation ... the present was an excellent time for selling pictures ... stored in the basement as they were not of sufficient merit ever to be hung in the Gallery.

PLATE 2: Daphne Taylor, *The Brazen Serpent*, c. 1928, oil on canvas, 1525 × 1835.

Roworth was authorised "to make a careful selection of such pictures and to arrange for their sale"[117] and began selling what he considered as inferior artworks, far below their real value and not in compliance with the legislation he quoted.

There was no mention of this in the *Annual Report*: accessions were recorded, but not de-accessions. Further selling sprees followed, in 1945, 1946 and 1947, and it was only in the 1946–47 *Annual Report* that the board made public its decision. The announcement was paired with a justification: "As no special grant for purchases had been received since 1936, the Board has tried to build up a fund for this purpose by exercising rigid economy in other directions, and by selling pictures which were considered not of a standard to hang in the National Gallery."[118] There were no guidelines about the "standards" to which they constantly referred, and it was left to the director to decide on the merit or demerit of artworks.

In 1946 Roworth sold sixteen pictures to the Pieter Wenning Gallery for £80. In the same year a sub-committee, comprising Roworth, Boonzaier and Bernard Lewis, was appointed to make "a careful selection" and this resulted in a list of 136 paintings. Considering their tastes and attitudes to art, this was a triumvirate that would guarantee that more rather than fewer works would be sold: Roworth and Lewis represented the reactionaries, while Boonzaier, being a founding member of the New Group, represented the "modern". One of the paintings sold had previously attracted Lewis' ire. In 1931 he described Daphne Taylor's *The Brazen Serpent* (c. 1928) as "a large canvas, without colour, without design ... which flaunts so cheap a symbolism" (Plate 2).[119]

Various dealers were invited to inspect the selection with a view to purchase, four responded, but only A. Krook of the Art Centre in Johannesburg made an offer of £1,200. As an alternative, the board engaged the services of a Johannesburg auctioneer, E. Lezard, who valued the collection at 900 guineas, estimated that they would fetch 1,400 guineas on auction and offered £1,100. He was willing to sell the works on auction, provided that the sale was advertised as "being reluctantly disposed of under direct instructions of the Trustees in order to make room in their galleries for the huge collection of pictures bequeathed by the late Sir Abe Bailey".[120] Lezard also wanted slips printed, signed by the director and pasted on the back of unsigned paintings, to confirm the authenticity of the work as stated in the catalogue. These demands, coupled with the expenses that an auction in Johannesburg would incur and the certainty of Krook's offer, encouraged the trustees to sell to Krook.

Lezard had raised the thorny issue of the arrival of Bailey's gift and its display. Bailey's will provided for a choice that the trustees accept the collection in its entirety, or that it be offered, in whole or in part, to any gallery or galleries in South Africa. Advised by Roworth, they accepted the entirety of the bequest. While they were reluctant to acknowledge the demands placed on space and the connection to the sale of pictures, it is clear that room had to be made. Many works on paper arrived in October 1946, with the oil paintings and watercolours following in January 1947.

Comprising over 400 artworks, the Bailey collection was hung in the three new galleries. It was opened on 5 March 1947 by Prime Minister Jan Smuts, whose Randlord-backed United Party was in the

FIGURE 8: Sale of works, 1947; collection National Library of South Africa.

twilight of its hold on power.[121] Smuts was generous in his appreciation of Bailey, the man and of his gift to the country, going as far as to say that Bailey "even stimulated a parsimonious Government to add to your gallery. Now Cape Town is quite well equipped with artistic wealth".[122] However, Smuts also described Bailey as a "son of the soil" who had few opportunities for education and who did not pretend to possess great discernment in art. Alluding to the British sporting and hunting pictures, Smuts conjured up an inspirational image of "the eerie loveliness of South Africa and the opportunities which its manifold and wonderful charm offers the artist of the future".[123]

It was at this point that the matter of de-accessioning finally entered the public domain, followed by an outcry and severe criticism and condemnation of the administration in the press. The chairperson of SANG's board called a special meeting on 3 April to discuss the matter and make a public statement. Ironically, in the same *Annual Report*, the trustees expressed their appreciation for the bequests, gifts and loans received, including more works from Alfred de Pass. They purchased paintings by Neville Lewis and J. H. Pierneef. Among those bought by Maxwell Reekie, their representative in England, was *Des Pins Parasol* (1925) by the French Impressionist Lucien Pissarro.[124]

Income from the sale amounted to £1,238.7.0, but £568.17.6 had to be spent on the recovery of works sold during 1947: £70.12.0 for the eight pictures presented by Lady Michaelis; £25 for *The Ever Open Door* (1918) by F. G. Roe; £400 for the sixteen paintings presented by SAFAA before 1895; and £73.5.6 on solicitors' and advocates' fees.[125] The trustees and Roworth showed complete disregard for their culpability and continued to find excuses and apportion blame, in short a deplorable lack of responsibility. At the time of the 1947 sale they had been "unaware" that some pictures were part of the fifty-nine presented by Lady Michaelis under a Deed of Gift that required them to be housed permanently at SANG (Fig. 8). Furthermore, Roworth had "inadvertently" included eleven works from the presentation in the 1944 and 1945 sales. It had proved impossible to recover ten of these, as they could not be traced and A. J. ter Beek, who had taken over the Pieter Wenning Gallery, returned a small painting without charge. Dr. Villet sternly criticised the administration at a meeting of the city council held in April 1947 and the grant-in-aid was suspended pending an inquiry.[126] It was subsequently reinstated.

Public art museums are not ideologically neutral, and once again the national art museum – perceived to be a mirror of society – could not remain impervious to profound political change in the country. The repercussions of the sales reached the highest levels of government. In this regard a member of parliament identified only as Naudé put a question to the acting interior minister, and requested that an "explicit statement" be made "to prevent a recurrence of this sort of thing in future".[127] This led to a formal parliamentary debate, held on 29 April 1947 and published in the *Hansard* of that date. It was primarily concerned with the circumstances and the facts of the sales, and the expectations among the people in the Cape, and in the country as a whole, that something should be done about it. However, the debate uncovered many simmering cultural and political issues. As recorded in the assembly proceedings, there was outright denunciation of SANG's administration and of the director, by both UP and NP members of parliament. The very purpose of the national art museum came under the microscope.

In a lengthy speech, MP Bertha Solomon, who was evidently well informed about what was going on, acknowledged that the institution was poorly supported by the government, but that it did not fulfil the purpose for which it was erected – it did not send works of art to country towns and did not share loan collections with other galleries. She reprimanded Roworth for having rejected the "functions for which the National Gallery should exist", when the main function was to "actively propagate all art knowledge amongst the public and not of one school only". Solomon maintained that there was no catalogue of the collection and that the books purchased with the Carnegie Institution grant were not accessible to the public. She criticised Roworth's hostility to modern art and his refusal to accept what was recorded in the *Hansard* as the "Cassierer [sic] Loan Collection" of French paintings, including works by Paul Cézanne, Honoré Daumier, Camille Pissarro, Auguste Renoir and Vincent van Gogh. According to Solomon, Anton Hendriks, director of JAG, snapped it up.[128]

Correspondence with Jillian Carman, an authority on JAG and author of in-depth publications on the collections, revealed that Solomon's information was not correct and that it was highly unlikely that the collection was offered to SANG. In the interviews Carman conducted with collector and dealer Reinhold Cassirer, he never mentioned that Roworth had rejected the collection. Cassirer took care of what was known as "The Hague Collection", on behalf of the extended Cassirer family. In 1935 he smuggled it out of Berlin in a train – the pictures off their stretchers, rolled up and thrown into the luggage rack. The collection's name derives from the Gemeentemuseum in The Hague where the collection was stored until 1939 when Reinhold Cassirer, by then living in Johannesburg, arranged with Hendriks to bring it to South Africa, where it was placed on loan at JAG (1939–61).[129] These dates do not tally with Solomon's reference to "a little while ago" in 1947.

Both Solomon and UP MP Humphreys were prepared to overlook the sales, but they were concerned about the method of the disposal – without public notification or a call for tenders. Humphreys admitted that it was "a bad policy and great pity", especially as regards selling works by South African artists, and further cautioned that private donors would be reluctant to give pictures to the gallery if this were to happen in future. Questions around the value and authenticity of some works sold had also put unsuspecting private collectors, who innocently purchased fakes, "under a cloud". South Africa had moved from a "pioneering stage" to the "cultural stage" and government needed to do more to protect and educate the public.[130]

NP member W. D. Brink described SANG as an "Imperial" gallery not a national gallery. For him, the greatest scandal was not that the artworks had been sold, but that "apparently they were sold at these ridiculous prices to make room for approximately 300 pictures which were imported from abroad and which do not appeal at all to South Africans". He noted that three rooms had been set aside for the Bailey collection, and that South African paintings, some of them of a high standard, were removed. The gallery was subject to "studious de-nationalisation with the object of promoting the process of Anglicism". Parliament was being asked to vote £4,000 for the art museum, added Brink, but there was no information about the works available in the gallery and he could not be attended to in Afrikaans.[131]

Humphreys agreed that the "racing pictures do not belong to a National Gallery. I have no fears. The racing pictures will not remain there very long ... Room will be found for them elsewhere".[132] Interestingly, he was echoing Jan Smuts' words as reported in the *Cape Times* (6 March 1947) that the pictures were to be held in trust for the South African people, "to be kept as one collection as a gift to the new Art Gallery subject to suitable accommodation being provided for their housing and display". The collection remained at SANG.

All the speakers urged the minister to pay attention and act on the matter and manner of the sales.

Shocked by the public and state disapproval, and in a bid to protect what was left of their reputations, the trustees requested an inquiry by a public service inspector. Government responded by appointing a commission led by James Stratford, chief justice of South Africa (1939–43), to enquire into and report on the affairs of the gallery. His findings are contained in the *Report of the Commission Appointed in Connection with the S.A. Art Gallery, Cape Town*, generally referred to as the *Stratford Report*.[133] It was a thorough investigation in every respect, its findings captured in a nineteen-page report that analysed the situation and made recommendations for future policy and administration. In addition to visiting the gallery, inspecting the records and interviewing board members, Stratford obtained a detailed report from the public service inspector, V. G. Chowles. He advertised the terms of reference of the commission and the sittings in the newspapers and requested submissions from interested parties; eighteen memoranda were received. Through diplomatic channels in London and The Hague, he sought information and suggestions from the National Gallery in London, the Frans Hals Museum in Haarlem and the Rijksmuseum in Amsterdam.

The board submitted a statement, focussing on and once again trying to mitigate their complicity in the sale; they additionally flagged the art museum's inadequate financial resources. They emphasised the need to appoint a full-time director (not a practising artist but a trained museum professional) and the principle that no sales of pictures (still ongoing seventeen years after the scandal of the opening of the new building) should be allowed at SANG. Additional office and cloakroom accommodation was requested.[134]

Stratford was somewhat ambivalent about the sale of works from the collection, but in their response to his report, the trustees finally recognised that the conduct by the governing body and director was unconscionable and needed to stop. They recommended that such sales be entirely prohibited.[135] To this day SANG is guided by the outcomes of the Stratford commission, its collections safe-guarded by a strict policy that no works may be alienated or de-accessioned unless they are damaged beyond repair. As this history unfolds, it will become clear (especially in the later chapters) that ongoing vigilance is required.

Against a backdrop of looming parliamentary elections in May 1948, which would usher in the NP and inaugurate a period of hard-line white nationalism, executive oversight of SANG was moved from the Union's interior ministry to the education department as early as April 1948. As a result of the *Stratford Report*, the government grant increased from £2,850 to £4,000 (when in fact £10,000 was needed) and immediate steps were taken to advertise for and appoint a fulltime director.[136] The board was impelled to act. Various decisions regarding better administration and management of the gallery were taken at the June 1948 board meeting. They included: the need to take cognisance of general trends in contemporary art and the promotion of exhibitions of South African art; a request that the Liberman Room be restored to its original purpose, which was the display of South African art; the need to appoint a registrar and establish a finance committee; an injunction against private work being undertaken by employees on the premises during working hours; and a prohibition against restoration work until a director was appointed.[137]

In what can only be described as a knee-jerk reaction to the negative press, it was agreed that art critics be invited to attend board meetings.[138] Following objections by Lycett Green and Dr. T. B. Davie, this was subsequently amended. Minutes from a board meeting in 1948 stated: "The public and press will be invited to the Annual Meeting of the Board, and may be invited to attend other meetings at the discretion of the Board."[139] Eighteen years after the scandal created by the selling exhibition with which the new building was opened, Boonzaier requested reconsideration of such exhibitions; fortunately he did not succeed.

A key protagonist in the whole saga, Roworth only resigned in 1949. Although the *Stratford Report* had declared a preference for a bilingual (Afrikaans and English) South African-born director, the post was widely advertised, locally as well as in Great Britain, France, Holland and America. The trustees saw this as the beginning of a new era in the history of the national art museum, which could provide services for the whole country.[140] Interviews were conducted with seven applicants, two in Cape Town (P. A. Hendriks and J. W. von Moltke, whose name was not on the original list), the remainder in London, the interviews handled by board members R. W. Wilcocks and T. B. Davie. They reported back on John Paris, then deputy director of the Walker Art Gallery in Liverpool, and A. C. Sewter, stating that "neither of them had exceptional personality" but that they were "first class men" and suitable for the position. However, they did not compare well with Hendriks, then director of JAG, who was highly thought of in Johannesburg. It was reported that he had "much more drive" than Paris or Sewter, he had both "long experience in South Africa" and was completely bilingual. Hendriks was the board's first choice, Paris second.[141]

However, Hendriks withdrew his candidature after inspection of the collections on exhibition and in storage, stating that "in view of the financial basis on which the Gallery is run at present it would be extremely difficult to turn the Gallery into an institution of truly national importance". He envisaged "years of work" for any director in shaping the collection given the institution's lack of funding: "only when generously supported financially would the Gallery become an institution worthy of its name". He communicated his wish to continue with his important work in Johannesburg, which, unlike SANG, was more generously resourced.[142]

In her contribution to the parliamentary debate on 29 April 1947, MP Bertha Solomon pointed out that the national gallery had received £3,650 in the 1945–46 financial year, that it would increase to £4,000, but that it was still much less than the £5,000 that the municipality allocated to the Johannesburg Art Gallery.[143] Writing in 1942, Lord Harlech stated that lighting, hanging and arrangement at SANG was far better than the crowded JAG, but that the national collection lacked the "generally high quality and interest" of the Johannesburg gallery.[144] While Harlech congratulated trustees and benefactors on assembling a collection of European art that offered much "to appeal and to give pleasure" to people familiar with larger collections abroad, he felt that there were "still many square yards of painted canvas that I would prefer not to look at. It may be that in a later age merits which it is hard for one of this generation to see may be rediscovered".[145]

It is pertinent to note Ruth Prowse's unhappiness that Von Moltke was not considered for the position. This discontent did not augur well for the future, as Prowse was against the new director from the onset and would lead the vendetta against him.

PLATE 3: Albert Adams, *Cape Town Harbour,* 1959, oil on canvas, 1220 × 910; courtesy of Edward Glennon; photographer Pam Warne.

2

Professional directors appointed – John Paris (1949 – 1962), Matthys Bokhorst (1962 – 1973) and Carel du Ry van Beest Holle (1973 – 1975)

1949 – 1975

THIS CHAPTER covers the tenure of three directors: John Paris, Matthys Bokhorst and Charles du Ry. It commences with the arrival of Paris, the first professional director. Visionary and controversial, Paris sets new standards for acquisitions, exhibitions, conservation, education, policy development and record keeping; he is dismissed after clashing with some board members, but leaves an important legacy. Bokhorst breaks new ground with the establishment of the Friends of the Gallery in 1968, programmes for blind and partially sighted adults and children, and overseeing some relief of the space constraints. Du Ry's tenure is brief. The role of assistant directors is highlighted, with particular focus on Bruce Arnott, who takes the initiative in the fields of acquisitions and exhibitions of the art of Africa and the aesthetic production of black contemporaries. South Africa's febrile political situation (1960 Sharpeville massacre, white republicanism) is absent from official documents. The grip of apartheid, as well as international reaction to it, nonetheless impacts policy and purchases, and the art museum's reputation.

What really happens next may be chance or miracle,
but like any other future it remains to be hoped for with
a high heart, prayed for and worked for.

JOHN PARIS[1]

John Paris arrives from Liverpool

FIGURE 9: Portrait of John Paris, August 1950; image courtesy of African News Agency/ANA.

JOHN PARIS ARRIVED in Cape Town in January 1949 (Fig. 9).[2] Journalist Eric Allen's description of SANG's new director was very different from the verdict of the board members who interviewed him in 1948:

> John Paris is electric with vitality. Brisk in speech and movement, but never brusque. Aggressive, but far from overbearing. Altogether charming, in fact, as all the artists whom I know have been telling me these 12 months. He has the knack of seeming to take you into his confidence from the start and the gift of giving the impression that he is interested in you – as I don't doubt that he is, for a man so very much alive himself could hardly fail to be interested in living people.[3]

As the preceding chapters have shown, the institution was badly in need of scholarship and professionalism, and Paris' vision and international experience would soon have an impact on all aspects of SANG's mandate and activities. He set about to develop policy for every function of the museum; his thirteen-page memorandum was adopted at a special board meeting held on 15 June 1949 and attached to the minutes. Paris' knowledge of art history and his extensive experience, combined with a sense of purpose, informed the document. It remains in all respects still valid in the twenty-first century, albeit that many of the ideas that are essential for sound and dynamic museum practice, have fallen by the way in public art museums in South Africa.

In the memorandum Paris outlined the purpose and tasks of the institution and analysed its current state. With respect to the organisation, he emphasised the importance of record keeping, organising and circulating exhibitions throughout South Africa[4] and publications – catalogues, books illustrating the collection, leaflets, reprints of lectures in a numbered series, monographs on South African art and artists, posters and a Quarterly Bulletin for the "Friends of the Gallery" (the organisation did not yet exist). These initiatives would advance the prestige of the gallery at home and abroad, as well as its educational role. His wide-ranging interests and taste were reflected in plans for lectures and demonstrations to schools; these would include design and applied art, home decoration, town planning and architecture, all with a view to stimulating critical interest in "every day things" in towns, cities and the countryside. To achieve this, the secondment of a qualified art teacher from the department of education was required. He outlined the professional staffing needs, from curatorial and cataloguing to security attendants, from conservation to technical, and the finances that were necessary to realise his ideas.

Paris' rearrangement of the gallery, as set out in his memorandum, was both visionary and controversial. It was visionary in the suggestion that a permanent collection be formed and displayed of original examples of "Prehistoric Art and Bushman rock paintings and engravings", together with copies, tracings and photographs "so that the Gallery may become the world centre for the study of this universally important section of art history" and that in time an archive would be created for the study of the subject and for the benefit of students and scholars throughout the world. He recommended replacing the casts of antique statuary in the atrium with indigenous historical art as an appropriate introduction to the Liberman Room dedicated to South African art. Thus South African art would be displayed in adjoining spaces.

The proposals contained in his memorandum were controversial regarding gifts and loans. Observing that a whole wing was occupied by the A. A. de Pass gift and the Lycett Green loan collection, Paris proposed that rooms no longer be devoted to individual collections, but that they be split up and integrated into arrangements according to schools and periods. This resulted in much opposition from donors and lenders, and contributed to the strife and witch-hunt to which Paris was later subjected.[5]

Although Paris did not mention it directly in the memorandum, this would also apply to the Bailey bequest. A number of the works were not on display, resulting in suggestions that sporting pictures not exhibited be offered to other galleries, for example to JAG and Durban Art Gallery (DAG). The Bailey trustees were agreeable, but held SANG responsible for the safety of the paintings should they be loaned; nothing came of the idea and the Bailey collection continued to exert pressure on gallery space.[6]

In order to build a collection that could "uphold the honour of the Union before the many overseas visitors" who were keen to ascertain and study the characteristics of South African art and culture, a coherent policy and purchase grant were essential. Compared to JAG, the financial situation at SANG was rather shocking. Where JAG was boosted by £9,000, followed by £5,000 annually for acquisitions alone, SANG received a total of £7,200 composed of £5,550 from government, £700 for cost of living allowance and £1,000 from the CTCC. The grant to the national institution, wrote Paris, should not be less and "the needs, considering the present state of the collection, are far greater than that of the already admirably stocked municipal Gallery of Johannesburg". Little wonder Hendriks declined the directorship.

Paris recommended that, in addition to the official grants and the gifts and bequests that enriched the permanent collection, an "art collection fund" should be created and that judicious tax concessions be sought. There was however a caveat attached, one that has continued to ring true through the decades since:

> But whatever can be done through private enterprise will depend entirely on the gesture the Government is prepared to make to show that it seriously means to undertake the development of the National Gallery as the main National institution and the pride of the whole nation.

This, combined with resolution shown by the board, argued Paris, would also stimulate interest in the public domain.

Paris' greatest priority was augmenting the collection, which he regarded as "extremely unrepresentative and haphazard" – the result of lack of money and a coherent policy. His acquisition policy was inclusive of South African artists and craftspeople, but he affirmed the importance of setting up and maintaining an international critical standard. He cautioned against being parochial: "a nation is judged by the excellence of its arts", and asserted that "purchase for the National Gallery is not by personal sympathy or lack of sympathy, but by objective consideration of the importance of the various contributions which the artists have made to the story of the country's art".[7]

PLATE 4: Mario Radice: *Composition*, 1940, oil on wood, 868 × 645.

Constrained by the financial situation, and in his effort to enhance the existing collection, Paris initiated an unusual practice – substituting less representative works of South African artists for more recent and better examples.[8] This is contrary to accepted practice, whereby an art museum strives to build a collection of an individual artist's oeuvre over time. This desire for modernising the image of SANG resulted in the purchase of the first abstract painting, in 1957, by the Italian artist Mario Radice: *Composition* (1940) (Plate 4).

Paris' memorandum of 15 June 1949, which was followed by many in the years to come, was submitted to the Museums Committee of Inquiry that had been instituted in the same year. Another substantial policy document, which expanded upon the principles and ideas stated in the first, was approved by the board on 27 January 1950 and detailed in the *Annual Reports*. Especially pertinent was Paris' call for the Gallery to collect "Pre-Historic and Native Arts Indigenous":

> Examples chosen for high aesthetic quality rather than for Ethnological interest should be acquired for an introductory section prefatory to the South African Exhibition rooms … The point to be made here is that many primitive and pre-historic objets d'art have very great and universally recognised aesthetic merit and are very important to the study of contemporary art. *It is pointed out also that in an art museum the line of demarcation between fine art and Ethnology should not be drawn too narrow* [my italics].[10]

Paris was acutely aware of the provincialism that prevailed in influential art establishments and circles in South Africa, and the focus on aspects that were hardly related to art:

> There are too many petty controversies, too much quibbling over inessentials, over distinctions between modern and traditional painting and so on. The South African National Gallery is interested in all painting, and in showing it as completely and accurately as possible. Its purpose is not to develop a painting industry but to foster a South African art.[11]

He resisted classification of art as "modern" or "old" or any label for that matter, as context was important and every work formed part of the whole history of art.[12]

At Paris' second board meeting Boonzaier again raised the vexed question of selling shows at SANG, nineteen years after the scandal of the opening exhibition; the new director advised that this was not how national galleries operated. The matter was forever laid to rest. As far as Boonzaier's enquiry about charging for exhibitions was concerned, the Regulations were clear: entrance should be free of charge. It was nevertheless agreed to approach the secretary for Education.[13]

In 1951, Joachim Wolfgang von Moltke, a specialist in old masters and prints, who had been teaching art history at Michaelis, and who had been shortlisted for the directorship, joined Paris as assistant director.[14] They served together for the next eleven years. Bokhorst described the period as a "two-masted ship [that] sailed on a stable course and with remarkable success,"[15] and that – for some time at least – could conceal the growing tensions between the director and certain board members, as well as the chairperson and the board. Minuted criticism appears just a year after Paris' arrival, about a matter for which he was not responsible.

The focus of the disapproval was the 1948 government-sponsored exhibition of contemporary South African paintings, drawings and sculpture, organised by the SAAA, and selected by a committee advised by John Rothenstein, director of the Tate Gallery in London, who came to South Africa for the purpose. It ran at the Tate Gallery from 21 September to 31 October, and then travelled to Paris, Amsterdam, Ottawa and Washington before opening at SANG in November 1949.

Dr. D. F. Malan led the NP to victory in the 1948 election with the promise of reinforcing institutionalised racial segregation and discrimination and safeguarding white supremacy in the country. The exhibition, a flagship international event for the new government, came in for some severe criticism, both in London and Cape Town. London *Sunday Times* art critic Eric Newton noted in an article on 26 September 1948 that the exhibition was "premature". He stated that there were "samples of all kinds of intermediate stages between childhood and adolescence, but that maturity was not yet in sight," and further that South African art did not yet exist.

Judgment in The Netherlands and Belgium was different. In an article in the *Cape Times* ("How Oversea [sic] Critics View South African Art," 7 February 1950), R. K. Cope analysed the different responses. The exhibition had been "a revelation" for a Dutch critic ("Art in South Africa is on the way to being South African art"), while a Flemish reviewer wrote, "The exhibition, which in many ways arouses interest, will undoubtedly be the starting point for the initiation of new manifestation in art." Cope pointed out that no-one from South Africa was in London to speak about the exhibition, and that Bokhorst, one of the selectors who was on leave in Europe at the time, was present in the Low Countries and in France. Bokhorst "established cordial relations with the Press, and interested the leading dignitaries of the countries. His work of a part-time and voluntary nature, was an outstanding achievement".

Locally, journalists and members of the public responded and engaged in heated for-and-against debates. Expectations of a school of South African painting had not been met and the exhibition was not seen as representative. The furore, however, also pivoted around the issue of the selectors, the followers of "the more decadent tendencies of modern European art" and the fact that it had not been shown in South Africa before going abroad.[16]

According to an article published in the *Cape Times* (1 November 1949) at the time the exhibition was being installed at the gallery, 85,000 visitors saw the exhibition in London and thousands of catalogues were sold. L. A. Sanderson, organising secretary of SAAA, reported that the exhibition attracted considerable coverage and reviews were not as unfavourable as imagined in South Africa, where people concentrated on negative criticism. The work of Walter Battiss, Moses Kottler and Gerard Sekoto received the most attention. The exhibition did not travel in South Africa as envisaged. A lack of funds was cited as reason, which is rather strange and short-sighted after the substantial investment in the overseas tour; negative criticism and local hostility must have influenced the decision.

At the forefront of a high-profile attack on the exhibition was Cecil Sibbett, the powerful trustee who in 1947 bypassed the board and wrote to cabinet ministers when Roworth was in charge. He repeated his action, condemning the selection in his ministerial letter; he also proceeded to blame Paris, who had inherited the project, for the selection and exhibition at SANG. This led to a special board meeting at which Sibbett was hauled over the coals. The board passed a resolution reiterating its "full confidence" in Paris; they further stated that "any criticism of the Director or works exhibited in the Gallery should be raised at Board meetings and not with Ministers or officials outside the Gallery, nor with the public and press."[17] This incident was the beginning of a protracted quarrel that marked Paris' tenure.

Paris acted on his vision and the department of pre-historic and indigenous art was inaugurated with a loan exhibition of transcriptions of rock art from South West Africa (Namibia) and Southern Rhodesia (Zimbabwe) by Henri Breuil (a.k.a. Abbé Breuil), a Catholic priest, archaeologist, anthropologist, ethnologist and geologist known for his studies and drawings of rock art in Europe, China and Africa. Loans of rock engravings were also secured from the Transvaal Museum (now Ditsong Museum of South Africa in Pretoria) and paintings from the University of the Witwatersrand. Abbé Breuil was present at the opening of the exhibition, which was accompanied by a catalogue.[18]

Under Paris' direction, SANG acquired a reputation as an ambitious and outward-looking institution. Added to his focus on South African art and artists, including a memorial exhibition for the expressionist painter Wolf Kibel, were important overseas exhibitions from many different countries, and international art curated from local collections. The permanent collection was catalogued and extensive publications and educational materials were produced.

Paris' catholic and eclectic approach impacts on the national art museum

IN 1952, white South Africans celebrated the tercentenary of the founding of a refreshment station at Table Bay by Jan van Riebeeck for the Dutch East India Company (VOC). The NP government used the opportunity to assert and demonstrate its power. The day of 6 April was declared a public holiday and named Van Riebeeck Day (later Founder's Day). Questions and discussions about the simmering racial tensions in the country are not documented in the minute books or Annual Reports. Clearly the board and director chose to be – or wished to be perceived as – apolitical.[19] They could surely not have been oblivious of the launch of the ANC's Campaign for the Defiance of Unjust Laws on the same day, and the start of the campaign on 22 June 1952.[20]

The former colonial powers were enthusiastic about participating in the 1952 Jan van Riebeeck Tercentenary Festival, as it was officially known. The Netherlands sent an important exhibition of seventeenth-century Old Masters and maps of the Cape from the Rijksmuseum and Mauritshuis, while Britain provided sculpture by Henry Moore and Old British Masters (1730–1840) (Fig. 10). Paris, the English internationalist, uttered nationalist sentiments as if born to the manner: he reiterated the slogan of the Festival ("We Build a Nation") and linked the achievements of the Dutch Old Masters to the arrival of "our founder". Of course, he also saw great value in exposing the local public to superb works of art, and to offer opportunities for comparison with SANG and Michaelis Collection holdings.[21]

FIGURE 10: SANG atrium as part of *The Meaning of Sculpture* exhibition, with works by Henry Moore, 1952.

These exhibitions attracted much positive publicity, as they were rare events. Brian Lello dedicated a large section of the *Cape Times Weekend Magazine* to the exhibition of Dutch Masters and Deane Anderson, an art historian and newspaper critic, wrote about the British School. Anderson commented on the "extraordinary simplicity and refinement of the portraiture, and the almost scientific approach of the landscape work," singling out Thomas Gainsborough's and Joshua Reynolds' portraits and the landscapes of John Constable and J. M. W. Turner. He concluded that the thirty-four masterpieces balanced "the great achievements of Dutch art on the opposite side of the courtyard. These two fine exhibitions set a standard of twin cultures which, combined, can form a sure foundation on which to build a nation".[22]

While Paris was seemingly caught in nationalist ideology, his ambit and vision for South African art and for the gallery were much greater. Taking the sculpture and drawings by Henry Moore and some of the older British works as sources of inspiration, he developed the watershed exhibition *The Meaning of Sculpture* that he regarded as the centrepiece for the 1952 Jan van Riebeeck Tercentenary Festival (Fig. 11). It comprised three parts: African sculpture juxtaposed with small Renaissance bronzes (from the Alfred Beit Collection) against a background of paintings and a tapestry in the entrance room; Moore's work, combined with textiles, in the atrium; and South African sculptors from the permanent collection and loaned from artists and private collections, in the Liberman Room, displayed in the context of *objets trouvés* from nature and different materials such as stones and woods used for three-dimensional expression. Not only did this arrangement speak of curatorial creativity and conceptual depth, it had a strong educational component. Paris selected specific sculptures by Lippy Lipshitz, Moses Kottler, Coert Steynberg and Anton van Wouw – all well-established South African sculptors by then – to reveal the way in which they used the grain and properties of stone or wood to express ideas or carve portraits.

FIGURE 11: *The Meaning of Sculpture*, installation of African sculpture with small Renaissance bronzes from the Alfred Beit collection, 1952.

Henry Moore's sculpture attracted much attention and controversy. Madeleine Masson, an aristocrat and author of minor repute, quoted the artist extensively in the *Cape Times* (29 March 1952). She regarded the exhibition as one of the most important seen in South Africa, and one that allowed the public, perhaps for the first time, to discover "the true meaning of sculpture". Many visitors, however, regarded the work as incomprehensible and in letters to the press applied labels such as "crude", "uncongenial" and belonging to the "kindergarten of sculpture". According to Masson, others were swayed and moved: "With a shock of surprise visitors who came to jeer remained speechless before the beauty of the Henry Moore figures. They have the beauty of trees and stones which have been animated by the hand of man."

One visitor complained about the absence of labels in the exhibitions. In a letter to the *Cape Argus* (31 March 31 1952) Paris offered a lengthy explanation that casts light on his approach to installations, the value of catalogues and the visitor's experience. Works of art were numbered, as labels, according to him, disfigured the walls and distracted the eye, and he wanted to encourage the public to use the catalogues systematically: "These catalogues contain full information in the form of prefaces, introduction, annotations and historical details with which repeated visits to the exhibitions may be greatly enriched." He added that catalogues did not generate income and that the sales of the English versions reduced the loss on the Afrikaans ones – in one weekend 390 in English were sold compared to twelve in Afrikaans, and this was for the Dutch exhibition.

Throughout his directorship Paris' choices reflected his catholic and eclectic approach – to what was appropriate for an art museum, and he consistently eroded boundaries of art and craft, high and low art. Highlights of the decade were *French Contemporary Paintings; Graphic Art of the 15th/16th century* and *Chinese Ceramics* from the South African Museum and private collections; photographs of Indian architecture and sculpture, *Japanese Prints and Contemporary Graphics*; sculpture by Gerhard Marcks; *Malaysian Art* (sculpture, textiles and silver from Dutch East-India) and *Middle Africa and Early Christian art* that drew on Irma Stern's private collection; Rembrandt etchings and Impressionist paintings from The Netherlands; etchings by Francisco Goya from Spain and *Modern Israeli Artists*; *Contemporary Italian Art*, prints from Austria and photographs of contemporary Swiss architecture; and *French Tapestries, Antique and Modern*. An exhibition of eight scroll paintings by Japanese artists Iri Maruki and Toshiko Akamatou, secured from Tokyo, proved a hit. The exhibition depicted scenes related to the bombing of Hiroshima in 1945 and attracted 5,900 people in one month; special admission of 1 shilling for adults and 6 pence for students was charged, and 1,690 catalogues were sold at 2 shillings each.

The *Annual Reports* (1949–60) were upgraded with illustrations of acquisitions and installations, which from the perspective of the researcher constitutes an invaluable resource. They were also indicative of Paris' embracing purview of aesthetic production – from pre-history to the present, from applied art to contemporary expression. The first issue, for 1949–50, featured sixth-century textile fragments gifted to SANG by Raymond Henniker-Heaton on the inside cover. For later editions Paris chose examples from gifts or loans, for example, from the Alfred Beit presentation and the Robinson Collection. There are images of an enamelled ceramic (1477) from the School of Faenza, Christmas cribs on loan from artist Pranas Domsaitis and acquisitions of work by contemporary South African artists such as Lippy Lipshitz, Irma Stern and Alexis Preller (Plate 5). Paris included installation shots of the 1952 Dutch and English exhibitions, as well as the much-debated *The Meaning of Sculpture* exhibition.[23]

As part of his professionalisation of the museum, Paris encouraged the board to create sub-committees to deal with specific functions, ensured the appointment of an education officer and created a children's club.[24] The work on compiling a checklist of the holdings, initiated in 1943, continued. In the 1950–51 Annual Report it is stated that library donations from eight countries had been received. Much of his directorship is remembered as one of stability and excellence, and for the move away

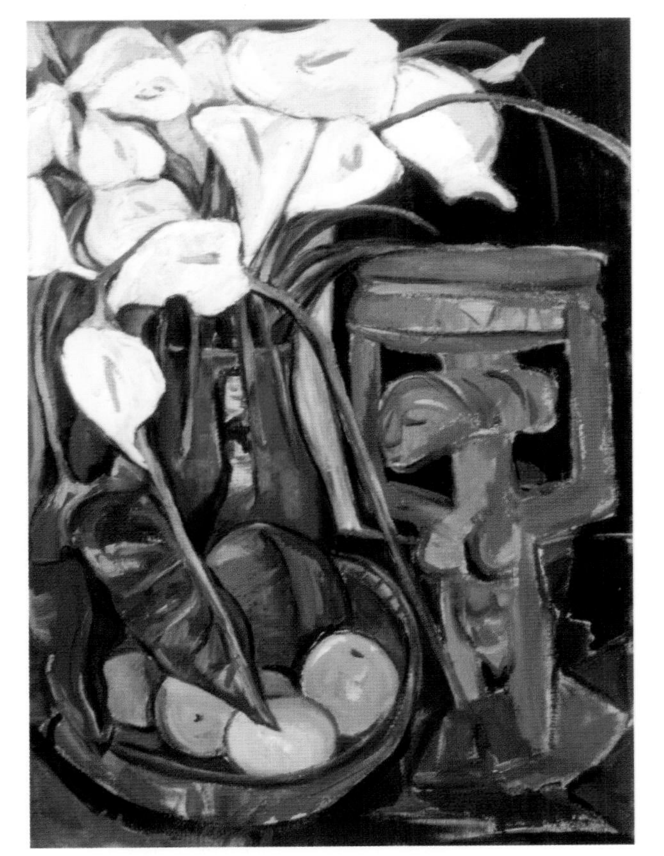

PLATE 5: Irma Stern, *Arum Lilies*, 1951, oil on canvas, 900 × 650.

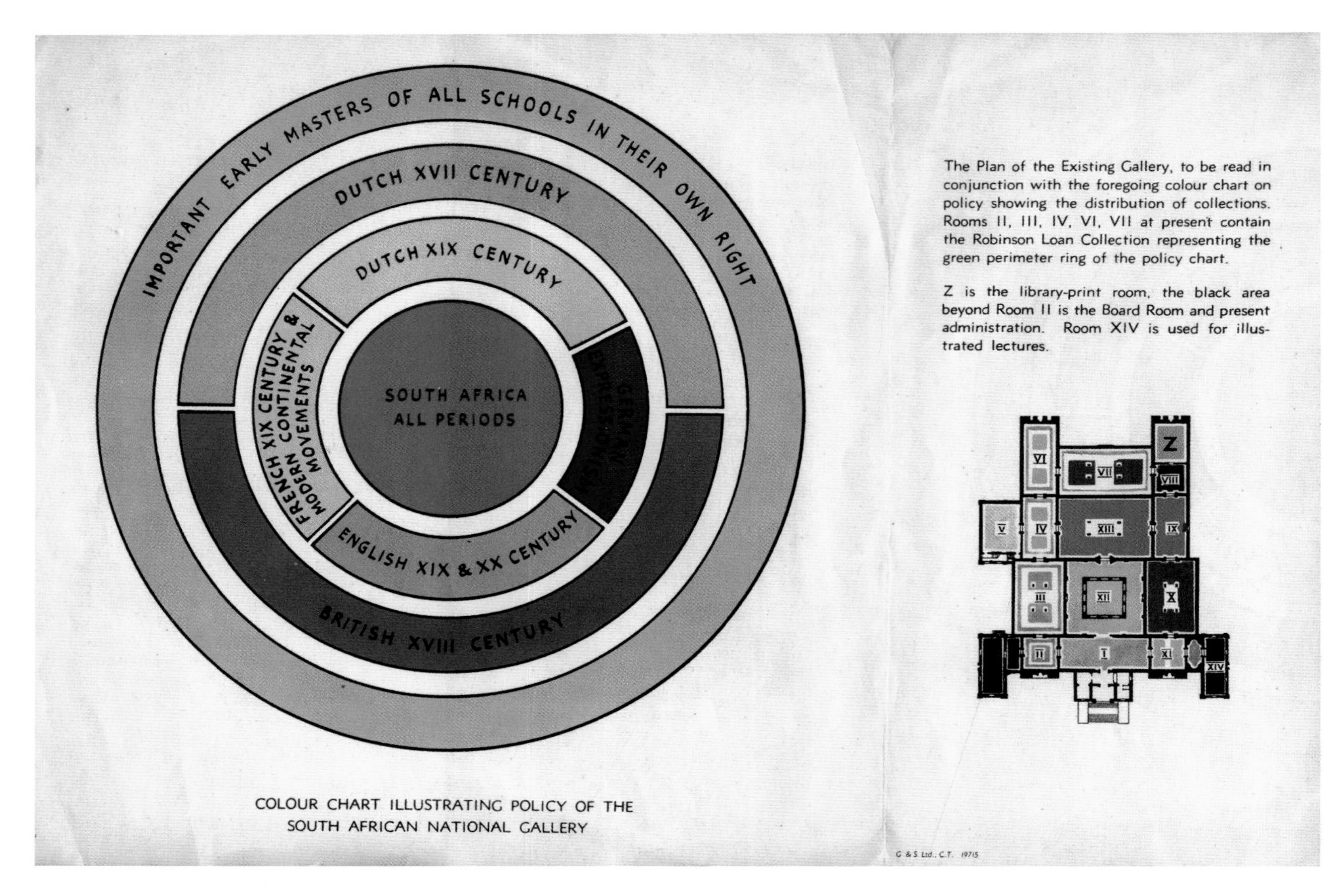

FIGURE 12: Alfred Honikman, *Colour Chart Illustrating Policy of the South African National Gallery,* 1958.

from the conservative personal tastes of the Michaelis directors towards a greater engagement with the art of the times, including a number of South African artists, including Walter Battiss, Eleanor Esmonde-White, Katrine Harries, Cecil Higgs, May Hillhouse, Maggie Laubscher, Gustave Preller, Jean Welz and Florence Zerffi.

The context in which South African artists' work was exhibited and interpreted was that of the "founder nations" in particular and European art in general. This is illustrated in a 1958 combined floor plan and *Colour Chart Illustrating Policy of the South African National Gallery,* compiled by CTCC representative and chairperson at the time, Alderman A. H. Honikman (Fig. 12).[25] In his handwritten Preface, Honikman expressed the hope that the diagram would assist visitors in a better understanding of the story told at the gallery, enrich their experience and encourage them to return. The plan of the gallery was to be read in conjunction with the circular colour chart showing the distribution of collections; at the time the Robinson Loan Collection represented "important early Masters of all schools in their own right". Apart from the Liberman Room and a gallery adjacent to it, which contained South African art of "all periods," artists were linked to the European art that influenced them and the countries in which they studied or were born. For example, J. H. Pierneef and Pieter Wenning were linked to nineteenth-century Dutch art; Pranas Domsaitis, Maggie Laubser and Stern to German Expressionism; Gwelo Goodman, Neville Lewis, Roworth and Rupert Shephard to nineteenth- and twentieth-century English art; and Bettie Cilliers-Barnard, Maud Sumner and Maurice van Essche to European modernism.

The vast improvements made in the display of artworks were possible because of the extensive renovations of the building. A request to extend the main building and upgrade the heat and humidity control – formulated in 1948, and presumably based on plans submitted by Kendall some years before – was approved and implemented. It provided for the introduction of air conditioning in certain parts of the building, cloakrooms and accommodation for the technical department. The additions above the atrium aisles, accessed by a winding staircase, housed the library and administration.[26] According to Bokhorst, the generous flat occupied by the director "remained a luxury considering the almost complete lack of facilities for a growing Administration".[27]

Paris' achievements speak clearly from the pages of the newspapers, *Annual Reports* and board minutes. Visitor numbers reached an all-time peak of 161,128 during the 1953–54 financial year. He visited other provinces and cities, gave lectures that were recorded and broadcast, opened exhibitions, wrote articles and letters to the press, and participated in committees and initiatives at local and national level. The Minister of Education appointed him, together with Von Moltke and Professor F. E. J. Malherbe, to organise South Africa's first participation in the XXV Venice Biennale in 1950. They selected painters Walter Battiss, John Dronsfield, Cecil Higgs, Irma Stern, Maud Sumner and Maurice van Essche, and sculptors Elsa Dziomba and Lippy Lipshitz.[28] Responding to an attack on the selection at a public lecture in Stellenbosch, Paris stated that the artworks were intended to "show some characteristic aspect" of South African art, and "something of the contact of South Africa with European and with indigenous primitive art".[29]

No acquisitions of work by black South Africans were made under Paris' directorship, which is surprising when assessed in light of policy statements and his pioneering curatorial initiatives. It would seem that he had not come to terms with this aspect of local art, and that painters like Moses Tladi and Gerard Sekoto did not fit into the classifications that he detailed in a memorandum to the trustees, dated 29 September 1950. In some instances he named specific artists: Africana (Thomas Baines and Thomas Bowler); pioneers (Frans Oerder, Pierneef and Pieter Wenning); groups and schools (for example South African impressionists, the New Group); trends and movements (contact with contemporary trends abroad and artists who have "sought out new idioms for themselves or tried to discover a style indigenous to the country"); predictions (accomplished young artists whose reputations were still to be made); and prehistoric and native, primitive and indigenous.[30]

Paris drew attention to the importance of collecting prints and drawings and applied arts, and he appended a list of seventeen painters and sculptors not represented or inadequately represented in the SANG collection. He listed Sekoto, but his declared interest came to naught. In 1953, nearly ten years after Sekoto's four paintings were rejected by the board, the trustees bid on a work at an auction, but the offer of £50 was too low. Considering that there was £4,970 in the special purchases fund, it says a great deal about the value they, and the director, placed on Sekoto's paintings.[31]

Moses Tladi was the first black artist to have his work displayed on the walls of SANG when he participated in the *Exhibition of National Contemporary Art* in 1931 (Plate 6). Tladi exhibited at the gallery again in 1933 and remained more or less forgotten until Hayden Proud included him on an exhibition, *The*

PLATE 6: Moses Tladi, *Spring*, c. 1931, 180 × 240, private collection.

Advancement of Art: The SA Society of Artists and its Exhibitors, 1902-1950, which celebrated SASA's centenary in 2002. Fitting recognition would come much later. Sekoto was the only black artist to be included in the 1948 Tate Gallery exhibition and had his first Paris exhibition opened by W. G. Parminter, the Union minister in France.[32] Did they perhaps not meet his criteria of international standards and non-parochialism? "Native" was used to describe the work of living black artists, while "Indigenous" referred to the rock paintings and engravings of the San. This may explain why the word "Native" was replaced by "Indigenous" in the minute books, as the former would encourage the acquisition of work by contemporary black artists. It remains a conundrum.

A vendetta against the director and his departure

THE 1950s are remembered for the loan collections which were obtained for considerable periods of time. Remarkable among these were the Alfred Beit Collection (1949–54), described by Bokhorst as "perhaps the most exquisite collection of old masters the Gallery ever had"; the collection of modern French and English paintings and drawings belonging to Mr and Mrs Peter Hughes (1953–54); and the

Robinson Collection, for which the Gallery had waited thirty years – it arrived in 1959, thanks to the Princess Ida Louise Labia, the daughter of mining magnate J. B. Robinson.[33]

The Lycett Green loan collection of European Old Masters, which was assembled in Britain in the 1920s and 1930s, was still on display when Paris arrived. Yorkshireman F. D. Lycett Green was badly injured in the First World War and struggled with poor health. He had summered in the Cape and moved there in the hope that his health would improve. Differences between the director and the collection's owner, who was also a board member, led to protracted controversies that would, in part, contribute to Ruth Prowse's move to indict Paris, and eventually to his departure. At this time, Prowse – a painter, teacher, keeper of the Michaelis Collection, member The New Group and representative of the SAAA on the gallery board – was a key figure in the Cape Town art and museum world. Attributions and display of the Lycett Green collection had been an issue since 1949.[34] It came to a head in 1952, with the director's well-reasoned report on and classification of the collection into an A, B and C list, which the board accepted. Paris did not wish to show the collection in its entirety: of the 113 pictures on loan, he proposed hanging forty permanently, with thirty-eight in reserve to be used from time to time; he rejected thirty-five. Acceptances were provisional to the review of what Paris described as "many extremely ambitious attributions," a process that he had started, and that concerned works wrongly attributed to masters such as Andrea del Sarto, Peter Paul Rubens, Antoine Watteau, Paris Bordone and Tintoretto.[35]

In September 1953, Paris expressed his concern to the board that many works in the collection were actively infested. Two months later Lycett Green proposed that Paris' qualifications and suitability for the directorship of the SANG be reviewed.[36] He was convinced that Paris, having come from the Walker Art Gallery in Liverpool, was not competent to judge Old Masters. Lycett Green was also unhappy with the director's report: he wanted part of his collection exhibited all the time and threatened to remove it if not satisfied with the hanging.[37] He solicited a report from John Pope-Hennessy, then assistant keeper of architecture and sculpture at the Victoria and Albert Museum (later director of the British Museum), which he submitted to the trustees. Pope-Hennessy declared Paris' assessment devoid of clear thinking, patronising and inept, and indicative of the limitations of his taste and the inappropriate nature of the aesthetic criteria applied. He stated that collections were not all either in uniformly good condition or unvarying in quality and that the educational value had been overlooked.

In his reply to the board, Paris pointed out that Pope-Hennessy's behaviour was not collegial, as no discussion had taken place with him, that Pope-Hennessy had no knowledge of the pictures, and that he was unaware of the conditions in South Africa. Paris frequently referred to these conditions and that the judgment of works of art by visitors could not be compared with those in Europe; consequently the quality of what was shown was extremely important.[38] Inaccurate and ambitious attributions could serve to misinform a public that would have no means of comparison with great works of art. Sibbett again communicated directly with the minister. Honikman was shocked at the tone of members conspiring against the director. Professor F. E. J. Malherbe, acting in his capacity as chairperson, asked trustees to submit written comments on the management of the gallery on or before 15 December 1953, "to ascertain whether the grounds for such complaints could be explained or rectified, before lodging any such complaints to any outside body".[39]

Honikman, who would be a sane and steady voice as the disagreement escalated, reminded the board that Lycett Green's demands were in conflict with a board resolution of 28 July 1950 that no gifts or loans should be accepted with conditions attached.[40] The lender agreed to withdraw the conditions, but instead of engaging with Paris on the rehanging of selected pictures, he tried to set Von Moltke up against the director. He then summarily withdrew the collection through a direct communication with the minister of education, rather than the board. He offered the paintings as a gift to the York Gallery while the pottery remained at SANG. Lycett Green was dissatisfied with both the director and the board, but he ultimately held the board, which stood by its policy, responsible. Prowse also intervened by bringing up the removal of the loan with the SAAA, the professional body she represented on the board, but which in fact had nothing to do with the running of SANG. She further fuelled public debate and condemnation of Paris in the press.[41]

All along the director defended himself against the accusations, reminding the board of his memorandum of 25 May 1949, which they had approved. He also reiterated his qualifications and pointed out his functions and responsibilities. He had done everything to avoid withdrawal of the collection and was subjected to an enquiry without warning. In 1953 he took a month's sick leave due to overwork, and to "replenish aesthetic sensibilities ... [that] may become blunted by long contact with local circumstances".[42] These few words speak volumes about the parochialism against which Paris guarded, and his need to balance local circumstances and demands with his professional, internationalist ambitions.

On receipt of the written comments requested by the chairperson on the management of SANG from Lycett Green (who remained a member of the board), Prowse and Buisman, Paris fought back in a thirteen-page document dated 31 January 1954.[43] The director was understandably troubled by the "perpetual controversy," lobbying, insinuations, arguments and highly personal attacks on his character and professional reputation, and was considering taking legal action against the individual trustees.

In the memorandum Paris outlined his achievements and challenges and described some of the personalities with whom he had to deal. They included A. A. de Pass, who would enter the gallery at will to hang and remove works from his presentation. He reiterated the board's support in his opposition to hampering restrictions that were attached to bequests, and in the gallery's exercise of absolute and unconditional control and use of the collections. Paris had transformed SANG, which had a high profile and positive responses from the public, but he was held back by the four board members who consumed his time and energy, local art controversies and lack of resources.

Under the heading "Possible Motivation for Malice" Paris took the four dissenting board members to task, pointing out that Prowse and Sibbett were trustees at the time of the sales and the Stratford Report, and further that Sibbett was in the chair. Sibbett was notorious for going behind the backs of the board and director, as well as writing about art under pseudonyms such as "Philistine" and "Scutator". Paris referred to articles like "A Noodle's Creations" and maintained that they had caused embarrassment in Liverpool and London, and that they were detrimental to the reputation of SANG. Both Buisman and

Prowse were SAAA nominees and the latter had a personal dislike of Paris, constantly contradicting him and interfering in purchases and with staff, while there was a conflict of interest in her roles as SAAA member and keeper of the Michaelis Collection.

Concluding his case for conspiracy and malice, and attempts to discredit and destroy his authority, Paris stated that complaints were never discussed with him and that steps needed to be taken "to expunge the calumnies from the records, for the prevention of the continuance of such ill will, and for giving me a free and reasonable opportunity henceforth for the pursuance of my work". It was all to no avail. The board minutes, instead of elaborating on Paris achievements, are filled with unremitting attacks against him, questioning his judgment, purchases, exhibitions (down to the labels) and management style, undermining him at every opportunity. Prowse insisted on a ministerial enquiry at board meetings. Honikman resisted. In October 1954 a resolution was passed that the matter "stand adjourned for six months and that thereafter if in the opinion of the Board there is sufficient fresh evidence to justify and inquiry, the Minister be informed".[44]

Professor T. B. Davie, UCT's principal and vice-chancellor, put his concerns about the "witch hunt" that had extended beyond individuals to the SAAA in a letter to the chairperson (9 June 1955). He confirmed that the Lycett Green loan was accepted in 1947 without any conditions and that the lender had subsequently imposed them. "His removal of the pictures was undertaken despite several efforts on the part of the rest of the Board to persuade him not to do so and to accept the fact that agreement seemed to be possible between him and the Director in respect of the great majority of the pictures," noted Davie.

The British press vindicated Paris' measured views of the Lycett Green collection when it went on display in York. He wrote to the chairperson in this regard on 23 May 1955 and the next day he submitted a lengthy memorandum in which he analysed the publicity under two headings: news (in the local York press, the *Times* and *The Illustrated London News*) and criticism (the *Burlington Magazine* and *The Listener*). He quoted from the *Burlington Magazine* of April 1955:

> There are no masterpieces; and though the collection is rich in minor masters, there are many pictures which do no credit to the collection as a whole. One wishes that there had been sixty pictures instead of 130: for it is all too easy to allow one's appreciation of the real merits of one half of the collection to be tarnished by consciousness of the shortcomings of the other half.[45]

Paris' basic positions had been upheld and he reiterated that he at no time advised that the collection be removed, but that he requested modifications to major attributions and divided it into the three categories. He remained convinced that withdrawal of the collection, rather than showing it in its entirety, was in the best interest of the country. He concluded:

> I still firmly believe that I served South Africa and the interests of the National Gallery to the best of my ability in these findings. Nor was this disagreeable controversy one of my seeking; but rather it was one thrust and hurried upon me, which I could not in honesty shirk, and which in the light of the responsibility with which you have honoured me as your advisor and executive officer, I have not shirked and do not.

Prowse, however, remained a pitched adversary. Malherbe tried his utmost to control her, warning her in a letter (8 August 1955) that by uttering and broadcasting possible libel she was laying herself open to action, based on the Regulations governing the institution. Her accusations were seemingly devoid of facts, evidence and witnesses, and he warned her that the persistent controversy was affecting the work of the director and the board. Prowse was undeterred, insisting in correspondence that she was acting in the best interest of the gallery, suggesting that Paris be given an opportunity to resign. She further made reference to two matters that she should report, although what these issues were was never communicated. She did, though, cast aspersions on the director's physical and emotional state: "On Saturday afternoon, I saw the Director wandering alone along St Georges Street, looking wretched, and I felt desparately [sic] sorry for him, he cannot help himself."[46] Whatever ailed the director, there is no record of anyone – even his supporters – trying to help him.

In 1955 the vendetta against Paris, instigated by Lycett Green and Sibbett, was taken up with renewed zeal by Prowse, who submitted a six-page indictment asking for an inquiry into the administration of SANG.[47] She communicated her concerns under specific headings, starting with the loss of the Lycett Green loan collection; she reiterated the lender's lack of trust in Paris' capabilities and judgment. She took issue too with the director's bilingualism, an aspect that would be farcical if it were not so inward-looking and counterproductive. Prowse further accused Paris of neglecting South African art and went into a detailed criticism of how inadequate his arrangements were, as well as the absence of the print room that he had promised. Her complaints against his management were similarly detailed: Paris had not reported on his attendance of meetings of the South African Museums Association (SAMA) and had not sought permission to join the committee of the heads of state-aided institutions.

Although the matter of the Michaelis Collection had long been put to rest, Paris' advice to the board once again came under fire in Prowse's document. Moreover, he had applied, albeit unsuccessfully, for positions at Natal University and the new Art Gallery in Salisbury, without informing the board. Meddlesome and interfering, Prowse also went into great detail about the proposed restoration of a painting by Gainsborough, commenting on the quality of the painting and giving advice on restoration. She complained that a bust of Winston Churchill by Jacob Epstein was not displayed, while the sketch for a tapestry by Edward Burne-Jones that had "no quality" held pride of place in the entrance gallery. Prowse's attack is filled with assumptions.

At the meeting held on 18 October, Malherbe expressed his concern that a committee investigating the charges against Paris would include his accusers; the board was uncertain about what to do and voted in favour of Honikman's proposal to seek legal advice. Two months later this was not yet available and therefore the matter could not be taken at the meeting of 20 December. However, in the absence of the chairperson, Davie, the indictment was discussed and the resolution to obtain legal opinion was rescinded. Subsequent legal opinion confirmed that the accusers were entitled to attend.

The board was deeply divided. A special meeting was set for 4 January 1954. Honikman was unable to attend but keen to assist the chairperson in ameliorating the situation. He was also deeply suspicious of what was going on and wrote to Malherbe to express his views for consideration. The chairperson read relevant extracts of the letter at the meeting and affirmed that he would "not be party to any illegal or irregular procedure".[48]

It is worth considering some pertinent views contained in Honikman's letter. He did not concur that the loss of the Lycett Green loan collection had set back planned development schemes, but attested that the persistent criticism of the director and concomitant loss of public confidence would be an impediment. "The attacks on the Director commenced long before the Lycett Green collection was removed. The nature of these attacks, the many trivialities and irrelevances they contain, are suggestive of persecution." He described Paris' memorandum as objective and courageous, considering Lycett Green's presence on the board; they had met and the board had imposed no conditions on the director regarding the hanging of the pictures.

Once again, Prowse inappropriately took an internal board matter to the annual general meeting of SAAA. She included a rather bizarre comment, from that meeting, in her indictment: Irma Stern had seen Paris at a hospital where he was having X-ray images taken of some paintings in the Lycett Green collection to assess their authenticity. In his letter Honikman conceded that removing works from SANG revealed a degree of indiscretion, but he did not see it as an offence. He asserted that Paris had made a serious effort to learn Afrikaans and that his limited knowledge "should not be used as a weapon with which to destroy him".

Honikman further pointed out that the director had persistently encouraged the board to acquire a more representative selection of quality works by South African artists. He rebutted the inference with regards the Michaelis Collection as unjustified, and stated that it was quite understandable that Paris would apply for positions elsewhere "in view of the unrelenting attempts that have been made to discredit him in the eyes of the Board and to obtain his dismissal that he should seek to safeguard his future and that of his family". This did not make him guilty of discourtesy, offered Honikman, and it did not provide evidence of bad administration of SANG. Rather, it was typical of the sort of criticism that had been levelled at Paris for the past three years. Honikman suggested that the director might be a victim of a personal vendetta. Honikman was clear that he held "no brief for the Director, nor has he requested me to take this course," but he had come to the conclusion that the indictment presented no basis for an enquiry into the director's conduct. He recommended that it be rejected.

As a result of Honikman's letter, the resolution adopted on 18 October – to seek legal advice – stood, the meeting was postponed, and those present proceeded with an informal discussion of Prowse's indictment.[49]

The saga of, and obsession with Paris' bilingualism (or lack thereof) is extraordinary, but it is also indicative of the increasing grip of the NP government on state institutions, and the ascendancy of Afrikaner nationalism. In terms of his contract, Paris had to develop some proficiency in Afrikaans within two years. It was discussed at many board meetings. In 1953, following a ministerial petition, Paris received an additional six months to learn the language. Legal advice to the board suggested that Paris' failure to become proficient could not be fairly described as misconduct, but that it related to contractual obligations. The board was told to act with great caution by its legal advisors: "It is a serious matter to impute misconduct to a person in the absence of reasonable and probable grounds."

The Deputy State Attorney also confirmed this opinion.[50] The indictment was, however, not a matter for the office of the State Attorney and he advised the board to consult their attorneys. He nonetheless expressed the opinion that there was nothing in the indictment that could lead to a charge of misconduct. The board's advocate set out the Regulations and urged the board to convene a meeting to determine facts in a bona fide manner, and to frame and deliver a charge, if deemed necessary. He came to the same conclusion as the Deputy State Attorney: "Unless other evidence is available, I fail to see how a charge of misconduct could possibly succeed," either in terms of Part V of the Regulations or the requirements of Common Law.[51]

The lengthy legal advice from the two independent sources was included in the board minutes of 21 February 1956. Vice-chairperson Prof. R. W. Wilcocks' proposal that the board should not ask for a government inquiry was carried (with the exception of Prowse), as was his second proposal that the board carry out no further investigation with regards the indictment, except for particular items and that points for discussion be forwarded to the chairperson. A copy of the indictment was to be placed in the minute book, next to Paris' reply, and any further action would depend on the chairperson.[52]

The indictment, and a memorandum from Paris acknowledging receipt (23 December 1955), were included in the minute book of 17 April 1956, but there was no document from the director. Prowse demanded a response from Paris in a letter and he agreed to circulate his reply to the trustees, but there is no record of such a document. It is relevant to note that while there were unsubstantiated accusations of mismanagement, SANG received a clean audit, with the exception of a query about the insurance cover for its collection.[53]

The issue was not discussed again in 1956, and Paris continued with his work in the face of formidable odds. In 1957, the minister of education, arts and science appointed a committee chaired by C. M. Booysen to enquire into the needs of institutions like SANG, and to establish how they could best serve the country as a whole. In reply to a questionnaire from the Booysen Commission of Enquiry, a board subcommittee was formed and Paris prepared a memorandum in which he detailed the functions and requirements of his institution.

The memorandum was attached to the board minutes of 2 June 1960 and included a motivation for an annual grant for the purchase of works of art, as well as a special grant towards the cost of publications. Other necessities were the appointment of an education officer and the purchase of a station wagon in order to send exhibitions to outlying towns. The statistics regarding lectures, concerts, loans in and out, and exhibitions and publications are impressive: in addition to the display of loan collections and gifts, Paris and Von Moltke had organised thirty-seven special exhibitions and produced thirty-three catalogues since his appointment in 1949.[54]

The Booysen Commission of Enquiry visited SANG in May 1961 and held a joint meeting with the board; a supplementary memorandum, expanding on the first, was submitted. The gallery's claim to national status, which at the time was still uncertain, was put forward. For thirty years SANG had been the only national institution and it had established an international reputation by negotiating major exhibitions with museums and embassies abroad. The board stressed:

> … the desirability for at least one recognised institution to be properly provided for, in the general interests of Art in South Africa, and that a major and balanced permanent Collection be insured; having sufficient specialised staff to maintain it properly, and to provide advisory, technical and educational services.[55]

A plea was made for having the classification of the gallery changed from a B to an A institution, which would enhance it status and funding. Considering its aims "at presenting South African art and its international context before the world," it required appropriate "recognition of due dignity and significance".[56]

SANG's board received the findings and recommendations of the Booysen Commission of Enquiry in June 1962. The most important immediate result was a purchase grant of R14,000 for the 1963–64 financial year, a huge improvement on the pitiful R600 previously allocated. The commission insisted that a strong policy, which differentiated South African and European art, be adopted for acquisitions. "Preference should continue to be given to the purchase of South African art as this is the primary purpose of the Gallery," noted the commission. Interestingly, it encouraged the acquisition of contemporary art of "our non-white races which form an integral part of the South African art movement". It supported the name and status of the institution, the purchase of a station wagon and the expansion of the reference library.[57]

In September 1961 Paris submitted a four-page report, accompanied by five letters in support, for the establishment of a department of conservation to serve SANG and various other associated and official institutions. It was followed by a report on gaps in the collection and a policy on which works would be suitable to loan to official houses. Despite the swirl of controversy around him, stoked in large part by Prowse, Paris was still very much in demand. He travelled to the William Humphreys Art Gallery (WHAG) in Kimberley, gave extramural lectures at UCT and stood in for painter Rupert Shephard during his absence as director at Michaelis.[58]

Little wonder then at his surprise and shock when Paris was requested to leave the board meeting of 27 November 1961. All previous resolutions were rescinded and a motion was tabled that Paris be informed he had lost the "confidence" of the board. The motion included a summary request that he tender his resignation by 5pm on 30 November 1961.[59] If he resigned he would be given maximum leave and the resolution would be rescinded and expunged from the records; however, if he failed to do so, he would be given three months' notice from 1 December 1961. Paris had the right to appeal to the minister within fourteen days. The board wished "to avoid unnecessary hardship, embarrassment or inconvenience," and Paris would have to take responsibility for publicity that might ensue, should he choose to appeal. On his return to the meeting Paris expressed surprise and agreed to consider the matter.

The December board meeting was poorly attended and little transpired. By the end of January 1962 Paris had not yet resigned. Once again he and Von Moltke, who was in attendance, recused themselves. Paris circulated a memorandum to the board. Dr. J. P. Duminy, UCT's principal and vice-chancellor, made a vital point: there were various complaints, but the board had not formulated any *specific* charges; he urged trustees to exercise caution and to review the previous resolution. This was not carried. The board was simply not prepared to compile a document and Paris would be given another chance to tender his resignation. Duminy objected. When recalled and informed, the director, after again expressing his surprise, referred to his track record and appealed to the board.[61]

The trustees were recalcitrant. Both this meeting and a further special meeting held in February 1962 were devoted to Paris' resignation/dismissal, including ancillary issues related to leave and his vacating the director's house. Paris decided against an appeal. His services terminated on 31 May. Von Moltke, who was designated acting director, had in the interim accepted a position as director of the Haus der Kunst in Bielefeld, Germany, starting on 1 July. In light of the perceived difficulties with Paris not acquiring sufficient knowledge of Afrikaans, it follows that the board would use the opportunity to look for candidates closer to home. Nevertheless, both vacancies were advertised in South Africa, Great Britain, Belgium, Germany, Holland and the USA.[62]

While all this was going on there is no reference to the aggravated political context in which the national art museum was functioning. The events on 21 March 1960, the eve of the fiftieth anniversary of the Union of South Africa, proved a fateful tipping point. The republican ideal – the NP's answer to British colonialism – had come to a head with Prime Minister Hendrik Verwoerd's announcement, two months earlier, that a referendum would decide on the country's future as a republic in the Commonwealth. This was a referendum for whites only and it exacerbated black anger at increasingly stringent pass laws. Sporadic violence in many places culminated in an anti-pass demonstration. In Sharpeville, a township south of Johannesburg, police shot and killed sixty-nine people. Public meetings were banned.

In Langa, a township near Cape Town, Philip Kgosana, regional secretary of the Pan African Congress (PAC), told some 6,000 men to leave their passbooks at home and surrender themselves, but to no avail. Police opened fire, killing two people; rioting broke out. The anti-pass march to police headquarters in Caledon Square took place on 24 March, followed six days later by one on parliament. Kgosana was arrested, a State of Emergency was declared on 8 April. Both the PAC and ANC were banned under the newly enacted Unlawful Organisations Act.[63]

Fifty-two per cent of white South Africans voted in favour of a republic in the referendum held on 5 October 1960. Fearing the embarrassment of expulsion from the Commonwealth, Verwoerd left the Imperial Conference in March 1961, and the country's membership expired with the proclamation of a republic on 31 May.[64] Politically isolated, the grip of apartheid tightened. The impact on SANG policy and purchases would soon be felt, as would international reaction to events in South Africa.

For the moment, however, many newspaper columns were dedicated to the departure of two art historians and museologists under whom the gallery had flourished. Paris enjoyed the support of the press. During the heat of the action against him he wrote a poignant opinion piece in the *Cape Times* ("Proud City Possession Needs Aid S A Gallery's Great Work Over 13 Years", 12 January 1962). His talents as a writer, his profound understanding of what was required and his love for the institution still speak powerfully from his article.

> As I look back what is it that I see? Certainly not a time where it has always been "five in the afternoon". I see a time of struggle and endeavour, of sunshine and shadow, of high hopes and disappointments, of storms and clashes, of times when we thought I had rounded the Cape, as it were, only to find we had not. There were periods of excitement and accomplishment and, over all, the unending struggle to establish a standard and give South Africa a National Gallery worthy to be called one.

He outlined the challenges of what had to be done, and undone, and the marvels of the great loan collections. He singled out the Alfred Beit Collection with its works by Francisco Goya, Jacob van Ruisdael and Johannes Vermeer, the Hughes Collection of modern French and English pictures and early Italian paintings, and the Gainsboroughs in the Robinson Collection, which South Africa lost when the government refused to buy it. These, together with the collections that were sent from The Netherlands and Britain for the Van Riebeeck Festival, "changed the whole balance and standard of criticism in South Africa and the way it all happened should not be forgotten". Among the thirty-nine special exhibitions, accompanied by catalogues, folders and brochures, Paris highlighted the memorial exhibitions of South African artists, the Chinese exhibition, the modern Italian exhibition "seized off a ship for us suddenly by the Italian Ambassador," the Hiroshima scrolls and French tapestries.

> We could see now what we had for ourselves that was good, and love it in perspective. It was all very nice, but a Gallery, however much it may interpret and teach from what it has, using everything it has to the full, dies gradually of a hardening of the arteries unless it is always acquiring, always revaluing, always reinterpreting and getting better and better things, and always "impassionating" its visitors.

Thirty years later, novelist and literary scholar André P. Brink also evoked a physiological image when he reminded those present at a panel discussion that in French the acronym for SANG means blood, and that the blood must flow and pulsate. As the arteries harden, the blood can no longer propel through them. Under Paris's directorship SANG received 1,361,118 visitors. In his article Paris appealed to "deep patriots" to give great gifts or endowments like in America, Canada and Australia. He concluded:

> After thirteen years I love it all deeply and I am not ashamed of any of it. There is a gay little programme of talks and exhibitions I am working on now. What really happens next may be chance or miracle, but like any other future it remains to be hoped for with a high heart, prayed for and worked for.

At a press conference to announce the departures of Paris and Von Moltke, Honikman, by then mayor of Cape Town, elaborated on the logistics involved but would not give any reasons for the board's decision to terminate Paris' directorship. Paris told the *Cape Times* (21 March 1962) that he could make "no useful comment". The situation was preposterous: the board had determined to get rid of Paris without revealing why.

Paris' artistic and complex personality manifested itself in his work and relationships with individuals. He was brave and single-minded, but at times he seemed to be somewhat self-destructive and unpredictable. According to artist Leon Rubens, who was a student at Michaelis in the late 1950s, and a frequent visitor to the gallery, the exhibitions and engagement with students were excellent, but the director was obstinate and aggressive. Paris' demeanor impacted on the community of artists – Gregoire Boonzaier and Lippy Lipshitz disliked him intensely, while Eleanor Esmonde-White admired him.[65]

Judging from his responses to the board's request for his resignation and the optimistic nature of his opinion piece in the Cape Times, he was in denial about the gravity of his situation. Unfortunately, when his name is mentioned, the loss of the Lycett Green collection comes up straight away. There is also the delicate matter of his drinking problem, which, according to Rubens, was common knowledge, and which might have been the main – albeit unstated at the time – cause of his dismissal. There is no record of Paris' doing after he left the gallery; it has been impossible to establish where he went and what happened to him.

Von Moltke, on the other hand, had a bright future ahead. His final exhibition of twenty-nine drawings, presented by Lady Michaelis three decades earlier, bears testimony to his scholarship. In consultation with specialists abroad he identified and installed them for the first time.[66] Von Moltke was reluctant to leave South Africa, but he could not refuse the challenge of building a new gallery in Bielefeld and acquiring works of art for it.[67] He was also clear in an interview (*Cape Times*, 28 June 1962) that the state did not provide enough funds for proper research in the visual arts, and that developments were dependent on individuals. "I am confident that in time they will give more and I feel they have accepted the matter in principle." History has sadly proved Von Moltke wrong.

Matthys Bokhorst's directorship

THE BOARD ACTED swiftly after Paris' resignation, placing an advertisement in *The Star* on 16 March 1962. The advert was for both vacant positions and listed various qualifying requirements: applicants had to show specialised qualifications, knowledge and preferably some art museum experience and not be older than fifty-five; a good knowledge of both official languages would have to be acquired within two years from the assumption of duties. The closing date for applications was 15 May. Five applications for the director's post were received and thirteen for that of assistant director. Von Moltke left for Europe in April 1962 to further his research and to interview candidates. His report was tabled at the board meeting of 28 May. He conducted interviews in Amsterdam, The Hague, Cologne and London, but he was not enthusiastic about the applicants. He remarked on the paucity of applicants, perhaps due to the low salary, and recommended that the posts be re-advertised.[68]

FIGURE 13: Günther Komnick, *Professor Matthys Bokhorst on the stairs of the Old Town House*, 1959-60; image courtesy of the artist.

A sub-committee was constituted to consider the applicants for assistant director and two meetings were held in June. They included architect and art critic Neville Dubow, painters Erik Laubscher and Larry Scully, and Ivor Pols, who had applied for both positions and been interviewed in The Hague. Nobody had exactly the right qualifications, except for Dubow and Pols, but in the end neither was found suitable. It was agreed to approach Matthys Bokhorst, part-time curator of the Michaelis Collection since 1956 (upgraded to a directorship in 1962), to act as part-time director for SANG, and to seek his advice on Dubow and Pols. Failing Bokhorst, the trustees would approach Maurice van Essche, a Belgian-born painter and professor at Michaelis.[69] Bokhorst was sixty-two at the time and Van Essche fifty-six, so the age requirement stipulated in the advertisement was not applied to them.

Matthys Bokhorst (Fig. 13) was born in Rotterdam and completed his doctorate in Leyden under the eminent historian Johan Huizinga. He came to South Africa in 1929 to occupy the new chair of the Institute of Netherlands Culture at the University of Pretoria (UP). Bilingualism, a subject of great dispute during Paris's tenure, was not an issue for Bokhorst. He agreed to combine the directorship of SANG and MC until April 1964, even after his permanent appointment to SANG the year before.[70] No assistant director was appointed at this time.

Sculptor Bruce Arnott joined the staff as temporary professional officer in March 1962, and a year later was made permanent staffer in charge of the departments of sculpture and prints and drawings. He rose through the ranks, first promoted to chief professional officer in 1969 and assistant director in April 1970, after the 1968 Commission of Inquiry, chaired by Dr. F. J. de Villiers, recommended that the post be re-instated.[71] Arnott's tenure impacted significantly on the institution before he left for Natal in 1972, to pursue his career as a full-time artist. He was succeeded by Dutch-born art and architectural historian Hans Fransen,[72] who had come to South Africa as a young man in 1955.

Arnott's influence in advancing Paris' interest in pre-historic and African art provides a fitting epilogue to his visionary but fraught directorship. In 1963, Arnott curated the exhibition *Rock Art in Southern Africa*, which comprised 274 paintings and engravings borrowed from SAM and the South African Archaeological Society. The intention was to present both the scientific and aesthetic aspects of rock art in an exhibition that occupied seven rooms and in the catalogue, which included extensive introductory notes to the different areas, followed by illustrations. It was the first time that South African rock art was exhibited in the context of neighbouring countries – Basutoland, Swaziland, South West Africa, the Rhodesias and Nyasaland – and was described in a gallery report as "the most important exhibition in the period covered".[73] Following on the 1946 exhibition mentioned earlier, *Rock Art in Southern Africa* was the result of national and international collaboration – with the lenders but also with UCT, the South African Public Library, the Cape Tercentenary Foundation (CTF) and many experts in the field.[74] The exhibition toured to Bloemfontein, Kimberley, Durban, Johannesburg and Windhoek.

The 1968 De Villiers Commission of Inquiry gave the board an opportunity of again stating its case and the recommendations for the following five years were welcomed: wiping out the expected deficit and an increase in the government grant-in-aid; the emphasis on educational services and the concomitant development of the reference library; a full component of staff at all levels, including a professional officer for restoration; improved salary scales to attract staff; the purchase of the adjoining property for the future extension of the gallery and adequate climate control for the storage basement.[75]

The decade from 1962 to 1972 differed from the preceding one in that the days of the long-term loans were over, with the exception of the Natale Labia Collection. This was replaced by close co-operation between the gallery and the combined Rembrandt van Rijn and Peter Stuyvesant Foundations, which resulted in major exhibitions such as *Rodin*, *Scultura Italiana Moderna*, *Homage to Irma Stern*, *French Tapestries* and the semi-permanent housing in the gallery of a number of major works of art belonging to the foundations. *Art of the Space Age*, featuring sixty examples of European and American Op and Kinetic art was very popular, attracting 57,681 visitors between August 1966 and January 1967.[76]

Bokhorst's vision was to promote South African art and artists while maintaining existing international contacts and seeking new ones. He cooperated closely with foreign diplomats and local organisations like the SAAA and the South African Institute of Architects. However, with the ideology and bureaucracy of apartheid invading every aspect of life in the country and drawing increasing denunciation from abroad, this was becoming difficult. Bokhorst noted as much: "Not unlike sports and other cultural organisations, the gallery sometimes has to run the gauntlet when trying to draw exhibitions from overseas, but the fact that there is no racial discrimination as far as admission of visitors is concerned is a strongly mitigating factor."[77]

Exhibitions largely sponsored by foreign governments came from Australia, Belgium, Britain, Canada and France. The open-ended approach to what is deemed appropriate for a national art museum that started with Paris, was explored and reinforced with exhibitions such as *Rock Art in Southern Africa*, *Rhodesian African Sculpture*, *African Art in Metal*, *Ceramic African Heads from Lydenburg*, *Indian sculpture through the Ages* (from the Stone Age to the seventeenth century, in collaboration with the Vivekananda Centenary Committee that celebrated the birth of the revered Swami in 1863), the art and architecture of Le Corbusier, seventeenth-century English furniture and *Sculptural Ceramics*. Exhibitions of tapestries were popular, ranging from *Contemporary Belgian Tapestries* to contemporary South African works from local collections, from *African Weaving* created at Rorke's Drift to historical tapestries from Aubusson in France.

Retrospective or memorial exhibitions of established South African artists began in 1955 (John Dronsfield) and 1956 (Strat Caldecott). This grew in importance with artists such as Pranas Domsaitis, Hugo Naudé, Ruth Prowse, Fritz Krampe, Irma Stern, Peter Wenning honoured; unusually for the time, living artists like Lippy Lipshitz (1968) and Maggie Laubser (1969) were the subject of survey exhibitions. At a time when South African art and artists were regarded as not good enough to form part of university curricula, and books were few and far between, many of them in Afrikaans, the national art museum participated in writing the first draft of our art history, albeit much limited to paintings by white artists.[78] One of the primary sources in Esmé Berman's research for her 1970 Art and Artists of South Africa, were museum accession lists. A key criterion for inclusion, underpinned by twenty-three variables, was "public encounter" which meant representation in museums and prestigious one-person exhibitions.[79]

The SANG was also contributing to a maturing art market that would be the focus of Berman's controversial self-published *The South African Art Market 1971/72*. The author devised a "star system" based on the outcome of carefully calculated tables and advanced the potential of South African art as having investment potential. However, such was the furore and character assassination that ensued from artists and in the press, that Berman destroyed most of the copies. Although a number of black artists were listed, the book reflected a market that was both white and conservative.[80]

Group exhibitions during Bokhorst's directorship included *Cape Art '67*, *Quinquennial Exhibition of South African Art*, *Aspects of Jewish Life in South Africa* (held in the Cultural History Museum), and works from the Boerneef and the Sanlam Collections. There were special exhibits of single works, accompanied by leaflets containing text and a reproduction, among them Jacques Lipschitz's bronze *Prometheus and the Eagle*, two prints from Francisco Goya's *The Disasters of War* (1810–20) and Kevin Atkinson's *Sound activated electronic box*.[81]

In 1971, celebrations marking SANG's centenary started with a wreath-laying ceremony on Thomas Butterworth Bayley's grave in Wynberg. The board produced two modest but informative bilingual publications: *South African National Gallery 1871–1971* and *National South African Art Collection*. The former described the founding of the collection, a short history of the gallery and its patrons; the latter referred to the history, but focused on the exhibition of its entire collection of South African art, for the first time in its history. Bayley's bequest was marked with an exhibition of paintings and graphic works in 1973, and Abraham de Smidt the artist was celebrated with an exhibition of paintings from SANG and other collections the following year.[82]

Bokhorst's commitment to promoting South African art speaks to the present from his 1971 article "From our own soil".[83] The SANG centenary coincided with the decennial anniversary of the Republic of South Africa's and its contribution to the Republic Festival was to fill the entire gallery "with art from our own soil, an exhibition featuring the entire collection of South African art".[84] In doing so, Bokhorst stressed the importance of South African art for the national art museum – an art that had, for him, particular qualities that distinguished it from that of other countries with colonial histories. He also drew attention to the country's political independence, thereby linking the Republic to its evolving art.

This uncritical acceptance of the political status quo did not mention visual artists who were taking a stand against the evils of apartheid, and the emergence of socio-political protest art that would in time be labelled "resistance art". In 1963 *Art: South Africa: Today*, a non-racial, juried exhibition and competition, opened at the African Art Centre in Durban. It evolved into a major national biennial, with subsequent editions hosted by DAG, and featured a number of artists whose work was unambiguous in its opposition to and condemnation of the apartheid regime, including Omar Badsha, Norman Catherine, Malcolm Payne, Cyprian Shilakoe, Paul Stopforth and Gavin Younge.[85] Bokhorst could not have been unaware of what was going on – he had served on the 1965 selection panel of the biennial.

Notwithstanding these shortcomings, Bokhorst advanced the importance and role of the national art museum in many respects, inside and outside the institution. A sculpture garden adjacent to Gallery Lane was opened in the mid-1960s, but in September 1969 the board was informed that new servants' quarters were to be erected for the Presidency, necessitating a boundary wall between the sculpture garden and the official grounds. The trustees had little choice and eventually the sculpture garden would succumb to further expansion from the Tuynhuys side.[86]

Bokhorst initiated the photographic documentation of South African artists, while catalogues, educational material, a monthly programme setting out forthcoming activities and postcards were published and many lectures, films and concerts offered. Building on Paris' legacy, Bokhorst early in his directorship manifested his vision that SANG was "not only to exhibit the works of South African artists of merit past and present and so to reflect in balanced form an art history of this country, but also that the Gallery should develop more and more as a 'living' centre of art appreciation and dialogue". At the end of the 1970s he could rightfully claim: "The Gallery's activities have continued to expand in accordance with its policy of becoming an increasingly vital centre of art appreciation and awareness in the community."[87] To this end, kindred arts organisations were offered the gallery facilities at a nominal fee, which resulted in abundant and wide-ranging musical events.

Bokhorst maintained that he, "by the closest and most intimate co-operation with the Board under the able chairmanship of Councillor Honikman, was successful in having the financial aid from the Government increased to such an extent that many activities, which could not have been dreamed of before, could now be realised".[88] In 1963 the acquisitions grant increased from R600 to R14,000 (it was later increased to R15,000 per annum), to which the CTCC added R3,000; the government grant was further augmented to R30,000 in 1967 and that of the CCTC to R10,000. This meant growth in staffing and departments for education (including public relations), restoration and documentation (in cooperation with the documentation-training centre at the University of Stellenbosch) and photography.

From the 1950s travelling abroad was de rigueur for the director and senior staff – generous study leave, sometimes combined with vacation leave, allowed for doing research on the permanent collection, making contact with international institutions, attending conferences and meetings, and conducting own research.[89] This support from the board would cease in the 1990s, when financial constraints militated against international and even national travel.

The profile, presence and influence of directors in the broader art and museum sectors, as well as scholarly and other activities in the broader community, were important components of a director's professional life. Like Paris, Bokhorst was much in demand on important selection committees, for example, South Africa's participation in the 1964, 1966 and 1968 Venice Biennales, the 1965 and 1967 São Paulo Biennales and the 1965 *Art: South Africa: Today* exhibition in Durban. Interestingly, the thirty-six works in various media selected for the 1967 São Paulo Biennale were displayed at SANG, in association with SAAA, thereby giving the public an idea of how the country was being represented internationally. Fifteen artists participated in 1965, but not a single black artist was included; two years later draughtsman and sculptor Dumile Feni and Sydney Kumalo, widely considered South Africa's most accomplished sculptor of the 1960s, were selected.[90]

Bokhorst motivated for the introduction of art history as a major subject for BA and BA (Fine Art) students at UCT and US; this was already available at Wits, the University of Pretoria (UP) and the University of South Africa (UNISA). He regarded the subject as "most essential for filling vacancies at Art Galleries and Cultural History Museums".[91] Unfortunately the teaching of art history – as Bokhorst, his predecessors, contemporaries and some of his successors understood the subject, and the concomitant value that it had for professional museum staff – has lost its importance and is increasingly threatened by disinterest and retooling of the discipline under the rubrics of "visual studies" and "decolonisation" of curricula.[92]

Taking his cue from Paris, Bokhorst motivated for a national restoration centre to serve SANG and the country. Following his retirement from JAG, P. A. Hendriks settled in Cape Town and agreed to do restoration work and training on an ad hoc basis.[93] Hendriks trained E. C. L. Bosman, before the latter went overseas in 1968 on a bursary provided by the Department of National Education (DNE) and qualified as a painting conservator and restorer. The SANG offered regular three-week courses for students from UCT and US, consisting of the director and staff giving short lectures and practical training in museology: "The object of this is to interest students in gallery work and it is hoped to develop this into a full course

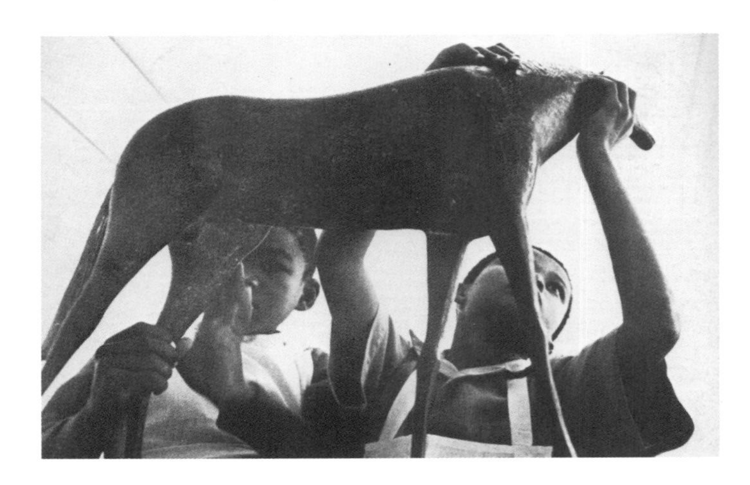

FIGURE 14: *Discovering* Young Horse by *Mascherini*, 1977; photographer Chris Jansen.

as part of the training for the Museums Diploma."[94] The SANG library grew exponentially as a resource and all the acquisitions are listed in the *Annual Reports*. Catalogues, which were prepared for all special exhibitions, were exchanged internationally with between 200 and 300 art museums, and the hundreds of books and catalogues presented far exceeded purchases for the library. The first of a series of catalogues on the permanent collection – on South African paintings and sculpture – was published in English in 1969, and was followed by drawings and prints and similar ones of foreign works.[95]

The question of charging the public for entrance to the national art museum was raised again. It was agreed to charge entry fees for people over eighteen, except for students on some days. This led to a considerable decrease in attendance figures, from 102,540 in 1963–64 to 89,649 in 1964–65. However, numbers increased the following year to 91,452. It was concluded that visitor figures fluctuated in relation to the popularity of temporary exhibitions. In the 1966–67 *Annual Report* Bokhorst claimed that the attendance figure of 103,080 (including 19,779 non-Europeans) was higher than ever before, but it was still far below the 161,128 recorded in 1953–54 during Paris' time at SANG.[96]

A groundbreaking initiative during Bokhorst's directorship was the focus on blind and partially sighted people and other forms of disability. Sandra Eastwood recounts how Bokhorst had heard of a tactile exhibition at the Gemeentemuseum in The Hague and brought the challenge to South Africa.[97] Eastwood joined SANG in 1964 and she devoted herself to giving tangible expression to his vision under his "empathetic generous mentorship".[98]

In 1967, the newly created education post was split between Eastwood and Elsa Verlooren van Themaat; together they curated the first *Sculpture for the Blind* exhibition in November that year. The sculptures were chosen to offer varying tactile experiences and were on view at the same time as a big exhibition of contemporary Italian sculpture, *Scultura Italiana*. The Rembrandt van Rijn Art Foundation allowed selected works to be touched and blind adults were offered guided tours. Bokhorst reported on the first special sculpture exhibition:

> This, our first pioneering exhibition in this field, can be regarded as a milestone in the history of the Gallery because it marked the start of our special activities on behalf of the blind. Few galleries anywhere, it would seem, have taken into account their very particular needs as far as the provision of exhibitions designed specially for them is concerned.[99]

Over time adults of all races with visual impairments were invited, as well as learners from the Pioneer School for the Visually Impaired and Athlone School for the Blind. Mobil Oil (now Engen) took on the programme as sponsors, teacher volunteers came to the fore and SANG's education department was very much involved.

From 1969 the Annexe would be used for ongoing exhibitions and workshops, multi-sensory approaches to art and an annual tactile exhibition. It comprised a working area, a study room and exhibition space.[100]

A special art collection was gradually assembled. Artists such as Bill Davis, Jill Joubert, Eduard Ladan and Cecil Skotnes created and presented works to the Touch Gallery. Skotnes donated the Shaka woodblock from the *Assassination of Shaka* portfolio in 1974.[101] By 1973 more than 65% of the blind community in the Cape Town region had visited the facility and at the end of the decade an exhibition of the Touch Gallery permanent collection could go on display. The catalogue *Touch Gallery,* in which the programmes and achievements were detailed and placed within a theoretical context, was published in 1977 (Fig. 14).[102] Richly illustrated and with a plastic cover overlaid in Braille, it draws attention to the numerous achievements of Eastwood, her colleagues and many supporters, as well as the talents and enthusiasm of the participants. A number of projects were linked to exhibitions in the main building, music was introduced and there were collaborative activities with UCT College of Music and sculpture students from Michaelis, as well as students from the University of Natal (UN) and well-known artists who created ceramic sculpture.

William Rowland, director of the South African National Council for the Blind and an avid supporter of the initiative, wrote an in-depth article for the catalogue, titled "The Sense of Touch and Beyond." Told from the perspective of a blind person, Eastwood paid tribute to Rowland's "refined critical faculties" and the role he played in the development of the Touch Gallery. In his "Appreciation", H. Raymond Singleton, director of museum studies at the University of Leicester, reflected on the changes that were occurring in museums, with the focus of attention shifting from collections to the community. He concluded:

> It is in the context of these changes that the Touch Gallery has for some time been leading the way. From an initial concern for those whom many museums unthinkingly exclude, it has developed a philosophy of accessibility which transcends physical access and opens up new levels of aesthetic appreciation. In its understanding provision of facilities which enable all visitors to enjoy, together, the pleasures and revelations of tactile contact with works of art and their constituent materials, and to appreciate the subtle links between music and the sculptural arts, the Touch Gallery has thrown open its doors wider than perhaps any other museum in the world. The muses are being welcomed back.

When things change and stay the same

OVER TIME, as the political dispensations, status of the country, its socio-economic conditions, aesthetic production and the approaches of different boards and directors changed, so did the nature of acquisitions. However, the one element that all directors had in common was the awareness of – and desire to fill – gaps in the collection. For Bokhorst the priority was the South African collection and the inclusion of young artists, photography and new directions. He was concerned about the absence of rock paintings and engravings, and commended Arnott's knowledge of and interest in both the historical and modern African art that was being acquired.

PLATE 7: Dumile Feni, *Woman and children*, c. 1968, conté on paper, 830 × 650; presented by the artist; courtesy of the Dumile Feni Foundation Trust; image provided by Iziko Museums of South Africa; photographer Nigel Pamplin.

Bokhorst further noted: "There is a large development in the non-white domain: 23% of our visitors are non-white and the time is not far off when the non-white artists will be represented by an equal percentage ... on the same basis as the whites, and this is exclusively: quality."[103] But this large gap was hardly reduced under his directorship. The *Annual Reports* (from 1963–64 to 1973–74) reveal that among the hundreds of paintings, sculptures and works on paper acquired, few were by contemporary black South African artists, and in some years there were none (1970–71).

Acquisitions were predominantly in Arnott's departments – prints and drawings and sculpture – and included a number of Rhodesian (Zimbabwean) stone sculptures and works by Sydney Kumalo and Michael Zondi. Ceramics and tapestries from the Evangelical Lutheran Church Art and Craft Centre at Rorke's Drift were purchased, with additional works presented by the Centre, the Friends of the Gallery (founded in 1968) and artists such as Peter Clarke and Dumile Feni, who generously augmented acquisitions of their work (Plates 7 & 8). Feni's drawings, *Resurrection Triptych* (1965) and *Railway Accident* (1966), constituted major additions to the collection, as did Julian Motau's *Man in Gaol* (1967) and three linocuts by Azaria Mbatha. Thanks to Arnott, of the 129 works illustrated in E. J. de Jager's 1973 volume, *Contemporary African Art in South Africa*, thirteen were from SANG – the only public collection featured.[104]

A single painting by a black artist was purchased in the 1960s: Gerard Sekoto's Street Scene (1945); it was acquired seventeen years after he left the country. By that time Sekoto was well established, far more so than in 1944 when the SANG board declined to purchase his work: his painting *Yellow houses: A street in Sophiatown* (1940) had been bought by JAG twenty years earlier, and he was included among the 500 "serious artists" in Harold Jeppe's 1963 book, *South African Artists 1900–1962.* The minuted discussion about the price of Sekoto's Street Scene, considering what was being spent on South African and international artists, is an appalling reflection on Bokhorst and the acquisition committee. It was noted that the seller, Mrs Bernadt, wanted R320 for the painting, but the committee – never shy to haggle – offered R160; she came down to R200, and it was agreed to pay R210.[105] Another painting by Sekoto, *Four men and a guitar* (1944) was purchased in 1971. The lack of respect for Sekoto is even more glaring in light of Bokhorst's report on acquisitions in 1971, after an increase in the purchase grant:

> The result was the acquisition of hundreds of works of art, about two-thirds of them South African of all periods, including the most modern ones, although those of the Cape are, on the whole, still better represented than those of the other provinces. Leading artists from oversea [sic] were, as a rule, represented by graphic works, the cost of paintings being prohibitive in most cases, with a few exceptions such as a Matta, a Clavé, a Landuyt tapestry and the well-known Vasarely "Vega Fel" for which R17,000 was paid.[106]

The acquisition of an op-art piece by Hungarian-French artist Victor Vasarely was a clear indication of the gallery's internationalist and progressive ambitions in the face of local conservatism and parochialism. However, Bokhorst's notion of works "from our own soil" remained conservative and excluded contemporary black artists. This is particularly puzzling, as he wrote many art reviews, and must have been aware of the increasing presence of black artists in solo and group exhibitions, as well as in publications. He must have known of the success of Louis Maqhubela, who won first prize in the Adler Fielding Gallery's annual "Artists of Fame and Promise" competition in 1966 with a conté crayon and mixed media drawing *Peter's Denial* (1966). The panel of judges – Walter Battiss, Esmé Berman and Nel Erasmus – considered 900 entries from all over the country and Maqhubela triumphed over white artists such as runner-up Stanley Pinker, and many other well-known names.

Bokhorst's bias towards what constituted "quality" becomes evident if one compares his responses and those of Neville Dubow to Albert Adams' exhibitions. Writing about Adams' first one-person show in the *Cape Argus* (30 October 1959), Dubow picked out two features that he regarded as remarkable and rare in first exhibitions: "the pronounced technical ability to express himself fluently in several media, and more particularly the tremendous emotional intensity behind that expression". He recognised "a talent well above the ordinary and a training to match".[107] In his careful analysis of the paintings, drawings and prints, Dubow identified and articulated all the characteristics that would unfold and manifest in Adams' career. In his review in the *Cape Times* (30 October 1959) Bokhorst wrote of "the beginning of a new era in South African art" connected to "a new, often undisciplined, but passionate expressionism".

PLATE 8: Peter Clarke, *Night Bird*, 1963, colour woodcut on paper, 340 × 330; presented by the artist; © 2019 Succession Peter Clarke | DALRO; image provided by Iziko Museums of South Africa; photographer Nigel Pamplin.

A year later Dubow reviewed an exhibition of Adams' etchings in the *Cape Argus* (22 November 1960) and commented on his "brilliant expressionist technique". Bokhorst was more circumspect in his the *Cape Times* (21 November 1960) review. While acknowledging Adams' mastery of graphic techniques and large self-portraits in watercolour, he chose to focus on the difficult times "the young Coloured artist" was having in London, rather than on his work. Considering Dubow's in-depth analysis, Von Moltke's interest in printmaking and Bokhorst's knowledge of Adams' work when he took over the directorship of SANG, it is astounding that it took another two decades before a painting by Adams, *Cape Town Harbour* (1959), was acquired (Plate 3).[108] One can only wonder about the content of Bokhorst's illustrated lecture, "Fine Arts and the Racial Groups in South Africa", delivered at the annual general meeting of the Nederlands Zuid-Afrikaanse Vereniging in Amsterdam in 1967.

After an extended trip abroad in 1969, Bokhorst reported about the success of his visits to:

> ... all those American museums which now collect traditional primitive art and integrate it into their collections of contemporary art by the same people. This was being done in the cases of American Indian, Mexican, South American Indian and Eskimo art. This strengthened his opinion that the same integration could be applied to traditional Bantu art and contemporary Bantu art in the S. A. National Gallery.[109]

However, the significance of pioneer black modernists – like Ernest Mancoba, George Pemba and Moses Tladi – escaped Bokhorst.[110] As chairperson of the selection committee for the South African participation in the 1968 Venice Biennale, he stated: "The composition of the entry was intended to breathe the spirit of Africa and so two of the Zulu tapestries acquired by the Gallery from the E.L.C. Art and Craft Centre, Rorke's Drift, were included."[111] Like Paris, Bokhorst was more interested in the distant past, and in historical African art. He bemoaned the fact that no department existed for "our world-famous rock paintings and engravings" and made a firm policy with regard to historical African art. His and Arnott's vision and achievements in this regard are discussed in chapter four.

Neville Dubow joined the board and acquisitions committee as UCT representative in 1971. In a 1996 interview with Emma Bedford and Jane Taylor, he recalled how business was conducted in the early 1970s, which clarifies Bokhorst's attitude and behaviour towards acquisitions:

> Yes, broadly speaking, there was an assumption that members of the Board were civilised representatives of the sort of ruling constituencies who knew what is right. What was chosen was what the National Gallery should have but, of course, these things weren't ever spelt out in those days. Those sorts of assumptions were implicit. There was a general consensus among most of the members of the Board about what was good taste and what was not and I think that there were hierarchies of values which were generally not challenged. This does not mean to say, and I must be quite clear about this, that those hierarchies were necessarily always wrong or that some of the acquisitions were not good and informed of their kind, but there was generally not an atmosphere of contestation, of the thrust and parry of ideas. People were very anxious not to be confrontational. It was assumed that we all knew

> why we were there and 'let's get on with the job in the most polite and civilised way', even though it was well known that there were wide differences in political opinion on the part of some of the members of the Board. Board meetings were conducted, as they continued to be until very recently, alternately in Afrikaans and English. I think that when there were issues that were discussed which were perceived to be weighty issues which involved State funding and that kind of thing, the voices that one heard were very much those of the Afrikaans establishment speaking in their mother language.[112]

The ceiling paintings in the first room of the main building were removed in the mid-1960s. Owing to leakages the ceiling was in a bad state of repair and the paintings, executed in distemper on canvas, and originally created as a memorial to Mrs F. K. Wiener, could not be saved for presentation to another institution. The executors of the Wiener estate agreed to the removal and Mrs Wiener was instead commemorated by showcases displaying memorial plaques.[113] Paris had raised the appropriateness and desirability of the decorations in 1958, when he was installing the Robinson Collection that would be on loan for two years; the large paintings by François Boucher were designated for the entrance gallery, but Paris found the ceiling to be out of keeping with modern methods of display and suggested that they be covered up or removed. Nothing happened at the time.[114]

There can be no doubt that SANG flourished under Bokhorst, and added to its well-being and development was the founding, on 2 April 1968, of the Society of Friends of the South African National Gallery, with its own council and representative on the board of trustees. By 1971 it had nearly 400 members, had published colour reproductions of well-known South African paintings, exhibited works from their private collections and was "rapidly becoming a tower of strength for the Gallery, and actively or financially supports many schemes undertaken by the management, and – at the same time – provides many attractive functions for its members".[115] And this was only the beginning. Through all the changes, challenges, achievements and upheavals in the history of SANG since then, the Friends would be there to promote, support and enhance the work of the institution.

The national art museum was going from strength to strength, but space constraints were critical and once again the spotlight fell on the artistic quality and display demands of the Bailey bequest – in particular the sporting and hunting pictures. History was about to repeat itself. From 1969 the board engaged with Sotheby's of London – initially to publish a "first class catalogue" of the collection for promotion abroad. The Bailey Trust had no objections but declined to contribute to the costs.[116]

However, soon the auction house's interest was revealed to be in line with that of SANG trustees and director. Honikman approached the Bailey Trust to request permission to sell some of the pictures in order to buy new British, European and American works "to enhance the status of the Bailey collection". Needless to say, the response to this disingenuous move was negative, but it is a blot on the otherwise exemplary roles of the chairperson and director. Undismayed by the rebuke from the Bailey trustees, Honikman sought their permission to loan works to art museums abroad, "in order to get other worthwhile works in exchange".[117] Nothing came of this idea.

In response to the recommendations contained in the 1968 Commission of Inquiry, the secretary for cultural affairs Dr. J. J. P. Op't Hof secured the purchase of the adjoining property. The building, which had housed the first Marist Brothers School in Africa from 1867 to 1970, was occupied in January 1971.[118] This provided much relief and accommodation for the Touch Gallery, education and conservation departments and administrative staff. Bokhorst was, however, clear that it was a temporary solution and that there was no question that an additional building, a permanent extension of the gallery, was required. To this end a board sub-committee was appointed to remain in touch with the Department of Public Works (DPW).

Efforts continued after Bokhorst left in 1973, but the socio-economic climate would soon have a negative impact. The chairperson commented as follows in the 1975–76 *Annual Report*:

> Having regard to the National economy the Board has temporarily deferred activity in regard to the proposed extensions to the Gallery buildings. Shortage of exhibition, storage and workshop space, however, remains acute. Some space in the main building was made available by transferring the Administration Department to the Annexe and with reluctance, partitioning off part of the exhibition space in the Annexe for use as storage.[119]

The ongoing challenges and struggle, a leitmotif in the history of SANG, has so far been documented in some detail. As the chapters of the book unfold, they will expose the numerous representations to the authorities in succeeding years to provide an additional building for exhibitions, educational activities, conservation and adequate facilities for the public, all of which proved to be futile.

Bokhorst had reached retirement age before he left in April 1973, but the trustees agreed to retain his services on an annual basis, until his successor could take up the post. In a tribute to Bokhorst, chairperson Honikman thanked him for gaining the trust of artists, the government and the public, and for enlarging the grant-in-aid that meant new staff, departments and acquisitions. He commended the director for his role in encouraging the government to purchase the Marist Brothers property and for his "seemingly endless energy" that ensured important national and international support and outstanding special exhibitions for SANG.[120]

In a short obituary on his passing in 1982, the chairperson of the Friends, Cees Wolters, paid tribute to Bokhorst, his important role in founding the society and his continued involvement on the Friends' council after his retirement.[121]

The brief directorship of Carel du Ry van Beest Holle

THE DIRECTORSHIP vacancy was advertised in South Africa and abroad, and after "the only possible local candidate" accepted and then withdrew, another Hollander, Carel (a.k.a. Charles) J. du Ry van Beest Holle, was appointed. He took up the position in May 1973. The candidate to whom Honikman referred was Albert Werth, first curator of and, until 1991, director of the Pretoria Art Museum (PAM).[122] There was substantial expenditure involved in Du Ry's appointment, which included his relocation from The Netherlands, and

Bokhorst's departure. Financially the institution was in dire straits – the government grant of R165,000 for the 1973–74 fiscal year was divided, leaving only R30,000 for acquisitions (including library books), plus R3,000 from the CTCC, and a shortfall of R5,768. Trustees were optimistic about a gradual increase so that the subsidy formula could be properly applied.[123] They succeeded in achieving a liquid position in the following two years, but only because the director's post was vacant from August 1975 to March 1976 and Hans Fransen stepped in as acting director.[124]

Considering the financial situation, one has to question the wisdom of purchasing two landscapes by German-born Namibian artist Adolph Jentsch, which took up two thirds of the budget. The works were offered at R20,000 each, but in their inimitable way the trustees knocked down the asking price to R10,000 each and arranged to pay the amount in installments over two years.[125] It was still expensive, and it is unclear why two were needed (albeit two for the price of one). The balance of the R30,000 acquisition budget was spent on a painting by the minor French Impressionist, Albert Lebourg. Clearly the director and his acquisitions committee were somewhat at sea.

Paintings by South Africans Enslin du Plessis, Erich Mayer, Fred Page, Stanley Pinker, Marianne Podlashuc and Douglas Portway were also purchased, as well as an assemblage by Judith Mason and a soapstone sculpture by Dörte Berner. The paintings were mostly oil or mixed media on paper, including an untitled work by Louis Maqhubela who, by this time, was represented in many public and private

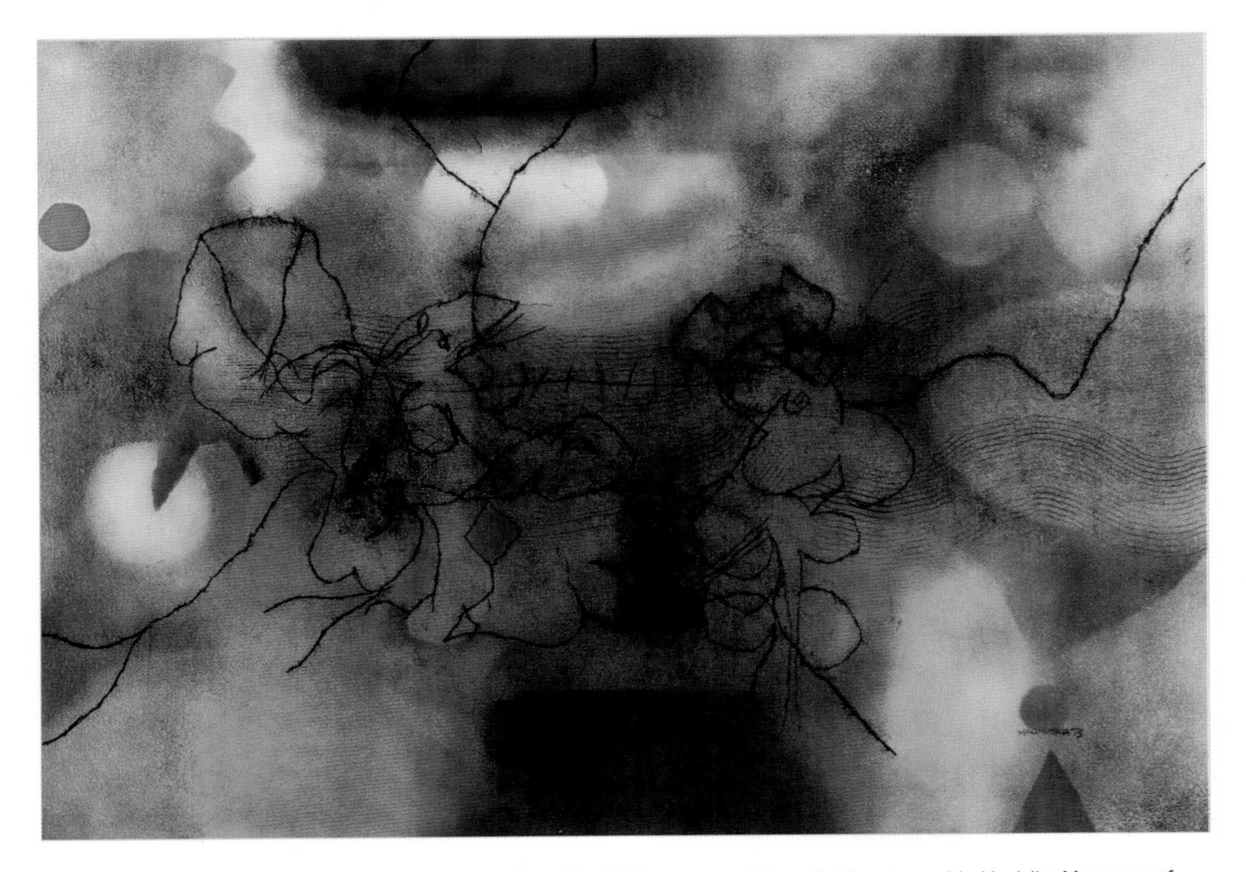

PLATE 9: Louis Maqhubela, *Untitled*, 1973, oil on paper, 510 × 728; courtesy of the artist; image provided by Iziko Museums of South Africa; photographer Nigel Pamplin.

collections (Plate 9).[126] Works by minor international artists Otto Nebel and Takis entered the collection, as did many graphics, both local (such as a linocut by Peter Clarke) and international.

In the 1975–76 financial year, the government grant increased to R195,000 but acquisitions were again limited to R30,000; fortunately the CTCC raised its allocation to R10,000. Du Ry's successor, Raymund van Niekerk, signed the *Annual Report* and referred to the purchases made:

> As will be seen, by far the majority are South African works of art (also in terms of the amount of money spent). It is felt that the Gallery is still just managing to act as the "memory" of our own art in its successive developments, though more depth and a better representation of important figures are needed for a truly National collection. Acquisitions of overseas art, however, are now totally insufficient to illustrate in any detail the antecedents of our own art in the mother countries.[127]

It was a long list all the same and enhanced by many gifts. Only one black artist was added to the collection: Lucky Sibiya's portfolio of fifteen woodcuts.

The policy that Bokhorst formulated – to show South African art in an international art historical context and to promote SANG as a dynamic centre for art appreciation and awareness – remained the same under Du Ry. He seemed to be particularly interested in forging links with Rhodesia and thirty-eight paintings by South African artists were sent to Salisbury (Harare) and Bulawayo; he envisaged sharing touring international exhibitions with them – to keep the arts alive in that country.

The restoration department offered a national service and expanded to accommodate a paper restorer from parliament in rooms in the Annexe. Not only did Bosman conserve paintings in SANG and municipal and provincial museums, he travelled extensively to other centres in South Africa and as far afield as Windhoek. Institutions were charged for his time and expenses, but it did impact negatively on his ability to deal with the backlog that existed in the gallery. Professional staff was available on Wednesday mornings to assist the public with enquiries on works of art related to authorship, authenticity, technique, state of repair and assessment of value or damages (for insurance, legal or estate purposes only).[128]

Care of the physical condition of a collection is important, but the director and curators did not neglect other critical aspects – research, the full documentation of each work and artist, and the publication of this information. In 1973 SANG joined the International Council for Museums (ICOM).[129]

In addition to the Natale Labia loan collection, which contributed a great deal to public interest in the gallery and short-term exhibitions exploring the history of the permanent collection, there were retrospectives and commemorative exhibitions by South African artists such as Cecil Higgs, Moses Kottler, Maggie Laubser, Charles Peers, Maurice van Essche, Jean Welz and Pieter Wenning. Small exhibitions of work by artists like Cecil Skotnes, Reginald Turvey and photographer Jansje Wissema were organised. The Michaelis School's fiftieth birthday was celebrated and the centenary of the first permanent art display in Cape Town, from which SANG's collection grew, was marked in 1975 by *One Hundred Years Ago*.

Over the 1975–76 holiday period the gallery arranged an exhibition of historical art from various parts of Africa, drawn from the permanent collection and from that of collector and dealer Peter Miller.

Entitled *African Motifs*, it included work by Walter Battiss, Alexis Preller, Cecil Skotnes and Peter Webber. This offered the possibility of interesting comparisons between an African past and South African present, as well as between ethnography (a term widely used to describe historical African art) and contemporary aesthetic production. The exhibition was well received, especially by visitors from abroad.[130]

Foreign shows came from the usual diplomatic sources and the Peter Stuyvesant Foundation: they featured contemporary French paintings and the ever-popular tapestries, contemporary British art, graphic art from Germany, The Netherlands and Spain (etchings by Francisco Goya) and a collection of cartoons and poster designs by Wim Muller, a Dutch artist who worked in Pretoria at the beginning of the twentieth century. Important sculpture exhibitions featured Giacomo Balla, Antoine Bourdelle and Henry Moore. The Goodman Gallery presented an exhibition of work by Victor Vasarely.

One of the highlights during Du Ry's directorship was *Three centuries of French painting: François I – Napoleon I*, on loan from the Wildenstein Foundation; it ran from May to July 1974 and attracted 20,000 visitors. Considering the fame and importance of the artists on show, this was not surprising – among them were the Le Nain brothers, Simon Vouet, Antoine Watteau, Jean-Baptiste Simeon Chardin, François Boucher, Jean-Honoré Fragonard, Marie-Louise Elizabeth Vigée-Lebrun, Jean-Baptiste Greuze, Jacques-Louis David and Théodore Géricault. The director wrote a scholarly, historical survey of the period and each image was extensively annotated. The exhibition was followed by a selection of French art at the turn of the twentieth century from the same lender, who also provided an exhibition of paintings by Camille Corot.

Du Ry's tenure was short and the director's position was left vacant unexpectedly when, at the end of July 1975, he took up the chair of the Department of Netherlandish Culture History, later the Department of Western Cultural History at UCT, before his contract expired. In view of the protracted issue and costs of advertising, Albert Werth was approached to assume the directorship, while Von Moltke was asked to serve as interim director.[131] The latter refused, as he was not prepared to pay for his travel from and to Germany at his own expense. Hans Fransen was appointed acting director.[132] Werth was interested in the position, but there were problems with the transfer of his total pension benefit from PAM and his requirement that there be no salary reduction; in the end this transfer could not be arranged.[133] The post was advertised, but only in South Africa to ensure the bilingualism of the next incumbent. Of the nine applicants, Valerie Leigh and Murray Schoonraad were interviewed; neither was found suitable.[134] Members of exco were requested to submit names of potential candidates. Raymund van Niekerk was interviewed and appointed at the November 1975 board meeting.[135] He took up the directorship on 1 March 1976.

Under the leadership of professional museum directors, assistant directors and staff, SANG was well connected internationally, and acquired a reputation as outward-looking and ambitious, while at the same time fulfilling its mandate as an educational institution. Their achievements during the years 1949 to 1975 affirm the necessity that the national art museum be run by knowledgeable art historians, who conduct research and write and publish extensively, and who contribute to the discourse on, and history of art in South Africa and further afield.

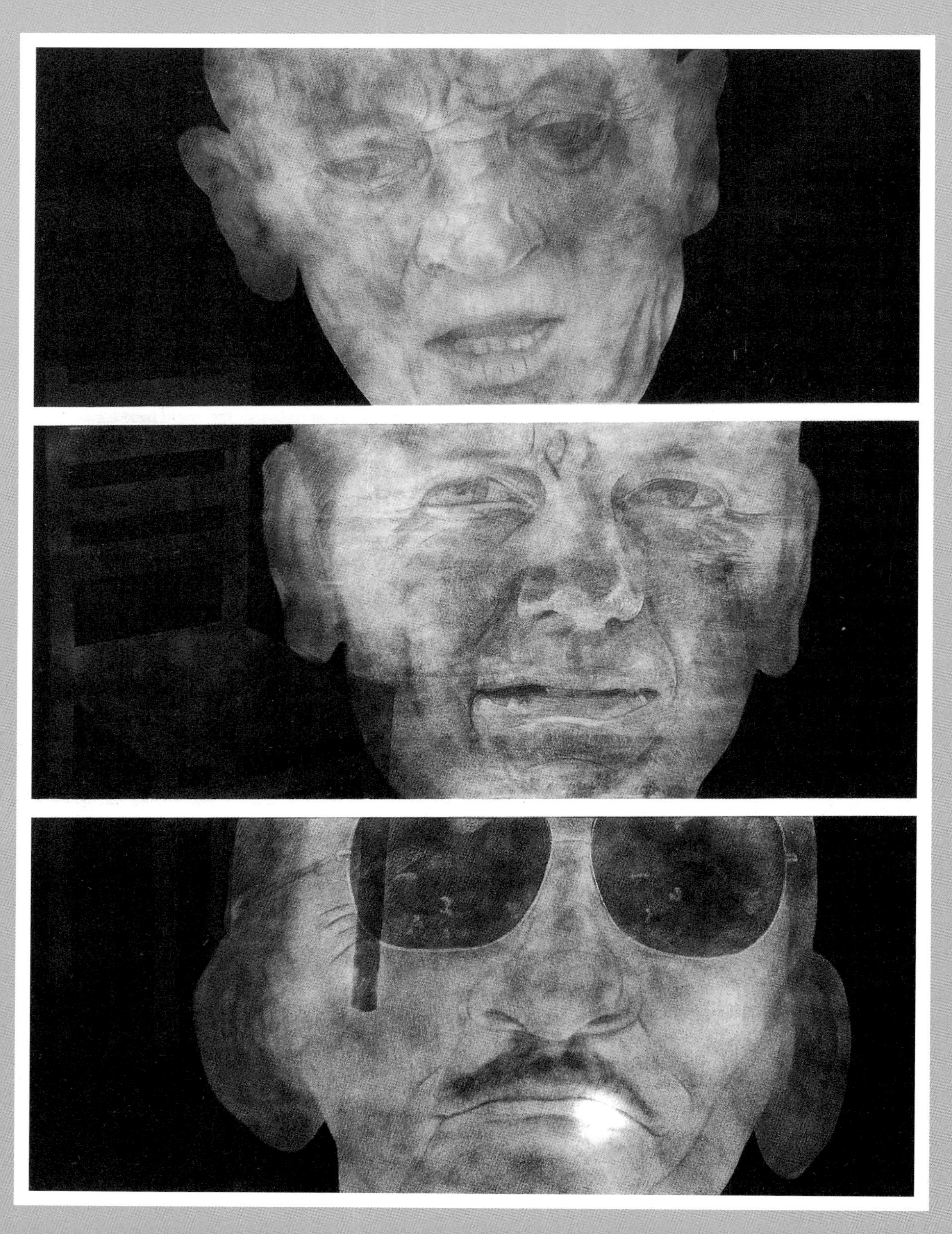

PLATE 10: Paul Stopforth, *Interrogators*, 1979, wax and fine grained graphite on paper mounted on wood panel [765 × 1830 each panel of the triptych]; courtesy of the artist; photographer Kathy Grundlingh.

3

The winds of change – Raymund van Niekerk's directorship

1976 – 1989

THIS CHAPTER is book-ended by two pivotal events: the 1976 Soweto rebellion and demise of the apartheid system in 1990. Politically engaged, new director Raymund van Niekerk is ideally placed to steer the national art museum through this turbulent period. He understands the need to balance local demands with international ambitions. Supported by trustees and staff, Van Niekerk establishes the highest standards in museology and scholarship, and takes SANG to new levels of influence. Van Niekerk's consistent lobbying, advocacy and public criticism of the state ensure an increased acquisitions allocation. Important purchases follow, notably of black artists and art inspired by socio-political conditions. The grip of the cultural and academic boycott tightens in the 1980s and requires innovative partnerships, changes in policies and activities, and exchanges with sister institutions. Extensions to the main building are delayed by the establishment of the Natale Labia Museum in Muizenberg. SANG is closed for extensive renovations in 1989, when Van Niekerk unexpectedly also opts for early retirement.

In the end we shall see a National Gallery
which is no credit at all to
the cultural life of this country.

RAYMUND VAN NIEKERK[1]

FIGURE 15: Portrait of Raymund van Niekerk; photographer Kathy Grundlingh; collection Marilyn Martin.

RAYMUND HUGO VAN NIEKERK[2] (Fig. 15) arrived at SANG in March 1976, just three months before high school students in Soweto initiated a nationwide rebellion against the Department of Bantu Education's decree imposing Afrikaans as the medium of instruction in half the subjects in higher primary and secondary school. Apart from the fact that Afrikaans was regarded as the language of the oppressor, African teachers and learners lacked the required fluency in the language, resulting in further disadvantage within a system that was devised to be to their detriment. Through their sacrifices, the young people of Soweto instigated profound changes in the socio-political landscape of the country.

For the national art museum, Cape Town and the country, Van Niekerk's appointment meant new energy and innovative approaches to how things were done in the museum, and the visual arts sector more broadly. In addition to being fully bilingual, SANG's first South African-born director was also fluent in French and in every respect an internationalist. In his obituary in *Die Burger* (19 March 2005), art critic Melvyn Minnaar described Van Niekerk's lively charm and colourful personality, which won over both the establishment and a younger generation soon after his appointment. His authoritative eloquence swayed opinion in his favour, particularly while performing the "cultural egg-dance of the time (predominantly determined by the ruling party establishment and its hegemonic cadres)".[3] Kim Siebert, education officer at the time, also conjures the image of Van Niekerk's ability "to walk on eggs" and how he gained the trust and respect of the board, the Friends, staff, art community and the general public.[4]

Curator Joe Dolby recalls Van Niekerk's exceptional aptitude for public speaking, his high scholarly and writing standards, and his knowledge of art and architectural history, which he conveyed to staff. His museological demands were rigorous and further afield he raised the bar of teaching art and architectural history by giving talks and lectures to organisations and at universities throughout South Africa.[5] Like his immediate predecessors, he was the face of the national art museum: he opened exhibitions, participated in selection committees and was a council member of the South African Museums Association (SAMA), serving two terms as president.[6]

Van Niekerk travelled extensively in South Africa and abroad, the latter often on invitation, and he used his connections in London to alert him to possible purchases. Dolby asserts that Van Niekerk maintained "a much wider national range than at present" through his contacts in Johannesburg and Durban, and buying regularly at auctions. "Dealers like Linda Givon mentioned that it was easier to sell a work if the gallery had acquired a work by that artist."[7]

Assistant director Hans Fransen, who was also curator of prints and drawings, ably supported the new director. After Fransen's departure in 1980, Lynn McClelland became the assistant director in 1983, while remaining curator of paintings and sculpture. She resigned from the position in the same year for personal reasons, but returned from 1985 to 1991. The capable and dedicated A. H. Honikman remained at the helm of the board until 1980 when he handed over to Justice L. de V. van Winsen. Cees Wolters, appointed as FONG representative at this time, played an important role as vice-chairperson, and as guide to the director and administration staff in matters of finance.

As discussed in chapters one and two, SANG has its origins in civil society – in the vision of enthusiastic individuals and organisations, whose taste was expressed in the collections they endowed the institution. Their founding initiatives would continue to influence purchasing policy during Van Niekerk's tenure. It has, however, also become clear that alongside these civic efforts there is a parallel history of official indifference and neglect. Unlike Paris, Bokhorst and Du Ry, who appeared to tacitly support NP segregationist policies, disdain for and opposition to the apartheid government was one of the defining hallmarks (and achievements) of Van Niekerk's directorship.

True to his convictions, Van Niekerk acquired art inspired by socio-political conditions; in this he had the unqualified support of the chairperson of the acquisitions committee, Neville Dubow, and staff. Acquisitions occupied a central role at the quarterly meetings. The story of how Dubow and Van Niekerk conspired to purchase Paul Stopforth's *Interrogators* (1979) is told in the 1997 catalogue to the exhibition *Contemporary South African Art 1985–1995*, but it is worth repeating here (Plate 10). The work depicts the three security policemen who interrogated the anti-apartheid activist Stephen Bantu Biko, and the chair to which he was bound. Van Niekerk titled the work "Triptych" for the purposes of the board meeting. As Dubow tells it:

> I think that only the Director, Raymund van Niekerk and myself really knew what the work was about and what its real provenance was. There was a lot of uneasy humming and hawing amongst the members of the Board and I got the sense that those members of the Board who were there as State representatives had a kind of an uneasy feeling that they had seen these people before and they more or less knew who they might be but they were not prepared to say so, and there was a general feeling of unease. Nobody was prepared to say an outright 'no'; nobody quite knew what the work was about; nobody was prepared to say 'yes'. In the end that particular decision was referred to me and I was asked to give a view and I said that yes, I definitely thought the work should be acquired by the Board because for many reasons I found that the technique of its presentation was rather interesting. I phrased this in a way to allow those members of the Board who actually had their doubts to think that I was simply referring to

> the techniques whereby the work was realised. This was partly true, but I was also thinking of the technique whereby the real title of the work was withheld and was submitted under a rather more bland title. In the event, the work was acquired; it went on display.[8]

Gallery staff understood the meaning of the work. Curator Emma Bedford, then an education officer at the gallery, conducted tours for large school groups:

> And so this piece became a springboard to us talking about very important people and events in our history, things which weren't being talked about in their school history texts or in other ways; and so it enabled education staff at the Gallery to engage in people's education at the very time in which the cultural boycott was also building up and being directed against the national Gallery as a State institution.[9]

Education was a crucial element in subverting and opposing apartheid. Bedford's radical education programmes landed her and the gallery in trouble:

> I organised a small display of works made by the Zamani Soweto Sisters in conjunction with a screening of a Kevin Harris documentary. I think it was *This we can do for Justice and for Peace* which gave expression to the standpoint of the South African Council of Churches in opposing Apartheid in South Africa through the concerned perspectives of General Secretary Bishop Desmond Tutu and SACC President Peter Storey. Unfortunately, the Minister of Education took exception to this and to my use of the word 'regime' to refer to the government and the director was advised to fire me. He managed to argue against that but the message was clear.[10]

Van Niekerk openly opposed the classification of SANG as a proscribed "own affairs" public space, and succeeded in securing the institution's status as a "general affairs" venue, while fighting for the maintenance of "arm's length" funding.[11] According to Dolby, SANG was "punished" in subtle ways, but Van Niekerk "rigorously resisted efforts by the Department of National Education to promote whites-only policy" – all activities were open to everyone.[12]

Curator Hayden Proud, who joined the institution in the 1990s, was friendly with Van Niekerk and he disclosed private conversations confirming that SANG was penalised financially. As head of a declared institution, Van Niekerk would have been privy to the budgets of sister "white own affairs" museums. Moreover, "Raymund was quite explicit in conversation with me and others like [art historian] Evelyn Cohen in his post-retirement years that F. W. de Klerk had tried to have him sacked several times, and his dislike for and cynicism about the man seemed to know no bounds."[13] That none of this is minuted reveals much about the modus operandi at the time – De Klerk would have called the chairperson of the board, who in turn clearly protected the director. The Michaelis Collection did not escape the "white own affairs" classification.

Van Niekerk appointed the first coloured professional: Emile Maurice, an education officer, in 1988. Former SANG employee Jo-Anne Duggan called to mind Van Niekerk's request to read through the pile of applications and make a recommendation:

> I was delighted to find Emile's letter among these. As a highly qualified and respected art teacher, he was an obvious choice. The fact that he was a 'person of colour' was a bonus … I was convinced that Emile would play a role in transforming SANG's educational programmes. Van Niekerk was most indignant when I reported back to him. "I can't appoint him", he said. "Not after he wrote me that rude letter". I returned to the Annexe to search the correspondence files. There I found a letter from Emile berating SANG for running a Matric Art Programme during the 'white' school holidays, effectively excluding the participation of 'coloured' and black students. I marched back to Van Niekerk's office brandishing the letter. "This", I told him firmly "is *exactly* why you should employ Emile". To his credit Van Niekerk backed down, conceding that Emile's determination to access the resources of SANG for his students was in fact commendable.[14]

Duggan spoke to Maurice about his time at SANG.[15] He told her how he had been heavily criticised for his move into an apartheid institution, how he was regarded as a "sell-out", but that he was convinced he could contribute to transformation from the inside:

> Emile explained that he had been driven by the desire to open SANG up to artists and others who had been previously excluded on the grounds of race or class, what he termed, 'ordinary' South Africans, and he wanted to give these people a voice, accord them the dignity and recognition they deserved by writing them into the broad narrative of South African art history. Reflecting on the exhibitions which he curated or co-curated, the programmes he initiated or participated in and the publications he authored or contributed to and the people whose lives he had touched, or been touched by, Emile was able to say quite humbly, that looking back, he felt that he was satisfied that he had made a small difference.[16]

It is important to remember that at the time professional staff was appointed at different levels, providing career advancement, and that Maurice was on a par with his colleagues of the same rank and qualifications. He immediately joined the acquisition committee and, as the following chapters will tell, made an invaluable difference to all aspects of the gallery's advancement.[17]

Van Niekerk appointed Faeza Allie to a senior administrative position in 1989. She was responsible for financial management and a team of staff; she made a huge contribution to the financial well-being of the institution in various capacities until 2001, and subsequently to Iziko Museums, until her retirement in 2015.[18] Allie recalls going for an interview and having to arrange with a colleague to meet her in the Company's Garden as she had never been to the gallery, an institution associated with white people and apartheid in her community: "I was early for the appointment and saw two benches which I had to assess to ensure that I sat on the correct bench allocated for 'Non Whites/Nie-Blankes' until I was collected to go to the gallery for my interview with the director." Once inside, she found the atmosphere and stillness eerie and was tempted to leave.[19]

After a daunting interview with Van Niekerk and board member Cees Wolters, Allie left feeling that she would not get the job – not as a "coloured" woman at that time. But a telephonic interview with the gallery auditor followed, after which she was appointed. "My view immediately changed and I was optimistic, hopeful and inspired about the revelation ... the beginning of transformation of SANG." She reported directly to Van Niekerk and worked closely with Wolters while he was on the board.

Boycott, policy changes and the impact on exhibitions

IN THE 1960s, the ANC began to call for a cultural and academic boycott in order to end apartheid in South Africa. In his first report to the board of trustees, Van Niekerk foresaw the impact that a December 1980 United Nations general assembly resolution titled "Cultural, academic and other boycotts of South Africa" would have on the institution: "Although, once again, the exhibitions schedule of the National Gallery provided a varied fare of the art of this country and abroad, of present and past, and of all the main mediums, the absence of major exhibitions from overseas is becoming more and more noticeable." [20]

He gratefully acknowledged modest exhibitions by nineteenth-century American lithographers and photographs by Arthur Rothstein provided by the Government of the United States, as well as those made available by the Peter Stuyvesant Foundation and the Rembrandt van Rijn Art Foundation. The latter, *Rodin and his Contemporaries*, attracted a vast public and nearly 1,000 catalogues were sold.[21] These foundations, together with some foreign embassies, institutions and cultural agencies such as the British Council and Pro Helvetia, as well as South African commercial galleries, continued to play a role in ensuring on-going exposure of international art.

Chief among these were exhibitions of work by renowned artists Yaacov Agam, Michael Ayrton, Richard Hamilton, Friedensreich Hundertwasser, Eduardo Paolozzi, a tribute to John Piper and watercolours by J. M. W. Turner. *Gold from Peru*, hosted in 1981, attracted some 10,000 visitors over a two-week period. *Forty Years of British Sculpture* and *De Renoir à Kisling* (The School of Paris) were made available by the British Council and the Petit Palais in Geneva respectively, while eleven paintings and eighteen drawings from the estate of Pablo Picasso's granddaughter, Marina Picasso, was organised in collaboration with the Goodman Gallery, Johannesburg.

Drawing on local collections and expertise resulted in remarkable exhibitions. Van Niekerk liked to host or present a retrospective exhibition every alternative year and to fulfil the role of SANG as a national institution by sharing major exhibitions curated by gallery staff with sister art museums in Durban, Kimberley, Johannesburg, Pietermaritzburg, Port Elizabeth and Pretoria. The gallery in turn received shows from these art museums, such as the Stanley Pinker retrospective from the King George VI Art Gallery (now the Nelson Mandela Metropolitan Art Museum, NMMAM) in Port Elizabeth. Joe Dolby remembers the importance Van Niekerk placed on participation in the National Arts Festival in Grahamstown, while, on the local front, Dolby curated and organised exhibitions for the Worcester Museum every year. Continuing the tradition of showing works from FONG's private collections, education staff, with input from artist and dealer Joe Wolpe, curated two exhibitions.[22]

The practice of generating catalogues for important exhibitions continued unabated. McClelland and Lucy Alexander curated *Women artists in South Africa* (1985), which included a catalogue; in the same year, McClelland and Liz Biggs curated *Focus on Bloomsbury*, with a catalogue written by Marion Arnold.[23] Bedford singled out the *Paris and South African Artists* (1988) exhibition and publication, and the way in which Van Niekerk developed and fore-grounded South African art through high-profile travelling exhibitions such as the *Cape Town Triennial* (CTT), which not only captured the extent and quality of recent South African art but also enabled SANG to make important acquisitions.[24]

Nurturing existing partnerships and forming new ones remain essential for any museum. The role of the Standard Bank Gallery in Johannesburg and the Standard Bank African Art Collection has been central to the success story of major exhibition exchanges. Since 1984 this large banking group has sponsored the Standard Bank Young Artist Award, a prestigious early-career prize that includes a travelling exhibition and catalogue. SANG hosted the Standard Bank Foundation Collection of African Tribal Art in 1984.[25]

By the mid-1980s, the grip of the cultural and academic boycott was tightening. It was exacerbated by the burden of insurance costs of art brought into South Africa. Van Niekerk mentioned an innovative American law whereby the value of the contents of an exhibition was, at the time, indemnified against loss or damage to the tune of $250 000. SANG funds, as well as this kind of support for museums, were (and remain) hopelessly inadequate. In 1982 he remarked on the disequilibrium in funding: "Large sums of money are found to import performing artists and sportsmen. When will something be done for the visual arts and our art museums, languishing for lack of support?"[26]

To make matters worse, the Department of Trade and Industry imposed a 60% import surcharge. Van Niekerk's objection to government that works of art were "neither capital goods nor raw materials," supported by the heads of Declared Cultural Institutions, was to little avail.[27] Responding to representations by commercial galleries, the astonishing 60% surcharge on sculptures and prints remained, while a levy on paintings, drawings and pastels was reduced to 10%.[28]

The mid-1970s marked the beginning of a decline in the visitors to SANG, which Van Niekerk correctly diagnosed as signs of economic downturn, political uncertainty and upheavals; the growth of suburban shopping centres also contributed to the decline of the city centre. The long overdue introduction of television in 1976 further negatively impacted on all cultural and art activities, at least until the novelty wore off and people tired of the poor quality of the offerings. However, for SANG, high-profile exhibitions and associated education activities brought many positive results.[29] A small museum shop was created in 1981 and immediately proved popular with tourists, while the gallery benefited from the profits.[30]

If the growing shortage of international exhibitions contributed to the downward trend in attendance figures, it also resulted in a policy change to make better use of the permanent collection. In 1976 already it was reported: "Whereas in the past these works were hung in the form of 'room changes' only, grouped according to schools but otherwise selected at random, attempts are now made to present them in the form of thematic exhibitions, logically arranged and accompanied by detailed catalogues."[31]

The dearth of international exhibitions also led to a modification of the policy on retrospective exhibitions:

> The previous policy that such exhibitions should only take place towards the end of a long career has been changed to allow for recognition of conspicuous achievement at earlier stages of the artists' lives. The Trustees have consistently agreed that the gallery should play a vital role in the contemporary artistic life of the country.[32]

Kim Siebert recalls how she motivated for the Invited Artist Programme in order to introduce a more flexible approach to the retrospectives dedicated to established artists, as well as to support contemporary aesthetic production. It grew into an important event at the gallery and ran until 2000, when it was replaced by the Artists-in-Residence initiative. Open studios were set up in the Annexe (or on occasion in the main building) for two weeks and the public could engage with the invited artists, who would lead workshops and sometimes curate exhibitions from SANG's permanent collection – all without payment.[33]

Public, students and learners alike had the privilege of engaging directly with some of South Africa's foremost artists, including recipients of the Standard Bank Young Artist Award, as well as many invited by the institution and some who visited Cape Town from abroad. Often invited before they had achieved acclaim, some of these invited artists included Willie Bester, Andries Botha, Alan Crump, Keith Dietrich, Ângela Ferreira, William Kentridge, Peter Schütz and Penny Siopis.[34]

From the mid-1970s photography was taken seriously as an art form and regular exhibitions were organised, ranging from a variety of group shows to South African photographers such as Jansje Wissema, and Irish-born Alfred Duggan-Cronin, who undertook several photographic expeditions across the sub-continent in the earlier twentieth century. In 1980 SANG's Geoffrey Grundlingh and photographers Gavin Furlonger and Dan Roberts invited photographers working in the fields of advertising, editorial and fashion to submit portfolios for selection. They endeavoured to show the quality work produced by professional photographers who were also concerned with creating independent artistic statements.[35] David Goldblatt was honoured with his first retrospective in 1983, covering thirty-five years of his work; it travelled throughout the country. SANG visitors were also exposed to international luminaries, for example Constance Stuart Larrabee, Ansel Adams, Ezra Stoller and photographic works by Paul Nash. By 1984 there were enough photographs in the collection to warrant a special exhibition.

Van Niekerk maintained the catholic and eclectic approach to exhibitions initiated by his

PLATE 11: *Ashanti gold weights* from Ghana, bronze, c. 15th to 19th century; photographer Pam Warne.

predecessors. SANG's shows under his tenure included *Inuit Art – Art of the Canadian Eskimo*, French theatrical posters and illustrations curated by JAG, musical instruments from the Kirby Collection and *Never-Never-Land – The Golden Age of Illustrated Children's Books*, which consisted of 350 books from the Victorian and Edwardian eras assembled from private collections. *Silver from Five Centuries* and *The Arts of China and Japan*, a showcase of porcelain, glass, ivory, fabric and precious metals, were arranged in co-operation with the Antique Collectors' Society of South Africa.

In addition to the exhibition of African art from the Standard Bank collection, work from SANG's permanent collection, including the Ashanti gold weights, recent acquisitions and textiles loaned from SAM, were exhibited and accompanied by an audio-visual programme (Plate 11).[36] Historical African art from the permanent collection was also shown in the Touch Gallery, as were musical instruments from SAM's collection, together with workshops and demonstrations. It is important to note the initiatives from SANG to work with the "ethnographic" collections at SAM.

What to acquire in a rapidly changing South Africa?

LIKE HIS PREDECESSORS and successors, Van Niekerk immediately and consistently referred to the inadequate budget for acquisitions and the impact this had on the permanent collection: "It is felt that the Gallery is still just managing to act as the 'memory' of our own art in its successive developments, though more depth and a better representation of important figures are needed for a truly National collection."[37] He saw the need for collecting artists throughout their careers, as well as in the broader art historical and educational context. Just like Paris, he also wanted to avoid parochialism:

> Although there is an emphasis on the acquisition of local art, the Gallery's acquisitions policy aims at the presentation of a representative picture both of South African art and of the art, past and present of the mother countries in Europe. Without this background picture, our own art development cannot be fully understood. One must also consider the aesthetic and educational value which a good European collection, in its own right, has for the South African public.[38]

Although a national art museum, SANG still played second fiddle to JAG, a municipal institution, "which had the good fortune of being able to buy excellent European works at a time when this was still possible in the years immediately after the war, years during which the National Gallery's purchasing allocation was negligible".[39] Nevertheless, it is extraordinary what could be purchased in the mid-1970s, nationally and internationally with SANG's meagre budget of R30,000, supplemented, of course, by R10,000 from Cape Town's city council and small additional amounts from the Montagu White Bequest.[40]

Writing in 1980, Van Niekerk compared SANG's acquisitions budget with that of national galleries in Australia and Canada; he described as "shameful" the funds available to the gallery. "In the end we shall see a National Gallery which is no credit at all to the cultural life of this country." His policy document of the same year stated that art from the European founder countries, Africa and South Africa would be purchased, but it was becoming increasingly difficult to make significant additions to the modern western or older European collections.[41]

It is important here to pause and briefly consider the acquisition of South African art in general and work by black artists in particular. In Johannesburg in the late 1940s, the Local Committee for Non-European Adult Education established the Polly Street Recreational Centre; under the leadership of Cecil Skotnes it became known as the Polly Street Art Centre, the first large-scale urban art centre in the country. It enabled black artists to learn their craft, participate in practical and theoretical discussions and read art books and magazines. White artists could meet their black compatriots and share their skills as volunteers; some of South Africa's greatest artists found their creative home and a platform to break into a serious art market there.[42]

University education was to a certain extent already segregated and discriminatory when the NP came into power in 1948, but some, for instance the universities of Cape Town, Natal and the Witwatersrand, accommodated black students. In 1959, the NP applied apartheid principles to higher education through the Extension of University Education Act No. 45, and the universities were forced to comply. This was followed by the establishment of separate institutions for Coloureds, Indians and the different African ethnic groups; art departments were rare.[43] The South African Native College, founded in Alice in the Eastern Cape in 1916, was racially inclusive, but in 1959 it was renamed the University of Fort Hare (UFH) and it was designated for Xhosa speakers only.[44] It had an art department, but most black artists relied on, and benefited from, the missionary schools such as the Evangelical Lutheran Church Art and Craft Centre at Rorke's Drift and a few formal and non-governmental facilities.

The 1970s saw the founding of the Community Arts Project (CAP) in Cape Town (1977–2008), and the Funda Arts Centre (1976) and Federated Union of Black Artists (FUBA) (1978) in Johannesburg. Bill and Fieke Ainslie bought a large home in Saxonwold in 1977 and formalised the Johannesburg Art Foundation as a non-governmental organisation (NGO) in 1982. It was a non-racial hive of creativity and experimentation in a white area and as a result the owners and participants were subjected to night-time searches and arrests.[45]

John Peffer has written extensively and authoritatively about Ainslie's and artist David Koloane's roles in fostering FUBA and the Thupelo Workshops. The workshops had emerged from the Triangle Workshop, which had been launched by art patron Robert Loder and artist Anthony Caro in New York in 1982. The South African iteration followed in 1985 – it created much controversy and debate, as it disrupted prevailing notions of "committed" and "resistance" art by the introduction of abstraction, which at the time was under aesthetic as well as political pressure. Peffer's reference to the exhibition Koloane curated for the ANC Zabalaza festival in London in 1990 confirms that many of the participants in the workshops were harbingers of things to come: "While the politicians were busy trying to figure out what the new post-apartheid South African culture might look like, artists like Koloane were able to show what had been going on all along in the grey areas of art during those black-and-white years."[46] Bongiwe Dhlomo-Mautloa, Sfiso Ka Mkame, Billy Mandindi, Kagiso Pat Mautloa, Sam Nhlengethwa, Toni Nkotsi and Mmakgoba Mmapula Helen Sebidi and Durant Sihlali have indeed left their mark on South African art – as artists, curators and teachers.

Foreign donors, anticipating that a democratically elected government would support these initiatives, as well the Alexandra and Katlehong Art Centres, gradually withdrew their funding. This never happened, as there was and still is little or no understanding – at any level of government – of the vital role that these initiatives could play post-1994 and particularly today, when the country is overwhelmed by educational and cultural challenges.[47]

At the time white universities offered a thorough education in the history of western art and architecture, but South African art – whether produced by black or white artists – was largely absent from the curriculum. Artist and academic Walter Battiss introduced rock art and some historical African sculpture into the curriculum at the University of South Africa (UNISA) in the 1960s. Wits University followed in 1978.[48]

In 1973, E. J. de Jager, a professor of anthropology at UFH, mapped and described the wealth and depth of black art in his book Contemporary African Art in South Africa. Thirteen works from SANG's collection were referenced, the only public collection represented. There was little reaction in the press at the time and no reviews of De Jager's book in UNISA's journal, *De Arte*. Frieda Harmsen reviewed the first four volumes of the South African Art Library from Bouman to Berman, published by Struik under the auspices of SANG, and traced the history of books on South African art, but she mentioned neither De Jager's book nor the absence (or presence) of black artists.[49] This neglect might partly be attributed to the fact that De Jager was an anthropologist, not an art historian, and his understanding and analyses may therefore have been considered unworthy of academic consideration.[50]

The lack of engagement with De Jager's book was symptomatic of a broader lack of scholarly engagement of black artists. It is possible to speculate that the white academy either knew little about or were simply not interested in the pioneering work of painters such as Ernest Mancoba, John Koenakeefe Mohl and George Pemba. Much has been written about the importance and impact of Esmé Berman's 1970 *Art and Artists of South Africa*. For the first time in South African art history, she integrated primary source material, drawn from catalogues, gallery and institutional records and museum accession lists, with historical research. Her selection of artists was based on objective criteria that are disclosed in all the editions of the book: "public encounter" – representation in museums and public galleries – underpinned the twenty-three variables. These included participation in major national and international exhibitions, winning significant national competitions, presence in publications, and awards; Berman required a minimum of three criteria for individual inclusion.[51] Her methodology was undermined by apartheid and its institutions, as few black artists had the opportunity of a career, and her uncompromising adherence to the criteria resulted in the exclusion of well-known and important artists. Berman was aware of the necessity for further, detailed research and the first to acknowledge that there were lacunae in her books. Successive editions of *Art and Artists* saw an increase in the number of black and emerging artists.[52]

The 1980s marked a period of revision and significant changes. In 1985, artist and curator Ricky Burnett presented his ground-breaking exhibition *Tributaries: A View of Contemporary South African Art* at Museum Africa, followed in 1988 by curator Stephen Sack's *The Neglected Tradition* at JAG. These two events had a profound impact on the way exhibitions would be curated and collections assembled, but it has to be noted that both had their origins in foreign initiatives: Burnett was commissioned by German car manufacturer BMW, as part of their *Kulturprogramm*, to curate an exhibition for a European tour, while Christopher Till, then director of JAG, was inspired by an exhibition and seminar held at the Alliance française in Pretoria in 1986, titled "Historical perspective of black art in South Africa".[53]

The reluctance of South African art museums to acquire work by black artists, particularly those resident in cities and living in townships, some directly connected to white artists and administrators through their involvement in community arts projects, is often raised. Once again the issue of quality is relevant. Looking back on his years as a member and chairperson of SANG's acquisitions committee, Dubow in 1996 remarked:

> It was rather seen as the kind of stuff meant to supply a commodity that would be of interest to certain commercial art galleries, notably in Johannesburg, who were interested in what was becoming known in their terms as 'the township style'. Artists were very happy to supply what was being demanded of them. The National Gallery at that stage had a particular mindset. It did not see that as the kind of art that necessarily should be inside a national art gallery – it was the kind of stuff that was being flogged in Johannesburg commercial galleries.

Referring to the role of SANG, Dubow continued:

> I think that there is the realisation now amongst practicing black artists generally that there is more to making art than the kind of thing that is readily disposable in commercial art galleries in the northern suburbs of Johannesburg. But keen-eyed buying on the part of the National Gallery can, in fact, stimulate art production where artists themselves do not make incorrect assumptions about the kind of art that can end up on the walls of a gallery. So, I think that in this sense it becomes very much of an interactive process and there is a new dynamic at work, which I think is an important one.[54]

Dubow is, of course, here referring to the phenomenon of "township art," a category of urban art practice that depicted everyday activities in black urban environments created under apartheid. Commenting on the "unremitting success" he achieved as a young artist in the early 1960s, painter Louis Maqhubela remarked: "Township art was in demand and there was no need to first hold an exhibition in order to sell your work. The novelty as a whole led to lots of sales and I quickly became the main breadwinner at home."[55]

No national art museum would buy art mass-produced for the market, not then and not now, but SANG had not kept up with complex developments in art by black South Africans, which had its foundation in the 1940s, notably through the activities of painters Mohl, Mancoba and Sekoto. As discussed in chapter two, Paris and Bokhorst were either incapable of, or unwilling to seriously engage with such art; it

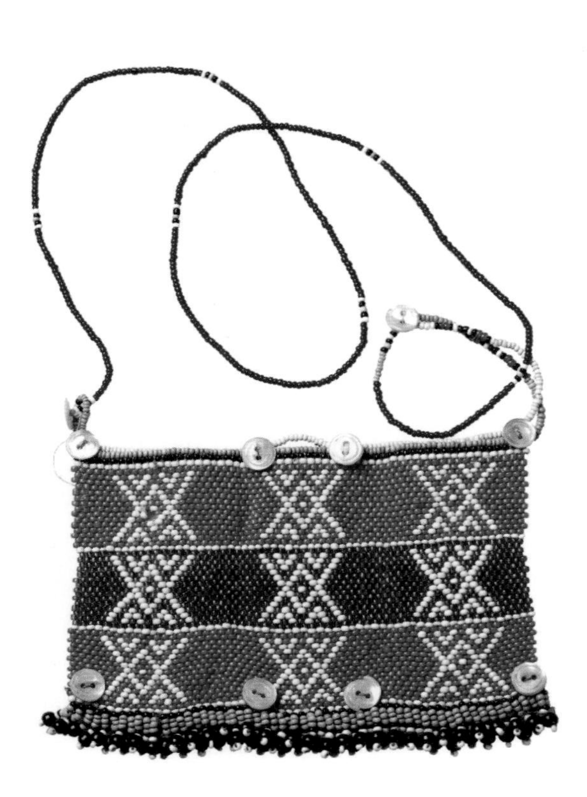

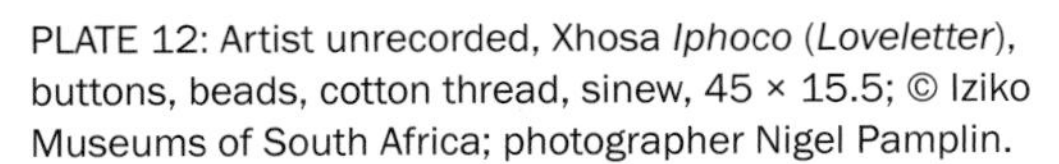

PLATE 12: Artist unrecorded, Xhosa *Iphoco* (*Loveletter*), buttons, beads, cotton thread, sinew, 45 × 15.5; © Iziko Museums of South Africa; photographer Nigel Pamplin.

PLATE 13: Artist unrecorded, Xhosa *Iphoco* (*Loveletter*), buttons, beads, cotton thread, sinew, 34 × 6.5; © Iziko Museums of South Africa; photographer Nigel Pamplin.

was left to Arnott to make some amends as curator of prints and drawings and sculpture. Artists change and grow, and many, such as Dumile Feni, Ezrom Legae, Sydney Kumalo, Maqhubela and Durant Sihlali, always had a personal essence and style. It was inevitable that they would break out of the conventions and stylistic mannerisms of what became a clichéd genre. Moreover, they took a stand against white commercial expectations of artists living in townships – to depict only township scenes.

Seen against this background, there was indeed "keen-eyed buying" happening at SANG during Van Niekerk's tenure. Works by contemporary black artists – from the townships, cities and the rural areas – were added steadily to the permanent collection and slowly historical African art from other parts of the continent, as well as South Africa, was acquired. In addition to the purchase of the first beadwork from South Africa in 1987[56] (Plates 12 & 13), the following contemporary black artists entered the collection: Albert Adams, Tyrone Appollis, Sipho Hlati, Austin Hleza, Jackson Hlungwani (three sculptures), Ezrom Legae, Thami Jali, Sfiso Ka Mkame, David Koloane, Sydney Kumalo, Noria Mabasa, Richard Mabaso, Fikile Magadlela, Billy Mandindi, Johannes Maswanganyi, Titus Matiyane, Tommy Motswai, Bekhi Myeni, Roy Ndinisa, Tony Nkotsi, Lucas Seage, Johannes Segogela, Dr Phutuma Seoka, Sithembiso Sibisi and Lucky Sibiya.

In 1986 the acquisitions committee agreed to recommend to the board that the gallery purchase so-called "transitional art".[57] Dubow urged that "every effort be made to acquire further works by contemporary black artists," and he specifically mentioned Titus Matiyane, who was having an exhibition

PLATE 14: Sfiso Ka Mkame, *Letters to God*, 1988, oil pastel on paper, 1280 × 910; courtesy of the artist; photographer Kathy Grundlingh.

at UCT's Centre for African Studies.[58] This resulted in the acquisition of Matiyane's tin and wire sculpture Concord in September.[59] Moreover, gallery staff advised the artist's agent on stabilising the ephemeral nature of some the materials Matiyane used.

More often than not the paintings, sculptures, drawings and prints – like those of many of their white compatriots – were openly or covertly critical of the government. Paul Stopforth's *Interrogators*, already discussed, offers one example, but many other works exploring history and resistance to oppression and malfeasance were purchased. A few examples will suffice: Tyrone Appollis' gouache *Recalling Caledon Square March 1960* (1988); Norman Catherine's assemblage *Animal Instincts* (1985); Claire Gavronsky's pastel triptych *Plus Ça Change, Plus C'est La Même Chose* (1988); Sfiso Ka Mkame's pastel *Letters to God* (1988) (Plate 14); William Kentridge's triptych *Dreams of Europe* (1985) and the screenprints *Art in a State of Grace, Art in a State of Siege, Art in a State of Hope* (1989); David Koloane's abstract painting *Emergence* (1988); Billy Mandindi's painted tin, wire and wood *Fire Games* (1985); Johannes Maswanganyi's painted wood portraits *PW Botha* and *DF Malan* (1988); Karel Nel's pastel and sprayed pigment *Accelerating Field* (1986); Penny Siopis' *Piling Wreckage Upon Wreckage* (1989); Diane Victor's triptych *Judgement of Parys* (1988) and Gavin Younge's sculpture *Botha's Baby* (1981) (Plate 15).

The small individual pictures and glowing colours of the densely-worked oil pastel in Ka Mkame's *Letters to God* belie the turbulence, pain, anger and helplessness that the artist is communicating to God – cries for deliverance from the violence and police repression that characterised the townships outside Durban in the 1980s. Younge's *Botha's Baby* is a chilling reminder of the fear, white paranoia and militarisation that intensified under the hard-line leadership of P. W. Botha; crafted in welded steel, a baby's high chair becomes an ominous object, complete with a revolver carefully laid into the tray.

In 1978, the SANG trustees commissioned Bruce Arnott's monumental bronze sculpture, *Numinous Beast*, which was installed facing the main entrance of the gallery two years later. Arnott's sculpture stands on axis with Sydney Harpley's statue of Jan Smuts (back cover). It is a magnificent and enduring physical and spiritual sentinel and guardian of the institution, but also a commemoration of the annihilation of the indigenous San people. It is worth including the description of this work from the *Quarterly Bulletin* here:

> *Numinous Beast* was conceived and made in the foothills of the Natal Drakensberg which, within living memory, was one of the last havens of the Southern Bushmen [San], preserving countless reminders of their presence. The image of *Numinous Beast* arose in a dream and is, for the artist, an archetypal evocation of the spirit of that place – awesome, threatening and protective. In a sense this sculpture can be seen as a paradoxical reference and monument to the tragic passing of the Bushmen, a creatively spiritual and ecologically balanced people destroyed by other acquisitive races.[60]

As with exhibitions, there was a positive side to the lack of funds: the extraordinary vitality and power of the art which emerged in South Africa during the 1980s contributed to the move from buying work by international and well-established South African artists, to younger artists. This produced a more open-ended and pluralistic approach to the appraisal of work originating from formerly marginal contexts. While there was only one formal policy statement in 1980,[61] the shifts are recorded in the *Annual Reports* in the words of both the chairpersons and the director. Taking into consideration the policies of other art museums, Van Niekerk said of the purchase of contemporary art from abroad:

> The desire not to overlap with the purchasing activities of, for instance the Johannesburg Art Gallery, has been a factor in the decision. The agreement on loan exchanges between the various art museums in the country will mean that acquisitions in different fields will help the public in several centres to arrive at a broader view of art production today.

JAG was buying American art and it was therefore regarded as a "constructive policy" at SANG "to concentrate on the acquisition of British and European works when additions to the modern collection are contemplated".[63] An exhibition of American art from JAG was displayed at SANG the following year.[64]

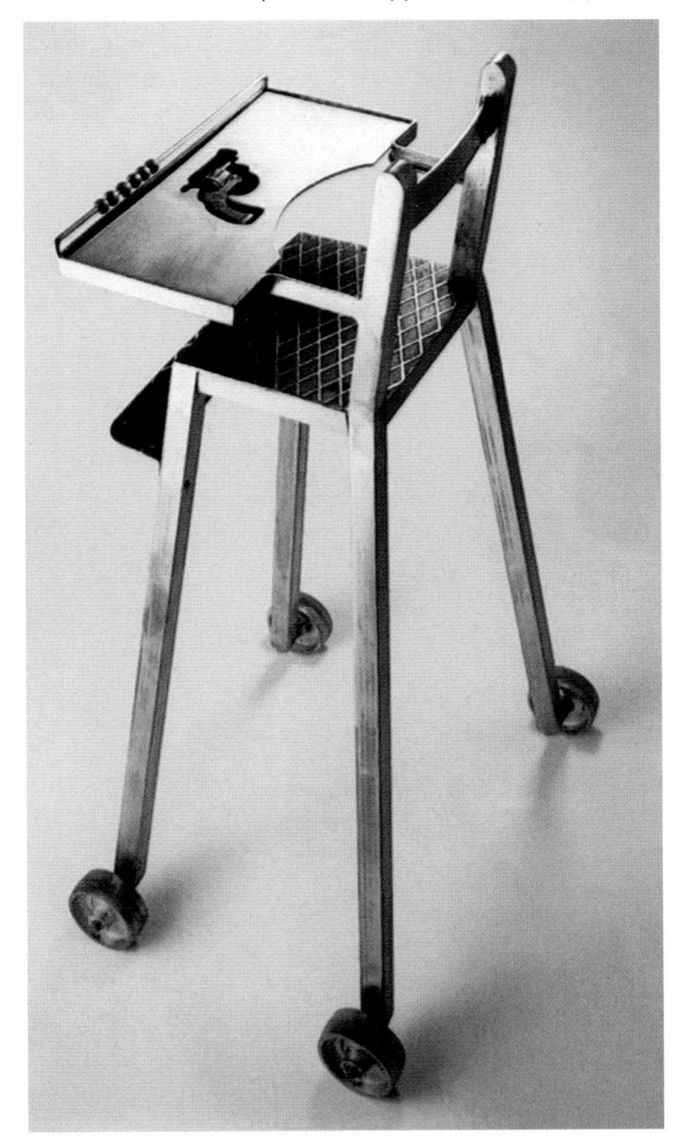

PLATE 15: Gavin Younge, *Botha's Baby,* 1981, cast iron and welded steel, 1186 × 590 × 515; image courtesy of the artist.

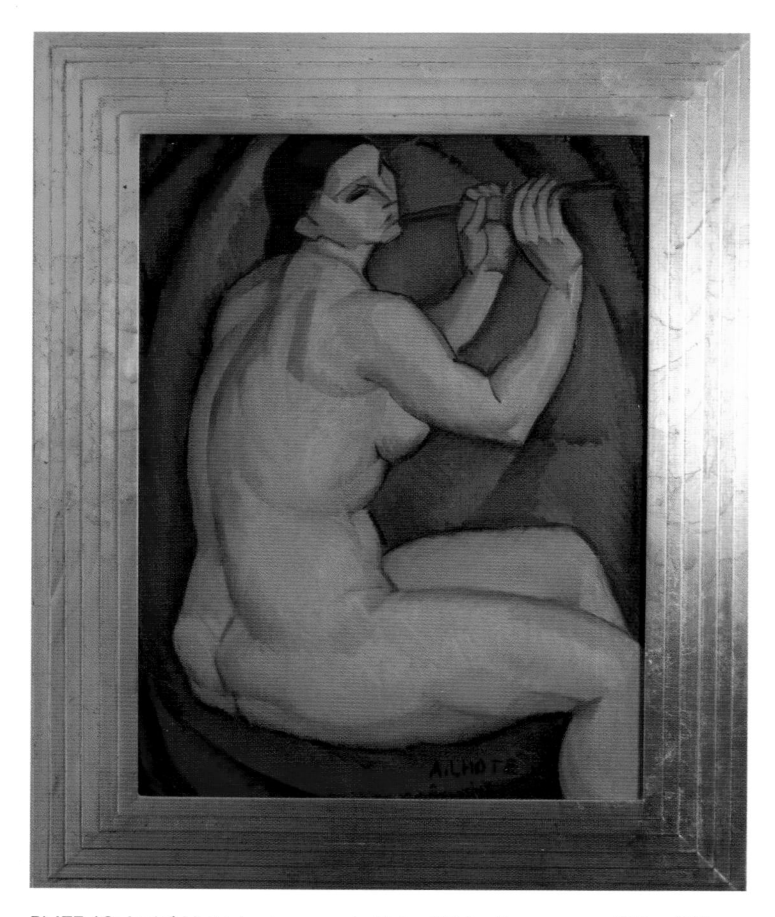

PLATE 16: André Lhote *La Joueuse de Flute*, 1911, oil on canvas, 813 × 595.

In order to increase support of younger South African artists, it was agreed that works would be commissioned from "an up-and-coming generation who show particular talent". This would become standard practice at the national art museum.[65] To return to the matter of quality, artists – irrespective of their identity – had to make their mark before entering the permanent collection. FONG stepped into the breach and established a sub-committee of the association in 1975 to purchase works by young, untested artists; over time most of them would be transferred to SANG and accessioned.[66]

Van Niekerk, supported by the trustees, was relentless in his efforts to address the untenable financial situation with DNE and he frequently turned to the press to gain support.[67]

Representations to the department eventually paid off. In his director's report of 1983–84, Van Niekerk referred to the welcome increase in the acquisitions fund that enabled the purchase of contemporary international works by R. B. Kitaj, Gary Wragg and Alan Davie, which in turn stimulated public interest.[68] Compared to the acquisition fund of R5,621 in March 1975, this was a major achievement.[69] With hindsight, SANG was doing extremely well – in some years to come there would be no acquisition budget and the allocation for the 2017–18 financial year was R290,850, a mere R40,850 more than thirty years ago.[70] The board minute books from 1986–1990 reveal government grants for acquisitions ranging from R192,000 to R250,000, and these were augmented by R10,000 from the city council, various small bequests and interest on investments. Government grants were paid throughout the financial year and specific amounts were allocated for the bi-monthly meetings. From 1986 a brief written motivation was submitted to the acquisitions committee for works costing R20,000 and more.[71]

However, as prices rose and the rand lost value, these amounts ultimately proved inadequate. The last important international acquisition was French late-Cubist painter André Lhote's *La Joueuse de Flute* (1911) in 1987 (Plate 16). The work was acquired for R110,772, and cost R110,923 including shipping. "It is seldom these days that a painting of this quality and importance by an internationally known artist can be acquired," noted the chairperson.[72] At a meeting on 25 November 1987, the acquisitions committee had R606,932 in the reserve fund and had paid for the painting from a purchase allocation of R143,000. Irma Stern's oil on board, *Bullfight*, cost R6,000; it augmented the already substantial holdings of twenty paintings, thirteen drawings and twelve prints by the artist.[73]

In addition to maintaining a modicum of its status as the national art museum, Van Niekerk regarded it as "imperative that the gallery continues to collect in the area of up-and-coming international artists, particularly in light of the cultural boycott". The acquisition committee agreed that, as a guideline, half of the grant from the DNE be reserved for such works.[74]

By the time of the Lhote acquisition the socio-political situation in South Africa had worsened. An economic boycott was taking effect and the value of the country's currency was in decline. Matters were exacerbated by State President P. W. Botha's infamous "Rubicon" speech, an intransigent statement of nationalist resolve and dedication to apartheid's logic of separate development, delivered to the National Party Congress in Durban on 15 August 1985. The country had indeed reached a point of no return, but not in the way Botha had intended.[75]

While the major bequests to SANG may have been a thing of the past, *Annual Reports* testify to the munificence of many artists and members of the public. This was all the more appreciated because the publicity around the monetary value of artworks could cause reluctance to part with valuable inheritance or investments. In the mid-1970s it seemed that "all gifts and bequests to this institution have now been exempted from tax – as they had been for educational institutions – which, it is trusted, will encourage increased generosity on the side of the public".[76] Unfortunately this policy was not implemented.

Different conservators cared for the collection during the period under discussion, with Thomas Rebok replacing Bosman. Paris' dream of a national restoration centre in reality consisted of one painting restorer who had to reduce the backlog of work on the permanent collection, as well as treat paintings for numerous small and big art museums and other public collections throughout the country, and also South West Africa (Namibia). SANG was paid for the work and this covered the restorer's salary.[77]

In an overview of the history and contribution of SANG in 1983–84, Van Niekerk pointed out that the character of the institution had changed considerably over the past three or four decades. It was now being called upon to perform a number of functions that were not usually housed under one roof in similar museums in London and New York, "certainly never under so exiguous a roof". SANG in fact combined the tasks undertaken by several London institutions, including the National Gallery, the fine arts section of the Victoria and Albert Museum, the Tate Gallery and the prints and drawings department of the British Museum.[78] Not to mention the collection of historical African art that was also under the roof and growing.

Publications and the growing role of the education department

PRODUCING INFORMATIVE catalogues for most exhibitions had been part and parcel of the work at SANG for decades, but it was becoming increasingly expensive. The situation was exacerbated by the policy of full Afrikaans and English bilingualism for publications, where possible. Catalogues in English were in much greater demand. It was also noted that "one rand is the maximum the public seems prepared to spend on a catalogue". While this was an added strain on the finances, the practice of sending all publications to some 150 international art museums and various libraries as exchange materials helped "to achieve an image of the gallery as a serious and scholarly institution".[79] The director and staff were committed to informing the public and it was decided to make use of photocopied information at a reasonable price (30 or 50 cents) for smaller shows. A monthly agenda, giving full details of exhibitions and all activities were sent to Friends and to libraries, galleries, schools and tourist bureaux.[80]

Travel was integral to the working life of Paris and Bokhorst, as it was too for the assistant directors and some key staff. In February 1989 the board approved Van Niekerk's proposal that professional officers be supported to travel abroad, as it was essential for them to keep abreast of what was happening. Well-motivated applications had to be submitted for board approval. However, times were changing for the worse financially and this policy decision would only apply once: when Patty Hardy, who was responsible for the newly acquired Natale Labia Museum, discussed below, visited relevant museums abroad.

Personal research was also negatively affected. Van Niekerk highlighted how the workload imposed by the exhibition and education programmes left no room for scholarly research into general topics, only on specific exhibitions.[81] A great deal of information was prepared for the catalogues and the documentation of the permanent collection, but the institution was disadvantaged in terms of the subsidy formula for publications that did not take catalogue essays into account. In this regard Van Niekerk wrote to the DNE, stating that it was unfair and not conducive to stimulating research in museums. He cited the *Paris and South African Artists* (1988) catalogue as an example: three staff members spent two and a half years on the publication, it was highly regarded in academic and museum circles and won the Volkskas Prize for art historical publications.[82] This was another matter that militated against SANG that would never be resolved, in spite of many representations made to the authorities.

In order to address this Van Niekerk initiated the *Quarterly Bulletin* in June 1980; it was edited by Lucy Alexander and sponsored by the private sector.[83] In spite of the DNE's refusal to grant the publication the status of an accredited journal, which would contribute to its demise in December 1984, it attracted contributors such as Jillian Carman, Rory Doepel, Dubow, Phil du Plessis, Nadine Gordimer, Diana Kenton (now Hulton), Clinton Harrop-Allin, Marilyn Martin, Elizabeth Rankin, Anna Tietze, Keyan Tomaselli and Van Niekerk.[84] Sadly Van Niekerk's brilliant insights into historical and contemporary art, and his knowledge of architectural history were not conveyed in any serious publications, apart from his contributions to the *Quarterly Bulletin* and the book on public sculpture in Cape Town that he wrote with Alan Crump.

Bokhorst had established the education department and he was clear about the role of the gallery in the community. The *Annual Reports* spanning many decades reveal how the institution moved away from the idea of the museum as mainly a repository for objects ("object-centred") to one which placed more emphasis on exhibitions, people and education ("people-centred"). This was lucidly stated by Lucy Alexander in 1986:

> Today the South African National Gallery pursues a vigorous exhibition policy with regular exhibition changes. Educational activities are an important feature and range from children's workshops and organised guided tours to ensure that less privileged members of the community are able to visit the Gallery on a regular basis. That the South African National Gallery is not content to be a mere

> repository of art objects is evident from … the fact that the Gallery actively encourages artists by commissioning works of art. It is prominently involved in the organisation of national exhibitions such as the Cape Town Triennial.[85]

Dolby has noted how the programmes and scope of the education department grew over the years, "and by the 1990s it was as influential as the curatorial departments and enjoyed equal status with them. This has not been maintained by Iziko."[86] Time and again Van Niekerk, Fransen and staff affirmed the vital educational role that an art museum plays, not only in adult education and as a source of intellectual enrichment for the young, but by giving public lectures and practical seminars to students involved in museological studies at US and the then Cape Technikon.[87] Numerous workshops were held for adults, learners from schools under the different apartheid education departments, community organisations, and clubs and associations.

In a talk delivered to a group of FONG members circa 1983–84, Van Niekerk reflected on the contribution of the gallery across the years:

> If I say that its major function has been an educational one that might raise eyebrows – it certainly would in Pretoria where there has always been a steady refusal to recognise the educational function of museums of all kinds. Still that is our conviction. And we do not mean education of a rigid or formal kind but perhaps in the sense of expansion of interest, stimulation and in so far as possible an enhancement of life. The odd discomforting, even irritating stimulus would be part of the process. As would the simple provision of pleasure.[88]

In 1981 Dolby wrote about the efforts that had been made to attract people who would not normally visit the gallery:

> In this regard it may be mentioned that the film shows … include everything from Chaplin and Hitchcock to religion and mountain-climbing. Children's workshops are held on a regular basis, concerts and poetry readings are arranged, and visitors to the gallery may also benefit from the conducted tours led by trained volunteer guides. Close contact is also maintained with schools. The South African National Gallery is, therefore, not a passive or static institution but a dynamic organisation that actively encourages artists and seeks out works of art.[89]

Van Niekerk's resolve that education staff participate in all aspects of museum work was ground-breaking. Siebert called to mind that this "showed deep insight and forward thinking in the central role of museum outreach programmes to every generation".[90] The director supported and encouraged exhibitions curated by the educators and he praised them in the *Annual Reports* for the excellent shows they planned and mounted. In addition, and most importantly, staff could occupy curatorial posts when opportunities arose. This happened in many instances, which in turn meant that curatorship was enormously enhanced by experience in education. The two became inseparable in the DNA of the institution. The thorny question of a hierarchical division and perceived superiority of museum curatorship to education is raised in chapter seven particularly with regard to the race and colour of staff appointed.

As discussed in chapter two, the Touch Gallery was unique in South Africa and SANG became a world leader in the field. After 1978 different education officers took charge of the space and it was decided that shows that stimulated other senses and that were geared towards the general public would also be arranged.[91] This resulted in an extraordinary range of exhibitions: *Touch Wood, Transformations – an exhibition of Wearable Art, Maskerade, African Art and Music, Tactile Tunnel,* and *Luminous Lunar Lumpland,* a white, wavy world with ultra-violet lighting and ghostly sound effects designed by Peter Cazalet from the design department of the then Cape Performing Arts Board (CAPAB). There were exhibitions by students from the Michaelis School, Ruth Prowse School of Art, Cape Town Teachers' College and University of Stellenbosch students.

The name of the Touch Gallery changed to the Annexe in 1987, in line with a decision to reach beyond people with disabilities and to include non-formal education, specifically geared towards Xhosa-speaking and coloured people in the broader community.[92] SANG offered education programmes in the three main languages of the province, and art teacher Noni Sipuye, who was seconded by the Department of Education and Training in 1986, worked with Xhosa-speaking pupils. There was a great commitment to this part of the education programme and in the same year a sponsored scheme for black art teachers was started.[93]

The context of these programmes has to be viewed in relation to the legislated inequities in the national education of school-going students, says Siebert:

> … we inherited an established museum policy, sanctioned by the director, that placed most of our budget and resources for education at the feet of the elementary students from the townships, where no art was offered in school hours. By intention it was fundamental that these students would … visit the gallery in an affirming context and [have] an opportunity for art-making and personal creativity, as well as experiencing original artworks first hand. Students would always be spoken to in their mother tongue, they would be transported to and from the museum by commissioned buses, they would be unhurried and have nutritional refreshments provided for them, and they would be able to work with quality materials and have programmes specifically designed with child-friendly approaches, as well as follow-up projects.[94]

For Bedford the "Art for Schools" exhibitions curated by the education officers in the main building and the annual history of art lecture series for matrics held in September were important. A programme called "A Shared Vision" brought learners from the racially segregated education departments together.[95]

Extensions attempted and thwarted, and a new art museum added

THE STORY OF South Africa's national art museum is one of neglect of its collections since the earliest days. It is a story about inadequate facilities for display, conservation and storage, a situation that endures to this day. Needless to say, Van Niekerk raised these issues. He devoted almost a page to "the condition of the buildings and its effect on the collections housed and the work performed there" in his first report to the board.[96] Leading up to the fiftieth anniversary celebrations of SANG on 3 November 1980, extensive renovations were carried out.[97] However, environmental conditions were deteriorating – ten years after cables to provide climate control in the basement storage area were installed, the system no longer worked.

Van Niekerk re-activated the sub-committee concerned with extensions to the main building and prepared a document with staff, which took into consideration optimum functioning of the museum until 1990.[98] By 1982 exhibition spaces in the main building had to be sacrificed for storing art works, while office, library and workshop accommodation was also under pressure.[99]

In the 1985–86 *Annual Report* the new chairperson of the board, Professor H. van der Merwe Scholtz, thanked Minister of National Education F. W. de Klerk for discussions around the dire space situation at SANG.[100] A response must have been slow in the coming because the following year the chairperson re-iterated trustee anxiety regarding the safety of the collections and the proper functioning of the museum. Van Niekerk stated that the building was in a deplorable state of dilapidation, and included a report from the department of paintings and sculpture. He again referred to the "massive indifference" of the national education department, in spite of articles in the press.[101]

In July 1987 Scholtz informed the board that he would meet with De Klerk to discuss the desired extensions, and that he would use drawings prepared by architect Hannes Meiring & Partners.[102] While he emphasised that there would be no contractual obligation with the architect and that the choice of architects to undertake work at Declared Cultural Institutions would reside within the board, Meiring's concept drawings were handed in to the DNE.[103]

On-going representation resulted in a further visit from De Klerk, now State President, along with Dr. R. Venter, the director general of the DNE. They recognised the urgency of the matter, undertook to address it, and requested the following information: a document of costs for urgent repairs; costs for a conservative twenty-year building plan; an indication of the institution's "acquisition philosophy" and whether works which were no longer "relevant" would be alienated.[104] This was dangerous territory, particularly in light of the sale of artworks in the late 1940s and the unsuccessful efforts to dispose of sporting pictures from the Bailey bequest in 1970. The board decided unanimously that the collection was national cultural patrimony and therefore inalienable; it confirmed the national role and responsibilities of the institution and the historical meaning that resides in the permanent collection.

In response to the request from the DNE, the director, chairperson and architect board member, Hannes van der Merwe, proposed R250,000 for immediate requirements and R41 million for the period 1988–99 for a new building. Van Niekerk undertook an extended trip to America, England, France and Germany to view new art museum buildings.[105] Nothing came of the building plan, the renovation programme, which included disabled access and the installation of climate control, was approved, and in the end the renovations cost R634,000.[106]

Another project and priority intervened when, in 1982, the Public Works Department accepted The Fort in Muizenberg from Count Natale "Luccio" Labia, on behalf of the government, while the furniture, objects and paintings were donated to SANG. An eminent Keynesian economist and leading figure in South Africa's art and cultural history, Count Labia's maternal grandfather was the Randlord and art collector Sir Joseph Robinson, while his father, Count Natale Labia, was the first Italian ambassador to the country.[108]

In the 1988–89 Annual Report, the chairperson acknowledged with gratitude the gift from the Labia family: it would make an important contribution to the cultural life of the False Bay area and the Peninsula.[109] These developments meant that focus and government expenditure shifted to the renovations of the newly-acquired property, while the proposed extensions were forgotten.

The architect in charge of the renovation, refurbishing and adaptation was Paul Righini, and on 22 October 1988 De Klerk opened the Natale Labia Museum (NLM), named thus in honour of Count Luccio Labia's late father. Van Niekerk was enthusiastic about the acquisition of this satellite museum, regarding it as "one more act of notable generosity towards the arts in the history of his family. What is more the house came not alone but with much of the original furniture and a group of fine paintings from the Labia collection". He saw it as an expansion of the SANG activities and a vibrant cultural centre, adding:

> One trusts that the museum will prove attractive to holiday makers in the area and will focus attention on the distinctive and distinguished domestic architecture that characterizes this section of the False Bay coast. As a declared national monument it will stand as an example of preservation that is likely to be followed, as people come to realize how valuable the whole area is in terms of architectural and social history and, consequently, how great our responsibility is.

Every effort was made to fulfil the expectations of the family, the board and the director. SANG education officer Patty Hardy took on the responsibility as curator of the new museum. In addition to documenting the collection and museum interior, Hardy initiated exciting programmes of exhibitions, functions, workshops for children and adults, concerts, school tours and poetry readings in collaboration with staff at SANG and different individuals and organisations in the art community. Memorable exhibitions at this time were *The Brilliance of Cartier* and *Decorative Arts of the West 1900–1940*.[110]

The NLM was indeed a great asset to SANG, but unfortunately – like the gift from Max Michaelis – the museum came without an endowment by the donor or financial provision by the national education department, in effect placing increased strain on SANG. Efforts to address the situation culminated in Count Labia's offer in 2002 to contribute R3 million if the Department of Arts, Culture, Science and Technology (DACST) met the amount; needless to say, such support was not forthcoming.[111] By 2005 it became unsustainable, and unfortunately the satellite had to be closed. The contents of the building were returned to the Labia family.[112] The Public Works Department's sale of part of the property resulted in a court case, which in turn brought about many reports in the press, both illuminating and factually incorrect.[113] Such challenges were of course nothing new in the history of the national art museum.[114]

A new subsidy structure, building closure and Van Niekerk's departure

TOWARDS THE END of the 1980s, shortly before Van Niekerk's unexpected early retirement, the DNE initiated major developments in the administrative structures of national museums. Known as Framework Autonomy, it provided for autonomous boards, with directors of Declared Cultural Institutions as full members.[115] The structure, which was implemented in April 1988, was a welcome affirmation of the principle of arm's-length funding, although it was impossible to foresee all the implications it would have for the museums. Down the line, the consolidated subsidy meant that there was no separate grant for acquisitions.[116] Government funding did not keep up with escalating and new costs such as the addition of the NLM and computerisation, and the core functions of the national art museum – care of the collection, acquisitions, exhibitions and education – would suffer most.

In order to acknowledge the increased responsibility of board members under Framework Autonomy, the DNE offered remuneration for services, but trustees decided not to apply and to devote their time and expertise to SANG free of charge; all travel and accommodation costs were covered by the institution.[117] This was maintained until Iziko Museums came into being.

Funding opportunities from government outside the annual grant became available. In 1981 F. W. de Klerk appointed Dr. Jan Schutte, retiring director general of the South African Broadcasting Corporation (SABC), to chair the Commission of Inquiry into the Creative Arts in South Africa, both state and public. It became known as the Schutte Commission and its findings were linked to the Niemand Commission of Inquiry into the Performing Arts of 1977. The report led to a white paper accepted in parliament in 1986. Seeking further input from the arts community, De Klerk called for and attended a conference in Stellenbosch in 1988 and as a result the Foundation for the Creative Arts (FCA) came into being the following year. It was a not-for-profit company that provided public support to all the creative arts not supported through the existing Performing Arts Councils. Chapters four and five bear testimony to the great benefit that the gallery derived from the FCA for projects and publications during the 1990s. In terms of the 1996 White Paper on Arts, Culture and Heritage, the National Arts Council (NAC) was established; the FCA was de-registered and its infrastructure (including a building in Newtown, Johannesburg) and resources were incorporated into the NAC in 1997.[118]

The main SANG building was closed in April 1989 for renovations and the installation of climate control and a new lighting system. Four board meetings were held instead of six. The move to temporary premises at 42 Keerom Street required a great deal of planning and preparation: works of art remained in the building, but the library relocated, a task undertaken by SANG librarian Josephine Andersen and the South African Library.[119] The building contractor moved onto site the following January, with a projected date for handing over in June 1991, but the museum remained closed for a period of two-and-a-half years. The director attended monthly site meetings and special meetings regarding the building operations. The chairperson commented on the renovations:

> The move to temporary premises of the Library and staff who are normally housed in the main building, as well as the shifting of art works in order to accommodate the building works, have highlighted the serious shortage of space which has plagued SANG for some time and which is reaching critical proportions. The problem will have to be addressed as soon as the work now in progress is complete.

Conservation work and the compilation of a catalogue of the permanent collection were maintained, while exhibitions and other activities took place in the Annexe and at the NLM during this period. The Invited Artist Programme continued to grow and attract public interest.

In May 1989, Van Niekerk, who was approaching sixty, applied for early retirement. He cited reasons of a personal nature and the board accepted his decision with regret.[121] Van Niekerk had submitted a letter of resignation to the board three years earlier with a notice period of six months to see the NLM project well advanced.[122] The reasons for his decision were neither minuted nor reported in the *Argus* or *Die Burger* (both 1 August 1986), but it is pertinent that Van Niekerk had recently taken fifty-four days leave, that the chairperson excused himself from the discussion and that the matter was referred to the executive committee.[123] The post was advertised in the South African Sunday press and the London *Times Educational Supplement*, but at the eleventh hour Cees Wolters, the vice-chairperson whom Van Niekerk held in high regard, requested that he withdraw his resignation in light of the demands of Framework Autonomy. Van Niekerk agreed.[124]

While he did not make any public statements about his personal reasons for taking early retirement, Van Niekerk shared some thoughts with colleagues and friends. Dolby recalls a meeting with Van Niekerk, who said that "he was not the right person to lead the gallery into the 1990s; the new director required a better knowledge of contemporary South African art; he was not the right person for the close engagement with the relevant stakeholders which had to take place". Proud explains the decision in relation to the first acquisitions of beadwork in 1987; while supporting the general consensus that such material should be collected, Van Niekerk had his reservations:

> The other thing that I sensed underpinning things was his fear that "community art" in all its manifestations … would move into centre-stage at SANG in the new dispensation and supplant the international vision that he had for the collection. Implicit in this for him was yet another version of the amateurism, artistic mediocrity and inward-looking insularity that characterised much (white) South African art in the twentieth century, and he obviously wanted no part in it, and saw no role for himself in it.[126]

Van Niekerk would have agreed with lawyer, writer and long-time activist in the ANC, Albie Sachs, whose landmark paper "Preparing Ourselves for Freedom" reappraised the role of culture in a country on the brink of democracy. In 1989, at an in-house seminar in the Zambian capital Lusaka, Sachs called on his fellow ANC members to desist from saying that culture was a weapon of struggle. The paper was published in the *Weekly Mail* on 2 February 1990. With a real weapon, Sachs argued, "there is no room for ambiguity: a gun is a gun is a gun, and if it were full of contradictions, it would ... be useless for its purpose. But the power of art lies precisely in its capacity to expose contradictions and reveal hidden tensions".[127] His call for the autonomy of the arts was a radical break with many of his comrades and it stimulated crucial and often heated debate in South Africa, and beyond. Some interpreted Sachs' words as an entreaty to stop making political art, but this possibility would soon dissipate in the face of new challenges.

A proper handover from one director to another was important at the time. Van Niekerk was due to leave at the end of 1989, and so the post was advertised immediately, with an application deadline of 30 June 1989. In light of the requirement that the director be fully bilingual the advertisement appeared in local newspapers only.[128] The names of the applicants were not revealed in the board minutes – the executive committee reported on the candidates, but the minutes could not be located in SANG's archive. Two candidates were interviewed on 25 October; on 29 November I was appointed to this august post.[129]

In his 1989–90 report to the DNE, the chairperson announced Van Niekerk's retirement and commended him for his "sterling services".[130] I was elected president of the SAAA in 1989 and as such represented the organisation on SANG's board. It was a brief period, but it allowed me to gain insight into the nature and workings of the board and the museum, and provided some preparation for the big task ahead.[131]

This chapter bears witness to Van Niekerk's visionary directorship, and his opposition to the apartheid government that sometimes put him on a collision course with the ruling powers in Pretoria, and indeed with members of the board. All the same, he worked tirelessly and closely with the DNE, his board, the staff, national and international stakeholders, sponsors and FONG to advance the status, profile and significance of the national art museum far beyond its walls. He was made an honorary member of the society of the Friends. In a letter to the council Van Niekerk expressed his appreciation for "the support and friendship" he had received, adding:

> I grew to depend on the energetic co-operation and loyalty of the Council of the Friends and the members from quite early on. It seems to me, now, that there is much that would not have been achieved for our institution had we not always been able to work so well together. I know that I was the envy of my colleagues in having such a committed and hardworking support group. And together we added some very important works of art to the Gallery collection. My friendship with the Friends is one of the best things that remain with me after my time at the Gallery.[132]

Some time after his retirement from SANG, Van Niekerk left South Africa and settled in England. He died aged seventy-five in Eastbourne, in 2005.

PLATE 17: Jane Alexander, *Butcher Boys*, 1985-86, reinforced plaster, oil paint, bone, horns, wood, 1285 × 2135 × 885; © Jane Alexander / DALRO; image courtesy of the artist; photographer Svea Josephy.

4

Facing the challenges of transformation

1990 – 1994

THIS CHAPTER covers the period of the political interregnum, from 1990 to the first democratic elections on 27 April 1994. It also sees a shift in the narrative style to the first person, this as I take up the role of SANG director in January 1990. It is time for change and transformation for the country, and in this chapter I describe how the staff and board of trustees tackle the monumental tasks at hand, on many fronts. SANG, which was closed for renovations and installation of climate control, re-opens with the Cape Town Triennial in 1991. The exhibition is mired in controversy. The cultural and academic boycott comes to an end. Integral to SANG's renewed vision is the acquisition and exhibition of African art, here discussed within the context of the history of African art in museums in France and America. Political and cultural differences between some trustees and director, coupled with the fallout from the Triennial, result in a formal charge of misconduct against me; it is discussed in detail for the first time.

There is no such thing as an art object
or an ethnographic object;
it all depends on how objects are regarded
historically and how they are classified.

JOHN MACK[1]

SOUTH AFRICA WOULD CHANGE FOREVER on 2 February 1990 when State President F. W. de Klerk, speaking in the parliament building next to the temporarily closed national art museum, announced the unbanning of thirty-three political organisations, including the African National Congress and South African Communist Party, and release of Nelson Mandela and other political prisoners from jail. A new future awaited the country and its institutions.

The closure of SANG's main building enabled me to get to know the gallery's forty-three staff, its collection, as well as the board, and to work with all concerned on a mission statement and policy documents.[2] While the renovations were welcomed, the new climate control and lighting systems brought with them a crippling electricity account and many teething problems were experienced in moving back into the main building. Repeated flooding in the storage basement meant that two exhibition rooms had to be used for this purpose. Like our predecessors, the chairperson and I raised the lack of adequate accommodation in the 1991 *Annual Report*.[3]

In order to bring important exhibitions to Cape Town while the main building was closed, we cooperated with the Irma Stern Museum (ISM) on the retrospective exhibition *Gerard Sekoto: Unsevered Ties*, which was organised by JAG.[4] Japanese prints and nineteenth-century French prints and drawings from the permanent collection were respectively shown at the Michaelis Collection and SAAA in Bellville.

Initiatives continued in the Annexe: *People's Parks*, curated by Steven Sack, then director of the Johannesburg Art Foundation, photographic documentation of self-funded public gardens and sculpture parks made by townships residents of the Transvaal (now Gauteng), 1985–86; *Graffiti on the Berlin Wall*, photographs by Ralph Gründer taken between 1983 and 1989 documenting graffiti that reflected the feelings of East and West Berliners; and *Put to Paper*, a showcase of recent work by diverse calligraphers and paper artists from the Western Cape that included fifty workshops run by a member of Calligraphers and Paper Artists.

I shared my vision for SANG in a talk at the AGM of the Friends on 21 March 1990.[5] My approach to the topic of "The South African National Gallery in the 1990s" was governed by the major functions of the museum: conservation, research, publication, acquisition, exhibition and education. While it was premature to present firm statements, I touched on the financial challenges faced by the museum, as well as different museological aspects, in the context of discussions taking place in a working group comprising members of staff and the board, which would formulate ideas around a philosophy, vision and policies for the institution.[6]

The process culminated in a comprehensive Draft Policy Manual, which was submitted to the board on 27 February 1991; it was approved the following May.[7] I urged the board to address the long-standing space crisis "if the SANG is to continue to acquire works of art and to contribute meaningfully to the promotion and development of the visual arts in South Africa".

The board approved two significant recommendations: the institution would henceforth be trilingual (Afrikaans, English and Xhosa), meaning its education programmes, as well as publications, would be made available in all three languages, where possible;[8] and admission to the museum,

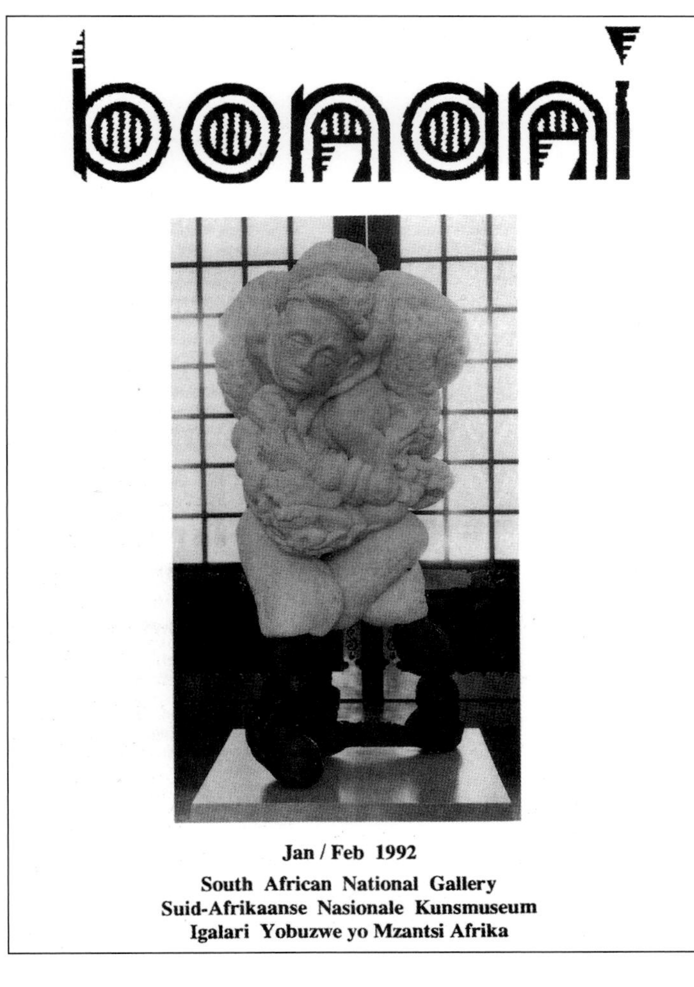

FIGURE 16: *bonani*, Jan/Feb 1992, cover featuring Willem Strydom, *Dorslandboom*, 1989, marble, bronze, 1100 × 650 × 600.

library and education services would be free. I announced this important decision in the first issue of a new bi-monthly newsletter, *bonani*: "We believe that access to collections of publicly-funded museums is an important and integral component of the nation's academic, educational and cultural life."[9]

Launched in January 1992, the title of the newsletter is a Xhosa word meaning "people are looking" (Fig. 16). The publication was sent free of charge to Friends, and over time it grew into an important vehicle for communicating with the public. The first issue included the gallery's mission statement and presented its new logo, which was the result of a nationwide competition won by Jinny Heath, an artist and lecturer from Pietermaritzburg (Fig. 17). The July/August 1992 issue incorporated the Friends' newsletter; they provided sponsorship and contributed information and articles in a special section. In his first "Letter from the chairperson," Melvyn Minnaar wrote:

> When *bonani* came onto the scene with such verve, the Friends' Council decided that we would support it all the way … the Friends will have a regular space in this exciting new gallery publication. Information which previously appeared in our quarterly newsletter, will now appear more frequently as part of *bonani*.[10]

In my talk to the Friends, I acknowledged the curatorial and educational legacy of my predecessors and the role of the Friends. I also shared my dreams and pointed out new directions: growing the small collection of African art, photography and cartoons; giving consideration to new policies with regards to ceramics, textiles, the decorative arts and architecture; addressing the critical shortage of space by revitalising the need for a new building on the parking area adjacent to the main

FIGURE 17: Jinny Heath, Logo, South African National Gallery.

building; expanding the purview of SANG with satellite and mobile museums in addition to the Natale Labia Museum; making renewed representation in respect of tax deductions for donors to museums; and achieving recognition for museums as educational institutions that would allow them to receive subsidies for publications, like universities. It was an extensive list. In reality, only the changes in acquisition policies regarding historical African art, photography and cartoons materialised.[11]

Seeking tax relief for donations and bequests from government was nothing new. Matthys Bokhorst had reported that a resolution to this effect was adopted at the 1968 SAMA conference, and in the years to come many representations were made.[12]

In a paper delivered at the 1979 conference, *The State of Art in South Africa*, a watershed event attended by white artists, academics, students, educators, museum professionals and public intellectuals held at UCT,[13] education officer Pat Kaplan raised an important question in her paper titled "The South African National Gallery as an Educational Institution?". Board chairpersons and Raymund van Niekerk referred to Kaplan's paper in a number of *Annual Reports*.[14] There was a firm recommendation in the Schutte Commission Report (1984) concerning the educational status of museums and active engagement from SAMA. Many pages were dedicated to different perspectives on the matter in the 1985 *South African Museums Association Bulletin*.[15] Van Niekerk confirmed that the Committee of University Principals had made their support known to the DNE, which was also taking the matter seriously.

Victor Kröhn, the DNE's director-general, outlined the role of the Human Sciences Research Council (HSRC) in researching the field of non-formal education. He added that the educational value of museums would not be ignored:

> For museums in South Africa, more than ever, the time has come for them to claim their rightful place as educational institutions provided that they very clearly overcome various constraints and outline the definitive role they can and must play, especially in the field of non-formal and informal education.[16]

Unfortunately, successive governments from both the apartheid and post-apartheid eras were not prepared to acknowledge this role and offer crucial tax relief to museums. In 1993 SANG submitted a detailed report and motivation to the Katz Commission on Taxation, all to no avail.[17]

The end of the cultural boycott and a reassessment of SANG's role

IN 1991, I gave a talk at the AGM of the Friends titled "South African Culture at the Crossroads – Where are we? Where are we going?"[18] It was an overview of the cultural boycott and its effects on South Africa, the emergence of internal structures to implement and monitor the cultural boycott, with words such as "cultural Stalinism" and "cultural commissars" having entered the vocabulary, and the conflicting views on how and when the cultural boycott would come to an end. There were concerns that independent, critical voices were becoming endangered. I quoted poet Mzwakhe Mbuli, who presided over the cultural boycott as head of the United Democratic Front's cultural desk: "The days of sitting behind desks are over. I have an international career to pursue. I have created an audience and a market the world over."

I explored the meanings and interpretations of culture to different South Africans, particularly as a key site of struggle for liberation in South Africa. In the words of the academic and anti-apartheid activist, Jakes Gerwel: "Our understanding of the anti-apartheid struggle had always been that it at the same time involved a process of nation-building. And to say that is essentially a cultural statement and a challenge to our thinking on issues related to the building of a national culture."

It was time, I argued, to consider the role of the national art museum in a changing South Africa, to acknowledge cultural expressions other than Eurocentric ones, as well as broader concerns:

> It is crucial that – as we stand at the crossroads – a national cultural organisation be formed, which can bring together all the players, all the factions and all those who care about the future of culture in this country. Only through debate, the exchange of ideas and action can we move forward and overcome the real threat, that culture – which was shamefully neglected in the 'old' South Africa – will not find its rightful place in the new.[19]

In the years to come every function of the institution would be reassessed and re-tested against the needs and requirements of a changing South Africa. The acquisition, exhibition and education policies, and the numerous exhibitions and publications that showcased the collection, contemporary and historical aesthetic production, as well as collections from abroad, enabled staff and the board to begin to redress the imbalances created by South Africa's history of exclusion. There was a desire to participate in the re-examination of South African history, and in particular its art history, and to use the context of art to address the historical problem of cultural difference in the country. SANG would challenge perceived culture and counter the separation between heritage and contemporary cultural production, between history and current expression.

To implement the new directions and mission it was necessary to respond to, and work directly with, the different constituencies that comprised the community; to share facilities and expertise with more organisations and individuals; and to create a cultural centre for debate. We met with the Community Arts Project[20] and negotiations with progressive cultural groups culminated in the formation of a Joint Working Group (JWG), comprising members of staff and the board, and representatives of the Federation of South African Cultural Organisations (FOSACO), an initiative to establish a representative national structure for cultural workers.[21] In Cape Town, visual arts organisations included the Visual Arts Group of the Cultural Workers' Congress.

At the national level, I was elected to the SAMA council in 1991 and attended the National Arts Policy Plenary in December 1992. The Convention for a Democratic South Africa (CODESA), a negotiating forum to broker a new political direction for the country, was established in December 1991. Political parties, organisations and interest groups were invited to make written submissions to one of the five working groups by 2 March 1992. We encouraged the board to make a representation to CODESA in order to ensure that culture would be placed on the agenda.[22]

I noted in *bonani* that the country was on the brink of a truly historic moment that would signal a shift from 350 years of white domination:

> We are privileged to be part of the transformation of South African society. That culture has never been higher on the agenda is evidenced by the number of seminars, conferences and cultural and educational investigations that are currently taking place. Staff members of SANG are participating in many of these initiatives, thereby honouring our vision that, after fulfilling all our functions and after contributing to learning in all its facets, we also have a responsibility to the national well-being. This is essential at a time when South Africans are so dominated by fear and pessimism that we are in danger of creating a self-fulfilling prophecy.[23]

There was a nationwide call for peace and silence at noon on 2 September 1993. We gathered with visitors to form a circle, followed by song on the front steps, and the release of white and blue balloons – and staff member Yusuf Masoet's pigeons.

Writing about the scope of the 1993 exhibitions and activities – creating a balance between the imaginative and meaningful display, and interpretation of the permanent collection and significant temporary exhibitions – I considered what the new approaches meant to the gallery:

> We are learning that, in many cases, the process is as important as the end result: we are exploring new ways of curating and presenting exhibitions; we are tempering and altering our authority with community interaction. The whole process of consulting with individuals who are an integral part of a culture which is represented at SANG, as well as the act of welcoming – rather than resisting – the overlap with discourses and disciplines other than our own, is contributing enormously to the broadening of knowledge, perspectives and to the revitalisation of the institution.[24]

Acknowledgment of SANG's achievements came from an important source in 1993: Dr. P. van Mensch, president of the International Committee for Museology, a committee of ICOM, visited South Africa and, according to the DNE, he considered SANG to be the best museum of the twenty-five he visited – at all levels.[25]

Art historical perspective on SANG's policy of acquiring and exhibiting African art

THE HISTORY OF SANG's collection of African art begins in the late 1960s, but the art historical roots of African art in major art museums run deep. In 1827, under the reign of Charles X, the Louvre Museum in Paris housed a maritime and ethnographic collection in a section called the Dauphin Museum (Musée Dauphin), where visitors could admire "exotic" pieces – "curiosities" brought back by explorers such as Captain James Cook and Jean François de Galaup, Comte de Lapérouse. Labelled "ethnographic specimens", in the 1880s, it was decided to separate the history of traditions and customs from the field of art. The scientific value of the objects prevailed and they went to the Trocadero Ethnography Museum (Musée d'Ethnographie du Trocadéro), established in 1878 to house the collections of the Dauphin Museum.

Artists and writers enter the narrative in the first years of the twentieth century. Pablo Picasso, Henri Matisse and Georges Braque, among others in France, as well as the Expressionists in Germany, set out consciously to redefine African and Oceanic objects (what in French was called *l'art nègre*) as art.[26] In 1909, the French poet, playwright, novelist, art critic and champion of non-western art in Paris, Guillaume Apollinaire, demanded that the art of Africa and Oceania be transferred from the Trocadéro to the Louvre. He criticised the Louvre for being behind the times, and for the absence of artistic works from Australia, Easter Island, New Caledonia, the New Hebrides, Tahiti and diverse African regions: "The Louvre should collect certain exotic masterpieces, whose appearance is no less moving than that of the beautiful specimens of western statuary."[27]

Apollinaire lambasted ethnographic collections in France for their pell-mell display of such works among the everyday objects and natural products of the regions, as well as the Trocadéro, which had become too vast, with open days few and far between and visitors rare. The art of Egypt and Asia was housed at the Guimet Museum (Musée Guimet), "at the same time museum, temple, library and laboratory".[28] Apollinaire emphasised the necessity for a big "exotic" museum to replace the Trocadéro, which could become an ethnographic museum. His pronouncements anticipated the opening of Quai Branly Museum (Musée du quai Branly) in 2006 by almost a century.

Writing in 1917, the visionary Apollinaire articulated the growing aesthetic interest in the "idols" from Africa and Oceania in a catalogue published by Paul Guillaume. He bemoaned the fact that the critical and analytical means of classifying and attributing were lacking, with the result that they could not be presented in the same manner as a collection of artworks executed in Europe, the "classical civilisations" of countries in Asia, and the Roman regions of North Africa or Egypt. He saw the publication of the "album" as a contribution to research and celebration of African art, and concluded:

> It is by a great audacity of taste that we arrive at considering these *idoles nègres* as veritable works of art. The present album will assist in recognising that this audacity has not surpassed its objective and that we find ourselves here in the presence of aesthetic realisations of which their anonymity removes none of their ardour, their grandeur, their genuine and simple beauty.[29]

The Trocadéro was demolished and replaced by the Palais de Chaillot in 1937. In the 1930s, under the leadership of the novelist and art theorist André Malraux, who later became an influential minister in Charles de Gaulle's post-war government, science and art were separated. The scientific artefacts went to the Musée de l'Homme, housed, among other museums, in the Palais de Chaillot.[30] In official circles the word "art" was first applied to these collections only in the 1960s, and in 1990 they were moved to the National Museum of Arts from Africa and Oceania (Musée nationale des Arts d'Afrique et d'Océanie, MNAAO), built for the Colonial Exhibition in 1931.

The year before MNAAO's closure, in 2003, the museum hosted *Ubuntu: Art and Culture in South Africa*, a major exhibition of South African art, with objects on loan from public and private collections. It was the first time a French national museum held an important exhibition of this kind. The exhibition focused on everyday, personal and utilitarian objects based on four themes: authority and power, everyday life, cult of the ancestors, and individual and collective identities.[31] In the early stages of organising the exhibition, director Jean-Hubert Martin offered SANG the exhibition, but we had to decline because the amalgamation of national museums, discussed in chapter five, had become a reality in 1999. SANG had no operating budget and it would certainly not be in a position to pay the required exhibition fee.

Malraux and a host of other French intellectuals and scientists, including André Breton and Claude Lévi-Strauss, called for the creation of a museum in Paris dedicated to the arts and cultures of non-European societies. Nothing happened until Jacques Kerchache, an art expert, dealer, defender of non-European art and co-author of the book *L'art africain* (1988), stepped in decades later. On 15 March 1990, Kerchache issued a manifesto entitled *Pour que les chefs-d'oeuvre du monde entier naissent libres et égaux* (For the masterpieces of the whole world to be born free and equal). Signed by 150 artists and intellectuals, including former Senegalese president Léopold Sédar Senghor, Kerchache demanded that an eighth section be opened in the Louvre, devoted to the arts of Africa, Asia, Oceania and the Americas.[32]

In 1995, President Jacques Chirac set up a commission to reflect upon the place of what was still referred to as "primitive" art in French museums. The following year he decided on the creation of a museum of arts and civilisations in Paris, and on assigning rooms at the Louvre to exhibit the masterpieces of which Apollinaire wrote. This was easier said than done. Chirac, the *New York Times* reported in 2006, "overruled objections from Louvre officials that their museum was for European art, not a universal museum and he ordered the Louvre's Pavillon des Sessions turned over to one hundred historic works of African, Asian, Oceanic and American art. They were installed in a setting of pure aesthetic bliss". [33]

The attitude of Louvre officials is preposterous, unless one regards Egyptian and Oriental antiquities and Islamic art as European. Chirac appointed Kerchache as scientific advisor to the public establishment of the future Quai Branly Museum. Kerchache's dream, and that of Apollinaire before him, was finally realised in the Pavillon des Sessions at the Louvre in April 2000.

Six years later architect Jean Nouvel's magnificent Quai Branly Museum opened in Paris to much admiration and condemnation.[34] What's in a name? Originally mooted as a Museum of Arts and Civilisations, then "arts primitives" (politically incorrect), then "arts premiers" (controversial and meaningless), *quai Branly* does not mean anything except the place where the museum is situated on the river Seine. On 13 April 2016, *Le Figaro* announced that the museum would be "re-baptised" Musée du quai Branly-

Jacques Chirac on the occasion of the tenth anniversary of the opening of the museum, 20 June. The next day an exhibition dedicated to the former French president opened with 150 objects linked to him.

The museum is at the same time a bridge museum: Quai Branly Museum is a museographic, scientific and cultural institution dedicated to the dialogue between cultures and civilizations. It is a multi-faceted cultural institution. In the words of Chirac:

> The creation of the musée du quai Branly is the result of a political desire to see justice rendered to non-European cultures, to recognize the place their artistic expressions occupies in our cultural heritage, and also to acknowledge the debt we owe to the societies that produced them, as well as to their countries of origin, with many of which France has especially close ties. We are putting an end here to a long history of disregard, and giving just consideration to art forms and civilizations too long ignored or misunderstood – giving back their dignity to peoples too often dismissed, looked down upon, sometimes even annihilated by arrogance, ignorance stupidity and blindness.[35]

Across the Atlantic, much was happening during the early decades of the twentieth century, but as late as 1984 Kurt Varnedoe, then chief curator of painting and sculpture at New York's Museum of Modern Art (MoMA), wrote:

> There is a need for a full account of the shifting treatment of tribal arts in displays of the 1920s, 1930s and 1940s. The role played by dealers in their isolating concentration on tribal objects as aesthetic objects ... was crucial in disseminating the kind of nonethnological formal approach implicit in, for example, many Cubists' appreciation of tribal art.[36]

According to writer Evan Maurer, Alfred Stieglitz, an influential photographer and promoter of modern art, presented the first commercial exhibitions of African and pre-Columbian art in America at his New York gallery in 1914, and again in 1916.[37] MoMA organised an exhibition of *African Negro Art* in March 1935. Art critic and author James Johnson Sweeney selected 602 objects for the exhibition, drawn principally from West and Central Africa, and from numerous international public and private collections. "The art of negro Africa is a sculptor's art," he is quoted in a MoMA press release. "As a sculptural tradition in the last century it has had no rival. It is as sculpture we should approach it."[38]

And it was as sculpture that African art would initially be approached at SANG. As I noted in chapter two, John Paris envisaged a department of prehistoric and indigenous art for the national art museum as early as 1950. Nothing however came of it. In the early 1970s Bruce Arnott initiated the process of acquiring sculpture from West and Central Africa, with the support of director Matthys Bokhorst. In an unpublished article Arnott detailed his interest in and research on the subject abroad, engaging directly with some of the luminaries in the field. He was also familiar with collections in Cape Town and Johannesburg. "As a result of my studies in Europe I was attuned to African sculpture, my guiding interests being aesthetics and art history."[39] Arnott presented works for acquisition, but there was no budget for such a collection, and purchases were occasional.

PLATE 18: Artist unrecorded, *Lydenburg Head*, c. 750 CE, fired clay, specularite and pigment, 380 × 260 × 250; Iziko Museums of SA, Social History Collections, UCT loan collection (UCT701/1).

Nevertheless, in an *Annual Report*, Arnott listed twelve acquisitions of "Traditional African" sculpture.[40] A fine collection of 290 bronze objects and gold weights from the Ashanti in Ghana was added in 1971, the year in which Bokhorst made a clear policy statement regarding the desirability of collecting African art:

> The last decade has seen an ever-growing number of works by contemporary African artists added to the collection. A few years ago, the Board of Trustees accepted the consequences thereof, by giving the green light for collecting traditional African Sculpture, which in the past, had almost solely been the domain of ethnographical museums.[41]

To support and supplement the acquisitions, a series of important and wide-ranging exhibitions was organised: *Rock Art in Southern Africa* (1963); tapestries and printmaking from Rorke's Drift (1967 and 1972, including acquisitions); and *African Art in Metal* (1970), which featured African music and was extensively discussed in overseas journals – it was described as an unusual and appealing exhibition.[42] "As an adjunct to this exhibition ... the newly reconstructed *Lydenburg Heads* [c. 750 CE] were shown to the public for the first time – as art (Plate 18)." [43] The exhibition featured art from different parts of the continent, from the collection of Peter Miller and that of the gallery. It drew "favourable comments over the holiday season, especially from visitors from overseas".[44] In 1981 SANG hosted the Standard Bank Foundation Collection of African Tribal Art. Two years later it showed work from the permanent collection, including the Ashanti gold weights, recent acquisitions and textiles loaned from the SAM; an audio-visual programme accompanied the exhibition.[45]

Acquiring historical African art was not a priority for Van Niekerk and after Arnott's departure the collection stagnated. The first beadwork pieces from South Africa were acquired in 1987: an Ndebele beaded blanket; ten Xhosa Love Letters (beaded necklaces) and a beadwork dress, followed by Mfengu and Shangaan beadwork in 1989.[46]

It is evident from these acquisitions that the focus was no longer on West and Central Africa – the works that most resembled western sculpture – but had shifted to acknowledging and celebrating the visual culture of southern Africa. Associated with this was a process of assessing and challenging definitions, categories and standards, and of shifting boundaries, all in order to include a wider range of expression. Re-invigorating gains made in this area by Paris, Bokhorst and Arnott, the national art museum became pro-active in stimulating debate about distinctions between "art" and "craft," and "high" and "low" art. It also sought to erode traditional boundaries and categories that had invariably been imposed from outside. The new acquisitions policy was first manifested in 1991 when the DNE responded positively to SANG's request to purchase a large and comprehensive collection of Ndebele beadwork and regalia. Produced by women mainly during the decades 1940 to 1970, it was showcased in the groundbreaking exhibition, *IGugu lamaNdebele/Pride of the Ndebele* (1994–95), to which I return later in this chapter.

Many more items of beadwork would be acquired to illustrate the regional diversity of the medium in South Africa.[47] The collection for which SANG became best known came from the Eastern Cape, represented all nine Xhosa-speaking groups, and was produced during the middle decades of the twentieth century.[48] The scope and beauty of this collection was celebrated in the exhibition *Ezakwantu: Beadwork from the Eastern Cape*, curated by Emma Bedford and Carol Kaufmann in 1993 (Fig. 18). Bedford edited the catalogue, which contains essays by specialists in art history, linguistics, ethnography, anthropology and archaeology, thereby affirming the multi-disciplinary approach that informed the curatorial concept.[49] The exhibition evolved through dialogue with many groups and individuals, as well as the involvement of Xhosa-speaking staff members Noni Sipuye and Vuyile Voyiya, in order to draw on knowledge and lived experience.

Sponsorship was crucial to the implementation of this and all other large-scale initiatives:

FIGURE 18: *Ezakwantu: Beadwork from the Eastern Cape*, installation, 1993; photographer Kathy Grundlingh.

The subsidy which the institution receives from the State is such that no provision is made for major exhibitions and educational programmes. Having a vision and the expertise to concretise the vision was one thing; having to raise the funds with which to achieve it is another. At times we seemed to battle against all odds, and it was only the total dedication and perseverance evinced by Emma Bedford and Carol Kaufmann that made this exhibition happen.[50]

Albertina Sisulu, then head of the ANC Women's League, opened *Ezakwantu*. It was a morning of poetry, storytelling, song, dance and deep emotion. Lindiwe Bacela's rendering of Mteto Mzongwana's poem *Malibongwe*, which praises the women of South Africa, was rousing and memorable, and audiences were treated to *umqomboti* (a traditional maize beer). Storyteller and academic, Abner Nyamende, who participated in the event, sent us a card: "Congratulations on an excellent opening ceremony and thank you for bringing the Art Gallery closer to ordinary people."[51] The exhibition culminated in a workshop and performance by Amampondo as part of the "Shared Vision Project", and brought youths from diverse communities together in an exploration of music and culture.

Ezakwantu included a wide range of beadwork: from rare items dating back to the nineteenth century, through to contemporary pieces using plastic and found objects. The curators went to great lengths to provide information and documentation that elucidated works on display, while mediating the tension between social meaning and aesthetic contemplation. Items of beadwork, blankets and three-dimensional pieces were displayed for their formal qualities as well as for their affinities with other works in the same room, for example, videos, photographs and paintings featuring colonial images and bead-sample cards used by early traders.

An interactive map, designed by artist and facilitator Roger van Wyk, situated the objects in historical and geographic contexts, and allowed visitors access to sites, the history of the African and Islamic bead trade, European expansion and the scramble for the continent. The map incorporated images, including a floor plan of a slave ship, and objects such as shackles and samples of the kind of beads used to trade in human beings.

Two invited artists, Tembeka Lucy Ntamo and Nosayizi Virginia Nzilana, worked in the exhibition space and engaged with the public through a translator. They made items that reflected the continuation of beadwork traditions, available materials and their particular sensibilities. In a review of the exhibition, art historian Nessa Leibhammer pointed out that problems arose when a translator was not present.[52] Art critic James Garner praised SANG in his *Cape Times* review (24 February 1994):

Particularly interesting are the ways in which European fashions and materials were adapted and included. These instances of cultural interaction play a positive role in a country as divided and segregated as ours. Far from mere ethno-bongo bleeding-heart bathos, this exhibition is proof that South African cultural institutions are capable of moving with the times and away from the position which presented black people as exotic specimens and curio-mannequins.

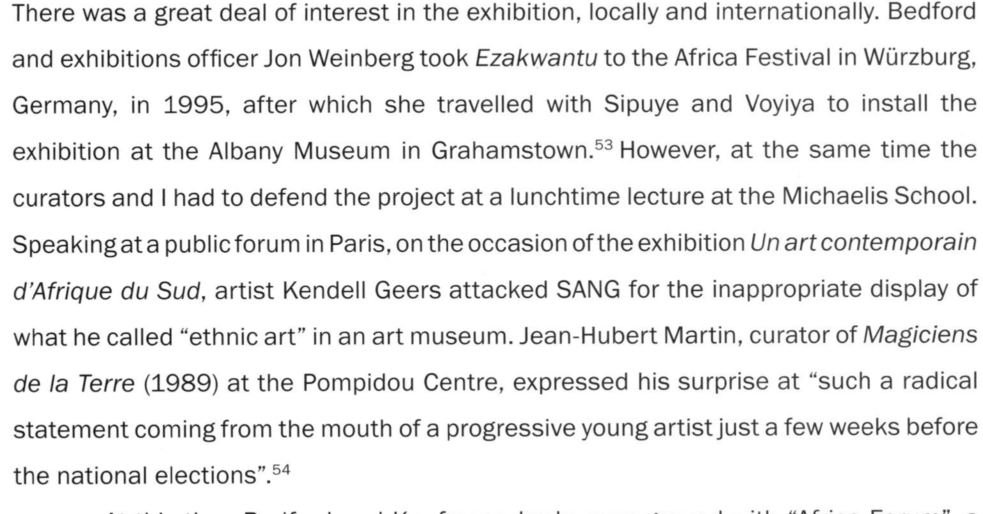

There was a great deal of interest in the exhibition, locally and internationally. Bedford and exhibitions officer Jon Weinberg took *Ezakwantu* to the Africa Festival in Würzburg, Germany, in 1995, after which she travelled with Sipuye and Voyiya to install the exhibition at the Albany Museum in Grahamstown.[53] However, at the same time the curators and I had to defend the project at a lunchtime lecture at the Michaelis School. Speaking at a public forum in Paris, on the occasion of the exhibition *Un art contemporain d'Afrique du Sud*, artist Kendell Geers attacked SANG for the inappropriate display of what he called "ethnic art" in an art museum. Jean-Hubert Martin, curator of *Magiciens de la Terre* (1989) at the Pompidou Centre, expressed his surprise at "such a radical statement coming from the mouth of a progressive young artist just a few weeks before the national elections".[54]

At this time Bedford and Kaufmann broke new ground with "Africa Forum", a series of lectures, debates and films around exhibitions and related issues. Organised in conjunction with the Western Cape branch of the South African Association of Art Historians (SAAAH), they were designed to redress imbalances in our knowledge of African history, art and culture. Participants included Martin Hall, John Parkington, Andy Smith, Melanie Hillebrand, Tim Maggs, Duncan Miller and Gary van Wyk.

As Kaufmann points out, collecting soon branched out geographically into "regions with which Bantu-speakers in South Africa historically shared cultural, linguistic and trading links" and into work done by men in wood, metal and other materials.[55]

In 1994 we made a commitment to the repatriation of artworks that were taken out of the country, principally during the nineteenth and twentieth centuries. The first formal demonstration of this vision was the "African Art Heritage Collection", acquired in 1995 by the government of the Federal Republic of Germany and gifted to the people of South Africa. The fourteen works were augmented by presentations from other sources: a rare Northern Nguni maternity staff from the new Department of Arts, Culture, Science and Technology (DACST), a Tsonga staff from the Friends and Jackson Hlungwani's *Angel Walking Stick*, which was presented by art dealer Linda Givon.

Gary van Wyk, a New York-based South African dealer and researcher in historical African art, and Norman Hurst, an American dealer, assembled the "African Heritage Collection" abroad between 1989 and 1993. The objects were acquired with emphasis on the aesthetic qualities appropriate for a national collection, and with the

PLATE 19: Artist unrecorded, attributed to the nineteenth-century maker known as the "Baboon Master", KwaZulu-Natal, *Maternity staff* (staff surmounted with a relief carving of mother and child), wood, pokerwood, 1120 (detail); presented by the Department of Arts, Culture, Science and Technology; © Iziko Museums of South Africa; photographer Nigel Pamplin.

specific intention of repatriating some fine works. They included masterpieces of great rarity, such as a "maternity" staff by the internationally renowned "Baboon master" active in the KwaZulu-Natal area circa 1897 (Plate 19).[56]

On-going initiatives in the field of historical African art are discussed in subsequent chapters, but it is appropriate at this point to commend the vision, resilience, innovation and ability of the chairpersons and members of SANG boards and acquisition committees, FONG, directors and staff in finding the money and support required to make Paris', Bokhorst's and Arnott's dream of an African art collection a reality. These big dreams were, however, thwarted by two issues that recur throughout this history of SANG, and to which I will return in greater detail in subsequent chapters: the housing and display of the collection remain unresolved, as do its lack of funds. Writing in 2006, the art historian Steven C. Dubin capably summed up the latter dilemma:

> To be completely candid, the commitment to black African art that South African museums have increasingly demonstrated since the 1980s reflects awareness and appreciation of its importance, but at the same time signals that these institutions are not financially able to compete in the world market for either modern Western or older European works.

The 1991 Cape Town Triennial and its aftermath

THE RENOVATED main building was scheduled for handover on 7 June 1991, but when the time came only two rooms were ready. It was decided that the building would not be opened, but for a section devoted to the Cape Town Triennial. We had invited State President F. W. de Klerk to officiate, but with the change in plans Dr. Mamphela Ramphele, then deputy vice-chancellor at UCT, opened the triennial exhibition on 9 October.[58] The response of the public was enthusiastic, with 12,317 people visiting the gallery between its opening and 17 November. We were confident that the new gallery shop and café, as well as the exciting programme that was planned for 1992, would capitalise on the encouraging attendance figures.[59]

In her opening speech Ramphele charted the challenges faced by the South African art world during the transition from authoritarian rule towards a more democratic and egalitarian society. The exhibition was a reminder that we could not live on political bread alone, but that we needed to stop and smell the flowers as we struggled through the process of transformation. The notion of a national culture was top of mind among many. On this, Ramphele noted: "It would have to reflect South Africa's richness and poverty, its strengths and weaknesses, its hopes and dreams. A national culture ought to be infused with a common value system for human dignity and the opening up of opportunities to all South Africans to learn, live, work and play together."[60]

Since its inception in 1982, each Triennial competition had been controversial, albeit in different ways. Much had to do with the mechanism of, and individuals responsible for the selection, the range and quality of the work and – in a rapidly transforming South Africa – representivity. In order to address the difficulties, the 1991 exhibition was the result of a process of consultation and debate, of publicly electing

PLATE 20: William Kentridge: still from the film *Sobriety, Obesity and Growing Old*, 1991, 16mm colour print, 9 minutes; image courtesy of the artist.

judges and allowing for greater regional representation on the final panel. This seemed to both offer a solution and be at the root of subsequent criticism, particularly from the regions that selected works only to be rejected by the national panel. Files of correspondence in SANG's archive, as well as endless columns in the national press, bear testimony to the controversies, which included the reluctance of the sponsors to engage with the public.[61]

Many reviews were scathing. The headlines in the Afrikaans press captured the tone of reviews: "Van koel realisme tot slymerige 'angst'" (From cool realism to slimy 'angst'), "Triënnale net draaglik as mens bietjie dronk is" (Triennial only bearable if one is a little drunk), "Chaotiese tentoonstelling verdien nie sy status" (Chaotic exhibition does not deserve its status) and "Triennale still can't shed Eurocentrism". In his review in the *Weekly Mail* (11–17 October 1991), Neville Dubow described the exhibition as "a tame affair", conservative and cautious within established conventions: "There is a prevalence of realism, little of it challenging, hardly any of it able to exploit the one thing that the realist canon can do which is pointedly to focus on issues of social concern."[62]

While the triennial judges' decisions met with the disapproval of many, there was universal praise for William Kentridge, who received the gold medal for his animated film, *Sobriety, Obesity and Growing Old* (1991). There was disagreement on the cover of the catalogue. We had selected a still from

Kentridge's film that depicted a scene of a crowd surging through the streets of Johannesburg carrying red flags (Plate 20). The sponsors would not allow the image. After much debate and acrimony, the cover was printed black with the letters of the competition and date in Afrikaans and English.

The following year I published an article in the *South African Arts Calendar* in which I examined reactions in the press (up until the end of the run in Cape Town in November 1991), interpreted some of the works and stated the position of SANG as regards the competition. I asked the question: Does the Triennial still have a meaningful role to play in South African art? Its greatest achievements had been to draw attention to the visual arts in the 1980s, to encourage other sponsors to initiate art competitions, and the fact that it travelled throughout the country, which contributed a great deal to the breaking down of regional isolation.[63]

I maintained that the watershed exhibition of the 1980s was not one of the three Triennial shows, but Ricky Burnett's curated exhibition *Tributaries A view of contemporary South African art* (1985). Commissioned by automaker BMW to tour Germany before opening in Johannesburg,[64] Burnett – a painter and teacher who briefly ventured into art dealing – travelled the country to find work. He settled on 111 artists, his final selection drawing on the assistance of art historian Karin Skawran and sponsor's representative Marina von Koerber. Burnett presented the work of established black and white artists alongside that of sculptors and bead artists from the rural areas, many hardly known at the time, as well as figurative works in every possible medium, and abstract paintings that spoke to viewers in another visual language. Burnett summed up his broad and inclusive approach as follows:

> We believe that we have unearthed some compelling images, revealed some intriguing parallels and re-affirmed the irrepressible energy of human creativity. South Africans cannot, and ought not, to lay claim to a common culture. But there is, we hope, in this collection a sense of a common humanity.

Museum Africa, the exhibition's host venue in Johannesburg, was still half derelict when I visited the exhibition with Raymund van Niekerk. Burnett's exhibition was a revelation to both of us. Not only did *Tributaries* challenge accepted views and offer new perspectives and possibilities for South African art, it confirmed the vitality and power that were stirring in art throughout the country, this at a time when the political mood was in tailspin. As artist Andrew Verster put it in a review: "I've just had a look into the future and it's a great deal more exciting than the past."[66]

I had always supported the Triennial, written reviews, and even opened the 1988 iteration at SANG, but seeing it from inside the museum raised serious issues. I inherited something of which the parameters were unclear from the outset, yet we did whatever we could to make it a success. This included facing the public, engaging the press and returning works to angry artists who had been rejected by the judges.

The challenges involved in hosting the competition and exhibition had already become complex by May 1991, and I placed these before the board following the end of the exhibition's run in November 1991. I stated that it was impossible to continue with the competition in its current form, as it made huge demands on gallery space and involved staff at regional and national levels for months on end. There was also the indelicate matter of the museums receiving no financial compensation from the sponsors – all the institution received were R2,500 and invitations for the opening. In order not to lose the event, I proposed rethinking of the format. Furthermore, I suggested that an internal working committee be constituted to draw up suggestions.[67]

My criticism of the Triennial gave rise to correspondence between Dr. Anton Rupert, chairperson of the Rembrandt Group, and me in January 1992, which culminated in him writing to the chairperson. Rupert, after referring to the good relationship that existed between Rembrandt and Bokhorst, expressed his concern about the "unnecessary controversy and minefield of political undertones" that they were experiencing. The total cost of the triennial was R882,740, Rupert stated. He further communicated his foundation's desire to use this amount for job creation for disadvantaged people in future.[68] The focus was entirely on me with seemingly no sense of accountability to the national organising committee, chaired by Christopher Till, the judges and art museum directors who had worked tirelessly to make the competition more representative.

I convened a meeting with staff and board members to discuss ideas on 7 February 1992, but matters took another turn: the staff was summarily dismissed and not recalled as promised. That same morning, *Die Burger* announced that the Rembrandt Art Foundation had terminated its sponsorship of the CTT. At an ad hoc meeting of the full board, held on 10 February, chairperson Van der Merwe Scholtz tabled a document outlining the reasons why he and other board members felt that I was directly responsible for the termination of the sponsorship, and whether the board should consider disciplinary action. The board decided against this course of action. Instead, a statement expressing disappointment and thanking the sponsor was formulated. It was also decided that only the chairperson would be allowed to speak on behalf of the institution in matters concerning the *Triennial.*

Scholtz wrote to Rupert, to inform him that all relevant correspondence had been discussed at the special board meeting. He conveyed his regret that the sponsorship had come to an end, and further expressed his appreciation for the support of the Rembrandt Group to the visual arts, music, theatre and conservation of the built and natural environments. Scholtz, emphasising that there were no problems between Rupert and the trustees, requested a meeting with representatives of the board.[70]

As I have outlined in previous chapters, political and cultural differences between trustees and directors, and directors and state officials were not unusual. Simmering disagreements and dissent among the trustees, and dissatisfaction with my directorship, at least from certain quarters, were coming to a boil.[71] From correspondence between Scholtz and me, dating back to September 1991, it is clear that he and some board members were unhappy with my approach and initiatives. I had the sense at the time that I was more highly regarded outside SANG than inside, particularly among some trustees. The situation escalated to the point that I was even held responsible for the delays in the reopening of the building, despite having attended numerous meetings with the architect and public works.

The letters Scholtz and I exchanged in March 1992 are filled with accusations and rebuttals. I tendered explanations about working with FOSACO and CODESA, my relationship with the Friends and the department, my views on Own/General Affairs and funding of the art museum, as well as many articles in the press. Possibilities for discussion and cooperation – a meeting with poet and ANC stalwart Wally Serote, and contact with Gordon Metz of the Mayibuye Centre at UWC – became bones of contention. Deputy chairperson Danie van Niekerk queried whether SANG "should be represented on an ANC Commission". It was pointed out that the institution was represented at these meetings in the same way as on those of the Department of National Education and the Simon van der Stel Foundation, and not as a member of any commission.[72] Among the many issues that were raised in the correspondence was a reminder that Scholtz had to submit all correspondence between him and the DNE to SANG for filing.

In my welcome address at the opening of the last Triennial in 1991, I said that there were more representatives of the ANC present than the De Klerk government and its national education department, who were invited but failed to attend. Officials denied receiving an invitation, so there were evidently miscommunications, but everything I said was reported in the press. The chairperson felt that I was "driving a wedge between SANG and the public and the Department".[73] I was instructed to attend meetings of the Heads of Declared Institutions and those of a new Association of Heads of Declared Institutions, although I had earlier gained the full support of the board to distance myself from such meetings. As discussed in chapter three, Raymund van Niekerk had successfully opposed the 1983 constitution's artificial distinction between "own" and "general" affairs in public life, and the classification of SANG's functions as the "own" affairs of the white population. The negative impact of the legislation on museums was particularly felt in the splitting of the original committee, which I regarded as retrogressive and untenable.[74]

Like John Paris before me, the achievements of all at SANG were largely ignored in board meetings. I had to constantly remind the chairperson that the board had approved my policy document, that I was acting upon it, and that nothing was done without the knowledge of the board and the staff. Like Paris, I alerted Scholtz to the workload I carried, that the wellbeing of the institution was everyone's priority, and that the time-consuming efforts to discredit and undermine my work and status were disruptive and counter-productive.[75]

A paper I delivered at the 1991 SAMA conference highlighted the delicate nature of this difficult relationship. Entitled "The South African National Gallery and accountability – some efforts and experiences", it set out my vision for SANG. I deeply regret that Raymund Van Niekerk misinterpreted the paper, which alienated him from the institution and from me. He wrote to Scholtz stating that I had been critical of my predecessors, trustees who approved past policies and acquisitions, the chairperson and members of the acquisitions committee. He withdrew his association with an exhibition that would have paid homage to his directorship. At the May 1991 board meeting, Dubow expressed his support for me and indicated that he did not feel threatened by the content of my paper. He added that it was "a good and pragmatic paper," and further highlighted that it had received an award for the best paper at the SAMA conference. Clive Keegan added:

> ... one of the Director's solemn duties was to be provocative, controversial and to introduce some kind of challenging thought into the national debate about the role of this Gallery and art in our society. The Board should encourage the Director in that direction. In responding to Dr. van Niekerk, the Board should express confidence in the Director and the way in which she has run the Gallery in recent months.[76]

The trustees decided not to proceed with the exhibition but to show recent acquisitions instead.

The simmering resentments came to a head on 2 April 1992 when the chairperson laid a formal charge of misconduct against me, thereby initiating disciplinary procedures. I was charged with having committed "certain acts" which "caused prejudice to the administration and efficiency of the institution". The details of the charge were entirely concerned with the Triennial: correspondence between Rupert and me that jeopardised the sponsorship to the extent that it was withdrawn, and which was exacerbated by statements I made to the press. I was given two weeks to admit or deny the charge.[77]

Deeply shocked, hurt and disappointed, I sought legal advice, which resulted in a sixteen-page response.[78] I denied the charge and provided relevant explanations, referring specifically to the chairperson's statement at the meeting of 10 February: "I emphatically do not want to initiate any such disciplinary procedures until I have consulted the Board ... the purpose of this meeting is to place all relevant facts before the Board and obtain member's [sic] points of view in regard to the matter." He repeated this several times. After a wide-ranging discussion, Dubow said: "My opinion is that it is not appropriate to institute disciplinary measures against the Director. I am hoping that a more constructive sequence can then arise after we have disposed of this." Scholtz agreed and I was informed accordingly. This earlier decision, followed two months later by the baseless charge, amounted to unfair labour practice.

I continued my defence by asserting that the consequences of my conduct on the efficiency and administration of the art gallery had never been called into question, either directly or indirectly. In fact, when Scholtz introduced the matter of the Triennial at the February meeting, he gave me a glowing testimonial in both official languages:

> The way in which the Director took up her duties here amazed and astounded. She took to it like a fish to water. Her flair and complete devotion to duty which at times went beyond the call of duty, impressed not only the Board but many members of the public ... I have differed from her on a few occasions, but on every occasion I told her so myself, as she will recall. So before we start to talk I want to have this put on record: my admiration ...

At this point Scholtz switched to Afrikaans and expressed his appreciation for the way in which I brought new life to the institution and involved the broader community. The minister of national education had written to commend SANG on the *Annual Report* and the educational initiatives. In my defence I mentioned that a delegation from the DNE, which had checked on the implementation of framework autonomy, was extremely favourable and concluded that we were operating well within the administrative and financial guidelines. I analysed the nature and content of the 1991 newspaper articles; they affirmed that I had spoken in my personal capacity, that it had never been my intention to "defame" Rembrandt or terminate the competition, and that I was held up as the scapegoat for the withdrawal of the sponsorship, which was on the cards anyway.

The charge was not defensible. It completely failed to distinguish between the interests, administration and efficiency of SANG, and those of the Triennial, a national competition with its own organising committee. I concluded with the hope that the matter be laid to rest, that we put all this behind us, and work together for the benefit of the institution, its sponsors and friends, and the wider community.

At the board meeting held on 22 April 1992 – it had been brought forward a month to deal with the charge – it was disclosed that Dubow, a member of the executive committee, had been excluded from the board delegation who met with Leo Kruger of the Rembrandt Group. Instead, FONG chairperson Melvyn Minnaar accompanied Scholtz and Danie van Niekerk. Dubow was justifiably displeased.[80]

This came as no surprise. According to a letter Minnaar wrote to Scholtz in preparation for the 10 February meeting, he felt a kind of ownership of the Triennial: "As one of the people originally involved in the mounting of the Cape Town Biennial, which in turn became the Cape Town Triennial, and as the person who specifically at the time suggested the sponsorship by the Rembrandt Arts Foundation, I am shocked at the withdrawal of the sponsorship and the events which led to it." He added what would become a pertinent point in the charge against me: "It is a fact that Dr. Rupert was provoked to cancel the sponsorship. Can the Director's responsibility in this matter be questioned?" Minnaar also had a problem with our decision to acquire works not selected for the Triennial exhibition, which in his eyes registered as a rebuke, "a vote of no confidence in the judging and the Triennial itself".[81]

Articles in *Die Burger*, and perceived tensions between Minnaar and me, generated acrimonious discussion. At the 22 April board meeting Keegan referred to the "deep divisions and antagonisms" within the board that would have to be resolved if the efficacy of the board were not to be destroyed. He emphasised the context of the debate as that "of a society which is deeply divided and riddled with tensions". Several members requested that the charge against me be discussed, and I was asked to recuse myself. Joe Dolby, who was taking the minutes, asked to be excused. The proceedings were recorded and subsequently transcribed into ninety-six pages.[82] A summary of the discussion follows.

Scholtz asked the board to allow him to outline the situation, asserting that there was no antagonism from him towards the director and that he was committed to seeking the board's opinion at a special meeting before initiating the disciplinary proceedings. He had waited two months before laying the charge. This resulted in a lengthy and legalistic document that raised the status of the chairperson as *functus officio* (having performed his office) when he laid the charge, as he had indicated at a meeting that he had no need to take disciplinary action against me; furthermore, that the regulation under which he laid the charge was *ultra vires*, in other words, he had acted beyond his legal power or authority.

Dubow wanted to know why the chairperson had changed his mind, when he had emphatically stated that he did not want to institute disciplinary measures against the director. "We all left that Board meeting feeling that this ... could be resolved, was resolved to the extent that you had agreed and you even gave the impression that you were very happy to agree ... that no good purpose would be served to initiate a charge." Dubow then repeated his question: "What made you change your mind. Were there new circumstances? The Director in one of her letters to you suggested that pressure was put on you. Is this so? And if it is true, from what direction did the pressure come?" As a member of the executive committee Dubow had been left completely in the dark and he was not happy with the relationship between the chairperson and the board, or the chairperson and members of the executive committee.

In a lengthy response, Scholtz agreed that he had been under pressure for many months, but that there were no special pressures. He was unmoved by Karin Skawran's opinion that I had not brought harm intentionally, and that lessons had been learned. Scholtz raised the issue of my not having apologised, notably to Rupert:

> The whole correspondence about the Rembrandt affair is in the hands of *Die Burger*. I was instrumental in stopping it from getting published, but many people have read it. Those things were creating a very bad impression, amongst other things of the Board, because we have never, never responded to it in public.[83]

Time and again Dubow returned to the crux of the disagreement and division in the Board: "I am gravely perturbed at the fact that you did not come back to the Board and that you did not allow the Board to advise you, or at least enlighten the Board, as to why you felt impelled to go ahead with this." While much was left unresolved at the April meeting, it was agreed that the chairperson would get legal advice in order to establish whether the charge could be thrown out on technicalities.

Throughout the disciplinary procedure, which lasted for four months (2 April to 22 August), a public vendetta was pursued against me in *Die Burger*. Johann Botha wrote an article entitled "Kunsmuseum se onderrok het uitdagende kleur" (Art museum's petticoat has a provocative colour, 20 July 1992) in which he made extensive reference to the June/August issue of *bonani*. He took issue right from the start, with my director's message. Adopting a sexist metaphor, he wondered: "Is it one's imagination, or is there a petticoat protruding at [SANG] in Cape Town? And it is not any old petticoat, but its colours are provocatively green, yellow and black." Botha was referring to the colours of the ANC. "One sees it hanging out under the skirt of Bonani, the SANG newsletter."

While Botha expressed excitement about the space given to the Friends in the publication, and the many activities at SANG and Natale Labia Museum, his feelings of "discomfort" and "irritation" stemmed from the way in which I interpreted "national" and "people" when writing about an exhibition opening. Here, in fuller terms, is the passage that irked him:

> The people came to [SANG] on Saturday morning, 16 May. The singing could be heard as the buses arrived in the parking area, some came in slowly for they were old, others came toyi-toying through the front door,

> through the atrium into the Liberman Room. Their presence, their joy and their appreciation were equalled in our hearts and in our minds only by the beauty and vitality of the 'lappies' which they had contributed to the exhibition *Where we live – panels by the People of Cape Town*. The SANG will never be the same, for we succeeded in bringing together for the first time (but not the last!) works from a cross-section of groups from various social layers and walks of life. The participants, with few exceptions, were not practising artists, but 'ordinary' people with no art background or training whatsoever. But they gave deep insight into the social and personal realities of life in Cape Town. We are deeply grateful to all who contributed.[84]

Botha was furthermore disturbed by the fact that Serote was "welcomed with pride" as speaker at the opening of the exhibition *Art from South Africa*. For Serote, the 1987 Culture in Another South Africa Conference marked the return of the people into history. "Now we enter history," he said in his speech. The recent Zabalaza Festival, held in London in July 1990, was another significant event in the return of the oppressed, a return that was irreversible. (Both exhibitions are discussed below.)

By the time Botha reached pages 10–11 of *bonani* "the petticoat was beginning to wave like a flag". The offending information, on which he commented at length, related to the films and videos (and the way in which they were described) that were shown to supplement *Art from South Africa*.[85] Minnaar did not escape invective. His announcement of the incorporation of the Friends' newsletter with *bonani* provided Botha with ammunition to rehearse factually incorrect details about the withdrawal of the institution's "biggest sponsor" – where in fact the Rembrandt Art Foundation sponsored the Triennial, not SANG. Botha also indulged in casting aspersions, fear mongering (he referred to recent cases of vandalism in the streets of Cape Town), jingoism (by accusing SANG of identifying its "salvation" with the "mass democratic movement") and political expediency (by currying favour in the hope of landing an administrative post in "Another South Africa").[86]

The space *Die Burger* was prepared to devote to me, and perceptions of my politics, were quite extraordinary, with articles starting in 1991. In his PhD thesis, "Manufacturing cultural capital: Arts journalism at *Die Burger* (1990–99)", Gabriël "Gawie" Botma sheds a great deal of light on what transpired: not only between the newspaper and me, but between the newspaper and the Rembrandt Art Foundation. I summarise relevant information from his thesis.[87]

Writing about the "early hegemonic struggles in *Die Burger* around the so-called Africanisation of culture", Botma referred to a 1991 speech about cultural transformation that I gave at the Afrikaans-language Jan van Riebeeck High School. The "political" nature of the speech caused an outcry and the principal subsequently informed the learners that individual speakers did "not necessarily reflect the views of the governing body or school" (*Die Burger*, 27 April 1991). The newspaper published my response on 4 May, as well as an op-ed article "Suid-Afrika moet besin oor kulturele prioriteite" (South Africa must rethink its cultural priorities, *Die Burger*, 10 May).[88]

Dealing with the economic field and ANC policies that might have negative implications for white-owned businesses, Botma turned to Rembrandt and the Triennial.[89] He expressed surprise that

Die Burger did not comment editorially when Rembrandt withdrew its sponsorship from the Triennial. A front page report by the arts editor (*Die Burger*, 7 February 1992) confirmed what Rupert had written to the SANG chairperson: the R882,740 spent on the Triennial would in future be used for job creation for disadvantaged people. Botma questioned whether *Die Burger* quietly supported this move, because "the powerful position of Rembrandt as one of the major advertisers of Naspers and *Die Burger* over decades deterred the newspaper from criticising Rembrandt for the suspension of its major support to the fine arts in this format". Surely greater inclusivity in post-1990 South Africa "was arguably just as pressing and deserving as supporting the fine arts during apartheid"? Botma surmised that Rembrandt's shift from supporting the fine arts to poverty alleviation may have been politically inspired: a few months later, Rupert contributed R250,000 to the Naspers initiative to establish a foundation for the promotion of Afrikaans (*Die Burger*, 6 June 1992).[90]

Back at SANG, Skawran had been on an extended trip abroad and missed the board meeting of 22 April. At the following meeting, held on 19 August, the chairperson opened the matter of the charge against me by offering her a brief summary of what had transpired. Scholtz concluded: "When I finish this I am going to ask you for a motion of confidence. It was quite clear to me in our previous meeting that a number of members emphatically disagree with me on the action initiated." He had obtained legal advice from DNE and confirmed that his actions were not beyond his powers, and that he had acted within the capacities of his office on 2 April, as he had not committed himself to not laying a charge at the special board meeting. The next step would be to appoint a person to conduct the disciplinary inquiry, but Scholtz wanted to establish the majority view of the board. "In the event of the majority deciding that they disagree with my decision to initiate and proceed with the inquiry, I shall resign as Chairman of the Board and hand the matter, the portfolio, to my successor."[91]

Danie van Niekerk proposed a motion of full confidence in the chairperson and his handling of the charge, which was seconded by Hannes van der Merwe. These conflicting and confusing proposals led to much discussion, in which statements made at previous meetings were reiterated: the fissure in the board, and the sides taken, were revealed. In the end Van Niekerk's motion was voted on: three for and five against, with two abstentions.[92] Scholtz capitulated. Dubow agreed to take the chair for the November board meeting, and further expressed his appreciation to Scholtz for his services as chairperson. Van Niekerk resigned soon thereafter. It was an ungraceful end to Scholtz's term as chairperson. He was devoted and committed to SANG, and we worked together well in a spirit of mutual respect. There is little doubt in my mind that he was placed under enormous pressure to act against me and that he could not resist.[93]

The trustees asked Dubow to write to *Die Burger* in response to all the articles it had published. His substantial text appeared on 29 August 1992. Dubow was clear that he was not writing on my behalf, or in my defence: "Martin is eloquently able to do this herself. Rather do I write as a long-standing member of the Board; but essentially I am writing as one who has long been interested in the more crucial of the issues raised in *Die Burger*." In inimitable fashion, he analysed an article in the newspaper that dealt with totalitarian propaganda in Stalinist Russia; he quoted Nazi propagandist Joseph Goebbels, the 1933 German Art Report and an extract from the "Actuality of Cultural Advancement" in the DNE journal *Education and Culture* of June 1979. They were not from the same source, but they followed each other with "inexorable logic".

He also quoted the administrator of the Cape who closed down a play at the Nico Malan Theatre (now Artscape): "We need drama that will give us steel in our bones for the battle that we will still have to fight." Dubow came to the conclusion that the justification "sounded chillingly like passages in the reports of the Führer's Council", and pointed out that this was not criticised by *Die Burger* at the time. He continued:

> I hope I shall not be thought to be making simplistic equations between Russia and Germany of the 1930s and South Africa in the 1980s. I am aware of the differences. But so should we continue to be aware of those parallels where they exist. In the new South Africa, when it finally comes about, we should continue to be vigilant. I have consistently urged that we be wary of calls to the blood (always by politicians who invoke the name of the people). Above all we should be wary of Art by Edict – and this applied to right, left and what may try to pass for centre.

FIGURE 19: Liberman Room in 1992, with destroyed sculpture: Gael Neke, *Eugène Terre'blanche and his two sidekicks*, 1989, ceramic, dimensions variable; photographer Kathy Grundlingh.

Dubow returned to the accusations against SANG, which had changed from being insufficiently Afrocentric to being anti-Eurocentric. He suggested that both charges be carefully examined to establish exactly what they mean:

> As I understand it, the task of the Gallery is to redress imbalances and to find a meaningful balance. Under its new Director, the Gallery has consciously positioned itself at the cutting edge of the redefinition of what South African art can really encompass. This will always be a difficult and controversial process … but it must be done. In my view this process will only succeed if we stop our hollow polarising cries of Euro- and Afrocentrism, and strive to make the search for quality central to our task.

Vandalism, exhibitions and activities

THE YEAR 1992 had started dramatically in more ways than one. That art can play a powerful role in society, and that it can challenge and rouse strong emotions and actions was brought home to us in a devastating way when, at 10h15 on 15 January, four uniformed members of the Afrikaner Weerstandsbeweging (AWB)[95] walked into the exhibition *Recent Acquisitions 1990–1991* with two people who had identified the location of a sculpture in advance, and proceeded to destroy it with hammer and boot (Fig. 19). Thanks to the vigilance and prompt action of the security staff, and the assistance of the police on duty at nearby Tuynhuys, the state president's Cape Town office, all six persons involved were arrested and charged. The police collected the shards as evidence.

Gael Neke's ceramic sculpture *Eugène Terre'blanche and his two sidekicks* (1989) was a powerful comment on a politically bellicose minority social group in South African society at the time. The AWB members smashed this likeness of their leader in order to "defend" his "honour". I was warned that they would not tolerate monstrous images of Terre'Blanche and would escalate their attack from hammers to using explosives, and "blow the place up". In the event, that threat didn't come to pass. SANG was awarded damages in the court case, but the work itself was irreparable. Neke "reconstructed" the work as *Untitled (Remains)* (1994–95).[97]

In the wake of the Triennial, I turned my attention to curating my first exhibition at the national art museum. Coming from Wits, where historical African art was acquired and exhibited in the university art gallery – then named the Gertrude Posel Gallery, now the Wits Art Museum (WAM) – alongside modern and contemporary art, and inspired by Burnett's *Tributaries*, I curated *Affinities*. It featured works from the permanent collection that cast a spotlight on similarities rather than differences, on the confluence of approaches rather than divergences, on the cross-pollination between traditions and transitions of past and present, western and African sources. It told new stories and stimulated debate regarding the art/craft hierarchy. But it also sparked alarm and the censure of SANG stakeholders and some artists.

Responses from abroad were most encouraging. Writing from London, art historian Susan Loppert reported on attempts to create a national culture in South Africa. She kept returning to SANG as an example of tangible possibilities:

> It is an exhilarating experience going to the National Gallery in Cape Town these days. Where once separate development and the emphasis on separateness were paramount, there's now an exhibition called *Affinities* deftly illustrating the relationship and crosspollination between western European and African art. Where once all signs were in Afrikaans and English only, now Xhosa has been added.[98]

Achille Bonito Oliva, director of the 1993 Venice Biennale, visited the gallery. "The different exhibitions there – especially *Affinities* and the exciting Eastern Cape beads of *Ezakwantu* – would provide him with much food for thought regarding his theories about the interdependence among 'cultural languages'," reported *Die Burger* (20 November 1993). Oliva went on to ensure South Africa's participation at the Venice Biennale for the first time in twenty-five years. The resulting exhibition, which featured Jackson Hlungwani and Sandra Kriel, was titled *Affinities*.[99]

In 1995, Jean-Hubert Martin, then director of the MNAAO, favourably remarked on the "iridescently coloured textiles made in local black communities which are hung right next to paintings. The aesthetic element is deliberately emphasized to the detriment of the work's function. I do not recall ever having seen an installation so firmly asserted in Europe".[100]

The diversity of projects and exhibitions ranged from *British Sporting Paintings*, drawn from the Abe Bailey Collection, to photographs from *Drum* magazine, Neville Dubow's *Sequences, Series, Sites 1971–1992*[101] and *Art Meets Science: Flowers as Images*.[102] An exhibition by Sephardi artists Francine Scialom-Greenblatt, Stella Cohen and Reggie Bardavid marked the culmination of the "Sepharad '92" programme organised by Cape Town's Sephardi congregation to commemorate the five-hundredth anniversary of the expulsion of Jews from Spain.

We organised a public debate at the time of the exhibition *Recent Acquisitions 1990–91*, which was chaired by author André P. Brink and attended by 208 people. It was characterised by a great deal of criticism, as was usually the case with public discussions. Brink referred to the acronym SANG as meaning "blood" in French and the arts as the lifeblood of a nation. In light of the controversies surrounding this exhibition, it was decided to share new acquisitions with the public every three months, immediately after the board meetings.[103] We were criticised in the public forum, but there were glowing reviews in the Afrikaans and English press.[104]

Where we Live – panels by the People of Cape Town resulted from a public project designed to encourage community involvement and participation in our activities, as well as to generate and express ideas and feelings about living in Cape Town, a divided city – then and now. We wanted to build bridges between the gallery and various communities, and amongst participants themselves. The "lappies" (an endearing Afrikaans diminutive for cloths, in this context work in fabric) included crafters' guilds, a literacy group, hospital patients, self-help cooperatives, women's groups, the Domestic Workers Association, the Monwabisi Seniors Club and prisoners from Polsmoor, who expressed themselves in beading, felting, embroidery, appliqué, quilting, weaving, sewing, crocheting, pasting, printing and knitting. Many works

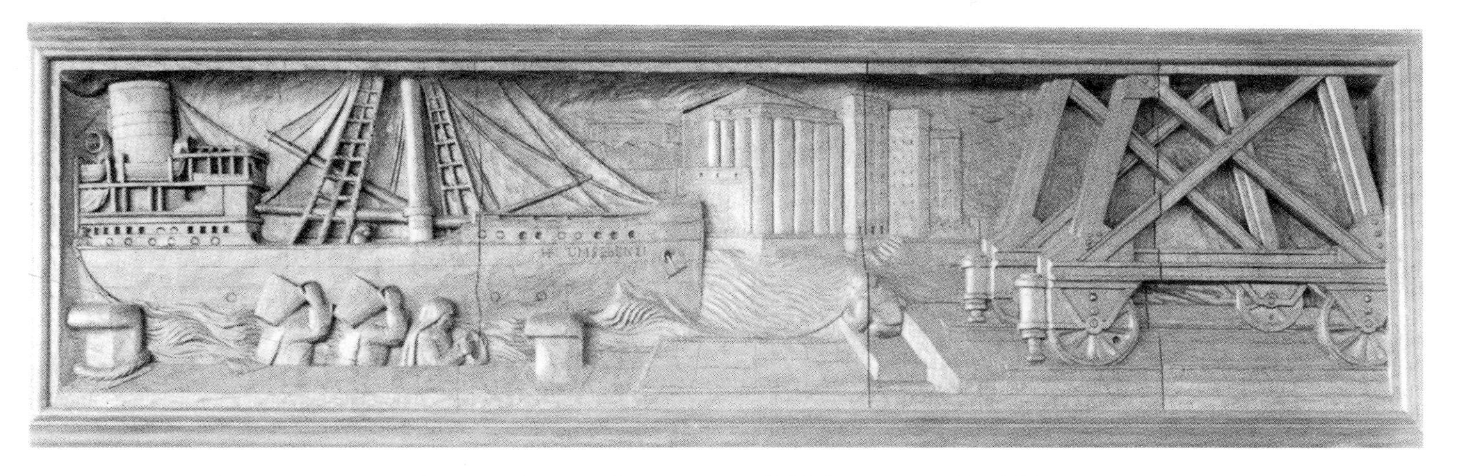

PLATE 21: Herbert Meyerowitz, *Dockside, Crane and Ship*, completed 1934, Burma teak, 580 x 1820; photographer Kathy Grundlingh.

were created in workshops in the Annexe and were returned to the communities in which they were made or donated to public service centres chosen by the makers. Jo-Anne Duggan recalled the noisy, joyful opening:

> One group of women arrived proudly bearing a banner and marched triumphantly through the gallery singing loudly. They were soon joined by others, taking ownership of a space that they may previously have been too intimidated to enter. Once the formal speeches were done our visitors tucked into platters piled high with samoosas and koesisters – not the usual gallery fare. For Emile, Fatima and I who had spent a year travelling between the groups, supplying materials, practical advice or moral support it was a heart-warming affirmation that SANG's transformation agenda, spearheaded by our 'new director', was firmly on track![105]

The year 1992 saw the first architectural exhibition at SANG. The series, which would continue until 2009, had its origins in the Sophia Gray Memorial Lecture and Exhibition, organised by the architectural school at the University of the Orange Free State. The series commenced with a show devoted to Gabriël "Gawie" Fagan, followed by Roelof Uytenbogaardt, Myra Fassler-Kamstra, Willie Meyer, Revel Fox and Jo Noero. In the absence of a collection of architecture, this was a way to foreground some of South Africa's most celebrated architects and provide the only museum platform for exhibiting architecture.

Made in Wood comprised sculpture in wood from the permanent collection, from workshops organised by education staff and work submitted for exhibition after an open call. The project was sponsored by Dr. Victor Hesse of the Hans Merensky Foundation and was shown in the main building and Annexe. The generous funding enabled education officers Duggan, Maurice and Siebert to expand the Invited Artist Programme into three dimensions and to schedule a series of workshops with foremost sculptors and lecturers Andries Botha (his visit coincided with his exhibition as the 1991 Standard Bank Young Artist), Ângela Ferreira and Peter Schütz. Duggan outlined the didactic approach to educational projects: "Exhibitions at the Annexe are intended to be interactive, engaging viewers directly in dialogue with the artwork as information. This dialogue can help us perceive our own life-world more critically, thereby revealing new possibilities for understanding our experiences and ordering our responses."[106]

The opening was attended by hundreds of people. Critical reaction, though, was mixed: for Benita Munitz (*Cape Times*, 28 January 1993) "inclusiveness" required limits, while Caryll Shear (*Weekly Mail,* 12 February 1993) commended the exhibition for exposing the public to a new generation of sculptors in the Western Cape. The exhibition in the main building and the catalogue also drew attention to Meyerowitz's Liberman Memorial Door and the carved wooden panels inside the gallery. Albie Sachs, who a year later was appointed a justice to the Constitutional Court of South Africa, provided interesting historical information regarding one of the panels (Plate 21) in a letter to *bonani*:

> For those people who are worried that [SANG] is being subverted, the position is worse than they thought. When Herbert Meyerowitz crafted the panels which now grace the exhibition halls, he gave one of the ships in the Cape Town Harbour the names HM Umsebenzi. At that time *The Umsebenzi* (meaning *The Worker*) was a revolutionary newspaper directed principally at dockworkers and other members of the black working class. According to my mother, Meyerowitz's political joke was widely applauded in the Left circles to which he belonged. If you look in the catalogue *Made in Wood: Work from the Western Cape* you can see the inscription clearly in the photograph on page 37. Otherwise those with good eyes can make it out in the panel above your head as you enter the room leading off from the bookshop. For many it must seem that their worst fears are being realised and the revolutionary ship has at last anchored in what was once considered the safest of harbours.[107]

A number of important shows were held with international cooperation and support: *Bloomsbury Artists at Charleston, Reader's Digest Collection*, and *Knots and Nets Spiritual Connections*, an exhibition of fibre art, curated by Nancy Neumann Press as part of the celebration of the year of American craft in 1993.[108] A major show intended to fill gaps in South African art history, *Hans Ludwig Katz (1892–1940) A Retrospective of a Neglected German Expressionist*, was drawn from German museums and local private collections.[109]

Practising artists can play a vital role in the process of rewriting history and transgressing cultural and disciplinary boundaries. Malcolm Payne's exhibition *Face Value: Old Heads in Modern Masks – a visual, archaeological and historical reading of the Lydenburg Heads* did exactly that by creating a context in which the inter-disciplinary discourse could be problematised. He conceived the installation, made works of art for it and carried it out in the last detail. For the first time since 1971 the seven terracotta *Lydenburg Heads*, c. 500-700 CE were displayed at the art museum, together with seven of Payne's own sculptures – the *Mafikeng Heads* – a series of etchings, seven supermarket trolleys and seven aluminium structures (containers of information), and a hand-printed book and catalogue on the project.[110]

The *Lydenburg Heads*, which UCT gave to SAM on permanent loan in 1979, were on display at a museum of natural history that included the ethnography collections. This presented a number of obstacles, as I noted in Payne's catalogue:

> In negotiating the loan of the *Lydenburg Heads* [from SAM], there was a condition that associated pottery and other artefacts from the site would be included in the exhibition; staff of the institution felt that it was important to provide viewers with the contextual material. This created an interesting situation and the dynamics and complexities peculiar to SANG were once again thrown into relief, demanding discussion and evaluation.[111]

SANG staff members held differing positions as to omitting the archaeological past of the works, but the artist had the last word, and he was adamant that such fragments not be included in his installation and that there would be no explanatory text on the walls. Graham Avery of the archaeology department at SAM graciously conceded that the artist-curator's demands in the context of the art museum were different. Information about the history and archaeology was made available to the public. Payne wrote in the exhibition catalogue:

> South African cultural histories have, in recent times, become the focus of much critical debate. Indeed, the debate itself may be considered to be a vital form of cultural expression. No exhibition, artist, artwork, political grouping or museum collection is free from its complex scrutiny. The debate aims to restructure representation, rewrite history, to transgress stylistic and cultural boundaries all in the search for dialogue that is meaningful. "History" is its focal centre. It is in this context that this volume will enter the fray, examine the production of meaning and, hopefully, itself become a site of meaning.[112]

An important sub-text for both the artist and the art museum was the question: Where do the *Lydenburg Heads* belong? Payne emphasised his position that "meaning is contingent, which supports the notion that the hierarchical grading of objects or material culture should be provisionally suspended".[113] In the catalogue I observed:

> … the first public showing of some of the *Lydenburg Heads* at SANG in 1971 did not seem to alter or affect their status as art; it did not make them part of the mainstream of the history of South African art … But from now on the status of these sculptures as timeless, enigmatic and irreplaceable works of art can neither be challenged nor revoked. This raises questions about the history of South African sculpture – as it is currently told – and about the proper home of the *Lydenburg Heads*.[114]

I was wrong: more than twenty years later, the sculptures have still not found their rightful place, and many parts of the history of our sculpture remain untold.

At the time of *Face Value: Old heads in Modern Masks*, two other exhibitions dealt with African aesthetic production: *Textiles from Africa*, curated by Rayda Becker, and *Transformed Fibres*, curated by Nessa Leibhammer – both drew work from the Standard Bank Foundation Collection of African art.

Dolby, Duggan and Maurice curated *Picturing Our World: Contemporary Images of the Western Cape* for the Grahamstown Festival, where it was shown at the Dakawa Art & Craft Project, and subsequently at the Standard Bank Gallery in Johannesburg and SANG.[115] The show comprised work drawn from SANG's permanent and education collections, CAP, Mayibuye Centre at UWC and from individual artists. It pictured the diversity of the physical and social world, and the domain of ideas that characterise the province. It built on *Where we live: Panels by the people of Cape Town* and *Made in Wood: Work from the Western Cape*, challenging "the prevailing notion of 'community art' as a category different and separate from other categories of art".[116]

A particularly moving and important event was the display of the Second Cape Town Aids Memorial Quilt. It was the first in a series of exhibitions and activities that would use art to engage and conscientise the public about the HIV/Aids pandemic. The source of inspiration was "The Names Project" in the United States, founded in 1987, which soon became an international manifestation. The organisation stages more than one thousand quilt displays each year in a variety of venues across the nation. In the words of Robert Munk: "The Quilt to me in terms of art is perhaps the most real kind of art – it's the most directly connected to people's emotions – it's not fine art and it's not school art. There are no rules for making panels."[117]

In 1994 the photo-documentary exhibition from the Anne Frank Centre in Amsterdam, *Anne Frank in the World: An international exhibition to promote tolerance and understanding*, was brought to South Africa by the Embassy of the Netherlands and the Jewish Board of Deputies, and presented in association with several church groups. It was organised by Myra Osrin, then director of the Cape Town Holocaust Centre together with Duggan, who represented SANG on the organising committee, and Jon Weinberg. It was not an art exhibition, but we were interested in bringing the story of Anne Frank closer to home and in exploring issues of discrimination, racism and the need to uphold tolerance and understanding. Duggan recalls the process and outcome:

> While the relevance to the South African context was unequivocal, the organisers had to be forcefully persuaded … to include a component that dealt more directly and specifically with conditions in South Africa. The complementary exhibition [curated by Gordon Metz and André Odendaal of the Mayibuye

PLATE 22: Herbert Meyerowitz, *Quayside* (arrival of Sheikh Yusuf), completed 1934, Burma teak, 580 x 1820; photographer Kathy Grundlingh.

> Centre] was hastily put together on a low budget. The simple black and white panels – made up of black and white photocopies rather crudely cut and pasted onto board – sat incongruously alongside the sophisticated, high-tech panels from the Netherlands. Ironically, the Anne Frank exhibition came and went. The apartheid and resistance exhibition was installed at the Mayibuye Centre, where it remains on display today, over twenty years later. According to the Centre's staff it has played a seminal role in telling the story of South Africa's dark past and has been drawn on as a resource for a host of subsequent exhibitions and publications.[118]

The exhibition *Muslim Art from the Western Cape* opened in April 1994, the month that saw South Africans vote in the first democratic elections. Curated by Duggan, Dolby, Maurice and I, with the active participation of education assistant Fatima February, it marked the three-hundredth anniversary of the arrival of Sheikh Yusuf of Makassar at the Cape.[119] Achmat Davids of the Sheikh Yusuf Tricentenary Commemoration Committee (SYTCC) approached us to organise an exhibition as part of the commemoration. Interestingly, Sheikh Yusuf has had a place in the Gallery since 1934 – in Herbert Meyerowitz's carved panel above one of the doors, depicting his arrival (Plate 22).

We were opening opportunities for participation and it was indeed heartening that members of a particular community, who previously felt excluded from the national art museum, were interested in working with us in the presentation of their culture, history and aesthetic production. Artists were invited to submit works for selection by a committee comprising SANG staff and members of the SYTCC, Dr. Cassiem D'Arcy and Sheikh Seraj Hendriks. The exhibition consisted of paintings, photographs, prints, calligraphy, minstrel carnival stands, copper and mirror work and fabrics loaned by artists, crafts-people and collectors in Cape Town.

We were faced with a lot of cultural and emotional learning and we were privileged to have D'Arcy – thinker, writer, artist and collector – on the team to share his knowledge of Muslim culture and to facilitate the participation of many artists. In addition to the extensive education programmes, invited artists worked in the exhibition area: Achmat Soni, Ayesha Gasant, Suleiman Nordien, Achmat Fish, Ebrahim Abed and Hadjiera Creighton displayed and shared their skills in media ranging from calligraphy and silk painting to copper work and the pinning of medoras.[120] Members of the public joined the creative process and worked on a commemorative fabric panel.

Six hundred people attended the opening, which was an extraordinary event. By the end of the day, 2,032 visitors had been through the gallery, many to view the *Anne Frank in the World* exhibition; they found their way to the Muslim art and the Muslims present showed great interest in Frank's world and other exhibitions. Duggan described a personal moment:

> We all understood that this exhibition marked another step forward in SANG's move towards becoming an inclusive space for all South Africans, but it took a brief encounter to remind me of the pain exacted by a lifetime of exclusion. While the crowds at the opening jostled their way happily through the exhibition, calling out their greetings and pointing out works in tones of great excitement,

> D'Arcy, almost overcome by emotion and struggling to hold back his tears, said: "I never thought the day would come when I would see one of my works in this place." It was a profound moment, and one I carried it with me through the years of negotiating cultural policies and discussing institutional transformation. When all is said and done it is not the systems and the structures that matter but the potential that they have to drive change: to give substance to the Constitutional injunction to "heal the divisions of the past and establish a society based on democratic values, social justice and fundamental human rights". [121]

The press was enthusiastic. Gawie Botma described the morning as "an ants' nest of activity – a lively living museum" (*Die Burger,* 25 April 1994), and James Garner commended the curators for their decision not to draw distinctions between different forms of expression (*Cape Times,* 25 May 1994):

> The result is an exhibition which highlights the multi-faceted nature of Muslim culture in the Cape – a picture which differs remarkably from the kind of Western media stereotypes which encourage the view that all Muslims are intolerant and unchanging fundamentalists. Notable, too, is the decision to concentrate on work produced since the 1940s – an effective way of challenging the Western tendency to lock Muslim culture into the distant past.

The year ended with another groundbreaking project. King Mayisha II Mabhoko opened *IGugu lamaNdebele: Pride of the Ndebele* on 3 December 1994. Architect Peter Rich was appointed to design the structures and general layout, and to work with Kaufmann. Rich and I were colleagues in the architecture department

FIGURE 20: *IGugu LamaNdebele* installation, 1994; photographer Kathy Grundlingh.

at Wits during the 1980s, and since 1991, when the board approved my proposal to establish a collection which would reflect the aesthetic production of all the people of South Africa, Rich had played an invaluable role as advisor. In that year – on his recommendation – the DNE acquired a major collection of Ndebele beadwork for the gallery. Soon thereafter discussions around a comprehensive exhibition of Ndebele art and architecture, which would reveal the culture in all its complexity and beauty, commenced.

Rich was instrumental in securing the support of the Ndebele Royal House for the project and the participation of six Ndebele women – Isa Kabini, Emma Mahlangu, Betty Masanabo, Lia Masilele, Sophie Masiza and Anna Matshiye – who represented six distinct regions. They were directly involved in aspects of the exhibition: they painted the structures and individual panels, made sculptures and chose the colours for the walls (Figs. 20 & 21). Anna Matshiye's sculptures were installed in the small niches on the façade, while Isa and Johannes Kabini returned to complete the painting of the big niches – enduring reminders of initiatives inside that aimed at positioning SANG as belonging on the African continent. The direct involvement of the Ndebele women provided new and unusual insights into their art, culture and architecture, and in turn they were given employment and exposure. Isa Kabini executed a major commission for Truworths, one of the corporate sponsors.

Historical and contemporary Ndebele art and architecture were presented in the context of the present and illuminated with depictions of the people and their art by Margaret Courtney-Clarke, David Goldblatt, Thomas Kgope, Constance Stuart Larrabee, Peter Magubane, Karel Nel, Stanley Pinker and Alexis Preller. The exhibition attracted 47,000 visitors during its run (3 December 1994 to 30 April 1995), and numerous school groups and students benefited from exposure to a culture that is geographically

FIGURE 21: *IGugu LamaNdebele* installation, 1994; photographer Kathy Grundlingh.

distant from the Western Cape. Academics in the field were commissioned to contribute essays to a peer-reviewed catalogue, but due to lack of resources it was never published.[122]

In a 1995 review published by Art in America, art historian Linda Nochlin referred to how:

> ... members of the Ndebele nation had enlivened the Neo-Classical facade [sic] of the building with colourful architectural decoration. Within was a striking show of remarkable art and architecture, beadwork and exterior decoration, produced by a group ravaged by the dislocations of colonialism and apartheid who nevertheless rebuilt their national traditions, mainly through the cultural productions of women.[123]

Reflecting on the Bailey collection in relation to *IGugu lamaNdebele*, Nochlin continued:

> In the next gallery, fortunately tucked away in relative obscurity, was a memento of colonialism's contribution to the great Western tradition in South Africa ... It was just a reminder that the Western tradition is not always so great; it contains a lot that suffers in comparison with the production of so-called minorities and the cultural workers of the "Third World."

The gallery, together with the Michaelis School, collaborated on a commemorative exhibition of works by Patricia Pierce-Atkinson. The exhibition drew from SANG's collection and from corporate and private collections, as well as work by Pippa Skotnes, the 1993 Standard Bank Young Artist Winner. For the first time in many years, the complete collection of works presented by Alfred de Pass between 1926 and 1949 went on display, accompanied by a catalogue written by art historian Anna Tietze. Her research revealed that on 29 July 1949 trustees had decided that a room in the building would be named after De Pass.[124] After his death this lapsed. The board addressed the matter on 18 November 1994 and room three was named the "Alfred de Pass Gallery", a name it retains to this day.

Patty Hardy organised a wide range of activities at the NLM. There were exhibitions from the permanent collection and elsewhere, including works from the Friends' private collections, lectures, concerts, art classes, storytelling, poetry readings (including regular meetings and events by The Poetry Society) and a café. The intimate spaces at this satellite museum were ideal for showing a wide range of decorative arts, ceramics, glass and textiles, such as *Kalahari-ware*; *The Women of Olifantsfontein*: *South African Studio Ceramics*; *The New Look*: *Art Glass of the 50s and 60s*; and Japanese "Ukiyo-ye" woodcut prints from the permanent collection, together with a selection of contemporary Japanese prints. A highlight was *The Hand is the Tool of the Soul: Works by Peter Clarke,* accompanied by special tours, discussions, demonstrations and poetry readings by the artist and selected friends.

While placing much focus on local matters, operating at national and international levels was important. A major event in 1992 was the exhibition *Art from South Africa*. Curated by David Elliott, then director of the Museum of Modern Art in Oxford, in association with the Zabalaza Festival held in London in 1990, the exhibition travelled to a number of venues in the United Kingdom before agreement was reached to cooperate with SANG. The exhibition was curated under the terms of the selective cultural boycott, and it included work by more than sixty individuals, mixed with beadwork, community group projects and wire toys. Wally Serote opened the exhibition.[125]

A joint project between the Délégation générale de l'Alliance française en Afrique du Sud and l'Alliance française de Soweto resulted in a travelling exhibition of watercolours, drawings, etchings, lithographs and paintings on handmade paper and canvas by Soweto artist Durant Sihlali, who was still largely absent from our art history books in 1994.

In Paris in the same year, I saw an exhibition at l'Institut du monde arabe (Arab World Institute) titled *Rencontres Africaines* (*African Encounters*), which brought together the art of nine contemporary artists then working on the African continent. Curators Jean-Hubert Martin and Brahim Alaoui devised an exciting new curatorial approach to start a dialogue between the Arab-speaking Maghreb and sub-Saharan Africa: they entrusted the selection of works to two artists, Farid Belkahia (Morocco) and Abdoulaye Konaté (Mali) to choose artists from the each other's regions.[126] I immediately approached Martin, l'Association française d'Action artistique (AFAA), and Laurent Deveze, then French cultural attaché and director of the l'Institut français d'Afrique du Sud (IFAS), to make the exhibition available to SANG. More than a decade before curator Simon Njami's synoptic pan-African showcase *Africa Remix* opened at JAG in 2007, we were able to offer our visitors an extraordinary encounter with contemporary art from the continent. The artists, little known at the time, are all famous now.[127]

International and continental links were further created with the exhibition *Asafo! Fante Flags from Ghana 1850–1957.* It comprised fifty appliquéd and embroidered flags from collections in Europe and the United States that were originally presented at the London Festival Hall. The exhibition travelled to several centres in South Africa.

Gifts, presentations, acquisitions and commissions

BEQUESTS and presentations to the gallery were shared with the public on a regular basis, while at the same time honouring and thanking individual donors for their generosity. In the early 1990s the largest presentation comprised the personal collection of Marjorie Reynolds: it contained works by her mother, painter Dorothy Kay. Shown on the exhibition *Bequests and Presentations*, Reynolds shared her wonder in a letter published in *bonani*:

> The first sight of the interleading rooms, each quite outstanding was a sight never to be forgotten. It was an enormous success as an overall view and each room most effectively judged and hung and really it was altogether and amazing experience. With no feelings of consanguinity intruding, I thought Dorothy Kay spoke loudly and clearly and with great integrity enhanced by the attention that had been given to each work.[128]

A substantial donation by retired art dealer and collector Fernand Haenggi of the Pelmama Art Foundation added to the holdings of work by black artists, as well as prints by well-known American Pop artists, and a ceramic piece by Sonja Zytkow. The *Cape Times* Lecture Fund, organised by Gwen Mills, donated the *Maquette for the Gandhi Memorial Statue*, Pietermaritzburg (1992) by Anton Momberg (Fig. 40).

In 1993, the Friends celebrated its twenty-fifth anniversary with the acquisition of two major ceramic works for the gallery: *From Here to Eternity* by Hennie Stroebel and *Veldfire* by Wendy Ross. This coincided with the opening of the Gallery Café, to which FONG made a substantial financial contribution. The increasingly diversified cultural production and open-ended approach to acquisitions resulted in the termination of the *Friends' Choice Collection*, which had been initiated in 1975 with a view to acquiring work by younger, lesser-known or unknown artists. In the ensuing years some works gradually entered the permanent collection, and in 1991 many more were acquisitioned and celebrated with an exhibition, *Friends' Choice*, curated by Joe Dolby and Deon Viljoen, and a catalogue.[129] This did not mean the end of the Friends' involvement in this area of SANG's activities; on the contrary, FONG has continued to purchase works on request and at times their support has been the only means of augmenting the collection. Catalogues and *bonani* are filled with expressions of gratitude for the sterling support the institution received from the Friends and from many different sources, not only for exhibitions but also for educational projects.

The early 1990s were bumper years for acquisitions. Unlike now, South African art was affordable and our global budget for the 1990–91 financial year was R2,063,000; a sum of R196,973 was available for acquisitions at my first meeting.[130] The acquisitions committee was chaired by Dubow and comprised members of the executive committee and those with a particular interest in the mandate of the committee, as well as staff members appointed at the different levels of professional officers.[131] A viewing of works put forward for purchase was arranged for all board members prior to the meeting.

Acquisitions were made from many different galleries, art centres and artists throughout South Africa, and occasionally from London. The historical African art collection grew exponentially, as did the collections of photographs, and prints and drawings. The wide range of paintings included Daphne Taylor's *The Brazen Serpent*, maligned by Bernard Lewis in his review and sold by Roworth. Dubow spotted it at Collectables in Kronendal and it was purchased for R12,995. Some fifty years after Lewis' vitriol Taylor was vindicated. Zirk van den Berg reviewed the exhibition of recent acquisitions for *Die Burger* (8 January 1992), which published an image of Taylor's painting. After recapitulating the history of the "captivating work", he noted: "More than six decades after its creation the painting looks surprisingly contemporary."[132]

In 1986 I attended sculptor Jane Alexander's Wits MFA-degree show at the Market Gallery, which included her well-known sculpture *Butcher Boys* (1985-86) (Plate 17). The sculpture, which is composed of three seated figures, is at once shocking and deeply moving. Life-size and alive in their presence, the three figures speak of the human condition, metamorphoses and mutation – in the mid-1980s, and beyond. It was always top of my list for acquisition and was acquired for R8,500 at the first meeting. It has endured as a most compelling work for specialists, art lovers and the general public – visitors requested to see it, even when not on display.[133]

Other important sculptures, paintings and works on paper and cloth or in mixed media, were purchased. They are listed in issues of *bonani* and are reproduced in the catalogue of the exhibition *Contemporary South African Art 1985–1995 from the South African National Gallery Permanent Collection* (14 December 1996 to 31 March 1997), which is discussed in the next chapter.

One of the works listed in this catalogue is a triptych by Joyce Ntobe (aka painter and sculptor Beezy Bailey), *Get Home, Cook Supper, Go to Sleep* (1991).[134] Bailey submitted two works to the 1991 Triennial: a painting under his own name, and the linocut by the fictional Ntobe. Neither was accepted for the exhibition, but we saw merit in the triptych and purchased it on aesthetic grounds. Bailey, who was already represented in the gallery's permanent collection, had invented his so-called alter ego "in response to political correctness where artists are chosen on their skin colour in an attempt to rewrite our sad history". Bailey further stated, "I regard this as racist and hence Joyce Ntobe. Joyce's works were promptly bought by the National Gallery, causing a heated controversy about the inverted racism of art world institutions."[135]

It was not an original idea. Painter Wayne Barker had challenged perceived imbalances in judging art competitions by entering two works in the 1990 Standard Bank Drawing Competition, one in his own name and another in the name of Andrew Moletse. The latter, fictional artist's drawing was accepted, but not Barker, who capitalised on the judges' decision. He received huge amounts of attention and press coverage.

Continuing the tradition of commissioning artists, SANG invited sixteen eminent local photographers to submit project proposals of their own choice. The submissions were of such an excellent and interesting nature that a single commission could not be identified. The selection committee decided that six photographers – Geoffrey Grundlingh, Ingrid Hudson, Lesley Lawson, Roger Meintjes, Guy Tillim and Paul Weinberg – should be funded to complete their projects over a period of two years. The FCA supported five of the photographers. The commission culminated in the exhibition *Through a Lens Darkly.* [136]

In an effort to enliven the area in front of the gallery and attract the attention of pedestrians in the Company's Garden, we initiated the competition and commission "Flags by Artists" in 1994, also funded by the FCA. The country was at the time considering proposals for a new national flag, so the project had a resonance beyond the precinct of the gallery. There was neither a specific theme nor complex rules, yet designing flags presented unusual challenges to artists, resulting in several calls for entries. A professional flag-making company turned designs by Kevin Brand, Isa Kabini, Craig Masters, Samuel Mglombane, Andrew Putter and André Vorster into flags. The artist flags were first flown on 24 September 1996 (Heritage Day). The nature of the project was ephemeral, but copies were taken into the SANG collection.[137]

Education at the forefront

CONTINUING WITH and expanding on the programmes that my predecessors initiated, highly trained volunteer guides offered guided tours and the education staff organised lectures covering wide-ranging topics. The talks included the popular *Cape Times* lecture series, held in the Annexe and at the NLM, with proceeds used for special presentations to SANG and to support the *Cape Times* Fresh Air Fund. There were regular lunch-time film and video screenings and special film festivals, not only about the visual arts but also music and musicians, and topics of general interest to the public. Duggan would periodically provide details and express gratitude in *bonani* for the extraordinary support her department received from organisations, groups, individuals and foreign missions. Fundraising fashion shows organised by Elsie Menasce of La Boutique Yvelle, raised money for educational activities.

In order to address the lack of art education in many schools, the educators had initiated an outreach programme in 1987; we saw that it required revision and a more intensive cycle of activity than one workshop and a tour. A new art education programme, sponsored by FONG and the FCA, was initiated: "Shared Vision Project" involved standard three (grade five) learners and their teachers from eight primary schools. It provided an opportunity for young people of diverse groups to meet, share experiences, perceptions and values through a series of art activities and discussions. Participants were drawn from a cross-section of inner-city schools and the programme fostered an understanding of the shared but diverse cultural heritage of the various communities of central Cape Town.[138]

The nature and quality of engaging with Xhosa-speaking teachers, learners and members of the public were hugely enhanced by the appointment of information officer Vuyile Voyiya in 1991. Duggan remembers excited learners "who would spend half the morning in the imposing space of the main gallery with Noni Sipuye or Voyiya looking at the artworks with big eyes and listening in rapt attention before returning to the Annexe for a practical session" and sandwiches.[139]

An annual highlight, funded by the FCA, was the Gerard Sekoto Children's Day. Sekoto, who left South Africa in 1947 to pursue his career in France, wrote to us from Paris. He described the 1992 event and the exposure it afforded children to "this wonderful world of fine art" as "an unbelievable dream!" He added: "I could never have imagined such heights, and I am feeling more and more proud of my land of birth ... I am enclosing my full excitement into the feeling of all those children on that day."[140]

In addition to the workshops offered for adults and the children's holiday workshops, the Annexe had a full exhibition schedule that was of a more specifically educational nature and that appealed to younger audiences. The popular annual December children's participatory exhibition, initiated under Van Niekerk's directorship, continued. Exhibitions included *Graffiti on the Berlin Wall* to *Shelter*; *City to Maze*; and *Design Works* to *Made to Move*, which consisted of puppets made by the Bamana people from Mali, masks mainly from Central and West Africa, dancing maces and articulated toys from southern Africa.

The talented and dedicated educators contributed enormously to the transformation agenda, and to reaching and building diverse audiences. "For many, SANG became a place where art happened, not just where it could be viewed, breaking away from the notion of the art museum as an elite space reserved for an elite few," said Duggan, adding that this "played an important role in revisioning the role of the SANG in public life at a critical point in the history of the institution, and the country".[141]

In January 1994, Malangatana Ngwenya, the renowned Mozambican artist and associate of Portuguese-born architect Pancho Guedes, visited Cape Town as part of a programme organised by the educators, Mayibuye Centre and the Bellville Association of Arts. Funded by the FCA and the DNE, Ngwenya created a mural in the library at the University of the Western Cape. He returned in March as part of a group of international artists and curators for a public discussion and meeting, requested by Christopher Till and facilitated by SANG, about the proposed Johannesburg Biennale.[142]

The reference library was ably and enthusiastically run and promoted by librarian Josephine Andersen, who believed that a museum art library acted as an intermediary between artists and society. She directed information programmes externally and internally to museum staff and shared her vision and groundbreaking practice in publications and at national and international conferences.[143] The SANG library contained a list of catalogues produced by the museum since 1904 and newspaper cuttings dating back to 1916, while the library exchange programme ensured that both national and international exhibition catalogues, including those from approximately ninety art museums in other countries, were systematically acquired. SANG subscribed to 120 current journal articles and when money was scarce, Andersen raised funds to sustain the subscriptions. The library was a hive of activity and energy, used by researchers, academics, students and learners. In order to assist schools and art teachers in accessing the resources, Andersen, together with her assistants and the educators, initiated the "Art Boxes" project: they contained information on different themes and in different materials and were loaned to schools for periods of four to six weeks, while copies remained in the library. Art Kits and flip files of news cuttings were prepared and ready for school and individual visits.

It was time for the permanent collection to be computerised. Peter Dennis was an assistant librarian and it was clear that he had a good understanding of databases and information systems, so in 1994 he was appointed as data and systems officer - and later as registrar.[144] Dennis described the registry of the collection as "in a haphazard state and the documentation partially digitised".[145] Using the latest technology (Microsoft Access version 1.0) and assisted by a volunteer, it took a year to check every record in the acquisition registers and capture the data. This formed the central resource for the collection and a valuable management tool for SANG.

Dennis also recalled that he developed a website for the gallery - the first art museum in South Africa to possess such a utility - in conjunction with Global Electronic Messaging (GEM). It was basic, but soon became a useful form of communication, and gradually became an archive of SANG's exhibitions, newsletters and events. Considering the dearth of funds, Dennis produced excellent results with sub-standard equipment. His knowledge and initiatives left a legacy for Iziko Museums, as well as for other museums. Unsurprisingly, his skills were in demand and Dennis left Iziko to establish his own business developing and selling database software. He now supplies a range of products used by museums, galleries, universities, municipalities, private collectors and some corporates.

Engaging internationally

FUNDS FOR TRIPS abroad, once readily available, were rapidly diminishing, this at a time when the end of the cultural boycott saw a flood of invitations and opportunities. I travelled to the United Kingdom and United States in 1990, delivered a paper and acted as chairperson of a panel at the thirty-third AGM of the African Studies Association in Baltimore. The German Ambassador invited me to visit his country on a study tour in September 1992.

It was always a balancing act, balancing travel with important duties locally. I was enormously proud to attend Nelson Mandela's inauguration as the first democratically elected president of South Africa in Pretoria on 10 May 1994, the same day I left for Paris as guest of AFAA and Art contemporain d'Afrique australe. We had assisted the organisers, Jean and Mathieu Nouzareth and curator Jean-Yves Jouannais, in putting together *Un art contemporain d'Afrique du Sud* at the Galerie de l'Esplanade, la Défense. In addition to planning advice and insight, I wrote an essay for the catalogue and participated in a panel discussion. I visited many museums and the studio of fashion designer Yves Saint Laurent, facilitated by Elsie Menasce, with a view to organising a retrospective exhibition of his work. Unfortunately the costs were prohibitive and the logistics too complex.

I was familiar with the history of Sarah "Saartjie" Baartman, the Khoikhoi woman who from 1810 onwards was exhibited in fair attractions in nineteenth-century London and Paris, but nothing had prepared me for the encounter with the plaster cast of Baartman's body made upon her death, displayed in a vitrine as part of an exhibition entitled *La sculpture ethnographique – de la Vénus hottentote à la Tehura de Gauguin* at Musée d'Orsay. I returned to South Africa determined that something had to be done to repatriate Baartman's remains to the country of her birth. An opportunity presented itself in 1996, which I discuss in chapter five.

President François Mitterrand visited South Africa in 1994. I was invited to his address in parliament, and to a small gathering of people from the broader world of art and literature for a conversation around the lunch table. Members of his delegation visited SANG, as did many foreign diplomats, curators, museologists, artists and writers, including artist and curator Rasheed Araeen, who in 1987 founded the critical journal *Third Text*.

This chapter ends at the momentous time in South African history, when on 27 April 1994, millions of black people queued with their white compatriots to exercise their democratic right for the first time. The intensity, exhilaration and difficulties of the transition for the country were keenly embraced and felt at the national art museum – traumatic as it was at times.

During the first four years of my directorship we started implementing the vision, mission and policy of SANG. At the local level, education programmes expanded, and we engaged with progressive cultural groups and different communities that were beginning to take ownership of their art museum. Staff joined the National Education, Health and Allied Works' Union (NEHAWU). Access was free and programmes and information were available in Afrikaans, English and Xhosa. While shining the spotlight on contemporary South African art and honouring the historical European collections, there was a desire to fulfil Arnott's and Bokhorst's dream of a substantial collection of African art. This included the repatriation of historical works that had been removed from the country in the preceding centuries, as well as works by artists who had left the country.

The cultural and academic boycott had come to an end and renewed contact with international museums, organisations, foreign missions and individuals enabled us to counter the parochialism that Paris, Bokhorst and Van Niekerk feared as much as encountered. Successful fundraising, increased visitor numbers and articles published nationally and abroad, confirmed the richness and diversity of the exhibitions and acquisitions. Staff contributed enormously by participating in conferences and seminars, and by engaging with other institutions and organisations. Often controversial, we were ploughing the ground and sowing the seeds for the future; during this interregnum we initiated public debates and generated new ideas of what was suitable for acquisition and display at the national art museum. Crucially, the transformation of the institution that had taken effect was way ahead of what politicians would soon demand of national institutions. After a period of negotiation, bluster and stasis, South Africa was ready to get on with the business at hand, in what would be a completely different social, political and museum environment.

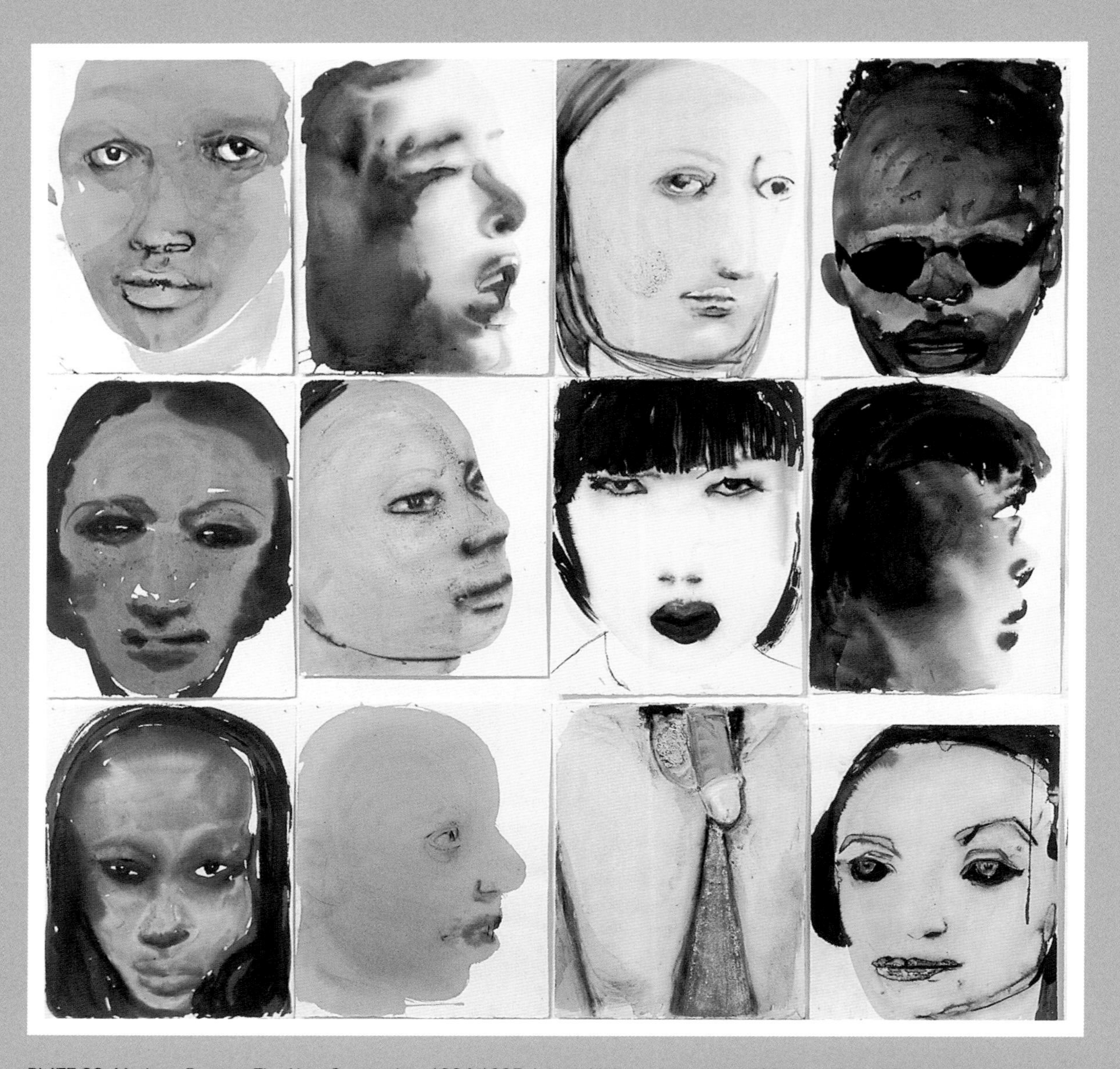

PLATE 23: Marlene Dumas, *The Next Generation,* 1994-1995, ink and ink wash on paper [45 parts, 66 × 50,5 cm each], detail; image courtesy of the artist; photographer Pam Warne.

5

A new dispensation for national museums

1995 – 1999

THIS CHAPTER charts a shift in mood following the 1994 elections as the new government's attitude towards South African history and SANG's work in particular becomes clearer. The government's overarching commitment to a neo-liberal macro economic strategy is discussed in relation to the art museum, and ministerial clashes with the director are revisited. This chapter documents the difficult but necessary process of restructuring South Africa's national museums in line with the White Paper on Arts and Culture, and efforts to engage and inform new ministers and officials in the Department of Arts, Culture, Science and Technology. Official indifference and neglect did not prevent trustees and staff at SANG from pursuing their ambitions and vision to impact positively on the lives of South Africans, and to repatriate cultural patrimony. The period is marked by important exhibitions, notably *Miscast* (1996), *Contemporary South African Art 1985–1995* (1996–97), *Graft* (1997) and *Lines of Sight: Perspectives on South African Photography* (1999). Thanks to fundraising efforts, the museum benefitted from significant acquisitions and fruitful partnerships, locally and abroad.

Democracy and art are a bit alike,
always striving, achieving, losing,
working towards an ideal.
CARLOS FUENTES[1]

Creating two flagship museums in Cape Town and Pretoria

FOLLOWING ON THE FIRST democratic elections held in April 1994, there was a sense of renewal and enthusiasm as the board of trustees and staff looked forward to a new era in which there would be interest in, and support for our national museums.[2] In an article that appeared in *New Nation* ("Conflict and confusion", November 1994), art critic Joyce Ozinsky sounded alarm bells about what was happening at the Department of Arts Culture Science and Technology (DACST), which had been nicknamed the "Department of Many Things". However, the confidence that things would change for the better was fuelled by arts and culture minister Ben Ngubane's constitution of an Arts and Culture Task Group (ACTAG), which was mandated to reconfigure the arts and culture landscape to redress past imbalances and reflect an inclusive democratic South Africa. SANG board chairperson, Karin Skawran, served on ACTAG, while Jo-Anne Duggan was appointed to ACTAG's Western Cape branch. The gallery made presentations to all relevant working groups.

Towards the end of 1995, DACST called for nominations for the appointment of new councils for Declared Cultural Institutions. On the one hand, this was a welcome departure from the way in which the DNE had directly appointed board members; on the other, it meant the loss of representation by the Cape Town City Council, the universities of Cape Town, Stellenbosch and the Western Cape, the SAAA and the Friends. We took the opportunity to nominate seriously. We met to discuss potential candidates, and forwarded a list of names to DACST; this was in turn submitted to an independent panel appointed to make the decision. We were fortunate in that some of our board members were reappointed for the sake of continuity, while being augmented with new members and a staff representative.[3]

ACTAG culminated in a national conference (31 May – 2 June, 1995), followed by the publication of a White Paper on Arts, Culture and Heritage on 4 June 1996. Reactions to the White Paper were mixed: it was hailed for initiating a cultural revolution, but criticised for lacking clear and practical guidelines. Both viewpoints were valid. The document offered a coherent and inspired vision for arts, culture and heritage, but many details as to how this vision would find concrete expression remained unanswered.

The White Paper called for an urgent review of the national museums to bring them in line with the new political dispensation, and DACST was required to carry out a review of the institutions.[4] In the interim, state-funded museums were encouraged to redirect their outputs to new activities that reflected the overall goals of the government. We had anticipated and already implemented the spirit and letter of many of these goals, particularly as they related to the Reconstruction and Development Programme (RDP), a socio-economic policy framework implemented by the ANC following its 1994 election victory and the single most important aspect of government policy.

In addition to the necessities of housing, electricity, running water, jobs and education for all, the RDP had a visionary context of nation building in an environment of peace and security, and of democratisation and empowerment.[5] We held public meetings at SANG on 13 May and 29 July in 1995 to gauge perceptions about, and expectations of the national art museum. Chaired by education scholar

Crain Soudien, a joint working committee comprising SANG staff and members of the community was formed, with on-going guidance and commitment from Soudien. Regular meetings of our RDP Forum, chaired by community leader Levona George, were held on Saturday mornings, the aim being to offer assistance to artists where possible and to apply for projects through DACST – not on behalf of, but together with organisations and groups in the community. We were creating the conditions for more equitable access to our resources and showing that arts and culture were integral to the RDP.

In exchange for lending paintings to the Anglo Farms homestead, Vergelegen, Anglo-American and de Beers Chairman's Fund presented SANG with a bus. The RDP Forum working committee took the bus on its first outing on 18 November 1995 – to visit facilities and organisations which formed part of the Forum.[6] The unexpected and moving ideas and dreams that we experienced on that day were summed up by board member Jane Taylor: "Such commitment to a metaphysical project under circumstances of such physical deprivation."[7]

Believing that democracy and empowerment began at home, the board and staff had embarked on our own process of internal assessment and restructuring in August 1994; led by Lynette Maart and Sue Soal of the Community Development Resource Association, every member of staff was encouraged to participate. The board ratified proposals for a vision and new management structure, as well as cogent draft policies of principles of management, staff development and affirmative action, in February 1995. This was followed by an outside review of job descriptions and salaries.[8] The advertising agency McCann-Erikson generously took on SANG as their client, pro bono, resulting in an exciting new brochure and posters.

The structural proposals contained in the White Paper were becoming a reality. The FCA metamorphosed into the National Arts Council, which continued to provide grants from public funds to support creative work. The Arts and Culture Trust (ACT) was launched, enabled by the support of founding parties Nedbank and Sun International, and Deputy President Thabo Mbeki initiated Business and Arts South Africa (BASA), to promote "mutually beneficial, equitable and sustainable business-arts partnerships for the benefit of the whole of society". The National Heritage Council (NHC), tasked to look after the interests and development of heritage institutions, followed in 2002.[9]

There was a sense that these commitments to the promotion and development of arts and culture would go a long way to dispel the feelings of insecurity and despair which pervaded many organisations and institutions during the time of transformation, and that Article 27 of the Universal Declaration of Human Rights would be realised: "Everyone shall have the right to freely participate in the cultural life of the community and to enjoy the arts."

As far as national museums were concerned, a long and tortuous, but also open and democratic, process followed. DACST, with the approval of the committee representing the new arts and culture minister and the provincial ministers with responsibility for culture, established a review committee to investigate and make recommendations. The committee prepared the document "Towards a New National Museums Service: a Vision for the Restructuring of Declared Cultural Institutions", which was made available to institutions in October 1996. The arts and culture minister later adopted the report.

On 31 January 1997, at an historic meeting on Robben Island called by Roger Jardine, DACST's director general, members of the Association of Directors of National Collections aligned themselves with the new vision and the framework for change, and made a commitment to its implementation.

A key recommendation was that two new flagship institutions be formed in Gauteng and the Western Cape by amalgamating the appropriate national museums; furthermore, that other museums funded by central government be funded by their provincial governments, and museum infrastructures and services be established in provinces that had none. DACST incorporated Robben Island as a heritage site, national monument and museum, with an interim management authority led by André Odendaal.[10]

Working groups and task teams, comprising staff in the institutions, excluding senior management, were constituted to investigate and make recommendations on the creation of the new entities. A great deal of time, commitment and energy were demanded from staff, but it was understood that museum workers had a unique opportunity to guide, inform and shape their future. Twelve technical working groups researched and reported on resources and approaches in the museums and tabled their vision. We were enormously proud when DACST appointed Emile Maurice as convener of the Cape Town flagship, and Duggan (who remained on the staff until the end of 1995) of the Gauteng flagship.

The working groups completed their research towards the end of 1997. The reports, which were the result of a broad and participatory process, outlined the potential capacity of the amalgamated institutions to deliver key national services. A management-consulting firm independently assessed their feasibility and implications for the museums. Directors and governing bodies were asked for input, and at a meeting called by Jardine, on 23 January 1998, they agreed to move ahead with the flagships, and to accept the organisational structure and implementation framework devised by the consultants. A new council would be established for each flagship, while sufficient flexibility was built in to deal with institutional issues and concerns.

This marked the start of a new process. A Transformation Committee, comprising representatives of DACST, directors and staff representatives of the two flagship institutions, was constituted with two sub-committees (for the museums in the north and south). Three technical committees were also created, tasked to analyse and refine the consultants' report and look into key issues, such as the creation of frameworks in which financial and human resources management could be located.

There were a number of problems and major delays, often caused by inadequate communication and dissemination of information. Early on in the investigations it was evident that salaries consumed virtually the entire combined subsidy of the flagship museums. Furthermore, it would be impossible to implement the proposed new management structures, and the institutions were only functioning because they had reserves and were able to raise funds for projects and activities. Reserves were, however, being depleted by day-to-day operational costs.

The original launch date for the proposed flagships was 1 April 1998, but was pushed back a year. As an interim measure individual institutions were allocated subsidies for the 1998–99 financial year. While our budget was not cut, and an allocation for the improvement of conditions of service was added, the budget was in real terms reduced by R1 million, as we had received an ad hoc grant at the end of the previous financial year. I commented on this in my director's message in *bonani*:

> We have not received increases for a number of years, making it increasingly difficult to budget even for our basic needs, let alone functioning meaningfully without raising large amounts of money with which to do our work. We trust that the new vision for national collections, and its implementation, will address the invidious position in which museum workers and Councils find themselves right now – a huge responsibility for the protection and security of collections which we hold in trust for the people of South Africa, and hopelessly inadequate funding with which to honour our commitment.[11]

The SANG board did not remain silent. Josie Frater, chairperson of the finance committee, wrote to the minister. I wrote to Jardine. Copies of all correspondence and documentation were sent to the chairperson of the portfolio committee.[12] There were no written responses to the letters; we were told that individual institutions had to work within the budgetary constraints and could not look to DACST for bailouts. A request to the department to respond to the information at hand, to present the museums with a vision and a plan for implementing the flagships, culminated in a meeting in June 1998. We were informed that a public process of establishing the two new councils would commence shortly; we were further told that there would be a transitional phase for the amalgamation of the budgets and the implementation of the new structures. I supported the restructuring and the vision for a national museum service, but expressed reservations:

> I still fail to see how this is possible within current subsidy levels: we are paying salaries and using reserves for running costs and maintenance. There is no money for museological, curatorial and educational functions. The responsibility for the safekeeping of our priceless heritage and the well-being of the workers in the sector lie with the government, but we see little commitment to our institutions. Instead there is a strong sense of the burden being shifted to museums – in the case of the future flagships, to councils that do not as yet exist. Until this happens, individual museums are expected to remain open and function without funds.[13]

Nothing came of the representations and pleas to the ministerial department. That nothing ever would is now clear given the new government's overarching commitment to a neo-liberal macro economic strategy, known as Growth, Employment and Redistribution (GEAR), and designed to make South Africa competitive in international markets. GEAR was hotly contested: commentators questioned whether it could meaningfully address, let alone transform, the inherited inequities of the apartheid system. GEAR also confirmed the substantive abandonment of the immediate post-1994 aspirations expressed in the RDP policy. The gap between rich and poor, which was already chronic in 1994, would grow ever wider and the lives of millions remain unaffected – in the years and decades after the first democratic elections.

Culture was – and still is – a concurrent national and provincial competency, and the notion of shifting responsibility to the private sector was felt early, when it became clear that the funding available for the ambitious restructuring and organisation of arts, culture and heritage was hopelessly inadequate. Jardine explained the decrease in the budget in a *Mail & Guardian* article ("Arts budget revealed", 15 April–1 May 1997): he stated that arts and culture would in future also be funded on local and provincial levels, and that the national budget would "be supplemented by initiatives co-ordinated by the department to extend the funding base for arts to the private sector".

At a press briefing on museum restructuring held on 4 August 1998, museums were told that DACST had suffered a budget cut for the financial year 1998/99, but they would receive the same funds as they had the year before. However, DACST's budget had in fact increased by 21.4% from R607.6 to R737.0 million (the sum represented 0.37% of the total national budget). The battle for a dynamic and adequately funded democratic institution for art, culture and heritage in South Africa was slowly being lost.

More than three months after the June meeting with DACST, museums had neither received minutes nor been informed about the department's vision and plan for the new flagship institutions. On 2 August 1998 an advertisement appeared in the Sunday press calling for public nominations of candidates for appointment to the two flagship councils. Badly worded, and marred by grammatical errors, the advertisement did not even mention the names of the institutions that would be amalgamated. It stated that the new councils would be announced on Heritage Day (24 September), and that there would be a transitional phase before the amalgamation of the budgets and the final implementation of the new structures on 1 April 1999. Heritage Day came and went, with no announcement. Meetings of the selection panel that was to advise the minister on the appointment of council members were scheduled for October and November, but never took place. They eventually happened in January 1999, in effect shortening the critical transitional phase to two months.

The new minister, Lionel Mtshali, an Inkatha Freedom Party (IFP) loyalist, made some controversial remarks in a press release prepared for the August briefing:

> We have to formulate for ourselves a principle of transformation and restructuring which as far as is possible will protect our policies from this principle of the reversal of previous entitlement. The principle by which we have to operate is the principle of 'pluralism'. We are a varied and multi-cultural society. Pluralism means that there should not be any kind of new 'dominance', except the dominance of variety and balance. If there is to be a new hegemony, it must be the hegemony of multi-culturalism and respect for difference.[14]

What did Mtshali mean exactly by a multi-cultural hegemony, and how would this play out in post-apartheid South Africa? The concepts of plurality, cultural diversity and tolerance he was exploring were certainly in tune with post-modern and post-colonial theory, which, in very broad terms, promoted an open-ended and pluralistic approach to arts and culture. However, the minister's concept of "pluralism" was met with suspicion: it reiterated a line of reasoning used by the architects of apartheid to emphasise difference in order to encourage fragmentation and to oppose an holistic view of culture. It bears noting that apartheid South Africa once had a minister of Plural Relations and Development, albeit briefly.

In an article in *Democracy in Action* political scholar John Sharp asked: "Does the language of multiculturalism provide a clean enough break with the past, or will it allow the old shibboleths that stressed ethnic separation to persist unchallenged?"[15] Ideas of ethnic or cultural separation, which lay at the heart of apartheid, had given way to a discourse of multiculturalism, but Sharp emphasised that South Africans had to make it work: "We have to ensure that our society offers all its members the opportunity to participate in, and draw benefit from, mainstream political and economic activity, as well as the opportunity to proclaim their difference."

With regard to the allocation of resources, Mtshali's pronouncement in his press statement was clear and fully in line with GEAR:

> In the new global economy the role of governments has changed as much as the structure of the economy. States can no longer be all-providing storehouses of resources. There is hardly a country in the world today in which governments are not reducing their welfare, social service and other support grants in order to release capital for investment. This applies even more to the arts, culture and aspects of science and technology than it does to welfare in general. A successful government in the fields of arts, culture, science and technology today is one which does not see its role as that of 'providing' resources, but rather the government which, while maintaining essential direct provision, is able to create a framework within which the private sector, civil society and local government can assume more and more of a role in providing resources.

DACST was by no means "maintaining essential direct provision", which was why museums were running on reserves and raising money for museological activities, exhibitions, projects, educational programmes and events. We were reminded of fiscal discipline, to the point of parsimony, and the need to reduce the deficit, yet the self-same government saw fit to allocate R65 million to host a summit of the Non-Aligned Movement in Durban in 1998.

After months in the dry dock, the flagships were getting ready to take to the water. At the back of the process were key changes in the department: Ngubane was reassigned to his former ministry after a spell as premier of KwaZulu-Natal, and Jardine resigned. The gallery faced a real and impending crisis: it would run out of reserves on 31 March, but by mid-January there was no word about either the flagship or the budget allocation for the 1999-2000 financial year. I called in to a radio programme featuring Jardine, Wally Serote and journalist Robert Greig to enquire about the allocation. Jardine undertook to provide the information, which he duly did.

His response was cause for further dismay: there was no word about the flagship; SANG's subsidy would remain the same, except for improvement of conditions of service; DACST was committed to funding a wider spectrum of arts, culture and heritage needs and if management of SANG could not fit expenditure to meet the amount of R4.2 million, activities had to be reduced and staff retrenched. The allocation would cover the salary bill, which was being reduced by keeping posts vacant, but the board came to a unanimous decision not to retrench staff – it would be the first time in the history of the institution. DACST employed 500 staff, while Cape Town's flagship institution had 280; DACST's budget had grown by 150% since 1994, from R329 million to R804 million, while the core funding of the national museums remained the same.

SANG's executive committee decided to act. Letters were drafted and sent to the director-general, the minister, the portfolio committee, the president and deputy president. Things started moving. At a meeting of directors and staff representatives held on 17 February it was confirmed that Rob Adam, the deputy director-general for science and technology at DACST, would be in charge of the process of implementing the new structures. The new councils would meet on 25 March.

DACST and the ministry of which it formed part were widely criticised as inefficient, inexperienced and over-ambitious. It also funded its own projects and organisations when in fact they should have applied to the NAC, which would have ensured impartial oversight of the merits. DACST had a habit of launching new projects and legislation without considering the financial implications, and for turning their backs on existing responsibilities.[16] In an article in the *Sunday Independent* (3 January 1999), playwright and arts administrator Mike van Graan analysed the high-level disputes and power struggles that were having crippling effects on arts, culture and heritage. He asked the question: "Does SA need an arts and culture department?"

To add insult to injury, Ngubane, in his March budget speech, blamed the way in which national museums were managed for the problems they experienced. This was a sweeping generalisation. Over the course of its entire history, SANG received clean audits from the auditor general (with only two queries in 1999). This would normally point to excellent management, let alone utilisation of resources and much fundraising, but DACST had never measured the output of the museums in relation to input.[17]

The gallery's board held its last meeting in February 1999. The implementation of the Cultural Institutions Act 119 of 1998 meant that the national art museum was set to become part of the Southern Flagship Institution (SFI). On 1 April 1999 the restructuring of national collections passed into law and the five main components (South African National Gallery, South African Museum, South African Cultural History Museum, Michaelis Collection and William Fehr Collection) were legally transferred to the new supervisory body. The legislation meant that the art, natural history and social history collections now belonged to the SFI rather than to individual museums, thereby erasing the colonial and apartheid classifications of objects in national museums with the stroke of a pen.[18]

Karin Skawran, the board's chairperson from 1994, provided outstanding leadership and unfailing wisdom and inspiration during a time of change. Her presence in the newly constituted council of the SFI, steered initially by Colin Jones and Kiren Thathiah, was invaluable.[19] While gaining a seemingly open and transparent way of appointing government representatives, both SANG and the SFI lost the experience and intellect of university representatives, the Friends, the SAAA and the City Council.

An interim management committee comprising directors of the SFI museums was formed and each was given specific duties within the new structures.[20] Council sub-committees dealt with diverse matters – finance, human resources and strategy – and members with special interests and expertise engaged with the directors in the different sections. The arrangement worked exceptionally well. A group of consultants and facilitators was appointed to join directors and staff in creating an institutional structure and to develop a strategic plan for the SFI. Financial management and administration, including a fully integrated budget, was centralised in preparation for 1 April 2000.

Sadly, the changes meant that *bonani* came to an end. The publication had documented all exhibitions and activities since 1992 to the first quarter of 2000. Not only did it keep readers abreast of events and shifts in the broader fields of arts, culture and heritage, it chronicled the changes, desires, challenges, achievements and disappointments at the national art museum. *Bonani* was modest, but it was read across the globe – in print and electronic form. Nicolaas Vergunst, the publications officer responsible for all the gallery's publications, had devoted himself to producing a newsletter and catalogues of great quality.

In my final editorial I took issue with the SFI council's decision to implement a fee at all the museums under its stewardship. While a uniform policy was being worked out, admission was by donation: a minimum donation of R5 (SANG) and R3 (NLM) was requested by staff at reception; pensioners, students and Friends, learners and children were allowed to enter free of charge.[21] Having done everything in our power to keep entrance to the national art collection free, this was indeed a painful blow to past and still-serving council members and staff. Inhibiting the public's ability to enter art museums at will and engage with the collections undermines their very purpose. As Neil MacGregor, then director of the National Gallery in London, wrote in *Time* (5 October 1998): "They are no more a luxury in modern life than literacy."

Under the new dispensation the nomenclature for managing museums followed the latest business models and employed the necessary jargon. Chief executives and managers were accorded defined status, salaries and beneficial allowances such as cars – this standardisation saw the salary gap between management, curators and scientists grow bigger. Museums also had to project a public identity, which in the language of commerce meant branding. The social role of museums remained part of the rhetoric of the SFI, but in reality much would change in the years ahead. Museums are no longer primarily at the service of the people of South Africa and contributors to creating a more equitable and just society; instead, they are managed as business units within a neo-liberal economic paradigm.

The role of civil society in the establishment and supervisory management of the national art museum is one of the leitmotifs of this book; another theme that runs through the narrative has to do with the state's enduring indifference to, and neglect of the collection. DACST, as well as its successor, the Department of Arts and Culture (DAC), established in 2004, would be relieved and pleased if our national gallery could sustain itself. It has, of course, done so for decades, but this is different from notions of self-sustainability and a museum as a business that relieves government of its obligations. Official responsibility for cultural patrimony – at all levels of government – should not be negotiable.

New initiatives, exhibitions and public forums

WHILE ALL THIS meta-level bureaucratic reorganisation was occurring, and in spite of DACST putting the national art museum in an untenable financial position, work went on. Numerous exhibitions, projects, public initiatives, forums and activities were held in the main building, Annexe and NLM. Like Paris, Bokhorst and Van Niekerk before me, I believed that national and international partnerships would enable SANG to initiate ground-breaking projects and to give concrete expression to our vision and mission.

South Africa's first official Heritage Day was held on 24 September 1995. It offered an opportunity to celebrate past and present events at the gallery, notably the centenary of the promulgation of the South African Art Gallery Act and repatriation of the "African Heritage Collection". German consul general Fritz Bruns officially handed over the collection to Minister of Arts, Culture, Science and Technology Ben Ngubane at an exhibition on the day.[22]

In an on-going commitment to nurture and encourage local artistic talent, curator of photography Kathy Grundlingh organised and curated a national photographic competition and exhibition, *People's Portraits*, in collaboration with the *Weekly Mail & Guardian*; it toured nationally. New media required attention and *Video Views*, the first exhibition of video art at SANG, was presented in collaboration with the Association for Visual Arts (AVA), with additional support from Linda Givon, artists and the German Consulate.[23] *Water in a dry place/Amanzi endaweni eyomileyo* explored the dense history and legacy of the Community Arts Project.

With sponsorship from the NAC and ACT, Grundlingh coordinated seven components, curated by different people, of the exhibition *Lines of Sight: Perspectives on South African Photography* and produced an accompanying catalogue.[24] The curators explored various aspects of South African photography and showcased works by some of South Africa's leading photographers as well as images by unknown amateurs. *Lines of Sight* received wide and enthusiastic press coverage, resulting in it travelling to the Centre de Musée national du Mali, Bamako, as part of "Recontres de la photographie africaine" in 2001. Journalist Chris Roper wrote an extensive review in the *Mail & Guardian* (23–29 July 1999) that highlighted the gallery's limited financial means:

> Given the budgetary constraints [SANG] has to work under, deciding to hold an exhibition of the history of South African photography this century seems a foolhardy venture. That makes the hugely successful *Lines of Sight* show even more laudable. I arrived to view it expecting, at most, one room of photographs, and those pretty much devoted to the usual idea of history. Photos of famous people, famous incidents and a bit of nostalgia – the choices forced on curators when they're trying to juggle limited funds with the demands of politically correct representation. What the visitor gets is five rooms filled with a rich, varied collection that documents, comments on and created multitudinous views of South Africa. These are *Lines of Sight* that, as with all effective photography, work both ways: often you notice the image staring back at you, accusingly, seductively, or uncaringly.

PLATE 24: Fatima February, Yasmina February and Fayrouz Mathews, *District Six, Where we Lived*, 1992, fabric, pebbles, sequins, ribbon, stocking, batting, wood, 1630 x 1270; image courtesy of the artists; photographer Kathy Grundlingh.

Museum historian Katherine Goodnow regarded the exhibition as "an especially explicit move in the direction of thinking about how images are constructed" and an encouragement to the public to look critically at the narratives that confront them – at a time in South Africa when versions of history were being challenged.[25]

The tradition of honouring artists with retrospective exhibitions was maintained. Painter and sculptor Cecil Skotnes, photographer Jürgen Schadeberg and painter George Pemba all received shows, the latter in collaboration with Barry Feinberg of the UWC Mayibuye Centre.[26] Pemba was present at the opening, as was the pioneering abstract painter Ernest Mancoba, who had come from France to spend time at his alma mater, the University of Fort Hare. At last, two great South African artists – long neglected – were able to meet and celebrate together at their national art museum. It was a personally rewarding, as well as an exhilarating moment in the history of SANG. We also paid tribute to Florence Zerffi and Ruth Prowse at the Natale Labia Museum.

SANG curators and educators worked with the District Six Museum Foundation for more than eighteen months to access paintings and drawings of District Six from private and public collections. They were documented and many were selected for the exhibition *District Six: Image and Representation*, which coincided with a parallel exhibition at the newly established District Six Museum.[27] A mixed-race neighbourhood east of the central city, District Six was the site of forced removals during apartheid. Still largely vacant, the area remains a potent symbol of dispossession and government's failure to implement land redistribution. The memorial exhibition at the gallery explored how the insiders (former residents, mainly self-taught artists) and outsiders (those fascinated with, or interested in District Six) represented the neighbourhood (Plate 24). But there was a broader thrust to it: the exhibition aimed to contribute towards rewriting and reclaiming displaced histories in post-apartheid South Africa. The opening, attended by more than 500 guests, was a joyous occasion filled with music, singing, poetry and an opening address by Colin Jones. A broad range of South Africans, not merely entitled white residents of the city, were increasingly laying claim to their national art museum as participants. Their contributions helped the institution to face and rewrite history, and to confront memories.

Presented in 1996, *Miscast: Negotiating Khoisan History and Material Culture* was a watershed exhibition at SANG and bore testimony to our commitment to redress and reconciliation. Curated by artist and scholar Pippa Skotnes, and presented in association with UCT and SAM, the exhibition looked at the various relationships that were established with indigenous communities following the arrival of European traders and settlers in southern Africa. These relationships were, in the main, severely imbalanced. This is witnessed, for example, by the extreme objectification of individuals cast as other in anthropological photographs from the late-nineteenth century. The encounters, across wide swathes of southern Africa, saw instances of genocide and over time have resulted in the death of multiple language groups. Skotnes shared with me what lingered in her mind twenty-two years after the exhibition.

During the two years that she travelled around the country, Skotnes scoured museum storerooms, image and document collections, and even visited colonial depositories particularly in British museums:

> At the centre of the exhibition was the desire to do two things: to expose a genocide and the prejudices implied in the term 'bushmen' that gave rise to it; and to call attention to the pervasive idea that they were defined by a physical type, living in an ahistoric condition that precluded ideas of property ownership or intellectual life.

The project was informed by the work she had undertaken in the previous decade and focussed on the traditions of "rock art, storytelling, cosmologies and healing practices, as well as on the evidence of encounter with pastoralists and farmers that survived in the archive". The core of her interests was:

> … the |xam and !kun texts recorded by Lucy Lloyd and Wilhelm Bleek in the 1870s, and a desire to recuperate and celebrate the astonishing work of Lloyd, a woman-scholar in a man's world, whose considerably larger contribution up to that point had been ignored and effaced by almost everyone who touched on the collection … Celebrating her lifelong dedication to the project to record the personal narratives of those who were amongst the most marginalised and abused in South African history became a powerfully motivating project of mine, along with the desire to make known the astonishing ideas that the |xam and !kun themselves expressed, in their own words. It was a project about death, sacrifice and redemption.[28]

Skotnes contested the rightfulness of the San (Bushman) diorama at SAM, which portrayed indigenous Khoisan people as stuck in a never-changing and distant past; her exhibition historicised it. She examined the enduring tensions in museums between what is displayed, what is in storage and what is available to study. Skotnes also edited the book, *Miscast: Negotiating the Presence of the Bushmen*, in which scholars were invited to explore the controversial term "Bushmen" (which was purposefully not used in the title of the exhibition)[29] from the perspectives of anthropology, archaeology, comparative religion, literary studies, art history and musicology.[30]

Collaborations with outside curators are invigorating and stimulating, and they can assist in expanding the museum experience and narrative, but they also present challenges to both parties

FIGURE 22: *Miscast* installation, Liberman Room, 1996; image courtesy of Pippa Skotnes.

and have to be conducted in a spirit of mutual trust and respect. Consensus rather than compromise is required, so that when the exhibition opens, curator and institution act and speak with one voice. Many discussions about access to material and Khoisan voices took place, as well as what and how material would be displayed. Skotnes detailed the challenges she faced in mounting the exhibition in her book: she made every effort to consult with groups on the nature of the displays during the preparation for the exhibition, but there were few voices around to articulate or even echo the past, and in the end consultation took place through legal advisers, anthropologists or organisations that represent San interests in South Africa, Namibia and Botswana.

Miscast, designed by Skotnes and architect Jos Thorne, occupied three rooms at SANG and had a compelling visual presence: "Every part was considered in terms of how visitors would navigate the spaces and how visual and affective contrasts would direct viewer attention."[31] A quotation from Greg Dening's *Mr. Bligh's Bad Language: Passion, Power and Theatre on the Bounty* set the scene in the Liberman Room: "There is no escape from the politics of our knowledge, but that politics is not in the past. That politics is in the present (Fig. 22)." [32]

In contrast to many archive photographs of the Khoisan in various situations of exploitation, thirteen cases – ten named for San individuals represented in the archive, one for Louis Anthing and one for Lucy Lloyd – contained objects labelled San or Bushmen brought together from museums around the country (Fig. 23). The dramatic focal point was a grey brick structure, based on a centrally planned Renaissance church, but at the same time evoking a fort, jail and a tomb; it was surmounted by a circle, twelve rifles and a tall metal flag. A "garden" of cacti partially concealed a box with a collection of cast human remains and five books, with the spines collectively spelling the word "truth". A semicircle of thirteen pedestals, each displaying a resin cast of a body section made from the painted plaster casts at

SAM, delineated the central space. Lit from below, they were translucent and otherworldly. Accompanying texts described incidents of violence against the Khoisan, as well as fragments of stories given in their own words.

Against the walls were chilling piles of unlit body casts, metal shelves with cardboard boxes and two tall glass cabinets containing casts, documentation and anthropometric implements associated with nineteenth- and early-twentieth-century physical anthropology. The labels on the cardboard boxes did not disclose the nature of the contents, but carried dates of significant events in the recorded history of the Khoisan – date of event and date of recording.[33] Viewers were implicated by the placement of mirrors, so that they could see their own reflections.

In the adjacent room they were forced to walk on history in the form of vinyl tiles screen printed with largely denigrating images of indigenous people from nineteenth- and early-twentieth-century sources. Cameras protected by vitrines were placed directly on the floor, as if to record reactions. Paul Weinberg's photographs of daily life, taken between 1984 and 1995 with the cooperation of various groups in southern Africa, removed the Khoisan from the timeless historical vacuum and placed them in contemporary society (Fig. 24).

The last room contained copies of Khoisan rock paintings produced by researches over time, and offered a comfortable, quiet space with a selection of the research materials that went into the making of the exhibition, as well as a visitors' book in which people could comment on their own experiences. Author Nadine Gordimer wrote: "A bold and necessary contribution to the rewriting of what has too long passed for our SA history. Beautiful in its restoration of human dignity."[34]

In an attempt to bridge the gap between the curator and institution on the one hand, and the Khoisan descendants on the other, nine Khoisan groups were brought to Cape Town for a preview of the exhibition, the opening and a public forum at which individuals and representatives of various Khoisan organisations could present issues and concerns. These activities were carefully planned, but none of us was prepared for the overwhelming public interest in, and intense reactions to the exhibition.

FIGURE 23: *Miscast* installation, Liberman Room, detail of objects in display cases, 1996; image courtesy of Pippa Skotnes.

FIGURE 24: *Miscast* installation, 1996; vinyl tiles and photographs by Paul Weinberg; image courtesy of Pippa Skotnes.

The opening, which included a representation by /'Angn!Ao/'Un from the Nyae Nyae Farmers' Cooperative, was attended by over 1,000 people, and the subsequent forum by more than 700. The latter had all the tension, emotion and excitement of a political meeting. Politically, the exhibition became a rallying point and focus of both Khoisan unity and disunity, and the forum was exploited for political grandstanding by some factions and individuals. It revealed the chasm between considered and implemented curatorial concerns and public perceptions and experiences, many of which were deeply painful and disturbing, particularly for the Khoisan groups. There was a keenly felt sense that the organisers had failed to comprehend the magnitude of potential disagreement and dissent.

On the positive side, attendees appreciated the fact that we brought together so many Khoisan descendants under one roof, and created the opportunity for raising issues around colonialism, dispossession, restitution of land and the politics of history and presentation. The buildings reverberated with the indigenous languages, which few South Africans know or have even heard (American anthropologist, Meagan Biesele, acted as interpreter at the opening), and the beautiful singing of Griqua attendees.

Further acknowledgment of the significance of the exhibition and forum came from the Griquas of Adam Kok V, who recognised an opportunity of drawing attention to regaining their land for the reburial of ancestral Griqua remains. The Khoisan Representative Council requested that the forty coffins containing skeletons excavated by renowned South African palaeoanthropologist Philip Tobias (and subsequently returned to the people by Wits University) be included in *Miscast* before reburial. The board of trustees ruled against it, fearing that SANG would become even further involved in post-apartheid contestations and politics. Personally I regretted their decision.

The controversy did not only originate from the Khoisan descendants, academics also entered the fray. Rustum Kozain and Yvette Abrahams (both tutors at UCT at the time), as well as archaeologist and anthropologist Carmel Schrire wrote reviews to which Skotnes was invited to reply.[35] In 2018 Skotnes revisited the controversy:

It was not entirely unexpected, though its scale was, and the criticism was not unjustified, except where (as was surprisingly frequent), scholars and reviewers made up observations of things that were not on display. And while this was never really critiqued or explored in reviews, the curatorial intention was to produce an art exhibition – an installation in an art gallery, rich with, and at times dependent on, art historical illusion, irony and references. It was always clear that parts of the exhibition would speak to some visitors and not others, offend some and challenge others. This was because it deliberately invited new publics into the art gallery who had different interests in the subject and different perspectives to bear upon it. Indeed, apart from one or two essays no attention was attributed to how the curatorial decisions – decisions of an artist – both facilitated the controversy and the outpouring of emotion that was reflected in its reception, and exposed (to quote an overly used phrase) the politics and poetics of the archive.[37]

The responses to and concerns raised by *Miscast* prompted the gallery to host a public forum, entitled "Negotiating the Way Forward" and held in the Annexe Hall in September 1996. I formally apologised on behalf of the art museum to individuals and groups that were hurt and angered, a gesture I still hold as important. Crain Soudien, always prepared to support and assist SANG, chaired a panel in the presence of 184 people, and members of the board and staff.[38] Once again the focus shifted from SANG to broader issues - the historical and legal rights of indigenous people and the ANC government's detachment from Khoisan descendants. A number of proposals were tabled, new voices were heard and new prospective friends and partners identified to assist us in mapping the way forward. The art museum was in the process of being opened and transformed in a manner which was profound and far-reaching. Soudien suggested that the time had come for the rewriting of the story of South African lives through the art museum.

Miscast was in many ways a harrowing and draining experience for Skotnes and staff at the gallery; we all learned a great deal about the cultural politics of indigenous movements, their claims and aspirations, and the need to be vigilant and sensitive. The exhibition offended and alienated many South Africans; at the same time comments in the visitors' book were overwhelmingly positive and full of personal comment. Moreover, it made possible new initiatives and enhanced the reputation of SANG as an institution of national and international influence and significance. From Skotnes' curatorial perspective:

Miscast tested what it meant to curate archival material in the context of an art institution in South Africa, and it did it at a particular time when much was at stake. When I think back on the project I think that the SANG took a significant risk with it, and, in the face of an outpouring of emotion, its director stood her ground. The gallery became a space where major issues of representation, marginalisation and post-apartheid identities were charged with a visual and affective experience of what they meant and might mean in practice ... This active and vital interaction between archive, history, audiences and artists, in an environment curated to be challenging, unstable and often destabilising, is, to my mind discouragingly rare these days. South African institutions are crippled by funding limitations

> (the national, provincial and municipal museums) or worse, disabled by a lack of imagination (for example UCT's continuing failure to imagine a role for its art collections), and the eye of too many an artist is focused solely on the global commercial prospects contemporary art practice offers.[39]

Art historian Steven Dubin describes *Miscast* as "a pivotal moment when the representation of the bodies of non-white South Africans triggered a firestorm".[40] Writing in his book *Transforming Museums* (2006), Dubin places the controversy around the exhibition in the broader context of transformation at South African art museums:

> By bringing installation art to this otherwise staid setting, and by so pointedly interrogating museum practice, SANG stepped beyond its conventional comfort zone and endorsed a groundbreaking exhibition rife with provocation. *Miscast* pulled SANG even further away from the manner by which it had so recently functioned.[41]

Caught up in indigenous rights movements, SANG was indeed being pulled away from the past into unchartered territory. In line with partnerships formed through *Miscast*, the Griqua National Conference (in alliance with the East Griqualand Pioneers, Nama Representative Council and Rehoboth Baster Government) organised a public forum on Human Rights Day (21 March 1997). Nearly a thousand people arrived to discuss the burial of Sarah "Saartjie" Baartman, whose remains were kept in the Musée de l'Homme in Paris.[42] It was the first such public forum, but the DACST minister and deputy minister had prior engagements and no representative of the French government responded to the invitation. It was clear from the choir songs, prayers and speeches that the repatriation process could no longer be discussed behind closed governmental doors.

Jatti Bredekamp, then UWC professor attached to the Institute for Historical Research, was the driving force behind a conference entitled "Khoisan Identities and Cultural Heritage" at SAM. It was necessary to draw public attention to the plight and aspirations of Khoisan descendants who were still being displaced from traditional lands. According to sociolinguist Nigel Crawhall, Namibian authorities seized land occupied by the Kxoe people in April 1997, and land-related civil rights abuses against the /Gwi, //Ana and !Xoo in Botswana and Zimbabwe were endangering these communities and their languages.[43] Twenty years on, the South African government's failure to address indigenous people's rights led to the Khoisan Liberation Movement staging a protest at the ANC's elective conference outside Johannesburg in December 2017.[44]

As discussed in chapter four, the gallery played an active role in the repatriation of South African cultural patrimony. One example of this is the 1997 exhibition, *Gerard Sekoto – a body of work repatriated.* Curated by Dolby, the exhibition celebrated the return of nearly 2,000 items (sketches, drawings, paintings and memorabilia dating from 1935 to Sekoto's death in Paris in 1993) by this important modernist painter. The Gerard Sekoto Foundation enabled the exhibition, which received financial assistance from DACST and the French government.[45]

That same day Nelson Mandela inaugurated the Robben Island Museum. The president used this public platform to express deeply felt emotions and lambasted South African museums for excluding and demeaning black (African, Indian and Coloured) people. He was specific: "Of our museums, all but a handful – three per cent – represented the kind of heritage which glorified mainly white and colonial history. And even the small glimpse of black history in the others was largely fixed in the grip of racist and other stereotypes." He indicated that redress had "barely begun" and that the heritage sector was being restructured.[46]

Considering all that had been achieved at art museums in the country up until this point, and not only at SANG, it was problematic to lump together the different kinds of museums, particularly since Mandela never visited the gallery. As the president spoke, television cameras turned to me; it was an embarrassing and deeply hurtful experience. In correspondence Patricia Davison maintained that there was no doubt that his remarks were aimed primarily at SAM, although, to her knowledge, he also never visited that museum. She surmised that members of the ANC cultural desk had likely drafted his speech.[47]

Dubin regards the exhibition *TRANCEsending time and space: Sacred symbols of the San* (2000) as one of the best examples reflecting a "post-*Miscast* mentality".[48] Original rock engravings and paintings, some dating from 6,000 BCE, revealed San cosmology. They were shown in the company of Craig Foster's large-scale photographs, which contextualised the works in the present. The closure of the exhibition was marked by a First Nations healing ceremony on Easter Sunday. Rebirth, unity, cleansing and celebration inspired the lighting of a peace pipe and intertwined sticks.[49] The art museum was impacting positively on the life experiences and aspirations of individuals and groups, particularly those who had been, and remained, marginalised and oppressed.

We have seen in previous chapters that SANG curators were interested in SAM collections, and in the possibilities of working across disciplines, while breaking down boundaries and ploughing new curatorial ground. This was the most exciting prospect offered by the amalgamation of the museums. Curators took advantage and explored the different approaches to, and interpretations of time and space in museums of science, culture and art in the show *Theory and Myth: Interpretations of Time and Space in the Visual Arts* (2000), in conjunction with the exhibition *Footprints in Time* at the SAM.

A number of exhibitions originated from sister institutions and other sources: Elizabeth Rankin, then head of the Department of Art History at Wits, curated *Images of Metal* (1995), while Nessa Leibhammer and artist Karel Nel assembled fertility figures from public and private collections throughout the country in *Evocations of the Child* (1998).[50] Elza Miles curated two exhibitions for JAG: *Hand in Hand* (1994), a retrospective of Ernest Mancoba and his Danish wife Sonja Ferlov, and *Land and Lives: Pioneer Black Artists* (1997). David Bunn, professor in the English Department at UWC at the time, opened *Land and Lives* and his address took the form of an open letter to Roger Jardine. At the end of an insightful discourse on the exhibition and the artists, Bunn concluded:

> We are desperate to know more about the complex interaction between black painters and sculptors, here and in exile, in the early twentieth century. However, in the very moment when we are beginning

> to rediscover our early "pioneers", this and other national [sic] galleries have all but stopped purchasing work by South Africans. Conservation is grinding to a halt; storage conditions are appalling. Great painters like Anna Mashinini have quietly faded away. And of her work, brittle gouache on paper, the same as that characteristically used by [Gladys] Mgudlandlu, who can tell how it will survive? Look now, before it flakes away completely.

Bunn further went on to consider the effects of a neo-liberal programme, which conflates arts and culture with commercial practice:

> Politicians – and I am sure you are as worried about this as I am – are driving us to define 'Heritage' mainly in terms of an ethnicized crafts industry, and this in the very hour of our first coming to understand the complexity of our artistic past. We call on you to dedicate more funds for acquisitions, preservation, storage, and research into works such as the ones on this show.[51]

We hosted DAG director Jill Addleson's *Azaria Mbatha Retrospective* (1999), and *Heart of Darkness* (1998), a collaboration between Cameroonian artist Bili Bidjocka and Kendell Geers, courtesy of the Goodman Gallery.

The fourth exhibition of architecture, *Reflections on the making of space* (1998), organised in partnership with the Department of Architecture of the University of the Free State, featured work by Revel Fox. Exploring the close link between architecture and memory, and between architecture and recollection, Dubow in his opening speech referred to the Greek word anamnesis: "What is anamnesis? Well at its simplest level it is about being able to remember the past. It is the opposite of amnesia. In our prevailing national mood of selective amnesia, that's something worth remembering."[52]

SANG curators were much in demand. In 1996 we received an invitation from the Standard Bank National Arts Festival to curate an exhibition of contemporary South African photography. Approximately one hundred photographers and other artists who used photography in their work were invited to submit slides or working prints for selection. There were no constraints, except that the photographs were taken after January 1990. The selection and curatorial process broke new ground: led by Grundlingh, it included SANG staff, Jane Taylor (chairperson of the acquisitions committee), Thobile Skepe (in his second year as Standard Bank technical trainee at the gallery) and Anele Ngoko (photographer and member of the SANG RDP Forum). *PhotoSynthesis: Contemporary South African Photography* (1997) was shown in Grahamstown, Johannesburg and Cape Town, at SANG; it included a catalogue.[53]

South Africa featured in different components of *Africa 95*, a festival of African art and culture in the United Kingdom. Of greater import for the exposure and development of contemporary South African art was the 1995 opening of the first Johannesburg Biennial. It included Emma Bedford's thought-provoking, visually stimulating and coherent exhibition, *Objects of Defiance/Spaces of Contemplation*, which was subsequently shown at SANG. Bedford considered how artists – both men and women – were shaping new discourses on gender by challenging patriarchal structures and values or proposing new constructions of femininity and masculinity. She highlighted concepts and experiences of silence, absence, lack and loss.

The second iteration of the biennial was co-ordinated by the Africus Institute of Contemporary Art under the artistic directorship of Okwui Enwezor. He appointed six curators to organise specific exhibitions on the general theme of "Trade Routes: History and Geography". They included artist and academic Colin Richards who mounted a group exhibition entitled *Graft* at SANG.[54] *Graft* explored the various meanings of the word – sometimes obliquely, sometimes directly – and the different ways in which the fifteen artists selected were figuring cultural contact and exchange in the historical moment that was South Africa in 1997. Richards characterised the period as "a time of intense historical crisis and change," further adding:

> The last decade of the twentieth century had had many auspicious moments, and 1997 proved no exception. The fragile post-apartheid era was in early consolidation. We were coming down to earth hard after the heady days of 1994. The bright afterglow of the first democratic elections was waning. Painful revelations surfacing in the Truth and Reconciliation Commission (TRC) hearings reverberated across the country and beyond.[55]

A further reminder of the effects of gravity spoken about by Richards occurred when the cash-strapped Greater Johannesburg Metropolitan Council decided, without consultation, to close the second Johannesburg Biennale overnight on 30 November 1997, nearly two months before its advertised closing date of 18 January 1998. Interested parties and stakeholders rallied to the organisers' call to save the exhibition – and save face – and succeeded, thanks to careful re-planning and funding that came from DACST, ACT and Gauteng Province, held in a separate account. The combined effort resulted in turning a major crisis around – the show reopened on 5 December and remained open until 18 January, albeit with a skeleton staff.[56] However, it marked the end of Johannesburg's ambitions to host and sustain a biennial.

South Africa received a magnificent gift from abroad in the form of artworks made in service of the struggle against apartheid. Over a long period of time, artists Ernest Pignon-Ernest and Antonio Saura had built a collection of eighty-five works of art on behalf of the Committee of Artists of the World against Apartheid, with substantial support from the United Nations Special Committee against Apartheid. Their intention was to eventually present it to the first democratically elected South African government. "The collection offered here will form the basis of a future museum against apartheid. But first, these works will be presented in a travelling exhibition to be received by museums and cultural facilities throughout the world."[57] Pignon-Ernest's and Saura's dream for the collection of international art did not materialise.

The collection was donated to the South African government in 1995. Mandela recommended that the collection be housed at the UWC-RIM Mayibuye Archives, based at UWC.[58] In 1996, under the custodianship of the Mayibuye Centre, the works found a temporary home in parliament. Frene Ginwala, the speaker of parliament, requested our expertise and assistance in removing official portraits of apartheid cabinet ministers and installing the collection. DACST requested the assistance of Jon Weinberg and two technical staff to install the exhibition for the opening of the Nelson Mandela Museum in Umtata (now Mthatha) on 11 February 2002. It marked the tenth anniversary of former president Mandela's release from prison and comprised gifts and awards presented to him.[59]

In the midst of the hard work on many fronts, some fun was had with the first helping of *Softserve* (1999), a multi-media art event co-curated by artists Andrew Putter and Sue Williamson that handed SANG spaces over to creative people in the city and attracted many young visitors. A second instalment, *Softserve 2 Play*, was held the following year. The events drew hundreds of visitors, but proved to be a strain on staff and the permanent collection.

Dynamic international engagement and exchange

ESTABLISHED PARTNERSHIPS were maintained and new ones formed, as the international art community was keen to engage with South Africa and SANG. In the process we all learned from and shared expertise with curators and specialists from abroad.

In 1995 we hosted a Royal College of Art and British Council touring exhibition of contemporary British painting, and in 1998 *3WAYS. A Changed World*, which featured contemporary British sculpture. In her opening address for the latter exhibition, artist and academic Marion Arnold compared the funding situation in Britain with that in South Africa:

> Britain has a highly visible and very well organised Arts Council; we, by contrast, have a ministry of culture that is paying lip service to our cultural vitality, as it is apparent if we consider the budget given to this, our National Gallery. It is a shameful disgrace. It has crippled the library and inhibited the growth of the permanent collection and it makes a mockery of the talk of an African Renaissance that rumbles out of Parliament. If politicians want to know about transformation they need to make the short walk from their building to this building – to see and feel the force of the work on *A Changed World*, and to understand that South African artists are also giving expression to our changed world. The British Council has generously shared British sculpture with us. Can we return the favour?

Arnold was unambiguous in her answer to the question: Yes. "We have the artists, and we have the curators with expertise and ideas, but we need political commitment and action in our art world to make our changed world a cultural reality."[60]

The photographic exhibition *Positive Lives: Responses to HIV* (1995) explored the complex, individual and social responses to HIV/Aids in Britain. Extensive funding enabled South African photographer Gideon Mendel, one of the contributors to the original British exhibition, to produce a portfolio about the pandemic in South Africa, as well as a duplicate edition that was used in community centres, both as an awareness campaign and educational tool.[61] Our work in the field of HIV/Aids led to a highlight of this period, when Wola Nani (an non-profit organisation offering support to people with HIV/Aids) launched their 1996 awareness campaign with a concert from the front steps of SANG, the first public building to be "wrapped" in a gigantic red ribbon, on 1 December.[62]

In 1998 N'Goné Fall, editorial director of the Paris-based magazine *Revue Noire*, approached us to host a photographic exhibition, *Eye Africa: African photography 1887–1998*. Curated and realised by *Revue Noire*, in partnership with SANG, William Fehr Collection, La Pinacoteca do Estado de São Paulo and la Maison Européenne de la Photographie in Paris, the exhibition ran simultaneously at SANG and the Castle of Good Hope; it was the first festival of African photography in Cape Town.

Another first was a major show of West and Central African art, *The Pierre Guerre Collection of African Art*, curated by Marguerite de Sabran. It comprised eighty works loaned from the Musée d'arts africains, océniens, amérindiens of Marseilles and the Vidal-Naquet family, and it offered South Africans a rare opportunity to become acquainted with objects of great significance and antiquity, and indeed to consider our place on and relationship to the larger African continent. It set new standards in design and museological practice, enabling us to show African art in all its beauty and power. De Sabran worked closely with Kaufmann and Weinberg, thereby exposing them and other staff members to contact with international museum professionals in the field. The exhibition was supported by AFAA and IFAS and included an illustrated catalogue and extensive education programme. France's foreign minister, Hubert Vedrine, closed the exhibition on 9 October 1997.[63]

Widely supported in South Africa and abroad, *Africa Meets Africa* (1999) offered visitors another opportunity to see some of the masterpieces of African art in European collections. Curated by Erna Beumers, it featured over one hundred works from the Museum voor Volkenkunde in Rotterdam. Historical and contemporary pieces were juxtaposed in line with the museum's policy: to reinforce historical collections, but also to look for relevant contemporary developments in the art of the countries – in western, central and southern Africa – from which they collect. It mirrored the SANG vision and mission perfectly.[64]

It was a great privilege to host an exhibition of drawings, prints, objects and multiples by the acclaimed German artist Joseph Beuys, made available by the Institut für Auslandsbeziehungen (Institute for Foreign Relations) and supported by the German Consulate General. Beuys created analogies between art and society, visible and invisible processes, by using materials such as fat, wax, felt and copper. His theory and practice of social sculpture still influences and inspires artists.

David Goldblatt's *Structures* (1999), the culmination of fifteen years of photography, research and writing by the artist, came to SANG after its 1998 première at the Museum of Modern Art, New York, and subsequent showing at the Netherlands Architecture Institute in Rotterdam.[65] Also in 1999, *Isintu Ceremony, Identity and Community* marked the first (and last) exchange and co-operation between SANG, Robben Island Museum (RIM) and Flinders Art Museum in Adelaide, Australia. Initiated by Doreen Mellor, an Indigenous Australian of Mamu/Ngadjan heritage, this "south-south" collaboration explored ideas around the notion of "blackness" and the challenges facing indigenous Australians and black South

Africans. It offered a unique opportunity to reflect on the commonalities and differences between these two southern countries with a shared British colonial history and appalling race histories. Curated by Tumelo Mosaka and Zayd Minty, *Isintu* was the first-ever exhibition at SANG to be solely curated by black South Africans. It meant taking another step in the direction of altering museum practice at the national art museum.[66]

South African artists, academics and museologists were taking their place in the international world. Numerous specialists visited SANG from abroad. There were also opportunities for travel, sometimes fully funded or when individuals raised money to attend an exhibition or event. In 1994 I was invited, together with author and literary scholar Njabulo Ndebele and sculptor Andries Botha, to attend a conference in Chicago. Organised by Carol Becker, then professor and dean of the School of the Art Institute of Chicago, it was based on her anthology *The Subversive Imagination: Artists, Society and Social Responsibility* (1994). While in the USA I went to New York, visited museums, attended a panel discussion on *The Italian Metamorphosis, 1943–1968* exhibition at the Guggenheim Museum and met the director of the Solomon R. Guggenheim Foundation, Thomas Krens, who was working on the Guggenheim Bilbao at the time.[67]

Afrique en Créations, a project of the French Institute that aimed at enabling creativity on the African continent,[68] invited me to curate an exhibition of two South African photographers for the *Premières Rencontres de la Photographie africaine* – the first biennial of African photography held in Bamako, Mali in December 1995. I selected works by Ingrid Hudson and Santu Mofokeng, and travelled to Mali for the exhibition. The exhibition subsequently featured as part of a selection from the biennial at FNAC, in Paris, and Mofokeng was invited to show at a special sitting of UNESCO, also in Paris, in February 1996.[69]

In the same year, DACST approached me to advise on South Africa's participation in the Third International Biennial of Photography in Tenerife, Canary Islands. The focus was on Africa and the nineteenth century, which presented a huge challenge, as Africans were mostly depicted as subjects for ethnographic studies or as part of the flora and fauna of the continent. I was familiar with Mofokeng's as yet untitled archive of black family portraits offering new perspectives on black urban life, aspirations and social history. Mofokeng studiously collected and documented these photographs on field trips across South Africa.

The department accepted my proposal and funded the process of making negatives of existing photographs and digitally reworking them. A selection of thirty-two images presented under the title *The Black Photo Album/Look at me: 1890–1900s* was exhibited in Tenerife, and later shown across South Africa. The exhibition travelled from Grahamstown, where it premièred at the National Arts Festival, to various institutions across the country, eventually reaching the Natale Labia Museum in 1997. An expanded collection (1890–1950) was shown in slide form on the second Johannesburg Biennale and has since received global recognition. The archive has been shown in major exhibitions and museums abroad and there is now also a book.[70]

Bedford was invited to visit Sweden and made a second trip in 1997, with a view to an exchange of exhibitions. A year later her trips resulted in the celebration of the relationship between the two countries with the exhibition *Transpositions: Five Swedish artists in South Africa*.[71]

In 1995, Bedford acted as courier for Jane Alexander's *Butcher Boys* when curator Jean Clair selected the work for his exhibition *Identity and Alterity: A brief history of the human body over the last century*, which coincided with the centenary of the Venice Biennale. Installed on the top floor of the Palazzo Grassi, a storied building rich with Venetian history, it was a great honour for Alexander to exhibit in the company of Pierre Bonnard, Giorgio de Chirico, Alberto Giacometti, Henri Matisse and Pablo Picasso. It was also a moment of great pride for SANG to have a work from its permanent collection recognised as part of that history. South Africa was officially invited to exhibit in Venice that year. Curator Malcolm Payne built a triptych of walls at the entrance to the Giardini and embedded them with artworks, his own as well as works by Randolph Hartzenberg, Pat Mautloa and Brett Murray. He included thirty-four funerary urns bearing the names of artists potentially excluded from previous Venice Biennales.[72]

Weinberg attended a three-month internship at the Travelling Exhibition Services department of the Smithsonian Institution in Washington, D.C. Not only did this expose him to the sixteen Smithsonian museums and more than thirty related projects, he also participated in the Festival of American Folklife and travelled along the Eastern Seaboard to Boston, New York, Williamsburg and Orlando.[73]

South Africa received many heads of state after 1994, but the request in 1996 for an exhibition to coincide with the visit of Queen Margrethe II of Denmark was the first of its kind. This was no surprise, as the monarch is an accomplished artist in her own right. Working with Mikael Andersen Galerie in Copenhagen, six contemporary Danish artists were selected, including Doris Bloom, who was born in South Africa and studied here before moving to Denmark; she was already represented in the permanent collection with a painting, *Miss Muffet I* (1986–87).

Copenhagen was the Cultural Capital of Europe in 1996 and I was invited as one of the curators for the project *96 Containers – Art Across the Oceans*. Curators from around the globe met twice to discuss and plan this unusual approach, which had as its focus port cities rather than big capitals. I was responsible for five shipping containers, one each from Luanda, Cape Town, Durban, Maputo and Mauritius. The organisers took care of all the expenses, but the curators had to secure the money for the artists and their work. The Department of Foreign Affairs funded the South African containers and contributed to the Luanda and Maputo installations. The following artists represented their cities: Billy Mandindi and Gavin Younge (Cape Town); Andries Botha and Sam Ntshangase (Durban); António Ole (Luanda); Malangatana Ngwenya, Titos Mabote and Reinata Sadimba (Maputo); and Khalid Nazroo (Port-Louis).[74] Ntshangase wanted to offer a song of praise for the Queen of Denmark and the Prince Consort at the opening: an *imbongi* (praise singer) outfit was improvised and his powerful voice rang out in Zulu against the pale grey sky and the stark whiteness of the pebbled site.

Interpreting, showcasing and augmenting the permanent collection

WE GUARDED against being overwhelmed by international interest and the plentiful exhibitions on offer, particularly since there was a need to interpret and showcase the permanent collection, which is the mainstay of any art museum.

In the contemporary field, the show *New Art, New Issues* (1996) shifted the focus away from familiar images that captured the political and social struggles of the 1980s towards artworks which addressed a range of issues that already faced South Africa early in the post-apartheid era. The tone was set by Marlene Dumas' magnificent series of portraits, *The Next Generation* (1994–95), which the artist and her dealer, Paul Andriesse, generously presented to SANG (Plate 23). The exhibition included Brett Murray's subversion of racial stereotyping (*Rich Boy*, 1995), Wayne Barker's delightful spoof on colonial art and institutions (*Blue Colonies*, 1995), Andrew Putter's *Gene Pool* (1994), one of several works that questioned more conventional gender identities and Colin Richards' etching *Childsplay* (1987/1992) that addressed violence against women and efforts to resist patriarchal domination.

The historical European collection, for which Hayden Proud was and still is responsible, was not neglected; on the contrary, he has devoted himself to interpreting and re-interpreting the collection and to giving new meaning to works long hidden in the basement. The central painting in *Architecture into Art: the Building as motif in works from the Permanent Collection* (1997) was James Ford's architectural fantasy *Holiday Time in Cape Town in the Twentieth Century* (1891–99) and included architect-artist William Timlin's fantasy *The Palace on the Sea* (c. 1930). Angela Zehnder, who succeeded Thomas Rebok as painting conservator, restored *Holiday Time in Cape Town* with information gained from infrared photographs and X-rays taken by Grundlingh and Rachael Alexander of SAM; a conservation display included the X-ray and cross-section.[75]

Following on a generous grant from the Abe Bailey Trust for the conservation and restoration of the Bailey Collection, much admired paintings by Thomas Gainsborough, Joseph Israels, Alfred Munnings, Joshua Reynolds and George Stubbs were exhibited. The tradition of making prints after paintings was also explored. The Alfred de Pass and Sir Edmund and Lady Davis presentations were highlighted in exhibitions and publications. The latter was shown at the same time as the Musée d'Orsay exhibited the British art that they gifted to the Luxembourg Gallery in Paris in 1915. Once again Alexander's X-ray told a story about a painting in the collection: in correspondence Zehnder remembered that an X-ray of *Charles Shannon's The Morning Toilet* (1912), revealed an earlier portrait; it was displayed and included in the catalogue.[76]

Staff's Choice (1997) took an internal view of the collection to answer a variety of probing questions: Who works at SANG? What are their roles and functions? What do they like? Private sensibilities and opinions were shared as each and every member of staff exhibited and described his or her favourite work in the collection. It was enormously popular with both staff and the public, and entirely unpredictable in the choices people made.

PLATE 25: Artist unrecorded, *Zulu Neckpiece*, c. 1879, glass seed beads, sinew, brass buttons, 190 x 130; presented by the Rowland and Leta Hill Trust; photographer Cecil Kortje.

After the political transformation, the richness of southern Africa's aesthetic traditions became the focus of international and local attention and acclaim. The restrained elegance and antiquity of works from South Africa captivated viewers at the Royal Academy in London, Martin Gropius-Bau in Berlin and Guggenheim Museum in New York. In order to present a plurality of perspectives on the collection and unveil the potential of cultural objects as living witness to the past and as vectors for understanding the present, we invited South Africans to select one or two works from recent acquisitions of historical southern African works for display and comment in the exhibition *Heritage Choices* (1997), curated by Kaufmann.[77]

Mtshali, the arts and culture minister, selected a piece of nineteenth-century Zulu beadwork, taken from a battlefield during the Anglo-Zulu war (Plate 25). He commented:

> I was deeply moved to see and handle the Zulu necklace worn by Zulu warriors. This artefact, which was repatriated into the country, is a reminder of the creative talent of Zulu women. They expressed their deep feelings and support for their beloved ones through beadwork. The dominance of red beads symbolises spiritual warmth and love. The necklace evoked heroic feelings to a person of Zulu stock. The necklace is a living symbol of a gallant amabutho who fell at Ulundi on 4 July 1879.

It was time to take stock of the contemporary South African art being collected and to share it with the public. Bedford proposed and co-ordinated the exhibition *Contemporary South African Art 1985–1995*, which featured a selection from the nearly 1,000 paintings, sculptures, works on paper, photographs, videos, baskets, beadwork and ceramics by more than 230 artists that had been produced and acquired during that decade.[79] It provided a comprehensive overview of recent art production in the country and enabled visitors to assess the extent to which political and cultural changes were reflected in the visual arts, as well as in the collecting policies and practices of the national art museum. As always, the museum and the public were enthusiastically and ably supported by the Friends and the volunteer guides.

The exhibition ran from 14 December 1996 to 31 March the following year. A public discussion forum was held in February 1997. It was a very different affair from the first such debate organised at the time of the exhibition *Recent Acquisitions 1990–1991*, held five years earlier. The first was characterised by anger, disapproval and criticism of the new directions we were taking – mostly by traditional stakeholders and some artists. While there were still many incisive questions and firm opinions on offer at the 1997 forum, the discussions were held in a constructive spirit. The public was becoming accustomed to, and indeed appreciative of the way in which the institution was changing and growing.

PLATE 26: Willie Bester, *Head North*, 1995, mixed media, 1750 × 2200 × 970; presented by the artist; courtesy of the artist.

In an extensive review in *Third Text*, Jacqueline Nolte described the exhibition as "a voluntary exposure in the spirit of national reconciliation" and a "grand tour of contemporary South African art". She commented on the successful and problematic juxtapositions of different works, on the abstract paintings by black South Africans, the impressive photographic collection and the "welcome admission of the art of satire and caricature into the gallery space". While critical of the overall quality of the ceramic works on display, and the absence of contemporary design, and questioning the criteria used within the rubric "reparation", Nolte stated: "One of the major accomplishments of this collection lies in its range of media and its attempt to erase boundaries between the categories of 'craft', 'popular', 'folk', 'community' and 'fine art'." She concluded:

> Despite the practice of fashionable simulations of infinite difference, despite receptions of imposed homogeneity and collective experiences of the devastation of loss, what was displayed in this exhibition was witness to artists' attempts to make sense of what has transpired in South Africa and what is still desired.[80]

The magazine *Time* identified Contemporary *South African Art 1985–1995* as a must-see exhibition on the African continent.[81] The supporting catalogue contained texts by Bedford (curator and editor) and

PLATE 27: Karel Nel, *The Island and the Dream of the Table House*, 1995, pastel pigment on bonded fibre fabric, 2110 × 1545; presented by the Friends of SANG; courtesy of the artist; photographer Cecil Kortje.

me, as well as an elaboration of acquisition policies (1980 and 1996) and exhibitions policy (1996), and a listing of the various board and staff members who served on the committee during the period under review. Bedford and board member Jane Taylor conducted an interview with Neville Dubow for the catalogue. His institutional knowledge was vast. Dubow was appointed as the UCT representative on the board in 1971 and had been a member of the acquisitions committee from that date too, having served as its chairperson and member of the executive from 1980–95; he had also served on selection panels for the institution's sculpture and photographic commissions.

The appointment of a new board in 1995 saw the end of Dubow's direct participation in SANG's decision-making process, but it did not mean the end of his involvement and support. In the difficult times encountered before and after 1994, Dubow was always there for the staff, individually and collectively.[82] One of the most telling testimonies to this role was captured in the published interview, from which I quoted in chapter three.[83] Dubow provided an historical overview of the shifts and changes that occurred over a critical period of his tenure. His philosophy for the national art museum – a philosophy that is embedded in a socio-political context, in which the role of the artist is paramount – is as appropriate today as it was then:

> The artist has to continue to question control and to challenge perceived conventional wisdoms. In fact, I think that after the revolution has been won the role of the artist becomes even more crucially important than in the pre-revolutionary phase. He's still got to formulate those very tough and very difficult questions that are going to somehow stop the 'fat cats' in their stride. The period that we are going through at the moment is a kind of interregnum. For me the role of the artist in this is very crucial and the role of the National Gallery and the role of the Acquisitions Committee in allowing artists who wish to ask difficult and awkward and challenging questions and the degree to which an Acquisitions Committee offers such artists a venue to confront and to challenge – I see that as being a very key role indeed. In other words, I would like to think that the National Gallery should buy work of a kind that might cause a future Director to wonder whether that work could still hang when the future Minister of Culture comes to visit the Gallery. I would like to think that the answer would be yes.[84]

My contribution to the catalogue reflected on the new directions and shifts in thinking and working taking place at the gallery:

> Definitions, distinctions and standards must constantly be assessed and debated among ourselves and in public forums, many of which are initiated by SANG. We are, in turn, challenged about what is suitable and appropriate for the collection of a national art museum – issues about 'art' and 'craft' and 'high' and 'low' are often raised, as we continue to erode traditional boundaries and eliminate categories which have invariably been imposed from outside our own borders and experience. They only serve to hinder the potential of interchange and the creation of our own theories and terminologies.[85]

We were no longer able to budget for major exhibitions, programmes or events, and we had to raise money for all big projects and catalogues. The gallery's staff was committed to and very successful in sourcing funds, and fortunately there was no lack of interest in or support for the visual arts in general and the national art museum in particular – if not from government, then from many different sources. The publications from this period abound with logos and expressions of appreciation for the benefaction.[86] We applied and were granted R50,000 by DACST for the casting and repatriation of sculptures by Dumile Feni, who had died in New York in 1991. The City of Cape Town and the Rowland and Leta Hill Trust funded the acquisition of *The Black Christ* (1962) by Ronald Harrison. The controversial painting, which depicts ANC leader Albert Luthuli as Christ on a cross being persecuted by Hendrik Verwoerd and John Vorster, led to Harrison's arrest. It was subsequently smuggled to the United Kingdom. Decades later the work was located in London and repatriated in 1997 – the artist offered it at a price well below what it would have fetched abroad.[87]

We did not solicit gifts from artists, but some were extremely generous and presented the following works: Willie Bester, *Head North* (1995) (Plate 26); Alan Alborough, *Heathen Wet Lip* (1997), a site-specific work he created for the Liberman Room as part of the exhibition *Graft* that formed part of the second Johannesburg Biennale; Colin Richards, *The True Image (Veronica)* and *Veronica Cloth* (1996); Cecil Skotnes, *Confrontation* (1996); Vivian van Blerk, *Autorittrato* (1994); Ian van Coller augmented purchases with *Rickshaw Boys (Suite*

PLATE 28: David Goldblatt, *Victoria Cobokana, housekeeper, in her employer's dining room with her son Sifiso and daughter Onica, Johannesburg June 1999. Victoria died of AIDS 13 December 1999, Sifiso died of AIDS 12 January 2000, Onica died of AIDS in May 2000*, 1999, digital print, 590 × 590; presented by Linda Givon; image courtesy of the David Goldblatt Legacy Trust.

of five) (2000); Ed West, *Casting Shadows* (1999); and Kevin Brand donated *So it goes* (1996) by Bridget Baker.

FONG also presented gifts: Keith Dietrich's *A Small Miscalculation in Sir Francis Galton's Eugenics Theory* (1996); Karel Nel's *The Island and the Dream of the Table House* (1995) (Plate 27); Nhlanha Nsundwane ceramic painted by Phumelele Nene (1997); Berni Searle's mixed media *Traces* (2000); Andrew Tshabangu's silver print *Joubert Park* (1997); and Joe Wolpe's *Broken Planes* (1994).

Funds raised from different sources enabled us to purchase major works: from Zonnebloem and BASA, Johannes Phokela's *As the Old Ones Sing, so the Young Ones Pipe* (1998); from the Board of Executors, Sue Williamson's *Messages from the Moat* (1997) (Plate 33); from the City of Cape Town, Williamson's CD-ROM *Can't Forget, Can't Remember* (2000); from the World Presidents Organisation (WPO) dinner, *Frontline Three with Centurion Models* (1997) by Sandile Zulu and *Mounds: scratched, poked, imped* (1995) by Jeremy Wafer.

Truworths donated a range of linocuts, while Linda Givon presented three mixed-media works by Peet Pienaar and added to the holdings of David Goldblatt's photographs with his moving portrait, whose title evokes an unfolding tragedy: *Victoria Cobokana, housekeeper, in her employer's dining room with her son Sifiso and daughter Onica, Johannesburg June 1999. Victoria died of AIDS 13 December 1999, Sifiso died of AIDS 12 January 2000, Onica died of AIDS in May 2000* (Plate 28).[88] It was a timely acquisition for the national art museum. In 1999, HIV infection rates in adults had soared to 22.4 %, up from 0.76 % in 1990.

Awareness about the need for diversity within the art museum, and the desire to train and engage individuals fully representative of all South Africans, resulted in rewarding outcomes. Bongi Bengu joined SANG as a trainee curator in 1997, while she was completing her MFA studies at Michaelis. In correspondence she recalled the privilege of being in the presence of "an outstanding collection of local and international art", the great pride she experienced in working with Kaufmann on *Musuku* and escorting the writer Lewis Nkosi to the opening of *PhotoSynthesis: Contemporary South African photography*.[89] Bengu had an opportunity to travel to Europe and terminated her internship early. In her view, the programme lacked real structure: "For example, it could have been really interesting for me to assist one of the curators from the conceptualisation phase to installation of the exhibition. But for me as a young artist I can say that was a true pivotal moment."

Generous financial support impacted positively on training and staffing, and enabled us to appoint the first black curator at SANG. The Deaf Federation of South Africa funded a three-year training programme in frame restoration and photography for Hanna-Marie Pheiffer. Thanks to funding from the Standard Bank trainee programme, Zola Mtshiza entered a curatorial traineeship. At the end of his first six months I could report that a detailed programme had exposed him to working with different curators and that he was an asset to the gallery. Standard Bank also funded him to undertake a research trip with Grundlingh. I expressed the hope that we would be able to offer him employment, which became a reality in late 2000, when he was appointed as assistant curator.[90]

PLATE 29: Walter Sickert, *Royal Hotel, Dieppe*, c. 1902, oil on wood, 140 × 240.

Extensive education programmes at SANG, NLM and beyond continued and were even expanded. Jo-Anne Duggan left in 1996 and Liesl Hartman, who had worked with her as a student while studying towards a Higher Diploma in Education, stepped in. She remembers the "daunting experience" of taking her first group of visitors on a guided tour of *Miscast* and Skotnes' openness to talk about the exhibition.[91]

As part of a focus on art education in high schools, Hartman and Jill Joubert (an art teacher representative for the Cape Town region) curated an exhibition in the Annexe of work made by the first Grade 12 art students registered in the newly constituted Western Cape Education Department (WCED). All three rooms were covered floor to ceiling, and it attracted many visitors and schools.

The exhibition coincided with a high school art teachers' conference on South African art history and was accompanied by an exciting programme in which artists discussed their work, as well as a series of practical workshops on art disciplines taught at school. According to Hartman, Emile Maurice was alarmed that there were so few black art teachers present – a reflection on the number of black schools that offered art at the time (estimated at about five). "Sadly this remains the case even today, almost twenty years later."[92] In their article in *bonani*, Hartman, Joubert and Gill Cowan (art subject advisor for the Cape Town region) expressed their appreciation for the strong links between SANG and the WCED, and further thanked FONG, the provincial department of arts and culture and the gallery's education department for financial support of the initiatives.[93]

The partnership between SANG and the Curriculum Development Project for Arts Education bore fruit at the graduation celebration for the teachers who completed the in-service teacher training (Inset) course, jointly offered with SANG during 1997, and run by Vuyile Voyiya. Our educators were playing a leading role in addressing the legacy of apartheid and providing relevant and exciting exposure to making and teaching art. Hartman took this example and lesson with her when she left SANG in 1997 to take up a position as principal of Battswood Art Centre. For her the need for Inset in the arts remains "overwhelming".[94]

The NAC funded the Museum Young Ambassadors Programme, initiated by Dammon Rice, an independent art teacher, who trained groups of grade eleven learners to give tours of the exhibition *Landscape in South African Art* (1999) to primary school groups at Natale Labia Museum. Twelve of them accommodated 821 learners over a six-week period and received their certificates at a "graduation" ceremony in October 1999.[95]

Caring for and safeguarding the permanent collection

SANG FORMED further links with Africa through PREventive conservation in Museums of Africa (PREMA), a conservation project initiated by the International Centre for the Study of Preservation and Restoration of Cultural Property (ICCROM) in Ghana. The programme ran from 1984 to 2005, with the aim of establishing a network of African professionals capable of taking charge of the conservation of collections and the training of colleagues, thereby giving sub-Saharan African museums tools for a long-lasting development. Kim Siebert, who had moved from education to become collections manager, spent nine months in the Ghanaian capital, Accra, and as an adjunct, museum directors were invited to attend a week-long seminar at the end of the training. I met museum directors from twelve so-called Anglophone (not one of us spoke English as mother tongue) sub-Saharan African countries and had the privilege of joining a trip to the Cape Coast Castle Museum, the site from which hundreds of thousands of slaves were shipped from the Gold Coast (as Ghana was known during the colonial period) to the Americas.[96]

Siebert took the opportunity and responsibility seriously and together with Angela Zehnder initiated the Safe House Project on her return. She sent out a call to attract volunteers to assist and she interviewed over forty people before setting up a motivated team. She made another trip to Ghana and this, as well as the acquisitions made in Ghana and further afield, resulted in an exhibition *Forging Links with Ghana and her Neighbours* (1997). It was an occasion for presenting the objects purchased, but also for acknowledging Bruce Arnott's contribution to the permanent collection in this area.

When Siebert left SANG, Kaufmann took over the Safe House Project to honour this extraordinary initiative of conserving and storing more than 2,000 objects made of beads, ivory, wood, animal skin and other fragile materials under extremely difficult circumstances. She paid tribute to the many volunteers in *bonani*.[98] In correspondence from 2016 Kaufmann commented on the status of the project:

> The Safe House Project has left a legacy with us all, in that we still practise Kim's recommended method of preventative conservation where applicable and are all far more aware of the care and management of our collections ... it has been *integrated into collections management practice* here.

> We have more staff, but no more storage space and fewer funds than before, so despite the numbers of staff the situation remains imperfect, with storage critical and impacting negatively on the collection – cramped, crowded conditions in inaccessible storage without any climate control and faulty air con. The collection remains dispersed in three locations at present and is less accessible than ever before.[99]

As far as the European and South African collections - historical and contemporary - were concerned, paper conservation was outsourced. Zehnder, who had a fine arts undergraduate degree and further masters degree in easel painting conservation from the University of Northumbria, Newcastle, brought her experience to bear on the collections in many additional ways: holistic collection management and care, environmental control, preparation of loans, condition reports and, on occasion, acting as courier for international loans. The latter experiences were greatly enhanced by contact with international couriers and conservators who travelled to SANG with exhibitions.[100]

Alerted by Dubow about the presence of sixty-two World War II Russian posters in the South African Library, our request that they be transferred to SANG was approved. These large, hand-painted posters are works of art in their own right, while also presenting a vivid picture of the history and course of World War II as experienced by the Russians. They required a long process of restoration before they could be exhibited and André van Oort, senior conservator of paper and photography at the Stedelijk Museum in Amsterdam and an internationally recognised authority on the restoration of posters, spent two weeks in Cape Town to undertake the task. Dolby organised a workshop at the conservation centres of the Library of Parliament, SAL and UCT while the work was carried out. Seventeen qualified bench restorers from around the country participated in the workshop and were afforded the unparalleled opportunity of gaining expertise in a highly specialised field.[101]

Lack of adequate security was but one of the effects of inadequate funding and the vulnerability of the national art museum was brought forcefully and painfully to the fore on 3 October 1998 when a painting by Walter Sickert, *Royal Hotel, Dieppe* (c. 1902), was stolen (Plate 29). A small but extremely valuable work (at the time it was valued between £15,000 - £20,000, or R150,000 - R200,000), formed part of the exhibition *Architecture into Art*; it was unscrewed and removed from the gallery by habitual criminal Shaun Prince.

While the electronic security was neither sophisticated nor pervasive enough, staff did not fail the institution. Security attendant Lucy Williams, on duty at reception that morning, noticed that the thief was concealing something under his jacket when he stopped at the desk on his way out. She alerted the security supervisor, Shamiel Fakir, who gave chase and picked up the sheath of the knife Prince dropped; this put the police on his trail immediately. Williams' commendable vigilance, coupled with the images captured on closed circuit television, the coverage by the media and information received from members of the public, led to the arrest of the thief. Johannes Swanepoel, who allegedly bought the painting from Prince, was bailed until the case went to court.

The painting was never recovered and the insurance claim was eventually paid out six years later. We acquired a number of works with this money, including graphic works by Sickert from The Fine Art Society in London: *The Old Royal Hotel* (c. 1910) and *The Orchestra of the Olympia, Shoreditch* (c.1920).[102]

The more things change ...

IN 1999 I was once again unpopular with the powers that be in Pretoria following the publication, in *Leadership* magazine, of an article titled "The Horn of the Art's Dilemma". The editor introduced it with the following statement: "The community of art fondly imagined that two decades of official indifference to it might end under the new government. Instead the despair has deepened ..."[103] DACST had been approached for comment and prior to the article going to press, I received a phone call from Carol Steinberg, then chief director for cultural development at DACST, asking me to reconsider publishing the piece. I refused.

Ngubane, who had replaced Mtshali and was now serving his second tenure as arts and culture minister, replied. He sermonised about the need for "a fundamental re-definition of the way museums see themselves, so that they become the property of all South Africans," and the "new paradigm" of museums being "people centred" instead of "object centred". He referred to the creation of the flagship museums "which will effectively *rationalise* [my emphasis] and co-ordinate the operations of clusters of smaller museums and galleries," the ample resources allocated for the establishment of the new entities, and the need for museums "to become adept at fundraising from a range of sources". In the minister's view this was not a bad thing. "It means that what is done is aligned with market needs." Funds, he argued, were available, but depended "on the creativity and competence of institutions". He cited the aquarium at the V&A Waterfront in Cape Town and La Villette in Paris as examples of "edutainment", of institutions that combined "scientific integrity" with "fun and commercial success". Museums, he reminded, should also consider the international agreements administered by DACST in seeking partnerships and funding.[104]

Ngubane's arguments, in all probability compiled by his officials, were specious and based on a limited understanding and knowledge of the history of SANG and its on-going initiatives – an institution for which the ministry and department were ultimately responsible. By 1999 DACST and its ministry were facing widespread criticism of their inefficient management of the arts and culture portfolio. Mike Van Graan's article in the *Sunday Independent*, quoted earlier, summarised the views of many. In a follow-up article published online, Van Graan further unpacked the crippling effects on arts, culture and heritage that had resulted from tensions between IFP and ANC officials in government. He also penetrated the "smokescreen" surrounding Jardine's resignation, followed by that of Steinberg, and the power-base they had built within DACST.[105]

Ngubane would try to punish me in 2003 when it was time to re-appoint members of the NAC board on which I served. Van Graan wrote about the demise of the board for the online platform Artslink ("The NAC: where to now?", 12 December 2004). He spoke of "the sheer incompetence of the management of processes around the NAC". His analysis of the main reasons bears quoting. Firstly, the minister changed the law so that board chairpersons would no longer be elected, but appointed. Secondly, a new board should have been appointed on 1 April 2003, but delays meant that the announcement was only made in mid-May. And thirdly:

> … despite being elected legally by the previous Board as one of three members to serve on the new Board to provide continuity, Marilyn Martin was specifically excluded from the Board by the Minister who had been criticized by Martin on prior occasions for some of his actions such as his "ringfencing" 20% of the NAC's funds for him to allocate as he chose. Even then, Martin had only been elected along with John Kani and Lisa Combrinck after the Minister had sent a letter to inform the Board that he had in fact appointed Kani, Kiren Thathiah and his adviser, Bongani Tembe, as the three Board members to serve on the new Board. Only when it was pointed out to him that the law required these three to be elected, did Ngubane relent, and Board members then chose Combrinck, Kani and Martin. Yet, even so, the Minister excluded Martin, which action was defended on national radio by the Department's Director of Art Institutional Governance, Sidney Selepe, "as the Minister's prerogative". This led to a public outcry that, coupled with legal opinion, had the Minister embarrassingly climb down and appoint Martin to the Board. Selepe has subsequently been promoted to Chief Director: Arts and Culture in Society, and nominations for the new NAC Board are to be sent to him.[106]

Endless internal and external factors impacted negatively on the work and administration of the NAC. I wrote to Ngubane in November 2003 expressing concern about these, but none of the matters I raised were addressed and the NAC was on a slippery slope. It was frightening to witness, helplessly, what amounted to the hijacking of the organisation. In September and November 2004 I wrote to Pallo Jordan, who had taken up the reins as minister of DAC. I provided details of the maladministration, lack of compliance with the Public Finance Management Act, the resignation of seven of the fifteen national members, and the illegal status of the executive committee. After many delays a company was appointed to perform an internal audit and I urged Jordan to access the relevant documents and information.[107] In November he lodged a request that we resign. I did so straight away, but some members resisted.[108]

The exhilaration and expectations that followed the first democratic elections, coupled with the promise of transformation, were turning into disbelief and despondency. We realised that the national government had little interest in advancing the arts and museum sectors and that the struggle would continue.

PLATE 30: Jonathan Shapiro, *HIV/AIDS Dissidents Highway*, © 2000 Zapiro, ink on cotton rag paper, 365 × 255. Originally published in the *Sowetan*; re-published with permission; image courtesy of the artist.

6

Museum amalgamation and the making of Iziko Museums of South Africa

2000 – 2008

TRANSFORMING national museums at macro levels, devising a structure for Iziko Museums and the far-reaching impact on SANG, as well as concerted efforts to address crippling space and financial constraints, are major themes of this chapter. The gallery loses its autonomy and becomes part of Iziko, with responsibility for managing the Michaelis Collection. Gradually, the professionalisation of the art museum is compromised and replaced by bureaucratisation. Jatti Bredekamp succeeds the first CEO, Jack Lohman. The Natale Labia Museum is returned to the Labia family. The collections are once again targeted for disposal. Against the odds, there are major achievements in all aspects of work, and the gallery continues its role as an instrument of activism and social justice, particularly with regards HIV/Aids. International exchange flourishes far beyond expectations, but there is a sense that Africans do not own their narrative.

What does it mean to say that an artist (or an art gallery)
'shows commitment'?
It means that he or she brings not only an engagement
to the subject of the display,
but an involvement in that it transcends
mere observation or representation.

JUDGE EDWIN CAMERON[1]

The Southern Flagship Institution tacks into the transformation wind

IN APRIL 2000 the first issue of the Southern Flagship Institution quarterly newsletter *Zanazo* appeared, replacing *bonani* and SAM's *Musenews* and combining information about activities at SAM, SANG, South African Cultural History Museum, Michaelis Collection and the William Fehr Collection (Fig. 25).[2] In his "Message from the Acting CEO", SAM director Mike Cluver announced that Jack Lohman, British educator, designer and museum administrator, had been appointed CEO.[3] He was tasked with the creation of the new museum institution and participation in the transformation of the national museum sector.

In the second issue of *Zanazo* the new CEO articulated his vision for what, at that moment, was called Museums of Cape Town. He outlined the work ahead, with emphasis on the relevance of museums to their time: "Getting this right, reflecting in all our displays and programmes the richness and diversity, which is the reality of urban Cape Town, will be a benchmark for my time at Museums of Cape Town." There were major projects in the pipeline that would "provide a fresh approach to the communication and interpretation of our past and present". He further described the institution as "an emerging world-class organisation":

> In the past we have explained our rationale by pointing out the variety of our responsibilities and the quality of our achievements. In the future we will be content to be judged by our visitors and our ability to live up to our mission.[4]

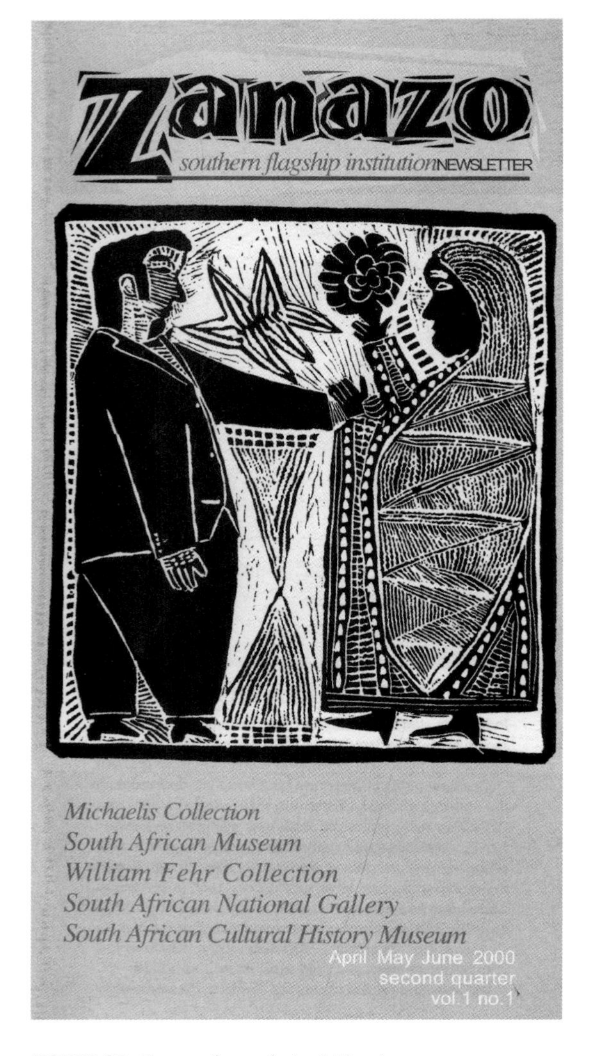

FIGURE 25: *Zanazo* 1, no. 1, April May June 2000, cover featuring John Muafangejo, *The Pregnant Maria*, undated, linocut, 280 × 245.

The reality turned out to be different. In a personal communication to me, Lohman offered his perspective on the transformation process and the national gallery. He described his beginnings in Cape Town as "disastrous":

> I had inherited consultants who had already been working with the Southern Flagship Institution … and running staff workshops based on that institution's vision and mission. They appeared to have strong traction with the board and management, and I felt somewhat reluctantly obliged to follow their lead. Indeed the three consultants were charming, smart people. Their workshops brought staff together – in some cases for the first time – in a very positive way. The mood was hopeful. Their constant advice to me was to push transformation through fast and launch a new organizational

> structure soonest, bringing the various museums closer together. Naively, I accepted their advice and this is where disaster struck and the mood of hope amongst staff turned to a mood of anger and disappointment. Clearly, bringing together fifteen museums and several hundred staff has its own resource and cultural challenges. But three rather militant unions were involved, keen to prevent any redundancies, and there was a layer of staff more concerned with antagonising authority than with enthusiasm. It seemed I spent much time in union meetings as they pushed back on the proposed leaner structure.

This institutional culture, said Lohman, pushed some staff across the museum group into depression and saw others resort to alcohol and violence. "Seeing a member of staff with a knife through her own hand was, and still is, one of the most frightening moments of my professional life," stated Lohman. He further added:

> The speed of change, encouraged by the consultants, was leaving people behind and frightened about their jobs. The consultants urged me to forge ahead and not to worry about bringing everyone along with me. This was South Africa I was reminded – everyone expects a revolution. I remember thinking that this speed of transformation could not be right and would not work. Feeling most concerned and genuinely panicked, in consultation with Patricia Davidson, Marilyn Martin and board member Sheryl Ozinsky, I paused all work on restructuring and effectively disengaged the consultants. I brought all the staff into the lecture theatre and explained I had made a mistake in progressing so fast and that we would do it differently: more transparently, more carefully. I was encouraged by watching Tony Blair similarly back down on the Iraq War. I have since been very cautious about allowing consultants into the organizations I have led.[5]

Lohman recalls that transformation was not just about staff structures, but also about approaches to presenting art and culture in a new South Africa. Much time was spent on how to rationalise the collections and find answers to the questions of what belonged where. For instance, where should the rock art in SAM go? Why were the *Lydenburg Heads* and baskets and beadwork in that museum and not at SANG? Why were Roman and Greek objects displayed in the context of cultural history, while African art was treated as natural history? The many discussions, papers and workshops led to the reimagining of the cultural history museum as the Slave Lodge. Twenty-seven years later, the former ethnological collections have been transferred to the Iziko Social History Centre and combined with artefacts from the colonial period, as well as collections of ceramics, furniture, coins and textiles. None of the other questions have been satisfactorily answered, though.

The workshops and discussions resulted in a new management structure with directors for the three main disciplines (art history, natural history and social history), and directors for finance, human resources and property services. Staff at every level had to apply for positions, which exacerbated the uncertainties and fear described by Lohman. Collectively, the national art museum, Michaelis Collection and Natale Labia Museum now comprised the Art Collections Division (later Department), and I was appointed director.

The amalgamated museums needed a name and a competition was initiated at the gallery to find an appropriate appellation. Vuyile Voyiya compiled a list from which *Iziko* was selected: it is a Xhosa word, meaning "hearth", the centre of a typical African homestead where people gather to cook, eat, talk and socialise. Thus Iziko Museums of Cape Town (Iziko) came into being and SANG was renamed Iziko: South African National Gallery (ISANG); in time the colon disappeared.[6] I have used the original acronym in this book.

The new name was meant to evoke the welcoming warmth of a fireplace but in practice, institutionally at least, it meant the cold reality of centralisation and bureaucracy. Librarians now reported to Central Services and the educators to Education and Public Programmes; they were therefore no longer integral to the internal decision-making and curatorial processes of the gallery. Education was also given responsibility for the technical staff and the dedicated groups of art, natural history and library volunteer guides.[7] Having educators and exhibition staff physically removed from the art museum did not work out in the long term – subsequently individuals were re-assigned to the site and the discipline, but the numbers were severely reduced. On the positive side, the amalgamated museums offered opportunities for staff members across the museums to apply for different positions and to grow through new challenges.[8]

Lohman described how he "took refuge" from his job stresses with gallery staff. "They were the most outward and best-connected of all my staff," he recalled. "They were also immensely good at what they did ... I still consider Carol Kaufmann, Hayden Proud and Emma Bedford amongst the best curatorial staff I have ever had the privilege to work with. They were brimming with ideas and enthusiasm."[9] We at the gallery often had a feeling that we were not necessarily welcome in the amalgamated museums; Lohman confirmed this. He praised our blend of "showmanship and scholarship", and described how he still relishes the vibrant and memorable openings of exhibitions such as *Musuku: Golden Links with our Past, Hoerikwaggo* and work by William Kentridge, as well as the "very timely display focused on HIV/ Aids at a time when President Mbeki was questioning its existence and how it spread". It seemed as if the whole South African rainbow nation was present at the openings and that the national gallery was a vector for change within the Iziko stable.

But to the then board, noted Lohman, the gallery "was not as advertised":

> There was a sense that it was now some kind of impostor in the new South Africa, impossible to pin down and unreliable in terms of toeing the government line. There were only ever one or two board members who would speak up for the gallery – it had its own authority and independent power, bolstered by its director. But SANG was never really disrupting our sense of a museum group, it was simply living in a process that was unfolding.[10]

Lohman's most sweeping public act was the closure of the San diorama at SAM. It occurred in the face of criticism coming from many different directions, particularly from parliamentary committees, DACST and some Khoisan groups, and afforded Iziko time to reflect on and to reconsider how the casts might be displayed in future. Lohman's description of the diorama is piquant and bears quoting at length. It was, he wrote, an "embarrassing and shameless tableau of indigenous people 'in the wild' and village scenes depicting various tribal groups":

> Narrow and dimly lit, the tableau had been a favourite of tourists brought in groups by white tour guides and had held a morbid fascination for generations of school children. In the nearby cultural history museum, the story of 'white' civilization made the lesson of racial contrast all too clear. The diorama was a lingering insult to the new South Africa. For a moment the closure made world news. In the transformation taking place in the country toward a shared future, the museum was transforming the way in which people saw themselves in the past.[11]

For social history collections director Patricia Davison, the closure of the diorama "opened a space for public debate about the diorama and more generally about the presentation of history in museums. It confirmed that representations of the past are always contingent on the politics of the present".[12] San groupings were against the closure, arguing that their history would become less visible.[13] Scholar and artist Pippa Skotnes agreed: "The challenge is not to get rid of the diorama, but to alter it ... to find ways to displace and replace the stereotype it perpetuates."[14] A failure to recast the diorama, she added, "makes the closing of the diorama yet another act of dispossession, of casting the San [Bushmen] out of the contemporary political and historical debate".

When the diorama was closed, plans were in the pipeline for a new rock art gallery that would counter the representation of San people as primitive hunter-gatherers and to highlight instead the richness of their mythology, cosmology and art. Project-managed by Carol Kaufmann, the exhibit opened in 2003 and was followed by exhibitions relating to rock art and the Wilhelm and Lucy Lloyd archive of |xam and !kun notebooks, curated by Skotnes. A public forum held in 2007 brought together indigenous groups and academics, but failed to result in any outcome other than the need to publicly acknowledge San dispossession. For Davison, this presented SAM with a unique opportunity to reflect on its own practice and to look critically "at how it had affirmed racial stereotypes through the cast project".[15] By the time Davison retired in 2010, the focus of Iziko CEO Jatti Bredekamp's attention had shifted to Robben Island; "the diorama was not an institutional priority".

The display of human remains is directly related to the diorama and Iziko worked through a series of policies, eventually agreeing that the more than sixty casts of San and Khoi people created by modeller James Drury were also part of human remains and should therefore not be exhibited. For Davison the casts were:

> ... artefacts of museum practice and part of the history of the SAM, including racial science. As such, they have the power to be used to raise awareness of this history and, with the participation of people of Khoesan descent, to educate museum audiences. Technology provides the possibility of multiple voices and dialogues – this could have been used to explore the history that is now 'archived', if not silenced.[16]

The possibilities for recasting the diorama and keeping San history and culture in the public domain were not explored and the ethnographic hall, an adjunct to the diorama, was finally closed in August 2017 after the Khoi-Boesman-Nguni Coalition performed a cleansing and re-dedication ceremony. A month later, Iziko's education and public programmes department – in collaboration with curator Kara Blackmore, artistic director Mandla Mbothwe and the Institute for Creative Arts at UCT – organised an interactive artistic intervention. They asked the audience to join in transforming and decolonising the static displays into "a collectively lived memory". The intervention, argued the curatorial team, aimed to recast the objects in the gallery as "evidence of colonial crimes" that required "decolonial investigation".[17]

Lohman initiated "legacy projects" for the collections and it gave me an opportunity of once again addressing the lack of space at the gallery, which was becoming more critical and untenable. I revised earlier documents for a contemporary art centre, but nothing came of it. In 2002 I worked with fifth-year architecture students at UCT as part of their simulated office team to design such a building. The team engaged the members of the curatorial staff, who provided input in what their respective departments required, as well as various administrative staff. Another key consideration was the need to speak to a wider public in the hope of demystifying "to ordinary people what art was all about," as participant Vanessa September put it:

> The SANG had already by then acquired a huge collection of contemporary works that it was obliged to exhibit alongside all the more staid and older artworks from the nineteenth century. The newer and younger artists who were creating more dynamic artworks would have a place that was equally young and dynamic to present their works to a wider audience.[18]

Drawing on these insights and the many conversations a vision was developed to, in September's words, "create a 'spectacle' amongst the cluster of neo-classical buildings on the SANG perimeter":

> … we proposed what we thought was a very lovely space that located the building in relation to the gardens, the mountain, and the surrounding built fabric; that took account of the movement of people to and through the gardens and the public facilities; that created links to the existing SANG building and allowed for seamless movement of staff, visitors and artworks; that used the natural light in a diversity of spaces whilst being cautious to shield the works from direct sunlight; that allowed for facilities like a café and rest spaces that could be used for a multitude of other functions even when the gallery was closed; and that provided a chance for the visitor to have an engaging experience.

For me personally, I envisaged that the design project could form the basis for a competition brief and fundraising drive, but it was overshadowed by the demands of the social and natural history collections, which Iziko management prioritised at the expense of the national art museum.[19] As the following chapters show, the consequences of this have been dire.

A spectre from the past returns to haunt the national art museum

AFTER ITS AMALGAMATION under the Iziko flagship, all the gallery's collections now belonged to Iziko, which presented opportunities for some within the organisation to resurrect talk of disposing these collections. Curator Hayden Proud revisited this vexed issue in a 2011 article:

> In the debates around the rationalisation of state-funded museums post-1994, surreal ideas of selling off the collection and using the SANG building as an 'international exhibitions venue' were bandied about. The expedient target of such talk was, of course, the supposedly 'irrelevant' art representing the European artistic tradition, as if some kind of mental, historical and financial enema applied to the SANG collection could retrospectively remove all guilt about the institution's colonial origins.[20]

I asked Proud to elaborate on his assertion, and he remembered a conversation in which Lohman and former JAG director Christopher Till discussed income-generation and future directions for the flagship. Although the conversation was speculative, Proud deduced that "logically implicit in this was the idea that the collection should be sold off as well".[21] In correspondence to me Lohman acknowledged that "selling off works from SANG was something that some members of the board often threw out there but were never followed up in meaningful conversations with outsiders to my knowledge".[22] He recalled talking with Themba Wakashe, the deputy director-general for heritage, archives and libraries at DACST, and council chairperson Colin Jones while exploring strategy options, but neither his interlocutors believed selling anything was an option. "They somehow respected the historic integrity of the SANG collection," stated Lohman and added: "No director or CEO wanting a future would ever have considered such an option."

Till recalled this conversation too, but not the details of what he described as an "abstract discussion" on how to secure private funding in the absence of government support, at national, provincial and municipal levels.[23] He had recently been appointed director of culture for the city of Johannesburg and he was assessing the sustainability of JAG and Museum Africa. Till affirmed that under no circumstances would he have either contemplated or advised selling off public collections.

I share these communications in the context of what had happened in the early years of the new century. Lohman left Iziko in August 2002 for a position at the Museum of London. I have a vivid memory of a call I received in February 2003 from his successor, Henry Charles "Jatti" Bredekamp, who was enquiring about an arrangement the gallery had with the London-based auction house Bonhams regarding the valuation, deaccessioning and potential sale of paintings from Iziko's collections. Bredekamp was reacting to a letter from Bonhams. I had no knowledge of such an arrangement. I only became acquainted with the full extent of the back-story to Bredekamp's call during my research towards this book. It goes as follows.

In 2001, the Old Town House was closed for refurbishment, particularly of its foyer, which Bonhams had agreed to sponsor following a request from Lohman. This reliance on private donors was not unusual. The OTH's ground floor air-conditioning was installed with a grant from the government of the Netherlands, in collaboration with Iziko property services and development, Department of Public Works (DPW) and the Friends of the Michaelis Collection. We were understandably delighted. In my contribution to the Iziko *Annual Report* (2002–2003), I wrote that "with this substantial investment the museum has been placed firmly on the road to excellence".[24]

In May 2017 I approached Lohman for clarification on his relationship with Bonhams, which in 2002 had merged with rival auction house Phillips. Concerned about the security of the Michaelis Collection and keen to get money for renovations, Lohman had asked Phillips about "valuing" the collection. "I had no intention of proposing to the board that we contemplate a sale but that we engage with Phillips in conversations," said Lohman.[25] He pointed to the new glass lobby as a tangible outcome of these discussions. The narrative captured in correspondence in the Iziko archive, however, reveals a different truth.

On 21 June 2001, Lohman sent a letter and draft proposal to Georgina Lawrence, Phillips' representative in the Western Cape.[26] In the first part of the proposed agreement Lohman outlined his vision for the Michaelis Collection, the refurbishment of the building and a framework for its implementation. He also defined a working relationship between Iziko Museums and Phillips: in return for the donation of £15,000 there would be "a full understanding" that in the event of any deaccessioning at Iziko Museums, Phillips would be "the sole auctioneer". It was additionally proposed that if the sum fell short of the project need, Iziko Museums would seek from Phillips a further amount up to £5,000 to complete the project.

In the second part of the draft agreement Lohman detailed the benefits for Phillips of this arrangement: the auction house would receive recognition as patron of the collection, with their name featured in the entrance and in printed material, special viewing privileges for their VIPs and free valuation days. But first and foremost, Phillips would be "the sole conduit for deaccessioned objects" within Iziko; a caveat demanded "total discretion" by the parties involved. Lohman further stated in his letter that a policy on deaccessioning was being prepared "under the auspices of the museum council" to address "areas of the collections which can be deaccessioned *across all fifteen national museums over the next five years* [my italics]". A list of the fifteen Iziko museums followed. There is no record in the 2001 minute books that the matter was formally brought before council. The chairperson was, however, integral to the plot.

After Lohman's departure in 2002 nothing further happened until Bredekamp met with Lynn Rowand, the Johannesburg representative of newly rebranded Bonhams. This was followed by correspondence from her and Lawrence in January 2003, which prompted Bredenkamp's call to me.[27] Bredekamp was utterly surprised and confused; he too was in the dark about Lohman's proposed agreement. Both Rowand's and Lawrence's letters were unambiguous in detailing what had transpired and who was involved, although it is not clear to what extent.[28] Lawrence attached the June 2001 draft agreement to her letter and described how Bonhams had been in contact with Lohman for about two years, during which time they "were involved at grass roots level with the planning of the intended deaccessioning". She revisited the donation towards the refurbishment of the OTH, and how, as a quid pro quo, the auction house had been "given the assurance that we would handle the de-accessioning programme".

The discussions towards deaccessioning had been extensive. When Bonhams' international director Paul Whitfield opened the refurbished museum in 2002 he had discussed various practicalities with Lohman, including commission rates. According to Lawrence, Whitfield had indicated that "Bonhams would be prepared to pay a percentage of the estimated proceeds up front prior to sale in order to create liquidity for Iziko" and had offered specialists from London in the various disciplines. In effect, Bonhams were ready to formalise the agreement with Iziko with a letter of intent and a progress schedule. According to Lawrence, Bonhams had been informed (it is not clear by whom) that the project would commence in April 2003 following the appointment of a new council. She referred to the "delicate nature" of the negotiations and listed the names of the "various people involved in the discussions". They included the council's chair Colin Jones, former arts and culture minister Ben Ngubane, Dr. B.O. Tema, who was chief director of public science and international liaison at the newly constituted DAC, as well as DAC functionary Vusi Ndima.[29] Lawrence's letter was faxed to all the names mentioned, as well as to council member Karin Skawran. Their responses are not recorded.

Following my conversation with Bredekamp, I registered my shock and surprise in writing. I referred him to two telephone calls in which Lohman had discussed deaccessioning with me, and my firm opposition to this proposal. I requested an urgent meeting of the directing team and expressed concern that we were working on another project with Bonhams.[30]

Rowand's letter served before council at the meetings of 20 and 21 February 2003. Jones was in the chair, but the minutes recorded that council members were unaware of the proposal to deaccession and that they, and the directors, dissociated themselves from the contents of the letter. Individual items had been deaccessioned in the past, but there was no intention of doing so on a large scale in future. It was agreed that Lohman be contacted for an explanation, and human resources director Denise Crous draw up a deaccession policy.[31] The latter request was indicative of how out of touch the council was with its own structures and policies: it is not the task of human resources to draft collection policies. As it stood, a council-approved policy already existed. Adapted from an older SANG policy, it offered specific guidelines on de-accessioning. It acknowledged that museums hold collections "in public trust with an expectation of permanency and there is an ethical case against de-accessioning, except under special circumstance". Further, it clearly stated that no object in the permanent collection could be deaccessioned without the permission of the council and subsequent approval by the minister of arts and culture.[32] These provisions dovetailed with the Cultural Institutions Act of 1998, which clearly stipulates that ministerial approval is required "to alienate any specimen, collection or other movable property".[33]

Although such a decision is not minuted, Bredekamp informed Rowand that council would refer the matter to Ngubane "for further guidance".[34] A meeting with the minister was followed with a letter headed, "Bonhams Johannesburg: de-accessing of some Iziko museums and warehouses".[35] This was an extraordinary move on Bredekamp's part. Why turn to the person with whom Lohman, Jones and Tema might have colluded in order to secure ministerial approval? After all, Lawrence named Ngubane as one of the individuals who was party to the discussions.

There are three letters on record acknowledging Bredekamp's correspondence, but it took three months for DAC's legal services to respond. In the absence of legal opinion and faced with meeting a delegation from Bonhams, Bredekamp acted unilaterally. "After a prolonged discussion on the matter we came to a good understanding that Bonhams would not pursue any legal action but rather seek ways and means for further cooperation with Iziko on the art landscape," he wrote in a letter to Ngubane. "Iziko has thus succeeded in putting the matter to rest."[36] In this same letter Bredekamp criticised the advice he received from DAC's legal services as "nothing more" than quoted extracts from the Cultural Institutions Act PFMA of 1999, "with which we should be relatively familiar". Quite clearly neither the CEO nor council had taken these into account in the first place.

In hindsight, it is frightening to think that for two years art collections staff and I had performed our duties unaware of the institutional malaise and real risk of deaccessioning. It was a risk brought about by a group of individuals who, while accorded the privilege and authority to safeguard and protect our national patrimony, had wilfully chosen to ignore legislation of their own making. As the next chapter will show, vigilance is required at all times.

In his book *Museums at the Crossroads?* (2013), Lohman recounts the traumatic nature of his last day in Cape Town, when he was involved in a car accident en route to the airport:

> My luggage, containing not only my personal effects but my collection of mementos and much treasured laptop were, in an instant, destroyed. I had lost three years of work and writing. My close friend and chairman of the board of Iziko, Colin Jones, collected me from the site of the accident. As we sat lamenting the broken pieces of my life in South Africa, strewn alongside the highway, he pulled from the debris a note to me from President Thabo Mbeki thanking me for my work. Mr Mbeki had been the first president of the new South Africa to set foot in the old South African Museum and had written on the occasion of his visit: 'The discovery of our past is a journey to a more human future. Your valuable work gives us the possibility to do both.'[37]

Mbeki had gone to SAM to see the diorama and the note was a response to his visit. It has accompanied Lohman on his travels, "a daily syrup of immense personal meaning reminding me of the mission driving my work".[38]

While interviews for the CEO position were conducted, the directors of natural history and central services, Anusya Chinsamy-Turan and Faeza Allie respectively, jointly served as CEOs.[39] Jatti Bredekamp was appointed, and in their message in the 2002–03 *Annual Report*, he and chairperson Colin Jones wrote: "In this, the beginning of the African century, it seems fitting that a son of this soil has been chosen to lead an organization that holds so much of our nation's heritage in trust for posterity."[40]

The professionalisation of SANG that started with the appointment of John Paris in 1949 was slowly but systematically compromised by bureaucratisation, in part due to DAC requirements, but also in service of Iziko executive management's wish to centralise power and control. A new management structure and reporting system implemented in 2005 further created distance between collections directors and council. Reports to council had to now be delivered through the executive directors for collections and operations. The *Annual Reports* changed from offering informative narratives to jargon-rich statements, often in table form, detailing activities, objectives, strategy, outputs, service delivery indicators and performance against target. In the process the main activities and achievements of the core departments, the raison d'être of the museums, were relegated to lists in appendices. The excellent design and many illustrations compensated to some extent for the loss in content.[41] In the absence of an informative newsletter and scholarly art catalogues, an incomplete record of some of the real work being done in art collections is now only discoverable on the Iziko website.

Facing and addressing the financial challenges

IN 2004 THE GALLERY hosted *A Decade of Democracy: South African Art 1994–2004*, a large exhibition curated by Emma Bedford from SANG's collection in celebration of ten years of democracy. Notwithstanding the multitude of gains democracy had brought to the country, South African society was still deeply flawed, its arts and heritage sectors in crisis and the transformation process stalked by official indifference and inadequate funding. I reflected on the gallery's funding situation in the exhibition catalogue:

> It is not so much that the national coffers cannot fund change, but that new initiatives such as Freedom Park ... are receiving vast allocations and are privileged at the expense of what are perceived as elitist, white-dominated, traditional institutions. This thwarts the ideal of a vital, representative national art collection for South Africa.[42]

The dilemma was that the amalgamated museums, although vastly different from one another, were uniformly perceived as untransformed. Yet, at the same time there was an unprecedented interest in South African art generally and SANG's activities more specifically. As described in previous chapters, the national art museum had benefited from the country's entry into the international community and in the essay I affirmed that we were making the most of a whole range of new opportunities:

> The list of exhibitions, loans, exchanges and participation in conferences, seminars and judging panels is long, exciting and far-reaching. We have received and curated major exhibitions, thereby exposing South Africans to works that they may otherwise never have seen and promoting our art nationally and internationally. The profile and influence of SANG has never been greater, and its struggle to fulfil that role has never been more difficult. Since 1990 a whole range of issues, touching directly on how the country and its museums are perceived and its artists – black and white – represented, has come into play. This is partly stimulated by the agendas of a stream of international academics, curators, culture-mongers and gallerists who come looking for inspiration, 'authenticity', 'relevance', art that is demonstrably African or internationalist and conceptualist, and a new market. We have had to learn to

resist cultural neo-colonialism and Eurocentrism, which is difficult considering the funding situation that prevails.[43]

Taking a broader view of the role of the institution in a globalised world, I made a plea for the kind of support that would address unequal access to resources, a strategy to secure South African participation in major biennials and to empower the national art museum to curate and tour major exhibitions:

> We need to seek partnerships on the basis of strength not weakness, as equals not beggars. Only then will South Africans involved in arts and culture be in a position to engage fully and take their place in the world, while doing the work that needs to be done at home. Only then will we be able to confront and interrogate a global system that wants to dominate and homogenise the world.[44]

In reality the core subsidies had not increased since 1994, except for annual adjustments pertaining to salaries. The permanent collection suffered most: between 1984 and 1997 the acquisition budget remained at R200,000 per annum, but between 1997 and 2003 there was no dedicated budget. In the 2003–04 financial year art collections received only R138,000 from the Iziko budget.

The scope and ambition of *A Decade of Democracy*, which is discussed in greater detail in chapter seven, speak clearly of our proactive approach to ameliorating the stagnation of the permanent collection. In 2002 Iziko was invited to bid for a portion of the R6 million transformation money that DAC made available. We motivated for R700,000, which was equally allocated to the repatriation of heritage objects and purchase of work by previously disadvantaged artists. In the subsequent financial year we secured another transformation grant of R850,000 for specific works, including those dealing with HIV/Aids. Money was raised from the National Lottery Board (NLB): R500,000 for repatriation, and the same amount for specific acquisitions. These sources would, however, come to an end for different reasons: special allocations from the department dried up and the excessive applications from other Iziko departments, on which not everyone was able to deliver on time, meant that the NLB door remained firmly closed to us for the rest of my tenure. Furthermore, the National Heritage Council has priorities that somehow exclude art.

There was indeed much for which to be grateful. In my contribution to the *Decade of Democracy* catalogue, I acknowledged artists, the Friends, individuals, gallerists, organisations, trusts, the Tosca Reynolds bequest, the City of Cape Town and corporations that contributed to augmenting the collection.[45] William Kentridge and the Museum of Contemporary Art in San Diego offered a significant gift: the museum auctioned a work by Kentridge and presented an amount of $10,000 for an acquisition, enabling us to acquire Minette Vári's video installation *Chimera (The Black Version)* (2001) and Tracey Rose's digital print *Lolita* (2001). Subsequently art collections received a donation of R102,945 from the Museum of Contemporary Art, Los Angeles, comprising 50% of the proceeds from the sale of a work donated by Kentridge; this amount was added to the acquisitions budget.[46]

FIGURE 26: rosenclaire, sketch submitted for the public art competition, 2004; courtesy of the artists.

Other artists were also generous and presented the following works between 2000 and 2008: Matts Leiderstam, *The Power and Pleasure of Breeding* (oil on canvas, 1999) (Fig. 41); Louis Maqhubela, *Inyoka*, (oil on canvas, 2002); Nicolaas Maritz, *Penis Valentine II* and *V* (enamel on glass, 2007); Santu Mofokeng, six photographs added to the four purchased (1996–2000); Malcolm Payne, *Rorschach Test* (screenprint on four geological survey maps, 1999); Martha Rosler, *Semiotics of the kitchen* (video, 1975); Ian van Coller, digital prints from the series *Rickshaw Boys (Suite of five)* (2000) and *Interior Relations* (2007); and Ed West, *Casting Shadows* (digital print, 1999). Struan Robertson entrusted his archive of negatives and silver prints to the gallery.

As part of a performance curated by art lecturer Andrew Lamprecht at a Michaelis School fundraising auction in 2002, I bid on Edward Young's *Bruce Gordon* (Found Object [Concept]) (2002), which saw the artist offer the owner of a well-known nightspot as a work. I was outbid by arts writer and curator Suzy Bell, who was prepared to pay R52,000 for Bruce Gordon; she immediately gifted her purchase to the gallery. Fortunately we managed to get this unusual work through the acquisitions committee and council, and an acquisition number (03/02) was duly tattooed on Gordon's arm at a special event presided over by artist Penny Siopis. The sale was national news.[47]

We successfully applied for R370,000 from the Lottery for a major national public art commission, which was conducted between May 2003 and March 2004. The primary objectives were to enliven and enhance the area in front of the gallery, to replace the unsightly tarmac with an artist's design in brick, and to encourage participants to break boundaries concerning what public art could be and mean in South Africa. The commission was meant to herald a much greater intervention, through art, in the Company's Garden and serve as a mechanism for generating new ideas and partnerships. The sharing and transfer of skills were integral to the process and collaborative entries were encouraged.

The entries of six finalists were exhibited and the public invited to comment; an adjudication panel selected four finalists to develop their proposals in digital and/or maquette form.[48] In the end the main award went to Matthew Hindley's text-based soundscape *Speak naturally and continuously* (2004), an LED display installed on the front façade of the gallery. He empowered two young artists, Vuyisa Nyamende and Lebohang Tlali, in the creative application of new technologies. Claire Gavronsky and Rose Shakinovsky (working together as rosenclaire) and Mark O'Donovan received commendations for their entries that were very different but equally innovative (Fig. 26).

Rosenclaire's *Soap Boxes* (2004) was the first of the four projects to be completed and was launched on 6 April 2005 with an evening of performances. Their work had a strong theoretical basis in the Duchampian question of what art is if it denies the hand of the artist and is neither sculpture nor painting.

FIGURE 27: rosenclaire, *Soap Boxes*, bronze, surveillance camera, plasma screen, ginkgo biloba trees, featuring Masai warrior Miyere Miyandazi who stood on the work for long stretches to raise awareness of his people in Kenya; image courtesy of the artists.

At the same time the bronze "soap boxes", surveillance camera and plasma screen inside the building invited public debate, performance, protests and exhibitions – it was one of the first participatory politicised public works dealing with themes that remain prominent fourteen years later (Fig. 27). In time the shade of the three ginkgo biloba trees will provide opportunities for togetherness and conversation. O'Donovan worked with Lawrence Manyakama and Ncebile Mabilokasi, as well as other artists, to build *Lion chasing a man* (2004), a giant moving sculpture. Made from a variety of media and modelled on mobile toys well known to South Africa, the work was activated by turnstile mechanisms. Roger van Wyk won the commission to design and realise the brick paving.[49]

There were other exciting developments. In 2000 South African-born painter Marlene Dumas generously allocated an award from the Stichtung Prins Bernard Cultuurfonds in the Netherlands to the art museum. Re-interpreting the Invited Artist Programme, Bedford devised the Fresh project (2000–03) whereby the museum hosted seven young South African artists – Dorothee Kreutzveldt, Moshekwa Langa, Senzeni Marasela, Robin Rhode, Tracey Rose, Berni Searle and Usha Seejarim – for month-long residencies, with studio and exhibition space in the gallery and a stipend while in Cape Town. Each artist received a catalogue, edited by Bedford and including an essay by a writer of the artist's choice, providing an additional significant platform for the artists. In a review of the project, art historian Liese van der Watt concluded:

> All in all Fresh introduces the public to refreshing art with both visual documentation and verbal interpretations. This is a wonderful project, with a wonderfully tangible product, a box set of seven slim volumes that will be invaluable in art libraries and will complement the field of contemporary art which is only now becoming more accessible."[50]

Information technology company IBM and the State Hermitage Museum in St. Petersburg entered into a multi-year partnership to make the priceless collections available to museums throughout the world, and installed a touch-screen kiosk at the gallery. By 2003 IBM had digitised 3,000 of this great Russian museum's holdings of three million works of art. Visitors to SANG had virtual access to the Hermitage's digital collection. IBM also provided an additional computer to be used for internet art and public access to the database. Nearly three decades after his scale-model airplane Concord was acquired by the gallery in 1986, Pretoria artist Titus Thabiso Matiyane was commissioned to create *Panorama of Cape Town* (2007), a large-scale drawing in mixed media on paper.

FIGURE 28: *Musuku: Golden Links with our Past,* 2000, installation featuring the wall built by Venda builders according to ancient traditions, and incorporating the Venda royal chevron snake-pattern; photographer Kathy Grundlingh.

Temporary exhibitions at home, and to and from abroad

ONE OF THE MOST complex and significant exhibitions in the history of the national art museum was *Musuku: Golden Links with our Past*, which was opened on Heritage Day in 2000 by His Royal Highness King Tshivhase of Venda. The collaborative project was the outcome of lengthy negotiations with the University of Pretoria (custodians of the Mapungubwe Archaeological Collection of metal, ceramics and beads), as well as Venda and Shangaan communities from South Africa's far northern provinces. It was sponsored by Anglogold, represented by Christopher Till and Sarah DaAvanzo.[51] The King and Venda people were consulted every step of the complex way, and among the 300 people who travelled to the opening from the Northern Province were musicians and Tshikona dancers, who enthralled those present with unfamiliar sounds and movements; there were sacred offerings to the ancestors.

Musuku celebrated the art and culture of a major trading empire situated along the Limpopo River and the north-eastern reaches of southern Africa. Gold (musuku in the Luvenda language) was panned from the Shashe and Limpopo rivers by the Vhavenda and their ancestors, who acquired significant knowledge working and trading gold. The inhabitants of sites known as Bambandyanalo and Mapungubwe (c. 850–1250), Great Zimbabwe (c. 1300–1750) and Thulamela (c. 1350–1750) built and inhabited intricate stone-walled settlements, and as the dates indicate, this did not necessarily happen simultaneously. The rulers of Mapungubwe lived in stone buildings located on a hill, while the rest of the population occupied adobe homes below. They crafted exquisite objects from gold and other metals, including ivory, stone and clay, and also imported luxury items such as glass beads, silk cloth and glazed ceramics from as far as Egypt and China.

Curated by Carol Kaufmann and Irene Mafune, the exhibition offered the public, for the first time, an opportunity of viewing a selection of this unique aesthetic production found in the royal burial sites. Included were clay figurines, earthenware bowls, a ceramic spouted vessel, tenth-century Oriental porcelain from China and the only original anthropomorphic soapstone bird from Great Zimbabwe in South Africa, held in the Groote Schuur Collection. The original golden rhinoceros from Mapungubwe, which was declared a national treasure in 1997, was shown with other objects in gold, including a bowl, sceptre, half moon and spiral plates, beads and anklets. When it was subsequently exhibited at the British Museum in the exhibition *South Africa: The Art of a Nation* (2016), this petit gold rhinoceros, made of many components of thinly beaten gold foil originally pinned to a carved wooden base with gold tacks, was heralded as the star of the show.[52]

Installing this precious heritage beautifully and securely presented many design challenges and the staff worked with Kruger Roos Architects and designer Gary Kinsman. Venda builders, who still worked in the ancient traditions, travelled to Cape Town and created a wall that incorporated the royal chevron snake-pattern (Fig. 28). Thanks to the cooperation of theatre designer at Artscape, Peter Cazalet, a large draped black cloth brought down the ceiling of the gallery space to create greater drama and intimacy. In a review in *Die Burger* (23 November 2000), Wilhelm Grütter commended the team for the scientific, multi-disciplinary approach that succeeded superbly in merging aesthetics with the practical demands of archaeology, geology, anthropology and writing history. Commenting on the stone walls and low lighting he described the effect as breathtaking and almost magical.

Anthropologist and academic David Brokensha reviewed the exhibition for *African Arts*:

> The exhibition was valuable both historically, in clarifying the record, and aesthetically, in demonstrating the high quality of the delicate works in gold, ivory and other media. It also was a model of how to involve not only academic specialists but all those concerned, especially those who, like the Venda, were often excluded in the past.[53]

The only two sites where the gold rhinoceroses (feline and bovine) are on permanent display – in the context of other contextual objects – is at the Mapungubwe Museum, University of Pretoria, and Mapungubwe Interpretation Centre, which is situated in the Mapungubwe National Park on the country's northern border.[54]

Concerned with history of another kind, Nicolaas Vergunst curated the praised and popular 2000–01 exhibition and book *Hoerikwaggo: Images of Table Mountain*, sponsored by the Netherlands Government and the British Council. It comprised old maps, travel books, colonial prints, paintings, photographs, postcards and work by contemporary artists. Vergunst wrote in *Zanazo*: "The iconography presented on this exhibition highlights the palimpsest nature of the mountain as a cultural landscape open to a variety of interpretations, and hopefully illustrates how the imaging of Table Mountain reveals changing relations and contrasting attitudes toward the Cape."[55]

In 2006, after Mtshiza's departure, Gabi Ngcobo was appointed as assistant curator. Ngcobo, the curator of the 10th Berlin Biennale in 2018, worked with artist and lecturer Virginia MacKenny of the Michaelis School on the exhibition *Second to None: Celebrating 50 Years of Women's Struggles*, which commemorated the anniversary of the Women's March to the Union Buildings, Pretoria, in 1956.

We partnered with the Skotnes family to host *Cecil Skotnes: A Private View*. Curated by Pippa Skotnes, the artist's daughter, and Thomas Cartwright, the installation focused on the life and work of this celebrated South African artist. The works on paper, portfolios, artist's books, woodblocks, tapestries, paintings, objects, letters, newspaper clippings and memorabilia were drawn from the Skotnes household and archive, carefully created by his wife, Thelma Skotnes, over a period of fifty years.

Opened in September 2005, *ReVisions: A Narrative of South African Art* showcased an impressive private collection of predominantly black South African artists started in the mid-1980s by Bruce Campbell-Smith. The exhibition was curated by Hayden Proud, who also edited the superb book, *ReVisions: Expanding the Narrative of South African Art* (2006), which includes extensive essays and texts on individual artists.[56]

In 2007 the gallery hosted Marlene Dumas' first solo exhibition in South Africa following her move to the Netherlands more than thirty years before. Sponsored by the Standard Bank Gallery and curated by Bedford, the exhibition, *Marlene Dumas: Intimate Relations,* was opened by David Goldblatt in the presence of more than 700 guests. Comprising some fifty paintings, drawings and prints, as well as personal letters, documents and photographs collected by the artist, the exhibition was in many ways a coup: in late 2008 New York's Museum of Modern Art presented the first major American survey of Dumas' expressive paintings, followed by the Tate Modern in 2015. The works shown in Cape Town were drawn from public and private collections in South Africa and abroad, and included *The Next Generation* (1994-95), a major work presented to SANG by Dumas. The exhibition was accompanied by an illustrated catalogue.[57]

The gallery occasionally hosted award exhibitions. The 2007 *Sasol Wax Art Award* exhibition was a short-lived competition that invited artists resident in South Africa to develop their concepts using wax as part of the process or as a medium in its own right. The beautifully

FIGURE 29: Joe Dolby, *Gerard Sekoto: From the Paris Studio* (Cape Town: Iziko South African National Gallery, 2005), cover.

presented exhibition featured work by Wayne Barker, Walter Oltmann (winner), Usha Seejarim, Andrew Verster and Sue Williamson; Barker challenged the art museum on many levels by installing live bees in the atrium. The Daimler-Chrysler Award (subsequently Mercedes-Benz) for South African art and culture was established in 1999 to give young people their first international exposure. All the visual arts exhibitions were shown at the gallery, as well as the 2007 award for South African architecture, which was won by Cape Town-based Heinrich Wolff, then part of Noero Wolff Architects.[58]

While the national touring exhibitions curated by sister institutions had virtually come to an end, JAG made available retrospective exhibitions of the work of Gladys Mgudlandlu and Dumile Feni, curated by Elza Miles and Prince Mbusi Dube respectively, as well as *Dungamanzi / Stirring Waters: Tsonga and Shangaan art from southern Africa* (2008), curated by Nessa Leibhammer. We also received Jill Addleson's *Cyprian Mpho Shilakoe Revisited* (2007) from the Durban Art Gallery. Publications formed part of all these exhibitions. The annual Standard Bank Young Artist Award touring exhibition is ongoing.

SANG's exhibitions also went on tour. Curator Joe Dolby's *Gerard Sekoto: From the Paris Studio* (2006), which was accompanied by a catalogue, travelled to Durban and Johannesburg (Fig. 29). The exhibition showcased a selection from the archive of over 2,000 items, notably works on paper, which DACST presented to the gallery in 2000. On request from the South African High Commission in Namibia, the exhibition was also installed at the National Gallery of Namibia in Windhoek in March 2008.[59]

Charles O'Brien of Bonhams agreed that the money left over from the foyer refurbishment could be used to restore the wood panelling in the Frans Hals room.[60] The Old Town House was festooned with banners inviting the public, and we were optimistic that the Michaelis Collection was entering an exciting new era. Since the amalgamation, Hayden Proud has been the designated curator for the site and he immediately took charge of rehanging and re-interpreting the collection. We inherited a dedicated group of Friends of the Michaelis, established in 1993, to stimulate interest in the collection and activities of the museum, and to channel financial and active support for its work, including education and conservation.[61] Like FONG, they contribute enormously to the well-being, advancement and profile of the small museum.

Although I was concerned about the potential threat to the collection, we accepted Bonhams' sponsorship – together with support from the French Embassy and IFAS – for *Ballet in Bronze* (2003), an exhibition of exquisite bronze and ivory figurines from a private collection. It formed part of the seventh World Congress on Art Deco, held in 2003 and brought visitors from all over the world to the museum.

Guest curators were integral to the Old Town House's programme. Art historian Michael Godby curated *Is there Still Life? Continuity and Change in South African Still Life Painting* (2007), a comprehensive view and interrogation of the still life genre, which was also shown at the Sanlam Art Gallery in Bellville. The scholarly catalogue offers a lasting contribution to an understanding of this genre.[62] Andrew Lamprecht curated the innovative exhibition *Flip* (2004), which displayed the backs of paintings in the collection. An important informational resource, the reverse side of paintings are of great interest to researchers, collectors and curators. Lamprecht viewed his "curatorial intervention" as a means to "radically transform an existing museum," further adding that the gesture of showing the paintings reversed "forces the viewers

FIGURE 30: Adrian Kohler and Basil Jones (Handspring Puppet Company), *Episodes*, installation; image courtesy of the artists.

to consider what it is that has become the subject of their gaze. The backs of the paintings now take on a different aspect. Three-dimensional features are highlighted and pictures begin to tell a new story".[63]

The Muse of History: Paintings by Helmut Starcke (2005) combined works from the collection with German-born Starcke's own critical and celebratory views on the Golden Age of Netherlandish painting, as well as the Dutch presence at the Cape from 1652. In 2006, the memorial exhibition, *A Woman from Delft: the Art of Marianne Podlashuc 1932–2004*, was devoted to this Dutch-born figurative painter, and *Sacred Cows Make Large Targets* featured original drawings by the political cartoonist Jonathan Shapiro, aka "Zapiro" (Plate 30).

Our international connections and partnerships, travel and projects, both institutional and personal, enabled the gallery to secure major exhibitions from abroad. We were privileged to present the first survey exhibition of William Kentridge in a South African art museum in 2002. Bedford initiated the proposal and collaborated with the artist, the Museum of Contemporary Art, Chicago, the New Museum, New York and the Hirschhorn Museum and Sculpture Garden, Washington, D.C.[64] Opened by Ben Ngubane in the presence of 647 guests, it was the most ambitious and expensive national and international project to date. It also tested Iziko's capacities, revealing strengths and weaknesses in different departments and functions that had been centralised. Concurrent to the Kentridge exhibition, Joe Dolby and Kathy Grundlingh curated the exhibition *Episodes*, which surveyed the work of the Handspring Puppet Company, founded by Basil Jones and Adrian Kohler, and well known for its collaborations with Kentridge (Fig. 30). *K2K (Kentridge to Kids)* in the Annexe Gallery comprised work by various learners who had participated in workshops. Dolby also installed works by Kentridge from the permanent collection at the South African Jewish Museum.

An extraordinary selection of African art assembled between 1916 and 1928 by the Swiss connoisseur Han Coray, and procured by the Völkerkundemuseum in Zürich, was displayed in 2001 under the title *Soul of Africa / Âme d'Afrique*.[65] Ngubane opened the exhibition in June 2001 and Kaufmann organised a programme of events involving local communities from Angola, Ghana, Mali, Mozambique, Nigeria, Tanzania and Zimbabwe. Another project with the Völkerkundemuseum resulted in *Iintsimbi Beadwork from South Africa* (2005), supported by Pro Helvetia,[66] while the concurrent show at the Old Town House, *Synergy: An exhibition of Contemporary Bead Art*, celebrated the collaboration between artists working in urban and rural contexts. Facilitators Jeanetta Blignaut and Elbé Coetsee invited twelve well-known South African artists to create works for transposition into bead art by women from the beading studios Qalo and Mogalakwena Craft Art Foundation.

The gallery hosted two exhibitions from Germany, one from the DaimlerChrysler Collection and another surveying landscape works in the Deutsche Bank Collection. *A Century of Landscapes* (2004) offered visitors a chance to see important German landscape paintings and consider them in the context of a genre that is integral to the history of South African art.[67] Landscape also featured in *Singing the Real* (2007), an exhibition of contemporary Irish art that was curated by Patrick Murphy, director of the Royal Hibernian Academy in Dublin. Murphy selected ten artists, working in contemporary and traditional media, who employed a combination of scientific method and art practice ranging from astrophysics to thermodynamics and from meteorological observation to chemistry and environmental science. Messages about pollution and global warming were subtle, but very much present.[68] The exhibition was the first in a planned exchange between the two institutions, but because of lack of interest and funds in South Africa the reciprocal exhibition did not happen.

Michaelis-trained, United Kingdom-based artist Shelley Sacks presented *Exchange Values* in 2001. The installation was formed by stitched "sheets of skin" from twenty randomly selected boxes of Windward Island bananas. Sacks traced each box back to its origin in the Caribbean and recorded the voices and stories of the growers, thereby suggesting the interconnections between producers and consumers in the global economy and stressing the role of the artist in re-envisioning the world. Also shown at the gallery in 2001 was *Inferno & Paradiso*, an exhibition by Chilean artist, architect and film maker Alfredo Jaar. Organised by the BildMuseet and Riksutstallningar in Sweden, the exhibition dealt with the effects that images of violence have on society and showcased eighteen of the world's most acknowledged photojournalists: each photographer was asked to choose two pictures – their most painful and their most joyful – which were presented as alternating slide projections.

An expanded version of *Positive Lives: Responses to HIV*, first hosted by the gallery in 1995, was opened on International Aids Day, 1 December 2001, by Zackie Achmat, a social activist and chairperson of the Treatment Action Campaign (TAC). At the heart of the exhibition was *A Broken Landscape*, documentary photographer Gideon Mendel's study of HIV/Aids in Africa. For Mendel the status of the art museum and its location near parliament offered an opportunity of creating a radical and stimulating project. For three months the Liberman room provided a "live documentary space", an evolving series of works created by Mendel in collaboration with TAC and people participating in an anti-retroviral programme in Khayelitsha, an outlying suburb of Cape Town.[69] An open letter to President Thabo Mbeki, an Aids-denialist, was integrated into the display but did not generate a presidential response. Far-reaching education programmes, workshops, film screenings and the presence of HIV-positive people as volunteer guides added significantly to the message and impact of the project.

Mendel launched his book *A Broken Landscape: HIV and Aids in Africa* (2001) at the closing ceremony in April 2002. Organised by the TAC and *Mail & Guardian* newspaper, the finissage had all the energy and power of a political rally. Judge Edwin Cameron delivered a hard-hitting and inspiring speech in which he outlined the nature of the crisis of HIV/Aids in South Africa. He also commended Mendel and the gallery:

> This exhibition has been a remarkable event. Its presence here represents a major commitment by SANG to people living with HIV and AIDS. The work on display itself shows deep commitment. What does it mean to say that an artist (or an art gallery) 'shows commitment'? It means that he or she brings not only an engagement to the subject of the display, but an involvement in that it transcends mere observation or representation.[70]

In the 2000s I expanded and deepened my personal commitment to dealing with the HIV/Aids scourge. Unlike Mendel, few visual artists in South Africa had confronted HIV/Aids until they were invited to participate in a 2000 project that I curated for pharmaceutical company Bristol-Myers Squibb and the Harvard AIDS Institute. Together with Chris Howard, then corporate associate of BMS's Secure the Future Art Project, I consulted with a small group of people before commissioning thirty-one artists from five southern African countries to tackle the subject of HIV/Aids.[71] The responses were extraordinary. We exhibited the collection of work at the XIII International AIDS Conference in Durban in 2000, after which it travelled to Washington, D.C., Brussels and Boston. I attended the charity auction at the Harvard AIDS Institute in late 2000, and this in turn opened the door to participating in the conference "Aids and South Africa: The Social Expression of a Pandemic" at Wellesley College. I subsequently worked with economic scholar Kyle Kauffman on exhibitions at Wellesley College, and at SANG.[72]

The author, actor and social activist Pieter-Dirk Uys opened the joint exhibition *AidsArt / South Africa* in November 2003. In his speech he confirmed the political power of art:

> If a political cartoon can rattle the foundations of fascism and a vicious punchline can send the perpetuators of evil running for their reputations, art becomes the ultimate weapon of mass destruction when it comes to the unspoken roar and the silent scream.[73]

AidsArt was the first exhibition at the gallery to go beyond photography. Kauffman and I selected existing work and asked artists to create images, thereby aestheticising a complicated and increasingly political public issue. The results were powerful; once again artists showed that the creative act could engage profound social issues in compelling ways.

Opening on the same day, and running concurrently at the Annexe Gallery, was *Long Life*, comprising life-size body maps, photographs and small paintings created as part of a collaborative participatory research and advocacy project involving Doctors without Borders, the Memory Box Project, Other-Wise Media and the art facilitator Jane Solomon. Life-size body maps told the stories of fourteen courageous Khayelitsha residents (thirteen women and one man) living with HIV or Aids and who, through Doctors without Borders and the Western Cape Province Health Department, had access to treatment. They recorded and shared their experiences by marking the areas where actual wounds held their feelings.

The country was in the deadly grip of Mbeki's Aids denialism, but some brave participants came forward to provide guided tours of their exhibition, to speak about how antiretroviral drugs changed their lives and how art helped them to regain their courage and dreams. All who attended were moved, inspired and humbled. The remarkable self-portrait body maps travelled abroad and a portfolio of prints and a book, *Long Life: Positive HIV Stories* (2003), were published.[74]

Throughout this period we continued our work on HIV/Aids in many ways, through exhibitions, education programmes and acquisitions. We showcased works from the permanent collection, many of which had entered the collection as a result of the commissions funded by Bristol-Meyers Squibb and Wellesley College, or were acquired through the transformation grant.[75] *Embracing HIV/Aids*, which opened in December 2006, drew criticism from some members of the public who felt that such an exhibition was not appropriate for the festive season. It bears noting that in 2007 one thousand people died of Aids-related illnesses every day, so there was little to celebrate, and the national art museum had to fulfil its role as an instrument of social justice.

The works included on *Embracing HIV/Aids* encompassed diverse media – photography, sculpture, drawing, painting, new media – and were metaphors for the range of views and voices in the struggle against HIV/Aids. They revealed a great variety of ideas and approaches to the pandemic, some hard-hitting and didactic, others thoughtful, poignant and enigmatic. Here art merged private and public experiences, and embraced social and activist domains, while transcending perceived and constructed boundaries regarding race, class, creed, gender and sexual orientation.

Outside SANG there was a large and colourful display by the children from the Nekkies Township, near Knysna, where Larry Gurney, a healthcare training professional living with HIV, had founded MADaboutART to fight stigma and empower children and youth through art. Supported by the Friends, they had come to Cape Town on International Aids Day, 1 December, to share their responses to the pandemic with their impressive *The Rainbow of Hope* painting that had been seen at London's Trafalgar Square the year before.

Interest in South African photography was growing apace. Responding to an invitation from the Neuer Berliner Kunstverein, Pam Warne curated *Reality Check: Contemporary South African Photography*, which travelled to four German cities before a selection was shown at SANG in 2008.[76]

In the years following *Miscast* the art museum's team, led by Kaufmann, continued to engage with the art and culture – past and present – of the indigenous people of southern Africa, whose plight and aspirations have to this day not been addressed by the government, in spite of the fact that the motto on the new South African coat of arms is written in the ancient language of the Cape San.[77] *The Moon as Shoe: Drawings of the San* (2003) comprised works from South African collections and was presented in partnership with the Ethnological Museum of the University of Zürich and Pro Helvetia. The exhibition featured the work of six San people, the youngest of whom was seven years old, who had been incarcerated by the authorities in Cape Town. Between 1875 and 1881 they were assigned to the home of linguists and philologists Wilhelm Bleek and Lucy Lloyd to convey their lives, environment and beliefs in pictures.[78]

At the end of the Angolan and Namibian wars of independence (1975 and 1990 respectively) and the South African Border War (1966–89), Catherina Scheepers-Meyer started a cultural project in the Northern Cape to provide therapy for displaced and traumatised San communities. German collector Hella Rabbethge-Schiller, who had inherited a farm near Kimberley in the 1970s, acquired more than 400 works and we showed a large selection of paintings and drawings under the title *Memory and Magic: Contemporary Art of the !Xun & Khwe* (2006).[79]

Even as the national art museum was negatively impacted by the amalgamation, staff at SANG participated – fully and energetically – in the transformation process. Partnerships, collaborations and international exchange flourished far beyond our dreams and expectations. Nonetheless, there was a growing sense that South Africans did not own the narrative around these projects. This detachment is discussed further in the next chapter.

PLATE 31: David Goldblatt, photograph of SANG staff, 1999, commissioned by *Leadership*; in the foreground is Jane Alexander's *Integration Programme: Man with TV*, 1995, plaster, oil, clothing, found objects, video, 1380 × 1000 × 2200; and in the distance Isa Kabini's *Obelisk*, 1994, acrylic on wood, 2750 × 630 × 630; commissioned by SANG. Image courtesy of the David Goldblatt Legacy Trust and Cape Media.

7

Negotiating our place in the world – as equals – and celebrating ten years of democracy

2000 – 2008

THE TIMEFRAME remains the same as in chaper six, but different aspects are discussed. Democratic South Africa continues to offer exciting opportunities for international exchange, but there is a growing realisation that cultural material is not in African hands; also that important debates are not taking place on the continent. At SANG, we begin to negotiate and engage as equal partners in major exhibitions. The permanent collection is promoted at home and abroad, and we celebrate ten years of democracy with a major exhibition of works acquired during that time. Staff contributes to Iziko by working across collections and in different sites, but crucial issues remain unresolved. The chapter concludes with my retirement.

Historically, because ... exhibitions were hosted in either Europe or the United States, the framing of the subject of African art is usually defined, written and determined by Western historians and curators.

CLIVE KELLNER[1]

Taking charge of international projects

THERE ARE NUMEROUS examples at the national art museum, and further afield, of how a democratic South Africa offered exciting new opportunities for international exchange. At SANG we had to be on our guard, as these opportunities often turned out to be flawed due to instutitional poverty. Curator Okwui Enwezor's *The Short Century Independence and Liberation Movements in Africa 1945-1994* was an ambitious project that started its global run at Munich's Museum Villa Stuck in February 2001, and subsequently travelled to Berlin, Chicago and New York. I was among many scholars and writers on the African continent who contributed to the catalogue. SANG also loaned works, including Jane Alexander's *Butcher Boys* (1985–86). We were sensitive to criticisms that the local public was seldom if ever exposed to major travelling shows of South African art curated abroad and enquired about hosting *The Short Century*, even if not in its entirety. It would have been possible, but the expenses were prohibitive. In 2003 artist Kendell Geers asked:

> Why is it that the Kentridge retrospective [discussed in chapter six] will visit South Africa last when all the works originated in Houghton? The irony is that if the retrospective had been organised and curated five years ago, by a South African museum, then all the huge fees and royalties for the show would have been paid into a South African museum rather than the other way around.[2]

These matters remain unresolved. In 2014, *The Rise and Fall of Apartheid: Photography and the Bureaucracy of Everyday Life*, an encyclopedic survey of apartheid and photographic practice co-curated by Enwezor and South African art historian Rory Bester, was shown at Museum Africa, Johannesburg. Supported and organised by the International Center of Photography in New York, the exhibition featured more than seventy South African photographers and artists and included over 800 images and twenty-seven films. It arrived in Johannesburg after successful runs in New York and London. Reflecting on the exhibition, critic Matthew Partridge rehearsed familiar questions:

> One of the issues is around ownership with the question who has the right to tell a history, to narrate our story being commonly asked. Overarching narratives thus become problematic when these different experiences of the past converge and meet in an exhibition. It's been a question on my mind. Why did an exhibition of photographs about apartheid by South African photographers start in the United States and stop twice in Europe before coming to South African shores? Money, I'm told. Resources. Costs. Funders. Travel and Sustenance. Big names. Curatorial fees.[3]

It is not just South Africans who are proprietary about who tells "our story". The back-story to the blockbuster exhibition *Africa Remix: Contemporary Art of a Continent*, which ended its run at JAG in 2007, is instructive.

Promoted as the largest exhibition of contemporary African art ever seen in Europe, *Africa Remix* was the result of an international collaboration among four countries and institutions: Museum Kunst

Palast in Düsseldorf, Hayward Gallery in London, Centre Georges Pompidou in Paris and Mori Art Museum in Tokyo.[4] In September 2004 curator Jean-Hubert Martin formally requested collaboration from SANG, as the curators wished to bring the show to Africa. Unlike the European museums that had been involved from the start and had curators assigned to the project under the leadership of Paris-based curator Simon Njami, SANG, one of the major art museums on the African continent, was only contacted weeks *after* the exhibition opened in Düsseldorf in July 2004. The nature of the proposed "collaboration" was simple: accept the show, in an edited form.

Notwithstanding our lack of resources it was a desirable project. We requested a budget and suggested that a selection be made that would be appropriate for the gallery's spaces and audiences. There was, however, no response. In February 2005, I informed Jean-Hubert Martin that we were no longer interested in the show. The exhibition went to JAG. Writing in the South African catalogue for *Africa Remix*, JAG's chief curator Clive Kellner observed:

> Historically, because similar exhibitions were hosted in either Europe or the United States, the framing of the subject of African art is usually defined, written and determined by western historians and curators. The ability to control the content and the way it is translated and ultimately perceived is not in the hands of Africans. Similarly, debates surrounding such exhibitions and the discourses of African art should be taking place in Africa and not only in the international centres where the exhibitions are held.[5]

While the exhibition was welcomed by many, it was, in my view, a missed opportunity for constructive engagement – from the inception of the project – between theorists and practitioners, between Europe and Africa. Njami described the show as "an interrogation", but on whose terms and for whose benefit?

Fortunately there were a number of excellent examples of international exchange that involved equal partnerships. In 2004 Bedford and I co-curated the exhibition *Tremor: Contemporary Art from South Africa* with Fabienne Dumont for the Palais des Beaux-Arts de Charleroi in Belgium.[6] I worked with assistant curator Zola Mtshiza[7] and Pam Allara, then associate professor of art history at Brandeis University in Massachusetts on *Coexistence: Contemporary Cultural Production in South Africa* (2003) for the Rose Art Museum at Brandeis; it was subsequently shown at the gallery. On her first visit to the country in 1997 Allara was "impressed with the commitment many artists demonstrated to active engagement with political and social problems resulting from the legacy of apartheid". With the support of her university she initiated *Coexistence*, which – in tandem with the catalogue – would embrace the many levels of creative production in the country in the new millennium.[8] The catalogue featured contributions by Rose Art Museum director Joseph D. Ketner and South Africans Kim Berman, Julia Charlton, Thembinkosi Goniwe, Steven Sack and Brenda Schmahmann, as well as Simon Njami. William Kentridge, in town for a lecture at Harvard University, went to see the show and created an amazing, torn-paper *Shadow Procession* for the museum's staircase.

The curatorial premise for *Coexistence* was simple: the arts were making a significant contribution to social transformation in South Africa. During the apartheid years politically-concerned artists working in the western tradition, the majority of them white, raised individual voices in protest through their powerful "resistance art"; after 1994 some engaged collectively to contribute to poverty alleviation and awareness of HIV/Aids. In the process, artist-initiated projects harnessed the untapped creative voices of some of the most disadvantaged of the country's citizens. The exhibition was reviewed by *New York Times* art critic Holland Cotter (25 April, 2003). After registering the general complaint that "too many exhibitions of African art are still conceived along simplistic, introductory-level lines, coasting on the reliable allure of charismatic objects rather than venturing fresh, stimulating and possible challenging ideas," Cotter singled out works by Willem Boshoff, Thembinkosi Goniwe, Moshekwa Langa, Given Makhubela, Christina Nkuna, Johannes Mashego Segogela and the Siyazama Project.

Cotter heaped particular praise on two sculptures: Walter Oltmann's *Larva Suit*, which he described "an outlandish fantasy of neo-colonialist body armor hand-woven from industrial wire in a traditional South African basketry technique," and a wooden figure by Johannes Maswanganyi. The latter work had been commissioned by a traditional healer and was "spiritually active," but, as Cotter observed, "the fact that Maswanganyi makes identical sculptures for the tourist market neatly throws western notions of authenticity, based on a perceived convergence of form and function, to the winds". This convergence, he concluded, was one of the strengths of the exhibition: "By bringing together traditional art and conceptual art, high art and tourist art, black art and white art, it scrambles easy distinctions and complicates the definition of 'South African art' in ways that other surveys too seldom do."

FIGURE 31: Remix Company, choreographed by Jay Pather, performs *Dancing with Shadows*, in response to the exhibition *Invoice: Photographs by Santu Mofokeng*, 2007; photographer Pam Warne.

In 2007 SANG hosted *Invoice: Photographs by Santu Mofokeng,* which coincided with the fiftieth birthday of one of South Africa's foremost photographers. It included images from virtually all Mofokeng's major bodies of work produced in the period between 1982 and 2006. Choreographer Jay Pather and the Remix Dance Project presented *Dancing with Shadows* in response to Mofokeng's photographs; it was a moving experience for all present (Fig. 31).[9] Originating in a partnership between Autograph ABP in London and the gallery, with the support of Standard Bank Gallery and Gallery MOMO in Johannesburg, Mofokeng's exhibition travelled to Johannesburg, Kimberley and Durban.

Touring exhibitions to sister institutions was for many decades a standard practice, but this soon became a thing of the past. Mofokeng's *Invoice* offers a useful case study of the financial uncertainty that now grips South African art museums. Notwithstanding the excellent infrastructure for the arts – art museums, commercial art galleries, a flourishing market, art fairs, auction houses and major shows – South Africa has been unable to sustain major art events such as the Johannesburg Biennale and the Cape Africa Platform. Putting together *Invoice* and travelling it brings this context in perspective.

By May 2006 a number of role players and potential funders agreed to support *Invoice*, but no money was forthcoming and it took extraordinary focus and energy from Pam Warne and me, along with the active participation of Mofokeng, to prepare the exhibition for its December 2007 opening. In addition to Johannesburg, Kimberley and Durban, other venues were considered, but once the (modest) financial implications became clear various institutions pulled out – they could just not afford it. The experience was exhausting, but also inspiring and rewarding. *Invoice* was a superb exhibition, an example of true reciprocity and equality in exchange. In a small coup, SANG was invited to organise Mofokeng's first solo exhibition in the United Kingdom, which was hosted by Autograph ABP, London, in 2009.

A high point in the history of the institution (and for me personally) was the exhibition *Picasso and Africa* (2006). Since 1990 there had been a constant stream of exhibitions of African art from European museums, as well as exhibitions by international masters such as Marc Chagall and Joseph Beuys, to mention a few. The difference with *Picasso and Africa* was that SANG was not at the receiving end of a show curated elsewhere; rather, the exhibition involved fully-fledged partnerships with the National Museums of France, Picasso Museum and Standard Bank Gallery.[10] Planning for the exhibition took three years. Negotiations were conducted in English and French, across great distances. It involved grappling with distinctive organisational cultures and politics, as well as understanding cultural differences and different ways of working in South Africa and France.[11] It required commitment, resilience and huge financial and logistical support to bring eighty-one works by Picasso to South Africa, as well as to organise loans of African art from a number of South African collections.[12]

I co-curated the *Picasso and Africa* exhibition with Laurence Madeline, who then worked at the Picasso Museum. We also co-edited the book, which included essays by the curators, African art scholar Peter Stepan and poet and administrator Wally Serote. Artist Peter Clarke contributed the poem *Guernica*. We reprinted Léopold Sédar Senghor's address ("Picasso en Nigritie"), which he produced for the opening of Picasso's exhibition in Dakar, Senegal, in April 1972.[13] Dolby assisted throughout the process and Kaufmann played an important role in the selection and sourcing of the African works, as well as their installation. All the gallery's staff had the experience of working with international museums, collection managers and curators as equals. They shared and learnt a great deal. While the exhibition originated at the gallery, it involved just about every Iziko department and many individuals, and it was enthusiastically embraced by council and the CEO, who in his end-of-year report described *Picasso and Africa* as "the Iziko exhibition that overshadowed all others on the calendar".[14] It confirmed that internal institutional cooperation was possible.

The exhibition opened at the Standard Bank Gallery in February 2006, where it ran for a month before opening in Cape Town in April, for a another month-long run. (Figs. 32 & 33) It was presented under the auspices of honorary patrons, presidents Thabo Mbeki and Jacques Chirac, and within the ambit of a cultural agreement between South Africa and France, but there was no financial support from DAC. Significant government assistance, however, came from different sources. When two major works proved too big for the domestic cargo aircraft from Johannesburg to Cape Town, teamwork, creative thinking and intervention at the highest levels solved the dilemma. Thanks to the preparedness of Standard Bank to foot the bill, and the cooperation and commitment of the then minister of arts and culture, Pallo Jordan, and the South African Defence Force, the works were delivered by military aircraft, accompanied by the French courier. We also benefited from a huge investment by the DPW in the upgrade of the climate control and security systems in order to comply with the rigorous international standards required.

The Friends organised a fundraising event with the curators ahead of the public opening on 11 April, which was attended by 1,600 people. The exhibition drew a total of 50,656 visitors, including 14,000 learners and people with different disabilities. Visitors even queued in the autumn rain (Fig. 34). *Picasso and Africa* was a resounding success, exposing visitors to the art of Picasso in the context of Africa for the first time. Thanks to the commitment of Standard Bank to the education aspect of the exhibition, Philippa Hobbs developed an excellent resource. A grant from Business Arts South Africa

FIGURE 32: *Picasso and Africa* installation, 2006; photographer Pam Warne.

made possible programmes with the Frank Joubert Art Centre and Sandra Eastwood. Dolby, Kaufmann, Eastwood and Jill Joubert of the WCED installed an exhibition for abled and differently-abled learners in the Annexe Gallery. Arguably the most extensive material for blind and partially sighted learners in the history of the national art museum was made available.[15]

The Friends and the French Institute co-hosted a public seminar. Organised by Jo-Anne Duggan of the Heritage Agency, it offered the general public insights into the background of the exhibition, the logistics involved, the selection process and the curatorial vision. There were excellent presentations, lively panel discussions and engagement with the audience, particularly from Neville Dubow, who delivered the opening address and Judge Dennis Davis, who chaired one of the panels.

Sandile Memela, spokesperson for DAC, kickstarted an intense public debate around cultural appropriation when, in a personal letter to *The Star* newspaper, he accused Picasso of "stealing" from Africa. This generated much publicity, in South Africa as well as abroad, with many columns devoted to the exhibition in newspapers, magazines, including *Art South Africa* which ran a special feature.[16] In certain respects the tenor of the commentary and criticism reflected on needs and desires beyond the remit of the show; in some instances the commentary was meaningless grandstanding. It was not the first time that we bore the brunt of general dissatisfaction with the state of the visual arts and discourse in the country, and the media sideshow affirmed perceptions that some academics, officials and critics simply did not like a success story.

FIGURE 33: *Picasso and Africa* installation, 2006; photographer Pam Warne.

FIGURE 34: *Picasso and Africa* exhibition, queue outside the gallery, April 2006; photographer Pam Warne.

Utilising and promoting the permanent collection at home and further afield

NATIONAL AND international partnerships expanded far beyond expectations and the permanent collection benefited greatly from exposure at home and further afield. The staff and I undertook many trips abroad, as couriers, curators or participants in conferences; we were exposed to the best international practice while at the same time promoting our museums and collections.[17] The lists in the Iziko *Annual Reports* of exhibitions at our sites, as well as requests for loans, are long and impressive. A few are highlighted here.

Angela Zehnder and Hayden Proud managed the preparation and packing of seventy-eight paintings and works on paper for an exhibition *Art from the Cape: Dutch and Flemish masterpieces from the Michaelis Collection in Cape Town* (2003) at the Bonnefanten Museum in Maastricht, the Netherlands. Curated by Rik van Wegen, Kees Schreuder of the Limburg Conservation Institute joined the local team for special conservation treatments and acted as courier. The collection received high-profile exposure in Europe and a restorer from the Institute worked on two paintings in a space accessible to visitors during the exhibition. It was installed at the Old Town House on its return.[18]

We acquired artist Andrew Putter's film installation *Secretly I will love you more* (2007) and exhibited it in the museum. Like painter and Michaelis lecturer Helmut Starcke, Putter also revisited seventeenth-century Cape Town in a work that considered the life of Maria de la Quellerie, Dutch colonial administrator Jan van Riebeeck's wife, albeit in a completely different way. Putter focused on the relationship between her and Krotoa, daughter of one of the Khoi chiefs, who formed part of the Van Riebeeck household as mediator and interpreter.

The Natale Labia Museum paid tribute to English artist Andrew Murray with a collection that was generously donated by Desmond Mcloghlan.[19] Another important project was *Crossing the Divide* (2000), an exhibition of work by artists who studied at the Evangelical Lutheran Church Art and Craft Centre at Rorke's Drift and the Polly Street Art Centre in Johannesburg, curated by Mtshiza. It included works by Azaria Mbatha, Gordon Mbatha, John Muafangejo, Lucky Sibiya and Durant Sihlali, and was designed to accommodate a specific section of the matric art syllabus by providing access to original artworks for teachers and students. Dolby drew from the permanent collection for *Telling Stories* while the future of NLM was being decided. (As discussed in chapter three, the museum was closed and handed over to Count Labia in 2005.)

A comprehensive selection of works from the Abe Bailey Bequest opened at SANG at the beginning of 2001. It featured examples of British sporting art, as well as portraits, landscapes, history paintings and works on paper in a variety of media. Informed by a special catalogue written by Anna Tietze, the exhibition emphasised the benefactor's personality and the story of his success.[20] Thanks to support from the Abe Bailey Trust, Zehnder carried out extensive conservation work.

Proud installed *Old Masters: New Perceptions* (2004) that highlighted new interpretations and acquisitions, particularly the presentation of four nineteenth-century French bronze sculptures presented by Donna Nicholas, as well as conservation work done between 1994 and 2004. A conservation website funded by the Bailey Trust was completed.[21]

Another significant focus on the permanent collection was produced in the form of *ReCollection: 130 Years of Acquiring Art for the Nation (1871-2001).* Kerryn Greenberg, then an Honours student at UCT, now curator of international art at Tate Modern, wrote in a review on *Artthrob*:

> *ReCollection*, by now almost a permanent feature of SANG's entrance room, continues to provide visitors with an impressive overview of the gallery's 130 years of collecting. It is also a highly unusual undertaking considering that public galleries do not normally stage exhibitions revealing their collecting policies. Presented both thematically and chronologically, this exhibition takes the viewer on a journey through the trials, tribulations and achievements associated with collecting art within a restrictive political and economic framework. By taking an honest look at the SANG's turbulent history, Proud bravely acknowledges the collection as a product of this history.[22]

Proud followed this exhibition with *Why collect? New Acquisitions made by the Iziko Art Department 2005–2006*, which thanked and honoured supporters and benefactors while raising questions about funding issues and collecting for the nation. He had been a judge in the competition for the monument to the four Nobel Peace Prize laureates – former President Nelson Mandela, Chief Albert Luthuli, Archbishop Desmond Tutu and former State President F. W. de Klerk – and the exhibition included the V&A Waterfront donation of maquettes by Noria Mabasa.

An important part of Proud's strategy with *Why collect?* was to draw public attention to the measly amount the national gallery was allocated for acquisitions. Even in South African terms the statistics were shocking: Art Collections received R141,000 compared to R280,000 by the NMMAM in Port Elizabeth and R776,966 by the WHAG in Kimberley (in 2005-06, of which 92% was spent on purchasing works by black

PLATE 32: Tracey Rose, *The Kiss*, 2001, lambda print, 1445 × 1435, image courtesy of the artist, the Dan Gunn Gallery, London and the Goodman Gallery, Cape Town and Johannesburg; photographer Pam Warne.

artists). Twenty-six years earlier Raymund van Niekerk was too embarrassed to tell overseas visitors that SANG had R30,000 for acquisitions, opting simply to say "nothing".[23] Proud included details of government expenditure on controversial projects,[24] and further underscored his curatorial concept by installing empty frames with labels featuring information about artists such as John Koenakeefe Mohl and Moses Tladi, whose work had not been acquired and was beyond the reach of the national art museum.

Chris Thurman reported on the situation in *The Weekender* ("National Gallery's pleas for funds fall on deaf ears", first published 7 April 2007, and again on 25 March 2017). He unsuccessfully sought comment from Iziko's CEO and executive core functions director, as well as from the department.[25] Ten years on from 2007 the acquisitions budget was R290,850, but in 2018 a boost in the budget enabled Proud to motivate for and finally fill Mohl's and Tladi's empty frames.[26]

Exhibitions, for instance *Beyond the Material: Conceptual Art from the SANG Permanent Collection* (2002) and *Subject to Change* (2005), profiled many recent acquisitions made with available and extraordinary funds, the latter including works purchased through the DAC transformation fund. *Ernest Cole: Chronicler in the House of Bondage* (2008) showcased a portfolio of photographs acquired at a cost of R288,000 with money raised from the Lottery.

Ten years into democracy it was time to take stock. *A Decade of Democracy: South African Art 1994–2004 from the Permanent Collection of Iziko South African National Gallery* opened in April 2004. Led by Bedford, the exhibition featured works of art made during the first ten years of democracy and acquired by the national art museum. Edited by Bedford, the catalogue contained essays by Rory Bester, Ashraf Jamal, Andrew Lamprecht, Moleleki Frank Ledimo, Zayd Minty, Andries Walter Oliphant and Liese van der Watt, alongside contributions by gallery staff. It offered a rich mix of perspectives.[27] A computer terminal provided access to the art and artists featured on the exhibition and Braille labels were added to selected works. Viewed in the light of the critical shortage of resources, both financial and human, discussed above, this major achievement bore testimony to the creativity, initiative and resilience of the staff.

A Decade of Democracy presented a visual record of the hopes and aspirations, the fears and concerns of South Africans during the years 1994–2004. According to art historian Steven Dubin it also formed part of "a series of warts-and-all exhibitions" that revealed how SANG once operated, why it once did so, and how it had subsequently changed. "This has been a way of putting itself under the microscope for a thorough self-examination," he noted.[28] Dubin offered a considered appraisal of the cover image for the exhibition's catalogue, describing Tracey Rose's *The Kiss* (2001), in which the artist re-enacts Auguste Rodin's *The Kiss* (1888) with Christian Haye, her (black) art dealer from New York, as a "scandalous visual refutation of the classic, Eurocentric orientation" and "a National Party nightmare" (Plate 32).[29]

Reviewing the exhibition, art critic Ivor Powell flipped a question frequently asked of artists, about how well art had served the needs of politics, asking instead how well politics had served art in ten years of democracy? His diagnosis was even-handed:

> The answer is: not very well at all, but about as well as could be expected under the circumstances. Or to put it differently, government's neglect of art in the new South Africa has been relatively benign in its effect – at least on the basis of what was on show at the South African National Gallery's *A Decade of Democracy* exhibition, and equally in the accompanying catalogue. Government might not have done very much constructively, but at least it hasn't interfered too much and art has been allowed, by default, to get about its business.[30]

Powell went on to discuss neglect and bureaucratic obstructionism of the arts, adding that "the arts and culture portfolio in government has regularly been used as a kind of dumping ground for politicians with no better position to go to". Pallo Jordan was, according to Powell, the exception. Powell criticised the opening speech delivered by Ntombazana Botha, then deputy minister, as a recycling of another speech by her predecessor and "about as appropriate to the occasion as a lap dance in a high Catholic mass". He described the deputy minister as ignorant of her context and added that "in many ways she is merely an emblem in this of the way government has approached art in the past decade".[31]

Compared to and in contrast with the speaker's utterances, stated Powell, "what has been achieved by SANG over the past ten years, from one viewpoint at least, is remarkable". He commended the staff and acquisitions committee, donations by artists and fundraising initiatives and described the collection as "genuinely authoritative" in terms of the decade under review:

> It is not only compelling in itself, not only confidently integrated into a global artistic discourse, but also, and maybe most importantly, evocative of both the issues that have dominated cultural discourse in this county, and those that have shaped our developing national psyche and our shifting position within the community of nations.[32]

Powell then developed this statement with reference to specific works and returned to another viewpoint that for him was less successful: an Ndebele beaded apron in a vitrine. Devoid of information about its creation, it was uncomfortable as it could not really be read in the context of discourses of "Art". For

Powell the fact that it could be approached as one would any work of art, in terms of material, colour, line and surface articulation, was not enough.[33] We were aware of the ambiguities and tensions created in the juxtaposition of objects from different collections that have their own histories and requirements, but as curators held to the point of view that they are not immutable and that meaning can be reconstructed in different contexts.

It is inevitable that comparisons would be made between the two major shows at Iziko sites: *A Decade of Democracy* and *Democracy X: Marking the present, representing the past*, mounted by social history at The Castle of Good Hope and led by Rayda Becker, Sandra Klopper and Lalou Meltzer.[34] In her joint review for *African Arts*, Lize van Robbroeck raised fundamental questions around national heritage, archives and the role of visual culture and art in the construction of South African cultural identity since 1994. Her weighty insights are worth quoting at length. Concluding her room-by-room analysis of *Democracy X*, Van Robbroeck noted:

> As any reasonably critical South African will verify, celebrations of the national body as one big, happy family can easily collapse into unconvincing kitsch and obscene sentiment. In this exhibition, however, visual culture is not reductively promoted as a reassuring link between peoples or as a mindless celebration of plurality and multiculturalism. The South African family that is here on view is a fraught one – traumatized by incest, sibling rivalry, divorce, betrayal and domestic violence – but also enriched by an intricate interweaving of languages, values and interests. The emphasis on connectivity and intimacy speaks of a common reciprocal legacy that always succeeded, even in the darkest years of apartheid and colonial history, in bleeding beyond the confines of enforced segregation and a pervasive culturalism that promoted cultures as irreconcilable isolates.[35]

Turning to *A Decade of Democracy*, Van Robbroeck described the exhibition as a showcase of "the redoubtable achievements of SANG in the face of considerable financial adversity":

> SANG's indomitable commitment to the promotion of quality art, despite severe budgetary constraints, is remarkable. The 'decade of democracy' exhibition cannot be evaluated without acknowledgement of the fact that this collection had to be acquired by means of assiduous fund-raising, through bequests and donations, and with a measure of corporate support.[36]

For Van Robbroeck this prestigious collection of contemporary art attested to the relevance of the national art museum in post-apartheid South Africa, both in "the dynamic diversity of the art it represents and in the polemical thematics it addresses". Above all, offered Van Robbroeck, the exhibition confirmed that "South Africa produces artists of high calibre capable of competing with the world's best. These artists need a national institution to support and validate them and to facilitate contact with the global arena."[37] She commented on the authoritative catalogue containing essays that trace major themes in the exhibition, and praised the gallery for the many quality publications produced during the decade under review. Without them, "the teaching and study of contemporary South African art would also be unthinkable".[38]

Fourteen years later, the catalogue was still receiving scholarly attention. In a call for chapters for the book *Public Intellectualism in the Arts and Humanities in South Africa*, editor Chris Broodryk gave examples of public intellectuals and activists, and wrote: "In the arts specifically, the essay collection *A Decade of Democracy* (2004) brings together visual art and public intellectualism."[39] This is praise indeed.

Writing in *Interventions*, a journal of postcolonial studies, education scholar Crain Soudien investigated a number of "key post-apartheid museum initiatives with a view to understanding the character of the new counter-apartheid identity forms they are beginning to generate". His enquiry was aimed at understanding the new and inclusive South African identity that was emerging. "What does it stand for and what are the politics that underpin it?" he wondered. Soudien mentioned new museums, such as the District Six Museum in Cape Town, the Robben Island Museum, the Nelson Mandela National Museum in Mthatha, the Apartheid Museum in Johannesburg and Constitution Hill at the Fort in Johannesburg, and considered and compared "innovative exhibitions" – namely *Democracy X* and *A Decade of Democracy.*[41] His article made reference to two works on SANG's show: Berni Searle's mixed media *Traces (*2000) and Minette Vári's *Chimera* (2001).

Crain observed of *A Decade of Democracy*:

> The tone of the exhibition, in contrast to the high-mindedness of many of the other museums, is at one level playful, but simultaneously deeply provocative. It takes one, in several instances, into the deep interior of life during apartheid. Touching as it does on the ravages of HIV/Aids, the pervasive anxieties of South Africans about crime, and the conundrums posed to both black and white people by boundary-transgressive gay and lesbian identities, the exhibition offered an opportunity for deconstructing the homogeneity of the new South Africa in important kinds of ways.[42]

A Decade of Democracy was followed by two concurrent exhibitions that celebrated traditionalist African art forms, both past and present. Pallo Jordan opened *Ilifa laBantu Heritage of the People* (2005) and *Voice-overs: Wits writings exploring African artworks* in November 2004. The latter comprised works from the Standard Bank Collection of African art housed at Wits, and included the "voice-overs" of people connected to Wits, including artists like Deborah Bell, William Kentridge and Peter Schütz, who chose pieces that had either inspired or were in some way related to their own practice.[43]

In a review and comparison of the two exhibitions, art historian Sandra Klopper compared the way in which the exhibitions complemented and differed from each other. She commented on the "indifferent quality" of some of the works on display because SANG only started actively collecting in these areas in the 1990s, while Standard Bank's collection was initiated in the 1970s: "It is a shocking indictment of publicly funded art institutions that most of them failed to purchase or display traditionalist art forms produced by indigenous communities prior to the unbanning of political organizations in the 1990s."[44]

Ilifa laBantu showcased objects we acquired during the decade 1994-2004 and celebrated the achievements of all involved in the extraordinary journey of acquiring African art that started with Arnott and Bokhorst in the 1960s. In addition to the richness of historical and contemporary southern

African cultural production, purchased locally and repatriated, the exhibition linked the collection to other countries on the continent. The exhibition included textiles and a fantasy coffin from Ghana, an elaborate beaded Yoruba crown from Nigeria, Kuba ceremonial beadwork from the Democratic Republic of Congo and a superb collection of over 250 figurative gold weights made in the late nineteenth or early twentieth century and presented to SANG by David Brokensha in 2001.[45]

Essays were commissioned and a catalogue designed, but unfortunately it was never published. Kaufmann found raising money for the publication difficult.[46] By contrast, it was "effortless" to access funds for the catalogue *Brushing up on Stern* which features work by Irma Stern from the permanent collection, and which Kaufmann collated in 2015.[47] We did, however, have an opportunity of foregrounding the art and social history beadwork collections when I proposed to the South African Post Office Philatelic Services that they feature on the eighth definitive series of stamps (Fig. 35). The stamps, as well as in the commemorative book *The Luminous Beauty of South African Beadwork on Stamps*, were launched in October 2010 at the Third International Philatelic Conference in Johannesburg, and exhibitions of the stamps and beadwork followed at Iziko's Bertram House and the national gallery.[48]

Exciting platforms for showing the permanent collection abroad were negotiated. *Head North: Views from the South African National Gallery Permanent Collection* (2001), marked the first time that a

FIGURE 35: 8th Definitive Series, 2010; image courtesy of Philatelic Services and used with the permission of the South African Post Office.

FIGURE 36: Hayden Proud, ed., *Scratches on the Face Antiquity and contemporaneity in South African works of art from Iziko Museums of Cape Town* (New Delhi and Cape Town: Iziko Museums, 2008), cover.

representative selection of contemporary works drawn from the collection was displayed abroad. It was the result of an international exchange programme titled "Visual Cultures in Dialogue" initiated by the BildMuseet in Umeå, Sweden, with SANG and South African partners Wits University, UWC and the Robben Island Museum. Jan-Erik Lundström and I managed the exhibition and the gallery co-ordinators were Grundlingh, Mtshiza and Voyiya. The project included a comprehensive catalogue, education programmes, seminars, lectures and exhibitions that ran over two years.[49]

A cultural agreement between the governments of India and South Africa resulted in an official museum exchange between SANG and the National Gallery of Modern Art in New Delhi. We hosted *Visual Trajectories: Art from India*, curated by the director, Rajeev Lochan, in 2008. It traced the evolution of the visual arts over a period of 150 years through the confluence of tradition and individual forms of expression and included leading twentieth-century schools as well as neglected artists of the previous century. The exhibition travelled to Durban and Pretoria (Ditsong Museums formed part of the project).

The reciprocal exhibition, *Scratches on the Face Antiquity and Contemporaneity in South African works of art from Iziko Museums of Cape Town* (2007–08), was curated by Hayden Proud and was seen in Mumbai and New Delhi, and subsequently at SANG. Proud and I travelled to New Delhi for the installation and opening by Pallo Jordan. A catalogue was prepared for the tour (Fig. 36).[50] Inspired by Mary Louise Pratt's 1985 essay "Scratches on the Face of the Country; or, What Mr Barrow saw in the Land of the Bushmen", Proud's curatorial concept encompassed the deep antiquity of meaningful mark making on the Blombos Ochre (c. 70,000 BCE), the successive layers of artistry on the Linton Rock panel (eighteenth or nineteenth century) and the way in which colonial, modern and contemporary artists recorded and commented on their times and scars left by colonialism and apartheid. Proud provided detailed contextual and historical analyses of the major works on the show.

The Indian art critic and curator Gayatrini Sinha favourably reviewed the exhibition:

> It suggested a stunning curatorial alternative in our cultural context. For one, it merged material distributed into anthropology, art history or contemporary collections and used it in a different way to posit a palpable feel of 300 years of South African history. For another, it told a story close to the Indian heart: of domination, of the scarring of a nation's psyche and the difficult complex routes to post-colonial freedom.[51]

Among the individual loans that were requested by international museums, were the *Butcher Boys* and twenty-five other works selected by philosopher and curator Pep Subirós for the exhibition *Apartheid: The South African Mirror (*2007) at the Centre de Cultura Contemporània de Barcelona, Spain. The exhibition dealt with apartheid in this country but also with its European legacy. "Apartheid in South Africa can be seen, not only as an extreme manifestation of old, deeply-rooted western racism, but also as a dramatic but clear precedent, metaphor and paradigm of some fundamentally inherent aspects of the current world order," elaborated Subirós.[52]

Behind the scenes and across Iziko collections

AMONG THE MANY loans that are listed in the Iziko *Annual Reports* during this period, several offered a long-term window on the collection in different venues. A fine selection was installed and remains at the Anglo American Farms historic wine farm and manor house, Vergelegen.[53] Works were on loan to Tuynhuys, the High Court and six paintings by Gerard Sekoto to the Constitutional Court. SANG accommodated, supervised and benefited from a range of local and international interns. Research culminated in new information, texts and re-attributions of historical works, updating of the database and information, and a complete revised checklist of the permanent collection with a view to uploading it online. Council ratified the revised and consolidated art collections policy in 2007.[54]

To alleviate space constraints, we agreed – in good faith – to the relocation and consolidation of the historical African art collection in social history. It was a joint project coordinated by Kaufmann, with the support of the Safe House Project volunteers, but in the long run it did not work out for SANG. Kaufmann made this observation, immediately prior to her retirement in March 2016: "The collection remains dispersed in three locations at present and is less accessible than ever before."[55] It has been without a curator since.

National museums have participated in the implementation of the Generally Recognised Accounting Practice (GRAP) required by the national treasury, which meant taking stock and establishing values for the objects in their collections with auditors. But this has not impacted positively, not on storage conditions nor access for the more than 3,000 works in the African art collection at SANG.[56] In answer to my question about the appointment of a curator of African art, Iziko executive director of core functions, Bongani Ndhlovu, replied in March 2017: "All vacant positions will be filled as soon as curators and the team have given their input. Iziko is hoping to have this finalised in the new financial year."[57] By December 2018 no appointment had been made.

Soon after the amalgamation the notion of "silos" within Iziko took root, particularly with top management. It was based on the perception that curators, collection managers and scientists were safeguarding their territories and battling for scarce resources. The structure was partially to blame, because the centralisation of many functions – education, libraries and technical, as well as general assistants, front-of-house and security staff – disrupted the seamless flow and exchange of information

PLATE 33: Sue Williamson, *Messages from the Moat*, 1997, engraved and stencilled glass, printed canvas, found fishing net and water pump, dimensions variable; installation view, Castle of Good Hope, Cape Town, 2004; image courtesy of the artist and Goodman Gallery; photographer Herschel Mair.

and the sense of collegiality and belonging that existed in the individual museums. But the "silos" existed mostly in people's minds – and would turn out to be one of the main considerations when a new management structure was devised and implemented by Iziko in 2016.

It is my hope that this book has affirmed the interest of individuals working at the national art museum in engaging with other disciplines over many decades and making moves to create new conversations. Rather than retreating into a windowless "silo", the amalgamation meant renewed commitment from staff at the gallery to work across the disciplines in Iziko, curating exhibitions, taking care of collections and organising projects, thereby contributing to the integration of functions and the utilisation of material in exciting and innovative ways. Like SANG staff, Lohman was aware of the negative implications of the amalgamation on "a successful gallery with world class exhibitions and openings rivalling anything the Tate was able to do". But he also understood that we would take a leadership role in creating "a sense of ensemble" and proactively supporting unfying projects across the fifteen sites.[58]

To celebrate the coming together of the three major disciplines and collections, I curated *Birds of a Feather* (2001) at the gallery for Heritage Day (24 September). Birds have fascinated scientists, ornithologists, writers and musicians, and have inspired works of art in which they feature as realistic images, objects of beauty and mystery, and symbols of another world. The theme offered a wonderful opportunity to embrace collaboration, to explore Iziko's diverse collections, to imagine unorthodox pairings and to integrate historical, modern and contemporary artworks from South Africa, Africa and Europe in two- and three-dimensions. In addition to paintings, sculpture and works on paper, the premise allowed me to include all manner of functional and decorative objects – ancient Greek silver coins, Chinese and Japanese ceramics, Meissen porcelain, Venetian glass and first-day envelopes from the social history collection. The natural history study skin collection drawers revealed the beauty of small birds and eggs, and large birds were suspended from the ceiling of one of the rooms. Many objects, seldom or never seen by the public, were presented within new and unfamiliar frames and live owls graced the atrium. Jill Joubert, of the Frank Joubert Art and Design Centre, led an education and creative project for learners. Kader Asmal, then education minister, opened an exhibition of the artworks they produced in the Annexe Gallery in December.

Kaufmann was seconded to project manage *IQe-the power of rock art: ancestors, rainmaking and healing* in 2003, a display from SAM's collection that celebrated the cultural and aesthetic production of the San and addressed the problems of the diorama, which had been closed in 2001. In 2009 she curated *The Loom of Life – African Attire from the Iziko Collections and Voices of the Ancestors: Musical Instruments from the Iziko Collections* that featured more than a hundred instruments from south, east and central Africa held in the art and social history collections. Many had not been exhibited before.[59]

I had been inspired by the intimate, domestic scale of the Musée Dapper of African art in Paris, and in 2007 I proposed that Iziko's moribund Bertram House (c. 1839), a Georgian-style red-brick home situated on the Michaelis campus, be designated as a venue for historical African art. Initially the idea of a joint project between art and social history was received with enthusiasm, but in 2008 it was deferred, never to be actioned. At the end of 2018 Bertram House remains closed for "maintenance until further notice".[60]

Our curators mounted exhibitions at other Iziko sites, for instance *Italy: The One and Only. A Century of Photography* (2002) at the Castle of Good Hope and Japanese colour woodcuts from the permanent collection at Rust en Vreugd in the same year. We acquired Sue Williamson's *Messages from the Moat*, first displayed at the 1997 Johannesburg Biennial, and installed it at the Castle of Good Hope in 2004. It was the ideal venue for this monumental work comprising engraved and stencilled glass bottles, printed canvas, found fishing net and a water pump that chronicled the more than 1,500 transactions involving the buying and selling of slaves at the Cape of Good Hope between 1658 and 1700. Williamson engraved each transaction on the side of a bottle (Plate 33).[61]

As one of the consultants (with Neville Dubow) for the artworks in the Cape Town International Convention Centre, I negotiated display windows for all Iziko collections. Mtshiza served on the adjudication panel for the major artworks and Dolby assisted with the acquisition of paintings and works on paper.

SANG was fortunate to have a succession of dedicated individuals who were key role players in all its activities and in liaising within Iziko with the public: publicists Heidi Erdmann and Ashraf Johaardien and administrative assistants Bertha Duncan, Adri Minnaar and Khanyisile Mbongwa.

Baggage and black curators

IN 2003, WHILE we were preparing *A Decade of Democracy* with great enthusiasm, Julie McGee, an academic at Bowdoin University in Brunswick, Maine, and Vuyile Voyiya released a documentary film *The*

Luggage is Still Labeled: Blackness in South African Art.[62] It engendered much controversy and many debates. The film gave voice to black artists, but it pitted black against white, without differentiation and without consideration of the hybrid nature of South African identities. It created the impression that the visual arts sector and its institutions remained untransformed and stuck in the apartheid past nine years after the first democratic elections. This is not the place to analyse the documentary; suffice it to encourage the reader to engage with Mario Pissarra's insights, Dagmawi Woubshet's American perspective and critique, and Michael Godby's response in *Art South Africa* under the rubric "Weighing ... and wanting".[63]

It is, however, useful to briefly set the record straight in certain respects. McGee and Voyiya interviewed me, enabling me to state the case on behalf of the national art museum. The film was initiated by McGee, edited by a sophomore at her university and made for international as much as South African audiences. Voyiya chose not to disclose that he had been a staff member at the gallery since 1991, that he served on the acquisitions committee, that he was involved in curating exhibitions and producing a number of video projects for the institution, nor that he completed his studies at Michaelis while working at the gallery. Together with Grundlingh, he wrote an essay in the 2001 catalogue *Head North: Views from the South African National Gallery Permanent Collection*.[64] In addition to his contribution to the art museum, Voyiya's many activities as an art educator and activist in the community, and his participation in national and international exhibitions as a practising artist, were great assets to SANG, and admired by all.[65]

One of the main criticisms of the film was the poor editing, which Woubshet also raised: "Having seen unedited versions of several interviews, it's unfortunate that artists aren't represented more generously in the final cut, because one discovers, in the unedited versions, how nuanced and different each artist's perspective is."[66] I do not know what Lionel Davis and David Koloane said other than what appears in the film. Both were appointed to the board of trustees in 1996 and were members of the acquisitions committee, together with Jane Taylor (chairperson), Bongi Dhlomo-Mautloa, Jacqueline Nolte, Karin Skawran and staff. Commenting on SANG, Koloane said that art museums were "run by elderly women about to retire" and evoked Madiba, who apparently refused to visit our museums because they were foreign to him. Davis emphasised quality as a criterion for acquisitions, but noted that art museums were influenced by the market. "This is how they buy," he said. Reflections on their time at the art museum, whether positive or negative, would have been more constructive and edifying.

Davis, Koloane and a number of other artists who appear in the film were members of the Thupelo Workshop, but there is no mention of the space that we made available in the Annexe, free of charge to the workshop participants, and the open days held there.[67] Nine of the fifteen artists interviewed were represented in the permanent collection and in the 1995 and 2004 exhibitions that foregrounded acquisitions of contemporary art: Tyrone Appollis, Peter Clarke (honoured with a small retrospective exhibition, *The Hand is the Tool of the Soul*, at the Natale Labia Museum in 1992), Thembinkosi Goniwe, Sipho Hlati, Lallitha Jawahirilal, Koloane, Moshekwa Langa, Berni Searle and Mgcineni Pro Sobopha.

Langa and Searle were part of the Fresh artists' residency programme and publication discussed in chapter six. It is further worth noting that Iziko Museums had a black CEO at the time, and that seven of the eleven council members were black.[68] In addition to the work of the RDP forum that we initiated after 1994, curators had over a long period of time offered support for artists such Billy Mandindi, Vuyisani Mgijima and Sophie Peters; the latter used the Annexe as a temporary work-space.

The Luggage is Still Labeled again raised the vexed question of the absence of black directors and black curators in art museums. While acknowledging this, I would like to draw attention to the limited view that only black curators and directors can make a difference to and transform an institution. Curatorship is seen as somehow superior to other activities and the demographic profile of governing bodies and people working within institutions, as well as collaborators and stake-holders, is ignored. Going back to Raymund van Niekerk's directorship, we are reminded of the appointment of Faeza Allie as the person responsible – together with the director and the board – for the financial well-being of the national art museum. He also appointed Emile Maurice as the first black professional officer. In the years that followed South Africa's racial diversity was increasingly reflected across the institution. As I have repeatedly emphasised from chapter three onwards, staff fulfilling different functions – curators, collection managers, educators, librarians and those responsible for information, publications and publicity – worked together on projects, and served on relevant committees.

Everything changed when Iziko Museums came into being and hierarchies were entrenched in the structure. Prior to 2000, we made every effort to train and appoint black curators. In straitened circumstances, when there was no money for new posts, we had to either wait for somebody to resign or raise money for internships in the hope that a vacancy would occur. A new generation of black fine arts graduates were coming to the fore, but they were not necessarily interested in museum work, which is very different from being an independent curator – it requires in-depth knowledge of art history and of a particular collection, as well as working behind the scenes on documenting, safe-guarding and maintaining the collection, which to some may be boring. Add the meagre salaries, absence of career paths and pervasive bureaucracy in Iziko, and such a position may not be desirable.

While we had some success in attracting black curators, retaining them was another matter. As discussed in the previous chapter, Bongi Bengu terminated her mentorship early because of travel opportunities abroad. A successful application to Standard Bank paid for Mtshiza's internship (1998–2000), he was employed as assistant curator in 2001 but left in that year.[69] Gabi Ngcobo joined the staff but departed to head up research for the Cape Africa Platform and co-curate Cape07. They were employed as assistant curators, which was also criticised, but so was Andrea Lewis, a young white curator, and for good reason – all had the relevant qualifications but no art museum experience, and I still hoped to introduce a career path. Lewis now capably occupies the post of curator of prints and drawings.

Ernestine White took up the temporary position of collections manager on a part time basis in 2003 while working on the Parliamentary Millennium Programme and completing her masters degree at the Michaelis. She reflected on her brief tenure as follows:

> The decision to leave SANG at that time was that I felt that the role was too limiting and did not provide me with the opportunity to engage fully with the collections at SANG and also with artists. I took on the role to see whether the position was indeed suited for me. At the end of the agreed timeframe I knew it was not. I also felt that the kinds of opportunities that I was exposed to in my work at parliament provided me with a broader and richer understanding of how I could utilise my interest and passion in art, exhibition making and project managing to benefit audiences beyond the arts community.[70]

In 2014, having obtained an honours degree in curatorship at the Michaelis, White returned as curator of contemporary art. In 2019 she took up the directorship at the WHAG in Kimberley. After working as collections assistant in social history and gaining experience as an art educator in Iziko, Robyn-Leigh Cedras joined the gallery as collections manager in 2007. She left for the Rupert Museum in Stellenbosch in 2013. Cedras described working at SANG as challenging, chiefly due to financial and staffing constraints and little support from curators (except Warne and Dolby) and some workshop staff. Even though she was part of a "passionate team" and appreciated the opportunities to work with the permanent collection, outside institutions and visiting curators, Cedras was often left to accomplish demanding physical tasks woman-alone.[71]

In 2006 Bedford took the initiative and applied for a DAC transformation grant amounting to R114,000 to mentor a trainee curator in contemporary art. Thembinkosi Goniwe opened a vociferous debate with an open letter to Bedford, posted on the *Asai* website on 29 July 2006.[72] He wondered how many potential candidates "from historically disadvantaged groups" would apply given the requirement of a BA degree in fine art or history of art, and what that would mean for graduates from community-driven initiatives and organisations. Goniwe also had a problem with the terminology, as all black university graduates could not be described as from historically disadvantaged groups.

Bredekamp sent a considered response via email on 1 September, but *Asai* was not given permission to post it online until 16 October. Iziko welcomed the debate and Bredekamp explained that the complex terminology was in line with the department's requirements for the grant. Bedford provided a detailed background to and intentions behind the proposal in a discussion document she presented at the first South African Curators Workshop, organised by the Visual Arts Network of South Africa (VANSA) at the Robben Island Museum in November 2006. She pointed out that all staff in the art collections department had the opportunity to comment on the language and content of the proposal, and that the profession of museum curator demanded tertiary education in the relevant subjects. A trainee without knowledge would be set up for failure.

We received eighteen applications for the traineeship and three were evaluated by a panel: the selection criteria were mainly aimed at identifying the candidate who would best fulfill the demands of contemporary art curating, who demonstrated the greatest commitment to curation and education, and who would stay the course. Loyiso Qanya was appointed for one year and the budget included a salary, further academic study of his choice and a fully-equipped workstation.

As part of the internship programme, Dolby and I curated *Imbacu – Art from the Inside/ Outside* with Qanya in 2007. "Imbacu" means "exile" in Xhosa. Taking the thirtieth anniversary of political activist Stephen Bantu Biko's death at the hands of security police as the point of departure, the selection from the permanent collection focused on the work of artists who were exiled, be it geographically through leaving South Africa, or psychologically by suffering alienation, discrimination, confinement and persecution. The artists included Albert Adams, Ernest Cole, Dumile Feni, Thamsanqa Mnyele and Paul Stopforth, who all left the country. Ronald Harrison stayed, but he was harassed and detained because of his painting *The Black Christ* (1962), which was inspired by the 1960 Sharpeville massacre. It depicts Chief Albert Luthuli as Christ and Prime Minister H. F. Verwoerd and justice minister B. J. Vorster as Roman centurions. Interestingly, given the context of the exhibition, Harrison's work itself went into exile; it was subsequently traced in London in 1997 and acquired by SANG following its repatriation.

Bedford left SANG in 2007 to join the Goodman Gallery Cape. A position was now available, but Qanya was not ready to be appointed as a curator.[73] I made a number of calls across the Atlantic to encourage South African Tumelo Mosaka, then associate curator of exhibitions at the Brooklyn Museum in New York, to apply for the vacant position, but to no avail. He was not willing to relocate and certainly not for the salary on offer. After months in which I was expected to also fulfil the role of curator of contemporary art, Nadja Daehnke joined the institution on contract in 2007. As an artist and part-time lecturer, she had little experience as a curator, but she settled in quickly and showed her organisational skills in every aspect of the work, involving the collections manager and interns in improving storage conditions at the gallery. We entrusted her to take an exhibition of paintings by Gerard Sekoto to Namibia, as well as to represent the institution in Berlin, at the time of discussing issues around *The Tropics: Views from the Middle of the Globe* (2009) exhibition that was on offer to SANG.

Reluctance on the part of Iziko to appoint Daehnke permanently led to the constant renewal of her contract and in 2010 she left to become the curator of the Michaelis Galleries at UCT. Daehnke shared some meaningful encounters, experiences and insights gained with me: the privilege of viewing, researching and touching works in the collection; learning from international curators and collection managers when big exhibitions reached SANG from abroad; the chance to engage with great South African artists. She recalled in particular Marlene Dumas' "warmth with cookies for staff in the kitchen", William Kentridge's "no-nonsense down-to-earth-ness" and Willie Bester's lack of airs and graces when he brought his sculpture to the gallery "on the back of a farm bakkie" (at the time of Bester's solo exhibition in dialogue with his birthplace, Montagu, in the Western Cape). Angela Zehnder "always tried her best to brush us up on etiquette and drilled us in how to create an illusion of perfection", but this was a source of frustration. Iziko's mandate is "to strive for perfection in representing and serving the nation, but the constrained resources and access available to do so" make it unattainable.[74]

FIGURE 37: *Pancho Guedes: An Alternative Modernist* installation, 2008; photographer Pam Warne.

Time to say *au revoir*

MY TIME AS DIRECTOR concluded with two major exhibitions. Another excellent example of international exchange and amazing international and local support was the exhibition of work by architect Pancho Guedes. I regarded architectural exhibitions as an integral part of what should be shown at a national art museum and I wanted to pay tribute to Guedes, a Portuguese-born Mozambican who influenced generations of practitioners as a teacher at Wits, but we did not have the wherewithal to initiate a retrospective. Alerted by his daughter Llonka Guedes about an exhibition commissioned and produced by the Swiss Architecture Museum in Basel, we successfully negotiated to host *Pancho Guedes: An Alternative Modernist*, curated by Portuguese architect and curator Pedro Gadanho. The exhibition and catalogue focussed on the period of nearly twenty-five years during which Guedes was active in Mozambique and his extraordinary achievements involving over five hundred projects.[75]

Both Guedes and I wanted more for the exhibition in Cape Town, so a second component was introduced: *Works After April 25th 1974*, the date a reference to his departure from Mozambique with his family. The projects related mostly to South Africa. It was curated free of charge by architects Henning Rasmuss and Dagmar Hoetzel, in consultation with Guedes, and was separate yet conceptually linked to the Swiss show. The two exhibitions celebrated Guedes in his many different guises as architect, designer, artist, teacher, mentor and patron (Fig. 37).

The Swiss Architecture Museum waived the exhibitions fee and I put together two fundraising committees, one in Cape Town and one in Johannesburg, with Herbert Prins, former Wits colleague, chairing the latter. We managed to raise almost one million rand. Support came from the Portuguese

FIGURE 38: Neville Dubow, Pancho Guedes and Guedes' Ambassadors of Electica at the opening of *Pancho Guedes: An Alternative Modernist*, May 2008; photographer Pam Warne.

Consulate-General, the Instituto Camões in Portugal, the Cape and Gauteng Institutes for Architecture, the Cement & Concrete Institute, Grand West Cultural Heritage Trust, Arup and BASA. The spirit in which the architects, former colleagues and students and benefactors responded was remarkable and inspiring – individual contributions ranged from R3,000 to R100,000. The exhibition was complex and demanding, with works arriving from different places in Europe and at the last minute; it required many hands working at all hours.

The May 2008 opening was a grand affair, orchestrated by Guedes and including a performance by the Zip Zap Circus. His Ambassadors of Electica were in attendance and Dubow delivered a characteristically astute opening address (Fig. 38).[76] It was a rare privilege to host a full retrospective of Guedes' oeuvre, to share it with students and learners through extensive education programmes, lectures and publications and to inspire new generations of architects. It revealed his capacity to seamlessly bring together Europe and Africa, art and architecture, dream and reality. The exhibition closed on 31 August 2008, the last day of my tenure at the national art museum. With the support of Steven Sack, then director of culture in Johannesburg, the show travelled to Museum Africa and years later an overview of Guedes' architecture would be seen in Mozambique, for the first time since his departure.

My final curatorial project was a survey of the career of Albert Adams, *Journey on a Tightrope* (2008), which I co-curated with Joe Dolby. We were assisted by Andrea Lewis and received invaluable advice and support from Edward Glennon, Adams' life-long partner in London. Dolby had worked with Adams and Glennon on a small exhibition in 2002, but this was the first comprehensive retrospective exhibition of paintings, drawings and prints from local and international private and public collections. The exhibition was opened by Albie Sachs and was accompanied by an illustrated catalogue that included essays by Colin Cina, Peter Clarke, Elza Miles, Crain Soudien and the curators. It would be the last exhibition catalogue published by Iziko Art Collections, until 2015.[77] Lewis, who was appointed as assistant curator of modern paintings and sculpture in January 2008, regards this exhibition, her first with Dolby and me, as a highlight in her time at SANG:

> … it gave me much understanding and insight into how to curate an exhibition. More importantly, it made me understand the importance of addressing the imbalances of the past and making the public know or remember the artists missing from South African art history (or not acknowledged enough). This is why I also consider *Moses Tladi Unearthed* (2014) as one of my highlights.[78]

Unable to study at the Michaelis School due to the race laws of the time, Adams secured a grant from the Cape Tercentenary Foundation to study at the Slade School of Fine Art in London (1953–56). Thereafter a scholarship took him to the University of Munich and master classes with Oskar Kokoschka in Salzburg. Adams returned to Cape Town where he exhibited widely and to critical acclaim, but in 1960 he settled in London, where he taught at schools and lectured in art history at the City University in London.

An instinctive expressionist, Adams' subject matter is evidence of a deep social commitment and he can rightly be seen as an heir to Francisco Goya. He was inspired by international events, but he always returned to South Africa for inspiration, depicting, amongst others, the homeless people of Cape Town, the darker side of the Cape Minstrels and – in a more allusive way – the "baggage" or legacy of apartheid. Although Adams exhibited extensively and, on more than one occasion was chosen to represent South Africa on international exhibitions, his long period of absence from South Africa had resulted in undue neglect. The retrospective exhibition contributed to him being recognised and established as a major South African artist.[79]

I cannot emphasise enough the vital benefits of collaborative projects and partnerships. Our partners – the Friends of the gallery and Michaelis Collection, museums, statutory bodies, trusts, universities, diverse organisations and associations, foreign missions and institutions, businesses and individuals – were essential to our programmes and delivery. They enabled access to projects of international standard. The percentage allocated from the Iziko budget for core functions was such that few exhibitions could be curated without huge investments from our partners, either in direct funding or in kind. As Lohman put it:

> Despite all the problems of past and present South Africa, SANG was able to remain relevant and present as a successful gallery connected to the world. What was fascinating from my outsider perspective was that the gallery consistently attracted a broad range of audiences, and not just tourists but a strong community of supporters.[80]

My departure coincided with the celebration of forty years of the Friends at a special lunch and they gave me a splendid send-off. Their commemorative publication, *Forty Years of Friendship*, contains contributions by Dolby, Lewis and Proud. It captures the history and activities of the association, the Friends' Choice Collection 1975–92, and a special tribute to artist and dealer Joe Wolpe, a founding and council member for some twenty seven years. In the foreword I paid homage to all the chairpersons, council members and secretaries who gave expression to the Friends' constitution, outlined the structural changes that had taken place and concluded:

> Whatever the changes, the Friends have remained close to the staff and the director of the gallery, while at the same time maintaining their autonomy. This is one of the strengths of the association; another is the spirit of true friendship that guides and informs our interactions and decisions. The principle of mutual benefit and benefit to the public through our actions and activities ensures that the Friends and SANG go from strength to strength.[81]

The SANG family

ON A PERSONAL and professional level, there was the relationship between the staff and me (Plate 31). Some of us had worked together since 1990 and my personal and professional life was changed, shaped and enriched enormously by our interactions, and by what I learned and experienced. I gave a farewell lunch in the SANG atrium and I invited every staff member who had worked at the gallery prior to Iziko, and who was contactable. As I indicated in the introduction to this volume, the contributions and voices of people were important in writing this history and many of the bonds that developed remain to this day.

I have often been asked about my style of leadership and management and I have no answer, save to say that what I understood by these terms I absorbed intuitively from Pancho Guedes, my head of department at Wits in the 1980s, who was clear in his direction but flexible, and who valued inclusivity, intellectual curiosity and trust above all else. He inspired enthusiasm, not fear, and he depended on goodwill, not authority. I choose to end this chapter with two unsolicited acknowledgements of my directorship and legacy, particularly regarding what it meant for people who worked with me.

Faeza Allie wrote to me:

> Marilyn Martin took the gallery to another level and opened so many doors in the art world and for the staff alike. In particular, the opportunities afforded me that contributed to my personal growth over the last twenty-five years (1989–2015). She spearheaded the transformation of the gallery, its people, collections, policies and procedures with vigour, commitment and resilience. This process was very challenging with heartache, tears and ultimately joy and happiness because of her perseverance and belief in changing for the betterment of all at the gallery. I am humbled and honoured to have been part of this and reporting to and working closely with her. She has been my confidant and mentor. I am immensely grateful to her for being part of my life, her acknowledgement, confidence in me, trusting me, her encouragement, nurturing and support have contributed to my development and personal growth that made my life at the gallery and later at Iziko Museums a pleasant experience and led to my work achievements over the years.[82]

Jo-Anne Duggan, who worked at SANG between 1986 and 1996, concluded her responses to my various questions while researching this book as follows:

> Twenty years later I am still regularly invited to join a small but close group of former colleagues to mark special occasions like retirements, or memorials to colleagues who have passed on. The ties that bind us stretch back over more than two decades, to a time when I and they were proud to be part of the 'SANG family'. Like all other families we have had our differences and exchanged heated words: we have our 'black sheep', our 'prodigal sons and daughters' and those we have turned our back on. But the core still holds and we still laugh and cry together. We *are* family, as one said to me recently. Our motley group includes 'professional' and administrative staff members, general assistants, attendants and workshop staff. The bonds that hold us together were forged at a time when we as individuals, an

> institution and a country were struggling to find a place for ourselves in a time of transition. We share a history and like any family we can look back on the 'bad old days' and speak nostalgically of the 'good old days', we can intellectualise the processes we went through but we can also remember the personal pleasures and the pains we shared. Marilyn, as director through these tumultuous times, must take some credit for creating an environment in which each one of us felt equally honoured and valued and where our unique contributions were equally appreciated.[83]

As is clear in Duggan's message, SANG creates enduring bonds and keeps people connected long after the formal arrangements of the workplace have lapsed. We get together for happy, memorable or sad circumstances.[84] It is a ritual that continues, and in some senses explains my ongoing interest in what happened at SANG after my departure.

PLATE 34: Penny Siopis, *Beast*, 2009, ink and glue on canvas, 695 × 600; courtesy of the artist and Stevenson; photographer Michael Hall.

8

A new CEO and art collections director, restructuring and destructive controversies

2009 – 2014

MAJOR INSTITUTIONAL CHANGES OCCUR. Rooksana Omar succeeds Jatti Bredekamp as CEO. Riason Naidoo is appointed director of art collections. The chapter opens with the exhibitions prepared in advance of the new director's arrival. Naidoo's inaugural show from 2010 is discussed, and his performance assessed in light of his statements and actions. Naidoo challenges Iziko's decision not to renew his contract after five years; the legal dispute, which is only resolved in 2017, is examined in detail. Iziko Council identifies the need to review exhibitions and re-interpret collections held at all Iziko sites, and initiates "The Big Picture" project. This period sees yet another restructuring, as well as controversies that impact negatively on the profile and position of SANG. Little is done to address the severe space and financial constraints.

Cape Town is known to be quite colonial.
So apart from being a new director,
I'm also the first black director in a museum
where there have never been black curators.

RIASON NAIDOO[1]

Riason Naidoo appointed director of art collections

UNLIKE PAST PROCEDURES, when one SANG director was immediately followed by another, Iziko did not advertise the position until 13 June 2008, and interviews were only conducted at the end of September, a month after I had left. Council ratified the appointment of artist and curator Riason Naidoo in February 2009 (Fig. 39). He began work on 1 May.[2] There was no possibility of a professional handover, but fortunately Joe Dolby – who had many years of experience working at different levels in the institution, deep knowledge and much wisdom – stepped into the breach as acting director until Naidoo arrived.

FIGURE 39: Riason Naidoo, image detail courtesy of *Art Africa*; photographer Sean O'Toole.

We had prepared a provisional exhibition schedule for 2009 and 2010, and negotiated projects with external partners. These included two Standard Bank Young Artist Award winners, Pieter Hugo and Nontsikelelo Veleko; *Past/ Present: Andrew Verster*, an exhibition of drawings, paintings, stage sets and costume design, curated by Carol Brown, which showed the diversity of a prolific South African artist; William Kentridge's eight-channel video installation *I am not me, the horse is not mine*; the gallery's final exhibition of architecture, *The Everyday and the Extraordinary: Three Decades of Architectural Design by Jo Noero*; and *The Tropics – Views from the Middle of the Globe*, a project of the Ethnological Museum of Berlin that was curated by Alfons Hug, Viola König and Peter Junge and facilitated by the Goethe Institute.[3]

Some exhibitions were long in the making: they included the ambitious and impressive *Dada South?*, which was initiated and realised by curator Roger van Wyk against considerable odds, and jointly curated by Van Wyk and Kathryn Smith. It opened in December 2009. Andrea Lewis, who was the internal project manager, remembers how staff had to co-ordinate hundreds of national and international loans, and the pleasure of having works by Hannah Höch and Man Ray in the gallery.[4] *Richard Long: Karoo Highveld*, finally materialised in November 2011 and *Opening 'Plato's Cave': The Legacy of Kevin Atkinson, 1939–2007* in September 2013.

In an interview with *Art South Africa*, Naidoo spoke of closer cooperation with African countries and the "global south" instead of looking to Europe and America. He was seemingly unaware, or omitted to mention, that in its long history the national gallery had hosted exhibitions from many different places, albeit not enough from our own continent, and that *The Tropics* had emanated from Brazil. He stated his vision:

> Given that the local art world is still dealing with the exclusionary effects of the apartheid era – has a black audience been adequately developed? – the National Gallery can play a critical role by being

> more inclusive in the audiences we appeal to, in the selection of our exhibitions, in the work that we acquire for our collections, in the people that make up our committees and in the staff that we hire. And we need to be more inclusive on a national level. Let's open up our National Gallery to new voices and ideas, making the gallery more relevant and representative and putting it at the forefront of change. The increased demand for local contemporary artists abroad has created a crisis for many local museum acquisitions. This makes corporate partnerships and government engagement increasingly vital. But difficult situations are often opportunities for innovation and creativity. We will need to be more proactive in identifying young talent and leading with innovative shows that will simultaneously inspire conversation and debate.[5]

Naidoo's first curatorial project, *1910–2010: From Pierneef to Gugulective*, opened in April 2010 (Fig. 40). The gallery was closed from 1 March to 15 April for the installation. The exhibition occupied the entire gallery and covered 100 years of South African history – from the establishment of the Union of South Africa to the hosting of the FIFA World Cup (11 June–11 July 2010) – through the lens of visual art

FIGURE 40: *1910-2010: From Pierneef to Gugulective*, installation view marking the start of the exhibition and featuring Anton Momberg, *Maquette for the Gandhi Memorial Statue, Pietermaritzburg,* 1992, resin, fibreglass, copper, 665 × 190 × 190; courtesy of the artist; and JH Pierneef, *Union Buildings*, undated, oil on board, 910 × 2130; collection and courtesy of Pretoria Art Museum; image courtesy of *Art Africa*; photographer Sean O'Toole.

production. Naidoo and Joe Dolby travelled around the country to select works from municipal, university, corporate and private collections. Of the approximately 650 works shown, only 280 were loans, so the exhibition was also a reflection of the history of the collection.

Naidoo's exhibition generated a great deal of media attention, both locally and abroad. The headlines used by various news outlets capture the mixed responses: "Iziko celebrates reopening with unusual art" (*Die Burger*, 16 April, 2010); "The place to be or not to be: Art and soul of SA" (*Financial Mail*, 11 June 2010); "South Africa's Forwards: High scoring centennial survey at National Gallery greets World Cup" (*The Online Journal of Art and Ideas*, 29 June 2010); "It's our art, warts and all" (*Sunday Argus*, 11 July 2010); and "A first for the National Gallery: Our own art through the decades" (*Cape Times*, 9 September 2010).

The Sunday Independent's art critic Mary Corrigall observed: "The fact that this brobdingnagian narrative begins with Pierneef's pastel-coloured landscapes and ends with conceptual work by a collective of artists, is some indication of the radical socio-political and art historical shifts that have occurred during the past century."[6] *The Mail & Guardian*'s culture critic Miles Keylock wrote (23-29 April 2010):

> Indeed, for too long [SANG] has been haunted by a putrid history: of colonialism, of apartheid, of post-apartheid apathy and stagnation. No more. In what can only be described as a revolution [SANG] has been entirely rehung. Gone are the hallowed halls ways [sic] of "putrid" colonial treasure. Gone are the same tired artworks eternally oozing out of the permanent collection.

Writing in the *South African Art Times*, art critic Lloyd Pollak stated:

> It is apparent that Naidoo, who has piteous little curatorial experience, is out of his depth. As none of his fellow curators have ever been responsible for a pratfall of this magnitude, one can only conclude that he refused to heed their advice, and consequently one entertains the gravest fears vis-à-vis the future of the gallery under the present incumbent.[7]

Art historian and academic Gerhard Schoeman made a scholarly contribution to the debate in a feature article in *Art South Africa*.[8] For Schoeman the "unfocused jumble that follows" was apparent in the first room, which had no real connection with SANG's permanent collection or a "reflective selection of art" from other sources – an opinion I shared. It was an appendage curated by Bettina Malcomess and Simon Njami titled *Us* for JAG; by Malcomess' own account, "the show was not a critical success".[9] Schoeman acknowledged that the exhibition made it possible for him to see great works of art and to make wonderful discoveries, but he was "fatigued, irritated, dejected and frustrated" by the crowded spaces of the "blockbuster":

> A reflective selection? What is all this clutter then? Where, beyond disingenuous platitudes about insight into 'the soul of our nation', is the lucid theme, the Ariadne's thread, the astute discernment, the rhythm or rhyme? The idea of showcasing art from 'the length and breadth of this country' sounds like political sentimentalism, hubris and blatant opportunism.[10]

Much was made of Naidoo's Indian origins – by sensation-seeking journalists and art writers, but also by him. In an interview with David Smith in *The Guardian* (1 September 2010) he stated:

> Cape Town is known to be quite colonial. So apart from being a new director, I'm also the first black director in a museum where there have *never* [my italics] been black curators. There is definitely resistance to change. There are a number of firsts in putting this exhibition on and there is bound to be reaction from certain conservative quarters to change.[11]

He fuelled the controversy by ignoring the fact that most of the reviews were favourable. As a result, responses to the exhibition where often couched in racial terms, rather than on its merits. Art historian Steven Dubin, whose books include *Transforming Museums: Mounting Queen Victoria in a Democratic South Africa* (2006), criticised Smith (and other reviewers) for "some of the worst reviews imaginable: dismissive, hart-hitting, even snarly" and for reducing the dispute to "simplistic, knee-jerk terms". Dubin further remarked:

> A show such as 1910–2010: From Pierneef to Gugulective is a reasonable gambit for someone new in a museum director's seat. Unfortunately, Naidoo takes Smith's bait and casts himself as a racial victim, attributing all the criticism to untransformed Neanderthals. But while there was much to applaud ... there was much to take issue with as well. One does not need to have a huge racist chip on one's shoulder to find fault with this exhibition.[12]

Race would set the tone for Naidoo's tenure. The other constants would be him chipping away at the legacies that staff, the SANG board, Iziko council and I had left. His lack of knowledge of, or interest in, the history of the national gallery was also palpable. The appointment of black curators and participation of black education staff in curating exhibitions, which are discussed in previous chapters, is one example.

The reviews mentioned had one thing in common: they all included Naidoo's inaccurate comments on the proposed schedule of exhibitions that had been prepared, and it that was much like those of other institutions:

> ... it was all about football. We also received numerous requests to show foreign artists and exhibitions. With a store of few thousand artworks, we cleared the schedule and decided to use the opportunity of the World Cup to turn the focus in on ourselves; that is to give visitors to the National Gallery, both foreign and local, a reflection of our own art stores.[13]

Of course, a new director has to put his or her own imprimatur on such an important position. Naidoo's concept of bracketing the period between union and the 2010 FIFA World Cup, and showing how artists experienced and interpreted the turbulent century, was a sound and innovative one. It also chimed with an earlier exhibition, *Strengths & Convictions* (2009), which shared a timeline of about 100 years of South African history. It is therefore all the more perplexing that he felt the need to trash the existing schedule and to repeat in interview after interview that it was "all about football". This was simple expediency, if not simply trash talking. The facts, for the record, are as follows.

In 2006, soon after South Africa's successful bid to host the 2010 FIFA World Cup was announced, Iziko executive management organised meetings and requested directors to come up with ideas to profile and promote our museums during this global spectacle.[14] DAC allocated R150 million for projects, and artists and organisations were invited to apply for funding – but nothing happened. In March 2010 it was announced that the money had "gone" and a judicial audit was instituted. It was subsequently reported that allocations earmarked for 2010 FIFA World Cup projects were "used by the DAC for unrelated purposes in contravention of section 6.3.1(c) of Treasury Regulations".[15]

Between 2006 and September 2008, when I left, we discussed numerous proposals about the best way in which to approach the international sporting event. We were clear that, while football should feature, it was a great opportunity to showcase the permanent collection. Six rooms were allocated for curators to develop thematic exhibitions. *Engraved in Time* (engraved objects such as horns, bones, tusks and ostrich eggs) and *Pipes*, both curated by Carol Kaufmann, would occupy three rooms.

Nadja Daehnke's *Viewer: Spectator,* with its clever allusion to sport, was intended to shift the focus to the gallery visitor, and to incorporate art other than sculpture, painting, prints and photography, such as performance, sound-works and new media. Eight artists would be invited to choose one or more works from the permanent collection – either in storage or on exhibition – and to respond in a manner that questioned the position and role of the spectator, as well as traditional hierarchies. The emphasis was on subtle engagement and playful interaction, rather than on confrontational disruption.[16] As far as football was concerned, Pam Warne proposed a small exhibition by South African photographers, with Buyaphi Mdledle's unusual images and Zanele Muholi's *Sokka Plight at the Chicago Gay Games* (2006), already in the SANG collection, as points of departure.

I had seen avant-garde German artist, filmmaker and author Haroun Farocki's football-themed *Deep Play* (2007), at Documenta 12 in 2007. I contacted the artist who expressed his enthusiasm about having the twelve-channel installation shown in Cape Town. Comprising diverse perspectives on the final of the 2006 FIFA World Cup, played at the Olympia Stadium in Berlin, Farocki used raw material from television networks together with many soundtracks; he focused on individual players as well as abstract computer-generated representations of the flow of the game. Farocki delved into and brought to light the desires of nations (France and Italy in this case), players, coaches, spectators, the police and surveillance. The result was enthralling, eerie, disturbing and utterly compelling.[17] The dark, unusual images of the stadium, originally built by Werner March for the 1936 Olympic Games, awakened the ghost of Adolf Hitler's opening of the games that looked more like a military parade than a sporting event, with participants from many nations acknowledging his presence with the Nazi salute. Deep Play would have appealed to football fans, but also to followers of simulation and documentation, film, television and computer games. It was about much more than football.

South Africa's hosting of the football World Cup generated a great deal of interest in the cultural sector, with a number of exhibitions curated in South Africa. They included *Halakasha!* at the Standard Bank Gallery in Johannesburg, which the national gallery hoped to host later in 2010.[18] Carol Brown, an independent curator and former director of the Durban Art Gallery, guest edited a special issue of the US-based journal *African Arts*, entitled "South Africa After the Ball: Art and the World Cup 2010". The volume is filled with football paraphernalia, memorabilia and costumes created by local enthusiasts and reviews of exhibitions held in Cape Town, Durban and Johannesburg; it also contains penetrating observations and critiques by academics and writers Steven Dubin and Federico Freschi.

Anna Tietze maintains that *1910–2010: From Pierneef to Gugulective* happened "without any funding".[20] This is inaccurate, and impossible. Naidoo and Dolby travelled to various museums, loans were made that would have incurred transport and insurance costs, and there were costs related to the show's installation. Iziko did not respond to a request for details of the budget, but the global exhibitions budget for art collections amounted to R623,900, excluding the R340,000 National Lotteries allocation for a publication, which Naidoo failed to produce.[21]

Naidoo organised a series of panel discussions to close his exhibition (1–2 October 2010).[22] It brought together artists, curators, scholars and activists, and offered an opportunity to explore the state of art museums, curatorship, education, audiences and art criticism. I participated in a panel with Omar Badsha, Irwin Langeveld, Gordon Metz and Jenny Stretton, chaired by Iziko council member Ciraj Rassool. I reflected on my directorship – our many achievements and disappointments, our dreams and realities – and how change can be contentious and difficult to embrace. I addressed Naidoo's on-going attempts to impugn SANG's reputation and that of his predecessors as best I could, as it was demoralising for those of us who did our best and for those who were still working at Iziko. There were timely reminders, comparisons and ironies, but I came away realising that nothing would change. Naidoo held fast to the prevailing belief that we had to forget the past in order to construct a future, and that only some have the right to do so. Caught in a space between identity politics and platitudes, complexity was reduced to black and white, and little room was left for an exploration of fundamental questions and the grey areas in between.

In May 2010 I was appointed to the Iziko council. Rooksana Omar, a museologist from KwaZulu-Natal, joined Iziko as the CEO (designate) at the same time. In preparation for her role she worked with Jatti Bredekamp until she took over in the November. Omar brought extensive experience in the heritage sector with her, through positions held in KwaZulu-Natal and local and international museum organisations.[23] During her tenure Iziko Museums of Cape Town was renamed to Iziko Museums of South Africa, in 2012, thereby affirming its national status. Although the *Annual Reports* remain mired in bureaucratic speak and layout, Omar's contributions provide some narrative to augment the precious few details about core function activities.

Is there a future for the Bailey Bequest at SANG?

THE BAILEY BEQUEST came under the spotlight once again with *1910–2010: From Pierneef to Gugulective*. In 2001, when we hosted the exhibition *Marc Chagall The Light of Origins La lumière des origins* in collaboration with Standard Bank Gallery, trustees of the Abe Bailey Trust readily agreed that works from the collection could be taken down. The two rooms with green and blue fabric-covered walls were ideal for Chagall's paintings, works on paper and tapestries. A selection from the Bailey Collection was rehung immediately after the show. The trustees granted Naidoo permission to temporarily remove the works for his exhibition in the short term, after he informed them that he intended doing so.[24] He stripped a temporary exhibition that marked the completion of Anna Tietze's comprehensive publication on the collection, which the Bailey trust had funded (some articles inaccurately suggested that it was permanent), and pulled the fabric off the walls.

In his interview with *The Guardian* (1 September 2010), Naidoo justified his decision as follows:

> For the first time I thought it wasn't really appropriate because it's a kind of colonial English collection and there are many of those around the world in the English colonies. It wasn't really showcasing any aspect of South African culture that was unique to the history of this period. It was a conscious decision to show contemporary work in those spaces.

Of course, the works were not appropriate for the period covered by Naidoo's exhibition, but this signalled the beginning of his resistance to and marginalisation of all the historical European collections. The Bailey collection's profile would never be restored: neither to the levels it enjoyed pre-1990, particularly in landscape and portrait shows, nor in the way in which Proud enhanced it from 1991 to 2008. Proud's strategy for the historical collections at SANG and the Old Town House was to integrate them in carefully conceptualised thematic exhibitions that speak to the colonial past and the transformative present, and in so doing, to new audiences.

According to an article in the *Cape Times* (26 October 2011) there were only two paintings from the Bailey Bequest on view at that time, one of them being *Thomas Ashton Smith and the Tedworth hounds* (1829) by John Ferneley (Senior), which formed part of the exhibition *Neither Man nor Stone*. Critic Lloyd Pollak confirmed this in an article with a provocative title.[25] I raised the matter with Omar, who had been faced with the situation when she became CEO. Omar assured me that she and executive director of core functions, Bongani Ndhlovu, were taking the matter seriously, and were meeting with the Bailey trustees.[26] There were suggestions that the oval room be dedicated to the collection, but it was unsuitable: it is small, its shape allows for few pictures to go on the walls and it would be detrimental to Proud's creative curatorship.

The trustees, together and Sir Abe Bailey's grandson, artist Beezy Bailey, were understandably displeased with the situation. Beezy Bailey was quoted in the press:

> I and some trustees of the Bailey bequest believe that SANG have not honoured the legal agreement, and in view of this the trust is considering taking the bequest away from SANG. We are also debating the possibility of retaining only the most valuable paintings and selling off the residue. The proceeds would accrue to the Sir Abe Bailey Trust, which awards travel bursaries on a non-racial basis to students with exceptional leadership qualities.[27]

Once again the possibility of getting rid of some works – the ever-problematic "residue" – from the collection was mooted. Who would decide on this, and what would the criteria be? In 2014, responding to suggestions made by the Bailey trustees that works be disposed of by sale, Proud penned a lengthy defence of the collection and its significance to SANG, and the people of South Africa. He was critical of the appropriation of the two rooms set aside from the historical holdings without "consensus involving any of the experienced members of the curatorial staff". It resulted in exacerbating, not solving the "problem" of the Bailey Collection, and in staff being forced to insert "a few Bailey pictures into each and every thematic exhibition that comes up on our exhibitions programme, just so that we meet the requirements of Bailey's will".[28]

In his document Proud made a compelling case for the retention of the bequest, "inferior" works and all, lest the sale of these lead to deaccessioning the entire collection in the future. Moreover, the "inferior" paintings provided opportunities for exploring the history of printing and printmaking techniques, as well as conservation, and served as valuable teaching tools. Iziko is involved in the post-graduate honours degree in curatorship at UCT and has received a grant from the Andrew Mellon Foundation for conservation.[29] Considering the national and international impact, Proud argued that our public art museums were in a precarious state and that they did not need to have their reputations undermined and public confidence diminished:

> The potential loss of the nearly 400 works that comprise the Bailey Collection, which includes oils by Gainsborough, Stubbs, Reynolds and Turner, as well as a spectacular collection of works on paper, will also be seen as a seriously retrograde step and the negative consequences of this for the entire art museum establishment in South Africa should not be underestimated.[30]

In 2012 Proud curated *Dialogues: Conversations between 'old' and 'new',* which brought together historical, modern and contemporary works. Of particular interest was Swedish artist Matts Leiderstam's installation using works from the Bailey Collection, including his copy of Abraham Cooper's *The Day Family* (1838) that he titled *The Power and Pleasure of Breeding* (1998). Leiderstam altered the "gaze" by closing the eyes of all the personages in the painting, including the horses – with the exception of John Day, the *pater familias*. For Proud, Leiderstam, a gay activist, provokes "discussion of the role of patriarchal power structures and gender role conformity in the capitalist enterprise, of which Sir Abe Bailey himself was such a sterling South African representative".[31] Moreover, Leiderstam's work "instantly confers 'contemporary and conceptual art status' on an old and much-denigrated and contested collection".

Proud makes the point that if the Bailey collection were to be deaccessioned and sold, Leiderstam's installation (in which the rest of the room is filled with artworks from the collection) would be rendered meaningless and Leiderstam's painting would also have to be deaccessioned: "Works like this prove how the Bailey Collection has – like it or not – become embedded in the history of SANG."[32] He added that the same would apply, in a lesser degree perhaps, to Beezy Bailey's painting *Love in Heaven* (1991) in the collection.[33] Bailey's mixed media work was created while he was an invited artist at SANG (Plate 35). In

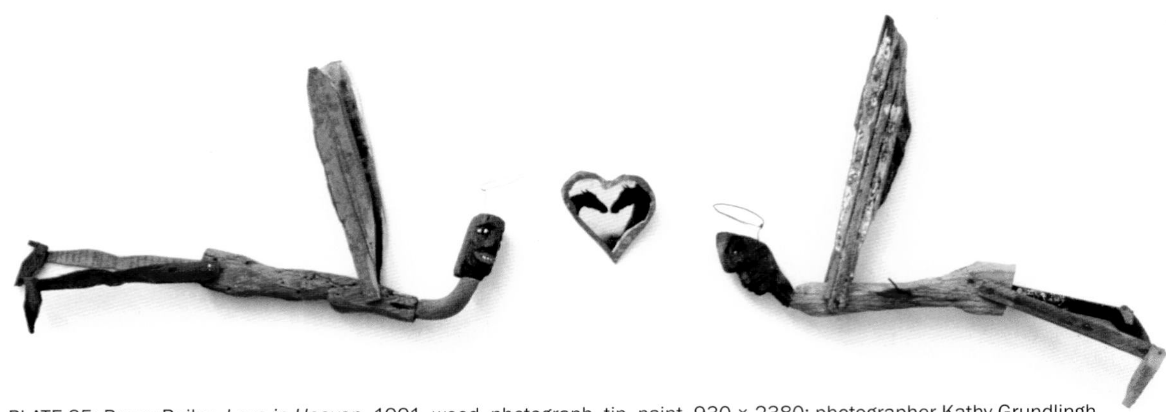

PLATE 35: Beezy Bailey, *Love in Heaven*, 1991, wood, photograph, tin, paint, 930 × 2380; photographer Kathy Grundlingh.

2018 Proud reconfigured Leiderstam's installation, under the title of his painting, which is also the title of the exhibition, *The Power and Pleasure of Breeding* (Fig. 41).

That the historical collections remain of interest to contemporary artists, was affirmed by Wim Botha's installation as Standard Bank Young Artist in 2005: the exhibition included landscapes and pastoral scenes from SANG's permanent collection as a backdrop for his *Mieliepap Pietà* (2004), a mirrored image of Michelangelo's *Pietà* (1499) executed in maize meal and epoxy resin, and mounted on a scaffold.

There is no record in the Iziko *Annual Reports* of exhibitions dedicated to the historical collections until *Selections from our Historical Collections* (March–October 2016). A year later Jane Alexander's *Butcher Boys* kept watch over a dismal sample of unlit paintings and a touch-screen display in a small space, no doubt to appease the Bailey trustees. This is in line with a decision to have rotating exhibitions of the Bailey Collection in this space and the oval room, which is even smaller and quite unsuitable for a meaningful display of two-dimensional works.[34] Echoing Proud, Anna Tietze summed up the situation succinctly in a 2011 *Cape Times* article (26 October 2011): "It would be a tragedy to break up the collection. It should be kept in its entirely until a different management team that looks on it more favourably comes into authority at the gallery." Such a team is not on the horizon and it is left to Proud and Zehnder to keep interest in the collection alive, and deaccessioning at bay.

In a 2017 email exchange, Beezy Bailey acknowledged Proud's love of the collection and the work he has put in, but he has not changed his position. Family members cannot make decisions regarding the collection, apart from Will Bailey, Beezy Bailey's cousin, who serves on the Trust and who oversees the bequest. According to Bailey, the trust is of the opinion:

> … that it should be sold considering the current climate of the Rhodes Must Fall campaign; a collection of hunting pictures of a Randlord is in potential physical danger and especially of no particular interest to the younger generation of South Africa. In the interest of it being sold the funds would be put into the Bailey Education Trust, which we believe would be of far greater benefit to the youth than the collection as it stands.[35]

The historical collections were not the only victims of Naidoo's interventions. The public artworks aimed at enhancing the space in front of the gallery (discussed in chapter six) were also interfered with.

Rosenclaire's *Soap Boxes* has stood the test of time, but the integrity of the work was destroyed with the installation of *1910–2010: From Pierneef to Gugulective*: the plasma screen, designed to be interactive and dissolve the walls of the gallery, was removed from the entrance room and not installed elsewhere; representations that the artists and I made fell on deaf ears.

Rosenclaire wrote to Naidoo on 9 March 2013, drawing his attention to email correspondence of two years earlier, in which he stated: "Just to let you know the monitor linked to the soap boxes is planned for a dedicated space in the Oval room at SANG."[36] The artists attached a lengthy explanation of the conceptual underpinning, meaning and function of the work to their email:

> We feel we have been more than patient in our request. We strongly object to the omission of the screen, which renders the work both visually but more so conceptually incomplete and arbitrary. At present it does not fully represent our concept which Iziko understood and wholly supported when the work was commissioned.

Naidoo responded to the artists explaining how difficult it was to keep the plasma screen in room one, but ensured them that, in spite of challenges with the re-routing of cables, the "artwork is still destined for the Oval Room, where we feel it will have a dedicated space. The work is highly appreciated in the

FIGURE 41: Installation featuring Matts Leiderstam, *The Power and Pleasure of Breeding*, 1998, oil on canvas, 970 × 1265 (presented by the artist) and Abraham Cooper *The Day Family* (1838), oil on canvas, 970 × 1265; © Iziko Museums of South Africa; photographer Nigel Pamplin.

gallery for its interactive quality and by students and learners who have had the chance to experience it in the past".[37] He promised to keep them informed. Despite his assurances Naidoo did nothing, and he did not seem to understand nor care that de-installing the plasma screen was like chopping off the arm of a sculpture or taking away a part of a triptych. Flattering remarks aside, the disrespect shown to the artists, the artwork, the sponsors and the visiting public was astonishing.

Four years later, I wrote to Ernestine White, curator of contemporary art, to enquire about the status of rosenclaire's *Soap Boxes*. She replied: "We are currently working with technicians to find alternative technology to reactivate this work of art as what was initially used is no longer viable. The screen is still with us."[38] On further enquiry in November 2017, White shared some positive news: the camera had been repaired, and some headway had been made with the new collections and digitisation department in finding "the best solution for upgrading the technology of this work".[39] But a hard truth prevailed until 2019, when Zehnder undertook to lead the restoration project.

Exhibitions: new director, new directions?

DUE TO THE SKELETAL nature of record keeping in the *Annual Reports*, it is not clear who was responsible for which exhibitions in the period under review and subsequently. Sources are not credited, and persons or organisations are not always mentioned. This creates the wholly incorrect assumption that all the exhibitions were generated internally: few were, except those from the permanent collection.[40]

Naidoo's interest in photography was evident in many exhibitions at SANG between 2010 and 2014, and as curator of photography Pam Warne was involved in all of them. They numbered: *The Indian in Drum Magazine in the 1950s*, an exhibition based on Naidoo's Master's degree research; *Ernest Cole, Photographer*, a rare collection from the Hasselblad Foundation that had never been exhibited internationally;[41] *Roger Ballen: Boarding House*, a show coinciding with a new book of the same title; *Borders: An exhibition from the 8th Bamako Biennale*, a showcase of work from Africa's premier photography biennial; *Ranjith Kally: Through the Lens of Durban's Veteran Photographer*, which was curated by Naidoo and also drew on his personal research; *A Nomad's Harvest*, a retrospective of photographer George Hallett's photographs spanning half a century; *Ever Young: James Barnor*, a survey of this pioneer of Ghanaian photography; and *Rotimi Fani-Kayode (1955–1989): Traces of Ecstasy*, the first museum retrospective in Africa of this celebrated Nigerian artist's portraits. The latter two exhibitions were both presented in partnership with Autograph ABP, a London-based institution founded in 1988 to support black photographic practices.

Exhibitions originating from other sources contributed greatly to the nature and quality of what was on offer at the gallery. Naidoo's divisive debut exhibition was followed by *In Context* in November 2010. First conceived by Goodman Gallery owner Liza Essers as a series of site-specific exhibitions and interventions in and around Johannesburg during the FIFA World Cup, *In Context* presented work by international and South African artists. It raised questions about space and geography, and about being "local" in a global world.[42] Emile Maurice, then working at UWC, returned to SANG in 2012 as curator of *Uncontained: Opening the Community Arts Project Archive*, on behalf of the Centre for Humanities Research. Retrieved from the Community Arts Project and Arts and Media Access Centre archives, Maurice's show brought to light the relationship between aesthetics and politics, as expressed by artists known and unknown. *Impressions of Rorke's Drift: The Jumuna Collection* (2014) was drawn from the Jumuna family's private collection and curated by Thembinkosi Goniwe; it put the spotlight on the importance of printmaking at Rorke's Drift, and its impact on South African art.

Umhlaba 1913–2013 marked the centenary of the Natives Land Act of 1913, a foundational apartheid statute that instituted territorial segregation, the legacy of which remains unresolved in 2018. Curated by Bongi Dhlomo-Mautloa, David Goldblatt, Pam Warne and Paul Weinberg, this exhibition, whose title means "land" in Zulu, included historical and contemporary images by more than thirty photographers drawn from eighteen South African archives.[43]

Against the Grain – Sculptors from the Cape (2013), curated by Mario Pissarra, founder of the Art South Africa Initiative (ASAI), showcased the work of five important but neglected sculptors: Thami Kiti, Isaac Makeleni, Shepherd Mbanya, Timothy Mafenuka and Ishmael Thyssen.[44] *The 8th Definitive Stamp Series: The luminous beauty of South African beadwork*, organised by Kaufmann in collaboration with the South African Post Office in 2012, featured the stamps and objects from Iziko collections that inspired the stamps. All these exhibitions were accompanied by catalogues. *Opening Plato's Cave: The Legacy of Kevin Atkinson, 1939-2007*, curated by Hayden Proud and Stephen Croeser, was a project of the Kevin and Patricia Atkinson Trust (Plate 36). It paid tribute to one of the most energetic, ambitious and influential artists who emerged in South Africa in the early 1960s. Heading the Michaelis School's Department of Interdisciplinary Studies from 1975, Atkinson became synonymous with a spirit of adventurous experiment at the School. Marlene Dumas, Ângela Ferreira and Shelley Sacks were among the many students he inspired.

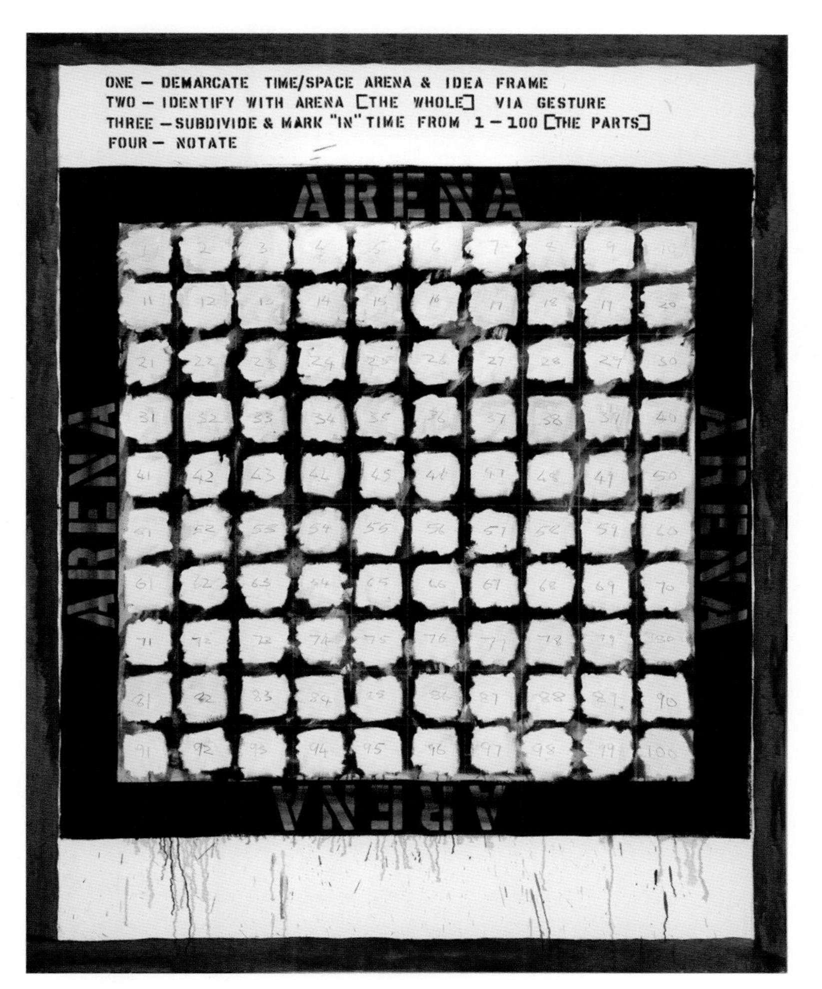

PLATE 36: Kevin Atkinson, *Arena*, 1975, oil and pencil on canvas, 2135 × 1685; courtesy of the Kevin and Patricia Atkinson Trust.

In addition to the annual Standard Bank Young Artist Award shows, the on-going partnership with the Standard Bank Gallery resulted in important exhibitions and publications. I curated the exhibition *A Vigil of Departure: Louis Khehla Maqhubela, a retrospective 1960–2010* for the Standard Bank Gallery (2010). The exhibition was produced with the support of the artist and his dealer, Clare Cooper of Art First in London, and included a catalogue. The sponsor generously agreed that money left in the budget could be used to travel the exhibition to Cape Town and Durban. Standard Bank also funded the exhibition *Listening to Distant Thunder: The Art of Peter Clarke* (2011), which profiled the career of this much-loved Cape Town artist and writer in the context of South Africa's social history from the 1940s to 2010.[45] Curated by Elizabeth Rankin and Phillippa Hobbs, the exhibition was accompanied by a sumptuous monograph.

For her Standard Bank Gallery commission, Berlin-based South African artist Candice Breitz created a single-channel video, *EXTRA!* (2011), in which she inserted herself as the white "intruder" in one of South Africa's most popular soap operas, *Generations*. Set against the backdrop of the advertising and media industry, this television production explored black African middle class aspirations in post-apartheid South Africa. Breitz's *Factum* (2010), seven dual-channel installations offering in-depth video portraits of twins, and her chromogenic prints Ghost Series (1994–96), highly contentious when first exhibited in the nineties, were also displayed.[46]

Kaufmann created a rich and varied framework from the permanent collection for *Imagining Beauty*, an exhibition for the 2010 Mercedes-Benz Fashion Awards winning designers. Her display included paintings, sculpture, video, textiles, beadwork, headdresses, regalia and recycled fashion and body adornments and celebrated the fusion of fashion and art (Fig. 42). Proud's *Objects in the Tide of Time* (2013) was a remarkable celebration of the depth and variety of SANG's 140-year-old collection. Proud was also responsible for *Baroque Meets Modern: The re-hang of the Michaelis Collection at the Old Town House* (2011) and *Rembrandt in South Africa: Pioneer Printmaker of Humanity and Modernity* (2014). The curator drew on fine etchings from the Michaelis Collection and SANG, as well as JAG, the NMMAM, the Rupert Art Foundation, the Rembrandt van Rijn Art Foundation and UCT.[47]

Two external curators added to the stature of exhibitions in 2010. Curated by art historian Michael Godby, in partnership with the Sanlam Art Gallery, *The Lie of the Land: Representations of the South African Landscape* was organised along five discrete and clearly described sections. Godby dug deep into the history of an ever-popular genre in South African art and the complex issues around land that artists continue to address.[49] Carol Brown's *Home and Away: A Return to the South* presented South African art from the apartheid years that had been repatriated by the Ifa Lethu Foundation.

A touching film entitled *Anathi Tyawa: A Painter from Khayelitsha* (2011), made by Swedish artist and educator Lena Boda was screened at the OTH. Tyawa was

FIGURE 42: *Imagining Beauty* installation; photographer Pam Warne.

a student at the Frank Joubert Art Centre (now the Peter Clarke Art Centre) in Rondebosch and had been nurtured in his studies via the Ibhabhathane Project.[49] Led by Colin Stevens, the project was responsible for many educational initiatives at the museum, funded by the Friends of the Michaelis. Teachers introduced Tyawa to oil paint, which had been out of his reach. The film illustrates his interest and feelings about the Michaelis Collection, and his dreams of becoming an artist. It was shown in the company of Frans Hals' *Portrait of a Woman* (1644), which inspired Tyawa's excellent portrait of his mother. Johannes Phokela's fascination with and utilisation of seventeenth-century Netherlandish painting is well known; his work *As the Old Ones sing, so the Young Ones Pipe* (1998) is held in SANG's collection. Boda's film affirmed the importance of the Michaelis Collection and other historical collections for exploration by contemporary artists.[50]

On the international front, the France-South Africa Seasons, a multifaceted bilateral collaboration between France and South Africa, took place in 2012 and 2013. It involved a range of more than seventy different projects, performances and events – encompassing science, education, tourism and sport – that took place across South Africa. SANG hosted *Rendez-Vous 12*, an exhibition from the Lyon Biennale that showcased work by twenty young international artists. It was, however, the second prize: the "flagship" art exhibition, *20th Century Masters: The Human Figure*, went to the Standard Bank Gallery. Supported by four art museums in the Région Rhône-Alpes, this exhibition brought together some sixty works of mainly French modern and contemporary artists. It included works by Gustave Courbet, Edouard Manet, Jean-Francois Millet and artists associated with French Impressionism.

Also part of the collaboration was the superb exhibition at SAM, *The King's Map, Francois le Vaillant in Southern Africa: 1781–1784*, curated by Ian Glenn of the Centre for Film and Media Studies at UCT, with Proud serving as project manager. Shown in the context of his fine watercolour paintings, Le Valliant's 2.67m × 1.83m painted map of southern Africa (c. 1790) was based on this explorer, author, naturalist and ornithologist's observations and constructed for King Louis XVI of France by M. de Laborde. The exhibition, mounted in the same space that housed the SANG collection many decades before, paid homage to Le Vaillant's scientific and artistic legacy.[51]

The national gallery was again somewhat short-changed with the reciprocal show in France, curated by SANG's art collections staff.[52] Entitled *A Portrait of South Africa: George Hallett, Peter Clarke & Gerard Sekoto*, the exhibition was shown at the Cité internationale des arts, a public foundation that offers residencies to artists from all over the world. It has a gallery space but is hardly an acknowledged venue for major exhibitions.

The Master of the Fallen Flower

TELLINGLY, NONE OF the aforementioned exhibitions, many of them excellent, attracted anywhere near the attention lavished on the exhibition *Tretchikoff: The People's Painter* (2011). Driven by fashion designer Marianne Fassler and curated by Michaelis lecturer Andrew Lamprecht, the exhibition generated thousands of words for and against it.[53] This was of course nothing new. Tretchikoff was a controversial artist during his lifetime. The respected art historian F. L. Alexander, who wrote criticism for *Die Burger* in the 1950s and 1960s, refused to use the painter's name in formal reviews, referring to him instead as "Die Meester van die Gevalle Blom" (The Master of the Fallen Flower). But it is Matthys Bokhorst's review in the *Cape Times* (16 September 1952) of a Tretchikoff exhibition in a department store that merits pause.

Headlined "Painter Expounds 'Lachrymose' Cheap Sensation for the Masses," Bokhorst offered *The Herb Seller* (1949) as an example of the artist's poor sense of colour. Bokhorst credited Tretchikoff for his drawing ability and wrote of *The Herb Seller* that it was "a good composition, also from the pictorial point of view". But, he added, the artist had "surrendered to the desire of the masses for cheap sensation and lachrymose sentimentality". In trying to be popular, wrote Bokhorst, Tretchikoff was "still hiding his light behind a bushel".[54] Angry letters in the *Cape Times* (20 September 1952) followed, attacking Bokhorst for his "disgusting criticism" and speaking out in defence of the "masses". One correspondent, Councillor A. S. A. East, who owned *The Herb Seller*, referred to a column by the "Man on the Spot" (*Cape Times*, 21 October 1949): "This painting by Tretchikoff of the old herb seller on the Parade, who died recently, demonstrates Tretchikoff's genius as a painter. He poses her between two old posters of the opposing political parties."

Some sixty years later, according to Lamprecht, *The Herb Seller* had acquired socio-political meaning:

> The painting depicts a well-known 'character' in Cape Town, disenfranchised because of South Africa's race policies, which were expanded to devastating effect soon after Tretchikoff arrived in his adopted land. Behind the direct gaze of the main figure are the torn posters of two political rivals: Smuts of the 'liberal' United Party and Malan of the apartheid-initiating National Party.[55]

This implies that the painting had anti-apartheid nuances, which is surprising, especially considering its provenance: the work was owned by Jan Haak, minister of economic affairs, in the late 1960s and later by R. F. "Pik" Botha, foreign affairs minister from 1977 to 1994. Lloyd Pollak suggested a different reading to Lamprecht in an essay: "Here a totemic, earth mother and fertility goddess ... surrounded by piles of big-bellied, uterine gourds and hairy, phallic tubers and roots, smiles in the certainty that her people will triumphantly outlive the ideologies of the Nationalist and United party whose election posters occur behind her."[56]

The presence of an artist in the national gallery of any country raises expectations of critical and scholarly attention to his or her work. In its publicity, SANG's communications team stated: "This retrospective exhibition aims to examine Tretchikoff anew and place him in contemporary perspective."[57] This was barely forthcoming. As in the past, many articles focussed on Tretchikoff's amazing life, his colourful character, his talent for managing his lucrative career and the powerful impact of his reproductions. Lamprecht, while stating that the time had come "for Tretchikoff to have his day in the

National Gallery", did not commit to a scholarly assessment of the artist's work. For him, the exhibition was not "about whether Tretchikoff was a good or bad painter (though I believe there are far worse in Iziko's permanent collection) or whether he was the 'king of kitsch'; he should be seen there because he changed the way that ordinary people relate to art, how they acquire it and take ownership of it, display it ... love it".[58] Tretchikoff's "importance lies beyond the canvases" and Lamprecht wanted visitors to decide for themselves just "how bad (or good)" the work was.[59]

To further legitimise and justify the exhibition at the national art museum, much was made of Tretchikoff's "phenomenal" success and fame abroad.[60] This was in fact limited to department stores in South Africa, Britain, America and Canada. Somehow the artist who, by 1969, was making "more money than any other painter with the exception of Pablo Picasso",[61] was cast as a victim of the politics of exclusion. Rejected by the SAAA's Cape Town gallery in 1947, he showed his paintings and promoted his prints in up-market department stores to "the people" who were in a position to frequent the stores and buy his work. These are hardly grounds on which to base a critical review. In his lifetime only two Tretchikoff paintings were exhibited in museums: *Zulu Maiden*[62] at the De Young Museum in San Francisco in 1953, and *The Herb Seller* that Naidoo included in the exhibition *1910–2010: From Pierneef to Gugulective* fifty-seven years later.

In a measured article in *Die Burger* (27 May 2011) artist and critic Cobus van Bosch searched for merit in Tretchikoff's paintings. Bokhorst would have agreed with his assessment of the obsessive attention paid to finishing the portraits at the expense of the individuality and vitality of the sitter. "Only two portraits show any spontaneity and character, and these are ironically two unfinished works, actually studies for his *Javanese Woman* and *Lady of the Orient*," noted Van Bosch. "If only Tretchikoff had brought his portraits to a close at this point." Like other commentators, Van Bosch wondered whether the paintings had their own raison d'être, or whether they were destined for reproduction from the beginning.

Van Bosch also pointed to the elephant in the room: "Not one of the organisers, from the curator to the director of SANG, has dared to explain that Tretchikoff's art belonged there purely on merit." Naidoo is quoted only as saying that the work from the 1940s and 1950s was "quite strong in terms of painting ... and quite strong, quite academic, and when I say academic, I refer to it being good draughtsmanship".[63] Lloyd Pollak echoed Van Bosch's concern in a review and summary of the "fiery and passionate" panel discussion held at the end of the show, noting that despite "the war of words, the question of why Iziko saw fit to glorify Tretchikoff's blend of sexist and colonial racist bigotry with a retrospective at the National Gallery, never received a satisfactory answer".[64]

I wrote to my then Michaelis School colleague, artist and historian Colin Richards, asking what he thought of the exhibition. He responded:

> With the most open mind I can muster, I still cannot see why a show (to dignify it in this way) that should be at Checkers [a supermarket] next to the cigarettes, or, if absolutely necessary in the foyer of the One and Only [an hotel] finds its way to a national institution with some credibility. An aesthetic

atrocity of the highest (or lowest) order, a political mistake (the people's painter??!!!), a betrayal of artistic values that we struggle for and over, and a waste of scarce resources. And to imagine that my colleagues lubricated the whole affair, and the institution I teach in and respect is associated with this sour confection! And to think, we have to expose ourselves to the originals nogal [quite], and them to us. Never, never, and never again ... The only value in the process is that the awful reproductions look almost dignified in their debasement of the popular, their sentimentally sexist stereotypes, their small-minded aspirations (to be camp in the city?). Is there no prophylactic against this? If one criticises this kind of show you dignify it with the attention and feed the monster that it is. Yet passing over it with silence seems an act of bad faith.[65]

What did SANG's curators think? Where were their voices? Kaufmann was quoted by Pollak in a review: she maintained that the studies of Africans portrayed "imagined generic types" clad "in an amalgamation of different styles of different periods from different geographical areas" that "feed colonial notions of anonymous romanticised subjects".[66] In private correspondence to me at the time, Proud complained about the way in which the Tretchikoff project was unfolding, and what it would do to the reputation of the national art museum. He quoted something writer and critic Edmund Wilson said in 1946: "The most immoral and disgraceful and dangerous thing that anybody in the arts can do is knowingly to feed back to the public its own ignorance and cheap tastes."[67]

In an article titled "Why president Zuma is like Tretchikoff", UCT constitutional law scholar Pierre de Vos offered an unusual reading of the exhibition that encompassed contemporary politics.[68] De Vos described some of the pictures on view as "charmingly and gratifyingly kitsch," but thought a series illustrating the biblical Ten Commandments as "so hideous and badly painted that I had to flee the room". The encounter was the source of further reflection:

Surely one does not have to be an art lover to see how bad, tasteless – even ugly – most of these paintings are? After all, most credible critics have panned Tretchikoff's work and have been horrified that it has remained so popular with the general public – despite the fact that it is so bad and so tasteless.

De Vos then pivoted to consider Jacob Zuma, whose controversial presidency was still in its relative infancy, likening him to Tretchikoff.

Both are really bad at what they do but remain relatively popular. Both have done rather well financially because of what they do best (painting kitsch Javanese women for Tretchikoff, singing and dancing for Zuma). Both can pull a few tricks out of the hat to please the crowds. Both have been panned by the "critics" and shunned by the chattering classes. And the careers of both can be explained with reference to their tumultuous pasts.

After describing their respective histories and personalities, De Vos wondered if Zuma's reputation might still be salvaged, as had apparently happened with Tretchikoff.

> After all Tretchikoff – whom no reputable art gallery ever wanted to exhibit during his lifetime – is currently being exhibited in [SANG]. And although most of us in the chattering classes still think that he is an unremarkable painter, some of us would consider hanging Tretchikoff's *Green Lady* in our homes (perhaps positioned next to three lovely porcelain ducks flying into the sunset), to show our appreciation – in an ironic sort of way, of course – for this kitsch artist. Who knows, one day long after his tenure as president has come to an end, some of us in the chattering classes might yet raise an ironic cheer to Zuma – the ultimate survivor and lover of women. Let's face it, amongst the chattering classes, fads and fashions change fast, so if only our president could get his paranoia under control, he might still emerge as a president who did better than we expected of him.

As it turned out, De Vos' speculative optimism was misplaced. Jacob Zuma did not serve out his tenure: he was ousted as ANC president in December 2017, a procedural nicety that prefaced Cyril Ramaphosa's swearing in as South African president on 15 February 2018.[69]

In a tribute to renowned auctioneer and art expert Stephan Welz, who had died in December 2015, the Afrikaans television channel *KykNET* aired an interview with him on 3 January 2016. Welz spoke about selling Tretchikoff's paintings at the auction house Strauss & Co, the artist's technical facility and how he was heartsore about the exhibition at the gallery. He concluded that in the end the public would decide on the artist's reputation. Welz was correct: the venerated "people" voted with their feet.[70]

Much has been made of the 28,500 visitors who saw the Tretchikoff exhibition during its four-month run. Both Karin Preller and Ivor Powell, for instance, referred to the large attendance in their reviews.[71] The reality is that the attendance figures pale in comparison to the 10,000 visitors who flocked to *Gold from Peru* during its two-week run in 1981 and the 54,000 who queued to see *Picasso and Africa*, presented over forty-two days in 2006. If time is the ultimate arbiter of that which has value, SANG's visitor figures do not measure up to the staggering attendance figures that this artist once enjoyed in the cities of South Africa, and further afield.[72] Whatever one's view of Tretchikoff, the artist endures. He continues to pit the academy against the true believers, critics against collectors, be they from older generations who bought his prints or an evergreen younger generation who love his retro-kitsch.

In 2014, South Africa's democracy was twenty years old. This milestone coincided with Cape Town being awarded hosting rights as World Design Capital, an honour that offered an opportunity to once again highlight the permanent collection and reflect on acquisitions. Having access to the schedule as a council member, there was little in the way of forward planning.[73] Andrea Lewis and Ernestine White curated *'Brave New World' ... 20 Years of Democracy*, which comprised a selection of works acquired between 1994 and 2014, but not necessarily created during that time. This allowed the curators to place diverse artworks from the permanent collection in conversation, with a view to presenting "multi-layered insights into South Africa's past and present" and gauging "whether we are upholding the principles of democracy and the Constitution of our country".[74] The exhibition built on *A Decade of Democracy: South African Art 1994–2004*, but there was no catalogue, only a learner resource prepared by the educators.

Symbols of South African Cultures, a World Design Capital exhibition that originated with the South African Philatelic Services and the Post Office, was displayed at SANG. In September 2013 the Post Office issued a set of ten stamps featuring artefacts drawn from museum collections, including the 70,000 to 80,000 year old *Blombos Ochre* and the earliest shell beads.[75]

Major additions to the permanent collection

EARLY INTO HIS TENURE Naidoo stated that he wanted the institution to be "more inclusive in the audiences we appeal to, in the selection of our exhibitions, in the work that we acquire for our collections, in the people that make up our committees and in the staff that we hire".[76] Major acquisitions were made from the Iziko budget:

Virginia MacKenny's painting *Songs of Innocence and Experience (Dog Days)* (2007–08); Georgina Gratrix's painting *Les Demoiselles d'Avignon* (2008) (Plate 37); Hentie van der Merwe's watercolour *Pegasus* (2003); Kudzanai Chiurai's *Untitled I & II* (2009, ultrachrome ink on photo fibre paper); Hasan and Husain Essop's C-print *Pit Bull Fight* (2007); Noria Mabasa's sculpture *Ndi Mukegulu a ne a khou thsimbila na vhaduhulu vhaue vhavhili/Grandmother and her two children* (2008); Pierre Fouché's crochet cotton *The Kiss* (2007) (Plate 38); Malcolm Payne's screen-print *Colour Test* (1974, re-editioned 2010); a selection of ten prints by Dan Rakgoathe; Athi-Patra Ruga's embroidery *In my mind the summer will last ...* (2009); and Vuyile Voyiya's four linocuts, *Rhythm in ¾ Time III, IV, V and VI* (1988).

These were excellent and varied additions to the permanent collection. At first glance Gratrix's painting, from the 2008 *Women Wallpaper Series*, appeared to be a take on modernist hard-edged geometric abstraction, but in fact she reduced Pablo Picasso's *Les Demoiselles d'Avignon* (1907) to vertical stripes in order to explore myths of representation, the flatness of the picture surface and his unassailable genius.[77] The size and medium of the original are respected and the colours are "true" but the subjects have disappeared. Fouché also finds inspiration in art history; his delicate

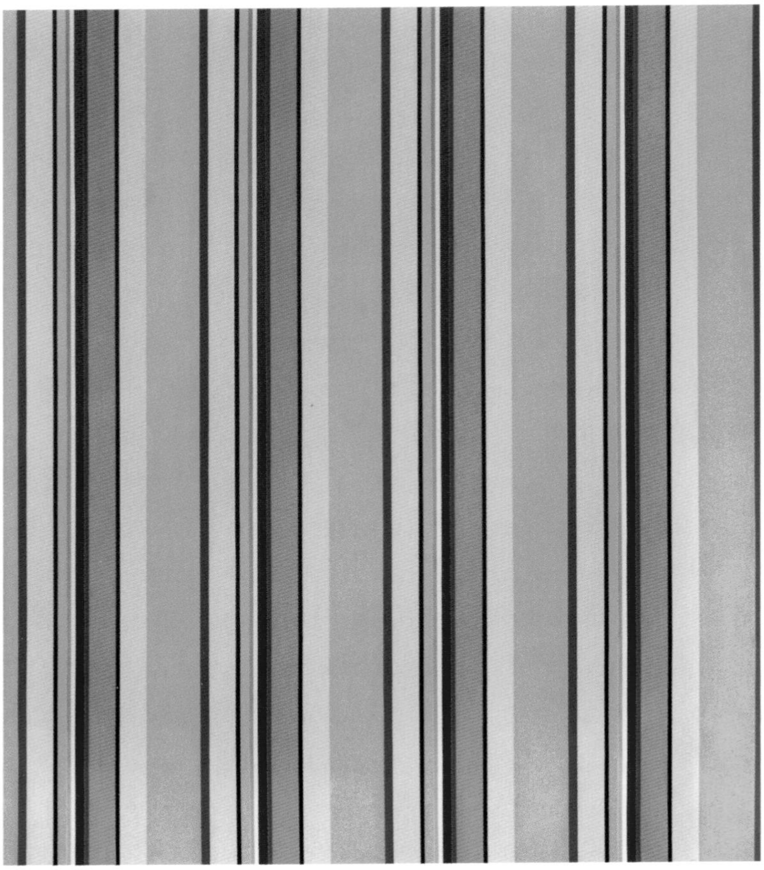

PLATE 37: Georgina Gratrix, *Les Demoiselles d'Avignon*, 2008, 1900 × 1300, oil on canvas; image courtesy of the artist and SMAC Gallery.

PLATE 38: Pierre Fouché, *The Kiss,* 2007, mercerised crochet cotton, 2000 × 1200 × 254; image courtesy of the artist.

mercerised crochet cotton piece evokes Auguste Rodin's famous marble sculpture, *The Kiss* (1882), as well as Tracey Rose's 2004 lambda print, which shares the same title. Like Rose, Fouché turns the original on its head and creates a multi-layered relief sculpture depicting two men kissing.

In a 2014 overview and history of photography at the gallery, curator Ingrid Masondo stated that between 2009 and 2011 purchases of photographs exceeded 40% of all artworks acquired. They included images by Graham Goddard, Fanie Jason, Svea Josephy, Jean Brundrit, Constance Stuart Larrabee, Zanele Muholi and Sabelo Mlangeni.[78] The video collection grew with works by Ed Young, Charles Maggs, Carol-Anne Gainer, Athi-Patra Ruga (*After he left*, 2008), Steven Cohen (*Chandelier*, 2001–2002), Gerald Machona (*Vabvakure (People from Far Away)*, 2012), and James Webb (*Le Marche Oriental*, 2009). The historical African art collection was augmented with purchases and gifts, including works presented by Alison Riley on behalf of the Elizabeth Newby-Fraser family.

SANG benefited from many donations from galleries and private individuals, including Betsy Younkins' large collection of prints by artists such as Azaria Mbatha, John Muafangejo, Dan Rakgoathe and Cyprian Shilakoe. Dr. M. Silbert presented a Wolf Kibel charcoal drawing *Church in Orange Street* (c. 1935), and Rhona Dubow gifted works on paper from the 1970s and 1980s by different artists. Alec and Lillian Rosenberg bequeathed paintings by May Hillhouse, Pranas Domsaitis, Cecil Higgs and Matthew Whippman, as well as two woodcuts by Wolf Kibel. Mark Coetzee offered a large number works in different media by David Brown, Isaac Julien, Khanyisile Mbongwa, Nandipha Mntambo, Andrew Putter and twelve of Sue Williamson's 1981 series of images, *The Last Supper, Manley Villa*. Michael Stevenson presented Churchill Madikida's mixed media installation *Status* (2005), and Samson Mudzunga's *Masindi* (2005), *Mmbe Ngwa Venda* (2006) and *Vivho Venda* (2007), while Zhané Warren of Warren Editions gifted a large collection of prints by various artists.

Artists were also supportive of the gallery. Michael Goldberg recreated his *Monument to the Nationalist Government* (1978/2009) for the *Strengths & Convictions* (2009) exhibition curated by Gavin Jantjes; the work was donated to SANG and the Friends covered transport costs from Australia. Kurt Campbell, Cameron Platter, Peter Clarke and Victor Gordon, among others, also donated work.

The South African Heritage Resources Agency (SAHRA) presented two unusual oil paintings on wooden roundels by George Pemba, *Men and Oxen Ploughing and Harvesting in the Wheatfields* (both undated), while the Roland and Leta Hill Trust purchased Tamlin Blake's woven glass beadwork piece *Standardised Mail, Nguni Bull* 1997 (2004) and three Iznik enamel on copper jugs. Albert Adams' *Portrait of an Afghan student* (1958) was acquired through the DAC repatriation budget.

The Friends bought important works by, for example, Jan-Henri Booyens (*Measuring Myth*, 2012), Brendhan Dickerson (*Cannon Fodder*, 2006), Diane Victor (*Disasters of Peace*, a portfolio of thirty etchings, 2001-2008), Trevor Coleman (*Untitled,* no date), six cartoons from Zapiro's *Lady Justice* series (2009), Gavin Younge *(Bonnie and Clyde (Remix)*, 1975/6–2009), Helmut Starcke *Ritual*, (2011) and assisted in the purchase of Mary Sibande's monumental sculpture *The Reign* (2010). After my retirement the Friends asked me to identify a work that they could purchase in my honour; I chose Penny Siopis' *Beast* (2009) (Plate 34). I have admired Siopis' work since the 1980s and this small ink and glue painting captures for me all the seductive and emotive qualities of the medium, as well as the enduring leitmotifs that characterise her oeuvre – allegory, ritual, sexuality, vulnerability, estrangement and the uncanny. The Friends of the Michaelis Collection acquired Clare Menck's oil painting *Young woman in a Dutch interior* (2014) in honour of Hans Fransen, who founded the association in 1993 and served on the committee until 2014.

Big picture plans and proposals yield nothing

AT A COUNCIL LEVEL, there was a need to review exhibitions and re-interpret collections held at all Iziko sites. According to Iziko council chairperson Ciraj Rassool, "the development of a coherent and detailed thematic plan and framework for the redevelopment of our various museums" was the most significant initiative of the council that served from 2010 to 2013. Other key issues included institutional redress, a financial review of Iziko's sustainability and a revision of its structure. The 2012–13 *Annual Report* identified the disciplinary "silos" as a problem:

> The purpose of restructuring is to integrate previously separate and even segregated collection-based departments into an organisation that is driven more purposefully and programmatically, and not worn down by genre-based 'silos' tainted by colonial collecting histories. The new structure will unlock the strength that lies in the variety of our museum sites and the vitality of our collections that have the potential to weave a new and uniquely South African narrative that embraces our interconnectedness and that of our collections.[79]

Iziko had been approached by a Dutch company prepared to invest €24,000 to re-envision the museums, but council was in agreement that such a significant project needed to be undertaken by South Africans. In 2011, a tender was put out for a "Big Picture" assessment and proposals. Executive management approved the relevant committee's recommendations and Mike Bruton, a marine biologist and designer of interactive science centres and museums, was appointed as consultant. Council members were requested to study his proposals and to comment on them. In my response I expressed concern that there were worrying gaps in the research, information and understanding of the nature and requirements of art and art collections.[80]

Bruton proposed the building of a maritime museum while ignoring the critical needs of SANG. His suggestions were frankly irresponsible: because millions were being spent on additional facilities for social and natural history collections, he suggested that plans for the Iziko Centre for Contemporary Art be shelved and that the beautiful heart of the building, the atrium, be closed in for the display of historical African objects, which by their very nature are fragile and light-sensitive. A drawing suggesting that the former library upstairs be used for exhibitions was deceptive, as it comprises offices and stopgap storage space. According to Bruton, the Michaelis Collection was under threat, and I agreed – it would indeed be the case if it were not for the Friends and their commitment to keep the site alive with activities and education programmes. Naidoo wanted to create a "museum of resistance art" at the Old Town House, which meant that the collection would go into storage.

I supported the principle of "cross-cutting" in the core functions departments, but noted that it would require a major mind-shift within Iziko, as previous attempts by art collections, described earlier in this book, had been received with little enthusiasm and had elicited no tangible responses from other collections. Restructuring alone had failed to achieve the desired integration of disciplines. Fortunately, council did not agree with Bruton's recommendations and appealed to the senior management team, which had embarked on visits to various sites, to present new views and a final report for ratification.[81] My council term ended in 2013 and, according to Bongani Ndhlovu, "the new council wanted to first understand their responsibilities as they were not ready to commit themselves to a project they did not fully understand".[82] DAC ignored the necessity of continuity from council to council in their appointments, and nothing happened with the development of a coherent strategy for core functions across Iziko. The next major restructuring would occur in 2016.

"Blood on the walls" when director is dropped

ONE OF THE LEITMOTIFS in this book is the relationship between directors and the national gallery's governing body. Naidoo's story is analogous yet different, because he reported to levels of Iziko executive management and was at some distance removed from the council. Naidoo had been employed on a five-year fixed-term contract that expired on 30 April 2014 – it was not renewed.[83] The decision not to keep Naidoo on as director was a bombshell. Iziko's handling of the matter was disastrous. Apart from stating that, in terms of his contract, Naidoo could not have had expectations of a renewal, the governing body kept mum. Not so the ousted director. On 8 May he addressed an email to "colleagues, partners, members of the media and friends" to thank them for their support.[84] He further informed the recipients of his email that he had been requested by Iziko to vacate his position. Naidoo left his readers with no doubt as to his opinions on the matter:

> I do believe that the actions of Iziko are unfair in this regard and will be looking to contest this decision further. This is regrettable especially since I believe that we have achieved a lot at [SANG] and the Iziko Art Collections department over the last five years under some very challenging conditions.

Naidoo attached a long, detailed and self-promoting media statement, and a list of highlights about exhibitions, acquisitions, fundraising and partnerships during his tenure. Naidoo's obfuscation of facts and appropriation of the achievements of others were staggering. As discussed at the beginning of this chapter, many of the partnerships were longstanding, or at least formed before he became director in 2009; the exhibitions were mostly curated by others, some inside the gallery, and others from outside. Working across collections and timelines was nothing new, and the credit he took for taking down the Bailey Collection ("a standalone, dedicated and permanent exhibition that had been constantly shown since 1947") and "finding creative solutions to this longstanding dilemma" was unwarranted and factually incorrect.

In his email petition, Naidoo stated, "it was important for us to address the imbalances of the past by acknowledging important and often overlooked artists in local art history". He proceeded to list and take credit for the career survey shows of Atkinson, Clarke, Cole, Maqhubela, Preller and Tretchikoff when, in fact, they were neither initiated nor curated by SANG staff, nor did he acknowledge any outside curators. He showed the same mendacity in relation to some of the group exhibitions, and the fundraising and partnerships claimed. As to the more than R2.5 million raised for *A Portrait of South Africa: George Hallett, Peter Clarke & Gerard Sekoto* (2013) shown in Paris, this sum was allocated as part of the France-South Africa exchange – it was not "raised" by SANG's ousted director.

Naidoo curated two international exhibitions: *Peter Clarke: Our artist, Our Poet*, which was presented at the Dak'Art Biennale in Dakar, Senegal (2012), and *Peter Clarke: Wind Blowing on the Cape Flats*, shown at the Institute of International Visual Art in London (2013). Interest in *1910–2010: From Pierneef to Gugulective* saw Naidoo invited to make presentations at many forums abroad.[85] As this volume has shown, invitations to the director of the gallery and staff were not unusual. What Naidoo did not do was to give back in the form of lectures, engaging with the public and, above all, publishing.

Naidoo viewed his directorship as an opportunity to showcase art from the African continent and shift the focus away from "the historical North-South relationship to a South-South one". *Rendez-Vous 12* from the Lyon Biennale featured work by young artists from, for example, Australia, Brazil, France, India, Mali, Russia, Thailand, Turkey, United Kingdom and the United States. Again the claim that "we raised more than R1.1 million in sponsorship to make this important exhibition possible" is misleading; it was part of the bilateral project with France and the funding came from France and the NAC.[86] Naidoo also claimed that they had been working with partners in Haiti and the United States to present an overview of Haitian art. The exhibition was planned for December 2015 and funding of €500,000 had been confirmed. According to Ndhlovu, Iziko had not received written confirmation of the funding and the project never materialised.

Visitor numbers had indeed increased during the runs of *1910–2010: From Pierneef to Gugulective* exhibition (67%) and *Tretchikoff: A People's Painter* exhibition (106%). Naidoo blamed the slump that followed on budget cuts.[88] In spite of the cuts and fluctuations in the acquisitions budget – from a high of R450,000 in 2010–11 to zero in 2012–13 and R50,000 in 2013–14 – significant works were added to SANG's collection. Naidoo, however, made no distinction between purchases and donations in the supporting document to his 8 May email. Noting that the South African art market had changed drastically and that contemporary art from Africa was attracting much international interest, Naidoo stated:

> … it was our strategy to acquire contemporary work by promising emerging artists … No longer could we sit back and wait for an artist to be established before we acquired an artwork by them. With very limited resources we had to be more proactive and look out for talented emerging artists before the markets celebrated them.[89]

Here, once again, Naidoo revealed his ahistorical approach to the gallery and its past policies and directions.

With regard to staff, Naidoo boasted about the appointment of a black curator of contemporary art (Ernestine White, who had worked at the gallery before) and a collections manager (Nkosinathi Gumede, who replaced another black collections manager, Robyn-Leigh Cedras, who had joined the staff in 2007 and left for the Rupert Museum in 2013). He referred to their "senior positions" as "unprecedented". Factually speaking, there are no "senior" positions in the art department and Gumede was appointed at the same level as Cedras. The external members of the acquisition committee remained the same until November 2017 and new members only accepted their appointment in October 2018.[90] Naidoo also omitted to mention that the first curator he appointed was white: Anthea Buys, who stayed for twelve months; she regarded the gallery's management as "too unyieldingly bureaucratic to see the results of hard work" and decided to become independent.[91]

For Cedras, this time at SANG was characterised by stifling "political agendas":

> At times it felt as though we simply couldn't work to any common purpose. In the end I struggled with all the last minute changes and shuffling around of our exhibitions schedule, which was mostly due to budgets being cut … or funds completely reallocated. Power struggles between [Naidoo] and the curators, not to mention the higher echelons of Iziko, made the job more of a dance on hot coals than a steady and planned progression towards the department's goals (whatever they were). Increasingly our departmental and interdepartmental issues, not to mention fallouts with outside institutions, became an embarrassing public display of egotistical disputes.[92]

The non-renewal of Naidoo's contract attracted a great deal of publicity. *The Guardian*'s headline screamed "Blood on the walls as South Africa's national gallery axes first black director". The writer Marianne Thamm, a veteran South African journalist with little investment in the art community, revisited *1910–2010: From Pierneef to Gugulective* and the "bold and risky endeavour" that replaced the "football exhibition" – when

Naidoo "felt the first sting of the so-called 'white art establishment' in Cape Town in 2010".[93] Details from Naidoo's media statement followed, as well as futile attempts by the *Daily Maverick*, for whom Thamm usually writes, to obtain answers from Bongani Ndhlovu and Melody Kleinsmith to a list of questions. The CEO released the following statement on 9 May 2014: "Naidoo was employed by Iziko Museums of South Africa on a fixed term contract. From the outset, [Naidoo] was aware that his contract would expire at the end of April 2014. Iziko has no further comment. Iziko will continue in future to provide the same exceptional quality art exhibitions that the public have always enjoyed." Unhappy with the response, Thamm concluded: "Those on the outside of the matter are left wondering: why the fear and loathing?"

The glowing, self-serving testimonial that Naidoo distributed, combined with a lack of information on the part of Iziko, prompted journalist Matthew Blackman to pen a follow-up editorial on *Artthrob*. He criticised Rooksana Omar for not responding to his questions; these included whether an acting director had been appointed, whether a new director had been selected and whether exhibitions would proceed without Naidoo.[94] These questions were premature, as such arrangements are not made in less than two weeks, and there was no reason to doubt that exhibitions and other activities would carry on as usual – these are the result of teamwork and not dependent on the presence of an individual. Besides, Naidoo had filed a complaint with the Commission for Conciliation, Mediation and Arbitration (CCMA), and Iziko was in no position to answer.

Like Thamm, Blackman uncritically accepted Naidoo's points of view, going so far as to write: "One major outcry concerned his taking down of the Bailey Collection and its inclusion into the rest of the gallery's collection. However, some see this now as one of Naidoo's greatest victories, allowing for more of the diverse collection to be seen." Victory? This was a disturbing lapse from a highly respected journalist and regular visitor to the gallery. Had he missed Proud's creative use of the collection in numerous thematic exhibitions and its virtual absence from the walls of SANG since 2010? Naidoo's departure was consistently linked to the budget, as if this were a sign of Iziko's attempt to undermine him. Having budgets slashed was nothing new. The pressure under which every director has had to manage and raise money is well documented in this book and elsewhere.

Naidoo's dismissal was the source of contretemps among critics. Melvyn Minnaar saw the situation differently to Thamm and Blackman. Writing in the *Mail & Guardian*, he said "Naidoo and his acolytes stirred up a flurry of arty political outrage" as a result of Iziko's "unfair" action.[95] Minnaar shifted the spotlight from Naidoo to the state of SANG, maintaining that the gallery was a victim of the Iziko structure. He wondered whether the museum's future was in doubt:

> … despite the huffing and puffing, the smoking gun isn't what the noisy ones think it is. The issue is not really about firing the man responsible for the institution. It's about a system and scholarship. It's about expertise and execution – and the lack of it.

Minnaar outlined the history of the national art museum and blamed the "real crisis" at the gallery on the bureaucratic Iziko structure and lack of adequate media management, dissemination of information and presentation of exhibitions. He also questioned the argument, put forward by Naidoo and his supporters, that bringing previously neglected artists and art into the canon had only happened during the preceding five years. In Minnaar's opinion Naidoo's appointment was arguably part of a system that failed the national art museum:

> How much he contributed to expertise, insight and erudition, is questionable. He opted to play to public appeal, choosing populism to draw people. He offered little curatorial motivation for those shows, no insight – critical for an institution that should chart current art history, especially one like the SANG. 'Feet through the door' is no counter to artistic discernment.

Adding to the polyphony of opinion and speculation, artist Kendell Geers, now based in Brussels, contributed his own extraordinary missive. Responding to Naidoo's entreaties for support, Geers wrote an open letter to the same people whom Naidoo had targeted. He expressed his sadness at learning that the director's contract had not been renewed, as it was unpleasant to lose one's job; he sent his condolences but affirmed that he would not support Naidoo, as he was "in complete solidarity with the decision to not renew his contract".[96] Geers went on to describe his futile attempt to collaborate with the art collections director on a retrospective scheduled to open in November 2010. He believed that SANG was on a par with international art museums and, together with his international galleries, had secured international museum partners, R1 million in funding and a publisher for the catalogue.

Geers blamed Naidoo for the exhibition's failure to occur. Naidoo's "blinding arrogance," he wrote, "prevented him from seeing that he lacked the experience needed to make such an exhibition open on time and so the show was postponed a number of times and eventually cancelled". It opened at the Haus der Kunst in Munich in February 2012, but South Africa was deprived of the opportunity because Naidoo "was unable to deliver on the most basic of professional museum requirements as demanded by the Haus der Kunst". To make matters worse, Geers' contract with Iziko stated that he would only liaise with the curator on curatorial decisions. Geers wondered how the director imagined it possible to put together a retrospective without the involvement of the artist. According to Geers, Naidoo's arrogance and lack of respect – for the artist personally, his work, sister institutions and sponsors – plunged him into a yearlong depression. Geers concluded:

> I have waited until now to speak out for I believe that the South African art world would be a better place without scandal. I believe that South African artists and curators need to support one another and collectively try to place South Africa on the international art map, in spite of the lack of basic government support and funding. I now feel compelled to speak out and make public that I fully support the decision to not renew Naidoo's contract and I will not be lending him my voice of support.

Veteran art critic Ivor Powell did not take sides in his article in the *Weekend Argus*. He referred to Naidoo's "glittering catalogue of achievement", considered the problems endemic to Iziko and expressed his sympathies for whoever would be appointed.[97] Powell quoted Geers, and added that he had been commissioned to write for the catalogue. It had ensnared him in "the Byzantine cycles of dilatoriness" of the institution. The nature of the official contract with Geers was, according to Powell, not "an aberration":

> While most co-curators and other partners in projects by the gallery are reluctant to be quoted on the subject, the accounts are legion in the art world of this kind of intellectual property predation. For instance, one curator of a major partnered project – who had similarly conceptualised the show, secured funding and arranged for it to travel abroad – was more than a little surprised to discover that the sole curatorial credit on promotional banners was given to SANG.

Naidoo filed a complaint with the CCMA, while Iziko threatened with a court interdict should he make any further public statements. Dissatisfied with the CCMA findings, Naidoo took his case to the Labour Court. What was it really all about? The litany of allegations and counter-allegations, denials, defensive responses, inconsistencies and bewildering statements is captured in case number C876/2015, held at the Labour Court in Cape Town. In the following paragraphs I attempt to distil the essence of the case from the forty-one-page pleadings bundle and papers prepared for the trial hearing.[98]

As mentioned above, the art collections budget was slashed in 2011 and 2012. Naidoo, interpreting this as victimisation, took legal advice. Prior to the expiration of his contract, Naidoo had received a request from Bongani Ndhlovu to host an exhibition of photographer and activist Omar Badsha's work. The exhibitions committee turned it down because SANG had featured his work previously; there was also a potential conflict of interest as Badsha was a council member at the time. This proposed exhibition became a "hot potato". In an unprecedented move, Ndhlovu attended a gallery meeting and instructed SANG staff to host the exhibition. It was clear that pressure was being exerted, although from where was unclear. The CEO got involved, but Naidoo stood his ground. He was convinced that this added to his woes within the institution. In the event, *Seedtime: A Retrospective of Omar Badsha*, curated by Badsha and Carol Kaufmann, went ahead. Iziko denied that staff had been instructed, but stressed in the court papers that the "CEO and its [sic] Executive Directors at all times retain the prerogative to make executive decisions" on behalf of Iziko.

According to Naidoo, the letter in which Rooksana Omar informed him of the non-renewal of his contract contained "no cogent reason" for this, instead offering a vague indication that she was "not sure about the future of the position" that he occupied. This would ultimately become a core issue in the case; it was intuited as betraying "an ulterior and unfair motive" for not renewing the contract. Naidoo's attorney at the time, however, decided not to raise this ground for non-renewal at the CCMA. At the hearing Ndhlovu maintained that Naidoo had been a poor performer, but the latter produced performance evaluations conducted by Ndhlovu that indicated "precisely the opposite". Ndhlovu allegedly also "dissembled" in the arbitration when testifying about a meeting held in June 2013 at which he promised Naidoo a permanent appointment; this time, however, Ndhlovu was contradicted by the council minutes.

The restructuring of core functions at Iziko did come up, with Naidoo casting doubt on Iziko's evidence that the process had started in October 2012. Minutes of the meetings held that month, and again in January and May 2013, were, claimed Naidoo, tailored to suit Iziko's executive director of operations Denise Crous' contention that her institution did not require a director of art collections. Naidoo felt that this, on the one hand, negatively influenced the CCMA commissioner's arbitration award of a one-year renewal contract back-dated from 1 May 2014 to 30 April 2015; and, on the other hand, the commissioner was seemingly influenced by the extension of education and public programmes director Wayne Alexander's contract for a further five years, thereby re-instating Naidoo for a short period.

Naidoo's return to work was accompanied by chaos and confusion. He claimed that he was subjected to victimisation, harassment, bullying and unfair discrimination and instituted grievances against executive directors and the CEO. The chairperson of council was involved and tried to resolve the grievances, but Naidoo apparently did not furnish the specific information that was requested. The R340,000 National Lotteries allocation for a catalogue for *1910–2010: From Pierneef to Gugulective* had not been spent. Naidoo accused Iziko of "impulsively" returning the money. Iziko maintained that the money was returned on instruction from the Lotto board in order to ensure that the funding proposal for the upgrade of the planetarium would not be compromised. The reality is that Naidoo had been at the gallery since May 2009, the exhibition opened a year later but by the end of 2014, when he started contacting potential contributors, there still was no catalogue.

Iziko's actions vis-à-vis Naidoo and the restructuring process are riddled with inconsistencies, particularly in their planning, and are difficult to unravel. Pam Warne had passed away in March 2014. In October Naidoo was interviewed for a permanent position as curator of photography and new media, at entry level with six months probation. He rejected the offer as it was an obvious demotion; besides, accepting it would have implied his agreement with and complicity in the scrapping of the post of director of art collections. Naidoo also had expectations of being reinstated.

By January 2015 the final form of the new structure was under review and Naidoo once again approached the CCMA. On 27 March, two hours before conciliation, Iziko offered Naidoo a three-month post as director of art and social history, a move that is described as "penurious", as the two departments had not been combined and there was no such post. That Iziko executive management could contemplate merging two vast collections, including the already neglected social history satellite museums, strains credulity and speaks to a fundamental lack of understanding of its responsibilities as custodian of the nation's patrimony. Naidoo declined the offer, the mediation failed and he was out of contract and unemployed for five months. He lodged two more disputes with the CCMA, mainly based on unfair dismissal and unfair discrimination. At issue were Iziko's ulterior motives, expressed through their offer for him to participate in restructuring consultations, and bad faith in the various short-term extensions of his contract. Naidoo also contended that a grievance Proud had instituted against him stemmed from the fact that he (Proud) had unsuccessfully applied for the directorship. He also accused Proud and Kaufmann of both undermining his leadership and colluding with Crous. Furthermore, the internal auditor had investigated acquisitions without Naidoo's knowledge and he was required to merge four job descriptions into two.

In the midst of this bitter legal wrangling, the state broadcaster, SABC 3, aired a programme titled *Riason Naidoo, Change Agent*, on 14 June 2015. Billed as an exploration of the life of "the boy from Chatsworth, Durban," it provided Naidoo with an opportunity to affirm that he had "done a very good job" by taking SANG "to another level", breaking "geographic parochialism" by, among other things, making the art museum "national rather than just provincial" and placing it in a "dialogue with the rest of the world".[99] Once again Naidoo massaged the truth with his comments on the Bailey Collection, the World Cup and the negative impact of the budget cuts on his directorship. Ironically, many of the works shown on the programme were acquired before his arrival. Iziko colleagues were absent but Antoinette Murdoch, then chief curator at JAG, art critic Mary Corrigall, curator and writer Khwezi Gule and artist Lionel Davis commented positively on Naidoo's work. Davis, for instance, stated that as "a person of colour" Naidoo had brought a "breath of fresh air" to the gallery.

The arbitration proceedings ultimately went against Naidoo. Dissatisfied with the outcome, he took his case to the Labour Court. This ushered in a period of even greater uncertainty at the gallery, during which curators took turns to head art collections on a three-monthly basis. Lodged on 24 July 2017, the nature of Naidoo's dispute hinged on two claims: the first related to his unfair dismissal and non-renewal of a fixed-term contract or failure to be made permanent; and the second averred unfair discrimination and/or harassment and/or victimisation and/or bullying in terms of the Employment Equity Act.[100] Naidoo's lawyers proposed three remedies: firstly, that he be reinstated indefinitely, or on a fixed-term contract for five years consistent with other directors and executive management; secondly, that he be reinstated to the position of director of art collections on a permanent basis with effect from 1 June 2015, alternative to which he receive two years' remuneration as compensation; and thirdly, that he receive twenty-four month's gross remuneration as compensation for damages and that Iziko be responsible for all the costs of the legal proceedings arising from the non-renewal of his contract in April 2014 on an attorney/client scale; and any further and/or alternative relief as the court may deem fit.

Iziko's response to the details of Naidoo's case and claims were summed up in twenty-five paragraphs. They revealed a great deal about Iziko management's attitudes towards SANG, in particular through their denial that it is the foremost institution of its kind in the country. Shocking as this may be, coming from those who are meant to value and advance the art gallery, the statement in fact confirms the prevailing mind-set of the gallery's overseers. It also sums up Iziko's successes in diminishing the national art museum's role and status. The denial constitutes a slap in the face for all who have worked tirelessly to establish and maintain the reputation of the institution as the national art museum and foremost of its kind in the country, if not the continent.[101]

In its pleadings Iziko admitted to some of Naidoo's allegations and refuted others. While admitting that Naidoo had been advised that there was "uncertainty regarding the future of the position that he occupied", all other allegations in that regard were denied. Naidoo was not in the top ten percent of employees, as he claimed, but merely an "average performer" who had not received a performance bonus. Iziko denied that Ndhlovu "dissembled" in the arbitration.

The case was set down for hearing from 1 to 4 August 2017, with John MacRobert acting for Naidoo and advocate Frans Rautenbach and attorney Glen Cassells of Maserumule Incorporated for Iziko. On the second day of proceedings the parties reached an agreement and issued the following joint statement, which Iziko posted its website on 10 August: "Pursuant to a restructuring exercise, the position of Director: Art Collections was abolished. An alternative position was offered to the Director, Riason Naidoo, which he declined. The parties have reached a settlement, the terms of which are confidential between them." The terms are, however, part of the public record: Iziko paid Naidoo a severance package of R832,090 (excluding statutory deductions, if any) and applied to the South African Revenue Services for a favourable tax dispensation. Both litigating parties paid their own costs.

The Naidoo matter was now settled, but awkward questions around institutional culpability remain. Was anyone at Iziko, a public institution funded by taxpayers, held responsible for creating and/or exacerbating the problems with Naidoo? What about the very significant costs incurred by the extended legal dispute that involved court time? The 2016–17 *Annual Report* blithely acknowledged two "unrelated labour cases by a director and an Iziko employee, which may result in liabilities for the entity". When the report was signed off, at the end of March 2017, the outcomes were unknown and no provision had been made in the financial statements. However, the legal costs associated with these legal matters were pegged at just over R3 million, an enormous sum given that in 2016 it had been R200,000.[102] No mention is made of the case relating to "a director" in the 2017-18 Annual Report and the agreement reached with Naidoo; the other case "involving misconduct ... was successfully concluded in 2017/18. The judgement was in favour of Iziko". [103] Elsewhere in this report it is stated that "Legal fees were spent strategically, resulting in no judgments made against Iziko." [104]

One may deduce from Naidoo's case against Iziko that the restructuring was an *ad hominem* attack, one directed against the person rather than the position. Mario Pissarra raised this in an article.[105] Pissarra compared the two statements issued by Iziko: one when Naidoo's contract was not renewed, and the other when the Labour Court case was settled out of court. He concluded that the reasons given did not add up: in 2014 Naidoo's contract had expired and was not renewed; by 2017 the joint statement specified that he had been offered another position, which he declined. The situation had in fact been the subject of open speculation for a long time. We will never know what led to the settlement, but it is a bitter and costly irony that a person whose contract was not renewed ended up with a huge severance package. More pressingly, Iziko management risked the future of its three main collections, and the reputations of its museums. This was a mind-boggling gamble, and the source of real dread given Iziko's commitment to restructuring. The negative impact of this policy is the subject of the next chapter.

PLATE 39: Hendrik Stroebel, *Port of Plenty*, 1987/1991, fabric, thread, ceramic, 2505 × 1460; courtesy of the artist; photographer Kathy Grundlingh.

9

The impact of the new Iziko collections structure and the lack of leadership at SANG

2014 – 2017

THIS CHAPTER details the implementation of the new organisational structure and its negative impact on SANG, which is stripped of what remained of its vision and autonomy. The restructuring process and "re-imagining" Iziko's collections occur during a period of uncertainty around the former director's position. The fault lines in the structure and the lack of leadership at the gallery are soon exposed. Fortunately, curators are not deterred from organising excellent exhibitions and the first, hugely successful Museum Night. Important gifts are received and acquisitions made. The Old Town House is closed due to lack of maintenance of the electrical system. Things kept changing in 2018 while the manuscript was edited and revised, and significant occurrences are recorded and analysed.

One of the truest tests of integrity
is the blunt refusal
to be compromised.
CHINUA ACHEBE[1]

Uncertainty and uneasiness persist

THE CLIMATE OF UNCERTAINTY caused by Riason Naidoo's legal dispute with Iziko exacerbated working conditions in the art museum, which was also ensnared in the mesh of disempowering bureaucracy and confronted by lack of proper funding and management. Nevertheless, work continued. Ingrid Masondo was appointed curator of photography and new media, and Sepadi Moruthane as registrar. Curators participated in conferences and panel discussions and published in the popular media. Masondo's appointment followed on the death of Pam Warne, on 15 March 2014, from a rare autoimmune disorder. Warne had been seriously ill with kidney failure by June 2013, but characteristically she worked throughout her dialysis treatment, often to her own detriment.

Warne had a long and distinguished career in the domains of photography and museums. Prior to her appointment as curator of photography and new media in art collections in 2003, she worked at the former South African Cultural History Museum and, in fact, proposed its new name – "Slave Lodge" – after the amalgamation. Her legacy runs deep, and extends to the memorable photograph she made of Tracey Rose for her work *The Kiss* (2001), created during Rose's Fresh residency at the gallery. Warne left prints by Hardy Botha, Lionel Davis, Tiemie Rosser and Manfred Zylla to SANG. Photographer David Goldblatt spoke warmly of Warne's importance to South African photography:

> If Pam Warne was shy and unassuming in an exceptional degree, she was equally firm in her convictions and in the quiet but determined ways in which she followed them. Photography and its archive at SANG have lost a passionate supporter and defender, and I, a colleague for whom I had a warm and high regard.[2]

Acquisitions were also made during the difficult early years of Iziko and Naidoo's litigation proceeding, and SANG benefited from the Friends' on-going support, as well as from many bequests and donations. Iziko's successful registration as a Public Benefit Organisation was significant, as bequests and presentations would qualify for tax benefits.

Purchases included work by many young black artists who were enjoying increasing exposure by local art dealers. Among them were Leonce Raphael Agbodjélou, Hasan and Husain Essop, S'Bonelo Tau Luthuli, Rafiq Mayet, Sethembile Msezane, Simphiwe Ndzube and Musa Nxumalo. The gallery also acquired the Wits History of Art Print Portfolio 2 (2014) and fifteen linocuts by Alexander Podlashuc (1977–79). The Friends added three inkjet prints by Thania Petersen (2015), Gerald Machona's photograph *Millennium Bar* (2010), Athi-Patra Ruga's photograph *The Intervention on the Anglo-Boer War Monument by the F.W.W.O.A. in 2012* (2015), ceramics by S'Bonelo Tau Luthuli (2015) and Maurice Mbikayi's major sculpture, *E-Mukishi* (2015), crafted from computer parts, fibreglass, resin cloths and found objects. Undocumented works from the Old Town House were absorbed into the collection. Since Carol Kaufmann's retirement in March 2016 the post of curator of African art has remained vacant, and the absence of purchases of historical African art is conspicuous.

Sue Robinson bequeathed Edoardo Villa's bronze *Untitled* (no date given) to the gallery, while the Michaelis Orthopaedic Hospital donated early twentieth-century French and British paintings. Artists George Hallett (through Gallery MOMO), Stephen Inggs and Thania Petersen generously presented their work, and art critic Lloyd Pollak gifted Mark Coetzee's six *Penis Prints* (c. 1998) and two paintings from Clive van den Berg's *Frontier Erotics* series (c. 1999). Photographer Tom Pierce presented sixteen portraits of white males who objected to mandatory conscription to the military during the apartheid regime's war on the border of Namibia and Angola.[3]

The challenges are great, but the gallery remains a beautiful, desirable venue – in spite of Iziko management's unenthusiastic attitude to its status, as expressed in the Naidoo court papers. Artists still dream of survey or retrospective exhibitions in their national gallery, and, as this book has amply demonstrated, good curators achieve in spite of adverse conditions. On a visit to The Netherlands, curator Andrea Lewis experienced Museum Night Amsterdam, during which some fifty museums in the city open their doors from 19h00 to 02h00. She brought the idea to Iziko. In 2015, working with First Thursdays, a monthly event where Cape Town galleries and stores in the central city are open until late, Lewis initiated Museum Night. More than 12,000 people attended the first event and it now occurs annually.[4] The 2017 iteration featured poetry, music, dance and live cartoon drawing by Brandan Reynolds whose work was displayed in the exhibition *Alternative Press: Works by Derek Bauer.*

There were a number of exceptional exhibitions during the years 2014 and 2017. The gallery hosted *Time and Again*, the first retrospective exhibition by globally recognised South African artist Penny Siopis, in December 2014. Working closely with the artist and drawing on institutional and personal collections, the exhibition celebrated thirty-five years of Siopis' remarkable aesthetic production in painting, sculpture, video and multi-media installations. The exhibition traced processes of change and the human condition that in Siopis' work is deeply personal and political. *Time and Again* was accompanied by a comprehensive, scholarly book edited by Wits academic Gerrit Olivier and published by Wits University Press; it offered an opportunity for students and learners to engage with Siopis' oeuvre on an unprecedented scale.

Moses Tladi Unearthed opened on 24 September 2015, Heritage Day. The exhibition and the book, *The Artist in the Garden The Quest for Moses Tladi*, were the result of Angela Read Lloyd's personal mission to tell the story of the gardener who worked for (and was also patronised by) her grandfather, and who in 1931 became the first black artist to have his paintings displayed in the national gallery.[6] Initiated by the South African Society of Artists (SASA), the *First Annual Exhibition of Contemporary National Art* included Tladi's *Witwatersrand Winter* and *Spring* (c. 1931). He was the only black artist on this nominally inclusive exhibition.

According to Hayden Proud, the 1931 exhibition was organised "in the hope of mollifying the outrage of SASA over SANG's inaugural exhibition" – the selling show, discussed in chapter one, which had disgraced the much-anticipated inauguration of the building in 1930. Commenting on Tladi's work on the 1931 show, board member and critic Bernard Lewis described the artist as a "Basuto houseboy" with "a naïve technique all his own" that told "the stark truth about the atmosphere of the Transvaal 'in a poetic way'".[7] Thanks to the UCT-Mellon Fund that is linked to the Honours in Curatorship degree at Michaelis, and Lloyd's commitment to rescuing Tladi's reputation and reintroducing him into South African art history, the curators unearthed some thirty superb paintings, predominantly landscapes.

In February 2015, SANG hosted William Kentridge's complex work *The Refusal of Time* (2012). Commissioned by Documenta 13 artistic director Carolyn Christov-Bakargiev and premièred at Documenta 13 in Kassel, Germany, Kentridge's five-channel film installation was produced in collaboration with science historian Peter Galison, video filmmaker Catherine Meyburgh, composer Philip Miller and dancer Dada Masilo. Kentridge's work captured the loss and disruption, and the fragmentation and coherence, which came with the standardisation of time in the 1800s. Inspired by science and early cinema, *The Refusal of Time* included film animation, a soundscape and wooden "time machine" that expanded and contracted, endlessly moving and breathing. The work showcased Kentridge's prodigious imagination and fields of interest and knowledge. He participated in the performance amid different scenes, processions, maps, texts, chairs, ticking clocks, megaphones, mechanical instruments and projected metronomes that metamorphosed into threatening structures on the gallery walls.

While Kentridge's work seamlessly straddled art and science, the disciplines were only partially integrated in *Shared Sky*, an exhibition initiated by Square Kilometre Array (SKA), a joint Australian-South African project that explores the universe with the world's largest radio telescope. The exhibition celebrated ancient cultural wisdom and visual motifs, and brought together Aboriginal Australian and South African artists under one sky in two cities: Cape Town and Perth. South African archaeologist John Parkington and Australian curator Chris Malcolm worked with the First People Centre of the Bethesda Arts Centre, established by poet Jeni Couzyn in the rural Eastern Cape settlement of Nieu Bethesda, and artists from the Yamaji Art Centre in Geraldton, Western Australia. Heritage, museum and education consultant Sandra Prosalendis curated the exhibition at SANG.[8] The Yamaji paintings were executed in the traditional dot style, whereas South Africans of |xam descent created images in a variety of textile techniques. Here indigenous astronomy and art merged, but the straightforward nature of the information about the SKA project on the exhibition jarred in the context of the gallery. *Shared Sky* could have worked well and crossed disciplines at the natural history museum, particularly in the space in which the art collection was accommodated for many years.

Two photographers were honoured with retrospectives during this period. Jodi Bieber's *Between Darkness and Light* (2015) was presented in partnership with the artist and the Goodman Gallery, and covered the years 1993 to 2010. It included nearly 100 photographs from eight of Bieber's key projects and a multimedia installation from her "Survivors of domestic violence" series. *Seedtime: A Retrospective of Omar Badsha* (2015), which created so much controversy with Naidoo and within Iziko, comprised four photographic essays spanning the years 1976 to 2010, as well as drawings, woodcuts, mono-prints and sculpture. The title of the show was inspired by a Mafika Gwala poem written in the wake of the 1976 Soweto student uprising. It set the tone for an exhibition by an artist-activist whose aesthetic production is inseparable from the cultural and political history of South Africa and its people. This was particularly powerful in the large section "Narratives of a Time of Revolution," but Badsha's ambit was wider, with images from Denmark, Ethiopia and his grandparents' ancestral village in Gujarat, India. His subject matter is, in the first instance, people and as Sean O'Toole put it, his portraits are "marked by great affection" that "capture the dynamic interplay of history and personal circumstance".[9]

Michael Godby's thematic exhibition, *Home Truths: Domestic Interiors in South African Collections* (2016), followed on two earlier exhibitions, *Is there Still Life?: Continuity and Change in South African Still Life Painting* (2007) and *The Lie of the Land: Representations of the South African Landscape* (2010). Like its predecessors, *Home Truths* was destined for the Old Town House, but in 2016 the site was closed for an unspecified period; lack of maintenance of the electric wiring resulted in serious and escalating problems and the collection was moved to the gallery. By December 2018 the site remained closed.[10] As to be expected from Godby, the exhibition was an excellent example of what a curator with a comprehensive field of reference and profound knowledge of art history can achieve.

Godby's leitmotif for *Home Truths* was Walter Benjamin's notion that the security, comfort and individuation offered by the home can assume positive as well as negative connotations. Drawn from public and private collections, the exhibition offered visitors an opportunity of seeing, perhaps for the first time, important but unseen paintings from the foundation collections of South African art museums. Many Victorian paintings – dismissed by modernists as conservative and today regarded by many as unwelcome colonial heritage – were liberated from their basement graves and given new life, interpretations and significance in the company of works that ranged from the seventeenth century to 2016.[11] There were unfortunately gaps. Paintings destined from the JAG collection did not arrive, despite curator Stefan Hundt's renewed efforts to secure them when the show moved to the Sanlam Art Gallery. Inefficiency is now a hallmark of our art museums; escalating insurance costs and the depreciation of the rand have further added to the difficulties of mounting shows.[12]

Collaborations remain a feature of SANG's exhibition programme. In 2017 Kim Siebert, former educator and collections manager at the gallery, and now collection and conservation manager at the Taiyuan Asian Puppet Theatre Museum in Taipei, Taiwan, returned to the gallery with *The Magic of Asian Theatre Puppets: Beauties, Heroes, Villains, Gods and Clowns*, an exhibition of puppets and related artefacts covering most Asian traditions and countries.

The permanent collection was not neglected. *Brushing up on Stern* (2015) combined SANG's holdings of Irma Stern's oeuvre with loans from a number of private collections. Curators Kaufmann and Lewis, in collaboration with art consultant Phillippa Duncan and the Irma Stern Museum, created a rich environment for oil paintings, gouaches and drawings by including the proofs of Stern's first German publication and the African sculpture, fabrics and ceramics that the artist loved to paint. Stern's intense, painterly expressionism and her interest in Africa were initially met with disdain by South Africa's parochial art cognoscenti, and it was only in her midlife that she achieved great success. This exhibition and its accompanying catalogue provided an occasion to reassess Stern's legacy, her on-going popularity and status as one of the top-ten most valuable woman artists sold at auction globally between 2005 and 2015.[13]

In 2016, Proud curated *Selections from our Historical Collections*, and for their exhibition *The Art of Disruptions* Lewis and Masondo augmented the permanent collection with loans of contemporary works. *The Art of Disruptions* opened on 16 June 2016, and marked significant political events in South African history: the sixtieth anniversary of the 1956 Women's March to Pretoria against pass laws; the declaration of District Six as a whites-only area in 1966; the fortieth anniversary of the student rebellion that started in Soweto; and the 1986 declaration of a second state of emergency, intended to suppress and control mass action. While reflecting on these ground-shifting moments in our history, burning current issues – racism, sexism, homophobia, inequality and privilege, corruption, migration and environmental degradation – were also confronted and explored. A large chalkboard enabled visitors to air their views about protest and social activism. I will discuss the brouhaha caused by artist Dean Hutton's contribution to Lewis' and Masondo's show later in this chapter.

Curated by Ernestine White and independent curator Olga Speakes, *Women's Work: Crafting stories, subverting narratives* (2016) was a memorable exhibition that juxtaposed historical and contemporary works from public and private collections to tell a fascinating and superbly constructed story spanning three centuries. Starting with a seventeenth-century Belgian tapestry, the curators presented works that engaged subjects ranging from colonial exploitation to land and identity, and also religion, sexuality and gendered power relations. It revealed how techniques such as knitting, crocheting, embroidery, quilting and beadwork – traditionally associated with domesticity and women – were being utilised by contemporary male and female artists alike (Plate 39). Artist Lisa Grobler transformed the atrium into a site-specific, mixed media installation. As in many past exhibitions, boundaries between art and craft were interrogated and shifted. The exhibition had no catalogue.

It is unfortunate that two very good exhibitions, *Women's Work* and *At Face Value* (2016), which probed the longevity of the genre of portraiture and the range and complexity of works in the permanent collection, were overshadowed by another controversy at the art museum in December 2016. Before unravelling what transpired, it is necessary to discuss what had been happening behind the scenes during Naidoo's legal dispute with Iziko, as this had a direct impact on these events.

Re-imagining and restructuring Iziko museums

WHILE SANG STAFF and board had supported and advanced the establishment of Iziko Museums, this new supervisory body and administrative structure did away with directors of individual museums, thereby eroding the autonomy of institutions like the national gallery. The next phase of restructuring abolished the posts of directors of collections. In terms of international best practice the director of a museum is a highly qualified and respected specialist in his or her discipline, an excellent manager and fundraiser, and someone who is the face of the institution. Not only were the power and influence of the national art museum eviscerated, the symbolic damage remains considerable. Prior to the amalgamation of national museums, directors contributed to a committee that met regularly. They constituted a powerful lobby group that, for example, participated in writing legislation for post-apartheid cultural institutions.

The "re-alignment" was confirmed at a workshop held on 22 March 2016 at the Cape Craft and Design Institute, to which Iziko invited relevant participants. Attendees received an anonymous discussion document that outlined the scope of the proceedings:

> Iziko is in a process of re-imagining its museums to make them respond to the challenges/themes of the present century. In general, difficult questions have been asked regarding Iziko's exhibition approach. Iziko would like to tackle these questions and incorporate the input to be generated during a workshop on its conceptual documents as it plans for the next generation of exhibitions.[14]

Steven Sack, a respected curator, administrator and former director of the Wits Origins Centre, was appointed as facilitator of the workshop. His discussion document was based on information provided by Iziko, including Mike Bruton's proposals, and interviews with some staff.[15] The different voices came through in the text. The document revealed much about the lack of knowledge of and attitudes to the national art museum that are current in Iziko. The institution was presented as an unrehabilitated colonial remnant that only had white curators until Naidoo came along. The document, which was very much Cape Town focussed, stated that SANG had to move from a "one-sided view of world art histories and developments" to embrace Africa and the Global South, and acquire "indigenous traditional African art and artefacts from other parts of the continent". The latter statement demonstrated an ignorance of the histories of collections within Iziko and the richness of the former SAM ethnographic collections. There was advice on research, online presence, conservation, acquisitions, exhibitions, funding and a sculpture garden extending into the Company's Garden. There was also agreement with my idea, first proposed in the 1990s, of an additional building "to extend the capacity for storage of the collection and increase possibilities of display of exhibitions".

Rooksana Omar opened proceedings with a broad summary and council's dissatisfaction with Bruton's proposals. The many site visits and workshops that followed had culminated in the workshop, she explained. Omar also informed the gathering that a new structure was to be implemented. Carolyn Hamilton, a cultural scholar from UCT, and Leslie Witz, a historian from UWC, chaired the breakaway session for the visual arts, which included Iziko staff. Pressing issues were raised in the lively discussion: the stifling effects of the lack of adequate space, not only on the collections and core functions, but also on the imaginations of staff; the desire to work across disciplines; bureaucratic constraints; art education; the absence of career paths and opportunities; the need to reach marginalised people in society; and – above all – free entrance. The discussions distilled a question: "Why museums?" Witz responded by referring to the success of the exhibitions *Ezakwantu*, *Miscast* and *Face Value: Old heads in modern masks*, all held at the gallery in the 1990s.

The plenary covered a lot of ground and was dominated by the relationship of humans to the environment, and whether people belonged in the natural history museum, or not. Andrea Lewis presented a concept document outlining the way forward for the art museum over the next five years. She drew attention to a series of exhibitions and a substantial publication in the build-up to the 150th anniversary of the founding of the collection in 2021. Lewis also identified key aims: maximising the potential of the existing building, preparing a comprehensive document for extensions to the gallery to be included in the DAC's User Asset Management Plan schedule by 2021, and increasing digital access to the collections. The latter was non-existent, as was preparation for revitalising the decades-old need for expansion of the national art museum. I return to this in chapter ten.

In his summary, Sack indicated that the way forward would be further communication with participants in the form of a conceptual framework, and the possibility of establishing an advisory committee. What followed, though, was complete silence – a sign of the lack of communication and transparency with which Iziko has become synonymous, and a lack of respect for the individuals who have given their time and expertise. Sack wrote a report after the workshop with various recommendations about further actions that Iziko could take. He did not hear from Iziko management again.[16] The document was not shared with participants.

A year after the workshop, Ndhlovu informed me that the inputs were part of the "Re-imagining Iziko" process and that art collections had begun "to implement some of the recommendations contained in the document".[17] It was not clear to which document and recommendations he was referring. In December 2017 Hamish Robertson confirmed that the workshop was the instigator for ideas that would result in a document scheduled for completion in September 2019, and that internal and external consultation would follow; nothing came of it.[18] Iziko's decolonisation rhetoric features prominently on the back cover of the 2017-18 *Annual Report* and there is an acknowledgment that the museum is "not equipped to do it alone. We therefore value active discussions and debates with all stakeholders and interested parties, and are open to re-imagining our museum spaces in an inclusive manner". In light of the lack of action almost three years after the workshop, these are just more empty words.

The workshop once again highlighted the uncomfortable position of the art museum within Iziko's structure. It also revealed this governing body's attachment to the narrative that the museum was untransformed, and had to be "re-invented" to fit in with DAC imperatives regarding social cohesion and nation building. Within the broader definition of what museums are and what they do, the three major discipline museums have vastly different histories, practices and roles, and by constantly labelling all with the same tag, their individual challenges and achievements are ignored. This, of course, enhances the rhetoric that is repeated, year after year, in the *Annual Reports*. In reality, though, Iziko has allowed the gallery to sink into the shadows.

What made the new structure possible, and how does it look? At the same time as Naidoo's case was rumbling on, his future at Iziko uncertain, social history director Lalou Meltzer retired; this left only Hamish Robertson as natural history director. Iziko management did away with the role of director for collections and created two new positions: a director role for research and exhibitions, and another director position for collections and digitisation. The posts were advertised externally, but two Iziko employees were appointed in 1 April 2017: Robertson to the former post, and social historian Paul Tichmann to the latter. The static exhibitions and halls that have remained unchanged for decades at SAM and the Slave Lodge did not inspire confidence that an exciting programme was about to emerge.[19] Whatever their achievements in their respective fields, neither Robertson nor Tichmann has any knowledge of art relevant to the positions to which they were appointed.

In a self-published article on his website, Mario Pissarra recalled the opening of Lionel Davis' retrospective exhibition at SANG, at which Robertson acknowledged that he did not know anything about the artist:

> Since Davis is one of the best known figures in the arts and heritage sectors in the Cape, one can only wonder what else Robertson does not know about the visual arts that he should, certainly if he is now the de facto director of SANG.[20]

William Kentridge articulated the risks to the gallery, both reputational and real, in a 2018 television interview.[21] Journalist John Perlman asked Kentridge about his views on the calamitous grand plans that threaten South Africa, and the world. Kentridge shifted the emphasis from politics to the arts and the prevailing inclination to unify a multiplicity of institutions: he used as an example a museum director who is an expert on ants and the reality of other museums – such as the "national gallery of art," which does not specialise in ants – finding themselves in a "catastrophic situation". A year into the structure it also proved catastrophic for Robertson, an entomologist specialising in ants, who resigned in February 2018.

The custodian of knowledge, the art library, now falls under collections and digitisation. Once upon a time it was a well-staffed, lively, living space teeming with learners and researchers. When the budget was tight, librarian Joey Andersen raised funds to keep journal subscriptions and other crucial aspects of this great intellectual resource going. As discussed in chapter four, she shared her vision and innovative practice at national and international conferences, as well as in publications. But her ideal was not honoured and the library has been allowed to atrophy; it is now virtually dead, with the odd researcher signing the visitors' book. Thanks to the lone presence and sterling efforts of Shaheeda Dante, the art library remains a viable and efficient place for researchers.[22] In 2018, for the first time in decades, there was no book sale in the SANG atrium on International Museum Day (18 May).

There are plans to move the library facility from the Annexe to SAM, no doubt to further "maximise limited resources", but such a move will only make it less accessible. According to Ndhlovu:

> Iziko is consolidating the use of its spaces and the management of its libraries and collections. As such, library collections will be centrally located but catalogued as per international best practice. In addition, a staff member will always be present to give maximum service to library users. In brief, all collection libraries will be moving to a central space, SAM. The library space at the Annexe has shortcomings.[23]

I had been aware that the lifeblood of the art library – the international exchange programme that Bokhorst initiated – was at risk. In 1977, under Van Niekerk's directorship, the practice of sending publications to some 150 international art museums and various libraries as exchange materials relieved the economic strain of stocking a library and also supported the image of the gallery as a serious scholarly institution.[24]

Over the last decade the number of catalogues produced by the gallery has been abysmal: since 2008 only two catalogues have been published, *Brushing up on Stern* (2015) and *Painted Surfaces* (2017). SANG offers little nowadays as a partner in this exchange. Robertson assured me that it was continuing "despite budgetary challenges with regard to postage".[25] Pissarra related a different story in a stinging 2017 rebuke: having gone to great lengths to raise money for a book on Lionel Davis to accompany his retrospective at SANG, Pissarra offered to donate sixty copies for the exchange programme, but shortly learnt that Iziko no longer allocated money for postage.

The exchange has not been terminated and books still trickle in. The website is poorly maintained and it is unclear how many of the twenty-four books catalogued in 2015 came from abroad.[26] This is a truly shocking state of affairs, for not only does this decision deprive the art library and its users of free access to costly international publications, it fails to promote South African artists at home and abroad. A few statistics from past *Annual Reports* indicate the extent of the loss: 1972–73: 180 received (47 purchased); 1989–90: 226 (83 purchased); 1994–95: 327 (101 purchased).[27] Ndhlovu's reasons for no longer allocating a postal budget were twofold: "budget constraints and books are increasingly becoming available through online resources".[28]

Was the "re-alignment" of Iziko's collections born of ignorance of museum practice, or was it simply a case of expediency? In her report on the process, CEO Rooksana Omar cited the breaking down of the "historic silos and boundaries" as a significant achievement. But more than that, "relinquishing the outdated, collections-based directorships will unleash the potential of an inter-disciplinary approach, specifically in the areas of exhibition and education, aligned with best practice internationally".[29] No explanation was given about how museum directors, a commonplace species across the globe, had become "outdated"; nor was there any explanation forthcoming about how this structure aligned with international best practice. And by January 2019 there was still no sign of such interdisciplinary potential being unleashed.

In response to my questions, Ndhlovu confirmed that staff had been consulted about the restructuring, and echoed the CEO's outlook on the need to break down silos. He noted that the new structure would maximise the use of limited resources and deliver more exhibitions with limited staff. For example, exhibition team members would work across sites. It bears noting that this approach was tried early on in Iziko; its failure saw individuals re-assigned to sites. Furthermore, staff would "grow intellectually" and advance career prospects "horizontally and vertically," added Ndhlovu; and the structure would "bring about *consistency and standardisation*" (my italics) across Iziko. The latter rationalisation speaks plainly of the desire to further strip the national art museum of what remained of its vision and autonomy. According to Ndhlovu, curatorial leadership, direction, knowledge and experience would be provided by a head of art collections, and "in a phased in approach" by Robertson.[30] How can any individual acquire the necessary knowledge, adequately fulfil the tasks across three disciplines and 2.26 million objects, and provide the leadership desperately needed at eleven museums?

By dividing and disrupting the immutable unity of collections and exhibitions, Iziko has created two new silos: the collections and digitisation department includes conservators, collections managers, librarians, archivists and positions relevant to digitisation, while curators reside in research and exhibitions. According to Robertson:

> There needs to remain a strong link between the curators and the collections staff and we are sorting out how this will work in practice. The curator is more involved with growth, interpretation, research and exhibitions associated with the collection whereas the collections staff will be concerned with access, digitization, loan management, conservation and other duties associated with management and conservation of collections.[31]

It soon became evident that "sub-heads" for collections were needed. By April 2018, a year after the implementation of the new structure, these appointments had not been made, procedures for doing so were also unclear and, to further complicate matters, Robertson had resigned. At the beginning of 2019 art curators are still taking turns on an annual basis to chair core-functions meetings related to, for example, acquisitions and exhibitions. One would have thought that Iziko management would have considered the practical implications of such invasive and untested restructuring before implementing it. Good processes will not guarantee a good outcome, but bad ones will guarantee a bad outcome.

The fault lines in the new structure were soon exposed.

"We are not your ladies"

IN DECEMBER 2016 a storm broke out around an exhibition with the genteel title, *Our Lady*. Curated by guest curators Kirsty Cockerill and Candice Allison of the New Church Museum (NCM), working together with Andrea Lewis of SANG, an introductory wall text explained that the exhibition had been "designed to interrupt the puritanical and patriarchal visual economy that surrounds imagery of the figurative female form". The exhibition juxtaposed historical and contemporary works by twenty-seven artists, only seven of whom were women (and of them only three of colour). The opening of *Our Lady* coincided with the start of an annual, government-led campaign against violence against women and children.[32] For some, the timing compounded the outrage at including a photograph (*Untitled*, from the *Hope Chest* series, 2012) by Zwelethu Mthethwa, who at the time was on trial for the murder of sex worker Nokuphila Kumalo in April 2013.[33] Mthethwa's work depicted an anonymous woman in a blue dress, seated – seemingly waiting – on a chest outside her neat, thatched adobe dwelling; it was paired with an undated portrait of a white woman in a blue dress by Glasgow School painter George Henry, drawn from the gallery's collection.

The origin of the show goes back to May 2016, when collector Piet Viljoen closed the doors to his private museum and decided to rather pursue strategic collaborations. What better strategy than a partnership with the national art museum? *Our Lady* originated out of a request by Cockerill, NCM's director, to SANG. In an article detailing the controversy that erupted over the exhibition, critic Chad Rossouw highlighted the complexities of the partnership:

> A museum show has value in the dialogue opened, thoughts generated, critique levelled, audience engaged and other important intangibles. However, there are other intangibles that go along with a space of a museum: legitimacy, relevancy, importance, reputation, prominence. This second set of intangibles affect the tangible value of a work, what it is worth. This asks a difficult question. The Mthethwa piece is part of the NCM collection, while it is styled as a museum, is a private collection. They are leveraging their collection to achieve the first set of intangibles, a laudable goal. Yet they are also leveraging the Iziko museums on the second set of intangibles. I'm not suggesting the curators and the owner of NCM are in an evil conspiracy. But this aspect cannot be ignored. We need to ask, when all the chips have fallen, who benefits?[34]

There is no easy answer to the question whether an artist's character and actions could or should be separated from his or her work. What transpired at the gallery confirmed yet again that the specific circumstances and context of an exhibition are of paramount importance.

In May 2016, curator Michael Godby presented the exhibition *Home Truths*, highlighted earlier. His wide-ranging survey of depictions of home included a photograph from Mthethwa's *Empty Bed* series. That nobody objected was probably due to Godby's curatorial concept: the work appeared in a room labelled "Behind Closed Doors", among works that variously portrayed injustice and violence. The context and framing of the Mthethwa work on *Our Lady*, however, prompted an outburst of anger, notably on social media. Participating women artists, the Sex Workers Education and Advocacy Taskforce (SWEAT), Sisonke National Sex Worker Movement of South Africa (Sisonke) and the general public all reacted vociferously to the inclusion of Mthethwa's photograph in *Our Lady*.

In response to the storm brewing in the public domain, Iziko and NCM issued a joint statement on 29 November.[35] The exhibition was "designed to interrupt the typical traditional moral attitudes and male dominated stereotypes that surrounds [sic] imagery of the female form". Artworks spanning more than 170 years would "celebrate empowered female capacity that counter and contextualise the current status quo", and Mthethwa's work presented an opportunity for "critical engagement". The curators took the moral high ground: not featuring the work would "betray women everywhere" and the two museums were "not prepared to pretend that the abuse of women does not happen". Denying suggestions of a cheap publicity stunt, the authors of the statement concluded: "Museums are places where we should feel the freedom and safety to have difficult conversations. We cannot remove the photograph by Mthethwa as it would silence a much needed dialogue." Little did they know how difficult and fraught the "conversations" would turn out to be.

On 1 December, Museum Night in Cape Town, members of SWEAT wearing white masks and holding placards with the names of murdered sex workers protested on the gallery steps. Artist Astrid Warren's portrait of Nokuphila Kumalo, commissioned by SWEAT, was installed at the entrance to the exhibition *At Face Value*. Over the ensuing days Iziko faced considerable pressure to host a public debate to discuss *Our Lady*. Two weeks after the exhibition opened, on 15 December, the eve of a public holiday, Iziko hosted a dialogue in a room where *Our Lady* was hung. The public event was packed (Fig. 43). Unsurprisingly the atmosphere was agitated and filled with emotion. Ukhona Mlandu capably facilitated

FIGURE 43: *Our Lady* public event, 15 December 2016, Candice Breitz leading the discussion; © Iziko Museums of South Africa; photographer Nigel Pamplin.

the public event. For Mlandu the crux of the problem and confrontation were the museum's claim to curatorial authority in the face of legitimate discontent, notably on the part of SWEAT and Sisonke, who distilled their anger in simple terms: Nokuphila Kumalo was dead; Mthethwa was enjoying life.

The anger and hurt of the participating artists, the sex workers and their supporters were palpable throughout the discussions. The insipid explanations and excuses offered by the curators further inflamed passions. Ernestine White, then acting director, read a statement on behalf of the gallery, while Allison spoke on behalf of NCM. Other speakers included Constance Mathe, coordinator of the Asijiki Coalition, and Dudu Dlamini, an organiser for Sisonke and coordinator for Mothers for the Future, a sex working mothers' support programme. White explained why the artists were predominantly men: "Women remain woefully underrepresented in our collection and, going forward, we must take this into account at every possible opportunity." This was a red herring: women artists are well represented in both collections.[36]

White raised the misgivings and concerns among art collections staff about the inclusion of Mthethwa's photograph, stating that partnerships were often about negotiation and compromise, which forced an institution to view things differently and to disrupt long-held practices. NCM's wishes ultimately prevailed, as it was Cockerill who lobbied for the inclusion of her institution's photograph by Mthethwa. During the negotiations Cockerill threatened to remove all NCM's works immediately prior to the opening. This was not mentioned in either the statement or at the public discussion – Piet Viljoen confirmed this with me, and that he had agreed to the removal of the photograph at a meeting with Iziko. In the end the curators decided against it. By way of a compromise, a label contextualising the court case involving Mthethwa was made to accompany the contentious photograph. At the public discussion White admitted that two labels had been made, and that it was Cockerill who had placed the label omitting reference to the trial on the wall. That the national art museum could give away its power and responsibility so cheaply is mind-boggling.

The driving force behind public anger was Berlin-based South African artist Candice Breitz. At the public discussion she outlined the process that had resulted in a letter addressed to Rooksana Omar and the curators. The letter communicated the collective views of participating artists Bridget Baker, Njideka Akunyili Crosby, Khanyisile Mbongwa, Deborah Poynton, Tracey Rose and Penny Siopis. The artists' aim was "not only to radically reconfigure the exhibition that is under discussion, but also to nurture and broaden a productive and forward-looking debate around the issues that it addresses." [37] The signatories demanded the withdrawal of their work, although this had already happened – NCM unilaterally decided to withdraw its works from the exhibition on the eve of the public dialogue, two weeks into the run of the show.

In the letter the artists also took issue with the press material and curatorial rhetoric that claimed that *Our Lady* was a celebration of the empowerment of women, which would interrupt male dominance and patriarchy and depict women as strong and in charge of their lives. For the signatories the exhibition fell "disastrously short of these claims," and they regretted that three women co-curators were responsible for making such a selection. The exhibition's timing was also seen as "expedient and insincere". The artists' anger was exacerbated by the fact that the exhibition took place at "the most prestigious art institution in this country":

> It would be hard to overlook the problematic nature of *Our Lady* in any context. It is all the more impossible for us to accept the curatorial conceits underlying the exhibition in view of the fact that it has been endorsed by an institution that has an official mandate to be representative of our society, as well as a special duty to redress – especially at the level of representation – the radical social inequity that continues to characterise South African society.

The greatest outrage was, however, the inclusion of Mthethwa's work. For me personally it is not a compelling photograph and its very nature was problematic in the context of the exhibition. The label stated that the image explored the relationship between women and the chests that function as objects of prestige, offered by their families before they get married. It also referred to the "unnamed subjects [that] read as a typological series, suggestive of an anthropological approach to documenting the 'other'. This type of photographic strategy has received broad criticism by many who view it as a violent approach to portraying the subject as a type rather than an individual". Cockerill is quoted as saying that, on the one hand, the photograph was beautiful, but "on the other hand it's very uncomfortable".[38] Why then include it?

The artists, who had not been engaged or consulted before the exhibition opened, refused to endorse the exhibition in its current form. Breitz ended the joint letter with the statement: "We are not your ladies."

At the discussion in mid-December the public were invited to make contributions, during a question and answer period. Their displeasure and disillusion were noticeable. The word "bullying" was bandied about. Breitz argued that her requests for information were ignored. Cockerill blamed Iziko's Institutional Advancement (IA), for editing and cutting texts. Interfering with curatorial texts is indeed unacceptable, and when I sought clarity from Bongani Ndhlovu, he replied: "All media releases for Iziko are done through IA, BUT the changes they propose should be done in consultation with the relevant curators. Of concern to IA was that NCM issued a media release, without informing Iziko about it, stating that museums are not courts and this was a matter taken on by IA."[39] Cockerill was quoted as saying, "curators are not judges, and museums are not courtrooms".[40]

Towards the end of the more than two-hour long discussion, Mlandu invited the collaborating museums to present closing remarks. Allison and Cockerill caused an uproar, with the former stating that she would do the same again, and the latter maintaining that she needed two weeks to critically review the decision, but that she believed it was the correct one. A member of the audience reminded the curators that an apology was called for. White said "sorry", followed by "but". Lewis was quiet throughout the event, but when she eventually spoke, hers was the only curatorial voice that rang true: she expressed regret that she did not stand her ground in the negotiations. Her statement was widely applauded. Lewis' courage to admit her mistake, for me, revealed much about the true nature of the public-private partnership, the blurred lines between a public and private collection and, ultimately, the consequences of depriving the national art museum of leadership. In the event, Cockerill, Allison and NCM only apologised after the fact, in an email circulated on 19 December.

The public meeting to debate *Our Lady* generated positive outcomes. It was invigorating to see artist-activists vigorously stating their demands, and to be reminded that, at its most effective, art and activism share a foundation of empathy, something sorely lacking in South Africa at present. The well-attended meeting was also noteworthy for the diversity of voices proffering demands and constructive suggestions. A French journalist observed that such a fiery public engagement would not happen in France; she also wondered what the future held for Cockerill's career as a curator. The entrance fees charged by Iziko were drawn into the conversation, a confirmation that only those who can afford to pay can enjoy, understand and benefit from what happens at SANG.

One of the many insights I gained during my time at the gallery was that, when faced with a crisis, you cannot over-communicate; Iziko, however, tends to favour using few words. Breitz, working in collaboration with the artists and sex workers, subsequently sent a letter that included various remedial actions that were easy to implement, such as a video documenting the public event.[41] Iziko's response was non-committal and anodyne.[42] Breitz's letter expressing the shared views of the six women artists would be displayed, while the "remnants" would remain open to the public during the summer holiday period. It was a hapless solution. No consideration was given to baffled visitors who were confronted with a largely empty exhibition. Iziko missed the opportunity of installing a video that would have sent a significant message to the public and offered access to the voices of SWEAT and Sisonke, as well as the many individuals who spoke at the debate.

The hurt and anger caused were acknowledged in the subsequent media statement, but considering Iziko's complicity, the seeming inability of curators to counter the pressure put on them from a private collection and the willingness to sweep the matter under the holiday-carpet astounded many people. To make matters worse, the didactic tone of the concluding paragraph was offensive:

> Museums cannot be static monoliths seated on the periphery of society. Museums have an important role to play and need to constantly engage and reflect the society we serve. As we chart our way forward in an

increasingly complex, rapidly changing, and often challenging environment, we endeavour to interrogate the full extent of how the role of museums have evolved – as vehicles of engagement; catalysts for social change; building an inclusive society and (hopefully) providing safe platforms for discourse.

Since when has the role of museums evolved, or is it only evolving now? And why had the institution turned a blind eye to the plight of vulnerable and marginalised communities? Why did everyone, whose salaries are paid by taxpayers, behave like civil servants and go on holiday amidst an institutional crisis? In the absence of action, Iziko's words had a hollow ring to them.

Breitz continued to spearhead the action to keep Iziko accountable in 2017. Inspired by John Berger's 1972 television series and book, *Ways of Seeing*, Breitz sent a petitionary letter titled "Ways of Seeing, Ways of Hearing" to Rooksana Omar and SANG curators on 9 January. The letter, which was endorsed by hundreds of signatories, summarised events. It also criticised the gallery for ignoring the women artists' request to have the collective statement placed where their works once hung; instead one copy of their statement appeared in the space left by the removal of male artist Cameron Platter's work, while Iziko's statement was placed on another wall.

Iziko posted the CEO's response to the letter and petition on 13 January. Omar confirmed that the curators would find an "inclusive and sensitive solution," but argued that demands for immediate action were premature:

> … internal processes and procedures … must be followed in order to render any action viable within a multifaceted institution such as Iziko … We sincerely acknowledge the urgency and momentum you expressed, but also request your tolerance of the processes and protocols required of institutions of our size and nature.[43]

Omar described the time frames specified in the artists statement as "operationally unfeasible". She further put it that a range of public and stakeholder views about the disrupted show were gathered and, while the institution was in favour of screening the recording of the public event, rights to privacy could not be infringed. The partnership with NCM had been terminated when the artworks were withdrawn. Iziko reserved the right, she noted, "to consider the very many opinions expressed thus far and to reconfigure the exhibition in due course, in a way we see fit, incorporating the various views of our constituencies".

When Robertson returned from leave in January 2017, I asked him what the future plans were. He indicated that he was sorry about the *Our Lady* situation, especially as he thought it a really good exhibition. "There are some lessons to be learned from it," he said.[44] The exhibition was glossed over in the *Annual Report* with a brief description of what had transpired, but without mention of the involvement of either NCM or the activist-artists; the whole painful and fraught debacle was couched in blandly upbeat terms:

> A valuable debate around notions of patriarchy and the role of art in society, that also foregrounded the plight of sex workers, was created through this exhibition. This engendered

greater empathy and tolerance in the public domain that may well have far reaching impacts and lead to further partnerships and collaboration as a result of the relationships forged.

There were many articles in the press, but for Breitz it was a lonely and distressing road, exacerbated by a sense that the curators had "no authority at all to make independent decisions".[45] Revealingly, she said this chimed with her earlier experience of working with SANG on her show *Extra!* in 2012, when "nobody was willing to make any decisions, nobody felt that they had any authority". She described the situation as "disastrous in terms of what we should expect from a national institution". Breitz subsequently turned her attention to her contribution to the South African Pavilion at the 2017 Venice Biennale – and with that the activism around *Our Lady* petered out.

Our Lady was eventually reconfigured. White tape marked the works withdrawn by NCM. After getting clearance from participants in the public event, the video footage was screened, accompanied by "Say Her Name" posters loaned from SWEAT, and an explanation and legal disclaimer protecting Iziko. Breitz's statement, written on behalf of the women artists, and the Iziko media statement were retained, as was the original and controversial *Our Lady* wall text. The partnership with NCM was no more, so keeping the text in an altered context added to the confusion.

Some good did come from the debacle. Following suggestions by Masondo and White, artist Donna Kukama developed the performance piece *Chapter Y: Is survival not archival?* that she performed in the space on 18 February 2017 as part of the Live Art Festival, a project of the Institute for Creative Arts at UCT. The curators also invited SWEAT and Sisonke to engage with the *Our Lady* exhibition on Museum Night on 20 April 2017, coincidentally the day scheduled for Mthethwa's sentencing. The legal hearing was postponed, but the art programme went ahead and the resulting exhibition remained for several days.

SWEAT intervened in the rooms with various installations, including an "Ask a sex worker" booth containing educational materials, and a jail cell with placards and associated performances inside. The most significant addition was a time-line installation that advocated for the decriminalisation of sex work. It featured a full-size skeleton behind a desk with a sign reading "Reserved for Department of Justice to work on South African sex work legislation" – a damning comment on a democratic South Africa that in twenty-three years had failed to address the plight and rights of sex workers.[46]

In 2018 an exhibition of photographs, voice and video installations by Robert Hamblin, titled *interseXion*, drew visitors' attention to sex work, in particular feminine identified transgender sex workers.[47]

Freedom of expression under the spotlight

A MONTH AFTER the *Our Lady* controversy made local and international news, another exhibition at the gallery unexpectedly became the source of heated public debate. Curated by Lewis and Masondo, The *Art of Disruptions* featured a provocative work by multi-disciplinary and genderqueer artist Dean Hutton. Titled

Fuckwhitepeople wall, chair and golden boots (2016), Hutton's installation was composed of a wall papered with a text motif reading "Fuck White People", a chair upholstered with the same design, and a pair of golden boots. On occasion Hutton appeared in the gallery dressed in a suit bearing the same stark text slogan. The installation went on display in June 2016, with little response either in the public domain or in reviews.[48]

In January 2017, members of the Cape Party, which promotes greater independence for the Western Cape, covered Hutton's work with a sticker stating, "Love Thy Neighbour". The party subsequently posted documentation of their act on Facebook and YouTube. The battle lines were drawn: support for the defacing on the one hand, and defence of freedom of expression on the other; few, though, engaged with and questioned the importance of the work. The action was the source of some news, with headlines writers whipping up the frenzy.[49]

The Freedom Front Plus, a party favouring freedom and fairness for Afrikaners, approached Iziko to remove the work after it received complaints from the public. In its submission the party argued that Hutton's work was "inflammatory" and it was "irresponsible" of the museum to display it. Iziko refused the demand. Omar released a statement defending Iziko's position: "Cognisant of the provocative nature of the language this work employs, Iziko displayed it along with an explanation (in the artist's own words) that contextualises the artwork and makes it clear that the artist is not trying to provoke racial hatred or violence."[50]

Dissatisfied with Iziko's response, the Cape Party, which viewed the work as hate speech, decided to take the matter to the Equality Court. They demanded that Hutton be fined R150,000 and also apologise. Chief Magistrate D. M. Thulare rejected their claim, stating in his judgment that the work drew South Africans to a moment of self-reflection and that the words were directed at white domination and structures rather than against all white people. The Cape Party was dismayed by the decision. Iziko's lawyer regarded the ruling as "a landmark decision," stating that it was both a defence of freedom of speech and "artistic expression".[51] The CEO also saw the case as an important milestone for Iziko:

> Significantly, over the past year, Iziko also set important national precedents for museums and artistic practice in South Africa by successfully defending litigations against our institution that challenged rights enshrined in our constitution. We are proud to have secured landmark rulings that protect freedom of expression.[52]

What was the work about and where was the artistic expression? The artist told the Daily Maverick, cited above, that the work was produced because:

> … white people in general tend not to feel racialised, or feel answerable for our actions in terms of a racialised identity. We exist in spaces where we very rarely 'feel white' … The discomfort of feeling racialised in spaces, to honestly ask ourselves if we belong, or how we achieve belonging, is a very necessary part of unlearning oppressive behaviours.

The source for Hutton's work was a photograph of Wits student Zama Mthunzi wearing a T-shirt with the words "fuck white people" painted on it, and "being black is shit" painted on the reverse. He was demonstrating against the presence of private security on campus during the Fees Must Fall student protests in February 2016. Mthunzi wore the T-shirt for a week, which led to a human rights complaint against him, a social media storm and other students wearing T-shirts with anti-white slogans in solidarity. Interestingly, Mthunzi offered his own critique of Hutton's appropriation: he told critic Laetitia Pople (*Die Burger*, 17 January 2017), that Hutton's work was not original, that it lacked ironical guts, and that its inclusion in *The Art of Disruptions* was a sign of SANG's sloppy political correctness.

Columnist Gareth van Onselen criticised the exhibition for being timid. He echoed Mthunzi, stating that the national gallery had been "a monument to political correctness" for some time; he added that Hutton had appropriated Mthunzi's idea:

> By its very nature, political correctness is boring. The closest Hutton gets to actual insight is this remark: "But I can do it – that is white privilege." I would say "white tolerance" is more like it (FF Plus excluded). Had the exhibition said, "Fuck Black People", the Third World War would have erupted. That would have been some real disruption.[54]

The intolerance and anger surrounding the display of Hutton's work recalls older incidences of vandalism. The year is not mentioned, but in 1972 Bokhorst described how a visitor to the gallery defaced George Crosland-Robinson's 1904 portrait of Boer political leader Paul Kruger; the vandal slashed Kruger's nose in half and then disappeared into the Company's Garden. Bokhorst described him as an unknown "politically-inclined young man".[55] In a way these acts of vandalism reflect the politics and flash points of the times.

Writing "with a slight trace of nostalgia," critic Melvyn Minnaar recalled another incident from the turbulent interregnum before 1994 (*Die Burger*, 21 January 2017). He described the minor skirmish between the supporters of the Cape Party and security staff of SANG in 2017 as a "feeble déjà vu" of 15 January 1992, when uniformed members of the Afrikaner Weerstandsbeweging (AWB) attacked a work of art. Hutton's weak and conceptually "one-line" work was hardly damaged by the biblical "Love They Neighbour" sticker, noted Minnaar; besides it did not come close to the dynamism and ingenuity of Gael Neke's ceramic sculpture *Eugène Terr'blanche and his two sidekicks* that the AWB destroyed with hammer and boot: "But the artist will have his [sic] moment in the media flash-light."

Few, if any, commentators on the debacle noticed that Hutton had also appropriated her key gesture from artist Kendell Geers' sculptures covered with the word "fuck", such as his Madonna sculpture *Holyfuckingvirgin* (2006), human skull piece *Fuckface* (2005) and 2007 self-portrait *Fuckface (Kendell Geers)*. Geers once described the context for the works as follows: "To me, Fuck always seemed to suggest somewhat more than just intercourse or copulation and somehow put a more animal or primal spin on the idea of coitus."[56] Hutton did not remotely approach Geers' iconoclasm. It was hard to imagine that things could get worse for the national art museum, but that they did – at institutional and national levels – is the topic of the next chapter.

PLATE 40: Dame Laura Knight, *Flying a Kite*, 1910, oil on canvas, 1498 × 1778.

10

New national policies for arts, culture and heritage, and a return to major themes of the book

2014 – 2017

SIGNIFICANT CHANGES happen at the metalevel with the introduction of more bureaucratic structures designed to centralise power and to erode institutional autonomy: they include a revised White Paper and a proposed new dispensation for arts, culture and heritage. Instead of speaking truth to power when required, Iziko Museums does DAC's bidding. In evaluating these changes and their impact on museums in general and SANG specifically, I return to major themes of this book: a lack of action regarding the crippling space constraints, staffing issues and disinterest in acquiring and displaying historical African art. As in chapter nine, I discuss important changes and that occurred in 2018.

In an attempt to be politically correct
an institution can fail its best intentions.

ASHRAF JAMAL[1]

A Revised White Paper and a new dispensation for arts, culture and heritage

AT THIS POINT it is appropriate to take stock of Iziko in the context of unfolding new national policies for arts culture and heritage. As playwright and cultural activist Mike van Graan points out, policies are products of their time; but conditions change, and therefore they require review and amendments.[2] Some observers commended Minister Paul Mashatile and DAC for initiating the revision of the 1996 White Paper on Arts, Culture and Heritage, and for inviting stakeholders to workshops on the draft in 2013; others, however, were circumspect. All the same, the sector took the document seriously and extensive comments and critiques were submitted and published, of which the DAC took heed. Many changes have been made over the years, and the most recent version, dated February 2017, is still "for discussion only". Implementation seems a long way off, but the effects are nonetheless being felt at Iziko.[3]

The fundamental differences between the 1996 and 2013 versions of the document were the levels of consultation; as discussed in chapter five, the 1996 version was the result of extensive consultation within the different sectors, captured in the AGTAG Report. The opposite was true in 2013. The Revised White Paper was drafted by DAC, either by officials and/or consultants, whose identities were shrouded in secrecy. The vision and ideas that inspired them were also divergent, and indeed indicative of how times had changed for the worse, and how government had failed the sectors. The 1996 White Paper aimed to address the historical legacies of colonialism and apartheid. It was informed by an adherence to Article 27 of the Universal Declaration of Human Rights, which states, "everyone shall have the right to freely participate in the cultural life of the community [and] to enjoy the arts". It was the objective and role of the new arts and culture ministry to ensure that this right, the right of all freely to practise and satisfy artistic and cultural expression, and enjoy protection and development of their heritage, be realised.[4]

The 2013 edition had little to do with strengthening and reimagining conditions that would encourage such participation and practice. Instead it was driven by the National Development Plan: Vision 2030 (NDP) of 2011, the Ministry's and DAC's own political imperatives and the market, with "South Africa's cultural and creative industries at the core of social and economic justice, security, growth and development, moral regeneration and national consciousness".[5] Forceful criticism resulted in a revised and much-altered vision: "Developing a dynamic, vibrant and transformed arts, culture and heritage sector, leading to nation-building, social cohesion and socioeconomic justice, equality and inclusion."[6] However, while stressing redress of the injustices and imbalances of the past, it ignored those created by post-apartheid macro-economic policy, endemic corruption and poor service delivery.

In 1996 arms-length funding, transparency and participatory democracy were founding principles; by 2013 funding was conditional, with the threat that government resources could be directed to achieve clearly defined objectives. This has resulted in institutions acceding to DAC's every demand, and it has raised the spectre of self-censorship and compromised artistic freedom. As if the flagships were not enough, further rationalisation and centralisation were contemplated. The rationale was that DAC was held responsible for qualified audits and that somehow the merging of institutions would address this, thereby reflecting positively on the department. However, research and analysis were lacking. The idea was also preposterous given what happened at DAC in 2014.

Reporting on the workshop held in Cape Town in September 2013, critic Matthew Blackman quoted director general Sibusiso Xaba as saying: "The bottom-line is this, that there isn't sufficient funding for the sector," and that cultural institutions would be closed down if they failed to meet certain "moral, social and economic" criteria.[7] In October 2014 Xaba was suspended following an "alarming" report by the auditor general (2013–14 financial year); the audit identified weaknesses as regards irregular expenditure, non-adherence to procedures and possible lack of action against officials who may have made or allowed such expenditure. It prompted the minister to instigate a forensic investigation and Xaba left the following January after reaching a settlement with DAC.[8] National institutions are subjected to the tyranny of bureaucracy, but there is no analysis of DAC and its management, implementation and evaluation of the 1996 White Paper. This militates against the positive elements in the document and its future implementation.

In November 2015 the new arts and culture minister, Nathi Mthethwa, appointed an eight-person reference panel to advise on the document (subsequently expanded to include a representative for the youth of South Africa). A national policy meeting followed. Consultations were held in all the provinces from May to June 2016, but there were problems within the panel: some members dropped out and only three members contributed, causing delays and raising questions about how one third of a panel was able to fulfil its mandate.[9] Who was responsible for the inadequate editing and the uneven structure and content? Neither the minister nor the unidentified individuals who failed to deliver anything of substance were held accountable. Apart from this, the process revealed the state of South African democracy: the 1996 arts and culture task group was appointed by then minister Ben Ngubane from nearly three hundred nominations received from the public; Mthethwa's reference group was constituted unilaterally.

The compilers claim that DAC has adhered to "the participatory and consultative principles on which South Africa's democracy and public policy development practices are founded". Van Graan, however, argues that the experience of stakeholders in the process "has generally been one of it being rushed, with inadequate time to interrogate the Revised White Paper and a feeling that the 'consultations' have been box-ticking exercises rather than genuine attempts to engage the views of stakeholders".[10]

One of the significant aspects of the 1996 policy was the transparent appointment of structures governing national institutions and arts bodies that dispense public funds. Public nominations are still called for but, considering the composition of councils, one is left wondering what happens after that. It would appear that nominations are either not forthcoming or that DAC has a heavy hand in the appointments. We are reminded of the 1895 South African Art Gallery Act in terms of which the Cape Government appointed three of the five trustees, as against two representing the South African Fine Arts Association. Control was wrested from the previous owners with grim consequences for the collection.

Van Graan cites the "illegal appointment of the National Arts Council in 2015" as an example: DAC contravened the NAC Act by conducting interviews behind closed doors, the public was not informed who the nominees were (leaving no room for objection) and the minister duly appointed the council members. Representations to the minister and department, the NAC and the Portfolio Committee on Arts and Culture in this regard were futile, and the council was inaugurated. A year later he had to terminate their services because of the contravention.[11] It is worth noting that, in terms of the amended Cultural Institutions Act of 2001, chairpersons of councils and boards are no longer elected by their colleagues (as was the case even under apartheid legislation), but appointed by the minister, thereby granting them disproportionate power and loyalty to the ruling party and the minister.

For Van Graan, the 2017 iteration of the White Paper is deeply flawed, both in terms of process and content:

> Notwithstanding the fact that the current version of the White Paper has been in development for nearly three times longer than the research and consultative process of the 1996 White Paper, it sorely lacks comprehensive research of the sector as it currently stands: the gains since 1996, the gaps, the new challenges of our society 20 years on, etc. Accordingly, it makes recommendations or statements that are often generalised and unsubstantiated by research.[12]

The revised document proposes a new name for the department (Department of Arts, Culture and Heritage), and it asserts the need for multilingualism and an integrated national dispensation aligned with the NDP. The level of centralisation envisaged for heritage is startling: all national museum councils are to be abolished and museums (and other national institutions, for example archives) are to be governed by the National Heritage Council. Where does this leave the national art museum? It is hard to tell, because there is another section in the Revised White Paper that deals generically with national, provincial and local art galleries and art museums. What is unambiguous is DAC's desire to control and ensure its interests, rather than those of the arts, culture and heritage sectors.

Ndhlovu responded as follows to my request for an opinion from Iziko:

> The Iziko Council has no opinion on this matter or at least I cannot comment on their behalf. The Iziko staff have engaged and protested about this new governance framework of a Super Council managing all the strategic and operational affairs of DAC's public entities. In fact, all museums will report to the National Heritage Council if the fourth Draft of the White Paper is tabled at Parliament.[13]

While the new dispensation is still up for discussion, DAC is surreptitiously developing and imposing policy, and there are noticeable shifts and emphases in how Iziko functions, particularly concerning the international museum world.

Bokhorst joined ICOM in 1973, but since 2014 Iziko is no longer a member of this organisation, which counts more than 35,000 members representing more than 20,000 museums, from 136 countries and territories. Instead it – like DAC – subscribes to the African Union Agenda 2063: "An Africa with a strong cultural identity, values and ethics, and ensuring Africa is a strong and influential global player and partner", as well as new United Nations Educational, Scientific and Cultural

Organization (UNESCO) frameworks that stress the need for museums to find strategies that "enable them to function and contribute effectively in a changing world".[14] This is all very well, but does it take account of the intersections between local and global art and art-market forces, and their impact on contemporary curatorial practices? Where does it leave an art museum when privately owned spaces and commercial venues have already usurped its role and prestige? The latter is examined in the following chapter.

Branding rather than marketing has since Jack Lohman's days been the panacea for all difficulties at Iziko, and this has recently been taken to an absurd extreme. The banners placed on the gallery's façade in 2018 do not promote the collections through appealing images and words, but rather feature "ISANG" in huge letters. This begs the question of what it might mean to passers-by who have no idea that the banner is promoting a house filled with art treasures. There is also the matter of co-branding with DAC. When DAC first announced the decision that publicly funded institutions were to be branded "agencies of the Department of Arts and Culture", Iziko council members were wary because this "would severely hamper its efforts at fund-raising, since its independence could be open to question". Iziko was an entity of DAC but an independent one.[15]

Real resistance would have amounted to Iziko taking a public stand, akin to what Van Niekerk did in the 1980s, but this did not happen – as an "agency" of DAC Iziko is not independent. In addition to being accountable for the funding they receive, institutions have to align their programming, strategies and implementation plans with the vision and aims of DAC. Iziko management is clearly taking its cue from government, and does its utmost to fall in with the national priorities outlined in the Revised White Paper – it is faithful to and uncritical of its "accounting authority".

Unavoidably questions arise as to the social responsibilities and independence of public art institutions. To exercise their role in a democracy and to be seen and heard as instruments of civil society, they have to be free from pressure to execute political agendas. In the current aggravated political climate this is simply not possible and the tacit support of government policies and programmes that prevailed at SANG before 1976 has now been revived. Gone are the days when art museum directors and curators in South Africa were creative negotiators and activists who desired to bring about societal change through exhibitions and education programmes and, when necessary, to speak truth to power. At least this is the situation for now. The commercial sector and privately funded museums are not going to assume this mantle.

In the main, it has been courageous individuals who have challenged the status quo. Matthew Blackman single-handedly took on DAC in order to reveal the murkiness that surrounded South Africa's participation in the 2011 Venice Biennale. DAC allocated R10 million of taxpayers' money to the exercise, which was subsequently marred by dubious expenses. Similarly, Mike van Graan, actor Pieter-Dirk Uys and cartoonist Jonathan "Zapiro" Shapiro have used satire to ask difficult questions. Artists have not been meek either: Laurence Lemaoana, Ayanda Mabulu and Brett Murray have all dared to address controversial issues through their art.

National priorities, museum education and student demands

IT MUST BE of some concern to those who care about youth empowerment and education that national policies and priorities are impacting education initiatives at SANG. In response to my request for his highlights, major challenges and vision for the art museum, Wayne Alexander, director of education and public programmes, reflected on the past and described an environment "in which curiosity, discovery, exploration, reflection, wonderment and contemplation" could be encouraged:

> The period 2009 to 2016 at Iziko was punctuated with many changes, so being involved in education one noted that neither quietness nor ease was among the reasons that one navigates museum education. So the issues of relevance and nation building at Iziko during the period precipitated new thinking regarding the meaning and role of art education. This propelled the Education and Public Programmes department at Iziko to offer varied programmes that would contribute to basic education outcomes, social cohesion and add value to classroom practice. Increasingly this period saw a move towards a more systemic and coherent art education programme … Art education in collaboration with internal and external partners continually aims, in relation to the changing exhibitions programme, to provide all visitors, regardless of age and background with inspiring and empowering experiences.[16]

These are fine sentiments, but the realities are challenging.

In 2017 there was one senior educator, Yentl Kohler, dedicated to the gallery; she was assisted by two volunteer guides, Barry Shipman and Hannelore Bouman, and a group of young people who helped with workshops and classes in the main building and Annexe, when they were available. National priorities are addressed through the art school programmes from junior to high school, heritage week and the art school club. For Kohler "a more systemic and coherent art education programme" means working in a "more integrated manner drawing on the expertise of staff".[17] The objectives are reached through strategic partnership with artists, facilitators, non-profit and non-governmental organisations such as Learn to Earn and Constitutional Literacy and Service Initiative, and Sandra Eastwood's Meaningful Access Programme for learners.

Collaboration between curators and educators, once taken for granted, has been revived. With the exhibition *Studio: Celebrating the Lives and Work of South African Artists* (2016), educators Kohler and Philippa Coleman joined forces with curators to view the permanent collection through the eyes of the youth, and to facilitate active engagement between art history and contemporary practice. *Studio* was the result of "ongoing pressure from art educators" to create an exhibition relevant to the national matric syllabus. Kohler wished to address what in her view was the "disconnect" between the Annexe and the gallery: a dedicated workspace in the gallery was set aside for workshops. For Lewis the project as "a fantastic way to connect with schools, teachers and school children. SANG was alive with so many kids for almost nine months".[18]

Iziko's important contribution to the educational project in the Western Cape has to be viewed against the challenges that prevail in the tertiary sector, particularly since the gallery is directly involved in the Honours in Curatorship degree at Michaelis. In 2015 South African students kick-started a revolution with their demands for free tertiary education, although it soon became evident that their demands involved far more than simply fees. They were also calling for a decolonised, Afrocentric education. The student movement gained a voice and gathered national momentum after a successful campaign at UCT calling for the removal of Marion Walgate's bronze statue of Cecil John Rhodes (1934) from its plinth on a central stairway. Student activists argued that the work was an offending image, symbol and celebration of colonialism and British imperialism. The protests kicked off in earnest after student activist Chumani Maxwele splashed Walgate's sculpture with human faeces in March. The statue became the site of intense activism and was removed in April 2015.

Photographer David Goldblatt, always interested in human values and fairness, applauded the students "sudden awareness" that "statues actually have significance. They are not simply blocks of stone, granite or whatever". But he expressed his opposition to the student's escalating demands, which after April 2015 were often expressed through "direct action":

> It precludes discussion and I think a democracy is based on the idea that when you have differences you can talk about it ... it's fundamental ... That students threw shit over Rhodes is a very important and significant event. The significance lies in asking what values were they expressing in those actions. Get to grips with those and I think you're beginning to understand some of the forces at work in this country.[19]

A November 2015 editorial in the *Mail & Guardian* commended the students for their diligence: "At every step of these protests, the students have eloquently articulated the sentiment, shared by many outside their ranks, that the decolonisation project is not finished and the time has come for a new kind of politics."[20] As the protests continued, however, they became increasingly marred by violence.

In February 2016 a group of UCT students burnt artworks displayed in university buildings, and a month later members of the Trans Collective vandalised a campus photography exhibition commemorating the first anniversary of the removal of Walgate's sculpture of Rhodes – the show included a work by Goldblatt.[21] This wave of iconoclasm was followed by student demands that various works be removed or covered up. Controversially, UCT's authorities acquiesced, on the grounds of "their vulnerability to potential damage" or because "some members of the campus community have identified certain works of art as offensive to them – for cultural, religious or political reasons".[22]

As soon as students began demanding free education, their movement became an important tool for exploitation by political parties. This culminated in President Jacob Zuma, then under severe personal and professional scrutiny, unilaterally announcing in December 2017 that there would be free education for deserving students from lower-income families. It was a surprise move, and wholly political: the presidency, national treasury and department of higher education were unable to indicate where the billions needed to fund such a scheme would come from.

Zuma's move, announced just as universities and public colleges were preparing for the 2018 academic year, threw the education sector into turmoil. Students allied to the Economic Freedom

Fighters (EFF) aggravated the situation by encouraging prospective students to simply turn up at tertiary institutions instead of registering online.[23] At the same time, Matamela Cyril Ramaphosa ousted Zuma as president of the ruling ANC in December 2017. Zuma shortly resigned as president of South Africa, and was replaced by Ramaphosa on 15 February 2018. The process of creating a free and equitable, decolonised education programme remains a work in progress.

Iziko plays a significant part in education at many levels in the Western Cape, and it will have to position itself clearly in relation to dramatic shifts and developments in all relevant sectors, without subservience to the ANC government's ideology. Instead of stimulating the discourse required from a knowledge-based institution operating in a democracy, Iziko management has uncritically heeded "the call to decolonise museums and heritage sites, and to remove national symbols of oppression like monuments and statues from public spaces".[24] More gloss without substance – the innovation that should go hand in hand with decolonisation is conspicuously absent from many Iziko spaces and crumbling or closed buildings. The SANG precinct and structure are in a deplorable state, the OTH is covered in bird droppings and disintegrating, but – thanks to its proximity to parliament – the Iziko Slave Lodge is a priority for DPW and gets an annual face-lift.

Conservation under the microscope

CONSIDERING THE POSITION of SANG and its future within Iziko, much may be wanting, but it can in no way be compared with the dysfunctionality that, for example, prevails at the Durban Art Gallery.[25] The Iziko *Annual Reports* detail the hard work that goes into being compliant with the legislation governing national museums, the excellent accounting procedures followed and the clean audits the organisation receives as a result. Furthermore, Iziko has had major recent successes in its flagship projects: the digital upgrade of the planetarium and the inclusion of artefacts retrieved from the shipwreck of the slave ship São José in the inaugural exhibition of the Smithsonian National Museum of African American History and Culture in 2016. An excellent exhibition titled *Unshackled History: The Wreck of the Slave Ship, São José, 1794* opened at the Iziko Slave Lodge in December 2018.[26]

The year 2017 ended on a high note in the field of conservation, due in large part to Angela Zehnder's commitment to international standards. Supported by a team of curators, a collections manager and registrar, Iziko's collections are as ever safeguarded and protected. She conducts the annual Bailey Collection conservation project and website that makes the collection accessible and keeps the public informed. Apart from working with colleagues on international shows, Zehnder acts as courier for international loans, and engages with museum professionals. In return she offers many tours and talks to the Friends, special interest groups, post-graduate students in curatorship at UCT and learners.

Zehnder's knowledge, experience and leadership in her profession culminated in a pioneering conservation project. A grant from the Andrew W. Mellon Foundation made possible the coming together of art and science in the fascinating exhibition and publication *Painted Surfaces* (2017).[27] Zehnder and

fellow conservator Bronwyn Leone showed how they used newly acquired technical examination methods – such as infrared photography, ultraviolet light, x-ray imaging and microscopic analysis – to expose what happens beyond the layers of paint (Plate 41). Their work spanned three years of focused scientific and technical exploration conducted at universities in South Africa and abroad. The results were juxtaposed with fifteen paintings by South African artists in the gallery's collection, and enlivened with illustrated texts, materials and objects, for example the artist's equipment from the Stanley Pinker studio archive at UCT.

Through the discipline of technical art history viewers were guided to an understanding of the painters' intentions and the conservation of artworks, and the foundation was prepared for future research. *Painted Surfaces* appealed to art lovers, academics, students and conservationists, but Zehnder and Leone also recognised the value for the general public, teachers and learners of all ages, and they joined forces with Yentl Kohler to offer workshops and walkabouts. Eastwood's access programme formed part of the outreach; of particular interest was the tactile interpretation of Pinker's *Figure with Bird* (1978) that visually impaired visitors were allowed to touch.

For Hamish Robertson the gallery was on an upward trajectory at the end of 2017, and he credited the new structure for some of the possibilities that were opening up. The CEO had allocated one million rand for acquisitions, and a new expanded acquisitions committee that includes experts from outside Iziko, would be appointed for the first time since 2008. The full committee was only constituted in October 2018 which meant that acquisitions were being made without either internal leadership or expert external advice.[28] The increased acquisition budget must be applauded; it is a reminder that the national art museum is a vital part of the advancement and career prospects of individual artists. The GRAP103 audit (a uniform accounting standard) had resulted in the complete documentation of the collections. Robertson envisaged greater focus on collection management and conservation, digital access to collections, a dynamic exhibition programme and much stronger marketing of exhibitions.[29] Omar was similarly upbeat about the future: "Going forward in 2018, Iziko will continue to build African museums of excellence that enhance the evolution of our democracy, support social and economic development, and promote active citizenship."[30]

This sounded encouraging, but the nagging question of the future of the national art museum and its different collections – in the context of social and bureaucratic change – remained unanswered. In February 2018, Robertson, not yet sixty years old,

PLATE 41: Louis Maqhubela, *Snake*, 2002, oil on canvas, 1300 × 285; presented by the artist; courtesy of the artist; detail under ultraviolet light, showing the fluorescence of the varnish interlayers; photographer Nigel Pamplin.

and seemingly disillusioned and exhausted by his experience of Iziko's bureaucracy and the burden of the job, resigned. The ant specialist had been director of research and exhibitions for less than a year.[31] Iziko was, once again, an institution in crisis. Wayne Alexander had also left. Bongani Ndhlovu briefly resigned at the end of 2017 to become CEO at Ditsong Museums of South Africa in Pretoria, but in April 2018 he was back in his former position at Iziko. Robertson departed at the end of March.[32]

The post remained vacant until January 2019 when Susan Glanville-Zini moved from institutional advancement. She has a fine arts degree and some experience in the field, but no post-graduate qualification or record of publications. Once again functionality (understanding how the bureaucracy works) triumphed over knowledge and scholarship.

Iziko continues to claim the work of others as its own: In the CEO's 2017-18 overview she states that "Over the past year, Iziko *curated* [my italics] 23 new, temporary exhibitions that responded to the imperatives of social cohesion and nation building."[33] She lists *Through Positive Eyes* at the Slave Lodge, without mentioning the roles of curator Carol Brown and UCLA professor David Gere. Carol Kaufmann, who left SANG in 2016, is not credited for curating *Hidden Treasures*. Omar's third example, El Anatsui's *Meyina*, curated by Bisi Silva, is discussed in the next chapter. The list of exhibitions across Iziko takes up a single page and provides no further information, while some details are given under the heading "Partners" that occupies ten pages and is clearly foregrounded to acknowledge Glanville-Zini's department and impress DAC.[34]

Robertson was vague on policy for the Michaelis Collection and the historical collections in general. According to Proud there is no policy for what has become the "hot potato" in art collections, but he has a clear vision.[35] Naidoo and the curators regarded the OTH as Proud's remit alone, a situation exacerbated by Naidoo's lack of interest, as well as executive management's and council's attitude towards historical collections – an attitude that is informed by political considerations and the decolonisation project rather than familiarity with art history. Proud advocates "a fundamental shift and sharing of responsibility": a reactivation of the site with changing exhibitions that include contemporary art, while a space is once again made available for the historical collections in the main building. He sees contemporary art integrated "in a more strategic and aesthetically-appropriate manner. Our buildings are, stylistically, the colonial frameworks in which we operate; we have a history and we will not be getting new architectural containers for our exhibitions and activities any time soon".

At some point Iziko senior managers, council and DAC will wake up to the fact that restructuring has separated leadership from knowledge. As this book has shown there were serious problems with the management of the national art museum prior to the appointment of a professional director, John Paris, in 1949. He and subsequent directors – supported by staff and members of the governing body – were integral to the public presence, profile and advancement of the gallery. Their achievements affirm the need for museum directors who are art historians, who have knowledge and awareness of contemporary art practice in South Africa and in the world, who research, write and lecture extensively, and who contribute to the making and writing of art history in South Africa and further afield.

A return to and assessment of major topics

AS THE NARRATIVE of this book draws to a close it is opportune to return to, and assess the status of important issues, and in particular two major topics that speak to the title of the book: dreams and realities. I pose questions that will only be answered in the years to come. Chief among these is the longstanding and critical lack of space. As discussed in chapter six, I worked with fifth-year architectural students at UCT in 2002 on a formal project to design an additional building, which could have formed the basis for a competition brief and fundraising drive. After I left Iziko, in 2008, the project faltered; it was reinstated in 2010–13 when I was a council member, only to be taken off the agenda again. The negative impact and stresses created by a lack of space are felt in many ways, notably by the collections, but also staff members, who do their utmost to maintain high standards against the odds.[36]

I had the privilege of being invited by architect Jo Noero, a former Wits colleague and emeritus professor at UCT, to participate in the 2015 honours programme. The brief to the twelve students was to design a centre for contemporary art adjacent to the important historic gallery building and to do so in a style that was situated firmly in the present and that would entice and welcome visitors. Refurbishing and reusing existing spaces in the main building and the Annexe were integral to the project, as was reconciling heritage and contemporary expression.

The project took the form of a competition and my role was that of "client" and external critic. I gave the students a lecture on contemporary art, provided the documents that I first prepared in 1993 and revised over time, while Noero added contextual and site information, as well as specific design considerations and an accommodation schedule with dimensions. Naidoo, who was still director at the time, declined to provide input, but Lewis generously guided Noero, the students and me on a site visit. Her tour drew attention to the dire lack of space and the rigorous museological demands that had to inform the design. Zehnder welcomed us in her conservation studio, which was previously the lounge of the director's apartment.

Such was the excellence of the solutions and presentations that I organised an exhibition of the drawings and models at the Association for Visual Arts. As part of the show, I chaired a panel discussion with panellists Matthew Blackman, Noero, Proud and Andrew Lamprecht.[37] Proud was keen to move the exhibition to SANG in order to conscientise Iziko's management and to further stimulate public interest in a building project, as well as in a debate around museums in general and the future of the national art museum in particular. Unfortunately the exhibition did not materialise.

The honours project affirmed my conviction that a new edifice, linked to the main and Annexe buildings, should be the result of an architectural competition. The Constitutional Court of South Africa is an excellent example of such a competition. Driven by Judge Albie Sachs and held in 1997, more than 500 entries were received and judged by an international panel led by Indian architect Charles Correa. The winning work was a partnership of young South African architects: Janina Masojada and Andrew Makin from Durban-based OMM Design Workshop, and Paul Wygers from Johannesburg firm Urban Solutions. Competitions create excitement and interest. Iconic art museum buildings across the world, and more recently in Cape Town, demonstrate that buildings are as important as the collections they house and programmes they offer.

At the March 2016 Iziko workshop, Lewis confirmed that extensions to SANG would be on the User Asset Management Plan schedule by 2021, in time for the 150th anniversary of the collection.[38] She also mentioned "operation atrium", a proposal to re-envision the heart of the building by covering it with glass. Robertson, who was committed to getting the gallery renovations and building project back on the agenda, and who had been in touch with Noero and me in this regard, shared enthusiasm for such an intervention. However, the notion of altering a single element outside of a holistic scheme designed by an architect sets alarm bells ringing.

The beautiful neo-classical entrance portico of the art museum is regarded by many as austere and unwelcoming. We tried to address this with the artists' flag project and Lotto-funded public art competition discussed in earlier chapters. In 2013 the gallery exterior prompted Iziko to reassure the public with the following words: "While it may seem like quite an imposing building, with its stark white façade, towering Greek pillars, and massive doors opening out onto the Company's Garden – the interior of SANG is as warm and familiar as a Xhosa mud hut."[39] This attempt at reconciling our colonial past with our African present is seriously flawed: the nomenclature applicable to the Greek Orders (Doric in this case) and the domestic scale of the Arts and Crafts-inspired wings, as well as acceptable terminology for adobe or vernacular architecture, escaped the writer. It is frankly an insult to call a vernacular structure a "mud hut" and one has to question the familiarity of the vast majority of South Africans – including Xhosa speakers born in cities – with such a dwelling. Besides, how did this help SANG's image and ambitions to be a state-of-the-art museum capable of hosting international shows?

Much discussion and reflection will be required to create an architectural dialogue between the old and the new, and between Africa and Europe. The students' wide-ranging solutions showed that this is indeed desirable, and possible. When extensions to the gallery were mooted in the late 1980s, the scheme that architect Hannes Meiring proposed was firmly rooted in the postmodern idiom fashionable at the time: it echoed the classicism of the main building and would have perpetuated notions of an art museum as an elitist place for the few.[40]

The second topic that requires attention is the future of African art at Iziko. The historical roots of African art in major art museums and the beginnings of SANG's collection in the late 1960s, as well as an ongoing commitment to repatriating, acquiring and exhibiting African art from 1990, are woven into this history. And yet, there falls a deep shadow between Iziko's rhetoric about decolonisation and being an African institution of excellence, and the reality that this part of our heritage and aesthetic production has failed to find its rightful place. The number of exhibitions showcasing the collection has dwindled. Until recently a banner on SANG's façade referred to "traditional" African art, terminology that we dropped in the 1990s in favour of "historical" to fall in line with how older European art is described. Naidoo was not convinced that such "artefacts" belonged within the fine arts context, a view shared by Anna Tietze who refers to pieces in the gallery collection as "African craft objects" and "crafted artefacts".[41]

In 1983 German art historian Reinhild Kauenhoven Janzen, then a visiting lecturer at the Michaelis, published an article in the SANG *Quarterly Bulletin*. While complimenting the gallery on its displays of works depicting the "troubled peace" in South Africa, by both black and white artists, she raised many questions and was critical of what was not shown:

> The rock paintings of the San people, the enigmatic Lydenburg heads, the abstract mural art of the Ndebele, the brilliant variations of beaded patterns of the Zulu, the flamboyant body arts of the Xhosa, to name but a few of the historical indigenous aesthetic expressions which are acknowledged as "African art" by all scholars in this field and by the leading journals on this subject.[42]

Janzen continued by describing the context in which this patrimony was displayed at SAM, where they were "squeezed in between whalebones, the planetarium and fossils," and "observed as natural rather than human history". She expressed her embarrassment at seeing the life casts in the diorama and suggested that the masterpieces of African art filling the storerooms could tell a different story. She then shifted her focus to a lengthy appreciation and analysis of the Irma Stern Museum (ISM) the one museum in Cape Town that offered (and still offers) a permanent collection celebrating what Janzen termed "classical African art".

Janzen's article elicited two harsh critiques in the form of letters to the editor. Bruce Arnott lambasted Janzen for her "rather pedestrian appraisal" of some of the works in the ISM and the poisoned barbs hurled at the Cape Town art establishment in particular and white South African attitudes in general. He described her stance as "the smug self-righteousness of the (privileged, white) liberal-minded European (or American), redolent of radical chic, fashionable social prejudices and the inverted sexism (and by implication racism?) of the Feminists".[43] Arnott defended the museums and reminded readers of the exhibitions *Rock Art in South Africa* (1963) and *African Art in Metal* (1970) that had the newly reconstructed *Lydenburg Heads* as an adjunct. There had been no resistance at SANG to acquiring African art, but rather a lack of funds, non-availability of good examples of art from West and Central Africa and lack of expertise in the field, which cumulatively were detrimental to "the systematic acquisition of good pieces of 'classical' African art".

E.M. Shaw, a revered former ethnologist at SAM, regarded much of Janzen's argument as unimportant. In her letter she pointed out the difference between the cultures of West Africa and South Africa, and the need to show the works in the context from which they stemmed: "To accept the art but object to it being shown in the context of the culture that gave it birth smack of contempt for that culture."[44] Shaw's opinion, and indeed Arnott's view that "the quality of each object determines whether it is art, not the context" in which it is shown, not to mention his use of terms "applied" and "functional" to qualify the arts of black South Africans, are still being debated.

It bears emphasising a key problem in relation to the above: the focus on caring for the objects by natural and social history departments, not curating and interpreting them. It may read as a bureaucratic nicety, but a major loan collection was lost because it was not exhibited. In 1992 Nicholas Penny, an adventurer and collector of African art, disappeared while river rafting on the Wit Els river in the Western Cape. His collection subsequently went on a twenty-year loan to SAM. It was well preserved and managed but hardly ever exhibited. When the loan was up Penny's family decided to auction off 520 pieces in October 2013. Iziko received a donation of 1,500 items of African and southern African beadwork, costume and personal items.[45]

What has changed for the visitor to Cape Town since the publication of Janzen's article thirty-five years ago? Not much. They may observe that the SAM diorama has been closed, but that the former ethnographic collections are still languishing in storage, the *Lydenburg Heads* and rock art have not moved across the Company's Garden to the art museum, and, with the exception of the temporary show *Hidden Treasures* at the gallery, the ISM is still the only museum that hosts a permanent display of African art. Iziko is ideally placed to exhibit and interpret its holdings in a curatorial framework where there are no more boundaries: between art and science, art and craft, art and religion, art history and anthropology, past and present. And the institution should be nurturing scholars in the field. But where are the vision and volition to achieve it? It is not discernable in management's project to re-imagine Iziko's museums.

African art in South African collections remains colonised without spaces dedicated to it. Lewis' presentation on behalf of art collections at the March 2016 workshop was vague about African art, suggesting that a room might be allocated for this purpose. Bertram House, unsuccessfully proposed by SANG curators as the ideal venue for the intimate display of African art, has been closed since August 2015. Not that it seems to matter to the public. The building on the Michaelis campus is a fine example of an early nineteenth-century Georgian red brick house, but the collection of furniture and porcelain it houses has rendered it moribund, with only 1,162 visitors in the 2014–15 financial year.[46]

John Paris had a vision of making the national gallery (and its related sites, now part of Iziko) the world centre for the study of the universally important San culture and aesthetic production. His dream to create an archive that would benefit local and international students and scholars will not be realised at Iziko.[47] As discussed in chapter two, Paris acted on his vision and he inaugurated the department of pre-historic and indigenous art with a loan exhibition of transcriptions of rock art from South West Africa (Namibia) in 1950. He broke new ground two years later when he juxtaposed African sculpture with small Renaissance bronzes against a background of paintings and a tapestry in *The Meaning of Sculpture*. Sadly he left before the department he envisioned could be created.

Storage and management of the approximately 3,000 pieces of African art in the gallery collection have not been resolved. In 2018 it was stored in part of the former art library. Nobody has replaced Kaufmann, who retired in March 2016 but came back to curate *Hidden Treasures*. According to Robertson, the African art curator position remains in the structure, but it has been redefined as curator of textiles, costume and adornment. African sculpture will fall under the curator of historical paintings and sculpture (Proud) or curator of contemporary art (White), "depending roughly on age". Curatorship and storage were divisible, he said. "How they are curated might be different to how they are stored – storage will factor in conservation considerations. This curator's collections of concern will also include relevant collections in social history (costume, textiles, beadwork, jewellery, etc.)."[48] How is African art defined and how can the evolving narratives proposed by Iziko's collections be activated in such a structure? The specialist knowledge and scholarship that are required to underpin acquisitions, research, interpretation and education relating to African art are overlooked in favour of some weird kind of functionality. The unintended consequences of what is being done, or not being done, will emerge over time.

This reorganisation of museum work raises the vexed questions of salaries and the absence of career paths for curators. New appointees come in on the same level as museum professionals with many years' experience. Curators' salaries at Iziko are virtually static and do not compare with what is on offer at private museums; besides, the gap between what a long-serving curator like Proud earns and what Robertson earned as director of natural history collections was huge.[49] While Iziko piles additional workloads onto staff (euphemistically described as enabling intellectual growth and improving career prospects), the question of career paths is not addressed. There is a senior educator, but no senior curator.

My efforts to rectify this – as art collections director and subsequently as council member – were futile. Responding to my request at a 2012 meeting that the matter receive attention, Ndhlovu agreed with the principle, took note of the issue and indicated that senior management "should be revising all policies and would be looking at this process from all angles". The following year I broached the subject again at a sub-committee meeting of council. Chairperson Ciraj Rassool supported me and said that Iziko would provide space for "professional development and professional fulfilment". Omar indicated that career tracks for curators would be evaluated after the then consultative process had been completed.[50] Nothing has changed. Moreover, at the end of 2018, art collections was without a curator of African art, the collections manager and registrar had resigned, and the curator of contemporary art was taking up another position in February 2019.[51] Posts take a long time to fill.

Now more than ever art collections is desperately in need of creating a professional, stimulating and enabling environment for curators, who are given opportunities to travel, participate in conferences, publish, lecture and become active members of professional organisations. Compared to their counterparts abroad, curators in South African art museums have seldom had the privilege of specialisation. On the one hand this has expanded the scope of interest and study that has contributed to the breaking of classificatory boundaries; on the other it has tended to prevent expertise in a particular field. The collection categories at SANG have always been broad and imprecise and could do with revision: the options are chronological for some (historical, modern and contemporary), medium-specific for others (paintings and sculpture/prints and drawings/photography and new media), and/or geographical (African).

To alleviate the wide gap between historical and contemporary collections, staff identified the need for a curator of modern paintings and sculpture. Lewis was appointed in this capacity, but after Dolby retired she was moved to prints and drawings and her previous post was scrapped. Robertson was keen to revive the long-standing gallery practice of publishing catalogues and to having them peer reviewed. How would this ever be possible if there is no curator to fill the art-historical gap between Proud and White, who are given additional responsibilities for thousands of objects in the art and other Iziko collections of which they have little knowledge? Eschewing the specialisation at the heart of collections could result in fine curators becoming dilettantes.

With Robertson's departure Glanville-Zini will probably be given the task of drafting the "Re-imagining Iziko" document in consultation with core functions staff, but there can be no vision or imagination without expertise in the disciplines, and familiarity with the complex world outside Iziko. Where are the ambitions for curators to engage internationally and for the national art museum to make its presence felt by, for example, submitting a proposal to DAC for the South African Pavilion at the Venice Biennale, now that such a pavilion exists? The institution is systematically being isolated from professional museological and curatorial best practice.

While collections are being built, conserved and interpreted, the threat of deaccessioning may rear its head at any time. The fact that Iziko acts under financial constraint leaves it vulnerable to institutions abroad and their agents who may wish to prey on the collections. In December 2015 Robert Greig, a South African-born journalist who now works as a performing and visual arts consultant in London, wrote to the CEO and reminded her that in 2011 he had assisted Penlee House Gallery in securing a five-year loan of Dame Laura Knight's *Flying a Kite* (1910) (Plate 40). The tour that followed was very well received and Greig had discussions about the painting with senior officials of two British art institutions.

"I have been asked to explore the possibilities of establishing a mutually agreeable arrangement balancing British heritage (repatriation) with Iziko's artistic funding priorities and development needs," wrote Greig.[52] Because of the sensitivity of such a proposal, Greig was not specific, but suggested that Knight's work carried "primary significance and emotional resonances" in Britain, that as an artist she was committed "to social justice and principled action," while Iziko was limited "in nurturing the roots of future heritage by acquiring modern and contemporary South African work or expanding outreach programmes". A year later, Greig wrote again, asking whether he should direct the request to council.[53]

Greig's somewhat patronising and curious arguments (imagine suggesting "repatriation" when so much of the world's patrimony finds itself in museums in the UK) did not sway Omar. In her reply she emphasised that Iziko valued its heritage assets and partnerships, and that it nurtured working relations with museums around the globe, including loans to and from like-minded institutions. "Through this, we hope to promote social inclusion, global citizenry and social justice," she wrote, adding:

> As an institution, we are not intending to exchange *Flying a Kite*. But if those unnamed museums are willing to engage the South African government through the British government on this question, and on the repatriation of the many South African heritage assets presently in various institutions in the UK, this may be a discussion you would like to enter into with our national DAC. Our participation in such a national discussion with global relevance will therefore be guided by DAC and the heritage prescripts of the country.[54]

The threat of deaccessioning *Flying a Kite* was averted, and Omar's defence of South Africa's complicated material heritage at Iziko is to be applauded. Greig's attempt does, however, serve as a reminder that our collections are vulnerable, and that approaches to alienate works may come from unexpected sources.

The Friends celebrate fifty years in 2018

SINCE THE ASSOCIATION was constituted under Matthys Bokhorst's directorship, the Friends have proved to be friends indeed and in need. This book bears testimony to this civic organisation's enormous contribution to the well-being and advancement of the national art museum in a multitude of ways, as well as the close relationship that existed between the Friends and directors. Sadly, though, Iziko management and council have in recent years tested their loyalty, as well as that of the Friends of the Michaelis Collection. Not understanding their love for and commitment to specific collections – art and natural history – Bredekamp in 2005 mooted the plan to amalgamate the three groups of Friends into a single body to facilitate more efficient liaison. The individual groups declined and expressed themselves satisfied with the status quo; they were encouraged to nominate individuals for the next council.[55] The situation was exacerbated by Naidoo's disinterest and by the perception of some individuals in management and on the council that the Friends were a burden rather than a blessing, and that they should be "diversified" in line with Iziko's transformation agenda.[56]

The fissures that deepened over time were revealed by six students of the Henley Business School in a 2013 report titled "Analysis of Iziko Museum's relationships with Friends Organisations".[57] Based on the premise that there were serious issues of trust and mutual respect, and that "the underlying subtext of the white and non-white cultural differences" would test the "more traditional structures and approaches" of the Friends of the gallery, MC and SAM, the students recorded their research, conclusions and solutions in a forty-three page document. According to the research, new members of the management team not only questioned the contributions of the societies, but imposed new rules on limiting parking and doing away with free entry to the museums. As might be expected the Friends were affronted and frustrated by the reduction of Friends' access benefits and lack of discussion about the policy changes; they concluded that Iziko did not wish to cooperate with them, but to control them instead. Lines of communication were unclear, their skills and contribution were not recognised and the bureaucracy placed limitations and uncertainty on organising events.

For Iziko management the SAM Friends – the more passive group – were the least problematic, while they feared the art collections' Friends. Their distrust was partly based on the influential individuals who were well connected to the press and the absurd complaint that a council member was teaching at an art school, but in the same breath members were also regarded as no more than "hobbyists looking for prestige". Such committees do of course attract individuals who may look for prestige, but – trickier – may have hidden ambitions and agendas that they want to put into effect. This had happened in the past and was dealt with without jeopardising the organisation and its aims, or alienating its members. The situation is likely to change for the worse, because without the presence and leadership of a director who works closely with the Friends' council, assertive members could try to push gallery staff around. It could mean the end of decades of friendship. In 2018, for the first time – as far as anyone can remember – the FONG council refused to buy a painting that the curators proposed.

According to Iziko, FONG created costs (related to office space and meeting venues), they had the audacity to propose exhibitions and artists for residencies (this had been encouraged prior to Iziko) and ultimately Iziko did not regard a relationship with the Friends "as essential in the future". This was a cynical attitude considering the financial and other contributions on which the art museum depends. Also at issue were the age and demographics of the Friends, which had not been satisfactorily resolved, despite efforts over many years.

The solutions offered in the document drafted by the six business students were based on evidence, but was also adrift of reality. They proposed a governance model that would formalise communication with all the organisations (more meetings and bureaucracy), and the creation of "Young Friends of Iziko". The logical outcome of the former would be to ultimately bring everyone together under an Iziko Friends umbrella, which simply reiterated Bredekamp's failed proposal of 2005. The students were unaware or ignorant of the fact that associations such as FONG were not initiated by the museums, but were an expression of certain communities or individuals with special interests. They also overlooked the time, commitment and hard work required of council members, who often invest personal resources in the programmes and events of the Friends. The recommendations were not implemented. While parking at SANG was limited to two bays, the Friends argued for retaining the valuable attraction of free entrance, which Iziko conceded.

While the students' troubling analysis was being conducted, appreciation for FONG's support was recorded in the minutes of a core functions and institutional advancement meeting held in 2013. The Friends received high praise for the "momentous role" it played in contributing half the purchase price of R280,000 for Mary Sibande's sculpture *The Reign* (2010). "The long-standing and mutually beneficial partnership was cemented via this purchase," it was noted.[58] With Naidoo's departure, the strained relationship with FONG improved.

The Friends' fiftieth birthday celebrations commenced on 15 April 2018 with *Friends50*, a selection of the more than 300 artworks the association acquired since 1968. The exhibition was jointly curated by Phillippa Duncan and Winnie Sze, representing FONG, and Lewis and Proud for SANG. The exhibition explored two aggregated themes: people and places, and history and myths. Considering the significance of the Friends' contribution to the collection, it was a modest show, occupying only two rooms, and there was no publication.

In his welcome address at the opening Bongani Ndhlovu affirmed FONG's importance in the life and welfare of the gallery: "Since the formation of the Friends in 1968, much has changed; the South African social and political landscape has been altered, but the Friends have shown remarkable resilience and loyalty. They remain a separate, parallel, yet indispensable support agency of SANG."[59] He applauded the association for identifying with the ideals, mission, priorities and activities of the national institution, and for enabling things that might otherwise have been difficult or impossible to achieve. In addition to the acquisitions, FONG supports education and conservation, and their lectures bolster attendance figures and interest. Ndhlovu acknowledged the dedication of chairpersons and council members past and present. He gave a fitting tribute to the Friends:

> In looking back over the statistics of the past fifty years of achievement and support, we at times forget that the Friends are a voluntary organization. We must not forget to acknowledge the many hours of selfless and unpaid work put in by Friends' council members that have made so much possible. For this, Iziko Museums, and especially the curatorial staff of SANG, and indeed the nation, must remain in their debt.

Critic and scholar Ashraf Jamal was the main speaker at the opening. He offered incisive insights and raised a number of pertinent questions about South Africa and the national art museum. Two of them stood out for me. The first dealt with the need to guard against political correctness. Referring to the decision of the Baltimore Museum of Art to sell seven works by some of America's best-known twentieth-century artists – Franz Kline, Kenneth Noland, Jules Olitski, Robert Rauschenberg and Andy Warhol – in order to buy art by women and "artists of colour",[60] Jamal had this to say:

> It is the anonymity and the generalisation that irks. What is a woman artist? A black artist? In an attempt to be politically correct an institution can fail its best intentions. Which is why I feel one must approach art in the singular, evaluate the particular worth of an individual artist, and refuse the easy framing notion which not only denies an individual artist their complexity, but which keeps them in check.[61]

Jamal made another salutatory observation in his concluding remarks:

> SANG is a national institution, in a time when what can be said to define South Africa is uncertain. To whom must the museum speak, and on whose behalf? How does one ensure an inclusive and culturally heterogeneous spirit? And, in relation to the strident and flashy aura of the Zeitz Museum of Contemporary Art Africa – with its embrace of the millennial – and the commanding austerity of Norval Foundation – with its enshrining of the great South African modernists – what I wonder, is the national gallery's place and role?

It is a fair question, and one that forms the basis of this book's final chapter.

FIGURE 44: Zeitz MOCAA atrium with Nicholas Hlobo's *Iimpundulu Zonke Ziyandilandela* (All the Lightning Birds are After Me) (2011), rubber inner tubing, ribbon, animal skull, mixed media, pink theatre lights, sound, 2500 × 4600 × 10000; image courtesy of Zeitz MOCAA.

11

Fundamental changes in the South African art and museum ecosystem

2017 – 2019

THIS CHAPTER reflects on fundamental changes in South African art and museums, and the place and role of the national art museum within this evolving ecosystem. It discusses the opening of the Zeitz Museum of Contemporary Art Africa, in Cape Town, and related controversies, as well as lists other recent private art initiatives. The still-new relationship between public and private art museums in South Africa is examined. The prominence of male figures in the museum sector is considered in relation to the historical contributions of women; museum ethics in an increasingly market-dominated landscape are also examined. Two important and related questions are addressed in this chapter: Have privately owned art spaces and commercial venues supplanted publicly funded art museums, and if yes, why?

Without a living past, we have only
an inert present and a dead future.

CARLOS FUENTES[1]

A new art museum for Africa – Zeitz MOCAA opens in Cape Town

MORE THAN A DECADE AGO, the owners of the Victoria & Alfred Waterfront (Waterfront), a portside mall development in Cape Town that is also the most expensive piece of real estate on the African continent, turned their attention to a derelict industrial site near Duncan Dock on the Foreshore. The site was home to a grain elevator system, completed in 1924, but long since abandoned. Waterfront CEO David Green and his team identified this complex of forty-two storage silos and grain-elevator tower as central to an urban renewal project that would connect the isolated mall with the revitalised lower city, in particular the Cape Town International Convention Centre.[2] Drawing inspiration from the model of the Frank Gehry-designed Guggenheim Museum Bilbao in Spain, the Waterfront contracted the services of British designer Thomas Heatherwick to develop an architectural plan to reinvent the 118 round, square and cruciform tubes cast in concrete into a museum space. Central to the success of this project, though, was the need for an art collection of recognisable stature.

Johannesburg art collector Gordon Schachat expressed interest in placing his collection with the new museum following a proposal, but eventually pulled out of the project after the protracted negotiations stalled. At the same time, German collector Jochen Zeitz, a former CEO of sportswear company Puma, and his South African curator Mark Coetzee, had begun looking for a suitable city and site in Africa to build an art museum for his collection. For Zeitz "it all started with football" when he commissioned African-American artist Kehinde Wiley to paint portraits of African footballers to celebrate the 2010 FIFA World Cup.[3] Zeitz and Coetzee found strategic synergy with the Waterfront's museum project, and a joint venture was signed in November 2013. The project was billed as a R500 million "philanthropic" undertaking. Following on the official launch in November 2013, there was much speculation about and anticipation of what would transpire. A temporary pavilion opened at Bascule Bridge in the Waterfront to showcase work from the collection and to make public Heatherwick's design. There were fashion balls, museum nights, talks, fundraising and requests for artists and galleries to donate works.[4] Initially Zeitz committed his collection "in perpetuity", but that changed subsequently to a loan for at least twenty years or Zeitz's lifetime, while Coetzee and his acquisition committee built its own collection.

Opened in September 2017, the Zeitz Museum of Contemporary Art Africa (Zeitz MOCAA) is a contemporary art museum that collects, preserves, researches and exhibits artworks produced in the twenty-first century in Africa and her Diaspora, and hosts temporary exhibitions. The centres for art education, curatorial excellence, performative practice, photography, the moving image and a costume institute established by Coetzee spoke to a broad and inclusive notion of contemporaneity that set a benchmark for the continent and further afield. Green and Zeitz co-chair a fourteen-member board. According to Coetzee, there were no precedents for the museum: it was brand new and therefore did not come with the baggage of colonial and apartheid inheritance that all too often bedevils the national gallery and other major art museums.[5]

That did not, however, safeguard the museum from questions and criticism. Lack of transparency about policy, the actual size of Zeitz's collection, and acquisition budgets and procedures, surfaced early on; it remains an issue. Zeitz MOCAA is a corporate project; it is privately funded and therefore not obliged to account to the public.[6] The museum has free lease of the floors for ninety-nine years and is named after Zeitz, who according to the November 2013 agreement is responsible for underwriting the running costs. The museum is dependent on fund-raising and sponsorship (the tension between its private-public status is discussed below).

The Waterfront and its partner, Zeitz, together with Coetzee, could have minimised criticism and speculation around the museum's opaque finances and the extent of its collection by answering questions and providing information. Coetzee raised huge amounts of money during his tenure, and sought partnerships inside and outside the arts sector and the country. He established a source of job creation and training, in South Africa and further afield, and focussed on education at all levels.[7] Many observers welcomed Zeitz MOCAA's vision of raising museum standards in South Africa, encouraging the growing interest world wide in African art and making or attracting major acquisitions. Coetzee's achievements could not protect him from the flaws inherent in the structure and governance, and in the end, hyperbole and hubris on the part of the museum and its director sullied the institution's early promise.[8] In May 2018, the trustees suspended Coetzee and launched an inquiry into his professional conduct following complaints from staff. Coetzee resigned, although his action was rejected in a labour court finding; he was subsequently fired in July 2018.[9] Adjunct curator Azu Nwagbogu took over the role of acting director and chief curator in a temporary capacity, until the appointment of Koyo Kouyo in May 2019.

None of this can diminish the significance of the museum building. The exterior of the grain silo has been respectfully and lovingly restored, while the concrete walls of the grading tower were cut away to create new honeycomb glass lattice windows that reflect Table Mountain and the sea, and glow like a beacon in the harbour at night. The spectacle and surprise that is Zeitz MOCAA is focussed internally, in the way in which a monumental cathedral-like space, inspired by a single grain of corn, is carved out of the silos and runs up to glass circles that form both the ceiling and the floor for the sculpture garden. Togolese artist El Loko fritted the nine laminated glass discs with his abstract and universal *Cosmic Alphabet* (2016). Nicholas Hlobo's enormous *Iimpundulu Zonke Ziyandilandela* (All the Lightning Birds are After Me) (2011) may detract from the architecture, but it adds to the drama upon entering the atrium, which provides access to some 100 galleries (6,000 square metres) spread over nine floors, the sculpture garden, café and other functional spaces. Here the silos of the mind that occupy Iziko management have manifested in the splendid transformation of real silos (Fig. 44).[10]

The building is as much part of the exhibit as the art it contains: its origins as a loved landmark in Cape Town predetermined Zeitz MOCAA's iconic status as an art museum that can take its place with edifices like Herzog & de Meuron's M. H. de Young Memorial Museum in San Francisco (2010) and Frank Gehry's Louis Vuitton Foundation in Paris (2014).[11]

Zeitz MOCAA opened to an invited public on 21 September 2017 and hyperbole took on a whole new meaning. The museum was labelled "Africa's Tate Modern"[12] and "The eighth wonder of the world ... promising to be to Cape Town what the Tate is to London, or the Met is to New York".[13] Speaking at the launch, Archbishop Emeritus Desmond Tutu channelled Nelson Mandela by pretending to take a phone call from the former president in heaven: "Yes! This is what we were fighting for!"[14] *Dezeen* described it as "home to the world's most important African art collection" and the by-line of an article in the Waterfront magazine offered the following absurdity:

> Cape Town's most famous landmark has always been its beloved Table Mountain. Then, this September, Zeitz MOCAA opened. The result of a partnership between the V&A Waterfront and renowned art collector Jochen Zeitz, and suddenly the mountain was no longer the biggest thing in town.[15]

When the project was first announced, critic Sean O'Toole wrote a thoughtful and probing article in the *Mail & Guardian*.[16] Amidst the enthusiasm for the initiative, he pointed to "the need for sobriety in a cultural backwater belatedly entering the era of the mega-museum". I was asked for a comment about the potential strengths and weaknesses of the new museum, and in the article responded by welcoming a project that spoke of vision and volition, elements that are sadly lacking, if not altogether absent, in public museums in South Africa. I added:

> A threat to ourselves may be our cultural insecurity and parochialism. On the one hand, this will negate many benefits while, on the other, we may be so overwhelmed by the presence and power of the Zeitz MOCAA that we follow trends and ideas blindly and neglect to engage critically with the museum and its projects.

These cautionary notes now ring true and need to be amplified by in-depth assessments and reviews of the management structure; the building, such as the nature of the white boxes, circulation and lighting; the quality and importance of Jochen Zeitz's loan collection, as well as the role of loans in the inaugural exhibition; curatorial rigour; printed wall texts and the availability of general information and publications. If not, we – both Africans and the millions of tourists who visit the Waterfront, and the city – may believe the frenzied nonsense that some writers are perpetrating.[17]

A week before the public opening of Zeitz MOCAA, hundreds of people – artists, curators, writers, patrons, collectors and gallerists – came from all over the world for the preview viewings, special events, lectures and tours of the exhibitions and the building. I was privileged to receive an invitation from Coetzee to what was indeed a memorable weekend. Sadly, the experience was clouded by conversations with diverse people from South Africa and abroad, who inevitably asked me about the state of the national gallery. Comments and questions about the absence of a director at SANG and a profile in the world also emerged in a public discussion with Coetzee. One of the foreign visitors wanted to know what the implications of Zeitz MOCAA were for the national art museum. Coetzee asked me to respond.

My short answer was that the responsibility lay with Iziko Museums and that it was up to its senior management to embrace the opportunity for collaborating with Zeitz MOCAA (an attempt at providing a longer answer follows below). Coetzee in turn mentioned that he was doing all he could to help, but that action from Iziko was not forthcoming: he had, for example, encouraged the institution to host a group from Art Basel at a dinner, but the offer was declined.

Heatherwick exacerbated the situation with his statements in the press. "This is like the missing piece in the jigsaw. South Africa has incredible artists and private galleries but it had no major public institution," he told *The Times*.[18] "There are all these incredible artists and galleries, but there hasn't been a major institution to bring them together. Even if no one likes the design, it was an important strategic moment," he is quoted in the *Sunday Times*.[19] This was an epic blunder by the architect, and indeed sloppy journalism on the part of the enthralled South Africans who interviewed him, and who left his remarks unchallenged. Even so, writers like Melvyn Minnaar, who remembered SANG, referred to its serious troubles: "lacking funds, expertise and leadership".[20] Sean O'Toole observed in the Sunday Times, that:

> … in a country where the biennale idea has proved unworkable, both in Cape Town and Johannesburg, and our public museums are frail, faltering and – in the case of the Johannesburg Art Gallery – physical wrecks, projects like the Joburg Art Fair have emerged as unlikely but durable pillars. Maybe the Zeitz MOCAA will match this outcome.[21]

We are left with troubling questions: have the national gallery, Johannesburg Art Gallery, the Durban Art Gallery and the Pretoria Art Museum ceased to exist, except in the minds of a few who still care?[22] Were management and curators at SANG aware of the impact that Zeitz MOCAA would have on the art community and general public? What did they do to attract the local, national and international visitors?

The answer to the first question is not evident right now and it will ultimately depend on whether our art museums can find ways out of the wilderness of official indifference, internal and external bureaucratic structures, and lack of knowledge, scholarship and vision. As I argued in previous chapters, at the national gallery this outcome is also a consequence of the restructuring process that has done away with the director and put in charge highly qualified individuals in their own disciplines, but who have neither knowledge of art and its history, nor experience in building art collections and conceptualising and implementing exhibitions and associated programmes.

With the exception of Susan Glanville-Zini, who has replaced Hamish Robertson as director of research and exhibitions, there is no art or art history knowledge in either the executive management structure or the Iziko council. The symbolism of not acknowledging the importance of museums and their collections by appointing directors is as damaging as is the shift from professionalisation to bureaucratisation, from creativity to functionality. Officials at DAC, who saw fit to appoint a former ambassador and three advocates to the council of 2017, are complicit in the evisceration of appropriate knowledge at the highest levels of Iziko and council members come at a huge financial cost to Iziko.[23] Without passion, underscored by knowledge and reputation, lobbying power is enfeebled.

Conditions inside and outside are difficult for the national gallery, but how much of the current problems are of Iziko's own doing, or *not* doing? Inaction is a position and has consequences. The cracks beneath the surface of compliance and subservience to DAC have widened steadily since amalgamation. The debacles involving Riason Naidoo and *Our Lady* detailed in earlier chapters, and the absence of engagement with and a creative response to Zeitz MOCAA, have revealed the extent of the fault lines.

Replying to a question about the challenges Zeitz MOCAA presented in late 2015, CEO Rooksana Omar said that Iziko viewed the new museum as a "positive development", that it would work with other institutions "to promote the arts and increase the footfall to South Africa and Cape Town," and that it had a "good working relationship" with Zeitz MOCAA.[24] In March 2017 Ndhlovu confirmed that staff members had been tasked to engage with Coetzee.[25] Nothing came of it: management, Robertson and curators were seemingly unaware of the activities at Zeitz MOCAA before the public opening on 22 September and complacent in thinking that people would automatically also visit SANG; as a result, the national gallery did not benefit from potential ripple effects. Moreover, they allowed Zeitz MOCAA to capture the art museum space.

It bears noting that by January 2019 nothing much had changed as regards collaboration. While Iziko management's focus is on decolonisation and re-imagining the museums, it took Haco de Ridder of the Mondriaan Foundation in Amsterdam to act as a catalyst for a workshop at Iziko entitled "Collaboration and Challenges: The Roles and Relationship of public and private art museums in contemporary society". Held on 4 September 2018, at Iziko, it featured informative presentations by a number of European and local role players, but neither the definitions nor the complexities of the relationships (or lack thereof) in Cape Town were addressed. A follow-up meeting was suggested.

The new art museum is by any standards ambitious and its popular uptake in the African context extraordinary. Zeitz MOCAA is unlike anything this continent has seen. However, it has been wrongly credited with all manner of innovations by notionally informed commentators and journalists who neglect to do their homework. One example will suffice. Writing for *Business Live* in 2017, art consultant Alexia Walker stated: "Today, photography is widely recognised as an important art form. Museums collect photography, major exhibitions, fairs and festivals are devoted to the medium, and collectors are actively committing to it."[26] Today? As this book has shown, interest in photography at the national art museum goes back many decades; it has hosted numerous exhibitions featuring photographers from Africa, and beyond. In October 2017 there were two major exhibitions of photography on at SANG: *The African Choir Re-imagined*, a superb installation that re-imagined The African Choir's first tour to Victorian England in 1891 using archival photographs and sound, as well as Andrew Tshabangu's *Footprints*.[27]

Zeitz MOCAA will never have the depth and scope of art practice and production in South Africa that resides in the national collection. The opening of this new museum presented a wonderful moment for the national gallery to create an historical and contemporary context for, and counterpoint to what was happening at the Waterfront: to conceptualise a comprehensive, coherent exhibition from the magnificent permanent collection. *The African Choir Re-imagined* could have been an excellent starting point. *Hidden*

FIGURE 45: *Hidden Treasures*, installation, 2017. In the foreground: Workshop of Paa Joe, *Fantasy coffin*, c. 1997, wood, oil paint, satin lining; collected and presented by Michael Heuermann; © Iziko Museums of South Africa; photographer Nigel Pamplin.

Treasures, featuring pieces that Carol Kaufmann selected, could have inspired a broader narrative of African art, although it was marred by the weirdly crammed and isolated presentation of Ndebele beadwork and painted panels in an otherwise carefully constructed exhibition (Fig. 45). In the event, a huge opportunity to draw attention to the country's premier art museum was missed.

The reasons for this were not strictly a lack of strategic vision. Incorrect, but politically correct main texts in two of the spaces occupied by *Hidden Treasures* stated that "the new democratic government of South Africa funded much of the collection, establishing it as a resource and visual archive for the nation," when in fact the Ndebele collection was purchased by the old Department of National Education and showcased in the exhibition I*Gugu lamaNdebele (Pride of the Ndebele)* in 1994–95.[28] Curiously, an example of the paintings by Isa Kabini, Emma Mahlangu, Betty Masanabo, Sophie Masiza and Anna Matshiye were absent from another exhibition that opened around the time of Zeitz MOCAA's launch, Hayden Proud's *Assessing Abstraction*, while a painting by an Australian Aboriginal artist was included. This omission removed the Ndebele artists from contemporary aesthetic production and relegated them to their "tribe" – an act that was exacerbated by the inclusion of Alexis Preller's painting *The Kraal* (1948). Preller's *Christ Head* (1952), in which the iconic oil on wood image is framed by white Ndebele beadwork, would have been more appropriate.

Few, if any, international visitors went to the national gallery during the festivities at Zeitz MOCAA, and it is just as well. Until 21 September, when *Alternative Press: Work of Derek Bauer*, a showcase of political cartoons, opened, five rooms were closed and the building was littered with notices explaining that forthcoming shows were being installed – with apologies for the inconvenience caused.[29] *Assessing Abstraction* in the first room had been taking shape for weeks, but was still unfinished – more apologies and many missing labels; the installation was only completed in December. Some visitors rightly demanded their money back and were refunded 50% of the R30 entrance fee.

Much was made of free access to all Iziko museums during heritage week (18–24 September), encouraging enjoyment of "a week of fun-filled family edu-tainment, exploring our shared heritage!" The irony of putting this notice up next to one apologising for spaces still closed on Heritage Day seemed lost on staff. In addition to the exhibitions mentioned above, there was *Lionel Davis: Gathering Strands*, a revealing retrospective of this artist and anti-apartheid activist's wide-ranging practice, organised with the District Six Museum. Jane Alexander's *Butcher Boys* kept watch over a small selection of unlit paintings from the Bailey bequest and a touch-screen display (no doubt to appease the Bailey trustees), but without any explanation why the sculpture was there. The website was hopelessly out of date.[30] Cumulatively, the art museum was the site of glaring oversight and embarrassing ineptitude at a time of intense focus and interest in South African art and museums.

Iziko let down our national art museum, our artists and our country. Its remedial actions are at best piecemeal. Since 1 April 2018 the museum now opens an hour earlier, at 09:00. Iziko's council took the decision to amend the hours of business "following public demand and a review of visitor trends at our museum sites and the competing destinations in Cape Town ... It is hoped that these new opening times will promote greater access to our museums, and have a positive impact on the visitor experience".[31]

Private vs. public museums

THOMAS HEATHERWICK'S ASSERTION that Zeitz MOCAA is a "public institution" was echoed by Jochen Zeitz, who described it as "a public museum with a private collection ... It's not my museum or the Waterfront's – it's for Africa" and "Africans need to come on board".[32] It is promoted as a public not-for-profit contemporary art museum on its website. In an article on *Artthrob* Sue Williamson points out that such organisations receive considerable tax benefits and that they are bound by the Nonprofit Organisations Act of 1997.[33] The Code of Good Practice issued by the Department of Social Development in 2001 requires that an organisation be "willing and open to public enquiry and questioning" and that it provides "timely, accessible and accurate information on the organisation and its activities to donors and others". To my knowledge there has not been the required annual general meeting at which "relevant information concerning goals, programmes, finances and governance" was shared with the public.[34]

Distinctions between public and private museums have not received much attention in South Africa. The national gallery and other public galleries in South Africa have their origins in private benefaction from civically minded people and eventually became public institutions funded by national government or municipalities. Unlike the new private museums named after their founders, most of the patrons gave selflessly and were not interested in having their names attached to the collections.

FIGURE 46 Norval Foundation; image courtesy of Norval Foundation; photographer Dave Southwood.

Until now single-donor art museums, such as the long-established Rupert Museum in Stellenbosch, have been the exceptions – they have been described as private, implying that they are not necessarily for the common good or a benchmark for one that is meant for public benefit. With Zeitz MOCAA and other museums such as the Norval Foundation, it is opportune to revisit a nomenclature that we take for granted.[35]

The New Church Museum is a recent example of a private museum founded by an individual person. Investor and art collector Piet Viljoen established the museum in a retrofitted Victorian home on New Church Street. He further appointed a director, Kirsty Cockerill, who assisted him in determining what would be acquired, how the collection would be exhibited, and who would be involved in curating exhibitions. It was billed as "South Africa's first privately owned contemporary art museum", accessible to the public and free of charge. It was Viljoen's prerogative to sell works, and also to close the museum, which he did in May 2016 after only two years of being open to the public.

Cockerill announced the suspension of the exhibition programme "for a period of sabbatical," although the "activation and development" of its permanent collection would continue. The New Church Street building still appeared on the website in August 2018, despite having been sold; the museum was effectively closed and silent after the *Our Lady* fiasco. Although modest in scale, the museum's closure was a great loss for Cape Town, and indeed South Africa.[36]

In April 2018, the Norval Foundation opened in the Steenberg area of Cape Town, adjacent to Table Mountain National Park. This museum houses the private collection of the initial founders and funders, property developer and art collector Louis Norval and his family. It is described as a centre for the research and exhibition of twentieth- and twenty-first-century visual art from South Africa and beyond, and it hosts exhibitions of both local and international artists. The aim of the Norval family is "to make art widely accessible to local and international visitors, by creating a self-sustainable centre for art. The proceeds from capital donations will be used to secure the foundation for future generations".[37]

Designed by dhk architects, the Norval Foundation offers state of the art exhibition, research and storage facilities, as well as a sculpture garden, outdoor amphitheatre, children's playground and hospitality services – they include the Skotnes restaurant, Sekoto bar and a bespoke shop (Fig. 46). Elana Brundyn, formerly of Zeitz MOCAA, is the director, while artist and Wits academic Karel Nel is adjunct senior curator. Nel visited many art museums with Louis Norval and Marelie Vorster, and has been integral to the development of the vision for the building and its materialisation in concrete and glass. Nel was responsible for the main inaugural exhibition, *Re/discovery and Memory*, which featured Ezrom Legae, Sydney Kumalo, Edoardo Villa and Serge Alain Nitegeka, as well as a catalogue that is a benchmark for South African museum publications.[38] (Zeitz MOCAA, by contrast, did not produce any publications in its first year.)

The Javett Art Centre, an independent art centre in which public and private interests intersect with the academy, is due for completion in 2019 at the University of Pretoria (UP). Designed by architect Pieter Mathews, the museum's director is Christopher Till. Javett's focus is the art of Africa, and the first exhibition surveyed the gold objects from Mapungubwe housed at UP, and the Javett family's private collection of twentieth-century South African art. It has been billed as "one of the largest philanthropic ventures and one of the most ambitious initiatives aimed at promoting the arts and cultural heritage in South Africa".[39]

The major distinction between private and public museums is the source of funding, although this is not decisive; another may be inherent in the nature and permanence of the collections. Private owners-donors like the Javett and Norval families and Jochen Zeitz may retain the right to sell works from their collections, and sell them for profit after much public exposure and loans to other museums. Unlike public collections that are usually assembled by expert committees and are subject to ratification by governing bodies, private collections often reflect the interests and tastes of charismatic and singular individuals and their advisors.

While diversity may be linked to staff members who are representative of South African demographics, white men have taken the gap left by established but floundering public art museums and are a major force behind these new private institutions. Unavoidably the collectors bring their own agendas and different kinds of baggage with them.

Stefan Simchowitz, a South African-born art advisor and collector based in Los Angeles, makes a case against the European system that explores history "with the cultural lens of race and post-colonialism" and for the "New Africa" that should instead lead cultural discourse:

> The problem in South Africa is that the collectors are white or CEOs or ex-CEOs of major companies and almost [all] have an unspoken subconscious mandate to fulfil this narrative through their engagement. Many of these "collectors" want to be seen as supporting the industry and artists, they want to be seen as "moral," "good" people. The results however often entrench this singular post-colonial cultural narrative.[40]

The dominance of males and money characterising the new museum landscape has witnessed a profound, if largely unremarked upon change: with a few exceptions, the soft power long wielded by women in art museums is, once again, in the hands of men. I was shocked into this realisation by an announcement of the appointment of Same Mdluli as gallery manager of Standard Bank Gallery: "Dr Mdluli represents a youthful and exciting voice in the contemporary art scene. She is part of a new generation of women taking on the historically male-dominated role of curator."[41] Historically male dominated? The writer clearly did not know their history; the previous curator of the Standard Bank Gallery was Barbara Freemantle, a woman.

As it is, the contributions of women to South African art museums is extensive: Pauline Mary Thomas, Florence Zerffi and Ruth Prowse were keepers of the Michaelis Collection for forty years (1916–56); Nel Erasmus, appointed in 1964 to lead JAG, was the first in a succession of women directors at this leading institution; elsewhere, Jill Addleson and Carol Brown headed-up DAG, Lorna Ferguson transformed the Tatham Art Gallery in Pietermaritzburg, Rosemary Holloway oversaw the WHAG in Kimberley and Melanie Hillebrand achieved a great deal with very little at NMMAM.

On the commercial front, Linda Givon, who founded the Goodman Gallery in Johannesburg in 1966, was a pioneer. The rest of the world has been trying to catch up with South Africa, and yet here we are regressing.[42] Male directors now oversee art institutions formerly run by women: at Iziko, Naidoo's tenure was followed by Robertson (replaced by Glanville-Zini in 2019) and Tichmann in the new structure; at JAG, Kwezi Gule replaced Antoinette Murdoch; and Mduduzi Xakaza heads up DAG after Jenny Stretton's selfless work. Brendan Bell at Tatham and Dirk Oegema, the "functional head" at PAM, have been in their positions for some time.

This is not to say that women do not occupy important posts. Emma O'Brien heads the NMMAM, Ann Pretorius was in charge of WHAG (she was succeeded by Ernestine White in February 2019) and the curator at the Oliewenhuis Art Museum, which forms part of the National Museum in Bloemfontein, is Ester le Roux. But a disconcerting trend is nonetheless discernible. Culture does not change unless women are part of the conversation at the highest levels. This unsettling turn of events deserves careful scrutiny and vigilance. Female museum workers everywhere must hold their own.

South Africans need time to fully assess the impact of these changes and new initiatives on the country and further afield, and to understand how the new museums will navigate the relationship between aesthetic experience and social utility, and between sustainability and accountability. In a 2018 interview in the *Mail & Guardian*, Matthew Blackman, who has consistently cast a spotlight on the machinations of officialdom and the art industry's dubious practices, broadened the discussion beyond Zeitz MOCAA and criticised other individuals and organisations.[43] A robust and public debate is required to lift the cloud that settled over the visual arts in the wake of Coetzee's dismissal, and to consider the bigger issues at stake, rather than point fingers at individuals and personalities.

In the meantime, the interpenetration of public and private art museums – neither truly private nor truly public – is a reality in South Africa. They are not-for-profit entities with permanent collections and endowments, and they seek patrons and donors to ensure sustainability. They are likely to have mission statements to which they adhere, follow legal and ethical standards of governance and join professional museum organisations like ICOM.

Promises of public benefit and access for all inevitably lead to questions about entrance fees, language policy and virtual access to collections. While internet images and virtual exhibitions can never replace a visit to a museum and an encounter with artefacts and works of art, all South African museums have a long way to go before they can compare with the Rijksmuseum in Amsterdam, which shares free, high-quality images without cost and restrictions.[44] As mentioned in chapter five, free access to the national gallery came to an end with Iziko, and the result is exclusion for those who cannot afford to pay, unless they visit on Iziko commemorative days.[45]

On the subject of entrance fees, Zeitz MOCAA is far more expensive than SANG; it is however free to everyone under eighteen and to South African and other African citizens on Wednesday mornings.[46] In its first thirty days Zeitz MOCAA had an astonishing 70,073 national and international visitors, of which 35,005 accessed the museum for free. By December the numbers were close to 110,000. Thousands of learners from the Eastern Cape and the Western Cape had attended guided tours in their mother tongue. By comparison, only 45,010 people visited the national gallery between 1 March 2016 and 28 February 2017 and the total visitors to Iziko's museums amounted to 459,634 including 64,746 described as "education".[47] The Norval Foundation is free to under-eighteens and to the general public on Mondays.[48] The attraction of free entrance is hard to dispute: queues at Zeitz MOCAA on Wednesday mornings, as well as the thousands who stream into SANG on museum nights, are ample testimony that South Africans are interested in visiting our art museums.

Language is integral to access, and Iziko's lengthy and great-sounding language policy – promoting South Africa's linguistic diversity and encouraging respect for language rights – is directly linked to broadening accessibility to "collections, historical buildings, exhibitions, education and public programme services as well as related information". External communication is in English, while Afrikaans and Xhosa feature "where there is a need".[49] With the exception of the new banner on the gallery façade, which is in four languages, no effort appears to have been made to diversify the language of the website, signage, invitations and information – the basic and most important level of engaging with the public. For all the rhetoric of transformation, decolonisation and inclusivity, Iziko has relegated a progressive policy of trilingualism, inherited from SANG, to the dustbin.[50] On the website Iziko Museums of South Africa appears in English only; by contrast, Zeitz MOCAA's name appears in English, Afrikaans and Xhosa, and is integrated with the logo, although that is where its multilingualism ends.

A perspective on the future of our art museums

THESE NEW INITIATIVES in South Africa's art and museum sector are showing what can be achieved with vision, passion and persuasion. At the same time they are throwing into sharp relief the rapidly changing landscape and concomitant plight of our art museums, and revealing the fault lines and ambiguities inherent in private initiatives. Threats and challenges to the national gallery are not new. In chapter three

I discussed how the mid-1970s marked the beginning of a decline in visitors to the gallery – a decline fed by the economic downturn, political uncertainty and upheavals of the time, as well as the introduction of television and rapid growth of suburban shopping centres. In the 1980s Raymund van Niekerk also had to contend with the strictures of the cultural and academic boycott. In response, the director and staff revised policies, curated significant exhibitions, published catalogues and organised ground-breaking educational activities. Some of these external influences on the life and functioning of the art museum have shifted in post-apartheid South Africa.

Corporate galleries and various associations throughout the country have continued to fulfil important functions. Similar to Linda Givon, dealer Michael Stevenson has made significant contributions. In 2003 he opened his Cape Town gallery with the exhibition *Contact Zones: Colonial and Contemporary*, in which past and present, tradition and contemporaneity, came together seamlessly. Since then the gallery bearing his name has presented many themed group exhibitions accompanied by catalogues.[51] The Goodman Gallery Cape opened in 2007 under the directorship of Emma Bedford and soon became known for ambitious shows, for example *Review Revue*, an overview of South African art over a period of fifty years (2009). Stellenbosch Modern and Contemporary (SMAC) has also staged exceptional exhibitions of abstract art and retrospective shows for their artists. The first Johannesburg Art Fair in 2008 included a curatorial component by Simon Njami and is now an important fixture of the annual art calendar; it is rivalled only by the Cape Town Art Fair.

There have been exciting additions to university campuses too. The University of Johannesburg (UJ) has a vibrant art gallery with a full programme, and the former campus-focused Gertrude Posel Gallery at Wits has transformed into a major public facility, the Wits Art Museum. The latter museum is the outcome of an intensive fundraising drive and occupies an award-winning building completed in 2011. Together with the Apartheid Museum and Constitution Hill, WAM has positioned itself as a premier tourist attraction in Johannesburg.

How can the national art museum adapt to these dramatic changes? In a 2009 column in *Die Burger*, I observed that curatorship was no longer the domain of art museums and biennials, and that serious curatorial practice had expanded to commercial galleries and art fairs that traditionally focused on marketing and sales.[52] I concluded the article with these words: "Museums are struggling with financial constraints and incapacity, and the business sector is increasingly contributing to the revision and rewriting of South Africa's art history."[53] Little did I foresee that the flourishing of the commercial sector would coincide with a downward spiral for South Africa's major art museums and that a new cultural ecology would evolve rapidly. This has adversely impacted staff. Unlike their counterparts in commercial galleries, who get to travel to art fairs and biennials all over the world, stay-at-home museum curators are deprived of first-hand experience and knowledge.

In a 2016 *Art Times* article, Sean O'Toole used the Robert Hodgins "bubble" in the auction market to look at broad issues in the visual arts sector. In an attempt to find answers to the many unanswered questions about Hodgins, he wrote:

> It would help if our public museums were not, to misquote Bacon, quietly stumbling from catastrophe to catastrophe. Functioning museums produce, among other things, reliable art scholarship. They temper dealer hyperbole, which is always rampant, and collate critical opinion, which is always conflicting. In short: they arbitrate on careers, sifting the wheat from the chaff. In South Africa, however, the balance between public museums and the vertically aligned retail trade (galleries, art fairs, private museums) is out of sync. Meaning: the soft exercise of power by public museums is non-existent. This has left it to auction houses, whose principle business is selling work offered by willing or distressed sellers on the open market, to fill the gap.[54]

Where museums have fallen short the market has indeed filled the gaps and we find ourselves in a world run by collectors. Role players have been aided enormously by increasing public interest in the spectacle of the art market, particularly as regards contemporary South African art. Connoisseurship declines as art is consumed by new buyers, who either tire easily of purchases and want the “latest” or invest in art with a view to making a quick turnover. Recent works by currently fashionable artists enter the auction market and are snapped up at hugely inflated prices; quality is not necessarily the benchmark and the market acts as an arbiter of aesthetic values and tastes.[55]

This situation raises the question as to how the lack of connoisseurship in turn influences the galleries and their choice of artists, when they need to sell in a competitive environment. The fallout is that too many committed and talented artists, whose work does not fit the fashionable and ever changing demands, remain under the radar. Not only has the curatorial narrative and influence on artistic production been ceded to the marketplace, which has its own limitations, but the absence of art museum publications means that commercial galleries, auction houses and the new public-private museums are writing a partisan first draft of our art history. That any art history is being written is, however, to be welcomed.

There are initiatives that seek alternatives to an art market that is driven by a neo-liberal economy. William Kentridge founded the Centre for the Less Good Idea in the Johannesburg arts precinct of Maboneng in March 2017. The venture is described as “an interdisciplinary incubator space” and a venue for showcasing “unconventional art experiences by established and up-and-coming local artists” – the less good idea is discovered through experimentation and the energy that is generated by unpredictable collaboration and the act of making.[56] In Cape Town, the A4 Arts Foundation, which opened in September 2017, is a privately-funded non-profit organisation established by the family trust of expatriate South African businessman Nathan Kirsch. The focus is on practitioners and exploratory creative processes, as well as connecting people, ideas and practices at local and international levels. A4 Arts Foundation offers a project space, private studio and workshop spaces, a multimedia library and an archive. The project is not without controversy.[57]

South African museums and collections – from the Apartheid Museum in Johannesburg to the West Coast Fossil Park, and including the private collection of Frank Kilbourn, executive chairperson of

Strauss & Co – were a key point of deliberation at the 2017 FynArts Festival, held in the seaside town of Hermanus.[58] To test perceptions of our publicly funded art museums, I chaired a panel with Stefan Hundt and Christopher Till. We discussed concerns about traditional custodianship: taking care of what our museums have inherited, building collections, doing research, educating and animating the museums, as well as their role as social entities for the common good. Our engagement as a panel and with those present was revealing and frankly depressing. In the face of government neglect (at all levels and by all political parties), poor leadership and deteriorating infrastructure, nobody offered solutions, except to suggest significant private-public partnerships or privatisation. Apparently we have come to expect that the private sector will step in where government fails; this is a cultural tendency that we must counter. As developments at Zeitz MOCAA have shown, private and corporate money is no panacea for advancing our art museums.

In this fluid situation, museum ethics are at stake. Of course, art museums and biennales the world over work with commercial entities – SANG is no exception. But a collaboration between SANG and Goodman Gallery in early 2018 was, in my view, just too cosy. The exhibition *Meyina* was a rare opportunity to see Ghanaian artist El Anatsui's work in South Africa. Curated by Bisi Silva, founder and artistic director of the Centre for Contemporary Art in Lagos, the exhibition was identical to a selling show held at the Goodman Gallery in Johannesburg at the end of 2017. Prior to the public opening, Goodman hosted a special event for "selected VIP guests".[59] Moreover, a detail of El Anatsui's *Fia* (2014), which is not in the SANG collection, graces the cover of the 2017-18 *Annual Report*. The Oliewenhuis Art Museum did it the other way round: Arlene Amaler-Raviv's exhibition *The Din of Daily Life* travelled from the museum to the Melrose Gallery in Johannesburg. Either way, this does not augur well for public institutions and their reputations.[60]

Our art museums are caught between their responsibilities to the general public and the commercial sector. They are frequently undermined by national or local authorities that are supposed to value them: the perception is that museums are not serving their diverse stakeholders successfully. Apart from the Friends, members of the public are not stepping up for the national art museum, as they have done many times in its long history. Reflecting on the 1988 exhibition *The Neglected Tradition* at JAG, Same Mdluli wrote in 2017:

> While the institution has … made great strides in encouraging greater inclusivity, not only in its collection and acquisition policies, the gallery nevertheless continues to occupy a precarious place in the lives of the majority of communities it aims to serve. The participation of these communities in the narrative of the history contained by the gallery is thus as implicit to its legacy as the exhibitions it has staged.[61]

This remains a huge challenge for the future for all art institutions in South Africa. Things change; they cannot stay the same. Our great art museums are at the crossroads and somehow they have to find ways of reclaiming the leadership role they once occupied. It will require a combination of political will, public pressure and advocacy, and involve vision, partnerships, networks of influence and the commitment to raise money for projects and publications. South Africa is brimming with creative talent and our art museums are in a unique position of looking backward and forward at the same time, and of presenting contemporary cultural production in the context of the past.

At Iziko history is being ignored and legacies constructed over many decades are being dismantled, but the South African National Gallery is bigger than any individual, structure, council and government department. One day, I am sure, it will once again achieve greatness and take its rightful place in the country, and in the world. It is all too tempting to give in to the prevailing attitude of resignation and indifference, even pessimism; our national gallery cannot become a lost cause. It is a basic point of belief, one that motivated the writing of this book. Sometimes we need to look back to find a roadmap for the future. It is my dream that this book will disrupt the prevailing narrative and apathy, alert the custodians of our heritage and cultural wealth to the problems and opportunities, and also galvanise them into action. This, combined with renewed public interest, participation and support, can contribute to the revival of the South African National Gallery, an august institution for all.

Notes

INTRODUCTION

1. T. S. Eliot, "The Hollow Men," *All Poetry*, https://allpoetry.com/The-Hollow-Men (accessed April 18, 2018). I am grateful to author Christopher Hope and to colleagues and confidants for their input.
2. Raymund van Niekerk, "Chat delivered to Friends sometime circa 1983-84?," 17. The real title of the speech, "The contribution of the S A National Gallery," is contained in the seventeen-page handwritten text in the SANG archives.
3. Government Notice, No. 668, May 23, 1932. A copy of an official guide to Cape Town, compiled by John Paris, July 27, 1951, carries the heading "The National Gallery of South Africa", but this is an exception.
4. SANG Board Minutes, March 27, 1961, 7.
5. Over time the term "art gallery" has come to include both art museums and commercial galleries, but Afrikaans still offers a distinction between "kunsmuseum" (art museum) and "kunssaal" (art gallery) for a commercial enterprise.
6. J. J. P. Op't Hof, letter and opinion to SANG board of trustees, May 10, 1962; Joachim von Moltke, letter to J. J. P. Op't Hof, June 6, 1962. It is interesting to note that the building inaugurated in 1964 to house the Pretoria City Council collection, was named the Pretoria Art Museum (Pretoriase Kunsmuseum). The design followed the International Style, thereby making a statement of renewal and modernity.

CHAPTER 1 – From colonialism to apartheid – the role of civil society and the battle for a building

1 Abraham de Smidt, "An Art Gallery for South Africa," *Cape Monthly Magazine*, April 2, 1871, 240.

2 "Public" usually meant the privileged classes, connoisseurs, artists and students, although the citizens of Urbino had access to the Ducal Palace of Federico da Montefeltro at Urbino (constructed 1470-75), with exception of the private apartments; the British Museum in London (1753) houses a vast collection of world art and artefacts and is free to all visitors. The Habsburgs' collection in Schloss Belvedere, Vienna, opened to the public in c. 1781, as did many collections in Italy. The Rijksmuseum in Amsterdam opened in 1808 and the National Gallery in London in 1824.

3 The Masters of the Orphan Chamber (the Board of Orphan Masters) was established at the Cape in c. 1673: "The Orphan Chamber originated through the necessity of making provision for the collection and administration of the property of persons who died intestate and left heirs absent from the Colony or were under age and therefore unable to take the duty upon themselves. Property of persons who died on the voyage to and from Europe and found on board was subject to its jurisdiction." *The History of the Orphan Chamber*. Ancestors South Africa, http://www.ancestors.co.za/the-history-of-the-orphan-chamber/ (accessed April 3, 2017). For the history of the Von Dessin Collection and the early history of the SANG collection, as well as a short biography of Butterworth Bayley and his role in this history, I am indebted to Robert Reginald Langham-Carter, "The Founding of the Public Collection," and "The Originator," in *South African National Gallery 1871-1971 Suid-Afrikaanse Nasionale Kunsmuseum* (Cape Town: South African National Gallery, 1971), 3-6. Known as R. R. Langham-Carter, he was a renowned genealogist and historian. For more on the fascinating life and many achievements of Von Dessin, see "Commemorating the first public library in South Africa," *The Heritage Portal. The Argus*, June 11, 2016, http://www.theheritageportal.co.za/article/commemorating-first-public-library-south-africa (accessed May 9, 2017).

4 The public could visit on Wednesday afternoons from 13:00 to 16:00 and subsequently by request. In time some of the paintings would be loaned to the South African Public Library.

5 The Von Dessin collection also included objects d'art, medals, coins, "curiosities", mathematical and astrological instruments and Chinese paintings; the whereabouts of the latter are not known. For more on the Dessinian collections, the neglect of the paintings and early attitudes to art collections, see Jillian Carman, *Uplifting the colonial philistine* (Johannesburg: Wits University Press, 2006), 14-24.

6 Quoted by Langham-Carter, "The Founding," 3.

7 Cape Town was taken and occupied by the British in 1795, briefly returned to Dutch rule in 1803, re-taken by the British in 1806; British possession was confirmed with the Anglo-Dutch Treaty of 1814.

8 Langham-Carter, "The Founding," 3. Butterworth Bayley was a member of the Legislative Council, a member of the Cape Roads board and president of the Cape Agricultural Society. Langham-Carter described him as "a most secretive individual" who "protected his private life most effectively and much conjecture must come in when posterity tries to unravel his story": Langham-Carter, "The Originator," 5.

9 Quoted in Marjorie Bull, *Abraham de Smidt 1829-1908. Artist and Surveyor-General of the Cape Colony* (Cape Town: self-published, 1981), 115. Bull was a senior technical assistant responsible for photography and various other duties related to publications and cataloguing at SANG, 1972-76.

10 The catalogue of extant works with owners, public and private, as in 1981, bear testimony to his often arduous journeys in South Africa and his trips abroad (England, Scotland, Wales, Switzerland, Italy, Austria, and Germany). Bull, *Abraham de Smidt*, 133-147. Both Bowler and Charles Bell, De Smidt's predecessor as surveyor-general, were active organisers of and participants in the SAFAA exhibitions.

11 De Smidt, "An Art Gallery," 240.

12 Giovanni Battista Salvi, called Sassoferrato (1609-85); such a painting is listed in the Ashmolean Museum collection and according to its website, Sassoferrato painted many versions of this popular subject: *Art UK*, https://artuk.org/discover/artworks/mater-dolorosa-142706 (accessed May 15, 2017). The painting was in Bayley's collection; many copies were made in Sassoferrato's studio and it is unclear whether this was an original or a copy. It was sold by Roworth in 1945: James Stratford, *Report of the Commission Appointed in Connection with the S.A. Art Gallery, Cape Town* (Pretoria: Government Printer), 12.

13 In 1945 SAFAA became the South African Association of Arts (SAAA) and in 1998 it changed to the South African National Association for the Visual Arts (SANAVA). It continues to function as a national non-governmental association for the promotion of the visual arts in South Africa.

14 Bull, *Abraham de Smidt*, 66.

15 Quoted by Bull, *Abraham de Smidt*, 69. For details of the "colonial" artists represented in the 1851-66 and 1871-79 exhibitions, see Bull, *Abraham de Smidt*, 148 & 149 respectively. She provides comprehensive information on the selection procedures employed and details of works selected for the 1871 exhibition, 19-24 & 36.

16 Bull, *Abraham De Smidt*, 72. De Smidt contributed £25 pounds to the fund.

17 Katherine Goodnow et al, *Challenge and Transformation Museums in Cape Town and Sydney* (Paris: EdUNESCO-BSI/PUB, 2006), 184.

18 Quoted in Carman, *Uplifting*, 23. There were other initiatives, for example, the Roeland Street Art School that opened in 1864; the following year it had 168 youths and adults enrolled, teachers were paid and it offered instruction in architectural drawing, freehand drawing and geometry. Ten years later R. B. Fowler Lowe, portraitist, drawing master and photographic colourist opened an Academy of Art: Bull, *Abraham de Smidt*, 47 & 79.

19 For more on De Smidt's involvement with the purchases and his relationship with SAFAA after his departure, including details of the first consignment bought, see Bull, *Abraham de Smidt*, 106-110.

20 Bull, *Abraham de Smidt*, 112. From 1902-05 Lord Carlisle and Samuel Pepys Cockerel were responsible for purchases: Bull, *Abraham de Smidt*, note 190, 153.

21 This situation did not improve with a succession of British painters and Royal Academicians who were entrusted to purchase British art prior to 1914; they included Samuel Pepys Cockerel, William Blake Richmond and, from 1910, George Clausen, who painted rural life in a naturalistic, often sentimentalised, manner.

22 Bull, *Abraham de Smidt*, 101.

23 It is not known when the collection was transferred to England: Bull, *Abraham de Smidt*, 99 & 110.

24 Matthys Bokhorst, "A Short History of the Gallery," *South African National Gallery 1971-1971 Suid-Afrikaanse Nasionale Kunsmuseum* (Cape Town: South African National Gallery, 1971), 8. In addition to primary research in SANG archives and *Annual Reports*, I accessed: Bokhorst's history of the first 100 years in this publication, 8-12; "From our own Soil" in *National South African Art Collection Nasionale Suid-Afrikaanse Kunsversameling* (Cape Town: South African National Gallery, 1971), unpaginated; Joe Dolby, "A short history of the South African National Gallery," *Lantern*, December 1981, 37-50; and Lucy Alexander, "South African National Gallery Brief History," *South African Arts Calendar*, 10, no. 4 (1986): 18-19.

25 Bokhorst, "A Short History," 8-9. The Act made provision for the management of the gallery and in a letter dated October 23, 1895 the prime minister undertook, on behalf of the government, to pay the association "Interest at the rate of 3 percent. per annum upon the balance of £6,000, the appraisal value of the New Street premises ... the payment to continue until the capital in the hands of the Government is expended in the construction of a permanent Gallery": *Reports of the Trustees of the South African Art Gallery and the South African Fine Arts Association for the Year ending the 31st December, 1912, 3*. The *Reports* of the trustees of the South African Art Gallery and SAFAA were combined and some individuals served on both structures, for example, at this time Sir Thomas Muir (superintendent-general of Education, Cape Province) was the chairperson of the South African Art Gallery and president of SAFAA, while John Fairbairn was secretary to both. The *Reports*, hereafter referred to as such, were published annually.

26 It was not unusual for art museums in the colonies to house and display plaster casts; De Smidt had been in favour of such casts, as these were seen to be part of the educational project. For more on the Alfred Beit bequest of plaster casts of Greek and Roman statuary, see Anna Tietze, "Antique Casts for a Colonial Gallery: the Beit Bequest of Classical Statuary to Cape Town," in *South Africa, Greece and Rome: Classical Confrontations*, ed. Grant Parker (Cambridge: Cambridge University Press, 2015); and Anna Tietze, *A History of the Iziko South African National Gallery* (Cape Town, UCT Press, an imprint of Juta and Company (Pty) Ltd, 2017), 42-46.

27 Stratford, *Report of the Commission,* 15.

28 The archives of the South African National Gallery are woefully incomplete; after 2001 the human resources department of the new museum structure removed the archives, carefully kept and managed by SANG staff in the Annexe, and dumped everything in spaces that the PWD had made available in Customs House. Patricia Davison, then director of core functions, alerted me to the situation and a salvage operation was launched. By that time filing cabinets had suffered water damage and some minute books and annual reports were missing. The earliest *Reports* referred to here, were those of 1905-1907; there is a gap between 1907 and 1912.

29 *Reports,* December, 1912, 2-6.

30 Bokhorst, "A Short History," 9.

31 SANG *Annual Reports*, 1970-1971 & 1971-1972 (published together), 6.

32 Iziko Museums *Annual Report*, 2017-2018, 153.

33 For more on the Randlords and the Michaelis Collection, see Michael Stevenson, *Art & Aspirations The Randlords of South Africa and their Collections* (Vlaeberg: Fernwood Press, 2002), 93-113. I am indebted to Stevenson for the research and insights he provides into the Randlords' attitudes to art deemed appropriate for South Africa, and the issues he raises regarding attribution, connoisseurship and the relationship between the Randlords and dealers. Randlords were the entrepreneurs who controlled the diamond (Kimberley in the Northern Cape) and gold mining (Transvaal, known at the "Rand", now Gauteng Province) industries in South Africa from the 1870s up to World War I. For in-depth information on the history of Dutch and Flemish paintings in this country, see Jillian Carman, *Seventeenth-century Dutch and Flemish paintings in South Africa* (Johannesburg: Johannesburg Art Gallery, 1994).

34 Dorothea Sarah Florence Alexandra was married to Sir Lionel Phillips, 1st Baronet, mining magnate and politician. He made his fortune on the diamond fields of Kimberley and the gold mines of the Witwatersrand. Known as Lady Florence Phillips she was a patron of the arts and instigator of major art, museum and architectural projects. She was central to the founding of JAG and getting Sir Edwin Landseer Lutyens appointed as architect; she was instrumental in the gift Max Michaelis bestowed on South Africa, having the OTH restored, as well as Martin Melck House and Koopmans de Wet House. In 1917 Lionel Phillips purchased Vergelegen for her and she restored and transformed the estate.

35 Thomas Bodkin, *Hugh Lane and his Pictures* (Dublin: Browne and Nolan, 1952), 29.

36 Some sixty years later, in 1998, the democratically elected second president of South Africa, Thabo Mbeki (1999-2008), spoke of two nations in the country, black and white, during a debate in the National Assembly on racism and nation building. He described the white "nation" as "relatively prosperous" while the black "nation" was "black and poor". This would counter Nelson Mandela's vision of a non-racial country and reinforce racism, as Mbeki continued to quote himself – as recently as March 2016: "Mbeki quotes himself on two South Africas: black and white," *News 24*, March 15, 2016, https://www.news24.com/Video/SouthAfrica/News/mbeki-quotes-himself-on-two-south-africas-black-and-white-20160315 (accessed February 19, 2018).

37 The term "black" in this book is based on current official usage: it refers to Africans, Cape Muslims, Coloured and Indian persons who were denied basic rights of citizenship before 1993.

38 "The Union of South Africa 1910," *South African History Online*. November 8, 2011, http://www.sahistory.org.za/topic/union-south-africa-1910; and "Coloureds are removed from the voters roll," *South African History Online*, March 16, 2011, http://www.sahistory.org.za/dated-event/coloureds-are-removed-voters-roll (accessed August 12, 2016).

39 Stevenson, *Art & Aspirations,* 102 and note 34, 184, cites the Afrikaans press as questioning the sincerity of the appeal to the descendants of the Dutch settlers, because the catalogue and labels were in English and the curator, Mrs P. M. Thomas, was English speaking. It is worth noting that many Afrikaans speakers did not descend from the Dutch settlers nor did they necessarily identify with the language and culture. For more on the history of the Afrikaans language see S. J. du Toit, "Patriot woordeboek: Engels-Afrikaans, 1902," *Digitale bibliotheek voor de nederlandse letteren (dbnl)*, https://www.dbnl.org/tekst/toit001patr01_01/toit001patr01_01_0002.php (accessed November 12, 2018); and W. Gericke, "Vroeë woordelyste en woordeboeke in verband met Afrikaans," *Lexikos Journals*, www.lexikos.journals.ac.za/pub/article/download/1151/667 (accessed November 2, 2018).

40 *Reports,* December, 1912, 1-2.

41 Ibid., 5.

42 SASA was founded in May 1897, but activities ceased during the South African War, to be resumed in 1902. It caters specifically to practising artists, and is the oldest surviving organisation of its kind in South Africa. *South African Society of Artists*, http://sasa-artists.co.za/ (accessed December 6, 2016).

43 *Reports*, December 1912, 6. The presence of the Mountain Club reveals much about Cape Town at the time: the important role of SASA and other societies, and the fact that there was an awareness of and interest in the future of the art collection beyond the confines of the art world.

44 *Reports*, December 1913, 6.

45 The name of the architect is not known. For futher information see Hans Fransen, comp., *Michaelis Collection. The Old Town House, Cape Town. Catalogue of the Collection of Paintings and Drawings* (Zwolle: Waanders Uitgevers, 1997).

46 *Reports*, December 1913, 6.

47 The trustees replied that they were not in a position to offer advice and suggested that expert opinion be sought in Europe. Acknowledging the problems attendant upon the painting, valued at £30,000, Hugh Lane took it back and substituted it with eighteen Dutch pictures.

48 They were Sir Thomas Muir, superintendent-general of education (chairperson); John Fairbairn, son of the newspaper proprietor, educator and financier (secretary); Sydney Cowper, mayor of Wynberg; Justice Searle; Sir Frederick Smith, deputy mayor of Cape Town; and Wilhelm Westhofen, civil engineer, amateur artist and illustrator of three books on the Cape Peninsula. Westhofen exhibited his work and was involved in SAFAA from 1914 until his death in 1925. "Westhoven, *Mr* Wilhelm (civil engineering)," *S2A3 Biographical Database of Southern African Science*, http://www.s2a3.org.za/bio/Biograph_final.php?serial=3108 (accessed November 12, 2016).

49 *Reports*, December 1913, 7.

50 Stevenson, "Art & Aspirations," 99.

51 Fransen, *Michaelis*, 20.

52 Lord Harlech, *Cape Town's Art Galleries* (Cape Town: Galvin & Sales, 1942), 7. His overview of SANG and the Michaelis Collection was reprinted from the *Cape Argus*, February 9 and 11, 1942. Interestingly, Harlech ended his review (10) of the MC with an analysis of the *Zaamenkanst slab*, a fragment of San painting from East Griqualand. He concluded: "The whole scene as well as the forms appear more vivid and real than life. Untutored, unsophisticated, he has grasped the actuality of the animals which played such a part in his people's struggle for existence; just as did the Palaeolithic artists of 20,000 years ago in the caves of Northern Spain and the Dordogne. Here is an "old" master indeed."

53 *Reports*, December 1916, 3.

54 For all the conditions attached to the presentation, see *Reports*, December 1913, 5.

55 Stevenson, *Art & Aspirations*, 99.

56 After Prowse's tenure, a succession of men was appointed: Matthys Bokhorst (1956-64), Willem Gravett (1964-75), Cecil J Haak (1975-89) and Hans Fransen (from 1990 until the Michaelis Collection became part of Iziko Museums' art collections department): Fransen, *Michaelis*, 24.

57 Both were founder members of the New Group (1937-53), which was initiated by professional artists. Membership was by nomination and the aims were, among others, to bring artists and craftspeople together to raise the standard of art in South Africa, to assist artists financially and to improve the circumstances of their profession. For more on the New Group see: Esmé Berman, *Art and Artists of South Africa* (classic edition, Cape Town: G3 Publishers, 2010), 307-309.

58 See for example, W. H. K., ed., *The Arts in South Africa* (Durban: Knox, 1933-1934) and Arie Cornelis Bouman, *Kuns in Suid-Afrika* (Cape Town: HAUM, 1935). JAG has had a succession of women in charge, starting with Nel Erasmus in 1964 and including Pat Senior, Rachelle Keene and more recently Antoinette Murdoch.

59 Resolution passed on July 14, 1913. *Reports*, December 1913, 3.

60 See SANG Board Minutes: September 24, October 5 & 22, November 25, 1953. Other members of the board were F. E. J. Malherbe (chairperson), R. W. Wilcocks and A. J. van der Merwe, F. D. Lycett Green, A. H. Honikman, G. A. Leyds (SAAA alternate for H. G. Buisman), Prof. Rupert Shephard (alternate for T. B. Davie, principal and vice-chancellor of UCT). Lycett Green, Prowse and Buisman comprised the sub-committee and compiled the minority report. They regarded the Michaelis Gallery as another national gallery.

61 Indictment of John Paris submitted to the board by Ruth Prowse, September 1955.

62 SANG Board Minutes, July 18, 1962, 67.

63 This process, as well as current attitudes to the collection, is discussed in subsequent chapters.

64 *Reports*, December 1914, 1-2.

65 *Reports*, December 1916, 1.

66 *Reports*, December 1917, 1.

67 *Reports*, December 1918, 1. Interestingly, visitor's figures reported for the year were still high: 79,681.

68 Staten was chairperson of the South African War Graves Commission, he conceived the idea of the Delville Wood Memorial, and made £15 000 available: Bokhorst, "A Short History," 9.

69 See *Herbert Vladimir Meyerowitz (1900-1945) The Hyman Liberman Memorial Door* (Cape Town: South African National Gallery, 1970) and Hayden Proud, "Arrival in a land of milk and honey: Herbert Meyerowitz and the memorial to Hyman Liberman, Mayor of Cape Town," in *Made in Wood Work from the Western Cape* (Cape Town: South African National Gallery, 1992), 17-33, catalogue of the exhibition. In his will, Liberman had envisaged a public archway at the junction of Adderley Street and Government Avenue; discussions between the trustees and J. S. Cleland led to the creative solution of the carved door leading into a gallery named after Liberman.

70 SANG Board Minutes, January 27, 1950, 4.

71 Alan Crump and Raymund van Niekerk (text), and Geoffrey Grundlingh (photographs), *Public Sculpture & Reliefs – Cape Town* (Cape Town: Clifton Publications, 1988), 50.

72 Kendall was also a foundation member and president of SASA and the Cape Institute of Architects: W. H. K., *The Arts,*164.

73 "Union's new Art Gallery," *Cape Argus*, December 23, 1926; see also "Cape Town's New Art Gallery," *Cape Argus*, December 22, 1926.

74 "South African Art Gallery," *The South African Builder*, February 1933, 11 & 13. For details of construction, materials and lighting I am indebted to this article. The builders and general contractors for the Delville Wood Memorial were Bakker Bros.

75 Bokhorst, "A Short History," 9.

76 Their avant-garde manifesto, *zerohour*, was issued on April 1, 1933 and produced as a memento of the 1985 Institute of South African Architects Congress (Johannesburg: Wits University, 1985). Hanson and Martienssen visited Europe in 1930, Martienssen made personal contact with Le Corbusier and they became friends.

77 Baker was active in South Africa from 1892-1913.

78 The diverse and rich plurality of modernity in South Africa in the 1930s was manifested in the segmentation of the architectural profession into different camps: Beaux-Arts classicism and revivalism (the "traditionalists" as Rex Martienssen called them), the International Style, Art Deco, regionalism and elements of expressionism. The "battle of the styles" was fought in the journals such as *The South African Architectural Record*.

79 Crump and Van Niekerk, *Sculpture*, 50.

80 Ibid.

81 According to the article, "South African Art Gallery," the work was carried out by the Michaelis School.

82 *Catalogue of Exhibition, South African National Gallery, Opening of the New Gallery* (Cape Town: Bon Accord Press, 1930). It is worth recording the names of the board members who were responsible for this fiasco: J. Wheatley (chairperson), H. A. Fagan, F. K. Kendall, Sir Thos. Muir, Lady Phillips; P. Thatcher was the secretary.

83 South African Society of Artists, *A Protest on Behalf of the Artists of South Africa against the slighting, and Belittling Attitude of the authorities on the Occasion of the Inauguration of the South African (National) Gallery on the Third of November, 1930* (Cape Town: South African Society of Artists, 1930). Apart from the selling of artworks and the display of the Fuller collection, a main complaint was that – responding to the SASA's visit to the gallery in October and their dissatisfaction with the paucity of South African representation, particularly in the Liberman room – Thatcher extended an invitation to artists on October 21, 1930 to submit works, deadline the 24th. This confirms a strategy to marginalise South African art. SASA bemoaned the omission of artists such as Strat Caldecott, Sydney Carter, Bertha Everard, Dorothy Kay, Erich Mayer, William Timlin, J. E. A. Volschenk and Florence Zerffi, among others.

84 SASA, *A Protest*, 15.

85 Many of the photo-copied newspaper clippings in the SANG Library are undated and do not give the name of the paper; this reference, dated 4 November 1930, comes from "A collection of newscuttings on the subject of art from 1904-1983 from English language newspapers published in the Cape", compiled by SANG librarian, J. Minicki and colleagues, part 1, 1928-1935, 13.

86 Minicki, "A collection," 14.

87 Ibid.

88 Ibid.

89 Originally called De Zuid-Afrikaanse Akademie voor Taal, Letteren en Kunst (South African Academy for Language, Literature and Art), the organisation was founded in 1909, with the aim of safeguarding and developing the Dutch (including Afrikaans) language, literature, art, history and study of antiquity. Today the Suid-Afrikaanse Akademie vir Wetenskap en Kuns (South African Academy for Science and Art) is a multidisciplinary organisation, encompassing a wide range of scientific and artistic fields. *Suid-Afrikaanse Akademie vir Wetenskap en Kuns,* http://esat.sun.ac.za/index.php/Suid-Afrikaanse_Akademie_vir_Wetenskap_en_Kuns (accessed November 5, 2016).

90 SANG *Annual Report*, 1945-1946, 4.

91 SANG *Annual Report*, 1946-1947, 4.
92 SANG *Annual Report*, 1934-1935, unpaginated.
93 SANG *Annual Report*, 1938-1939, 2.
94 Bokhorst, "A Short History," 10.
95 SANG *Annual Report*, 1945-1946, 3.
96 Edward Roworth, "The South African Art Gallery" (Cape Town: *Cape Times Annual*, 1910), 8-10.
97 "Work of Michaelis School praised," *Cape Times*, 25 September 1940.
98 Lippy Lipshitz, "A considered reply to Prof. Roworth," *Trek*, November 7, 1940; cited in Tietze, *A History*, 84, note 51.
99 Bernard Lewis, "Exhibitionism in the Avenue What Would Hitler Do?," *The Cape*, December 22, 1933, 13.
100 Sibbett was an enormously powerful individual: He was provincial Grand Master of the Irish Constitution of Freemasons and presented them with a portrait of himself to celebrate the 50th anniversary of his arrival in South Africa: *Cape Times*, September 29, 1948. Early in the century (1901-02) he was assistant policy secretary to Cecil John Rhodes – a devotee who is described as a "Rhodes Remembrancer" and avid collector of "Rhodes-ian"; he donated the bulk of his collection to UCT in 1932. *Google Books*, https://books.google.co.za/books?id=VbD_mokWhL8C&pg=PT138&lpg=PT138&dq=c+j+sibbett+biography &source=bl&ots=w6fTAaJeUh&sig=fDYcgalWaxw7V8BVAA2-PDCghpE&hl=en&sa=X&redir_esc=y#v=onepage&q=c%20j%20 sibbett%20biography&f=false (accessed December 9, 2016).
101 Bokhorst, "From our own," unpaginated.
102 I found Sekoto's name handwritten under General on the agenda of the meeting, but could not locate the minutes. I am grateful to Joe Dolby, who has done much research on Sekoto, for providing me with a copy of Lewis' letter to Roworth (the date is given as Tuesday night), as well as the first page of the minutes confirming the date and the list of four works that were not purchased.
103 The amount comprised £150,00 realised from the sale of pictures in Johannesburg (discussed later in this chapter) and £250,00 transferred from gallery funds: SANG Board Minutes, December 15, 1944, 1.
104 SANG *Annual Report*, 1934-1935, unpaginated.
105 SANG *Annual Report*, 1938-1939, 3.
106 SANG *Annual Report*, 1944-1945, 3.
107 SANG *Annual Report*, 1941-1942, 2. It took the City of Cape Town another four years before the grant was increased to £1,000.
108 For further reading on some of these bequests, see Anna Tietze, *The Alfred de Pass Presentation to the South African National Gallery* (Cape Town: South African National Gallery, 1995); Anna Tietze, *The Sir Abe Bailey Bequest: A Reappraisal* (Cape Town: Iziko Museums, 2001); Anna Tietze, *The Abe Bailey Collection in the South African National Gallery* (Cape Town: Abe Bailey Trust, 2008); Anna Tietze, "The Problem of Originality and Value in the Lady Michaelis Gifts to the South African National Gallery," *South African Journal of Art History* 25, no. 2 (2010): 161-176; Anna Tietze, "Artistically or historically important? The reception of the Abe Bailey sporting art collection in South Africa," *Journal of the History of Collections* 23, no. 1 (2010): 165-177; Hayden Proud and Anna Tietze, *The Sir Edmund and Lady Davis Presentation: A Gift of British Art to South Africa* (Cape Town: South African National Gallery, 1999).
109 According to Hayden Proud, this benefaction ceased after South Africa left the Commonwealth in 1961: Hayden Proud, "Our National Gallery: The 'Book' of our Art?," *Journal of the Helen Suzman Foundation*, 2011: 40. Helen Suzman Foundation, http://hsf.org.za/resource-centre/focus/focus-61/Hayden%20Proud_Our%20National%20Gallery.pdf (accessed August 16, 2015). Now known as the Art Fund, the NACF has helped museums and galleries buy great works of art since 1903 and continues to do so in the United Kingdom. Henry van den Bergh's bequest entered the SANG permanent collection through the NACF.
110 Thanks to the interest of Paul Mellon, American philanthropist and owner/breeder of thoroughbred racehorses, in sporting art, The Virginia Museum of Fine Arts is renowned for its fine collection of this genre. See Malcolm Cormack, *Country Pursuits British, American, and French Sporting Art from the Mellon Collections in the Virginia Museum of Fine Arts* (Richmond: University of Virginia Press, 2007).
111 See Tietze, *The Alfred de Pass*; and Tietze, *A History*, 56-60.
112 SANG *Annual Report*, 1940-1941, 4.
113 SANG *Annual Report*, 1942-1943, 3.
114 Jillian Carman, "Art Museums and National Identity," in *Visual Century South African Art in Context*, ed. Jillian Carman, vol. 1 1907-1948 (Johannesburg: Wits University Press, 2011), 21.
115 Bokhorst, "A Short History," 10.
116 Carman, "Art Museums," 21.
117 SANG Board Minutes, June 23, 1944.
118 SANG *Annual Report*, 1947-1948, 4. The sale of pictures was reported in detail, 4-6. At this time Sibbett was in the chair (until February 1960); S. Barlow succeeded C. T. te Water as vice-chairperson in May 1948; other members were: artists Gregoire

Boonzaier and Ruth Prowse; T. B. Davie, A. W. Falconer, W. C. Foster, Lycett Green (from February 1949), Bernard Lewis, C. T. de M. Villet, and R. W. Wilcocks.

119 Bernard Lewis, "The Libermann [sic] Room," *The Cape*, April 10, 1931, 12. Fortunately this painting was spotted by Neville Dubow and purchased by the SANG in the 1990s.

120 SANG *Annual Report*, 1946-1947, 6.

121 SANG *Annual Report*, 1946-1947, 4-5. 1947 was the year of the Royal Visit and Roworth provided two sculptures to decorate Government House: *Head of a Native Girl* by Moses Kottler and *Head of a Hottentot* by I. Mitford Barberton.

122 "Smuts Opens the Bailey Collection," *Cape Times*, March 6, 1947.

123 "Art in S.A.," *Cape Times*, March 6, 1947. There was criticism in the press about the large number of hunting and racing pictures that necessitated the removal into storage of South African and international artists: "Bailey bequest on show," *Cape Times*, March 5, 1947; "Too many long faces in art galleries," *Cape Argus*, June 19, 1947.

124 Hayden Proud, email to the author, April 21, 2017: the work by Lucien Pissarro is entitled *Umbrella Trees* (English translation); inscribed on the rear as 'les pins parasols le brusq(var)'. It is signed bottom right with a monogram, and dated 1925. Purchased from Mme L. Pissarro in 1946 for £150. I am grateful to Proud for this information.

125 SANG *Annual Report*, 1947-1948, 4-6. *The Ever Open Door* had been presented by the McDonalds in memory of their son who died in WWI; the SAAA, which succeeded SAFAA in 1945, served notice on the board on April 23, 1947, stating that the paintings presented to the gallery by its predecessor were inalienable and that if they were not recovered immediately, SANG would be taken to court.

126 SANG *Annual Report*, 1947-1948, 5.

127 MP for Pietersburg Naudé, in Parliament of South Africa, *Hansard*, April 29, 1947, col. 3504 (Cape Town: Government Printer, 1947). The names or initials of all the participants are not given in the *Hansard*. In all probability this was Tom Naudé who was later appointed as Minister of Post and Telecommunications, also Health and Finance during the 1950s and early 1960s; he was also acting State President in 1967-68.

128 MP for Jeppestown, Bertha Solomon, in Parliament of South Africa, *Hansard*, April 29, 1947, col. 3504-3506.

129 Jillian Carman, email to the author, May 25, 2017: "Parts of it were withdrawn during this period and finally in 1961 by Reinhold [Cassirer] under instruction from the family. This seems to have caused much bitterness; Hendriks was negotiating to buy one of the Cézannes, council baulking at the price, when the family demanded its immediate return. [Cassirer] said Hendriks never spoke to him again." The collection was exhibited in 1946: Tracy Murinik, ed. *CONSTRUCTURE: 100 years of the JAG building and its evolution of space and meaning* (Johannesburg: David Krut, 2015), 50. I am grateful to Sean O'Toole's question that led me to investigate further, as the incorrect information has become part of the literature on SANG; see for example Tietze, *A History*, 84.

130 MP Humpreys, in Parliament of South Africa, *Hansard*, April 29, 1947, col. 3509.

131 MP for Christiana, W. D. Brink, in Parliament of South Africa, *Hansard*, April 29, 1947, col. 3507-3508.

132 MP Humpreys, in Parliament of South Africa, *Hansard*, April 29, 1947, col. 3510-3511.

133 James Stratford, *Report of the Commission Appointed in Connection with the S. A. Art Gallery,* Cape Town (Pretoria: Government Printer, 1947).

134 SANG *Annual Report*, 1947-1948, 8-9. The additional office and cloakrooms were added as per Kendall's 1938 plan, as well as sliding rails for storing paintings in the basement: SANG Board Minutes, July 30, 1948, 3.

135 SANG Board Minutes, June 25, 1958, 1.

136 SANG *Annual Report*, 1947-1948, 9.

137 SANG Board Minutes, June 25, 1948, 1.

138 SANG Board Minutes, June 25, 1948, 2. Critic Bernard Lewis was already a board member.

139 SANG Board Minutes, August 12, 1948, 4.

140 SANG *Annual Report*, 1948-1949, 3.

141 SANG Board Minutes, August 12, 1948, 1-3.

142 SANG Board Minutes, September 23, 1948, 1-2. Hendriks' position at JAG was upgraded from curator to director in 1946 at his request: Jillian Carman, "Acquisition policy of the Johannesburg Art Gallery with regard to the South African collection, 1909-1987," *South African Journal of Cultural and Art History* 2, no. 3 (1988): 211, note 40.

143 Bertha Solomon, in Parliament of South Africa, *Hansard*, April 29, 1947, col. 3505.

144 Harlech, *Cape Town's Art Galleries*, 1.

145 Ibid., 6.

CHAPTER 2 – Professional directors appointed – John Paris (1949 – 1962), Matthys Bokhorst (1962 – 1973) and Carel du Ry van Bee

1 John Paris, "Proud City Possession Needs Aid S A Gallery's Great Work Over 13 Years," *Cape Times*, January 12, 1962.

2 John Paris (MA, BLitt) was born at Hove in Sussex in 1912. He graduated from Brighton College and spent time at the Brighton School of Art before graduating from Oxford University, where he worked for a while as assistant librarian at the Oxford University Examination Schools English Library. Prior to his appointment as deputy director at the Walker Art Gallery he lectured in art history at the National Gallery in London under Sir Kenneth Clark, and worked as John Rothenstein's exhibitions and research attaché at the Tate Gallery. Paris' field of expertise was English studies and eighteenth-century English watercolours. He served throughout WWII, first as a camouflage staff officer to the Scottish Command, then – with the rank of major – as head of the Army Formation College at Dalkeith, where he eased artists out of the services and back into civilian life. Paris was a painter and writer, and he played the violin. He had South African connections in that his father was Controller of Telegraphs in Natal for nineteen years. See Eric Allen, "Profile – John Paris," *Cape Argus*, November 3, 1950.

3 Allen, "Profile".

4 Organising travelling exhibitions throughout the Union was a priority for Paris. He envisaged that paintings, prints and drawings would be transported in a prefabricated "traveling art gallery" equipped with screens, fluorescent lighting and fitted into a big rail container. Concerned about the handling of works from the permanent collection, a pamphlet was prepared on the care of the works, which would accompany the exhibition. Paris identified three main groups: large, valuable works to travel to the major art museums in Johannesburg and Durban; a smaller version for small towns that had satisfactory facilities; a small group for church and town halls in the countryside. Major exhibitions would be exchanged with sister institutions and the exhibitions would first be shown at SANG. See "Art Exhibitions to Tour Union," *Cape Times*, December 9, 1950.

5 To begin with, De Pass was not happy, but the board changed its policy to the effect that it had the right to use gifts and bequests in any way it saw fit. In order to pacify the donor, a room in the Gallery was named after him. SANG Board Minutes, July 29, 1949, 2.

6 SANG Board Minutes, September 29, 1950, 4; SANG Board Minutes, January 26, 1951. Lady Bailey's suggestion that some of the pictures not exhibited be lent to members of the family was rejected and the board unanimously resolved not to lend works from the permanent collection to private individuals. SANG Board Minutes, January 27, 1950, 2-4.

7 The last part of the quotation is from a detailed policy for acquisitions that Paris submitted to the board on September 29, 1950. In this document he also recommended that a sub-committee be created to make recommendations on acquisitions.

8 *Cape Times*, November 5, 1953. For the effect of this policy on Irma Stern's work in SANG's collection, see Hayden Proud, "Irma Stern and the South African National Gallery," in *Brushing up on Stern, featuring work from the Permanent Collection of the Iziko South African National Gallery*, ed. Carol Kaufmann and Andrea Lewis (Cape Town: Iziko South African National Gallery, 2015), 53-54.

9 SANG Board Minutes, January 27, 1950, 1-2.

10 SANG Board Minutes, September 29, 1950, 2.

11 Allen, "Profile".

12 Paris quoted in a short report on his first public function after his appointment, when he opened an exhibition of paintings by Phay Hutton and Leng Dixon at the SAAA Gallery: *Cape Argus*, February 9, 1949.

13 SANG Board Minutes, March 23, 1949, 4-5.

14 Joachim Wolfgang von Moltke, DPhil, Frankfurt, was educated in Berlin, Munich and Frankfurt. He was the son of Countess Freya von Moltke, only daughter of Sir James and Lady Rose-Innes and Count Helmuth von Moltke (*Cape Times*, March 20, 1962). He arrived in South Africa in the late 1940s and taught art history at Michaelis.

15 Bokhorst, "A Short History," 10.

16 Eric Newton, "Prematurity," *Sunday Times* (London), quoted in the *Cape Times*, September 29, 1948; Also see: Letter from P. H. W. (*Cape Times* art critic), "S. A. art exhibition," *Cape Times*, October 8, 1948; letter from critic Bernard Lewis, *Cape Times*, October 6, 1948; letters from H. von Michaelis, *Cape Times*, October 7, 1948 and October 11, 1948; letter from F. D. Lycett Green, *Cape Times*, October 15, 1948.

17 SANG Board Minutes, February 24, 1950, 3.

18 SANG *Annual Report*, 1949-1950, 7; SANG Board Minutes, March 24, 1950, 3.

19 Contrary to the board's tacit support of the government, the SAAA – threatened with the withdrawal of a grant of £1,000 from the Department of Education – refused to comply when instructed to implement apartheid policies in its branches and affiliated bodies. But they escaped punishment by arguing that the branches were independent (some of them were already for whites only), and that the spaces in which the SAAA operated were governed by local regulations and restrictions. Funding for the running of the head-office in Pretoria was secured. See "Arts Society replies on Apartheid," *Cape Argus*, November 23,

1951; "Arts Body's Reply on State Grant," *Cape Times*, November 24, 1951; "Strict Art 'Apartheid' Ruled," *Cape Times*, August 26, 1952.

20 A "Day of the Volunteers" on Sunday June 22, preceded the opening of the campaign on the 26th. Volunteers, including Nelson Mandela, Yusuf Dadoo, J. B. Marks and Walter Sisulu, signed the following pledge: I, the undersigned, Volunteer of the National Volunteer Corps, do hereby solemnly pledge and bind myself to serve my country and my people in accordance with the directives of the National Volunteer Corps and to participate fully and without reservations to the best of my ability in the Campaign for the Defiance of Unjust Laws. I shall obey the orders of my leader under whom I shall be placed and strictly abide by the rules and regulations of the National Volunteer Corps framed from time to time. It shall be my duty to keep myself physically, mentally and morally fit. "Defiance Campaign 1952," *South African History Online*, March 21, 2011, http://www.sahistory.org.za/topic/defiance-campaign-1952 (accessed December 25, 1916).

21 John Paris, *Exhibition of XVII Century Dutch Painting* (Cape Town: South African National Gallery in association with the Van Riebeeck Festival, 1952). For insight into the realities of the Festival, see Ciraj Rassool and Leslie Witz, "The 1952 Jan Van Riebeeck Tercentenary Festival: Constructing and Contesting Public National History in South Africa," *The Journal of African History* 34, no. 3 (1993): 447-468.

22 Brian Lello, "Old Dutch Masters on View in Cape Town," *Cape Times Weekend Magazine*, February 23, 1952 and Deane Anderson, "Perfectly balanced exhibition of 'British school' art," *Cape Argus*, March 28, 1952.

23 SANG *Annual Report*, 1951-1952, unpaginated. See also Figs. 1-4 in this *Annual Report*.

24 SANG *Annual Report*, 1955-1956, 4; SANG *Annual Report*, 1957-1958, 5.

25 Alderman Alfred Harold Honikman, City Council representative and Mayor (1961-1963), was a great force for good on the board, both as a member and longstanding chairperson. He wrote a book, *Cape Town: City of Good Hope* (Cape Town: Howard Timmins, 1966).

26 SANG Report to the Minister of Education, incorporated in the Minute Books, 1959-1960, 4. Unfortunately the domical glass skylight above the Liberman Memorial Door was lost in the process; see: *Made in Wood Work from the Western Cape* (Cape Town: South African National Gallery, 1992), 16.

27 Bokhorst, "A Short History," 11.

28 Berman, *Art and Artists*, 474-475.

29 ""Huns and Vandals" of Art," *Cape Times*, April 13, 1950.

30 SANG *Annual Report*, 1951-1952, 5-6.

31 SANG Board Minutes, October 12, 1953, 2.

32 See "South African Native Artist in Paris," *Cape Argus*, December 10, 1948.For further reading on the black pioneers of modernism in South Africa and their quest for education and acceptance as artists, see Elizabeth Rankin, "Recoding the canon: Towards greater representivity in South African art galleries," *Social Dynamics* 21, no. 2 (1995): 56-90; Elizabeth Rankin, "Lonely Road Formative episodes in the development of black artists in early twentieth-century South Africa," in Carman, *Visual Century*, 92-113; and Lize van Robbroeck, ""That Magnificent Generation" Tradition and modernity in the lives, art and politics of the first modern black painters," in Carman, *Visual Century*, 114-133.

33 Bokhorst, "A Short History," 10.

34 Letter from John Paris to board chairperson, May 23, 1955.

35 Letter from John Paris to Lycett Green, March 7, 1952. The categories were as follows: A – to be hung permanently; B – to be hung at discretion occasionally and always to be held available; C – consisting of pictures Paris considered "frankly misleading, so altered as to have lost any aesthetic merit they once may have had": Paris, "Lycett Green Gift", May 24, 1955.

36 SANG Board Minutes, February 4, 1954, 2.

37 SANG Board Minutes, October 8, 1953, 2-4.

38 Ibid.

39 SANG Board Minutes, November 22, 1953, 1-7. Complaints were submitted by Lycett Green, Prowse and Buisman. Sibbett withdrew the charges against Paris.

40 SANG Board Minutes, February 4, 1953, 3-4.

41 See letters from Bokhorst, then president of the SAAA, in the *Cape Times*, June 13, 1953 and *Die Burger*, June 13, 1953, as well as one from Prowse and Buisman, her fellow representative of the SAAA, *Cape Times*, June 15, 1953.

42 John Paris' statement in his defense attached to SANG Board Minutes, November 22, 1953.

43 In addition to the three who wrote, Sibbett was the fourth trustee against Paris, but there were no complaints from other trustees.

44 SANG Board Minutes, October 28, 1954, 7.

45 John Paris, Memorandum to the Chairperson of the Board of Trustees, "Lycett Green Gift to York – U.K. Press in relation to the Director's advice to the Board," May 24, 1955.

46 Correspondence between Malherbe and Prowse, dated April 24, July 1, August 8 and August 10, 1955.

47 Ruth Prowse, "Undated document," described in the board minutes and correspondence as and "indictment", c. August 1955, copy placed on file on September 24. Paris received the document on September 24, 1955.

48 SANG Board Minutes, January 4, 1954, 2. Honikman's letter is dated December 28, 1955.

49 The board comprised the following members: F. E. J. Malherbe (chairperson, US academic and eminent literary critic); Rupert Shephard replaced T. B. Davie, who had passed away at the end of 1955; F. D. Lycett Green, A. H. Honikman, G. A. Leyds, Ruth Prowse, R. W. Wilcocks (US rector), A. J. van der Merwe. At the meeting of 4 January 1956 G. A. Leyds attended as SAAA alternate to H. G. Buisman.

50 Legal opinion submitted by Jan S. de Villiers & Son, February 16, 1954. This document and a response from the Deputy State Attorney were attached to SANG Board Minutes, February 21, 1956. In addition to correspondence and minutes mentioned, archival material with regard to Paris' bilingualism ranged from findings by the State Attorney to a testimonial from Sarah Goldblatt, dated October 29, 1953, in which she confirmed that he was continuing his studies, making satisfactory progress, and "learning faithfully and well": he could read and understand *Die Burger*, write a good short composition and read books. Subsequently Lycett Green raised the matter again, proposing that Paris pass an examination, but no-one seconded as the board as a whole was satisfied that the director was serious about learning Afrikaans: SANG Board Minutes and minutes of the AGM, July 17, 1956.

51 SANG Board Minutes, February 21, 1956, 50.

52 Ibid., 50-51.

53 The insurance cover for the collection was £100,000, but the State Auditor required written confirmation, not a verbal agreement, that the insurance company would refund any loss or damage of a single work according to the director's valuation: SANG Board Minutes, September 18, 1956, 136.

54 SANG Board Minutes, June 2, 1960, 27.

55 SANG *Annual Report*, 1961-1962, 5.

56 Ibid., 7.

57 SANG *Annual Report*, 1962-1963, 5-7.

58 See SANG Board Minutes, September 20, 1961, 108 for Paris' activities and for the attached memorandum on a department of conservation; SANG Board Minutes, November 27, 1961, 107.

59 SANG Board Minutes, November 27, 1961, 110. Present were A. H. Honikman (chairperson), J. P. Duminy (vice-chairperson), H. Buisman, M. de Villiers, G. A. Leyds, Magda Sauer; apologies recorded: S. Corder, W. E. G. Louw, H. B. Thom, D. J. Trümpelman.

60 It was neither attached to the minutes, nor found in the archives.

61 SANG Board Minutes, January 29, 1962, 133-134.

62 SANG Minutes of a Special Board Meeting, February 21, 1962, 136-138. Paris' services were finally terminated on 31 May 1962, he was paid his salary and a lump sum for balance of leave, and he vacated the house on June 15: SANG Board Minutes, March 26, 1962, 143.

63 "The Anti-Pass Campaigns 1960," *South African History Online*, November 25, 2013, http://www.sahistory.org.za/article/anti-pass-campaigns-1960 (accessed June 16, 2017).

64 "Becoming a Republic and withdrawal from the Commonwealth 1961," *South African History Online*, March 30, 2011, http://www.sahistory.org.za/topic/becoming-republic-and-withdrawal-commonwealth-1961 (accessed December 26, 2016).

65 Interview with Leon Rubens on October 13, 2017.

66 Bokhorst, "Old Drawings."

67 "Von Moltke to take up position in Germany," *Cape Argus*, March 21, 1962. He remained at Bielefeld until 1972.

68 SANG Board Minutes, May 28, 1962, 16-20. The director's salary was R3,960 per annum and the unfurnished house could be included at a rental of 12½ percent of the salary. The scale for the assistant director was R3,120 × R120 – R3,480.

69 SANG Minutes of the sub-committee, June 8, 1962 and June 27, 1962. The sub-committee comprised A. H. Honikman, J. P. Duminy and W. E. G. Louw. Pols, whom Von Moltke interviewed in The Hague, worked at SANG as professional officer from 1962 to 1966. Although his application was unsuccessful, Dubow would play a noteworthy part in the gallery's history, as board member and chairperson of the acquisitions committee from 1971 to 1995.

70 Matthys Bokhorst (1900-1982), DLittetPhil, Leiden University, was born in Rotterdam. He saw active service in World War II, returning to UP in 1946. Subsequently he taught in the Department of Netherlandish Cultural History at UCT. He was very much involved in the SAAA and served as its president (1951-58): *Cape Argus*, August 10, 1962. While at SANG he served on many official and selection committees, and was president of the SAMA for two years. He was the author of many catalogues and contributed to books on South African art, as well as three chapters in the two volumes *François le Vaillant in South Africa* (Cape Town: Library of Parliament, 1973).

71 SANG *Annual Report*, 1967-1968, 1968-1969, 1969-1970 (published together), 38. Bokhorst later contradicted the date of Arnott's appointment as assistant director, as January 1, 1971: SANG *Annual Report*, 1970-1971 & 1971-1972 (published together), 8.

72 Hans Fransen (1931-2017) was born in Amsterdam where he began studies of architecture; he came to South Africa in 1955 and completed a BA (UNISA) and PhD (University of Natal). He was curator of the Stellenbosch Museum and Groot Constantia. In 1972 he was appointed as assistant director and curator of prints and drawings; he left SANG in 1980 to take up a senior lectureship in art and architectural history at Natal University. Fransen returned to Cape Town as director of the Michaelis Collection and retired when the museum became part of Iziko Museums. Fransen was active in conservation and museum circles, a founder member of the Simon van der Stel Foundation, and served as national vice-president of the SAAA and on the council of SAMA. He was awarded a knighthood in the Order of Orange-Nassau by the Queen of the Netherlands.

73 SANG *Annual Report*, 1962-1963, 15-17.

74 Bokhorst acknowledged many individuals, including Dr. Ing. Edgar Denninger of the University of Stuttgart, who visited South Africa in 1962 and who allowed the gallery to show data and illustrations about the new method to date rock paintings, which he had developed: Matthys Bokhorst, "Foreword," in *Rock Art in Southern Africa* (Cape Town: South African National Gallery, 1963).

75 SANG *Annual Report*, 1967-1968, 1968-1969, 1969-1970 (published together), 4 & 6.

76 SANG *Annual Report*, 1966-1967, 12.

77 Bokhorst, "A Short History," 12.

78 Advised by Heather Martienssen, architect and Wits University lecturer, Esmé Berman wanted to do her PhD on South African art in the mid-1960s, but the university would not accept it as a doctoral subject: Sean O'Toole, "Modest Writer of *The* South African Art Book," *Business Day*, June 2007. By the end of the 1960s, the following general books on South African art had appeared: Friedrich Ludwig Alexander, *Art in South Africa since 1900 Painting Sculpture and Graphic Work/Kuns in Suid-Afrika sedert 1900 Skilderkuns Beeldhoukuns en Grafiek* (Cape Town: A. A. Balkema, 1962); *Register of South African and South-West African Artists 1900-1969/Register van Suid-Afrikaanse en Suidwes-Afrikaanse Kunstenaars* (Cape Town: South African Association of Arts, 1969); Arie Cornelis Bouman, *Kuns in Suid-Afrika* (Kaapstad: HAUM, 1935); Arie Cornelis Bouman, *Kuns en kunswaardering* (Kaapstad: HAUM, 1942); Arie Cornelis Bouman, *Painters of South Africa* (Cape Town: HAUM, 1949); Jan F. E. Cilliers, *Kuns in Lewe en Kultuur* (Kaapstad: Nasionale Pers, 1933); Alfred Gordon-Brown, *Pictorial Art in South Africa during three centuries to 1875* (London, Sawyer, 1952); Harold Jeppe, *South African Artists 1900-1962* (Johannesburg: Afrikaanse Pers Boekhandel) – the book was translated by Anna Vorster and published as *Suid-Afrikaanse Kunstenaars 1900-1962* in 1964; Petrus Johannes Nienaber, *Skone Kunste in Suid-Afrika* (Johannesburg: Afrikaanse Pers Boekhandel, 1951); W. H. K. ed., *The Arts in South Africa* (Durban: Knox: 1933-34).

79 For details about Berman's criteria, see Berman, *Art and Artists*, VIII. The importance and impact of this book are further explored in Chapter Three.

80 Esmé Berman, *The South African Art Market 1971/72* (Johannesburg: Art Institute South Africa, 1972). Black artists included Mslaba Dumile (Dumile Feni), Sydney Kumalo, Louis Maqhubela, Winston Saoli and Gerard Sekoto; Andrew Verster was the only artist under the age of forty-five to be allocated eight stars.

81 SANG *Annual Report*, 1967-1968, 1968-1969, 1969-1970 (published together), 14-24. The two prints from Goya's *The Disasters of War* are numbered eighty-one and eighty-two.

82 SANG *Annual Report*, 1972-1973, 10; SANG *Annual Report*, 1974-1975, 8.

83 Bokhorst, "From our own," unpaginated.

84 Matthys Bokhorst, "Foreword" in *National South African Art*, unpaginated.

85 "The 1971 Art South Africa Today Exhibition: Towards a Language of protest art," *South African History Online*, http://www.sahistory.org.za/archive/chapter-1strongthe-1971-art-south-africa-today-exhibition-towards-language-protest-artstrong (accessed December 26, 1916).

86 SANG *Annual Report*, 1967-1968, 1968-1969, 1969-1970 (published together), 14.

87 SANG *Annual Report*, 1964-1965 & 1965-1966 (published together), 4 and SANG *Annual Report*, 1967-1968, 1968-1969, 1969-1970 (published together), 6 respectively.

88 Bokhorst, "From our own," unpaginated.

89 Three examples will suffice: Bokhorst took study leave from April to July 1964 to study museums abroad and to do research for a book on François le Vaillant's South African watercolours; Arnott was awarded a British Council scholarship and spent twelve months at the Courtauld Institute of Art in London, where he studied the influence of West African art on European sculpture; this proved to be invaluable for his tenure at the SANG. SANG *Annual Report*, 1964-1965 and 1965-1966 (published together), 4. Bokhorst again took study leave, augmented with vacation leave, from May to September 1967; aided by a grant from parliament, he completed research on Le Vaillant among many other activities. SANG *Annual Report*, 1967-1968, 1968-1969, 1969-1970 (published together), 32.

90 Berman, *Art and Artists*, 382.

91 SANG *Annual Report*, 1966-1967, 4.

92 For more on this see Marilyn Martin, "The Baby and the Bathwater" (paper presented at the annual conference of the South African Visual Arts Historians, Michaelis School of Fine Art, Cape Town, September 5-8, 2013). "Visual Arts and Art History Now: What? How? Why?," *South African Visual Arts Historians*, http://savah.org.za/wp-content/uploads/2016/12/SAVAH2013-Conference-PROCEEDINGS.pdf (accessed December 26, 2016).

93 SANG *Annual Report*, 1966-1967, 6.

94 SANG *Annual Report*, 1967-1968, 1968-1969, 1969-1970 (published together), 8.

95 Ibid.

96 SANG *Annual Report*, 1964-1965 & 1965-1966 (published together), 10.

97 Sandra Eastwood, "The Touch Gallery," in *Touch Gallery* (Cape Town: South African National Gallery, 1977), III. According to Eastwood, the Gemeentemuseum in The Hague had in turn been inspired by Charles Stanford and the Mary Duke Biddle Gallery for the Blind at the North Carolina Museum of Art. Eastwood joined SANG staff in 1964, worked part time until the end of 1977, rejoined in a voluntary capacity in 1989 and in the new millennium coordinated Special Needs which became the Meaningful Access Programme (MAP), with museum and subsequently corporate funding; MAP is ongoing, in museums and beyond. Sandra Eastwood, e-mail to the author, May 5, 2016.

98 Sandra Eastwood, email to the author, May 1, 2016.

99 SANG *Annual Report*, 1967-1968, 16.

100 In an email message to the author, May 1, 2016, Eastwood recalled the enthusiasm and expertise of a variety of ingenious, dedicated art educators such as Victor Honey, August Hopley, Vernon Fisher, Bokkie Basson, Pedro Espi- Sanchis, Bevil Spence, Stanley Cohen, Van Zyl le Grange and teams from the Frank Joubert Art Centre (now the Peter Clarke Art Centre) and the Remix Dance Project. Volunteer Guides were also involved.

101 See the portfolio, Cecil Skotnes and Stephen Gray, *The Assassination of Shaka*, comprising forty-three original woodcuts with captions by Gray, 1973.

102 SANG *Annual Report*. 1979-1980, 8.

103 Bokhorst, "From our own," unpaginated.

104 E. J. de Jager, *Contemporary African Art in South Africa* (Cape Town: Struik, 1973). The works illustrated were sourced from the collection of the UFH, private collections in South Africa and abroad and SANG.

105 SANG Acquisitions Committee, March 19, 1964, 137.

106 Bokhorst, "A Short History," 11.

107 Albert Adams (1929-2006), a coloured man, attended art classes at Livingstone High School in Cape Town; his application to study at the Michaelis School of Fine Art at UCT was denied due to apartheid policies and he qualified as a teacher at Hewat College. He studied at the Slade School of Art in London (1953-56), the Munich Academy of Arts and attended master classes at Oskar Kokoschka's School of Vision in Salzburg (1956-57). He exhibited locally to critical acclaim, but left South Africa permanently and settled in London in 1960. He was honoured with a retrospective exhibition in 2008. See Marilyn Martin and Joe Dolby, eds., *Albert Adams Journey on a Tightrope* (Cape Town: Iziko Museums of Cape Town, 2008). I continue to promote Adams' legacy in museum exhibitions (the Rupert Museum in Stellenbosch, the Wits Art Museum in Johannesburg and the KwaZulu-Natal Society of Arts (KZNSA) in Durban), in collaboration with SMAC Gallery.

108 *Figure study I* and *Figure study VI*, both of 1979, charcoal on paper, were acquired in 1980.

109 SANG *Annual Report*. 1967-1968, 1968-1969, 1969-1970 (published together), 36.

110 Mancoba moved to Paris in 1938 to further his art studies and career, and became a prominent member of CoBrA, an avant-garde group of abstract painters from Copenhagen, Brussels and Amsterdam.

111 SANG *Annual Report*. 1967-1968, 1968-1969, 1969-1970 (published together), 32. Other artists selected were Eben van der Merwe (painting), Cecil Skotnes (graphics), William (Bill) Davis and Lucas Sithole (sculpture); 1968 was the year of intense student unrest in Europe, the South African entry was housed in the Italian Pavilion and in the face of protests against apartheid, the Vietnam War and other causes, the pavilion was closed on the opening day. Berman, *Art and Artists*, 474-475.

112 Emma Bedford, ed., *Contemporary South African Art 1985-1995 from the South African National Gallery Permanent Collection* (Cape Town: South African National Gallery, 1997), 28.

113 SANG *Annual Report*, 1964-1965 & 1965-1966 (published together), 10.

114 Paris mentioned that Mr. Wiener had paid the Wheatleys £1,000 for the work: SANG Board Minutes, November 24, 1958, 57. The Robinson Collection opened on April 9, 1959.

115 Bokhorst, "A Short History," 11.

116 The discussion was not minuted, but the board resolved "to spend about R400 on compiling an attractive catalogue of this important section of the permanent collection to boost the National Gallery's collection overseas": SANG Board Minutes, March 31, 1969, 13. Sotheby's would do the research, publish the catalogue and sell copies at cost to SANG: SANG Board Minutes, May 26, 1969.

117 Honikman reported on "informal talks" with the Bailey trustees, but there is no mention of his correspondence requesting permission to sell some of the works: SANG Board Minutes, March 23, 1970. The letter from the Bailey files 2/4/1/1 in the SANG archives, is cited in Tietze, *A History*, 131, note 68. From 2017 researchers were not permitted to work in the archives and Baheya Hardy, Iziko librarian who retrieved information for me, could not locate the file. In the end the total cost of the catalogue was R1,370.80.

118 SANG *Annual Report*. 1967-1968, 1968-1969, 1969-1970 (published together), 6. The main hall, holding more than 600 seats, was used for meetings, concerts, film shows and activities by outside bodies, while a large corner room became the office of the Friends; also upstairs were dressing rooms behind the stage, a kitchen and toilets, as well as five spaces dedicated to different departments; the ample downstairs space was dedicated to exhibitions; there were two classrooms and a small demonstration room at the disposal of the blind; the former chapel was used for conservation after Bosman's return from training in 1972; and downstairs toilets were for schools and coloured staff: SANG *Annual Report*, 1970-1971 & 1971-1972 (published together), 11.

119 SANG *Annual Report*, 1972-1973, 6; 1974-1975, 4-5; 1975-1976, 4.

120 SANG *Annual Report*, 1972-1973, 7.

121 Cees Wolters, "Obituary," FONG *Newsletter* no 6, December 1982, 3-4.

122 SANG *Annual Report*, 1972-1973, 7; "Gallery Director Appointed," *Cape Times*, February 3, 1973, 2. Du Ry was the director of the Rotterdam Historical Museum for ten years. He published the following books: *Art of the Ancient Near and Middle East* (New York: Abrams, 1970); *Art of Islam* (New York: Abrahams, 1976); *Wandering in western culture* (Inaugural lecture, August 5, 1976) (Cape Town: University of Cape Town, 1976) and the catalogue *Three centuries of French painting: François I – Napoleon I* (Cape Town: South African National Gallery, 1974).

123 SANG *Annual Report*, 1973-1974, 3-4.

124 SANG *Annual Report*, 1975-1976, 3.

125 SANG *Annual Report*, 1974-1975, 3.

126 Ibid., 15. Maqhubela's work was purchased for R495.00; *A Seated Child*, 1967 gouache on paper, was purchased in 2006. See Marilyn Martin, *A Vigil of Departure – Louis Khehla Maqhubela a retrospective 1960-2010* (Johannesburg: The Standard Bank of South Africa Limited, 2010), plate 18, 48.

127 SANG *Annual Report*, 1975-1976, 16.

128 Ibid., 10.

129 SANG *Annual Report*, 1973-1974, 4-6.

130 SANG *Annual Report*, 1975-1976, 7.

131 SANG Minutes of the Executive Committee, April 16, 1975, 69.

132 SANG Board Minutes, July 23, 1975, 105-106.

133 This went on from April to September: SANG, Minutes of the Executive Committee, April 16, 1975, 69; SANG Board Minutes, August 18, 1975, 141; SANG Board Minutes, September 9, 1975, 148.

134 SANG Board Minutes, August 8, 1975, 138.

135 SANG Board Minutes, November 24, 1975, 2. Fransen must have applied, because he was asked to recuse himself, and on his return he was informed of Van Niekerk's appointment.

CHAPTER 3 – Raymund van Niekerk's directorship

1 SANG *Annual Report*, 1979-1980, 5.

2 Born in the Free State town of Senekal in 1930, Van Niekerk qualified as a dentist at Wits University and went to work in London. There he developed an interest in and love for art history and in the 1960s he studied seventeenth-century French painting under Anthony Blunt at the Courtauld Institute of Art. In 1971 he was appointed Professor of Fine Art at the University of Natal, Pietermaritzburg.

3 "Waar hy soms versigtig moes trap in die kulturele eierdans van die tyd (hoofsaaklik bepaal deur die heersende party-establishment en sy hegemoniese kaders)..."

4 Kim Siebert, email to the author, March 12, 2016.

5 In the Western Cape this included lectures at US and UWC, and a series to students of the Department of Architecture at UCT.

6 At the time it was the Southern African Museums Association and drew in museums from Botswana, Malawi, Zimbabwe, and what was then still South West Africa.

7 The brief biographical details were amplified by Joe Dolby in an email message to the author, March 16, 2016. Dolby was employed in different capacities at SANG, including as assistant director, and at Iziko Museums from 1980-2012. In 1984 he received a British Council bursary that Van Niekerk supported and for which he motivated; this enabled Dolby to study at a

number of art museums in England and Scotland for a period of three-and-a-half months. He was honorary secretary of SAMA and, in addition to being curator of prints and drawings, acted as curator of works belonging to FONG.

8 Bedford, *Contemporary South African Art*, 30.

9 Ibid., 31. Emma Bedford was employed in different capacities at SANG and Iziko Museums, including as head of the curatorial department, from 1981-2006.

10 Emma Bedford, email to the author, March 27, 2016.

11 In terms of the Republic of South Africa Constitution Act of 1983, "Own Affairs" pertained to a particular ethnic group, controlled by that group through a chamber of the Tricameral Parliament (Coloured, Indian and White, excluding Africans). The groups made laws on Own Affairs and jointly legislated on General Affairs. Institutions at national and local levels of government were classified accordingly, for example, the former South African Cultural History Museum, now part of Iziko Museums, resorted under Own Affairs.

12 Joe Dolby, email to the author, March 16, 2016.

13 Hayden Proud, email to the author, April 6, 2017.

14 Jo-Anne Duggan, email to the author, February 6, 2017.

15 Maurice did not respond to my email request for input as he was seriously ill and passed away in August 2016.

16 Duggan shared her conversation with Emile Maurice in an email to the author, February 6, 2017. Maurice was employed in different capacities at SANG and Iziko Museums from 1988; Kim Siebert and Nicolaas Vergunst were also appointed at the time, and Jo-Anne-Duggan served in a part-time capacity from September to December 1987, all in education. Maurice and Vergunst were active in education at the highest levels outside SANG and acted as external examiners for Theory of Art at the Michaelis. Vergunst set the Matric Art Practical and Art History examinations for the Department of Education and Culture; he also served on the artworks committee, Centre for African Studies at UCT. Maurice's contribution to the national transformation project post-1994 was indeed substantial.

17 The categories were professional officer, senior professional officer, chief professional officer with specific duties after the title, for example education, paintings and sculpture, prints and drawings, and Touch Gallery (Annexe). There was a clear career path for curators and educators, related to experience and/or further qualifications. The input and participation of staff members in the acquisitions process were significant and valued, but they were not permitted to vote: SANG Acquisitions Committee Minutes, February 28, 1990, 141.

18 Faeza Allie was promoted to chief administrative officer in 1993; then head of administration and senior manager, 1998-2001; she served Iziko Museums first as director of central services and then chief financial officer until 2015.

19 Faeza Allie, email to the author, February 16, 2017,

20 SANG *Annual Report*, 1976-1977, 3.

21 Ibid., 5.

22 Joe Dolby, email to the author, March 16, 2016.

23 See Lynn McClelland and Lucy Alexander, *Women Artists in South Africa/Vrouekunstenaars in Suid-Afrika* (Cape Town: South African National Gallery, 1985); Marion Arnold, *Focus on Bloomsbury/Kollig op Bloomsbury* (Cape Town: South African National Gallery, 1985).

24 Emma Bedford, email to the author, March 27, 2016. See Lucy Alexander, Emma Bedford and Evelyn Cohen, *Paris and South African Artists 1850-1965* (Cape Town: South African National Gallery, 1988). Between 1982 and 1992 four CTT exhibitions were shown at thirty-three venues and were attended by more than 452,000 people. "Cape Town Triennials," *La Motte Museum*, March 18, 2015, https://www.la-motte.com/blogs/news/cape-town-triennials-exhibition-date-july-2013-to-june-2014 (accessed August 17, 2016).

25 The Young Artist Award started in 1981 and was sponsored by Five Roses, 1981-83. Now known as the Standard Bank African Art Collection, it was initiated in 1978 in collaboration with Wits University, where it is housed.

26 SANG, *Annual Report*, 1982-1983, 4-5.

27 SANG Minutes of the Acquisitions Committee meeting, February 22, 1989, 117 & 121. SANG Minutes were bilingual, English and Afrikaans, but not necessarily duplicated, so much of the information is in one language only.

28 SANG Minutes of the Acquisitions Committee meeting, May 24, 1989, 27.

29 The director attested to this, referring to the years 1979 to 1982, when attendance dipped from 75,190 to 66,625 and rose to 83,033: SANG *Annual Report*, 1981-1982, 4. However, there was a dramatic decline in 1982-83 to 56,167: SANG *Annual Report*, 1982-1983, 4; attendance would fluctuate until the Gallery was closed for renovations in April 1989.

30 SANG *Annual Report*, 1981-1982, 4.

31 SANG *Annual Report*, 1976-1977, 3.

32 SANG *Annual Report*, 1981-1982, 3.

33 Kim Siebert, email to the author, March 12, 2016.

34 Other participants are mentioned in relation to specific projects.

35 Geoffrey Grundlingh, then a recent Michaelis graduate, was appointed in 1978, raising the level of both the photography done at SANG and the organisation of exhibitions. Nigel Fogg took over from him three years later.

36 The recent acquisitions comprised a Bakongo Kifwebe figure and "nkisi" power figure; two masks from New Guinea; a Dogon ancestral figure and a Bambara doorlock with a metal key.

37 SANG *Annual Report*, 1975-1976, 16.

38 SANG *Annual Report*, 1976-1977, 16.

39 Ibid.

40 In the 1975-76 financial year SANG acquired the following South African works: five paintings, five sculptures, works on paper by twelve artists (including portfolios of woodcuts by Lucky Sibiya and Cecil Skotnes and a collection of photographs by Jansje Wissema); foreign works: two paintings, nine works on paper: SANG *Annual Report*, 1975-1976, 16-17. The following year eleven South African and seven foreign paintings and sculptures were purchased, as well as ten South African and three foreign works on paper: SANG *Annual Report*, 1976-1977, 16-17.

41 SANG *Annual Report*, 1979-1980, 5. For the full policy statement see Bedford, *Contemporary South African Art*, 38.

42 See Elza Miles, *Polly Street The Story of an Art Centre* (Johannesburg: The Ampersand Foundation, 2004).

43 For an analysis of the enrolment at South African universities from 1958, see The Ratcatcher, "Apartheid and the universities," *Politicsweb*, January 17, 2012, http://www.politicsweb.co.za/news-and-analysis/apartheid-and-the-universities (accessed August 5, 2017). UNISA was excluded from the legislation, as it is a correspondence university.

44 *University of Fort Hare*, http://www.ufh.ac.za/About/Pages/History.aspx (accessed August 5, 2017).

45 Among the white artists who worked at the JAF were Ricky Burnett, William Kentridge, Jenny Stadler and Jill Trappler.

46 John Peffer, *Art and the End of Apartheid* (Minneapolis & London: University of Minnesota Press, 2009), 129-190. Also see Marilyn Martin, "Is There a Place for Black Abstract Painters in South Africa?" *De Arte* 44 (September 1991): 25-39 and Marilyn Martin, "Abstract Art in South Africa: Then and Now," in *Practices of Abstract Art: Between Anarchism and Appropriation*, eds. Isabel Wünsche and Wiebke Gronemeyer (Newcastle upon Tyne: Cambridge Scholars Publishing, 2016), 225-247. The workshops moved to Cape Town in 1992. Year after year participants attest to the importance of the workshops, now associated with Greatmore Studios in Cape Town and The Bag Factory in Johannesburg.

47 Peffer, *Art and the End*, 171.

48 See Lize van Robbroeck, "The Ideology of Community Arts," *De Arte* 46 (1992): 49-57; Eben Lochner, "The Community Arts Project (CAP): The Role of the Arts in Building Community and Artistic Development," Rhodes University, no date. *Asai*, http://www.asai.co.za/jdownloads/Peoples%20Culture/Capepressclips/v__eben_lochner_asj_publication_final.pdf (accessed December 31, 2016); and Iziko Museums, http://www.iziko.org.za/news/entry/uncontained-opening-the-community-arts-project-archive (accessed December 31, 2016).

49 See Federico Freschi, "Other Views: Art History in (South) Africa and the Global South," *Diogenes* 58 no. 3 (2011): 93-101.

50 Frieda Harmsen, "The South African Art Library from Bouman to Berman," *De Arte* 18 (1975): 65-68.

51 For more on the subject see Marilyn Martin, "Esmé Berman: A Unique and Enduring Contribution to South African Art and Art History," in *Public Encounter: The Life and Work of Esmé Berman*, ed. Federico Freschi (Johannesburg: Raisonné, awaiting publication).

52 Esmé Berman, *Art and Artists of South Africa*, VIII.

53 The 1970 edition of *Art and Artists of South Africa* included entries on Bushman (San) art and Ndebele painting, and images of work by Amos Langdown, Louis Maqhubela, Azaria Mbatha, Gladys Mgudlandlu, Andrew Motjuoadi, Ephraim Ngatane, Zainab Reddy and Gerard Sekoto.

54 *Tributaries* is discussed in the following chapter. See: Christopher Till, "Foreword," in *The Neglected Tradition Towards a new history of South African Art (1930-1988)*, Steven Sack (Johannesburg: Johannesburg Art Gallery, 1989), 5. For a comparison of the two exhibitions, see Terry King, "Tributaries and the Triennial: Two South African Art Exhibitions," *African e-Journals Project*. Michigan State University Library, http://pdfproc.lib.msu.edu/?file=/DMC/African%20Journals/pdfs/Critical%20Arts/cajv5n3/caj005003004.pdf (accessed August 17, 2016).

55 Bedford, *Contemporary South African Art 1985-1995*, 32-33.

56 Maqhubela cited in Martin, *A Vigil of Departure*, 8.

57 The first beadwork pieces were an *Ndebele beaded blanket*; ten Xhosa *Loveletters* and a 'beadwork dress': SANG *Annual Report*, 1987-1988, 16.

58 SANG Acquisitions Committee Minutes, March 26, 1986, 17. The term "transitional art" was first used in South Africa in the 1980s, to describe the work of sculptors in Gazankulu and Venda, such as Jackson Hlungwani, Noria Mabasa and Johannes Maswanganyi. It was soon contested, as it created unsatisfactory hierarchies among black artists – those working outside the "mainstream" and in their communities as opposed to the "fine artists", who, for example, studied at the Polly Street Art Centre. For more on the term "transitional art" see Anitra Nettleton, "Myth of the transitional: Black art and white markets in South Africa," *South African Journal of Cultural and Art History* 2 no. 4 (1988): 301-310.

59 SANG Acquisitions Committee Minutes, July 30, 1986, 27.
60 SANG Acquisitions Committee Minutes, September 24, 1986, 40.
61 "A New Sculpture for the S A National Gallery," *Quarterly Bulletin*, September 1980, unpaginated.
62 For information on the 1980 policy statement, as well as the names of board members and staff who served on the acquisitions committee from 1985-1989, see Bedford, *Contemporary South African Art 1985-1995*, 38 & 44-45.
63 SANG *Annual Report*, 1981-1982, 5.
64 Ibid., 3.
65 SANG *Annual Report*, 1982-1983, 7.
66 SANG, *Annual Report*, 1981-1982, 3. Among the artists commissioned during these years were Jules van de Vijver, John Nowers, Nathan Margalit and Barend de Wet.
67 SANG, *Annual Report*, 1982-1983, 5.
68 See F. de Villiers, "Forget art, camping is culture," *Sunday Times*, April 27, 1980, 6; and Raymund van Niekerk, "Where are all the donors?," *Cape Argus Tonight supplement*, June 1, 1981, 1.
69 Unfortunately the archive of Board and Acquisition Minute Books is incomplete. With regard to the period under consideration in this chapter, all the Acquisition Minute Books from April 1970 to November 1985 and Board Minutes from July 1984 to July 1985 are missing. When Iziko Human Resources moved into the Annexe, where the SANG archive was stored, everything – from minute books to filing cabinets – was summarily removed and dumped in Customs House that belongs to DPW, without consultation with SANG staff. Patricia Davison, director of core functions at Iziko at the time, alerted me to the whereabouts of the books and filing cabinets; many of the latter suffered water damage and we salvaged what we could.
70 SANG Board Minutes, March 25, 1975, 149.
71 Hamish Robertson provided this figure and worked out that R250,000 in the 1980s would translate to about R3.4 million in today's terms. The picture looked better for the 2018-19 financial year, provisionally estimated at R1,520,000: Hamish Robertson, email to the author, March 14, 2018.
72 SANG Acquisitions Committee Minutes, July 30, 1986, 27.
73 SANG *Annual Report*, 1987-1988, 3.
74 SANG Acquisitions Committee Minutes, November 25, 1987, 70. Stern's *Bullfight* had been sold at Sotheby's for £3,500 on 4 July 1979. *Arts Sales Index*, https://www.artsalesindex.artinfo.com (accessed March 16, 2016).
75 SANG Acquisition Minutes, July 27, 1988, 99.
76 Padraig O'Malley, "Address by State President P. W. Botha, August 15, 1985," *O'Malley The Heart of Hope*. Nelson Mandela Centre for Memory, https://www.nelsonmandela.org/omalley/index.php/site/q/03lv01538/04lv01600/05lv01638/06lv01639.htm (accessed August 17, 2016).
77 SANG *Annual Report*, 1976-1977, 10.
78 SANG, *Annual Reports*, 1977-1978 & 1978-1979 (published together), 15.
79 Raymund Van Niekerk, "Chat delivered to Friends sometime circa 1983?4?," 15. The real title, "The contribution of the SA National Gallery," is embedded in the seventeen-page hand-written speech in the SANG archive.
80 SANG, *Annual Reports*, 1976-1977, 8. To my knowledge, this exchange programme was sustained until 2008; as discussed in chapter nine, it has not been formally terminated, but it was no longer operative in 2017.
81 SANG, *Annual Report*, 1976-1977, 9.
82 Ibid.
83 SANG Board Minutes, July 27, 1988, 37-38.
84 Lucy Alexander worked at SANG as an education officer and curator from 1976 to 1986 and part-time at the Natale Labia Museum until Patty Hardy was appointed as curator.
85 Gordimer opened the exhibition, *David Goldblatt: Thirty-five Years of Photographs* at SANG and her address was published under the title "David Goldblatt: So Far," *Quarterly Bulletin*, no. 13 (1983): unpaginated.
86 Lucy Alexander, "South African National Gallery Brief History," in *South African Arts Calendar*, 11, no. 1 (1986): 18-19.
87 Joe Dolby, email to the author, March 16, 2016.
88 There were three full-time education officers, one half-day and two education assistants, who carried out vigorous education programmes. The strong public and publicity presence of SANG meant monthly radio talks presented alternatively in English and Afrikaans, twice weekly films for the public, a full schedule of almost daily tours. Volunteer guides received extensive training and numbered approximately twenty. Contacts with the Worcester School for the Blind and Zonnebloem College were maintained: Joe Dolby, email to the author, March 16, 2016.
89 Van Niekerk, "Chat," 16.
90 Joe Dolby, "A short history," 37-50.
91 Kim Siebert, email to the author, March 12, 2016.

92 SANG *Annual Report*, 1978-1979, 15.

93 The Saturday afternoon art classes were particularly appealing to groups and individuals, such as St. Francis College in Langa, Coloured teachers, UCT students, a Xhosa-speaking UNISA art student, Friends and volunteer guides: SANG Board Minutes, November 25, 1987, 117.

94 SANG *Annual Report*, 1986-1987, 4.

95 Kim Siebert, email to the author, March 12, 2016. The chairperson of the board, The Hon. Louis van Winsen, acknowledged the Friends for initiating the bussing of school children to SANG and the Mayoress, Mrs Bettie van Zyl, for funding the project; teachers and pupils responded with enthusiasm and many letters of appreciation were received from principals: SANG *Annual Report*, 1982-1983, 4.

96 Emma Bedford, email to the author, March 27, 2016.

97 SANG *Annual Report*, 1976-1977, 10.

98 On that day a special issue of four commemorative stamps, which depicted four of the older paintings in the collection, appeared, as well as another work on the first-day covers.

99 SANG *Annual Report*, 1977-1978 & 1978-79 (published together), 12-13.

100 SANG *Annual Report*, 1982-1983, 3.

101 SANG *Annual Report*, 1985-1986, 3.

102 SANG *Annual Report*, 1986-1987, 10-11 & 4.

103 SANG Board Minutes, July 22, 1987, 2.

104 SANG Board Minutes, September 24, 1986, 33. Unfortunately I was unable to find these drawings – they were not kept at SANG and the response from Hannes Meiring's widow, Martie Meiring, who tried to assist, was negative: Martie Meiring, email to the author, April 2, 2018.

105 SANG Minutes, September 30, 1987, 107-108. The reference to the collection confirms the formal approach that the DNE made to SANG as regards alienating works in the collection. Hayden Proud maintains that "De Klerk recommended to Raymund van Niekerk ... that he deaccession and sell parts of the collection" to pay for the renovations required, but he does not substantiate this with a reference. Hayden Proud, "Our National Gallery," 41.

106 SANG Board Minutes, November 25, 1987, 118 & 120.

107 SANG Board Minutes, March 30, 1988, 8.

108 The Fort had been in the family since Count Labia's father, Prince Natale Labia, the first Italian Ambassador to South Africa, built and decorated it in 1929 to reflect the spirit of eighteenth-century Venice.

109 Count Labia died in November 2016, aged ninety-two. See: "Count Natale 'Luccio' Labia – obituary," *The Telegraph*, November 26, 2016, http://www.telegraph.co.uk/obituaries/2016/11/26/count-natale-luccio-labia-obituary/ (accessed July 31, 2017).

110 SANG *Annual Report*, 1988-1989, 4.

111 Raymund van Niekerk, "Foreword," in *Natale Labia Museum An account of the history of The Fort & its conversion to a museum and cultural centre*, Lucy Alexander and Patricia Hardy (Cape Town: South African National Gallery, 1988).

112 Iziko Council Minutes, August 23, 2002, 4. In the 2000/2001 financial year the NLM received only 12,000 visitors and it was clearly not viable in relation to the costs involved; the CEO was requested to convey this to DAC: Iziko Council Minutes, November 23, 2001, 7-8.

113 Iziko Council Minutes, March 3, 2005, 11.

114 See, for example, Shelagh Gastrow, "What can we learn from philanthropic mistakes?," *Daily Maverick*, April 8, 2015, http://www.dailymaverick.co.za/opinionista/2015-04-08-what-can-we-learn-from-philanthropic-mistakes/#.VyH-2zE098E (accessed April 28, 2016); and Shelagh Gastrow, "When can donors ask for their money back?," *Mail & Guardian*, August 8, 2008, http://thoughtleader.co.za/shelaghgastrow/2008/08/08/when-can-donors-ask-for-their-money-back/ (accessed April 28, 2016).

115 See Brent Meersman, "Casa Labia: Monumental reinvention," *Mail & Guardian*, October 26, 2012, http://mg.co.za/article/2012-10-26-casia-labia-monumental-reinvention (accessed April 28, 2016). Iziko issued an undated press statement in 2008 pointing out that the dispute between Count Labia and the DPW, which had recently been settled in the Cape High Court, had not involved Iziko in any way. The woodlands scene by James Stark that was presumed missing, formed part of the court proceedings, but the painting was found and returned to Count Labia. Since the return of the property and the collection, the family has created a vibrant and successful cultural centre, Casa Labia Cultural Centre.

116 Merwe Scholtz and Dolby attended an information session at the DNE on 20 and 21 January 1988, and Cees Wolters drafted a report: SANG Board Minutes, February 3, 1988, 133 & 135.

117 The first such subsidy amounted to R1 979 000: SANG Board Minutes, February 22, 1989, 81.

118 SANG Board Minutes, March 30, 1988, 8.

119 *Encyclopaedia of South African Theatre, Film, Media and Performance*, http://esat.sun.ac.za/index.php/Schutte_Commission (accessed February 1, 2017). Raymund van Niekerk and Albert Werth were approached to deliver the keynote address at the

1988 conference, but they were unavailable, and I was asked to step into the breach. De Klerk appointed me to the FCA board of directors (1989-97); I was chairperson of the specialist art committee. I was subsequently appointed to the new council of the NAC, 1997-2004, and served as chairperson of the visual arts and crafts panels.

120 SANG *Annual Report*, 1989-1990, 10.

121 SANG *Annual Report*, 1989-1990, 3.

122 SANG Board Minutes, May 24, 1989, 86.

123 SANG Board Minutes, July 30, 1986, 17.

124 A search for these minutes – if such a meeting did in fact take place – proved fruitless.

125 SANG Board Minutes, November 26, 1986, 2.

126 Joe Dolby, email to the author, March 16, 2016.

127 Hayden Proud, email to the author, April 6, 2017.

128 Albie Sachs, "Preparing Ourselves for Freedom," in *Spring is Rebellious*, Ingrid de Kok and Karen Press, eds. (Cape Town: Buchu Press, 1990), 19. Sach's paper and many of the responses were compiled in this volume.

129 SANG Board Minutes, May 24, 1989, 86.

130 SANG Board Minutes, November 29, 1989, 114.

131 SANG *Annual Report*, 1989-1990, 3.

132 Eunice Basson succeeded me as national president of the SAAA and as representative of the organisation on the SANG board after I was appointment as director.

133 Van Niekerk, FONG *Newsletter*, 1990, 12.

CHAPTER 4 – Facing the challenges of transformation

1 Professor John Mack, Sainsbury Centre for the Visual Arts, University of East Anglia, UK, speaking at a plenary session, June 21, 2016, held on the occasion of the opening of the Musée du quai Branly, Paris.

2 When I took over from Van Niekerk there were forty-three staff members: an assistant director (Lynn McClelland, who resigned in 1991), two curators (Joe Dolby and Emma Bedford), the curator of the NLM (Patty Hardy), three professional officers in the education division (Emile Maurice, Kim Siebert, Nicolaas Vergunst); Noni Sipuye, seconded to SANG by the education department; a librarian (Joey Andersen); six administrative staff, seven technical staff, including Kathy Grundlingh, designated industrial technician (photography), who would later become curator of photography; thirteen security officers and nine general assistants. Faeza Allie was in charge of administration and finances. Hayden Proud (curator), Jon Weinberg (exhibitions officer) and Vuyile Voyiya (information officer) joined the staff in 1992. It was the task of the director to arrange and attend meetings of the board, acquisitions committee, executive and selection committees, Friends council and weekly staff meetings. Committees were formed to deal efficiently and creatively with the running of the institution.
Vision: The South African National Gallery is an art museum which holds in trust an historical and contemporary art collection on behalf of the people of South Africa. We provide a cultural and educational resource, encourage involvement in the visual arts, and nurture a culturally diverse but shared national identity. *Mission*: 1. The Mission of the South African National Gallery (SANG) is governed by its function as a museum concerned with the visual arts. Activities include collecting, curatorship (documentation and conservation) and communication through exhibition, education, research and publication. 2. The goal of the SANG is to develop and maintain the highest standards of excellence in all its activities, and to be an art museum of the first rank. 3. The SANG acknowledges the multi-cultural nature of South African society; we strive to accommodate this diversity while recognising and supporting the building of a national culture. 4. We pursue a goal of non-discrimination with regard to race, class, creed, gender and sexual orientation. We are committed to equality of treatment and opportunity. The vision is published in: Emma Bedford, ed., *Contemporary South African Art 1985-1995 from the South African National Gallery Permanent Collection* (Cape Town: South African National Gallery, 1997), 9.

3 SANG *Annual Report*, 1991, 2 & 3.

4 Leslie Spiro, *Gerard Sekoto: Unsevered Ties* (Johannesburg: Johannesburg Art Gallery, 1989).

5 Marilyn Martin, "The South African National Gallery in the 1990s," FONG *Newsletter* 28, 1990, 3-8.

6 Since Paris' directorship the board had played an ever-increasing role in the work of the institution until, "by the 1990s, through its sub-committees, it was directly involved in all aspects of the Gallery's activities. This has not been maintained under Iziko". (Joe Dolby, email to the author, March 16, 2016). As an Iziko council member during the years 2010-13, I tried unsuccessfully to get members to visit the museums and, in particular, to view the acquisitions.

7 Marilyn Martin, "Draft Policy Manual submitted for consideration and comment to the Board of Trustees by the Director on 27 February 1991." I acknowledged the main source for the document: Hannes Oberholzer, "Durban Museums Policy Manual," 1988 and thanked the author for "his encouragement and his permission to draw on and learn from this work and to reproduce parts of his document verbatim". The nineteen-page Policy Manual comprised the following: preface, history of the

South African National Gallery; objectives and functions of SANG; organisation of SANG (including relationship with the state, composition and terms of reference of the board, director and staff); ethics, procedures, rules and guidelines: 1. institutional ethics and procedures (acquisitions, alienation and disposal of objects and loans, public access and use of buildings and equipment, the library, photography and reproduction rights, the gallery shop); 2. professional ethics and procedures (conduct, responsibilities to the collections and the public, professional confidence, outside employment).

8 Noni Sipuye was a part-time education officer at the time and Anne Munnik was engaged to offer Xhosa lessons to staff. Attendance was voluntary and numbers soon dwindled so that the lessons could not be sustained.

9 Marilyn Martin, "Message from the Director," *bonani*, January/February 1992, inside front cover.

10 Melvyn Minnaar, "Letter from the chairperson," *bonani*, July/August 1992, 16-17.

11 With the view to starting a collection of architectural drawings, Pancho Guedes, head of the department of architecture at Wits University during my tenure in the 1980s, presented SANG with a few drawings by Rex Martienssen; they were not accessioned and when it proved impossible to start such a collection, the were returned to Wits. Acquisitions and exhibitions policies were published in Bedford, *Contemporary South African*, 38-43.

12 SANG *Annual Report*, 1967-1969 & 1969-1970 (published together), 34.

13 Convened by Neville Dubow at the Michaelis School on the occasion of UCT's 150th anniversary, Raymund van Niekerk delivered a paper "The Administration of the Arts in SA". Black artists were invited, but they chose to boycott the event, as they felt that it was held at a white, elitist institution and that it would not change anything. See *The State of Art in South Africa Conference July 1979* (Cape Town: University of Cape Town, 1979).

14 SANG *Annual Report*, 1981-1982, 4; SANG *Annual Report*, 1985-1986, 3.

15 *Southern African Museums Association Bulletin*, 16, no. 8 (1985): 353-381. A special session, Museums as Educational Institutions, was organised at the 1985 SAMA Conference and was followed up later that year by the Museum Education Officers' Conference in Pietermaritzburg.

16 Victor Kröhn quoted by the editor, E. H. Bigalke, "Editor's note," Ibid., 357.

17 Officially known as the Commission of Inquiry into Certain Aspects of the *Tax* Structure of South Africa, it soon became known as the Katz Commission; recommendations were implemented from 1994 to 1999. See "Katz Commission Report into Taxation," *South African Government*, http://www.treasury.gov.za/publications/other/katz/3.pdf (accessed January 31, 2016).

18 Marilyn Martin, "South African Culture at the Crossroads – Where are we? Where are we going?," FONG *Newsletter* 31, 1991, 8-17.

19 Martin, "South African Culture," 17.

20 CAP was founded in 1977 by academics from the Michaelis School of Art, South African Institute of Race Relations, South African College of Higher Education and UCT's Extra-Mural Studies Department.

21 "Federation of South African Cultural Organisations," *Asai*, http://asai.co.za/peoplesculture/federation-south-african-cultural-organisations/ (accessed January 31, 2016).

22 S. S. T. van der Merwe and Mac Maharaj, "Codesa secretariat asks for participation," *Cape Times*, February 11, 1992. Staff submitted a draft proposal requesting the submission of a document to CODESA, February 26, 1992, resulting in a letter from the board chairperson to the CODESA secretariat, dated February 28, 1992. I encouraged the directors of art museums, directors of declared institutions and directors of 'own affairs' institutions to do the same in a letter, February 28, 1991. The initiative did not bear fruit.

23 Marilyn Martin, "Message from the Director," *bonani* July/August/September 1993, inside front cover.

24 Marilyn Martin, "Message from the Director," *bonani*, October/November/December 1993, inside front cover.

25 Martin, "Message," *bonani*, July/August/September 1993, inside front cover.

26 Terminology presents an ongoing dilemma; I use *art nègre* in relation to the early decades of the twentieth century, as the French does not translate satisfactorily into English. For reflections on the dilemma of terminology see Sally Price, *Paris Primitive: Jacques Chirac's Museum on the Quai Branly* (Chicago: University of Chicago Press, 2007), vii-viii.

27 Guillaume Apollinaire, "Sur les musées," *Le Journal du Soir*, October 3, 1909, 123.

28 Ibid.

29 Guillaume Apollinaire, "Sculptures d'Afrique, d'Amérique, d'Océanie," (written in 1917) in *Sculptures nègres et Sculptures d'Afrique, d'Amérique, d'Océanie*, Paul Guillaume, catalogue of the exhibition and sale of works from the collections of André Breton and Paul Éluard at Hôtel Drouot, July 2 & 3, 1931, first published 1931, 2nd ed. (New York: Hacker Art Books, 1973), unpaginated.

30 Gathered in one site was everything that defines the human being: evolution (prehistory), unity and diversity (anthropology), cultural and social expression (ethnology).

31 *Ubuntu: Arts et Cultures d'Afrique du Sud*, catalogue of the exhibition held at Musée national des Arts d'Afrique et d'Océanie (Paris: Editions de la Réunion des musées nationaux, 2002).

32 Vincent Noce, "Le Louvre s'ouvre enfin aux arts premiers," *Libération*, April 13, 2000, http://www.liberation.fr/evenement/2000/04/13/jacques-chirac-inaugure-aujourd-hui-les-salles-consacrees-aux-oeuvres-africaines-amerindiennes-et-oc_322640 (accessed February 18, 2016).

33 Michael Kimmelman, "A Heart of Darkness in the City of Light," *New York Times*, July 2, 2006, http://www.nytimes.com/2006/07/02/arts/design/02kimm.html?pagewanted=all&_r=0 (accessed February 9, 2016).

34 For more on the history and controversy, see Price, *Paris Primitive* and *Sally Price, Au musée des illusions: Le rendez-vous manqué du quai Branly*, translated by Nelcya Delanoë (Paris: Éditions Denoël, 2011); for reviews of both books, see John Warne Monroe, "Book reviews," *The Journal of Modern History* 86, no. 1 (2014): 193-196.

35 Jaques Chirac, Musée du quai Branly brochure, June 2006.

36 Kurt Varnedoe, "Abstract Expressionism" in *"Primitivism" in 20th century art Affinity of the Tribal and the Modern*, vol. II, ed. William Rubin (New York: The Museum of Modern Art, 1984), 615-657, note 20.

37 Evan Maurer, "Dada and Surrealism" in Ibid., 535-593, note 3.

38 Museum of Modern Art, *press release*, 1935, https://www.moma.org/momaorg/shared/pdfs/docs/press_archives/233/releases/MOMA_1934-35_0048_1935-03-09_11-3-9-35.pdf?2010 (accessed January 19, 2016).

39 Bruce Arnott, "Some recollections of the introduction of 'classical' African art at the SANG," unpublished essay, July 31, 2011, unpaginated. Arnott gained a British Council scholarship (not for degree purposes); his research at the Courtauld Institute of Art, London University, was supervised by Alan Bowness and he was tutored by John Golding. He held discussions with Anthony Blunt and William Fagg and visited collections of African art in France, Switzerland and Germany. Carol Kaufmann was appointed as SANG professional assistant/researcher in 1992, subsequently as curator of African Art; she retired in 2016. In 2011 Kaufmann started collating articles for a publication, *Ilifa LaBantu*, that would recognise and celebrate the journey of acquiring African art for the national art museum; it was unfortunately not published.

40 SANG *Annual Report*. 1967-1968, 1968-1969, 1969-1970 (published together), 84.

41 SANG *Annual Report*, 1970-1971 & 1971-1972 (published together), 12.

42 SANG *Annual Report*, 1970-1971 & 1971-1972 (published together), 7. Unfortunately there is no further reference to the overseas journals and I have not been able to trace them. The catalogue *Rock Art* (Cape Town: South African National Gallery, 1963) contains contributions by Ray Inskeep, Miles C. Burkitt, Jalmar Rudner, Townley Johnson and James Walton; introductions to different areas are followed by illustrations and descriptive details.

43 Bruce Arnott, letter to the editor, SANG *Quarterly Bulletin* no. 16 (1984): 7-8.

44 SANG *Annual Report*, 1975-1976, 7.

45 The recent acquisitions comprised a Bakongo Kifwebe figure and a "nkisi" power figure; two masks from New Guinea; a Dogon ancestral figure and a Bambara doorlock with a metal key.

46 SANG *Annual Report*, 1987-1988, 16. The Mfengu and Shangaan beadwork comprised: a Mfengu scarf (Fingo), Fingo beadwork (five loveletters, one large loveletter, one multiple loveletter), Mpondomise (chastity apron), two Mfengu aprons, a Shangaan pincloth: SANG *Annual Report*, 1989-1990, 16.

47 This included the De Bracey-Hopkins collection of nineteenth- and early twentieth- century beadwork, purchased for the SANG by the Rowland and Leta Hill Trust, and pieces, including some dating to the Anglo-Zulu War (1879), from Andrew Newall.

48 Between the years 1988-93 many fine examples were bought from dealer Stephen Long, who travelled to the Eastern Cape and brought back items that were no longer either produced or worn by the people. This area had seen many social and political upheavals, with the Transkei and Ciskei becoming "self-governing" Bantustans under the apartheid regime, and experiencing rapid cultural changes since the 1994 elections. The Ferreira and Van Rooyen collections of circa 1930s beadwork were also acquired.

49 Emma Bedford, ed., *Ezakwantu: Beadwork from the Eastern Cape* (Cape Town: South African National Gallery, 1993). A full page of acknowledgments of the catalogue and exhibition project, and the numerous organisations and individuals who contributed, bear testimony to the complexity and ambition of *Ezakwantu*; the word, literally translated, means "things from the house of the people".

50 Marilyn Martin, "Foreword," in Ibid., 7. The curators secured funding from Wooltru and the Friends to research the material culture of the different population groups of South Africa, in order to gain more knowledge about the new collections of beadwork that were being acquired. They travelled throughout the country and focused attention on work by the Southern Nguni in preparation for the exhibition. Many sponsors are listed in the catalogue, in particular the government of the Federal Republic of Germany that sponsored the specially designed display cabinets.

51 Marilyn Martin, "Message from the Director," *bonani*, January/February/March 1994, unpaginated.

52 See Nessa Leibhammer, "Ezakwantu Beadwork from the Eastern Cape," in *African Arts* (UCLA) XXVIII, no. 1 (1995), 81-82 for more on the invited artists, as well as other display issues raised by the exhibition. What Leibhammer overlooked was the history of invited artists at SANG, who worked either in the main building or the Annexe and engage with the public. Leibhammer also contrasted and compared *Ezakwantu* and *Face Value: Old Heads in Modern masks* in the review.

53 For a full report see Emma Bedford, "Travels with Art A case study?," in *bonani*, October-November-December 1995, 20-23.

54 Jean-Hubert Martin, "Art in a multi ethnic society," in *Africus: Johannesburg Biennale* exhibition (Johannesburg: Greater Johannesburg Transitional Metropolitan Council, 1995), 49.

55 Carol Kaufmann, "Report on status of holdings of Department of African Art as of January 1997". A collection acquired from Andrew Newall in 1994 comprised seventy headrests, clubs, staffs, seats, figurative sculpture, snuff containers, objects in horn, bone and ivory from southern Africa at the turn of the nineteenth century, as well as ceremonial regalia from Angola, East Africa and Zaire.

56 The collection comprises knobkieries, sticks and staffs, a Tsonga headrest, wooden milk vessels, an ivory fly-whisk, bone snuff-spoons, snuff-containers, a figurative axe-handle, a beaded Southern-Nguni pipe and a rare Northern-Nguni maternity staff. These are fine examples of functional objects which were transformed into artistic accomplishments – a principle that lies behind much of the nineteenth-century African art of southern Africa.

57 Steven Dubin, *Transforming Museums: Mounting Queen Victoria in a democratic South Africa* (Auckland Park: Jacana, 2006), 250.

58 The contractor for the climate control was declared insolvent, and as a result of the exposure of the walls to rain, the absence of both natural ventilation and climate control, the basement became exceedingly damp and fungus appeared on some paintings; conservator Thomas Rebok, two assistants and with the support of D. Smith from DAG, managed the situation professionally and quickly: SANG Board Minutes, August 28, 1991, 1.

59 Martin, "Message," *bonani*, January/February 1992, 1. The figure includes the opening of the exhibition (1,207 people), and the 910 adults and children who attended the Sekoto open day for children on 10 October. The FONG, together with the volunteer guides, had raised money for the café and the repair of the beautiful chairs that were part of the history of the institution. Elizabeth Benater ran the Gallery Café, but it proved to be a financial risk for her and her successors, as access and trading hours were limited; in time the facility was closed.

60 "Ramphele paints picture of a new South African culture," UCT *Monday Paper* 10 no. 33 (October 14, 1991); and "Forging a national culture in SA," *Cape Argus Spectrum*, October 14, 1991, 8.

61 An outline of the process, as well as comments, reservations and recommendation from the regions were published in the catalogue: *Kaapstadse Triënnale 1991/Cape Town Triennial 1991* (Cape Town: Rembrandt van Rijn Art Foundation/ Kunsstigting Rembrandt van Rijn, 1991). Kentridge won a merit prize in 1985 with his drawing *Conservationists' Ball*. The 1991 merit awards winners were Willie Bester, Sandra Kriel and Russell Scott.

62 The editors of the UNISA journal *De Arte* ran a special feature that incorporated some reviews initially published elsewhere, as well as individual responses to the invitation to contribute. The sponsors, the Rembrandt van Rijn Art Foundation, declined the invitation: "Special Feature: The 1991 Triennial," *De Arte* no. 45 (1992): 24-48; also see Antoinette du Plessis, "The Cape Town Triennial: a Phenomenon of the Eighties," Ibid., 15-24. For a positive review see Elza Miles, "Triënnale grense word versit," (Triennial boundaries moved) *De Kat*, November 1991, 84.

63 According to a report by the FCA, September 1989, there were thirteen national and seventeen regional competitions for the visual arts, for people of all ages. Marilyn Martin, "Issues, Reactions and Interpretations," *De Arte* no. 45 (1992): 35-44.

64 It formed part of the BMW Kulturprogramm destined for a European tour and was also shown at Museum Africa in Johannesburg. For a critique of both *Tributaries* and the Cape Town Triennials, see Terence King, "Tributaries and the Triennial: two South African art exhibitions," *Critical arts* 5 no. 3, (1987), 39-57.

65 Ricky Burnett, *Tributaries A view of contemporary South African art/Quellen und Strömungen Eine Ausstellung zeitgenössischer südafrikanischer Kunst* (Johannesburg: BMW South Africa, 1985), 1.

66 Verster quoted in Marilyn Martin, "Uitstalling van Suid-Afrikaanse kuns in Duitsland," in *South African Arts Calendar*, June 1985, 5.

67 SANG Board Minutes, November 1991, 4.

68 Letters from Rupert to Martin, January 15 and 31; letter from Martin to Rupert, January 21, 1992; letter from Rupert to Scholtz, January 31, 1992.

69 Bedford, Dolby, Grundlingh, Maurice, Proud, Siebert, Vergunst and Weinberg expressed their concern in a signed document, February 10, 1992, and requested an opportunity to discuss the CTT. This did not happen.

70 Letter dated February 12, 1992.

71 It is worth listing the names and affiliations of the trustees at this time: Government appointees: Karin Skawran, H. van der Merwe Scholtz, Danie van Niekerk (deputy chairperson), Kiren Thathiah, J. D. P. (Hannes) van der Merwe; university representatives: Ampie Coetzee (UWC), Neville Dubow (UCT), E. G. Meiring (US); Cape Town City Council: Clive Keegan; FONG: Melvyn Minnaar; SAAA: Louis Jansen van Vuuren (Head Office) and Jonathan Comerford (Western Cape); the director was a full member of the board and Joe Dolby was the secretary.

72 SANG Board Minutes, April 22, 1992, 73.

73 Ibid., 73-75.

74 My objection is noted in minutes from a 1991 meeting, where it was also stated that "there was no dissent from committee members other than Ms Martin". SANG Board Minutes, November 27, 1991, 23 & 26.

75 Letter from Martin to Scholtz, March 21, 1992; letters from Scholtz to Martin, March 11, 25, 27, 30 and 31. We encountered serious problems with FOSACO, which turned out not to be as representative as Omar Badsha and Mario Pissarra had claimed; in addition, they wanted to discuss a new management structure for SANG when a "transitional government" took over the country. While board members and staff were part of our JWG, I was blamed. Apart from many articles in *Die Burger*, those that most concerned Scholtz were: Pretrovna Metelerkamp, "Kaapse bohaai oor 'kuns vir 'n nasie,'" *Insig*, March 1992; interviews in the popular magazine *Rooi Rose*, February 1992; and Andrea Vinassa, "Between the old and the new," *Vrye Weekblad*, October 11-17, 1991, 32-33.

76 SANG Board Minutes, May 21, 1991, 1-2; Van Niekerk subsequently refused an invitation to open an exhibition at the NLM.

77 Scholtz charged me in terms of Regulation 19(b) (misconduct and inefficiency) of the Regulations promulgated under and in terms of Section 15 of the Cultural Institutions Act, No. 29 of 1969; the document was attached to the charge together with the relevant correspondence.

78 I called Albie Sachs, whom we had assisted at UWC with installing his collection, for advice; he referred me to attorney John MacRobert, who brought advocate Alec Freund on board.

79 The main press articles on the CTT were: a telephonic interview with journalist P. Naidoo, *Sunday Tribune*, December 8, 1991; Vinassa's interview cited above: it comprised a lengthy and wide-ranging interview. Some nine out of 600 odd lines were held against me months after the publication.

80 SANG Board Minutes, April 22, 1992, 66.

81 Letter from Minnaar to Scholtz, February 10, 1992.

82 SANG Board Minutes, April 22, 1992, 76-88.

83 This raises the question as to how correspondence, some of which was not filed at SANG, came into the hands of *Die Burger*.

84 Marilyn Martin, "Message from the Director," *bonani* July/August 1992, unpaginated.

85 These were: *Freedom Beat* (produced by Artists Against Apartheid in support of the Anti-Apartheid Movement, 1986); *Mzwakhe Mbuli, The People's Poet* (Afravision, 1989); *Before Dawn Culture for Another South Africa* (Dutch Anti-Apartheid Movement and the ANC, 1987); *Song of the Spear* (produced by the International Aid and Defense Fund (IDAF), and directed by Barry Feinberg, 1986); *Mapantsula* (Max Montocchio, directed by Oliver Schmitz, 1988); *Sounds for Mandela* (Parallax Films, 1986); *Apartheid* (A Doxa/Point du Jour/La Sept co-production, directed by Jean-Michel Meurice in collaboration with Joëlle Chesselet, 1992); *The Long Journey of Clement Zulu* (Open Door/Double Exposure for the BBC, directed by Liz Fish, 1992).

86 Archives, *Die Burger*, http://152.111.1.87/argief/berigte/dieburger/1992/07/20/4/1.html (accessed January 3, 2016).

87 Gabriël J. Botma, "Manufacturing cultural capital: Arts journalism at *Die Burger* (1990-1999)" (PhD diss., University of Stellenbosch, 2011), *Stellenbosch University Library, SUN Scholar Research Repository*, https://scholar.sun.ac.za/handle/10019.1/18065 (accessed January 3, 2016). Botma is a former arts editor of *Die Burger*, currently lecturer in journalism and head of the department at US. Botma accessed newspaper articles that are not readily available and I refer to them in the text; they are all drawn from an extensive footnote: Ibid., note xxi, 365-366.

88 On May 11, 1991 the newspaper published a letter from a reader who stated that SANG would no longer inherit his art collection because of the director's "political" comments – he feared that his artworks would be "handed back to the people".

89 Botma, "Manufacturing," 158-159.

90 De Nationale Pers Beperkt (National Press Ltd), now Naspers, was founded in 1915 by prominent Afrikaners to publish and print newspapers and magazines that would support Afrikaner nationalism: *Wikipedia*, https://en.wikipedia.org/wiki/Naspers (accessed August 12, 2017).

91 SANG Board Minutes, August 19, 1992, 89.

92 All Board members listed above were present, except for Comerford.

93 In spite of the outcome, I had to pay my legal fees of R8,000; the trustees agreed to an interest-free loan.

94 The drafts, original and translation, sent to *Die Burger* August 23, 1992, are in the SANG archive, as well as a handwritten note from Dubow to me suggesting that I do the translation as it would not be appropriate for Danie van Niekerk to do so; in the end Skawran translated it. The arts editor of the newspaper replied on August 29, again referring to his article of July 20, and warning the national gallery to guard against Art by Edict.

95 The Afrikaner Weerstandsbeweging (it does not have an English name but translates as the Afrikaner Resistance Movement) was formed by a group of seven young men in 1973, including Eugène Terre'Blanche, in Heidelberg, Transvaal (now Gauteng Province). It was launched in opposition to the ruling National Party and perceived threats to the future of Afrikaners: Padraig O'Malley, "Afrikaner-Weerstandsbeweging (AWB)," Nelson Mandela Centre for Memory, https://omalley.nelsonmandela.org/omalley/index.php/site/q/03lv02424/04lv02730/05lv03188/06lv03191.htm (accessed August 13, 2017).

96 See *bonani*, March/April 1992, 1-2 and Martin, "Introduction," in Bedford, *Contemporary South African,* 13 and Figs. 3 & 4, 16.

97 *Untitled (Remains)* was shown on the exhibition *Siyawela: Love, Loss and Liberation in South African Art* curated by Colin Richards and Pitika Ntuli for *Africa95* and mounted at the Birmingham Museum and Art Gallery.

98 Susan Loppert, "A real change of art: After years of apartheid, South Africa's galleries are adjusting their collections," *The Independent*, April 17, 1993, http://www.independent.co.uk/arts-entertainment/art-a-real-change-of-art-after-years-of-apartheid-south-africas-galleries-are-adjusting-their-1455717.html (accessed March 10, 2016). Loppert reports on the complicated attempt to create a new national culture.

99 For another interview with Oliva see Kendell Geers, "Critic needs a pig's eye view," *Business Day,* December 3, 1993. For information on the South African participation in the 1993 Venice Biennale, see Louis Jansen van Vuuren, "Preface," *Arts Calendar* 18, no. 2 (1993): 3; and Marilyn Martin, "The Venice Biennale 1993," Ibid., 4-5.

100 Jean-Hubert Martin, "Art in a multi ethnic society," in *Africus*, 51.

101 Neville Dubow, *Neville Dubow Sequences Series Sites Photographs 1971-1992* (Cape Town: self-published, 1992). The catalogue contains essays by Dubow, Karin Skawran and Marilyn Martin. The exhibition featured Dubow at the Standard Bank Arts Festival (July 1992); it toured to the major art museums in South Africa.

102 The exhibition was curated by Marion Arnold and sponsored by Standard Bank; it was a central feature of the 1992 Grahamstown Festival. Some 219 works were drawn from collections all over the country to examine the interface between the "fine artist" and the 'botanical artist", and ranged from seventeenth-century Dutch still-life paintings and contemporary South African works to the finest botanical paintings held in private collections and libraries. Marion Arnold, *Art Meets Science: Flowers as Images* (Johannesburg: Standard Bank, 1992).

103 Between 4 December 1991 and 31 January 1992, 14,594 people visited the main building.

104 My report on the debate in *bonani* (October-November-December 1992, 1) once again roused a columnist's ire: Pieter Spaarwater, "Museum-vriende word uitgetrap," *Die Burger,* March 20, 1992, 8. I replied: Marilyn Martin, "Gehalte van mense was glad nie ter sprake nie," *Die Burger,* March 24, 1992, 16; and Pieter Spaarwater, "Museum-vriende skuins uitgetrap," *Die Burger,* press cutting in SANG archive neither dated nor paginated. For reviews see: Andrew Putter, "Martin grabs bull by the horns," *Cape Times Tonight,* January 8, 1992, 4; and Zirk van den Berg, "Puik kunswerke, so reg uit die boek," *Die Burger,* January 8, 1992, 2.

105 Jo-Anne Duggan, email to the author, February 6, 2017.

106 Jo-Anne Duggan, "Made in Wood materials, processes and forms," in *Made in Wood Work from the Western Cape* (Cape Town: South African National Gallery, 1992), 38. There are also contributions by Martin, Maurice, Proud, Siebert, and photographs by Grundlingh. Also see *bonani*, March/April 1993, 10 and April/May/June 1993, 1; and Wilma Cruise, "Review," in *De Arte* no. 47 (1993): 39-41. Neville Dubow and Randolph Hartzenberg joined SANG staff on the selection panel.

107 Albie Sachs, letter to the editor, *bonani*, April/May/June 1993, 1. The gallery shop no longer exists.

108 Naomi Press, *Knots & Nets: Spiritual Connections – Noeuds et Filets: Liens Spirituels* (Washington D.C.: Arts America Program of the United States Information Agency, 1993). The exhibition travelled to Abidjan, Bamako, Dakar, Johannesburg and Harare.

109 Katz was among the 537 refugees from Nazi Germany who arrived with his wife Ruth on the steamer "Stuttgart" on 27 October 1936. It was greeted with an anti-Semitic demonstration. See Hayden Proud, ed., *Hanns Ludwig Katz* (Cape Town: South African National Gallery, 1994). The project was sponsored by Lufthansa and the German Consulate General. Katz was not represented in any South African public collection and unfortunately our attempt to raise money for the acquisition of a major triptych, *Selbstbidnis mit Franze und Affen (Self-portrait with Franze and Monkey)* (1934-35), was unsuccessful.

110 The exhibition was accompanied by two publications: Malcolm Payne, ed., *Face Value: Old Heads in Modern Masks: A Visual, Archaeological and Historical Reading of the Lydenburg Heads.* Edition 36/50 (Cape Town: Axeage Private Press, 1993): a hand-made book with fourteen copper plate etchings, plus seven etched renderings of the sculptural series, the *Mafikeng Heads*, and essays by Patricia Davison, Martin Hall and Payne; and Malcolm Payne, ed., *Face Value: old heads in modern masks. A visual, archaeological and historical reading of the Lydenburg Heads* (Cape Town: South African National Gallery, 1993): a catalogue with foreword by Martin, introduction by Payne and catalogue essay by Ivor Powell.

111 Ibid., 4.

112 Ibid., 6.

113 Ibid., 7.

114 Ibid., 5.

115 *Picturing our World: Contemporary Images of the Western Cape* (Cape Town: South African National Gallery & Foundation for the Creative Arts, 1993).

116 Jo-Anne Duggan, email to the author, February 6, 2017.

117 Quoted in *bonani*, July/August/September 1993, 8.

118 Jo-Anne Duggan, email to the author, February 6, 2017.

119 Fatima February is one of the national gallery's success stories: she was initially employed as a general assistant, but she soon joined the educators; she also showed a gift for objects and she is currently employed by Iziko Museums in managing social history collections. Her story is one of many that speak of our commitment to identify special skills and talents and to empower staff accordingly.
120 The Medora is a turban-like headdress that is pinned onto a Muslim bride's head on her wedding day as part of the traditional wedding ceremony.
121 Jo-Anne Duggan, email to the author, February 6, 2017.
122 They were Peter Delius, Manie Groenewald, Deborah James and Chris van Vuuren. The peer reviewers secured were Anitra Nettleton (South Africa) and Betty Schneider (America). The exhibition was supported by DACST, the FCA and many private sector sponsors: AGFA, Plascon, Truworths, South African Commission on Illumination.
123 Linda Nochlin, "Learning From "Black Male"," *Art in America* 83 no. 3 (1995): 91.
124 Anna Tietze, *Alfred de Pass Presentation to the South African National Gallery* (Cape Town: South African National Gallery, 1995). The exhibition and catalogue were sponsored by Phillips Auctioneers of London; they also sponsored a London exhibition of Old Master drawings given by De Pass to the Royal Cornwall Museum at Truro. Tietze and Crispian Riley-Smith gave a series of lectures.
125 The Zabalaza Festival, which was organised by the ANC, was intended to establish a basis for non-racial democratic cultural exchange for South Africa. Arguably the most comprehensive exhibition ever to leave South Africa, it was seen by 280,000 people during its tour in the UK. See David Elliot, *Art from South Africa/an exhibition organised by MOMA, Oxford, in association with the Zabalaza Festival, London* (Oxford: Museum of Modern Art, 1990).
126 The exhibition at SANG was made possible through the intervention of Laurent Devèze, then French cultural attaché and director of IFAS and Marie-Paule Serre (AFAA) in Paris.
127 Brahim Alaoui and Jean Hubert Martin, *Rencontres africaine: exposition d'art actuel du 6 avril au 15 août 1994* (Paris : Institut du monde arabe and Fondation Afrique en créations, 1994). The participating artists were Farid Belkahia, Frédéric Bruly Bouabré, Abdoulaye Konaté, Rachid Koraichi, Kivuthi Mbuno and Cyprien Tokoudagba.
128 Marilyn Martin, "Message from the Director," *bonani* May/June, 1.
129 *Friends' Choice* (Cape Town: Friends of the South African National Gallery, 1991). The catalogue contains a short history of the collection by Dolby and the directions that informed the collection by Deon Viljoen. It is a valuable document of acquisitions during 1975-1991, which included an early etching by William Kentridge (1980, acquired 1981), works by Simon Ford, John Kramer, Randolph Hartzenberg, David Hlongwane, Thami Jali, Percy Konqobe, Henriette Ngako, Sophie Peters, Velile Soha, Sarah Tabane and Lucas Seage's *Found object* (circa 1980, acquired 1981).
130 SANG Minutes of the Acquisitions Committee, February 28, 1990, 140.
131 For information on the acquisitions and exhibitions policies that would guide these functions of the SANG from 1990 to 2001 (when Iziko Museums was formed), and the Board and staff members who served on the acquisitions committee, see Bedford, "Contemporary," 39-47.
132 Van den Berg gave an overview of the contemporary works on display, including Jane Alexander's *Butcher Boys* and expressed his delight that Kevin Brand's *Nineteen Boys Running* and Paul Grendon's monumental *Ons vir jou, Suid-Afrika* would be safeguarded at SANG. He was most complimentary about the vitality of the institution that reflected the renovation of the building and he urged the public to support the art museum.
133 SANG Board Minutes, February 28, 162.
134 Bedford, *Contemporary South African*, 145.
135 Accessed February 8, 2017. http://www.home.intekom.com/beezybailey/new/joyce.htm. This was not the end of Bailey and Ntobe: exhibitions were held at the Market Galleries in Johannesburg and the SAAA, Cape Town in 1992; in 1995 they exhibited at the Goodman Gallery in Johannesburg. Bailey describes "Joyce's latest incarnation" as "a collaborative project comprising photographs and video with Zwelethu Mthethwa and Brian Eno" on his website.
136 The judges were Omar Badsha, Dubow, David Goldblatt, Dolby and Martin; the photographers were Geoffrey Grundlingh, Ingrid Hudson, Lesley Lawson, Roger Meintjes, Guy Tillim and Paul Weinberg. See *bonani*, October/November/December 1993, 22-23. In addition to the commissioned photographs, works by Lien Botha, Jean Brundrit, Neville Dubow, Benny Gool, Paul Grendon, Chris Ledochowski, Rashid Lombard, Gideon Mendel, Santu Mofokeng, Cedric Nunn, Jo Ractliffe and Anna Zieminski were bought.
137 Judges were Dubow, Gordon Metz, Louis Jansen van Vuuren and for SANG Bedford, Dolby, Martin and Maurice.
138 Jo-Anne Duggan, "New Art Education Programme," *bonani*, September/October, 1992, 18-19.
139 Jo-Anne Duggan, email to the author, February 6, 2017.
140 Marilyn Martin, "Message from the Director," bonani, July/August, 1992, 1. I secured funding from the FCA to sponsor this special day at nine art museums and organisations in South Africa.

141 Jo-Anne Duggan, email to the author, February 6, 2017.

142 Marilyn Martin, "Message from the Director," *bonani*, April/May/June, inside front cover.

143 Josephine Anderson, "Museum Art Libraries as a bridge between the artists and society with specific reference to the South African National Gallery Library," paper delivered at the sixtieth International Federation of Library Associations and Institutions (IFLA) Conference in Havana, Cuba, August 21-28, 1994. Accessed June 18, 2017. https://forge.fh-potsdam.de/~IFLA/INSPEL/94-4anjo.pdf.

144 Peter Dennis, "Computer database," *bonani*, October-December, 1994, 10.

145 Peter Dennis, email to the author, April 25, 2016.

146 For reports on the trip see: Marilyn Martin, "Message from the Director," *bonani* November/December 1992, 1 and "Documenta 9," 14-16.

147 Jean-Yves Jouannais, *Un Art Contemporain D'Afrique Du Sud* (Paris: Ed. Plume, 1994).

148 The Department of Arts and Culture decided on the spelling when Sarah Baartman's remains were returned to South Africa; her name is also spelled "Sara", "Saartje", "Saartjie" and her surname "Bartman", "Bartmann", or "Baartmen".

149 For a report on the trip see: Marilyn Martin, "A visit to Paris...," *bonani*, October-December 1994, 21-24.

150 The attendance figures at SANG were: 1992-93, 61,337; 1993-94, 72,493; 1994-95, 68,626. The Annexe attracted 13,682 during these years and the NLM 54,459.

CHAPTER 5 – A new dispensation for national museums

1 Mexican novelist Carlos Fuentes, keynote address at the conference "The Artist in Society: Rights, Roles, and Responsibilities," held at The Art Institute of Chicago, 13-15 October, 1994. Fuentes' address, entitled "Imagination and Historical Change," had as its source T. S. Elliot's notion of "the presence of the past", which enabled Fuentes to touch on many current concerns and debates. See: Carol Becker, ed., *The Artist in Society: Rights, Roles, and Responsibilities* (Chicago: Chicago New Art Association, New Art Examiner Press, 1995).

2 Much of this information is drawn from *bonani*; longer articles in *bonani* relevant to this text are referenced individually. All the exhibitions, events at the SANG and the NLM are listed in this publication, 1992 to the first quarter of 2000, after which the SFI newsletter, *Zanazo* came into being; after the second quarter of 2001 there were no more newsletters, only listings in *what's on at Iziko?*, still current. In 1997 and 1998 *bonani* was sponsored by Sappi War on Waste, thereafter with an advertisement; the SANG joined their "War on Waste" campaign and we started a recycling project.

3 Re-appointed: Bongi Dhlomo-Mautloa, Pat Gorvalla, Karin Skawran (chairperson), Kiren Thathiah (vice-chairperson), Patricia Kreiner (previously representative of the Cape Town City Council, in her personal capacity); new appointees: Lionel Davis, Josephine Frater, Vince Kolbe, David Koloane, Jacqueline Nolte, Jane Taylor, Pat Tebbutt. The FONG and the SAAA, head office, were accorded one representative each; they were Caryll Shear and Conrad Theys respectively. Kim Siebert was elected staff representative on the board.

4 Department of Arts, Culture, Science & Technology, *White Paper on Arts, Culture and Heritage*, 1996. Accessed March 9, 2016, http://www.dac.gov.za/content/white-paper-arts-culture-and-heritage-0. The document was revised in 2013. Accessed March 9, 2016. http://www.dac.gov.za/sites/default/files/REVISEDWHITEPAPER04062013.pdf.

5 The Reconstruction and Development Programme (RDP). Accessed December 26, 2015. https://www.nelsonmandela.org/omalley/index.php/site/q/03lv02039/04lv02103/05lv02120/06lv02126.htm,

6 These were: Battswood Arts Centre in Grassy Park, Joseph Stone Auditorium in Athlone, Ulwazi Centre in Langa, Zolani Community Centre in Nyanga, Islamic School in Manenberg, and Lingelethu West Training Centre in Khayelitsha. Photographer Anele Ngoko was given access to a SANG computer and mentored to acquire skills.

7 Jane Taylor quoted in Marilyn Martin, "Director's Message," *bonani*, first quarter, 1996, 1.

8 Dolby, curator of prints and drawings, was appointed assistant director, while retaining responsibility for the collection; a middle management structure was put in place with heads of departments: Faeza Allie (administration), Emma Bedford (curatorial), Emile Maurice (education), Jon Weinberg (exhibitions and technical) and Patty Hardy (NLM). For a complete list of staff at this point – forty eight at the SANG and nine at the NLM – see *bonani*, January/February/March, 1996, 25. The review of job descriptions and salaries was facilitated by Tim Hodson and Sabrina Lane of FSA-Contact.

9 Minister Lionel Mtshali appointed me to the NAC, together with Prof. Elize Botha, Lisa Combrink, Vanessa Cooke, John Kani, David Koloane, Corinna Lowry, Zakhe Ngqobe, Christopher Seabrook, Bongani Thembe, Kiren Thathiah, Musa Xulu and nine provincial representatives in February 1997. The names were selected from a short list of eighteen that was drawn up by the selection panel chaired by Judge Albie Sachs; the panel interviewed thirty two candidates in November 1996. Koloane and Thathiah were also members of the SANG board of trustees at the time. BASA was to be government's principal private sector partner in the field of arts and culture; there were forty nine founder members and a Board was appointed.

10 The museums that were incorporated in Cape Town were funded by central government and the process did not involve either provincial or local museums. The major museums were: South African National Gallery, South African Museum, South African Cultural History Museum, Michaelis Collection, William Fehr Collection.

11 Marilyn Martin, "Director's Message," *bonani*, fourth quarter, 1998, 3. Note: from the fourth quarter in 1996 the date referred to the quarter and the months were no longer used.

12 Roger Jardine had requested the SANG to give him an indication as to whether the museum would fit its anticipated expenditure to meet the allocation and what measures would be taken to stay within the limits of the budget. An edited version of my letter was published in *bonani*, July/August/September, 1998, 3-4. In summary: it provided a history of the funding situation since 1988; a Deloitte and Touche investigation had revealed that the SANG should have received in excess of R5 million, while the 1998-99 allocation was R3,974,000, with salaries taking up 98% of the subsidy; we had raised R920,000.00 from the private sector and various agencies, not including the cost of exhibitions fully funded by foreign governments; the negative effects on acquisitions; the security and storage of the collection was at risk, even after we had installed closed-circuit television with the support of board member Pat Gorvalla.

13 Marilyn Martin, "Director's Message," *bonani*, third quarter, 1998, 2.

14 The press release was entitled "Challenges and opportunities on the arduous road to a democratic, accessible, equitable and affordable dispensation: the Ministry's response". For a summary see *bonani*, fourth quarter, 1998, 2-4.

15 John Sharp, "Magic and a mix of cultures," *Democracy in Action*, August 31, 1994, 12.

16 For example, R3 million was allocated for promoting South African arts internationally (without using the expertise in museums and other structures), while the country remained absent from major international biennials.

17 For more details about the situation, see Marilyn Martin, "Director's Message," *bonani*, March-April-May, 1999, 3-5.

18 At the time there were forty one staff members and two trainees at SANG.

19 Other members were: Prof. T. M. Crowe, Prof. Jeanette Deacon, Ms. M. M. Isaacs, Mr. R. J. Monaisa, Mr. M. M. Mtembu, Ms. Sheryl Ozinsky, Dr. Franklin Sonn, Dr. B. O. Tema, Ms. E. A. Voigt and Prof. B. Warner; Prof. Roy du Pré was appointed subsequently.

20 Mike Cluver (SAM) headed operations; Aron Mazel (SACHM) was in charge of collections and policy development; Paul Grobbelaar (William Fehr Collection) directed information; I was responsible for public programmes; and Hans Fransen (Michaelis Collection) contributed to all the different sections.

21 *bonani*, first quarter 2000, 3.

22 Other nineteenth-century works repatriated at this time included beadwork, a Tsonga horn staff (purchased in 1996 by the FONG and South African Breweries), a pair of Sotho-Tswana ceremonial ladles in wood, a staff shaped like a stylised spear (possibly Ndebele) and a Swazi headrest: Carol Kaufmann, "Report on status of holdings of Department of African Art as of January 1997," unpaginated.

23 The series of eight exhibitions highlighted South African artists who used new technology such as video monitors, projections and laser discs: Kendell Geers, Randolph Hartzenberg, William Kentridge, Malcolm Payne, Tracey Rose, Penny Siopis, Greg Streak and Clive van der Berg.

24 Kathy Grundlingh, ed., *Lines of Sight Perspectives on South African Photography* (Cape Town: South African National Gallery, 1999) and *bonani*, third quarter 1999, 6-7.

25 Katherine Goodnow, with Jack Lohman and Jatti Bredekamp, *Challenge and Transformation: Museums in Cape Town and Sydney* (Paris: UNESCO, 2006), 177.

26 Hayden Proud, ed., *George Milwa Mnyaluza Pemba: Retrospective* (Cape Town: South African National Gallery & Mayibuye Centre, 1996).

27 *District Six: Image and Representation* (Cape Town: South African National Gallery, 1995).

28 Pippa Skotnes, email to the author, March 14, 2018.

29 We had many discussions about this and I sought advice from Jatti Bredekamp, then UWC professor attached to the Institute for Historical Research; he agreed that we use the term San to refer to the artists of the rocks, and Khoisan when speaking generally of the two major groups of indigenous southern African people, the San and Khoi. In 2003 I worked on a project with a San descendent /Toui Stefaans Samcuia at the Cape Town International Convention Centre. I asked him whether he preferred San or Bushman; he replied that it was irrelevant, that he did not mind what he was called, as the San people do not refer to themselves in generic terms, but to the specific group to which they belong.

30 Pippa Skotnes, ed. *Miscast: Negotiating the Presence of the Bushmen* (Athens: Ohio University Press, 1998). The *Miscast* archive, both digital and document, includes the documentary material collected as well as made for the exhibition, is held at the Centre for Curating the Archive at UCT. Accessed January 19, 2017. http://www.cca.uct.ac.za/projects/miscast-archive/. See analyses of and comments on the diorama and exhibition in Steven C. Dubin, *Transforming Museums Mounting Queen Victoria in a Democratic South Africa* (New York, NY, Palgrave Macmillan, 2006), 61-75; 78; 103.

31 Pippa Skotnes, email to the author, March 14, 2018. The description of the different rooms is based on the author's essay:

Marilyn Martin, "The Miscast Exhibition at the South African National Gallery," in Jack Lohman and Katherine Goodnow, eds., *Human Remains & Museum Practice*. (Paris: UNESCO, 2006, 33-41).

32 Skotnes, ed. *Miscast*, 15.

33 The double dating suggested that historians are characters in their own narratives, so "... history only begins to exist when its details are interpreted, and these interpretations are necessarily political": Pippa Skotnes, "Civilised off the Face of the Earth: Museum Display and the Silencing of the /Xam," in *Poetics Today,* 22.2 (summer 2001), 314.

34 Martin, "The Miscast Exhibition," 36. The visitors' book constitutes an extensive and invaluable resource.

35 *Southern African Review of Books*, 44, July/August 1996. Accessed March 24, 2018. http://web.archive.org/web/20010725193003/www.uni-ulm.de/~rturrell/antho4html/Miscast.html and http://web.archive.org/web/20010731110321/http://www.uni-ulm.de:80/~rturrell/antho4html/Skotnes.html.

36 See, for example, Anthony Morphet, "Miscast review," *Pretexts: Studies in Writing and Culture,* 6 (1), 1997, 95-99.

37 Pippa Skotnes, email to the author, March 14, 2018.

38 Panellists were Paulus de Wet (representing the Nama of the Richtersveld on the Namibian border), Martin Engelbrecht (spokesperson for the Khoisan Representative Council), Lavona George (member of the SANG RDP Forum) and Mansell Upham (mandated legal representative of the Griqua National Conference).

39 Pippa Skotnes, email to the author, March 14, 2018.

40 Dubin, *Transforming*, 257.

41 Dubin, *Transforming*, 250.

42 The Khoikhoi woman Saartje (Sarah) Baartman, known as the "Hottentot Venus", was exhibited in freak shows in Europe and died in Paris. President Nelson Mandela requested that the French government return her remains for burial and eight years later, on March 6, 2002, her remains were repatriated and buried near Hankey in the Eastern Cape on August 9. Accessed January 11, 2015. http://www.sahistory.org.za/people/sara-saartjie-baartman#sthash.bHoiJukt.dpuf.

43 *Mail & Guardian*, May 30, 1997: 22. At the time Crawhall was head of the Southern African San Institute. He is currently the Director of Secretariat for the Indigenous Peoples of Africa Coordinating Committee (IPACC) based in Cape Town.

44 The week before three Khoisan men had walked for three weeks from Port Elizabeth to the Union Building in Pretoria to submit a memorandum to then Deputy President Cyril Ramaphosa (elected president of the ANC at the conference, and subsequently as South Africa's president). Their demands included: Recognition as full citizens of the country; their language to be made official; scrapping or amending of the Land Claims Act that held them back from owning land; to be referred to/categorised as either Khoisan or Bushmen and not as Coloured: Nkateko Mabasa, "#ANCdecides2017: Khoisan Liberation Movement protesters want to meet with new Top Six," *Daily Maverick*, December 18, 2017. Accessed December 18, 2017. http://firstthing.dailymaverick.co.za/article.php?id=98434&cid=2017-12-18#.Wrl2gbiddh9. Their efforts were in vain and a year later the Khoisan 6 set up camp outside the Union Buildings; in February 2019 they were still there: Sakhile Ndlazi, "Khoisan want to be heard, demand land," *Cape Times*, February 5, 2019. Accessed February 6, 2019. https://www.pressreader.com/.

45 The exhibition travelled to the Standard Bank National Arts Festival and Standard Bank Gallery. The department donated the archive to the SANG in 2000.

46 President Mandela's full address is available online. Accessed January 20, 2015. http://www.sahistory.org.za/archive/address-president-mandela-heritage-day-robben-island-24-september-1997.

47 Patricia Davison, email to the author, April 13, 2016. Davison had been working with the ethnographic collections at the SAM from 1971 (first as assistant ethnographer to Margaret Shaw); after the amalgamation of the museums she was appointed director of social history collections and subsequently as director of core functions at Iziko Museums. Davison has a longstanding and continuing interest in the interface between art and artefact.

48 Dubin, Transforming, 75-76.

49 See J. Viall, "Pipes of peace lit as SA salutes San forerunners," *Argus*, April 25, 2004.

50 Elizabeth Dell, ed., *Evocations of the Child: Fertility Figures of the Southern African Region* (London: Lund Humphries, 1999).

51 David Bunn, "Open Letter," *bonani*, first quarter, 1999, 18-20.

52 For an extract of Dubow's speech, see *bonani*, third quarter 1998, 9.

53 Kathy Grundlingh, ed., *Photosynthesis: Contemporary South African Photography* (Cape Town: South African National Gallery, 1997).

54 Okwui Enwezor, ed., *Trade routes: History and geography: 2nd Johannesburg Biennale 1997* (Johannesburg: Africus Institute of Contemporary Art, 1997).

55 Colin Richards, "Curating Contradiction *Graft* in the 2nd Johannesburg Biennale," in Hans Belting and Andrea Buddensieg, eds., *The Global Art World Audiences, Markets, and Museums* (Ostfildern: Hatje Cantz Verlag, 2009), 334.

56 I am grateful to Bongi Dhlomo-Mautloa and Christopher Till for providing this information telephonically.

57 *Art against Apartheid*. Accessed December 30, 2015. http://www.chrflagship.uwc.ac.za/collections/art-against-apartheid-collection/. Parliament paid SANG for the work.

58 In 2010 independent curator Carol Brown selected twenty-nine works for a touring exhibition, *Home and Away.*

59 Letter from Steven Sack, then director: cultural development at DACST to the author, December 14, 1999.

60 For Arnold's full address, see *bonani*, third quarter 1998, 5-7.

61 Funders were The Terrence Higgins Trust, Levi Strauss & Company, The British Council, Old Mutual and the AIDS Foundation of South Africa.

62 In 1996 I was honoured as Wola Nani "Person of the Year." The citation read: "In recognition of her commitment and immeasurable support to Wola Nani and the community of people living with AIDS. Her unstinting efforts have contributed greatly towards the empowerment of many persons living with HIV and AIDS. A valued participant in this county's new struggle." I joined the Wola Nani board in a volunteer capacity in 2009 and currently serve as board chairperson.

63 Anon. *Art africaine dans la collection Pierre Guerre/African art in the Pierre Guerre collection* (Paris: AFAA, 1997). The exhibition was seen by 18,085 visitors and 1,415 learners who attended thirty five school tours.

64 Erna Beumers, ed., *Africa meets Africa: the African collection of the Museum of Ethnology Rotterdam* (Rotterdam: Museum of Ethnology, 1996). The exhibition was sponsored by the Museum voor Volkenkunde, the City of Rotterdam, the government of the Netherlands, the South African Embassy in the Netherlands, the Mondriaan Foundation, Dräger, Mercedes-Benz, Standard Bank and Vodacom.

65 David Goldblatt, *South Africa The Structure of Things Then* (Cape Town: Oxford University Press, 1998).

66 See Paul Edmunds' review "Isintu - Ceremony, Identity and Community," *Artthrob*, April 1999. Accessed January 23, 2017. http://artthrob.co.za/99apr/listings.htm.

67 My participation was made possible by the Centre for Science Development and The Anglo American and De Beers Chairman's Fund. See my report in *bonani*, January/February/March 1995, 20-23. Thomas Krens is currently the Guggenheim's Senior Advisor for International Affairs, overseeing the completion of the Frank Gehry-designed Guggenheim Abu Dhabi.

68 The project subsequently expanded to include the Caribbean. Accessed August 19, 2017. http://www.institutfrancais.com/en/creation-africa-and-caribbean.

69 For a report on the project, see *bonani*, April/May/June, 1995, 18-21.

70 Santu Mofokeng, *The Black Photo Album, Look at Me: 1890-1950* (Göttingen: Steidl Verlag, 2013) and *bonani*, January/February/March, 1996, 22-23; *bonani*, first quarter 1997, 6.

71 For reports on Bedford's trips and engagements with Sweden, see *bonani*, October/November/December, 1997, 17-19; *bonani*, April/May/June, 1998, 8; *bonani,* January/February/March, 1999, 22-23. *Transpositions* was curated by Bedford and Åsa Nacking, guest curator at the Modern Museum in Stockholm; it was presented under the auspices of Modern Museum International Programme, with additional funding from the Swedish Institute and the International Artists' Studio Programme in Sweden, Teljoy Television Services, Ericsson South Africa and FONG. See *Transpositions: Five Swedish Artists in South Africa, 28 March-10 May, 1998* (Cape Town: South African National Gallery, 1998).

72 See Bedford's report in *bonani*, October/November/December 1995, 20-23.

73 For Zehnder's report see *bonani*, first quarter, 1998, 15, and Weinberg's in the same issue, 16-17.

74 I had encountered António Ole's work at the Johannesburg Biennale; I selected the Maputo artists during a visit and in consultation with artists; unfamiliar with Mauritian artists, I consulted with Jean Loup Pivin, editor of *Revue Noire*. See *Container 96 Art Across Oceans* (Copenhagen: Kulturby 96, 1996) and my report in *bonani*, January/February/March, 1996, 19-23.

75 For more on the exhibition and restoration see *bonani*, second quarter, 1997, 4-5; and *bonani*, fourth quarter, 7. The Rowland and Leta Hill Trust made possible the purchase of *The Palace on the Sea*.

76 Angela Zehnder, email to the author, January 9, 2017. Anna Tietze, *The Alfred de Pass Presentation to the South African National Gallery* (Cape Town: South African National Gallery, 1995) and Hayden Proud and Anna Tietze, *The Sir Edmund and Lady Davis Presentation: A Gift of British Art to South Africa* (Cape Town: South African National Gallery, 1999).

77 Participants included Minister Lionel Mtshali, Wally Serote, Thami Ngwevela, Imbongi Zolani Mkiva, artist Zwelethu Mthethwa, board members Kiren Thathiah and Bongi Dhlomo-Mautloa, artist Anele Ngoko and other members of the SANG RDP Forum.

78 "Heritage Choices," *bonani*, second quarter, 1997, 2.

79 Many works are documented and reproduced in two major publications, so there is no need to list individual acquisitions: Bedford, *Contemporary South African Art* (the catalogue was also available on the internet at http://www.gem.co.za/sang, thanks to sponsorship by GEM); Emma Bedford, ed., *A Decade of Democracy South African Art 1994-2004 From the Permanent Collection of Iziko: South African National Gallery* (Cape Town: Double Storey and Iziko Museums of Cape Town, 2004).

80 Jacqueline Nolte, "Contemporary South African Art," *Third Text* 11:39 (1997): 95-103.

81 This was on the website http://www.museums.org.za/sang/SA_art/ that no longer exists.

82 Dubow remained involved in what was happening at the SANG until his death in August 2008: in March of that year he gave a lecture to the FONG entitled "In the Field of memory: The Berlin Holocaust Memorial"; he and Rhona Dubow kindly loaned a watercolour for the exhibition *Albert Adams: Journey on a Tightrope*. His collage of 1979, *Portrait of an egg-head contemplating*

the Future, was used on the invitation for the Pancho Guedes exhibition, *Pancho Guedes – an Alternative Modernist and Works after 25th April 1974*, which Dubow opened on 22 May, with characteristic flair, brilliance and wit, three months before his death.

83 Bedford, *Contemporary*, 27-37.

84 Bedford, *Contemporary*, 34.

85 Marilyn Martin, "Introduction," in Bedford, *Contemporary*, 18.

86 One example will suffice: *bonani*, January/February/March, 1997, 0-1. Special thanks went to Sappi (for sponsoring *bonani)*, De Beers, Kodak, Nedbank, South African Breweries, Standard Bank, Supreme Larson-Juhl; the Embassy of Denmark, the Consulate General of the Federal Republic of Germany, the Swiss Agency for Development and Co-operation, ICCROM, GEM; the many contributors to *Miscast*, including DACST.

87 For the history of the artist and the painting see *bonani*, first quarter, 1999, 8 and Ronald Harrison, *The Black Christ: A Journey to Freedom* (Cape Town: New Africa Books, 2006).

88 Hayden Proud, ed., *Scratches on the Face Antiquity and contemporaneity in South African works of art from Iziko Museums of Cape Town* (New Delhi and Cape Town: Iziko Museums, 2008), 61.

89 In addition to the important exhibitions received from abroad and the presentations/purchases listed in the text, there was local sponsorship for the Davis Presentation catalogue from Sotheby's; the Rowland and Leta Hill Trust paid for the restoration of the Liberman doors and carved panels in the building; Sanlam sponsored the Harry Trevor exhibition at the NLM; Scan Shop cut printing costs of publications; Herdbuoys McCann-Erickson provided design-input; thanks to Peter Dennis, MWeb linked the SANG into http://www.mweb.co.zactonline/museums; Zonnebloem Wines spearheaded the "Save the SANG" fundraising drive that raised R81,500.00; Rose Korber gave a percentage of her annual Salon sales, R30 000.00. This assisted with exhibitions, as well as maintaining journal subscriptions and buying books. Parking spaces were let, and the main building, Annexe and NLM made available for venue hire for special functions; a donations box was placed at the entrance.

90 Bongi Bengu, email to the author, March 31, 2017.

91 Letter from the author to Mandie van der Spuy, then manager: art sponsorships at Standard Bank, thanking her for "making a sound investment in this young man", May 3, 1999. We created the position of assistant curator, so that inexperienced appointees would not immediately be on the same level as curators who had many years of service behind them. Unfortunately things did not work out with Mtshiza in the long term, there were disciplinary procedures against him and he left Iziko. His training, however, stood him in good stead as curator of exhibitions at Museum Africa.

92 Liesl Hartman, email to the author, February 28, 2018.

93 Ibid.

94 See their full report in *bonani*, third quarter, 1997, 18-20. For the list of artists who participated, see *bonani*, second quarter, 1997, 6-7.

95 Hartman went on to excel in the field of education in different positions, for example as principal of the Frank Joubert Art Centre from 2009. In 2018 she was appointed as director/head of the education centre at Zeitz MOCAA.

96 For more information see *bonani*, fourth quarter, 1999, 21-22 and *bonani*, first quarter 2000, 22.

97 For more on our experiences see Kim Siebert, "How to be "street-wise" in Accra," and Marilyn Martin "A week in Accra," *bonani*, April-May-June 1996, 20 and 21-23 respectively.

98 *Bonani*, first quarter, 2000, 7. In a spirit of inter-disciplinary co-operation Kaufmann launched "The Bead Society of Southern Africa" in 1999.

99 Carol Kaufmann, email to the author, February 12, 2016.

100 Zehnder joined SANG in 1996 and remained in a full-time position until 2003 when she elected to go part-time. Considering her expertise and experience, the SANG could not pay her an adequate salary and she decided to undertake part-time contracts; she has been on a part-time contract with Iziko Museums since 2005, so the SANG continues to benefit from her presence. Zehnder recalled her highlights during the period under review in an email to the author on January 9, 2017: X-rays of Charles Shannon's *The Morning Toilet* and conservation of James Ford's *Holiday Time in Cape Town in the Twentieth Century*; attending an international symposium on the conservation of modern art in Amsterdam in 1997.

101 The project was funded by Dr. Mark Voloshin, director of the Marvol Group. The posters were displayed in 1999; see *bonani*, fourth quarter, 1999.

102 Other works purchased from the insurance money: two ink on paper drawings by Dumile Feni, *Whisper slight* (1970) and *Untitled* (1985); Simon Lekgetho's painting *Portrait of a Young Boy* (1958); Kathryn Smith's *Ennui 1:2 (after Sickert)* (2004), pigment print on cotton paper: Iziko Museums *Annual Report*, 2004-2005, 63.

103 Marilyn Martin, "The Horn of Art's Dilemma," *Leadership* 18 no. 1 (1999): 44-56.

104 Martin, "The Horn," 56.

105 For his analysis, see Mike van Graan, "To have a Department of Arts and Culture or not," *Artslink*, May 1, 1999. Accessed February 13, 2017. http://www.artlink.co.za/news_article.htm?contentID=10055. Van Graan was also targeted. He served as

special adviser on arts and culture to Ngubane (1994-1996) and produced and distributed *The Cultural Weapon*, a monthly publication monitoring the development of the post-apartheid arts and culture dispensation (1997-1998) under the auspices of "Article 27", which he founded. The principal sponsor was the Royal Netherlands Embassy but soon Van Graan's incisive criticism of DACST incurred Jardine's displeasure and the funder asked for their logo to be removed from the magazine. Van Graan was given to understand that Jardine had intervened, suggesting that it was inappropriate for a foreign government to fund a publication critical of government. Van Graan called it a day and issued a press release stating that this was "completely out of line and against the principles of democracy. To save themselves the embarrassment of having to account for their actions, they are happy to deprive the public of an invaluable resource. It is the kind of bureaucratic meddling which fills one with foreboding": "Cultural Weapon too sharp," *Artthrob* News. Accessed February 13, 2017. http://artthrob.co.za/july/news.htm#weapon.

106 I once again called on John MacRobert for legal advice, and he in turn involved advocate Alec Freund. This time they provided advice pro bono. A deputation from DACST met with us and tried to persuade me to step down from the NAC voluntarily; I refused.

107 I refer to my letter to Ngubane in my letter to Pallo Jordan, September 16, 2004; letter from the author to Jordan, November 18, 2004. Writer and NAC chairperson Gomolemo Mokae was indisposed and the deputy chair, advocate Mark Gordon, was in charge.

108 For details on the reasons for the demise of the board, who exactly resigned, who refused to resign and the ensuing legal action, see Mike van Graan, "The NAC: where to now?," *Artslink*, December 21, 2004. The court procedures went on for a long time and some years later I was called as a witness for DACST and against Gordon.

CHAPTER 6 – Museum amalgamation and the making of Iziko Museums of South Africa

1 Judge Edwin Cameron quoted in Marilyn Martin, "HIV/AIDS in South Africa: Can the Visual Arts Make a Difference?," in *AIDS and South Africa The Social Expression of A Pandemic*, eds. Kyle Kauffman and David Lindauer (Houndmills, Basingstoke: Palgrave Macmillan Lts, 2004), 125-126.

2 *Zanazo means* "give us the news, you who always know first"; there was a charge of R5,00 per quarter and a subscription form was included: *Zanazo* 1, April/May/June 2000. The first issue contained short articles by Medée Rall, "Museums in the Making" that told the story of SAM, 4-5 and Marilyn Martin, "The Making of a Flagship Institution," 6-7. The newsletter was described as "Cape Town's only trilingual magazine devoted to museums", *Zanazo* 2, July/August/September 2000, 2. *Bonani* had been trilingual, but everything was not translated – the languages were rotated; in *Zanazo* every article and entry was translated, which was overkill and not sustainable. There would be only one more issue of the newsletter, *Zanazo* 2, January/February/March 2001, after which it was replaced by the unilingual *What's on at Iziko* that contains lists of exhibitions, activities and events only.

3 In August 1999 Mike Cluver, director of SAM, took over from Colin Jones as acting CEO and Jones became chairperson, effective until the appointment of a CEO. Jack Lohman occupied the position until August 2002, when he left for the United Kingdom to become the director of the Museum of London. Lohman was educated at the University of East Anglia where he studied History of Art. He read architecture at the Freien Universität in Berlin and later obtained an MA at the University of Manchester. He won a British Council Fellowship Award to study architecture and conservation in Warsaw, Poland. He has received honorary doctorates from the Universities of Westminster, London (PUNO) and East Anglia: "Staff Profiles," *Royal BC Museum*, http://royalbcmuseum.bc.ca/staffprofiles/author/jacklohman/ (accessed December 25, 2015).

4 Jack Lohman, "Reinventing our Museums," in *Zanazo*, July/August/September 2000, 2.

5 Jack Lohman, email to the author, May 5, 2017.

6 Situating the institution firmly in Cape Town (in the vain hope of securing greater interest from the City authorities) would in time detract from its national status and the name was subsequently changed to Iziko Museums of South Africa.

7 The "directing team" comprised directors of art, natural history and social history collections; education and public programmes, human resources, central services and property services. There were more than 200 staff members in the amalgamated museums, but this figure would diminish as straitened financial circumstances worsened and posts were either left vacant for a period of time to save money, or not filled, leading to staff shortages. The government grant was R27,823,000 for the 2002-2003 fiscal year, total income R38,329,111 and staff expenditure R27,690,644. For details see Iziko *Annual Report* 2002-2003, 49-52.

8 There would be no career path for curators related to further qualifications, length of service and performance as in the past.

9 Jack Lohman, email to the author, May 5, 2017.

10 Ibid.

11 Jack Lohman, *Museums at the Crossroads?* (Victoria, Canada: Royal BC Museum, 2013), 9-10.

12 Patricia Davison, “Typecast: Representations of the Bushmen at the South African Museum,” *Public Archaeology* 1 (2001), 3. After another restructuring at Iziko Davison was appointed executive director of core functions.
13 Davison, “Typecast,” 3.
14 Pippa Skotnes, “Unmaking the San,” *Mail & Guardian*, April 6-12, 2001.
15 I am grateful to the insights provided by Patricia Davison, email to the author, April 15, 2016. For more on the Bleek and Lloyd archive, see: “The Digital Bleek and Lloyd,” *University of Cape Town*, http://lloydbleekcollection.cs.uct.ac.za/ (accessed September 20, 2017).
16 Patricia Davison, email to the author, April 15, 2016.
17 Patricia Davison made the description of the event, “Curating the colonial crime scene: between archive, archaeology and art,” available to the author in an email, September 18, 2017. According to a press statement, Iziko staff was consulting with a number of groups in planning a new exhibition that would focus on Africa and its people, as well as environmental, cultural and social issues. In 2018 the 2003 rock art gallery remains unchanged.
18 Vanessa September, email to the author, February 14, 2017.
19 These priorities were: the Iziko Social History Centre facility for the housing of the reserve collections and archives, completed in May 2010 and the “courtyard project” that consists of seven storeys within the courtyard of SAM; by 2019 this was not yet complete and it was taking longer than the two new art museums in Cape Town, Zeitz MOCAA and the Norval Foundation. While the Social History Centre (including the library) no doubt welcomes researchers, there are no visitors figures recorded in the *Annual Reports*.
20 Hayden Proud, “Our National Gallery: The ‘Book’ of our Art?,” 41, *Helen Suzman Foundation*, http://hsf.org.za/resource-centre/focus/focus-61/Hayden%20Proud_Our%20National%20Gallery.pdf (accessed March 16, 2016).
21 Hayden Proud, email to the author, April 4, 2017.
22 Jack Lohman, email to the author, May 1, 2017. From 2001 till September 2007 Wakashe was the deputy director-general for heritage, archives and libraries – responsible for the development of policy, strategic planning and oversight on legacy projects. In 2017, as CEO of the Film and Publication Board, he faced 279 allegations of misconduct; the matter was settled out of court. See: Charl Blignaut, “I was sacked cos I’m gay,” *Channel 24*, August 27, 2017, http://www.channel24.co.za/The-Juice/News/i-was-sacked-cos-im-gay-20170826 (accessed September 4, 2017).
23 Christopher Till, telephone interview with the author, April 20, 2017. According to Till, JAG received a gift of R6 million from Anglo American Corporation in 1984, two years before the city’s centenary celebrations: R1.7 million towards the extensions to and restoration of the building; an endowment fund of R4 million for purchases; the balance was spent on the centenary sculpture competition. In 2017 the endowment stood at R8 million.
24 Iziko *Annual Report*, 2002-2003, 34.
25 Jack Lohman, email to the author, May 1, 2017.
26 The proposal comprised two sections: “A high level approach to the development of the Michaelis Collection foyer” and “Proposed agreement between Iziko Museums of Cape Town and Phillips Auctioneers & Valuers”. I would like to express my appreciation to the Iziko CEO, Rooksana Omar, for her support in this research, and to her PA, Annelize Kotze, for locating the relevant documents.
27 Lynn Rowand, letter to Jatti Bredekamp, January 24, 2003; Georgina Lawrence, letter to Jatti Bredekamp, January 27, 2003.
28 Rowand mentioned Iziko museums and “warehouses” (I assume that she was referring to Iziko storage areas) and recommended that Bredekamp speak to “either the Rev. Colin Jones or Mr Vusi Nduna [sic, Ndima] who are fully aware of all the goings on up to the present date”.
29 In August 2002 DACST was divided into two new branches of government: Department of Arts and Culture (DAC) and Department of Science and Technology (DST).
30 Marilyn Martin, email to Jatti Bredekamp, February 18, 2003.
31 Iziko Board Minutes, February 20 & 21, 2003, 13.
32 The following criteria are contained in the SANG collections policy that was revised in 2004 and 2007:
- A lost or stolen object.
- An object that has deteriorated beyond any meaningful museum use or is damaged to a point where restoration is impossible.
- An object that no longer serves a useful purpose in the collection and that may be desired by another public institution or private collection.
- The closure of a museum that involves the return of an object or a collection to the donor in terms of a pre-existing agreement.

Examples of works that were deaccessioned were listed in a memorandum, dated April 9, 2008, that I prepared for council’s ratification:
- Unknown artist: *Portrait of Mr G. Moni* (undated), oil on canvas, presented by Mrs. Tosca Reynolds. In her will she left R100,000 for the conservation of the work; her niece, Patricia Gregory, requested that the painting be returned to the family.

The work had been conserved, the funds (far in excess of what is required for conserving one work) had been spent on acquisitions, and it was deemed appropriate to return the portrait to the family.

- Dumile Feni: five maquettes *Untitled* (undated): these were purchased with a grant from DACST in 2000. Made of plaster of Paris, they were deteriorating and an approach from Marriam Diale and Moeletsi Mbeki of the Dumile Feni Foundation Trust to have them cast in bronze was favourably considered. This did not materialise.
- Diana Hulton (exhibited under the name of Diana Kenton from 1973-1991): There were three paintings, oil on canvas, by Hulton on the 1991 Cape Town Triennial exhibition: *Mountain III* (1985) was acquired; *Mountain XI* (1985) and *Mountain XII* (1991) remained behind and were accessioned in error. They were deaccessioned and the artist donated the two works to the Constitutional Court.

33 Cultural Institutions Act, no. 119 of 1998, G*overnment Gazette*, December 4, 1998, http://www.dac.gov.za/sites/default/files/Legislations%20Files/act119_98.pdf (accessed August 26, 2017).

34 Jatti Bredekamp, letter to Lynn Rowand, March 6, 2003.

35 Jatti Bredekamp, letter to Ben Ngubane, March 6, 2003.

36 Jatti Bredekamp, letter to Ben Ngubane, June 16, 2003.

37 Lohman, *Museums*, 9.

38 Ibid., 10.

39 The short-listed applicants were: Jatti Bredekamp, June Bam, Y. Seleti and M. van Embden: Iziko Board Minutes, August 23, 2002, 2.

40 Iziko Museums *Annual Report*, 2002-2003, unpaginated. Jatti Bredekamp holds master's degrees in History from the Wesleyan University in Connecticut, USA (obtained as a Fulbright scholar) and UWC. He rose through the ranks at UWC's Institute for Historical Research, becoming the director in 1995. He has travelled extensively and published on topical historical issues, in particular on Khoisan revivalism and Khoikhoi identity. See: "Henry Charles (Jatti) Bredekamp," *On Set Productions*, November 2010, http://www.onsetproductions.co.za/english/OnSetProductions/Biographies/HenryBredekamp_Biography.htm (accessed August 12, 2017). Bredekamp did not respond to my request for the highlights and challenges of his time at Iziko.

41 I have relied on the information that I compiled for the *Annual Reports* for details about all SANG activities during the period under review.

42 Marilyn Martin, "The horn of the national art museum's dilemma," in *A Decade*, 60. Allocations to Freedom Park were as follows at that time: R50-million for the 2002-03 financial year, R100-million for 2003-04, R200-million in 2004-05 and R212-million in 2005-06. The subsidy for Iziko Museums, comprising fifteen sites, was R30,163,000 for the 200-04 financial year. Mike van Graan provided a detailed analysis of the 2003-04 DAC budget in "The Cultural Weapon", which was distributed electronically on *Artwatch South Africa*, March 21, 2003.

43 Martin, "The horn," 62.The details of these activities can be found in catalogue essays listed in the references and bibliography and in *Annual Reports*.

44 Ibid., 64.

45 Ibid., 58-59. For information on which works were donated or purchased from which allocations, see Bedford, "A Decade," 142-149 and Iziko *Annual Reports* 2002-2003, unpaginated; 2003-2004, xiii-xiv; 2004-2005, 61-64; 2005-2006, 84-85; 2006-2007, 70-71; 2007-2008, 76-78; 2008-2009, 98-91.

46 Iziko *Annual Report*, 2004-2005, 64.

47 For more on the auction and the acquisition see Andrew Lamprecht, *BRUCE GORDON: An Artwork by Ed Young* (Cape Town: South African National Gallery, 2003); Ivor Powell, "Ed Young: Bruce Gordon," *Art South Africa* 1, no. 4 (Ivor Powell, "Ed Young: Bruce Gordon," *Art South Africa* 1, no. 4 (2003): 62-63; and Paul Edmonds, "Bruce Gordon at the SANG," *Artthrob*, archive issue no. 68, April 2003, http://artthrob.co.za/03apr/reviews/sang.html (accessed March 1, 2017).

48 The adjudication panel comprised Andrew Lamprecht, Iain Low, Mokena Makeka, Michelle Robertson-Swift and SANG staff.

49 Exciting and innovative as the solutions were, three of them presented problems: Hindley's technology – the microphones, transmitters, software and outdoor LED display did not work as envisaged, it was expensive to maintain and was inactive for many years, to be restored only in 2019. The materials O'Donovan and his assistants used did not withstand the elements and the sculpture was subsequently reconfigured; in 2008 the artist agreed to replace the three-dimensional figures with two-dimensional ones in galvanised painted steel. Roger van Wyk's design was also intended to invite direct engagement from adults and children with a labyrinth and games, but the different colour bricks were not available and the process complicated; however, what he managed to do made a huge difference to the area in front of the gallery. We were grateful for our partnership with the Institute of Landscape Architects, represented by Michelle Robertson-Swift, for providing advice and the three ginkgo biloba trees for rosenclaire's *Soap Boxes*. This work has stood the test of time, except that its integrity was destroyed in 2009 when the plasma screen, which had been donated by Philips, was removed from the entrance room and not installed elsewhere. This is discussed in chapter eight.

50 Liese van der Watt, "Fresh: Seven artists' monographs," *Art South Africa* 2, no. 1 (2003): 61. Each monograph, with paper sponsored by Sappi, was published individually and boxed as a collection.

51 Two brochures accompanied the exhibition: Carol Kaufmann, *Musuku: Golden Links to our Past* (Cape Town: South African National Gallery, 2000) and an education brochure, *Musuku Golden Links with our Past*, produced by the Archaeological Resource Development Project, Wits in association with SANG and sponsored by De Beers.

52 The exhibition ran from 27 October 2016 to 26 February 2017. See Mark Brown, "South Africa's golden rhino to star in British Museum exhibition," *The Guardian*, August 7, 2016, https://www.theguardian.com/world/2016/aug/07/british-museum-south-africa-host-800-year-old-treasure (accessed September 20, 2016).

53 David Brokensha, Review, "Musuku: Golden Links with Our Past," *African Arts* 34, no. 1 (2001): 87.

54 Peter Rich Architects won the World Building of the Year Award for the Mapungubwe Interpretation Centre in 2009: Marcus Fairs, "Mapungubwe Interpretation Centre by Peter Rich Architects," *Dezeen*, November 7, 2009, https://www.dezeen.com/2009/11/07/mapungubwe-interpretation-centre-by-peter-rich-architects/ (accessed March 20, 2017). Once the Javett Art Centre at UP, discussed in chapter eleven, is completed in 2019, it will house elements of the Mapungubwe collection.

55 *Zanazo*, January/February/March 2001, 13. For more on the exhibition see Nicolaas Vergunst, *Hoerikwaggo: Images of Table Mountain* (Cape Town: South African National Gallery, 2000).

56 Hayden Proud, ed., *Revisions Expanding the Narrative of South African Art The Campbell Smith Collection* (Pretoria: South African History Online and UNISA Press, 2006). Also see Hayden Proud, *Revisions+ expanding the narrative of South African Art* (Stellenbosch: SMAC Gallery, 2008).

57 Emma Bedford, ed., *Marlene Dumas: Intimate Relations* (Amsterdam/Johannesburg: Roma Publications/Jacana Media, 2007). The catalogue includes essays by Bedford, Achille Mbembe, Sarah Nuttall, Marlene van Niekerk and Dumas' own writings. Other sponsors were the Mondriaan Foundation, the Embassy of The Netherlands and KLM.

58 The nominees were: Archilab, Thorsten Deckler, Heather Dodd, Andrew Horn, Ndabo Langa, Henning Rasmuss, Chris Wilkinson and Heinrich Wolff. See: Renate Wiehager, ed., *The Nominees* (Pretoria: Daimler-Chrysler South Africa, 2007), and Renate Wiehager, ed., *Heinrich Wolff* (Cologne: Seippel Verlag for Daimler-Chrysler, 2007). The exhibition travelled to DAG, Wits Art Galleries, DaimlerChrysler Contemporary in Berlin and the University of Bayreuth.

59 Joe Dolby, *Gerard Sekoto: From the Paris Studio* (Cape Town: Iziko South African National Gallery, 2005).

60 Marilyn Martin, email to Charles O'Brien, August 10, 2003; there was a balance of R130,000.

61 Hans Fransen was the driving force behind the establishment of the Michaelis Collection Friends and served the organisation for many years after his retirement. At the time of the amalgamation, the FONG chairperson was Margie Sedgwick and that of the MC Friends Wouter van Warmelo.

62 Michael Godby, *Is there Still Life? Continuity and Change in South African Still Life Painting* (Cape Town: Iziko South African National Gallery, 2007).

63 For Lamprecht's full curatotorial statement see "Flip," *Codart*, https://www.codart.nl/guide/exhibitions/flip/ (accessed March 6, 2017).

64 The substantial amount of money that was required for what was to date SANG's most ambitious and expensive project, was raised from the NLB, the Prince Claus Fund, the Goodman Gallery, the South African Jewish Museum, the NAC and supporters in kind: the Jupiter Drawing Room designed the invitations, posters and an advertisement for television, and secured airtime on KykNET and MNet.

65 Georg Bazelitz, Miklos Szalay and Peter Nebel, eds., *African Art from the Han Coray Collection, 1916-1928* (Zurich: Volkerkundemuseum, University of Zurich, 1998).

66 Carol Kaufmann, *Iintsimbi: beadwork from South Africa* (Cape Town: Iziko South African National Gallery, 2005).

67 Ariane Grigoteit, *A Century of Landscapes* (Frankfurt am Main: Deutsche Bank AG, 2002).

68 I had met Murphy when working *on Container 96 Art Across Oceans* in Copenhagen in 1996 and we began discussions about an exchange between our museums and artists. Funded by Culture Ireland, the exhibition was subsequently hosted by the Éigse Carlow Arts Festival: "Singing the Real," *Royal Hibernian Academy*, http://www.rhagallery.ie/exhibitions/singing-the-real/ (accessed March 4, 2017).

69 Mendel quoted in Martin, "HIV/AIDS in South Africa," 124.

70 Cameron quoted in Ibid., 125-126.

71 The group of advisors comprised artist and curator Bongi Dhlomo-Matloa, Goodman Gallery director Linda Givon and NAC CEO Doreen Nteta. The countries were Botswana, Lesotho, Namibia, South Africa and Swaziland and some of South Africa's foremost artists participated: Jane Alexander, Willie Bester, Norman Catherine, David Goldblatt, Lallitha Jawahirilal, Kagiso Pat Mautloa, Velaphi Mzimba, 'Wonderboy' Thokozani Nxumalo, Zwelethu Mthethwa, Karel Nel, Berni Searle, Durant Sihlali, Johannes Segogela, Penny Siopis, Clive and den Berg, Hentie van der Merwe and Sue Williamson. See: *Artworks for AIDS* (Cambridge MA: Harvard AIDS Institute and Bristol-Myers Squibb Company, 2000).

72 For more on the conference, collaboration and exhibitions see Kauffman and Lindauer, *AIDS and South Africa*; Kyle D. Kauffman and Marilyn Martin, *AidsArt / South Africa* (Cape Town: Iziko Museums & Wellesley College, 2003); and Marilyn Martin, "Curating HIV/AIDS at the Iziko South African National Gallery," *Kiosk* 1 (2007/08): 57-63 & 73-80.

73 Pieter-Dirk Uys, "Foreword," in *AidsArt*, 4. In addition to some of the artists commissioned by BMS, the following participated: Andries Botha, Lien Botha, Senzeni Marasela, Jacki McInnes, Sam Nhlengethwa and Jonathan Shapiro (Zapiro).

74 Jonathan Morgan and Bambanani Women's Group, *Long Life: Positive HIV Stories* (Cape Town: Double Storey-Juta, 2003). For more on the origins and history of the project see "Visual Body Maps and 'Mapping Our Lives'", *Centre for Social Science*, UCT, http://www.cssr.uct.ac.za/asru/outreach/visualbodymaps (accessed March 25, 2017).

75 Works by David Goldblatt, Penny Siopis and Sue Williamson were created and acquired through the BMS and Wellesley College commissions; others were purchased from the DAC transformation funds: Kim Berman, David Goldblatt, Churchill Madikida, Santu Mofokeng, Berni Searle, Clive van den Berg, Diane Victor, a selection of ten cartoons by Zapiro, and a portfolio of prints compiled and produced by Art for Humanity in Durban. When I retired in 2008 there were 150 individual images by forty-four artists in the collection. In 2007 Pieter Hugo donated four Lambda photographic prints, *The Bereaved*, the most challenging and difficult, as they depict individuals who had died of Aids, in their coffins.

76 For more on the exhibition see Pam Warne, "Reality check – Realitätsprüfung," in *Zeitgenössische Fotokunst Aus Südafrika* (Berlin: Neuer Berliner Kunstverein, 2007).

77 The motto *!ke e: lxarra llke* translates as "Diverse People Unite" in |Xam.

78 Miklos Szalay, ed., *The Moon As Shoe/Der Mond als Schuh*. (Zurich: Scheidegger & Spiess, 2002).

79 Hella Rabbethge-Schiller, *Memory and Magic: Contemporary Art of the !Xun & Khwe* (Johannesburg: Jacana Media, 2006).

CHAPTER 7 – Negotiating our place in the world – as equals – and celebrating ten years of democracy

1 Clive Kellner, "Preface" in *Africa Remix: Contemporary Art of a Continent*, ed. Simon Njami (Johannesburg: Jacana Media, 2007), 9.

2 Sean O'Toole, "The Vagaries of Transformation: The Case of the JAG," *Artthrob* archive no. 65, January 2003, http://artthrob.co.za/03jan/news/keene.html (accessed October 22, 2015).

3 Matthew Partridge, "Photography: The Rise and Fall of Apartheid," *Financial Mail*, February 20, 2014, http://www.financialmail.co.za/life/2014/02/20/photography-the-rise-and-fall-of-apartheid (accessed October 30, 2015); also see Matthew Partridge, "Weird scenes inside 'The Rise and Fall of Apartheid,'" *Daily Maverick*, February 12, 2014, http://www.dailymaverick.co.za/opinionista/2014-02-12-weird-scenes-inside-the-rise-and-fall-of-apartheid/#.VjnkPW4098E (accessed October 30, 2015).

4 This text is drawn from Marilyn Martin, "All encounters produce change Africa, Picasso and beyond," in *Picasso and Africa*, eds. Laurence Madeline and Marilyn Martin (Cape Town: Bell Roberts Publishing, 2006).

5 Kellner, *Africa Remix*, 9.

6 Emma Bedford, ed., *Tremor: Contemporary Art from South Africa* (Charleroi: Centre d'Art Contemporain and Iziko Museums, 2004).

7 Mtshiza was a curatorial intern funded by Standard Bank (1998-2000); on completion of his internship, he was appointed assistant curator, first on contract and then indefinite in 2001; unfortunately we had to institute disciplinary procedures against him, he left SANG and subsequently took up a position in exhibitions at Museum Africa. For reflections on his training and experience at SANG see Zola Mtshiza, "Crossing the Curatorial Rubicon," in *Coexistence: Contemporary Cultural Production in South Africa*, eds. Pamela Allara and Marilyn Martin (Waltham, Massachusetts: Brandeis University, 2003), 29.

8 Pamela Allara, "Introduction and Acknowledgments," in Ibid., 4. Allara described her experiences in the Introduction and her curatorial premise in her essay "Contemporary Cultural Production in South Africa: Jostling for Position," Ibid., 6-13.

9 Remix brings together people with different body histories, body types and abilities and creates innovative dance theatre performance and education programmes.

10 The exhibition was sponsored by Standard Bank and IFAS, with additional support from AFAA, BASA and Air France, while Iziko made a considerable financial contribution.

11 The idea originated with Bernard Malauzat, attached to the French Embassy. The roles played by Mandie van der Spuy of the Standard Bank, French representatives Ambassador Jean Félix-Paganon and Bénédicte Alliot, can be measured by the positive response from the directors of the Musée Picasso (the project spanned two directors: Gérard Régnier and Anne Baldassari, who succeeded him) and other lenders. After much exchange and correspondence between Laurence Madeline and me, her initial selection of thirty one works was increased to eighty four (seventy five from Musée Picasso, three from the Centre Georges Pompidou and three from South African collections).

12 For the Picasso section loans were sourced from the Musée Picasso; Musée nationale d'art moderne in Paris; the Fundación Almine y Bernard Ruiz-Picasso para el Arte; JAG; and SANG. The African art came from the Irma Stern Museum; University of Stellenbosch, Sasol Art Museum; Standard Bank African Art Collection (Wits Art Museum); Wits Ethnological Museum

Collection; Spier Collection of African Art; and Karel Nel's private collection. Collection managers Kirsty Cockerill (SANG) and Nhlanhla Ngwenya (SBG) had the matchless opportunity of travelling to Paris and working on the loans from the Musée Picasso.

13 Madeline and Martin, *Picasso and Africa*: the book contains messages from the presidents of France and South Africa, the ambassador of France and Derek Cooper, chairman of Standard Bank; acknowledgments of all the role players and lenders occupy two pages, 6-7.

14 Iziko *Annual Report*, 2006-2007, 8.

15 Iziko's EPP division organised additional visits and programmes and the fruits of the hard work and enthusiasm of learners were displayed in the Annexe in September 2006. The Annexe came to life again, as exhibitions in this venue had been few and far between since 2000. *Picasso and Africa* art boxes were created for the art library. All known (many retired) and trained guides were contacted and sixteen, ranging from ages 22 to 82 took care of numerous guided tours.

16 For the polemic and viewpoints generated by *Picasso and Africa*, see *Art South Africa* 4, no. 4 (2008), 30-40.

17 A few examples that are not mentioned in the text will suffice: Bedford travelled to Alexandria in Egypt, to present two papers; Grundlingh to Dakar for a seminar and to Malawi and Zimbabwe to install *Positive Lives: Africa*. I was invited as a curator and judge of Dak'Art, the Biennale in Dakar, Senegal in 2000 and again in 2010. I travelled to: the USA (as a member of the Africa Forum in 2000, as participant in a conference on HIV/Aids at Wellesley College, and with *Coexistence*); Brazil (as contributing curator to the 2002 São Paulo Bienal: *Five Johannesburg Artists*); The Netherlands, Germany (I opened Jane Alexander's exhibition in Stuttgart and visited Frankfurt, and participated in a conference on globalisation in Leipzig); India, France (as president of the Alliance française of Cape Town in 2004 and for the opening of the Musée du quai Branly in 2006); to Whitecliffe College, Auckland, New Zealand to examine the work of masters students and to give public lectures on South African art; and to Sydney, Australia to visit the Biennale and other exhibitions. All trips were paid for by the organising museum, institution or university. I attended the Venice Biennales and Documenta in Kassel largely at own cost; Iziko supported my presence at the International Committee for Museums and Collections of Modern Art (CIMAM) conferences in Germany and Spain.

18 For more on the exhibition see Derk Hendrik van Wegen, *Kunst uit de Kaap: Hollandse en Vlaamse meesterwerken uit de Michaelis collectie te Kaapstad* (Zwolle: Waanders and Maastricht: Bonnefantenmuseum, 2003).

19 Murray spent twenty-three years in South Africa as the managing editor of the Catholic newspaper, the *Southern Cross*. A self-taught artist, he developed the naïve style for which he became famous here and abroad, exhibiting regularly in Cape Town, London, Paris and Tokyo. Robert Murray, "Obituary: Andrew Murray," *Independent*, October 16, 1998, http://www.independent.co.uk/arts-entertainment/obituary-andrew-murray-1178497.html (accessed January 16, 2016).

20 Anna Tietze, *The Sir Abe Bailey Bequest: A Reappraisal* (Cape Town: South African National Gallery, 2001).

21 Iziko *Annual Report*, 2003-2004, 21.

22 Kerryn Greenberg, "ReCollection: 130 years of Acquiring Art for the Nation (1871 – 2001)," *Artthrob* archive: no. 69, May 2003, http://artthrob.co.za/03may/reviews/student_sang.html (accessed February 24, 2017).

23 Van Niekerk quoted in Fleur de Villiers, "Forget art, camping is culture," *Sunday Times*, April 27, 1980; the article is discussed in chapter three.

24 These were the vast sums spent on the controversial arms deal (R52 billion) and the president's security fence (R90 million). The Strategic Defence Package was a multi-billion-rand military acquisition project finalised in 1999 by the South African government. It was nicknamed "the arms deal" because of allegations of large-scale bribery and corruption: "The arms deal: what you need to know," *Corruption Watch*, January 22, 2014, http://www.corruptionwatch.org.za/the-arms-deal-what-you-need-to-know-2/ (accessed April 15, 2017).

25 Chris Thurman, "National Gallery's pleas for funds fall on deaf ears," *The Weekender*, March 25, 2017, http://christhurman.net/art-and-culture/item/national-gallery.html (accessed March 25, 2017). This website is no longer active.

26 The following works were purchased on auction from Strauss & Co: John Koenakeefe Mohl: *Serowe, Botswana*, 1954, oil on canvas laid down on board, 340 × 440, R40,000; Moses Tladi: *Farm Cottage, Driefontein, Jhb*, 1939, oil on board, 140 × 180, R130,000 and *Mountain Landscape (Mont-aux-Sources)*, oil on board, 335 × 445, R400,000. Hayden Proud, email to the author, November 26, 2018.

27 Warne joined SANG from social history and replaced Grundlingh as curator of photography and new media after Grundlingh resigned.

28 Dubin, "Transforming Museums," 248.

29 Ibid., 256-257.

30 Ivor Powell, "A Decade of Democracy: SA Art 1994-2004," *Art South Africa* 2, no. 4 (2004): 62.

31 Ibid.

32 Ibid.

33 Ibid., 64. For criticism about transformation at SANG in general and *A Decade of Democracy* in particular, see "This Day launches with a polemic against the SANG," *Artthrob* archive no. 74, October 2003, http://artthrob.co.za/03oct/news/thisday.

html (accessed April 3, 2017); and Joost Bosland, "'Amandla!': A critical assessment of 'A Decade of Democracy' at SANG," *Artthrob* archive no. 88, December 2004, http://artthrob.co.za/04dec/reviews/sang2.html (accessed April 3, 2017).

34 *Democracy ×* was seen by 60,000 visitors, it received the Western Cape Arts, Culture and Heritage Award for the best urban museum project in 2004 and was listed by the Royal Academy in London as one of the top fifteen exhibitions in the world: Iziko *Annual Report*, 2004-2005, 6-7.

35 Lize van Robbroeck, "Reimagining South African National Heritage Two Ten-Years-of-Democracy Exhibitions," *African Arts* XXXVII, no. 4 (2004): 45. Also see Lize van Robbroeck, "Democracy X," *Art South Africa* 2, no. 4 (2004): 65-67.

36 Van Robbroeck, "Reimagining," 46 & 47.

37 Ibid., 47.

38 Ibid.

39 Chris Broodryk, "Call for chapters for the book *Public Intellectualism in the Arts and Humanities in South Africa*," email dated August 24, 2018, distributed by Karen von Veh to South African Visual and Art Historians (SAVAH) members, August 27, 2018. This book forms part of a larger project on "The Public Intellectual in times of Wicked Problems" that is based at the Faculty of Humanities of the University of Pretoria.

40 Crain Soudien, "Emerging Discourse around Identity in new South African Museum exhibitions," *Interventions* 10, no. 2 (2008): 208.

41 Ibid., 209.

42 Ibid., 219.

43 Anitra Nettleton, Fiona Rankin-Smith and Julia Charlton, eds., *Voice-Overs: Wits Writings Exploring African Artworks* (Johannesburg: University of the Witwatersrand Art Galleries, 2004).

44 Sandra Klopper, "Ilifa LaBantu/Voice-Overs," in *Art South Africa* 3, no. 3 (2005): 65.

45 Brokensha bought the collection when he was teaching at the University of Ghana (1959-63). Of particular interest was the pair of scrimshaw decorated powder horns, one depicting a plan of Fort Cox and a mother and child, the other a two-storey house (c. 1846) that was purchased on auction from Bonhams in London.With permission from the CEO and with funds for repatriation from DAC allocation, I bid telephonically on the horns; there was little interest from other bidders and the hammer price was £500 (with charges: £617.50).

46 In response to my query about the status of the catalogue, Kaufmann wrote in an email on February 12, 2016: "With no budget for publishing and no interest from Iziko after your retirement it was impossible to proceed. There was also little interest from commercial publishers because of the Iziko red-tape that would have been involved if they took on the project." Kaufmann requested IA to put separate chapters under their topics on the web as a link to art collections, thereby providing access to the collection. This has also not materialised and a valuable, beautifully illustrated document with contributions by experts in the different fields remains incomplete and partially edited. Contributors were: Bruce Arnott, Tony Cunningham, Patricia Davison, Lindsay Hooper and Marilyn Martin; Carol Kaufmann interviewed collector and dealer Stephen Long.

47 Carol Kaufmann and Andrea Lewis, eds., *Brushing Up on Stern: Featuring Works from the Permanent Collection of the Iziko South African National Gallery* (Cape Town: Iziko South African National Gallery, 2015).

48 Carol Kaufmann, *The 8th Definitive. The luminous beauty of South African beadwork on stamps* (Pretoria: South African Post Office Philatelic Services, 2010). Landscapes from the SANG collection featured on a set of stamps issued by the Post Office in May 2005.

49 Jan-Erik Lundstrom, ed., *Head North: Views from the Permanent Collection of the South African National Gallery* (Umeå: Bild Museet, 2001). For details of participating artists and contributions by Grundlingh and Voyiya, Marilyn Martin and Colin Richards see: "Head North," *Media 1*, http://media1.mweb.co.za/iziko/sang/exhib/2001/headnorth/index.htm (accessed April 4, 2017).The project was funded by the Swedish International Development Cooperation Agency.

50 Hayden Proud, ed., *Scratches on the Face Antiquity and Contemporaneity in South African works of art from Iziko Museums of Cape Town* (New Delhi and Cape Town: Iziko Museums, 2008). For the virtual exhibition see: "Scratches on the Face," *National Gallery of Modern Art*, http://ngmaindia.gov.in/virtual-gallery-scratches-on-the-face.asp (accessed March 28, 2017).

51 Hayden Proud has not been able to trace the source of the words quoted.

52 Pep Subirós, ed., *Apartheid: The South African Mirror* (Barcelona: Centre de Cultura Contemporània de Barcelona, 2007).

53 The partnership established between SANG and Anglo American Farms has remained with Iziko, and it generates income. Proud is responsible for curating the site.

54 Iziko *Annual Report*, 2007-2008, 7.

55 Carol Kaufmann, email to the author, February 12, 2016.

56 Carol Kaufmann, email to the author, August 27, 2017: Kaufmann stated that she had repeatedly reported the broken air conditioning and when she was in the storeroom in August 2017, she ran a fan to keep the air moving so that works did not get mouldy.

57 Bongani Ndhlovu, email to the author, March 8, 2017. Appointed to the position in 2011, Ndhlovu has a Ph.D in history from

the University of the Western Cape. He started his museum career in 1996 as a cultural historian with the KwaZulu-Natal Museums Service. He has occupied various positions at Ditsong: National Museum of Natural History in Pretoria and was director of the Ncome and Msunduzi/Voortrekker Museums from 2004 to 2011.

58 Lohman, email to the author, May 5, 2017.

59 "Voices of the Ancestors," *Media 1*, http://media1.mweb.co.za/iziko/sang/exhib/2009/voices_ancestors.html (accessed March 28, 2017).

60 "Bertram House," *Iziko Museums*, https://www.iziko.org.za/museums/bertram-house (accessed, October 18, 2017). As the minutes record, the matter was first discussed in art collections on June 6, 2007 and deferred at a senior management meeting on April 4, 2008. The Musée Dapper first opened in Paris in 1986, but moved to larger premises in 2000: *Fondation Dapper*, http://www.dapper.fr/ (accessed October 18, 2017).

61 "Messages from the Moat," *Sue Williamson*, https://www.sue-williamson.com/messages-from-the-moat (accessed March 15, 2017).

62 McGee's interest in South Africa and details about the film are available on: "The Luggage is Still Labeled: Blackness in South African Art," *Bowdoin University*, March 21, 2003, http://www.bowdoin.edu/news/archives/1bowdoincampus/001236.shtml (accessed March 28, 2017).

63 Mario Pissarra, "Decolonise the mind," *Art South Africa* 2, no. 2 (2003): 37-41; Dagmawi Woubshet, "Staging the rainbow nation," Ibid.: 33-36; Michael Godby, "Responding to critique," Ibid.: 36. Also see Mario Pissarra, "The Luggage is Still Labelled But is it Going to the Right Destination?," *Third Text* 18, no. 2 (2004): 183-191.

64 Kathy Grundlingh and Vuyile Voyiya, "Towards a Democratic Museum," in *Head North*, Lundstrom, 12-17.

65 Voyiya's career at SANG: information officer (1991-1995); education officer (1996-2001); education liaison officer (2002-2003).

66 Woubshet, "Staging," 35.

67 I had taken a personal interest in the Thupelo Workshop since the late 1980s: I attended the 1989 workshop as "critic in residence", and spoke about the largely white and academic backlash against black artists creating abstract paintings at a conference of the South African Association of Art Historians and the African Studies Association in Baltimore, Maryland in 1990; the papers were published in: Marilyn Martin, "Is There a Place for Black Abstract Painters in South Africa?," *De Arte* 44 (1991): 25-38. David Koloane and Bill Ainslie initiated the Thupelo project in 1985 and their paintings were purchased in 1989 and 1990 respectively; works by participants were acquired from 1988: Thami Jali, Billy Mandindi, Sfiso Ka Mkame, Kagiso Pat Mautloa, Sam Nhlengethwa, Anthony Nkotsi, Mmakgabo Mmapula Helen Sebidi, Jenny Stadler, Kedibone Sarah Tabane and Jill Trappler.

68 For details of the council members as of May 1, 2003, see Iziko Museums *Annual Report*, 2003-2004, 3.

69 As mentioned in note 7 above, we had to institute disciplinary procedures against Mtshiza. Getting appointments confirmed was frustrating; a letter I wrote to CFO Rocco Human on October 26, 2000, reveals this, the mixed messages coming from management, regarding Mtshiza's position, as well as the full-time appointment of Kaufmann, who had submitted two letters of motivation to the CEO.

70 Ernestine White, email to the author, March 6, 2017.

71 Robyn-Leigh Cedras, email to the author, February 21, 2018.

72 For Goniwe's letter, Iziko's response and Bedford's paper, "Curating as a transformative practice," see: "Targeted Candidate," *Asai*, http://asai.co.za/?s=Targeted+Candidate (accessed May 22, 2017). Iziko submitted fifteen proposals to DAC in 2006; three, including Bedford's, were successful.

73 A prerequisite for the appointment was further study in art history, but Qanya did not attend lectures at UCT regularly (budgeted and paid for by the grant from DAC) and did not write the exam.

74 Nadja Daehnke, email to the author April 14, 2017.

75 *Pancho Guedes Ein Alternativer Modernist/An Alternative Modernist, SAM no. 03* (Basel: Schweizerisches Architekturmuseum, 2007).

76 The Zip Zap Circus School was an unrealised project by Guedes; together with Gadanho's exhibition design, it inspired artist Ângela Ferreira's installation for the Portuguese participation in the 52nd Venice Biennale in 2007: "Portugal Official Representation," *Instituto das Artes*, Universes in Universe, http://universes-in-universe.de/car/venezia/eng/2007/tour/prt/press-01.pdf (accessed April 1, 2017).

77 Marilyn Martin and Joe Dolby, eds., *Albert Adams Journey on a Tightrope* (Cape Town: Iziko South African National Gallery, 2008). The project was made possible by Grand West Cultural Heritage Trust, FONG, Scan Shop and Kuehne and Nagel, London.

78 Andrea Lewis, email to the author, September 28, 2017. This was another attempt by me to establish a career path for curators; Lewis had excellent academic qualifications and some museum experience, but she had not worked with a collection. In addition, we had identified the need for a curator of modern paintings and sculpture to care for and interpret the art that fell

between the historical and contemporary collections. She was appointed to this post and subsequently became curator of prints and drawings.

79 Dolby and I continue to promote Adams' legacy: in 2016, in collaboration with Stellenbosch Modern and Contemporary Art Gallery (SMAC) we curated *Albert Adams in Black & White* (Cape Town Art Fair) and *Albert Adams The Bonds of Memory* (SMAC, Woodstock, Cape Town). In 2017 Robyn-Leigh Cedras and I, with participation from Dolby, curated *Albert Adams(1929-2006) – A Fractured History* at the Rupert Museum in Stellenbosch. A retrospective of Adams' work will take place at the Wits Art Museum in April 2019.

80 Jack Lohman, email to the author, May 5, 2017.

81 Marilyn Martin, "Foreword," in *Forty Years of Friendship The Friends of the South African National Gallery1968-2008*, ed. Hayden Proud (Cape Town: Friends of the South African National Gallery, 2008).

82 Faeza Allie, email to the author, February 16, 2017.

83 Jo-Anne Duggan, email to the author, February 2, 2017.

84 Emile Maurice's death offers a poignant example of this coming together. Many former colleagues attended his funeral at St George's Cathedral, but there was a need to have a private moment to share our memories of a colleague who had left a footprint as a thinker, artist, activist, educator, writer and curator. This took place on 29 September 2016 – members of the SANG family were invited according to what Maurice would have liked; everyone was not available and the gathering was small: Esmé Adams, Rashaad Ajam, Faeza Allie, Baderoeniesa Bosch, Shaheeda Dante, Joe Dolby, Jo-Anne Duggan, Fatima February, Yusuf Masoet, Lorraine Mayekiso, Jon Weinberg and my daughter Catherine.

CHAPTER 8 – A new CEO and art collections director, restructuring and destructive controversies

1 Riason Naidoo in an interview with David Smith, "Gallery director defends decision to swap Gainsborough for African works," *The Guardian*, September 1, 2019.

2 Iziko Council Minutes: August 8, 2008, 2-3 (this meeting also decided that I would not be involved in the selection of my successor, as had always been the case in the past); October 30, 2008, 2; February 2, 2009, 4. Riason Naidoo (b. 1970) holds BA(FA) and MA(FA) degrees from Wits University. Prior to his appointment at Iziko, he was in charge of artistic projects at IFAS, he taught at Wits, and he worked as education officer at DAG. He directed the *South African-Mali: Timbuktu Manuscripts* project for the South African Presidency and DAC. He is known for his work on the photographer Ranjith Kally. "Riason Naidoo," *Independent Curators International*, http://curatorsintl.org/collaborators/riason_naidoo (accessed August 22, 1917).

3 I co-curated *Five Johannesburg artists* for Alfons Hug, chief curator for the 2002 São Paulo Bienal, and he approached me to bring *The Tropics* to Cape Town. The exhibition was first shown in Brasilia in 2007, then in Rio de Janeiro in 2008 and afterwards in Berlin; it was not possible to host the exhibition in its entirety at SANG, and a selection was made that contributed to the discourse of the "self" and "other". It was funded by the German Federal Cultural Foundation.

4 Andrea Lewis, email to the author, September 28, 2017. See Roger van Wyk, "Statement #1," *Art South Africa* 8, no. 3 (2010): 9.

5 Riason Naidoo, "View from the hot seat," *Art South Africa* 8, no. 1, (2009): 27.

6 Mary Corrigall, "Shoddy arts journalism and Riason Naidoo's Pierneef to Gugulective," *Incorrigible Corrigall*, September 11, 2010, http://corrigall.blogspot.co.za/2010/09/shoddy-arts-journalism-and-riason.html (accessed September 3, 2017).

7 Lloyd Pollak, "SA National Gallery's reputation trashed for 2010 show," *The South African Art Times*, April 30, 2010: 1& 3.

8 Gerard Schoeman, "Collected Works," *Art South Africa* 8, no. 4 (2010): 54-59.

9 Malcomess had this to say: "The exhibition was conceptualised as a response to the xenophobic violence of May 2008, and attempted to bring together a younger generation of South African artists to think through and question notions of group identity and belonging. The show was not a critical success, but made visible the work of several younger artists in the museum space, and also began a series of further collaborations between myself and these artists." "Luggage Limits: *US* and *23 Kilograms*," *Curatorial Talks*, May 18, 2013, https://curatorialtalks.wordpress.com/2013/05/18/bettina-malcomess-2/ (accessed October 17, 2017).

10 Schoeman, "Collected Works," 56.

11 David Smith, "Gallery director," *The Guardian*, September 1, 2019, https://www.theguardian.com/artanddesign/2010/sep/01/riason-naidoo-south-africa-gallery (accessed September 7, 2017). Naidoo's generalisations about history, art and culture, and the Bailey Bequest were not explored in any depth by the interviewer.

12 "Steven Dubin reacts to the Guardian's David Smith," posted on the Jacana Books website, October 4, 2010. I accessed the article via a collection of press articles on *1910-2010: From Pierneef to Gugulective*, distributed to Iziko council members.

13 Riason Naidoo, *The Making of 1910-2010 from Pierneef to Gugulective* (Iziko South African National Gallery, 2010), unpaginated. The introduction to the exhibition is in tabloid-format.

14 This discussion of the 2010 exhibition schedule at SANG and reference to the meetings are based on material in my personal archive. The exhibitions meetings to which I refer were held in art collections on September 18, 2006; May 16, 2007 and August 6, 2008 (my last meeting) and an Iziko 2010 planning meeting of the CEO and senior management on April 4, 2008.

15 "Poised to strike against corruption," *Special Investigating Unit Interim Report*, Politicsweb, April-September, 2011, http://www.politicsweb.co.za/politicsweb/action/media/downloadFile?media_fileid=2445 (accessed October 31, 2017). For an overview of initiatives in the country see Marilyn Martin, "Munisipaliteite kan trots wees of dié sokkerjaar-erfenis" (Municipalities can be proud of the soccer-year legacy), *Die Burger*, August 31, 2010.

16 Nadja Daehnke, exhibition proposal: "Working Title: Viewer: Spectator," undated, c. 2008, sent to the author on November 28, 2017. The following artists were listed provisionally: Alan Alborough, Bridget Baker, Alison Kearney, Shonisani Mapangwa, Brett Murray, Colin Richards, Usha Seejarim and James Webb.

17 For more on the installation see: "Deep Play," *Harun Farocki*, http://www.harunfarocki.de/installations/2000s/2007/deep-play.html (accessed August 16, 2017).

18 Fiona Rankin-Smith, ed., *Halakasha!* (Johannesburg: Wits Art Museum, 2010).

19 Carol Brown, ed., "South Africa After the Ball," *African Arts* 44, no. 2 (2011). In addition to Dubin and Freschi, Andrew Lamprecht wrote about Cape Town in 2010; and I reflected on South Africa after the event and reviewed the art in the Moses Mabhida Stadium in Durban and at the Durban Art Gallery, where acting director at the time, Jenny Stretton, curated *Art of the Ball*; she dug deep into the store rooms and devised a meaningful, interactive exhibition and project that included street children.

20 Anna Tietze, *A History*, 194.

21 Naidoo cited the amount for exhibitions in a document he circulated when Iziko did not renew his contract in May 2014. The Lotto allocation of R340,000 for the publication was still listed as unspent in the Iziko "financial performance" as at January 31, 2013, unpaginated; and in the consolidated annual budget, 1 April 2013 to 31 March 2014, 2.

22 For the full programme and names of participants see Naidoo, *The Making*, unpaginated. Naidoo circulated an email on October 6, 2010: "Please find for reference installation photos, materials, reviews, and events related to the show now online on our new micro-site: http://izikomuseums.com/blog/?p=248". The site is no longer active, so there is no visual record of the show.

23 Rooksana Omar has a BA(Hons) in History and an MA in Business Administration from the University of Durban-Westville. She has worked in the library and heritage sector since 1981. She is the former director of the Luthuli Museum in KwaZulu-Natal and prior to that the director of the Local History Museums and acting director of eThekwini Heritage. She is the a past president of SAMA and ICOM-South Africa, she has served as executive board member of the International Commission on Museums in South Africa and president of the Commonwealth of Museums. In June 2017 she was appointed to the ethics committee of ICOM.

24 Hayden Proud, email to the author, September 11, 2017.

25 Lloyd Pollak, "Why Sir Abe Bailey is turning in his grave," *South African Art Times*, March 2012, 8-9. Others entered the fray: "Painting of boys that look like girls, the Bailey Bequest and Iziko," *Panga Management*, https://pangamanagement.wordpress.com/2012/02/07/paintings-of-boys-that-look-like-girls-the-bailey-bequest-and-iziko/ (accessed October 8, 2017).

26 Email correspondence between Rooksana Omar and the author, October 31, 2011.

27 Pollak, "Why Sir Abe Bailey," 8.

28 Hayden Proud, "The Sir Abe Bailey Collection," document prepared for Iziko executive management, August 7, 2014, unpaginated.

29 Andrew Mellon, founder of the Foundation, shared a love of British sporting art with Bailey.

30 Proud, "The Sir Abe," unpaginated.

31 Hayden Proud, email to the author, October 23, 2018. Matts Leiderstam participated in the exhibition *Transpositions: five Swedish artists in South Africa* in 1998 and created the work for the exhibition. Often working from paintings in museum collections, he recreates historic artworks while exploring hidden stories and issues of identity and power relations.

32 Hayden Proud, email to the author, February 8, 2019. The original Cooper and the Leiderstam canvases both measure 970 × 1265mm.

33 Hayden Proud, email to the author, October 23, 2017.

34 Hamish Robertson, email to the author, October 6, 2017; interview with Robertson on December 1, 2017.

35 Beezy Bailey, email to the author, October 25, 2017. *Rhodes Must Fall (#RhodesMustFall)* is a protest movement that began on March 9, 2015, originally directed against a statue of Cecil John Rhodes at the University of Cape Town.

36 Riason Naidoo to Rosenclaire, February 12, 2011. Because I was the director at the time the work was commissioned, Rosenclaire forwarded all the email correspondence with Naidoo, as well as their explanation of the work, to me on March 19, 2013.

37 Marilyn Martin, email to Rooksana Omar, March 19, 2013; Riason Naidoo, email to Rosenclaire, March 19, 2013.

38 Marilyn Martin, email to Ernestine White, February 13, 2017; Ernestine White, email to the author, March 3, 2017.

39 Ernestine White, email to the author, November 16, 2017.

40 As a council member I expressed concern and asked questions: the art collections quarterly report was incomplete, it left council without relevant information and it was unacceptable in terms of the PFMA; there was not a single exhibition at SANG curated by a staff member, except for the director, and it was unclear what curators were doing, what research was being conducted, publications produced and participation in education programmes. Marilyn Martin, email to Rooksana Omar, May 19, 2011. A sloppy attitude to museum practice, exacerbated by the "sharing" of the SANG registrar, Lailah Hisham, with social history that had a huge backlog, resulted in unaccessioned works being shown on *New Additions* in 2011. After my retirement Hisham was moved to social history.

41 Characteristically the Iziko press release started with the institution being "more relevant" and ignored the fact that SANG had acquired a portfolio of Ernest Cole photographs at a cost of R288,000 from Clarke's Bookshop with money raised from the Lottery and that we paid tribute to him with a display of the works in an exhibition entitled "Ernest Cole: Chronicler in the House of Bondage" in 2008, curated by Pam Warne. "WC exhibition/photo – Ernest Cole, Photographer," *Artslink.co.za News*, February 25, 2011, from the author's digital archive.

42 "In Context/2010," *Goodman Gallery*, http://www.goodman-gallery.com/exhibitions/165 (accessed October 24, 2017). The project was sponsored by Goodman Gallery, the Goethe-Institut, Culturesfrance, IFAS, Galleria Continua, the British Council, and the Kirsh Foundation.

43 The exhibition was funded by the Institute for Poverty, Land and Agrarian Studies at UWC, the UCT Research Office, the Rosa Luxemburg Foundation, Gillian MacKay Graham and Georgina Hamilton. Paul Weinberg, "Umhlaba 1913-2013: Images from the exhibition commemorating the centenary of the Natives Land Act of 1913," 2015, *PLAAS*, http://www.plaas.org.za/plaas-publication/Umhlaba (accessed October 23, 2017).

44 Mario Pissarra, *Against the Grain* (Cape Town: Africa South Art Initiative, 2013).

45 As a council member I strongly supported the Peter Clarke exhibition, which needed funds and I asked Standard Bank and the Friends (the money had been paid into their account to avoid Iziko bureaucracy) to allocate the R15,000 left over from the Maqhubela exhibition to *Listening to Distant Thunder*.

46 The *Ghost Series* was at the core of an urgent debate about race and representation that took place in South Africa in the years immediately following 1994. Breitz and Brenda Atkinson responded: Candice Breitz and Brenda Atkinson, eds., *Grey Areas* (Johannesburg: Chalkham Hill Press, 1999).

47 For an in-depth review, see Michael Morris, "An unblinking, compassionate eye," *Weekend Argus*, February 7, 2015, 22.

48 Michael Godby, *The Lie of the Land: Representations of the South African Landscape* (Johannesburg: David Krut Publishing, 2010).

49 Ibhabhathane means "butterfly" in Xhosa.

50 Colin Stevens presented a copy of the film to the Michaelis Friends: "Old Master meets Young Master," *FMC News*, September 2011, http://www.iziko.org.za/images/uploads/fmc_sept_2011_5.pdf (accessed August 12, 2017). See the film: "Anathi Tyawa. A Painter from Kayelitsha [sic]," *Lena Bodabild*, http://www.lenabodabild.com/film-anathi-tyawa-a-painter-from-kayelitsha---2011.html (accessed August 12, 2017).

51 For more on the map and the exhibition see: Ian Glenn, "François Levaillant and the Mapping of Southern Africa," *Alternation*, University of KwaZulu Natal, http://alternation.ukzn.ac.za/Files/docs/14.2/03%20Glenn.pdf (accessed November 12, 2017).

52 "South Africa-France Seasons 2012 & 2013 FAQs," *Institut français d'Afrique du Sud*, http://www.ifas.org.za/index.php/south-african-season-france/222-france-south-africa-seasons-2012-2013/651-france-south-africa-seasons-2012-2013-faqs and "20th Century Masters at the Standard Bank Gallery (Johannesburg)," *Institut français Afrique du Sud*, http://www.ifas.org.za/index.php/visual-art/172-20th-century-masters-at-the-standard-bank-gallery-johannesburg (accessed October 24, 2017). The Iziko curators were Joe Dolby, Andrea Lewis, Riason Naidoo and Pam Warne.

53 I recommend Karin Preller's in-depth consideration of the exhibition and analysis of some of the interviews and reviews, "The Tretchikoff Conundrum," *Art South Africa* 10, no. 1 (2011): 42-48. See also: Lloyd Pollak, "More Agony than Ecstasy, The Tretchikoff Story – Now showing in vistavision at the SA National Gallery," *South African Art Times*, July 2011, 9-10; Sean O'Toole, "The Cake Shop: Vladimir Tretchikoff at the Iziko South African National Gallery," *Artthrob*, May 2011, https://artthrob.co.za (accessed May 31, 2011).

54 In this regard I agree with Bokhorst. I knew Tretchikoff and visited his studio in the 1960s – there, in the unfinished paintings and scraps of paper used for testing colour and tone, was the promise of a painter. Andrew Lamprecht approached me to contribute to the catalogue, but I would no doubt have written a text that was inappropriate for the occasion, and he did not pursue the matter with me.

55 Andrew Lamprecht, ed., *Tretchikoff The People's Painter* (Jeppestown: Jonathan Ball Publishers , 2011), 42.

56 Lloyd Pollak, "Tretchikoff: the supreme Schlockmeister of the 20th century," *Lloyd's Artbeat*, http://lloyds-artbeat.co.za/wp-content/uploads/2017/12/TRETCHIKOFF_v5.pdf (accessed January 23, 2018). In a lengthy illustrated article, based on a

lecture he gave to FONG, Pollak sketched the history and nature of Kitsch and applied it to his in-depth analyses of many paintings.

57 "Tretchikoff: The People's Painter," *Iziko Museums of South Africa*, https://www.iziko.org.za/calendar/event/tretchikoff-the-peoples-painter-1 (accessed November 12, 2017).

58 Lamprecht, *Tretchikoff*, 29.

59 Ibid., 30.

60 Ibid., 42.

61 Stuart Cloete, "Foreword," in *Tretchikoff, Howard* Timmins (Cape Town: Howard Timmins, 1969), unpaginated.

62 Boris Gorelik, "How the world was won: Tretchikoff goes international," in *Tretchikoff*, Lamprecht, 121. There are several paintings and drawings that share this title and Gorelik does not date the work nor does he indicate which one was shown in San Francisco.

63 Shanti Aboobaker, "'Vulgar' Tretchikoff exhibition draws flak and fans," *Cape Times*, September 30, 2011, https://www.iol.co.za/capetimes/vulgar-tretchikoff-exhibition-draws-flak-and-fans-1147975 (accessed November 10, 2017).

64 Lloyd Pollak, "A Bitter Farewell to Tretchikoff," *South African Art Times*, October 2011, 54. As a personal silent protest, and in memory of Matthys Bokhorst, F. L. Alexander and Raymund van Niekerk, I did not attend the opening or the panel discussion.

65 Colin Richards, email to the author, June 14, 2011. As for the scarce resources that threatened the realisation of the Peter Clarke and Moses Tladi exhibitions, "the people's painter" attracted funding from Iziko Museums; DAC; City of Cape Town; Rupert Foundation; Chinese Embassy; Tretchikoff Foundation; Elliott's International; GAC Laser; Lemnis Lighting.

66 Carol Kaufmann quoted in Pollak, "A Bitter Farewell," 54.

67 Hayden Proud, email to the author, June 8, 2011.

68 Pierre de Vos, "Why president Zuma is like Tretchikoff," *Constitutionally speaking*, July 4, 2011, http://constitutionallyspeaking.co.za/why-president-zuma-is-like-tretchikoff/ (accessed October 22, 2017).

69 Zuma had his first court appearance on charges of corruption, fraud, money laundering and racketeering in the Durban High Court on April 6, 2018.

70 Not all "the people" enshrined in the title welcomed the exhibition. Commenting on *Baroque meets Modern* at the OTH, a visitor wrote: "An outstandingly intelligent, sumptuous and immaculately hanged exhibition. It demonstrates how poorly & laughable is the presentation of the Tretchikoff at the National Gallery."

71 The sub-heading of Preller's article states: "Record-breaking visitor numbers at Iziko South African National Gallery speak volumes about the impact of Tretchikoff on the national psyche": Preller, "The Tretchikoff," 44. In the *Weekend Argus* (18 May, 2014), Ivor Powell wrote, "attendance figures dwarfed anything the gallery had recorded".

72 His first exhibition in Cape Town in 1948 drew 12,000 people and 30,000 went the following year, both in eleven days: "Tretchikoff," *Vladimir Tretchikoff*, http://www.vladimirtretchikoff.com/biography.htm (accessed November 1, 2017).

73 At the core functions meeting of October 24, 2012, I requested an exhibitions schedule; Ndhlovu assured the committee that the team was in the process of finalising a schedule for the following three years. In April and May 2013 I reminded the CEO that nothing was planned to showcase the permanent collection and only three exhibitions were confirmed beyond February 2014: *African art and design* and two exhibitions of photography.

74 "A Brave New World...20 Years of Democracy," *Iziko Museums of South Africa*, https://www.iziko.org.za/calendar/event/brave-new-world20-years-of-democracy (accessed November 2, 2017).

75 Louise van Niekerk, "Symbols of South African Cultures," *Setempe*, Virtual Post Office, https://www.virtualpostoffice.co.za/vpo/Downloads/pdf/Setempe_Sep-Dec_2013_VPO_1.pdf (accessed November 12, 2017). The *Blombos Ochre* and associated material were discovered in 1991 by Professor Chris Henshilwood, under whose direction the Blombos Cave, situated in a limestone cliff near Still Bay on the southern Cape coast, was excavated (1997-2009).

76 Naidoo, "View from the hot seat," 27.

77 The other two works in the series were Édouard Manet's *Olympia* (1863) and Willem de Kooning's *Woman V* (1952-53).

78 Art collections document "Collections background and strategy," c. 2014, unpaginated, provided by Hamish Robertson, October 6, 2017.

79 Iziko *Annual Report*, 2012-2013, 8-9.

80 Marilyn Martin, comments on consultant Mike Bruton's "Big Picture" proposals, January 20, 2012; personal archive.

81 Iziko Minutes of the core functions sub-committee, October 24, 2012; personal archive. In order to encourage thinking and working across collections, I gave a lecture on Documenta 13 held in Kassel, Germany – a curatorial project that seamlessly brought together many disciplines and chronologies – to all Iziko staff in May 2013.

82 Bongani Ndhlovu, email to the author, March 8, 2017.

83 Between April 2016 and September 2017, I wrote to Naidoo four times, asking him to share his highlights and challenges for inclusion in the book; he responded each time and thanked me, but did not provide any information.

84 Attached to Naidoo's email of May 8, 2014 were two documents from which I quote: Riason Naidoo, "Media Statement," May 8, 2014 and "Highlights: May 2009-April 2014," undated.

85 These included: Tate Modern, London; Virginia Commonwealth University, Qatar; ACASA Triennale, Fowler Museum, UCLA, Los Angeles; Museum of Modern Art, New York.

86 The funding sources of both exhibitions were confirmed by Bongani Ndhlovu, email to the author, May 4, 2018.

87 Naidoo's claim that a private collector had chosen SANG above Zeitz Museum of Contemporary Art Africa (Zeitz MOCAA) and the Tate Modern to donate a contemporary artwork valued at R3 million, also came to naught: Bongani Ndhlovu, email to the author, May 4, 2018.

88 According to Naidoo the art collections exhibitions budget was cut by 77% from R623,900 to R143,170 over the five years of his directorship.

89 Naidoo, "Media Statement," 3.

90 The committee had not changed since I left in 2008; at the end of 2017 external members were: Graham Falken (director, ZAG consultants, former director of CAP and AMAC); Andrew Lamprecht (Michaelis); Sipho Ndabambi (art collections manager at parliament); and Robert Mulders (representing the Friends). In October 2018 the following academics accepted the invitation to join the acquisitions committee for a period of five years: Nomusa Makhubu (Michaelis School), Desiree Lewis (UWC) and Lize van Robbroeck (US); the Friends were represented by Gcobani Sipoyo: Hayden Proud, email to the author, October 22, 2018. Reporting on acquisitions was inconsistent under Naidoo's watch and this sloppiness continued into 2018. Shockingly, from the 2009-10 *Annual Report* the prices paid for works are not revealed, nor are the sources; sometimes the Friends' purchases are not listed separately but under donations, at other times they are; the source of the donations is not always clear; purchases under and over R20,000 appear in the 2011-12 report; there were no purchases during 2012-13 fiscal year.

91 Nadine Botha, "The rigorous historian: Anthea Buys," *Mail & Guardian*, March 23, 2012, https://mg.co.za/article/2012-03-23-the-rigorous-historian-anthea-buys (accessed November 12, 2017). Buys worked at SANG from April 2011 to March 21, 2018: Bongani Ndhlovu, email to the author, May 4, 2018.

92 Robyn-Leigh Cedras, email to the author, February 21, 2018.

93 Marianne Thamm, "Blood on the walls as South Africa's national gallery axes first black director," *The Guardian*, May 16, 2014, https://www.theguardian.com/world/2014/may/16/blood-on-the-walls-as-south-africas-national-gallery-axes-first-black-director (accessed June 18, 2017).

94 Matthew Blackman, "Iziko Sacks Director Without Explanation," *Artthrob*, May 9, 2014, http://artthrob.co.za/News/Iziko_Sacks_Director_Without_Explanation_by_M_Blackman_on_09_May.aspx (accessed May 10, 2014).

95 Melvyn Minnaar, "National Gallery a victim of Iziko structure," *Mail & Guardian*, October 10, 2014, https://mg.co.za/article/2014-10-20-future-of-national-gallery-in-doubt (accessed September 25, 2017. Also see: Melvyn Minnaar, "Strydordes opgestel," *Rapport Weekliks*, June 8, 2014.

96 Kendell Geers, open letter to colleagues, partners, members of the media and friends, undated; the author received it on May 10, 2014. I saw Geers at the opening of Zeitz MOCAA on September 16, 2017 and he reiterated his anger and spoke about the suffering he endured as a result of Naidoo's behaviour.

97 Ivor Powell, "SA art: it's tough at the top," *Weekend Argus (Sunday Edition)*, May 18, 2014, https://www.pressreader.com/south-africa/weekend-argus-sunday-edition/20140518/282613145812235 (accessed November 12, 2017).

98 All the information, legal arguments and quotations contained in this section of the book were gleaned from case number C876/2015 held at the Cape Town Labour Court: the court file of the trial hearing set down for August 1-4, 2017; the forty-one-page pleadings bundle that details the background to Naidoo's three claims against Iziko; and a schedule of comments. They constitute documents of public record. Details of complaints that served before the CCMA are included in the file. The first statement of claim at the Labour Court is dated October 8, 2015, amended on June 26, 2017.

99 The programme was made by × CON Films for SABC 3. I was invited to participate, but declined.

100 Employment Equity Act, 1998, Section 6. (1): No person may unfairly discriminate, directly or indirectly, against an employee, in any employment policy or practice, on one or more grounds, including race, gender, sex, pregnancy, marital status, family responsibility, ethnic or social origin, colour, sexual orientation, age, disability, religion, HIV status, conscience, belief, political opinion, culture, language and birth; Section 6. (3): Harassment of an employee is a form of unfair discrimination and is prohibited on any one, or a combination of grounds of unfair discrimination listed in subsection (1): "Employment Equity Act," *Republic of South Africa Government Gazette*, Department of Labour, October 19, 1998, http://www.labour.gov.za/DOL/downloads/legislation/acts/employment-equity/eegazette2015.pdf (accessed July 23, 2018).

101 The Iziko website promotes SANG as "South Africa's premier national art museum": "Friends50," *Iziko Museums of South Africa*, https://www.iziko.org.za/calendar/event/friends50 (accessed April 17, 2018).

102 Iziko *Annual Report*, 2016-2017, 118.

103 Iziko *Annual Report*, 2017-2018, 65 & 117.

104 Iziko *Annual Report*, 2017-2018, 55.

105 Mario Pissarra, "Time to stand up for the South African National Gallery: or why no one cares any more...," *ASAI*, December 7, 2017, http://asai.co.za/time-to-stand-up-for-the-sang/ (accessed July 22, 2018).

CHAPTER 9 – The impact of the new Iziko collections structure and lack of leadership at SANG

1 Jarmel Bell, *The Quote* (Bloomington, IN: Authorhouse, 2011), 13.
2 David Goldblatt quoted in Emma Bedford, "Obituary: Pam Warne," *Artthrob*, April 1, 2014, http://artthrob.co.za/Feature/Obituary_Pam_Warne_by_Emma_Bedford_on_01_April.aspx (accessed December 19, 2017).
3 The End Conscription Campaign (ECC) was formed in 1983. See: "The Objectors," *Thom Pierce*, http://thompierce.com/the-objectors/ (accessed December 18, 2017).
4 Andrea Lewis, email to the author, September 28, 2017.
5 Gerrit Olivier, ed., *Time and Again* (Johannesburg: Wits University Press, 2014). The exhibition travelled to the Wits Art Museum in 2015.
6 Angela Read Lloyd, *The Artist in the Garden The Quest for Moses Tladi* (Noordhoek, Western Cape: Print Matters, 2009).
7 Hayden Proud, "Introduction," in Ibid., unpaginated.
8 Sandra Prosalendis, email to the author, December 1, 2017 – this clarified some confusing information on the Iziko and SKA websites.
9 Sean O'Toole, "One-Man Revolution: Omar Badsha's Latest Exhibition has been called a landmark," *Omar Badsha*, July 18, 2015, https://www.omarbadsha.co.za/node/1337 (accessed November 23, 2017).
10 In late 2017 Iziko made R4 million available for electrical work, lighting, air-conditioning and general refurbishment of the site, as well as upgrading of exhibitions at SANG. The problem was that the money had to be spent by the end of March 2018, which did not happen: Rooksana Omar, email to the author, December 14, 2017; interview with Hamish Robertson, December 7, 2017. According to Ndhlovu "Iziko is presently awaiting approval from heritage authorities to approve its maintenance project for the OTH. As soon as this is finalized, the institution will be able to concretize the date." Bongani Ndhlovu, email to the author, May 4, 2018.
11 The exhibition was also hosted at the Sanlam Art Gallery. See: Michael Godby, *Home Truths: Domestic Interiors in South African Collections* (Cape Town: Primavera Publishing, 2016) and a review of the catalogue: Marilyn Martin, "Home Truths: Domestic Interiors in South African Collections," *de arte* 51 (2016): 73-76.
12 Hundt remains in the dark about the reasons why the paintings never arrived: Stefan Hundt, email to the author, November 27, 2017.
13 Kaufmann and Lewis, *Brushing up on Stern*. The exhibition catalogue includes contributions by Lanitra Berger, Lewis, Proud and Hannah O'Leary; the project was supported by the Irma Stern Museum, Bonhams and Dramatic, Artistic and Literary Rights Organisation (DALRO).
14 Olga Jeffries, email to potential participants, March 8, 2018 with a formal invitation from the CEO attached.
15 Steven Sack, email to the author, October 12, 2018.
16 Ibid.
17 Bongani Ndhlovu, email to the author, March 8, 2017.
18 Interview with Hamish Robertson, December 7, 2017. At what cost might this happen? The 2016–17 expense category for consultants amounted to R944,790, and in 2017-18 to R1,018,871: Iziko *Annual Report*, 2016-2017, 109; Iziko *Annual Report*, 2017-2018, 55. In the latter report consultant fees are given as R799,421 for the previous financial year, and the increase is explained in terms of the need for heritage architects and implementing GRAP 103.
19 After describing the permanent exhibitions at the Iziko Slave Lodge a promise is made: "In the coming years we wish to transform these galleries to draw links to national heritage and history": "Exhibitions," *Iziko Museums of South Africa*, https://www.iziko.org.za/static/landing/exhibitions (accessed February 9, 2017).
20 Pissarra, "Time to stand up," unpaginated.
21 William Kentridge, television interview with John Perlman, "Under the Skin," *eNCA*, January 31, 2018.
22 Baheya Hardy, a social history librarian who is also in charge of the art library and archives, is physically removed, but always willing to assist.
23 Bongani Ndhlovu, email to the author, May 4, 2018. The reference to the availability of staff ignores Shaheeda Dante's presence in and knowledge of the art library. Dante is another of SANG's success stories – she started as a cleaner, was assigned to the art library to assist, and has established herself as the go-to person when staff dwindled.
24 SANG *Annual Report*, 1976-1977, 8.
25 Hamish Robertson, email to the author, October 6, 2017.
26 "New Acquisitions," *Iziko Museums of South Africa*, https://www.iziko.org.za/static/page/art-library-new-acquisitions (accessed December 31, 2017). See: Mario Pissarra, ed., *Awakenings: The Art of Lionel Davis* (Cape Town: ASAI, 2017).

27 South African National Gallery *Annual Reports*, 1972-1973, 19; 1989-1990, 10; 1994-1995, 47.

28 Bongani Ndhlovu, email to the author, May 4, 2018.

29 Iziko *Annual Report*, 2016-2017, 5.

30 Bongani Ndhlovu, email to the author, March 8, 2017.

31 Hamish Robertson, email to the author, October 17, 2017.

32 The 16 Days of Activism for No Violence Against Women and Children is an international awareness-raising campaign. It takes place every year from November 25 (International Day for the Elimination of Violence Against Women) to December 10 (International Human Rights Day). The period includes Universal Children's Day and World Aids Day. The theme for 2016 was "Count me in: together moving a non-violent South Africa forward."

33 The artist was subsequently found guilty of murder and in June 2017 sentenced to eighteen years in prison.

34 Chad Rossouw, "Dialogue and Value," *Artthrob*, December 2, 2016, http://artthrob.co.za/2016/12/02/dialogue-and-value/ (accessed January 3, 2017). Rossouw's critique of the curatorial statements and exhibition is a valuable addition to the discourse, including the reference to Jody Brand's work *#SayHerName*, which was shown at Michael Stevenson.

35 "Joint statement issued 29 November 2016 by: Iziko Museums of South Africa & New Church Museum," *Iziko Museums of South Africa*, http://www.iziko.org.za/news/entry/joint-statement-issued-29-november-2016-by-iziko-museums-of-south-africa (accessed January 3, 2017).

36 Having curated the exhibition *Thinking, Feeling, Head, Heart* for the NCM in 2014, I am familiar with Piet Viljoen's collection. See: Marilyn Martin, *Thinking, Feeling, Head, Heart* (Cape Town: The New Church Museum, 2014). Curators of other shows were, Penny Siopis, Rory Bester, Kirsty Cockerill and Candice Allison, curator at the museum.

37 "A letter to Iziko SANG and The New Church Museum," *Artthrob*, December 17, 2016, http://artthrob.co.za/2016/12/17/a-letter-to-iziko-sang-and-the-new-church-museum/ (accessed January 3, 2017).

38 Catherine Rice, "Curator defends exhibition of murder accused artist's work," *IOL*, November 28, 2016, http://www.iol.co.za/news/crime-courts/curator-defends-exhibition-of-murder-accused-artists-work-2094089 (accessed January 3, 2017).

39 Bongani Ndhlovu, email to the author, December 12, 2016.

40 Rice, "Curator defends exhibition"; see also: "#16DaysofActivism | Backlash for Iziko over Zwelethu Mthethwa," *Arterial Network*, November 30, 2016, http://www.arterialnetwork.org/article/iziko_zwelethu_mthethwa_fauxpas_2016 (accessed January 7, 2017).

41 Breitz put her and the artists' proposals for salvaging and transforming the exhibition in a follow-up letter, *Our Lady*/Moving Forward, to SANG curators dated December 19, 2016. It included the display of their collective letter of withdrawal; offer to edit, free of charge, the screening of the footage filmed during the event; and the acquisition of Warren's portrait of Nokuphila Kumalo from SWEAT. Breitz also listed the names of curators, scholars and feminists who were following the conversation and hoping for reconciliation: Bisi Silva, Sisonke Msimang, M. Neelika Jayawardane, Nana Oforiatta-Ayim, Zoe Whitley, Simone Leigh and Aruna D'Souza.

42 "Our Lady Arts Action Discourse," *Iziko Museums of South Africa*, December 22, 2016, http://www.iziko.org.za/news/entry/our-lady-arts-action-discourse (accessed December 21, 2016). The South African Pavilion at the 57th Venice Biennale comprised: Candice Breitz, *Love Story* (2016), seven-channel installation; and Mohau Modisakeng, *Passage* (2017), three-channel film installation.

43 "Iziko's response to Our Lady petition," *Iziko Museums of South Africa*, January 13, 2017, http://www.iziko.org.za/news/entry/izikos-response-to-our-lady-petition (accessed January 13, 2017).

44 Hamish Robertson, email to the author, January 5, 2017.

45 Candice Breitz, email to the author, January 8, 2017.

46 At the 2017 ANC Elective Conference (December 16-20, 2017) the organisation decided to fully decriminalise sex work, thereby further protecting women from abuse and stigma.

47 I am grateful to Ingrid Masondo, email to the author, January 23, 2018; and Andrea Lewis, email to the author, January 8, 2018, for providing information about initiatives before and after the *Our Lady* exhibition.

48 For a review of the show, in which Hutton's work is merely described, see Amie Soudien, "Past and Present Struggles: 'The Art of Disruptions' at SANG," *Artthrob*, September 21, 2016, https://artthrob.co.za/2016/09/ (accessed August 27, 2018.

49 "Art and Outrage: National Gallery under attack," (*Daily Maverick*, January 18, 2017); and "Om kuns aan te val", *Die Burger*, January 2017, 21).

50 Rebecca Davis, "Art and Outrage: National Gallery under attack," *Daily Maverick*, January 18, 2017, https://www.dailymaverick.co.za/article/2017-01-18-art-and-outrage-national-gallery-under-attack/ (accessed January 20, 2017).

51 Iziko lawyer, Jeremy Klerck, quoted by Petru Saal in "'F-k White People' exhibition is art, not hate speech – court," *Times Live*, July 5, 2017, https://www.timeslive.co.za/news/south-africa/2017-07-05-warning-explicit-language-f-k-white-people-exhibition-is-art-not-hate-speech-court/ (accessed July 10, 2017).

52 Rooksana Omar, "Reflecting on the past, looking forward to the future", *Iziko Museums of South Africa*, January 12, 2018, http://www.iziko.org.za/news/entry/reflecting-on-the-past-looking-forward-to-the-future-a-message-from-our-ceo (accessed January 12, 2018).

53 "In Pictures: the great f**king debate at Wits," *eNCA*, February 12, 2016, https://www.enca.com/south-africa/pictures-great-fcking-debate-wits (accessed December 26, 2017).

54 Gareth van Onselen, "'F**k White People': zero f**ks given," *Business Live*, January 16, 2017, https://www.businesslive.co.za/bd/opinion/columnists/2017-01-16-gareth-van-onselen-fk-white-people-zero-fk-given/ (accessed January 20, 2017).

55 Marianne Gray, "National Gallery is 100 years old," *Cape Times*, February 19, 1972. I am grateful to Marc Barben for alerting me to this incident: Marc Barben, "What does it mean to be a 'national' gallery when notions of 'nation' transform radically?" (MA diss., University of Cape Town, 2015), 121, note 117.

56 "Fuckface," *Kendell Geers*, http://www.kendellgeers.com/library/works/84 (accessed December 26, 2017). For more on Geers' intellectual and political iconoclasm, and how some works relate to Marcel Duchamp, see Paul Ingram, "Pissing in Duchamp's Fountain," *3:AM Magazine*, http://www.3ammagazine.com/3am/pissing-in-duchamps-fountain/(accessed December 26, 2017).

CHAPTER 10 – New national policies for arts, culture and heritage, and a return to major themes of the book

1 Ashraf Jamal, email to the author, May 16, 2018.

2 Mike van Graan, "Revised White Paper on Arts, Culture and Heritage – a critique," December 8, 2016, unpaginated, https://mikevangraan.wordpress.com/2016/12/ (accessed January 30, 2018). I am grateful to Van Graan for sending me his critique, and indebted to him for the way in which it informed this section of the book. I urge anyone who is seriously interested in the process and impact of the RWP to read this document.

3 *Revised White Paper on Arts, Culture and Heritage*, Department of Arts and Culture, October 2017, http://www.dac.gov.za/white-papers (accessed January 4, 2018). For in-depth analyses see: "Comment on the revised draft White Paper on Arts, Culture and Heritage," *The Archival Platform*, http://www.archivalplatform.org/blog/entry/comment_on_the_revised_draft_white_paper/ (accessed January 4, 2018); and Mike van Graan, "Oratio: A non-lawyer's views on the revised White Paper on Arts, Culture and Heritage," *Potchefstroom Electronic Law Journal/Potchefstroomse Elektroniese Regsblad* 16, no. 3 (2013), http://sayas.org.za/per/article/view/2352/3396 (accessed January 4, 2018).

4 *White Paper on Arts, Culture and Heritage*, Department of Arts and Culture, June 4, 1996, unpaginated, http://www.dac.gov.za/content/white-paper-arts-culture-and-heritage-0#CHAP3 (accessed January 4, 2018).

5 *Revised White Paper on Arts, Culture and Heritage*, Department of Arts and Culture, June 4, 2013, 30, http://www.dac.gov.za/sites/default/files/REVISEDWHITEPAPER04062013.pdf (accessed January 4, 2018).

6 *Revised White Paper on Arts, Culture and Heritage*, Department of Arts and Culture, February 2017, 8, http://www.dac.gov.za/sites/default/files/Legislations%20Files/Revised%203rd%20Draft%20RWP%20on%20ACH%20FEBRUARY%202017_0.pdf (accessed January 4, 2018).

7 Matthew Blackman, "Minister Mashatile's 'Teapot' Will Not Save Us!," *Artthrob*, September 17, 2013, http://artthrob.co.za/Feature/Minister_Mashatiles_Teapot_Will_Not_Save_Us__by_M_Blackman_on_17_September.aspx (accessed October 5, 2017).

8 "Arts and culture DG departs, *The Citizen*, January 29, 2015, https://citizen.co.za/news/south-africa/317362/arts-culture-dg-departs/ (accessed December 26, 2017). For an analysis of the challenges of compliance and service delivery at all levels of government, see Peter E. Franks, "The Crisis of the South African Public Service," *Journal of the Helen Suzman Foundation* 74 (2014), http://hsf.org.za/resource-centre/focus/state-and-nation/9.the-crisis-of-the-south-african-public-service-p.pdf (accessed January 4, 2018).

9 The reference panel comprised Prof. A. Oliphant (he chaired the ACTAG process), Dr. S. Fikeni, Prof. M. Nkondo, Ms. A. Joffe, Father S. Mkhatshwa, Dr. A. Beukes, Mr. T. Kgoroge, Ms. L. Mashile and Ms. T. Goso.

10 Van Graan, "Revised White Paper," unpaginated.

11 Ibid. This reminds me of the public interview before my appointment to the NAC, as well as Ben Ngubane's refusal, against the provision in the NAC Act, to re-appoint me after having been elected by my peers for a second term, because I had consistently raised critical questions; the process and outcome are discussed in chapter six.

12 Ibid.

13 Bongani Ndhlovu, email to the author, May 4, 2018.

14 Iziko *Annual Report*, 2016-2017, 12.

15 Iziko, Minutes of council meeting, November 6, 2012, 2.

16 Wayne Alexander, email to the author, March 2, 2017.

17 Yentl Kohler, email to Wayne Alexander and forwarded to the author, March 23, 2017. Kohler added that gallery walkabouts were related to the schools curriculum and that there were ongoing partnerships with schools, in order to serve their educational needs: "We hope to create an environment for learners in which they can make their voices heard through the medium of art."

18 Andrea Lewis, email to the author, September 28, 2017.

19 Jeremy Kuper, "The structures that David Goldblatt values," *Mail & Guardian*, April 24, 2015, http://mg.co.za/article/2015-04-23-david-goldblatt-structures (accessed April 25, 2015). I recommend novelist and poet Christopher Hope's account of a journey around South Africa that begins when the Rhodes statue was attacked, and that traces the fate and future of monuments in the country: Christopher Hope, *The Café de Move-on Blues In Search of the New South Africa* (London: Atlantic Books, 2018).

20 Editorial, "#FeesMustFall is shaking us up," *Mail & Guardian*, October 23, 2015, http://mg.co.za/article/2015-10-22-editorial-feesmustfall-is-shaking-us-up (accessed November 2, 2015).

21 Yusuf Omar, "Trans Collective stops RMF exhibition," *UCT News*, March 10, 2016, https://www.news.uct.ac.za/article/-2016-03-10-trans-collective-stops-rmf-exhibition (accessed July 28, 2018).

22 For an in-depth analysis of what happened and how this fraught situation would unfold over the months to come, see Ivor Powell, "Behind UCT's Removed Art: the Writing on the Wall," *Art Times*, August 2, 2017, http://arttimes.co.za/behind-ucts-removed-art-writing-wall-ivor-powell/ (accessed January 19, 2018); see also: "Art Under Threat at University of Cape Town," *Art Times*, August 1, 2017, http://arttimes.co.za/art-threat-university-cape-town/ (accessed January 19, 2018).

23 For details on the decision and consequences, see Dewald van Rensburg and Msindisi Fengu, "Zuma's fee-free higher education chaos," *City Press*, January 7, 2018, https://www.news24.com/SouthAfrica/News/zumas-fee-free-chaos-20180107-2 (accessed January 12, 2018).

24 Iziko *Annual Report*, 2017-2018, back cover.

25 This assertion is based on personal experience. I had co-curated an exhibition, *Albert Adams (1929-2006): A fractured history*, with Robyn-Leigh Cedras at the Rupert Museum in Stellenbosch (June 8 – October 5), after which it was going to travel to DAG (November 29 – February 15, 2018). It soon became clear that the responsible curator was not up to the task and I found myself trying to manage him long-distance. After working on the exhibition for eighteen months and then realising that the required loan agreements had not been sent, we decided to cancel the show, for the sake of all our reputations and the safety of the artworks. The lack of professionalism at every level deprived DAG and the people of Durban and KwaZulu-Natal of a major retrospective that was fully funded by SMAC Gallery. The KwaZulu-Natal Society of the Arts and the African Art Centre fill the vacuum to some extent, but it is depressing to see art museums with remarkable collections fall into such lamentable administrative states that they can no longer perform their core functions.

26 The Portuguese slave ship was wrecked near the Cape of Good Hope in 1794 and a research project, led by Iziko maritime archaeologist Jaco Boshoff, was launched in 2008. The Slave Wrecks Project, has since grown into Iziko's and the South African Heritage Resource Agency's collaboration with the Smithsonian and George Washington University.

27 Angela Zehnder and Bronwyn Leone, *Painted Surfaces: A Technical Study of Paintings from the Iziko South African National Gallery* (Cape Town: Iziko Museums, 2017). The educator and conservators did a great deal to promote the exhibition, the book and the programmes in the media and on the Iziko website; they prepared a "welcome brochure" and another in how to care for one's own collection in Afrikaans, English and Xhosa.

28 Hayden Proud, email to the author, October 22, 2018.

29 Hamish Robertson, email to the author, November 11, 2016.

30 "Reflecting on the past, looking forward to the future – a Message from our CEO," *Iziko Museums of South Africa*, January 12, 2018, http://www.iziko.org.za/news/entry/reflecting-on-the-past-looking-forward-to-the-future-a-message-from-our-ceo (accessed January 12, 2018).

31 It was common knowledge among museum staff, and confirmed by Robertson in a private conversation, that he was in such a state of distress that he resigned on impulse (instead of applying for early retirement) and that he sent an email to many colleagues detailing the reasons for his resignation. Unsurprisingly, other individuals saw the email. This was a big mistake and his subsequent withdrawal of his resignation and appeal to Iziko council to grant him early retirement were not approved. After decades of dedicated service to SAM and Iziko, at the end of March 2018, Robertson was told to be out of his office by 13:00 the next day. This was a message to staff not to commit the sins of bending under pressure, naiveté and transparency. While Robertson regretted his "unwise" actions, he did not regret leaving Iziko. He subsequently appealed successfully to Iziko council to consider granting him early retirement to mitigate the negative financial implications: Hamish Robertson, email to the author, June 21, 2018.

32 This information was apparently privileged: There was nothing on the Iziko website to inform the public. There is no acknowledgement of Robertson's contribution – over nearly three decades – to SAM and Iziko; he is simply a number in a table of "Terminations": Iziko *Annual Report*, 2017-2018, 60.

33 Iziko *Annual Report*, 2017-2018, 16-17.

34 Iziko *Annual Report*, 2017-2018, 138 & 128-137 respectively.

35 Hayden Proud, email to the author, 7 September 2018.

36 One example will suffice. In conversation with me, Sue Williamson mentioned that elements of her major installation *Messages from the Moat* (1997), which is composed of engraved and stencilled glass, printed canvas, found fishing net and water pump, had been lost and that it was incomplete. This untenable situation pointed directly to the space constraints that Iziko tried to solve by moving works to off-site storage in a DPW hangar. I followed up with Ernestine White who assured me that the work had been returned to the gallery, that Williamson and Zehnder had managed to acquire the missing components and that they were preparing the work for an upcoming exhibition, *Can't remember, Can't forget*, at the Apartheid Museum in Johannesburg: Ernestine White, email to the author, March 6, 2017.

37 "Public Architecture, Heritage, Art and the City" held on June 24, 2015.

38 Robertson was committed to taking the project forward and to this end he arranged a meeting with Noero and me in November 2016 to discuss the extensions; I provided all the documentation prepared for the honours course. A year later we met again and, although 2021 was a long way off, there was recognition at last that the decades-overdue space constraints at SANG were a priority that required action. With Robertson's departure, the future is unclear, and there is no policy regarding alleviation of the space constraints.

39 Quoted from Barben, "What does it mean," 145. The Iziko web page is no longer active.

40 I have not been able to trace the drawings; my search included contacting Hannes Meiring's widow, Martie Retief-Meiring who kindly tried to assist, but who could not find them: Martie Meiring, email to the author, April 2, 2018.

41 Anna Tietze, *A History*, 10. Tietze writes a great deal about classificatory boundaries and public art collections and ignores the history of African art in major art museums as discussed in chapter four of this volume.

42 Reinhild Kauenhofen Janzen, "African Art in Cape Town: Where is it, what it is? Irma Stern's African Art Collection in Context," *Quarterly Bulletin* 15 (1983): 1-7. When I served on the Iziko council (2010-13), I circulated copies of this article to members in order to conscientise them about the need to find a permanent home and appropriate context in which to display the Iziko collections of African aesthetic production – not a permanent display as in the ISM, but a space in which changing exhibitions could be curated.

43 Bruce Arnott, Letter to the Editor, *Quarterly Bulletin* 16 (1984): 7.

44 E. M. Shaw, Letter to the Editor, Ibid., 8.

45 For more on the Penny collection see Brent Meersman, "Adventurer's artefacts fall under the hammer," *Mail & Guardian*, September 20, 2018, https://mg.co.za/article/2013-09-20-adventurers-artefacts-fall-under-the-hammer, (accessed January 11, 2018). Details of the donation to Iziko were accessed in: "Progress report on Performance of the CEO in the 3rd Quarter of the Fiscal Year 2012/13," October-December 2012, 1.

46 Iziko *Annual Report*, 2014-2015, 154.

47 Thanks to Pippa Skotnes and the UCT CCA, a wealth of material is being safeguarded, researched and interpreted.

48 Hamish Robertson, email to the author, October 6, 2017.

49 Iziko staff is graded on the Peromnes system, but even before 2008 the salaries were falling behind the grades and this has not been addressed. Currently the salary scale for a curator is R341,508 – R462,060 per annum. Proud is at the top of the scale, but Robertson's remuneration cost Iziko R1,075,375 (including bonus, allowances, employer contributions and payments for subsistence and other expenditure): Iziko *Annual Report*, 2016-2017, 115. Paul Tichman's salary has increased from a basic R162,404 in 2016-17 to R511,572 in 2017-18. Zeitz MOCAA advertised for a curator of digital platforms (a three-year contract) on February 2, 2017 and a curator of costume on May 19, 2017; the salaries offered were R400,000 (cost to company with all deductions withheld from the amount). In an email dated July 3, 2017, Zeitz offered opportunities for sixteen assistant curators, for twelve months at different levels of support, a total scholarship amounting to R272,422 (Coetzee had established the programme in 2001). As of May 2018 the only figures for the Norval Foundation in the public domain were those for a curatorial assistant for one year: R192,000 (cost to company with all deductions withheld from the amount).

50 Minutes of the core functions meeting, October 24, 2012 (at the same meeting I reported on my recent trip to Documenta 13 in Kassel, Germany and agreed to give an informal talk on breaking down disciplinary barriers in 2013); Minutes of the core functions and institutional advancement sub-committee of council meeting, July 17, 2013, 2.

51 Sepadi Moruthane told me in conversation that he was leaving because he was on contract and he did not know from year to year whether his position was secure. Iziko is showing a propensity for contract appointments: of the thirty-four appointments made in 2017-18, five were indefinite and twenty-nine on short-term contract, a number at assistant level: Iziko *Annual Report* 2017-2018, 59. Iziko is not offering job security to staff and cannot expect loyalty and trust in return.

52 Letter from Robert Greig to Rooksana Omar, December 2, 2015.

53 Letter from Robert Greig to Rooksana Omar, December 15, 2016.

54 Letter from Rooksana Omar to Robert Greig, February 18, 2016.

55 Notes of a meeting chaired by the CEO with the three groups of Friends and the directors of art and natural history collections, February 15, 2005.

56 As a council member from 2010-13 I experienced this first hand many times, prompting me to write to the CEO to express my concern: Marilyn Martin, email to Rooksana Omar, February 17, 2011. The importance of "ensuring that the Friends are diversified to mutually explore continued involvement in Iziko's programmes, and avoiding the risk of alienating them", was raised by councillor Pearl Sithole: Minutes of the Iziko council, November 6, 2012, 3.

57 Henley Business School, "Analysis of Iziko Museum's relationships with Friends Organisations," 2013. The document was attached to the Iziko Council Minutes, July 31, 2013.

58 Minutes of the core functions and institutional advancement sub-committee of council meeting, July 17, 2013, minuted under "Partners 2012/13", 1-2. In November 2012 there was a special ceremony, followed by an illustrated lecture by the artist and a cocktail party.

59 Bongani Ndhlovu, "*Friends50* Welcome Address," April 15, 2018. The newly-elected FONG council comprised: Gcobani Sipoyo (chairperson), Phillippa Duncan (vice-chairperson), Winnie Sze (treasurer), Jilly Cohen, Claire Graaff and Robert Mulders. FONG no longer has a secretary to coordinate events and memberships.

60 Claire Armitstead, "Should a museum dump its Warhols to buy up work by artists of colour?," *The Guardian*, May 4, 2018, https://www.theguardian.com/artanddesign/2018/may/04/baltimore-museum-art-warhol-artists-of-colour?page=with%3Aimg-2 (accessed May 16, 2018).

61 Jamal spoke from a few notes, I did not want to misquote him, and so I approached him for comment on the matters that struck me; he kindly responded: Ashraf Jamal, email to the author, May 16, 2018.

CHAPTER 11 – Fundamental changes in the South African art and museum ecosystem

1 Carlos Fuentes, National Arts Club Speech (1988), quoted in William Least Heat-Moon, *PrairyErth: A Deep Map* (New York: Houghton Mifflin Harcourt, 2014), 303.

2 The silos became the catalyst and inspiration for the design of an urban precinct that echoes the silo circles. Designed by Van der Merwe Miszewski Architects (VDMMA) in association with Heatherwick Studio and Makeka Design Lab (MDL), there are six mixed use buildings, silo 1-6: "Silo Precinct," *VDMMA*, https://www.vdmma.com/silo-precinct (accessed June 13, 2018).

3 Jochen Zeitz, introductory remarks to Thomas Heatherwick's lecture during the first viewing weekend, September 16, 2017.

4 A major fundraising auction was held at Christie's in London on March 27, 2017. Fourteen artists – including El Anatsui, Kendell Geers, Frances Goodman, Antony Gromley, Isaac Julien, William Kentridge and Yinka Shonibare – donated work: "Zeitz MOCAA," *Christies*, https://www.christies.com/zmags?ZmagsPublishID=582110e7 (accessed May 5, 2018).

5 Unless otherwise indicated, Mark Coetzee's remarks and information about the museum are drawn from a lecture he presented during the first viewing weekend (September 16, 2017), information I receive as a member and the museum website https://zeitzmocaa.museum/. In addition to Green and Zeitz the board members were: Isaac Julien and Wangechi Mutu (artist members), Suzanne Ackerman, Jody Allen, Jonathan Bloch, Kate Garwood, Pulane Kingston, Gasant Orrie, Albie Sachs, Anton Taljaard, Roger Ross Williams and Mark Coetzee (ex officio).

6 Corporate sponsors include Bloomberg, BMW and Standard Bank. For more on the controversy, as well as other information about the museum see Sean O'Toole, "Are there blind spots in Zeitz MOCAA's permanent art collection?" *Sunday Times Lifestyle*, September 19, 2017, https://www.timeslive.co.za/sunday-times/lifestyle/2017-09-19-are-there-blind-spots-in-zeitz-mocaas-permanent-art-collection/(accessed September 21, 2017); Melvyn Minnaar, "Zeitz MOCAA-Museum open Kuns vir die miljardêrs," *Die Burger*, September 21, 2017; Sue Williamson, "Zeitz MOCAA is here," *Artthrob*, September 13, 2017, https://artthrob.co.za/2017/09/13/zeitz-mocaa-is-here/ (accessed October 2, 2017); and John O'Cealliaigh, "A re-imagining of a museum": the essential insider guide to Cape Town's newly opened Zeitz MOCAA", *Telegraph*, September 22, 2017, http://www.telegraph.co.uk/luxury/travel/zeitz-mocaa-cape-town-opening-date-guide-tips/ (accessed September 25, 2017).

7 The *Preview Week* welcoming booklet contained the names of fifty-two people who formed part of Coetzee's museum team. At the time the museum had seventy-six partner schools, with sponsorship for busses and refreshments.

8 According to critic Matthew Blackman, "Coetzee has recently failed to respond to questions about the institutional practices at Zeitz MOCAA. Instead he simply replied to an email stating that the questions sent to him [by *Artthrob*] 'seemed quite far removed from the reality of how the museum functions.'" The public was in the dark about that "reality". Blackman also stated that there "have been unconfirmed rumours for some months that abuses of power were taking place, the nature of which are [sic] not known": Matthew Blackman, "Inquiry launched into professional conduct of Zeitz MOCAA Director," *Artthrob*, May 16, 2018, https://artthrob.co.za/2018/05/16/inquiry-launched-into-professional-conduct-of-zeitz-mocaa-director/ (accessed May 17, 2018). For an excellent analysis of the museum's "unbalanced internal structure", a breakdown of the advisory board members and other pertinent issues, see Sue Williamson, "Zeitz MOCAA: The Way Forward," *Artthrob*, July 11, 2018, https://

artthrob.co.za/2018/07/11/zeitz-mocaa-the-way-forward/ (accessed November 12, 2018). An acquisitions committee has been appointed, but the absence of a South African art museum professional has not been addressed.

9 Francesca Villette, "Zeitz MOCAA fires its director after Labour Court battle," *Cape Times*, July 3, 2018, https://www.iol.co.za/capetimes/news/zeitz-mocaa-fires-its-director-after-labour-court-battle-15795752 (accessed August 8, 2018).

10 VDMMA was appointed as local executive architects together with Rick Brown Associate Architects (RBA) and John Pardy Architects (JPA): "Zeitz MOCAA," *VDMMA*, https://www.vdmma.com/zeitz-mocaa (accessed June 13, 2018).

11 In 2017 it was listed as one of the architecture and design magazine *Dezeen's* top ten museums and galleries.The list included the Louvre Abu Dhabi, Museo de Sitio C Tello situated on the edge of the Paracas National Reserve in Peru, Musée Yves Saint Laurent in Marrakesh, the Palestinian Museum on the West Bank and the Lascaux IV Caves Museum: India Block, "Dezeen's top 10 museum and gallery buildings," *Dezeen*, December 4, 2017, https://www.dezeen.com/2017/12/04/10-best-museum-gallery-buildings-architecture-2017-review-roundup/?utm_medium=email&utm_campaign=Daily%20Dezeen%20Digest&utm_content=Daily%20Dezeen%20Digest+CID_aadd0a73a97e709cd62af5b6fa77cafe&utm_source=Dezeen%20Mail&utm_term=More (accessed December 4, 2016).

12 "'Africa's Tate Modern' – Cape Town's Zeitz-Mocaa gallery opens," *The Guardian*, September 21, 2017, https://www.theguardian.com/travel/2017/sep/21/cape-town-zeitz-mocaa-art-museum-africa-open-september-2017?CMP=share_btn_link (accessed September 23, 2017).

13 Rebecca Davis, "Zeitz Mocaa: Cape Town's new art museum stuns and provokes," *Daily Maverick,* September 26, 2017, http://firstthing.dailymaverick.co.za/article.php?id=94799&cid=2017-09-26#.WcpKJ7iddh8 (accessed September 30, 2017).

14 Ibid. The museum featured as one of the "world's greatest places" in *Time*, echoing the hyperbole: Kate Rockwood, "A new home for African art," in *Time*, September 3-10, 2018, 79.

15 "The All-you-need-to-know guide to the Zeitz MOCAA," *V&A The Guide*, Summer 2018, 7.

16 Sean O'Toole, "Art brings home the grain drain," *Mail & Guardian*, December 13, 2013, https://mg.co.za/article/2013-12-12-art-brings-home-the-grain-drain (accessed August 8, 2018).

17 Such reviews are emerging; see for instance Lloyd Pollak, "The Zeitz Museum of Art Africa," *Lloyd's Artbeat*, http://lloyds-artbeat.co.za/wp-content/uploads/2018/02/AAAAA-MY-ARTICLE-ON-ZEITZ.pdf; and Lloyd Pollak, "Art at the Zeitz," *Lloyd's Artbeat*, http://lloyds-artbeat.co.za/art-at-the-zeitz/ (accessed February 23, 2018).

18 Claire Keeton, "Tripping on the Zeitz fantastic! Artists give new museum rave reviews," *Timeslive*, 15 September 2017, https://www.timeslive.co.za/sunday-times/lifestyle/2017-09-15-tripping-on-the-zeitz-fantastic-artists-give-new-museum-rave-reviews/ (accessed September 17, 2017).

19 Jackie May, "In Pictures: Inside Zeitz MOCAA, the museum everyone's talking about, "*Sunday Times Lifestyle*, September 15, 2017, https://www.timeslive.co.za/sunday-times/lifestyle/2017-09-15-in-pictures-inside-zeitz-mocaa-the-museum-everyones-talking-about/ (accessed September 17, 2017).

20 Melvyn Minnaar, "Great fanfare and setting, but will the Zeitz museum promote grassroots art?," *Business Live*, September 26, 2017, https://www.businesslive.co.za/bd/life/arts-and-entertainment/2017-09-26-great-fanfare-and-setting-but-will-the-zeitz-museum-promote-grassroots-art/ (accessed September 28, 2017).

21 Sean O'Toole, "...And while we're on the subject of art," *Sunday Times Lifestyle*, September 10, 2017, 10.

22 The major institutions seem to be beset by more problems than, for example, the Oliewenhuis Art Museum in Bloemfontein and the WHAG in Kimberley. The level of incompetence I experienced at DAG in 2017 is explained in chapter nine, note 77. JAG seems to have turned the corner after thirty years of wilful neglect by the Johannesburg municipality; after a period without a curator-in-chief, academic and historian Khwezi Gule was appointed in January 2018. Paging through *CONSTRUCTURE: 100 years of the JAG building*, one is aware of the rich history, as well as the many initiatives, projects and interventions made by staff, the Friends and artists to attract diverse visitors and animate the spaces. In 2017 the city committed R50 million for renovations: Murinik, CONSTRUCTURE, viii. For more on the saga see Luke Alfred, "Rocky road to Johannesburg Art Gallery's restoration," *Business Live*, May 18, 2017, https://www.businesslive.co.za/fm/life/art/2017-05-18-rocky-road-to-johannesburg-art-gallerys-restoration/ (accessed November 11, 2017).

23 In 2017 Themba Wakashe, former DAC director-general and former CEO of the Film and Publications Board, chaired council's core functions committee, joined by advocate Judith Leshabane; the Iziko council comprised: Ambassador Dikgang Moopeloa (chairperson), Advocate Judith Leshabane; Ms. Sijabulile Makhatihini; Mr. Andries Mooke; Mr. Tshimangadzo Nemaheni (resigned in January 2018); Prof. Sadhasivan Perumal; Advocate Rod Solomons; and Wakashe: Iziko *Annual Report*, 2016-2017, 8-9. Emoluments and honoraria to council members varied and increased from R113,214 in 2016-17 to R229,800 in 2017-18: Iziko *Annual Report*, 2016-2017, 114, and Iziko *Annual Report* 2017-2018, 113.

24 Michael Morris, "Warning of threat to National Gallery," *Weekend Argus*, November 29, 2015, 5.

25 In March 2017 I wrote to Bongani Ndhlovu to enquire about Iziko's approach to the Zeitz MOCAA opening; he replied that Iziko welcomed and supported the initiative and that "Our team members (including Susan [Glanville-Zini] and Ernestine White) are

in contact with the Zeitz and discussing some possibilities": Bongani Ndhlovu, email to the author, March 8, 2017. My emails to Glanville-Zini and White for details remained unanswered and it is clear that nothing happened. In an interview on December 7, 2017, Robertson said that Zeitz MOCAA had been a "wake-up call" for Iziko and that there would be cooperation.

26 Alexia Walker, "The Zeitz museum zooms in on African photographers," *Business Live*, October 5, 2017, https://www.businesslive.co.za/bd/life/2017-10-05-alexia-walker-the-zeitz-museum-zooms-in-on-african-photographers/ (accessed October 7).

27 Working with fourteen professional singers, composers Philip Miller and Thuthuka Sibisi re-invented songs based on programme notes from a concert by the touring South African choir, which took place in London during the summer of 1891. The exhibition, presented in partnership with Autograph ABP and Tshisa Boys Productions, comprised a multi-channel music recording and a body of large scale photographs by The London Stereoscopic Company, depicting the sixteen choir members in 1891; they were produced from original glass plates rediscovered at the Hulton Archive after 125 years. Supported by Gallery MOMO, Tshabangu's *Footprints* was curated by Thembinkosi Goniwe and shown at the Standard Bank Gallery in Johannesburg and at the National Arts Festival in Grahamstown prior to travelling to Cape Town.

28 This text is contradicted with the facts in a smaller text in the space, after I pointed out to Kaufmann that her information was incorrect; my attempts to have the text replaced have proved fruitless.

29 The exhibition was curated by Lewis and gallerist Heidi Erdmann, drawing on the works from the SANG and Bauer collections. It was a beautifully designed exhibition, bristling with his masterly drawings and the walls activated with the imagery, words and splashes characteristic of his approach; a video projection featured Zapiro in conversation with Brandan Reynolds. For Lewis it was "fascinating to work with Bauer's cartoons and to also consider the genre of cartooning (which is not often considered in a formal museum context)": Andrea Lewis, email to the author, September 28, 2017.

30 Anyone who went straight to https://www.iziko.org.za/museums/exhibitions/south-african-national-gallery as late as September 25, would have found a 2010 picture of the building and information that was completely out of date; and there was no reference to *Hidden Treasures* on https://www.iziko.org.za/calendar/exhibitions/current, *At Face Value*, advertised to close on December 15, was no more. By October 2018 works from the Bailey collection had been removed to a new exhibition in another room, and *Butcher Boys* left behind in what looked more like open storage than an exhibition space.

31 "Good Times Ahead," Iziko *Newsletter*, March 28, 2018, http://www.iziko.org.za/news/entry/good-times-ahead, (accessed April 16, 2018). The Michaelis Collection is listed, but remains closed in January 2019, as does Bertram House.

32 Jochen Zeitz, quoted by Maya Jaggi, "Zeitz Mocaa: a shining beacon for African art," *Financial Times*, September 20, 2017, https://www.ft.com/content/077bf3fe-9a2f-11e7-8c5c-c8d8fa6961bb (accessed September 22, 2017).

33 Williamson, *Zeitz MOCAA*.

34 For more on the Nonprofit Organisations Act see Ibid.

35 The ICOM definition (adopted by the 22nd General Assembly in Vienna, Austria, on August 24, 2007) applies across the board and does not distinguish between public and private museums: "A museum is a non-profit, permanent institution in the service of society and its development, open to the public, which acquires, conserves, researches, communicates and exhibits the tangible and intangible heritage of humanity and its environment for the purposes of education, study and enjoyment," http://icom.museum/thevision/museum-definition/ (accessed September 27, 2017). Distinctions exist in the United States, although the lines between private and public are not rigidly drawn – they may share characteristics and may be hybrids, with much depending on the "civic mindedness" of the private institution and its founders. For more on museums in the United States see, Madelaine D'Angelo, "Public vs. Private, Who Wins?," *Huffington Post*, June 10, 2015, https://www.huffingtonpost.com/madelaine dangelo/public-vs-private-who-win_b_8248518.html (accessed September 24, 2017).

36 Low visitor numbers and high costs were cited as reasons for the closure, but a number of factors led to the failure of the museum: a confusing name (named after the street), an isolated position with little pedestrian traffic, and lack of marketing and engagement with the public.

37 The Norval Foundation is the custodian of the Gerard Sekoto Foundation, Edoardo Villa Estate Collection, and the Alexis Preller Archive: *Norval Foundation*, http://www.norvalfoundation.org/ (accessed March 27, 2018). Karel Nel invited me to join a small group on a tour of the building site on February 14, 2018 and I was privileged to attend the opening private garden party fundraiser as a guest on April 27.

38 Elizabeth Burroughs and Karel Nel, *Re/discovery and Memory: The works of Kumalo, Legae, Nitegeka & Villa* (Cape Town: Norval Foundation and the Claire & Edoardo Villa Will Trust), 2018.

39 *Javett Art Centre*, http://www.javettup.org.za/ (accessed October 3, 2017).

40 Stefan Simchowitz, quoted in Brendon Bell-Roberts, "Africa is Open for Business," *Art Africa*, September 26, 2017, http://artafricamagazine.org/africa-open-business/?mc_cid=7487595ae9&mc_eid=4558813515 (accessed October 8, 2017).

41 "Dr Same Mdluli appointed as gallery manager of Standard Bank Gallery," *Arttimes*, February 13, 2018, http://arttimes.co.za/dr-mdluli-appointed-gallery-manager-standard-bank-gallery/ (accessed February 13, 2018).

42 For example, the National Gallery of Art in Washington announced with great pride that its first female director, Kaywin Feldman, would occupy the position from March 2019: Victoria Stapley-Brown, "National Gallery of Art in Washington hires

its first female director," *The Art Newspaper*, December 11, 2018, https://www.theartnewspaper.com/news/national-gallery-of-art-hires-its-first-female-director?utm_source=daily_december12_2018&utm_medium=email&utm_campaign=email_daily&utm_source=The+Art+Newspaper+Newsletters&utm_campaign=37de7eb7de-EMAIL_CAMPAIGN_2018_12 (accessed December 16, 2018).

43 Matthew Blackman, "How Mark Coetzee's resignation may lift the lid on the arts industry's practices," interview in the *Mail & Guardian*, May 25, 2018, https://mg.co.za/article/2018-05-25-how-art-world-truly-imitates-life (accessed May 30, 2018).

44 "The core goal of the museum is to get the collection out and known to the public as much as possible ... the digital reproduction of an item would pique public interest in it, leading them to buy tickets to the museum to see the real deal." For an analysis of and comments on this decision, see Timothy Vollmer, "Rijksmuseum case study: Sharing free, high quality images without restrictions makes good things happen," July 30, 2014, *Creative Commons*, https://creativecommons.org/2014/07/30/rijksmuseum-case-study-sharing-free-high-quality-images-without-restrictions-makes-good-things-happen/ (accessed September 21, 2017).

45 In October 2017 admission fees were: R30,00 for adults; R15,00 for children 6-18 (free for children during government school holidays, if accompanied by an adult); R75,00 for families (two adults and two children); R15,00 for students and pensioners (free on Fridays on presentation of valid cards); and free to all on Iziko commemorative days: "Admission Fee," *Iziko Museums of South Africa*, http://iziko.org.za/static/page/admission-fee (accessed October 7, 2017).

46 Admission is R180,00; half price tickets are available on the first Friday of the month from 16:00 to 21:00. Different categories of members benefit greatly from special privileges and invitations: *Zeitz MOCAA*, https://zeitzmocaa.museum/ (accessed October 7, 2017). As an annual member I had the pleasure of attending *Harbouring Expectations*, a site-specific musical performance by the Chanticleer Singers and classical guitarist James Grace, conducted by Richard Cock; it tapped into the cathedral-like atrium and its interstices and experimented with the acoustic qualities. It was worth the entire annual membership fee.

47 Iziko *Annual Report*, 2016-2017, 158. While total visitor figures to Iziko increased to 545,669 in 2017-18, SANG saw a further drop to 43,253: Iziko *Annual Report*, 2017-2018, 153.

48 Adult single admission to the Norval Foundation is R140,00 and there are various categories of membership; a donations box encourages donations to support the exhibition and education programmes: *Norval Foundation*, http://www.norvalfoundation.org/ (accessed May 1, 2018).

49 Iziko Museums "Language Policy, Taalbeleid, Umthetho-sisekelo Wolwimi," version 1.0, second draft, October 22, 2014. This is the version the author received on October 10, 2017. The policy is in English only.

50 The tri-lingual brochures prepared for the *Painted Surfaces* exhibition were welcome exceptions.

51 In 2018 Stevenson took a step closer to acting as a museum space with an exhibition *Both, and* to celebrate fifteen years of the gallery's existence. Having presented itself as a place of ideas that encompass art history and current discourse, the exhibition was an attempt to answer the question as to how the gallery could be "both dedicated to art history, and fully engaged with the market" and to "navigate this apparent paradox": "Both, and," *Stevenson*, https://stevenson.info/exhibition/3246 (accessed July 18, 2018).

52 Marilyn Martin, "Verrykende wending op kunsgebied" (Enriching turn in the field of art), *Die Burger*, April 13, 2009.

53 For an assessment of the situation eight years later, see Sean O'Toole, "The silences between," *Art Agenda*, September 21, 2017, http://www.art-agenda.com/reviews/%E2%80%9Cthe-silences-between%E2%80%9D/ (accessed September 29, 2017).

54 Sean O'Toole, "2016 Market Wrap Looking closely at broad issues through one artist," *Business Art*, December 2016/January 2017, 6.

55 For a perspective on the art market, collectors and galleries on the continent, see Nina Rodrigues-Ely and Vincent Kozsilovics, "The rising development of the contemporary art market in Africa," *Observatoire de l'Art contemporain*, February 24, 2017, http://www.observatoire-art-contemporain.com/revue_decryptage/analyse_a_decoder.php?langue=en&id=20120874 (accessed February 24, 2018).

56 *The Centre for the Less Good Idea*, https://lessgoodidea.com/ (accessed November 7, 2017).

57 *A4*, https://www.a4arts.org/ (accessed November 7, 2017). The A4 Arts Foundation has not escaped controversy: in 2017, artists and activists for Palestinian rights "became aware that the seed funding for the Foundation came from Wendy Fisher through the Kirsh Family Foundation, a family foundation with deep financial and ideological ties to Israel and its security apparatus": *The Daily Vox*, http://www.thedailyvox.co.za/the-ccd-collectives-response-to-participating-unwittingly-in-israeli-funded-cultural-activities-ccd-collective/ (accessed July 25, 2018).

58 FynArts Hermanus took place from June 9-18, 2017. Philanthropist, founding patron of the Ampersand Foundation and collector of art and books, Jack Ginsberg, attended the panel discussion "South African Art Museums – Quo Vadis?"; he spoke enthusiastically of WAM's success and has shown his faith in and commitment to the museum by donating his vast collection of Walter Battiss' work and archive.

59 *Iziko e-news*, February 2018, 2. *Meyina* was first exhibited at the Prince Claus Gallery in Amsterdam in 2017, after which it travelled to Goodman Gallery in Johannesburg. The Friends organised and funded a public conversation between Bisi Silva and Sean O'Toole on February 17, 2018.

60 "Arlene Amaler-Raviv – the Din of Daily Life," *Art Times*, April 9, 2018, http://arttimes.co.za/arlene-amaler-raviv-din-daily-life-oliewenhuis-art-museum/ (accessed April 16, 2018).

61 Same Mdluli in Murinik, *Constructure*, 92-93.

List of Illustrations

UNLESS OTHERWISE STATED, all works of art and photographs are in the collection of the Iziko South African National Gallery. The author accessed SANG slides, CDs, the database with Sepadi Moruthane and Nigel Pamplin, Iziko photographer, provided new images. Regrettably much of the historical SANG visual archive is nowhere to be found, the database is woefully incomplete and many artworks had to be scanned from publications. Photographers are credited when their identity is known.

Measurements are in millimeters, height before width before depth.

FIGURE 9: Portrait of John Paris, August 1950; image courtesy of African News Agency/ANA.
FIGURE 10: SANG atrium as part of *The Meaning of Sculpture* exhibition, with works by Henry Moore, 1952; source: *Annual Report*, 1951-1952, unpaginated.
FIGURE 11: *The Meaning of Sculpture*, installation of African sculpture with small Renaissance bronzes from the Alfred Beit collection, 1952; source: *Annual Report*, 1951-1952, unpaginated.
FIGURE 12: Alfred Honikman, *Colour Chart Illustrating Policy of the South African National Gallery*, 1958.
FIGURE 13: Günther Komnick, *Professor Matthys Bokhorst on the stairs of the Old Town House*, 1959-60; image courtesy of the artist.
FIGURE 14: *Discovering* Young Horse *by Mascherini*, 1977; source: *Touch Gallery* (Cape Town: South African National Gallery, 1977), X; photographer Chris Jansen.

CHAPTER 3

PLATE 10: Paul Stopforth, *Interrogators*, 1979, wax and fine grained graphite on paper mounted on wood panel [765 × 1830 each panel of the triptych]; courtesy of the artist; source: Emma Bedford, ed., *Contemporary South African Art 1985-1995 from the South African National Gallery Permanent Collection* (Cape Town: South African National Gallery, 1997), 26; photographer Kathy Grundlingh.
PLATE 11: *Ashanti gold weights* from Ghana, bronze, c. 15th to 19th century; photographer Pam Warne.
PLATE 12: Artist unrecorded, Xhosa *Iphoco* (*Loveletter*), buttons, beads, cotton thread, sinew, 45 × 15.5; © Iziko Museums of South Africa; photographer Nigel Pamplin.
PLATE 13: Artist unrecorded, Xhosa *Iphoco* (*Loveletter*), buttons, beads, cotton thread, sinew, 34 × 6.5; © Iziko Museums of South Africa; photographer Nigel Pamplin.
PLATE 14: Sfiso Ka Mkame, *Letters to God*, 1988, oil pastel on paper, 1280 × 910; courtesy of the artist; source: Emma Bedford, ed., *Contemporary South African Art 1985-1995 from the South African National Gallery Permanent Collection* (Cape Town: South African National Gallery, 1997), 69; photographer Kathy Grundlingh.
PLATE 15: Gavin Younge, *Botha's Baby*, 1981, cast iron and welded steel, 1186 × 590 × 515; image courtesy of the artist.
PLATE 16: André Lhote *La Joueuse de Flute*, 1911, oil on canvas, 813 × 595.

FIGURE 15: Portrait of Raymund van Niekerk, c. late 1980s; photographer Kathy Grundlingh; collection Marilyn Martin.

CHAPTER 4

PLATE 17: Jane Alexander, *Butcher Boys*, 1985-86, reinforced plaster, oil paint, bone, horns, wood, 1285 × 2135 × 885; © Jane Alexander / DALRO; image courtesy of the artist; photographer Svea Josephy.
PLATE 18: Artist unrecorded, *Lydenburg Head*, c. 750 CE, fired clay, specularite and pigment, 380 × 260 × 250; Iziko Museums of SA, Social History Collections, UCT loan collection (UCT701/1).
PLATE 19: Artist unrecorded, attributed to the nineteenth-century maker known as the "Baboon Master", KwaZulu-Natal, *Maternity staff* (staff surmounted with a relief carving of mother and child), wood, pokerwood, 1120 (detail); presented by the Department of Arts, Culture, Science and Technology; © Iziko Museums of South Africa; photographer Nigel Pamplin.
PLATE 20: William Kentridge: still from the film *Sobriety, Obesity and Growing Old*, 1991, 16mm colour print, 9 minutes; image courtesy of the artist.
PLATE 21: Herbert Meyerowitz, *Dockside, Crane and Ship*, completed 1934, Burma teak, 580 × 1820; source: *Made in Wood* (Cape Town: South African National Gallery, 1992), 37; photographer Kathy Grundlingh.
PLATE 22: Herbert Meyerowitz, *Quayside* (arrival of Sheikh Yusuf), completed 1934, Burma teak, 580 × 1820; source: *Made in Wood* (Cape Town: South African National Gallery, 1992), 37; photographer Kathy Grundlingh.

FIGURE 16: *Bonani*, Jan/Feb 1992, cover featuring Willem Strydom, *Dorslandboom*, 1989, marble, bronze, 1100 × 650 × 600.
FIGURE 17: Jinny Heath, Logo, South African National Gallery.
FIGURE 18: *Ezakwantu: Beadwork from the Eastern Cape*, installation, 1993; source: Emma Bedford, ed., *Ezakwantu Beadwork from the Eastern Cape* (Cape Town: South African National Gallery, 1993), 5; photographer Kathy Grundlingh.
FIGURE 19: Liberman Room in 1992, with destroyed sculpture: Gael Neke, *Eugène Terre'blanche and his two sidekicks*, 1989, ceramic, dimensions variable; source: Emma Bedford, ed., *Contemporary South African Art 1985-1995 from the South African National Gallery Permanent Collection* (Cape Town: South African National Gallery, 1997), 16; photographer Kathy Grundlingh.
FIGURE 20: *IGugu LamaNdebele* installation, 1994; photographer Kathy Grundlingh.
FIGURE 21: *IGugu LamaNdebele* installation, 1994; photographer Kathy Grundlingh.

CHAPTER 5

PLATE 23: Marlene Dumas, *The Next Generation*, 1994-1995, ink and ink wash on paper [45 parts, 66 × 50,5 cm each], detail; image courtesy of the artist; photographer Pam Warne.
PLATE 24: Fatima February, Yasmina February and Fayrouz Mathews, *District Six, Where we Lived*, 1992, fabric, pebbles, sequins, ribbon, stocking, batting, wood, 1630 × 1270; image courtesy of the artists; photographer Kathy Grundlingh.
PLATE 25: Artist unrecorded, Zulu *Neckpiece*, c. 1879, glass seed beads, sinew, brass buttons, 190 × 130; presented by the Rowland and Leta Hill Trust; source: Hayden Proud, ed., *Scratches on the Face Antiquity and Contemporaneity in South*

African works of art from Iziko Museums of Cape Town (New Delhi and Cape Town: Iziko Museums, 2008), 24; photographer Cecil Kortje.
PLATE 26: Willie Bester, *Head North*, 1995, mixed media, 1750 × 2200 × 970; presented by the artist; courtesy of the artist.
PLATE 27: Karel Nel, *The Island and the Dream of the Table House*, 1995, pastel pigment on bonded fibre fabric, 2110 × 1545; presented by the Friends of SANG; courtesy of the artist; source: Hayden Proud, ed., *Scratches on the Face Antiquity and Contemporaneity in South African works of art from Iziko Museums of Cape Town* (New Delhi and Cape Town: Iziko Museums, 2008), 61; photographer Cecil Kortje.
PLATE 29: David Goldblatt, *Victoria Cobokana, housekeeper, in her employer's dining room with her son Sifiso and daughter Onica, Johannesburg June 1999. Victoria died of AIDS 13 December 1999, Sifiso died of AIDS 12 January 2000, Onica died of AIDS in May 2000*, 1999, digital print, 590 × 590; presented by Linda Givon; image courtesy of the David Goldblatt Legacy Trust.
PLATE 29: Walter Sickert, *Royal Hotel, Dieppe*, c. 1902, oil on wood, 140 × 240.

FIGURE 22: *Miscast* installation, Liberman Room, 1996; image courtesy of Pippa Skotnes.
FIGURE 23: *Miscast* installation, Liberman Room, detail of objects in display cases, 1996; image courtesy of Pippa Skotnes.
FIGURE 24: *Miscast* installation, 1996; vinyl tiles and photographs by Paul Weinberg; image courtesy of Pippa Skotnes.

CHAPTER 6
PLATE 30: Jonathan Shapiro, *HIV/AIDS Dissidents Highway*, © 2000 Zapiro, ink on cotton rag paper, 365 × 255. Originally published in the *Sowetan*; re-published with permission; image courtesy of the artist.

FIGURE 25: *Zanazo* 1, no. 1, April May June 2000, cover featuring John Muafangejo, *The Pregnant Maria*, undated, linocut, 280 × 245.
FIGURE 26: rosenclaire, sketch submitted for the public art competition, 2004; courtesy of the artists; source: Emma Bedford, ed., *A Decade of Democracy South African Art 1994-2004 From the Permanent Collection of Iziko: South African National Gallery* (Cape Town: Double Storey, 2004), 87.
FIGURE 27: rosenclaire, *Soap Boxes*, bronze, surveillance camera, plasma screen, ginkgo biloba trees, featuring Masai warrior Miyere Miyandazi who stood on the work for long stretches to raise awareness of his people in Kenya; image courtesy of the artists.
FIGURE 28: *Musuku: Golden Links with our Past*, 2000, installation featuring the wall built by Venda builders according to ancient traditions, and incorporating the Venda royal chevron snake-pattern; photographer Kathy Grundlingh.
FIGURE 29: Joe Dolby, *Gerard Sekoto: From the Paris Studio* (Cape Town: Iziko South African National Gallery, 2005), cover.
FIGURE 30: Adrian Kohler and Basil Jones (Handspring Puppet Company), *Episodes*, installation; image courtesy of the artists.

CHAPTER 7
PLATE 31: David Goldblatt, photograph of SANG staff, 1999, commissioned by *Leadership*; in the foreground is Jane Alexander's *Integration Programme: Man with TV*, 1995, plaster, oil, clothing, found objects, video, 1380 × 1000 × 2200; and in the distance Isa Kabini's *Obelisk*, 1994, acrylic on wood, 2750 × 630 × 630; commissioned by SANG. Image courtesy of the David Goldblatt Legacy Trust and Cape Media.
PLATE 32: Tracey Rose, *The Kiss*, 2001, lambda print, 1445 × 1435, image courtesy of the artist, the Dan Gunn Gallery, London and the Goodman Gallery, Cape Town and Johannesburg; photographer Pam Warne.
PLATE 33: Sue Williamson, *Messages from the Moat*, 1997, engraved and stencilled glass, printed canvas, found fishing net and water pump, dimensions variable; installation view, Castle of Good Hope, Cape Town, 2004; image courtesy of the artist and Goodman Gallery; photographer Herschel Mair.

FIGURE 31: Remix Company, choreographed by Jay Pather, performs *Dancing with Shadows*, in response to the exhibition *Invoice: Photographs by Santu Mofokeng*, 2007; photographer Pam Warne.
FIGURE 32: *Picasso and Africa* installation, 2006; photographer Pam Warne.
FIGURE 33: *Picasso and Africa* installation, 2006; photographer Pam Warne.
FIGURE 34: *Picasso and Africa* exhibition, queue outside the gallery, April 2006; photographer Pam Warne.
FIGURE 35: 8th Definitive Series, 2010; image courtesy of Philatelic Services and used with the permission of the South African Post Office.
FIGURE 36: Hayden Proud, ed., *Scratches on the Face Antiquity and contemporaneity in South African works of art from Iziko Museums of Cape Town* (New Delhi and Cape Town: Iziko Museums, 2008), cover.
FIGURE 37: *Pancho Guedes: An Alternative Modernist* installation, 2008; photographer Pam Warne.
FIGURE 38: Neville Dubow, Pancho Guedes and Guedes' Ambassadors of Electica at the opening of *Pancho Guedes: An Alternative Modernist*, May 2008; photographer Pam Warne.

CHAPTER 8
PLATE 34: Penny Siopis, *Beast*, 2009, ink and glue on canvas, 695 × 600; courtesy of the artist and Stevenson; photographer Michael Hall.
PLATE 35: Beezy Bailey, *Love in Heaven*, 1991, wood, photograph, tin, paint, 930 × 2380; photographer Kathy Grundlingh.

PLATE 36: Kevin Atkinson, *Arena*, 1975, oil and pencil on canvas, 2135 × 1685; courtesy of the Kevin and Patricia Atkinson Trust.
PLATE 37: Georgina Gratrix, *Les Demoiselles d'Avignon*, 2008, 1900 × 1300, oil on canvas; image courtesy of the artist and SMAC Gallery.
PLATE 38: Pierre Fouché, *The Kiss*, 2007, mercerised crochet cotton, 2000 × 1200 × 254; image courtesy of the artist.

FIGURE 39: Riason Naidoo, image detail courtesy of *Art Africa*; photographer Sean O'Toole.
FIGURE 40: *1910-2010: From Pierneef to Gugulective*, installation view marking the start of the exhibition and featuring Anton Momberg, *Maquette for the Gandhi Memorial Statue, Pietermaritzburg*, 1992, resin, fibreglass, copper, 665 × 190 × 190; courtesy of the artist; and JH Pierneef, *Union Buildings*, undated, oil on board, 910 × 2130; collection and courtesy of Pretoria Art Museum; image courtesy of *Art Africa*; photographer Sean O'Toole.
FIGURE 41: Installation featuring Matts Leiderstam, *The Power and Pleasure of Breeding*, 1998, oil on canvas, 970 × 1265 (presented by the artist) and Abraham Cooper *The Day Family* (1838), oil on canvas, 970 × 1265; © Iziko Museums of South Africa; photographer Nigel Pamplin.
FIGURE 42: *Imagining Beauty* installation; photographer Pam Warne.

CHAPTER 9
PLATE 39: Hendrik Stroebel, *Port of Plenty*, 1987/1991, fabric, thread, ceramic, 2505 × 1460; courtesy of the artist; photographer Kathy Grundlingh.

FIGURE 43: *Our Lady* public event, 15 December 2016, Candice Breitz leading the discussion; © Iziko Museums of South Africa; photographer Nigel Pamplin.

CHAPTER 10
PLATE 40: Dame Laura Knight, *Flying a Kite*, 1910, oil on canvas, 1498 × 1778.
PLATE 41: Louis Maqhubela, *Snake*, 2002, oil on canvas, 1300 × 285; presented by the artist; courtesy of the artist; detail under ultraviolet light, showing the fluorescence of the varnish interlayers; photographer Nigel Pamplin.

CHAPTER 11
FIGURE 44: Zeitz MOCAA atrium with Nicholas Hlobo's *Iimpundulu Zonke Ziyandilandela* (All the Lightning Birds are After Me) (2011), rubber inner tubing, ribbon, animal skull, mixed media, pink theatre lights, sound, 2500 × 4600 × 10000; image courtesy of Zeitz MOCAA.
FIGURE 45: *Hidden Treasures*, installation, 2017. In the foreground: Workshop of Paa Joe, *Fantasy coffin*, c. 1997, wood, oil paint, satin lining; collected and presented by Michael Heuermann; © Iziko Museums of South Africa; photographer Nigel Pamplin.
FIGURE 46: Norval Foundation; image courtesy of Norval Foundation; photographer Dave Southwood.

Bibliography

The details of archival material accessed, for example minute books, reports and correspondence are cited in endnotes and are omitted from the bibliography, as are details of annual reports, newsletters, email correspondence, interviews and web sources; newspaper articles are either cited in the running text or in endnotes. Unless otherwise stated, all translations are by the author.

Primary Sources/Archival Material

Honikman, Alfred Harold. *Colour Chart illustrating policy of the South African National* Gallery. Cape Town: Trustees of the South African National Gallery, 1958.

Iziko Museums of South Africa minute books

Iziko Museums of South Africa *Annual Reports*

Iziko Museums of South Africa newsletters *Zanazo* and *What's On*

South African National Gallery archives

South African National Gallery minute books

South African National Gallery *Annual Reports*

South African National Gallery newsletter *Bonani*

South African National Gallery Library news cutting archives

Personal archives, printed and electronic

Reports of the Trustees of the South African Art Gallery and the South African Fine Arts Association, 1905-1907 and 1912 (there is a gap between 1907 and 1912); 1913-1918.

Legal Sources, Government Reports, Notices and Publications

African National Congress, *Reconstruction and Development Programme*, 1994.

Constitution of the Republic of South Africa, 1996 (Act No. 108 of 1996).

Cultural Institutions Act, 1996 (Act No. 29 of 1969).

Cultural Institutions Act, 1998 (Act No. 119 of 1998).

Cultural Laws Second Amendment Act, 2001 (Act No. 39 of 2001).

Department of Arts, Culture, Science & Technology, *White Paper on Arts, Culture and Heritage*, June 4, 1996.

Department of Arts and Culture. *Revised White Paper on Arts, Culture and Heritage*, June 4, 2013.

Department of Arts and Culture, *Revised White Paper on Arts, Culture and Heritage*, February 2017.

Department of Arts and Culture, *Revised White Paper on Arts, Culture and Heritage*, October 2017.

Department of Labour, *Employment Equity Act*.

Government notice, 1932 (No. 668, May 23, 1932).

Hansard, April 29, 1947, col. 3504-3511. Cape Town: Government Printer, 1947.

Labour Court, Cape Town, case C876/2015.

National Treasury, *Katz Commission Report into Taxation*, 1994.

National Treasury, *Public Finance Management Act*, 1999 (Act No. 1 of 1999).

Parliament of South Africa, *State-aided Institutions Act*, 1931(Act No. 23 of 1931).

Schutte Commission Report on the Creative Arts in South Africa, 1984

South African Art Gallery Act, 1895.

Stratford, James. *Report of the Commission Appointed in Connection with the S. A. Art Gallery*, Cape Town. Pretoria: Government Printer, 1947.

Published Sources

African Art in Metal. Cape Town: South African National Gallery, 1970.

Africus: Johannesburg Biennale. Johannesburg: Greater Johannesburg Transitional Metropolitan Council, 1995.

Alexander, Lucy. "South African National Gallery Brief History." *South African Arts Calendar*, 10, 1986, 18-19.

Alexander, Lucy, Emma Bedford, and Evelyn Cohen. *Parys en Suid Afrikaanse Kunstenaars 1850-1965/Paris and South African Artists 1850-1965*. Cape Town: South African National Gallery, 1988.

Alexander, Lucy, and Patricia Hardy. *Natale Labia Museum*. Cape Town: South African National Gallery, 1988.

Alaoui, Brahim, and Jean Hubert Martin. *Rencontres africaine: exposition d'art actuel du 6 avril au 15 août 1994*. Paris: Institut du monde arabe and Fondation Afrique en créations, 1994.

Allara, Pamela, and Marilyn Martin, eds. *Coexistence: Contemporary Cultural Production in South Africa*. Waltham, MA: Brandeis University, 2003.

Arnold, Marion. *Focus on Bloomsbury/Kollig op Bloomsbury*. Cape Town: South African National Gallery, 1985.

Arnold, Marion. *Art Meets Science: Flowers as Images*. Johannesburg: Standard Bank, 1992.

Art africaine dans la collection Pierre Guerre/African art in the Pierre Guerre collection. Paris: l'Association française d'Action artistique, 1997.

Artworks for AIDS. Cambridge, MA: Harvard AIDS Institute and Bristol-Myers Squibb Company, 2000.

Atkinson Brenda, and Candice Breitz, eds. *Grey Areas*. Johannesburg: Chalkham Hill Press, 1999.

Bazelitz, Georg, Miklos Szalay, and Peter Nebel, eds. *African Art from the Han Coray Collection, 1916-1928*. Zurich: Volkerkundemuseum, University of Zurich, 1998.

Becker, Carol, ed. *The Artist in Society: Rights, Roles, and Responsibilities*. Chicago: Chicago New Art Association, New Art Examiner Press, 1995.

Bedford, Emma, ed. *Ezakwantu: Beadwork from the Eastern Cape*. Cape Town: South African National Gallery, 1993.

Bedford, Emma, ed. *Contemporary South African Art 1985-1995 from the South African National Gallery Permanent Collection*. Cape Town: South African National Gallery, 1997.

Bedford, Emma, ed. *A Decade of Democracy South African Art 1994-2004 From the Permanent Collection of Iziko: South African National Gallery*. Cape Town: Double Storey, 2004.

Bedford, Emma, ed. *Tremor: Contemporary Art from South Africa*. Charleroi: Centre d'Art Contemporain and Iziko Museums, 2004.

Belting, Hans, and Andrea Buddensieg, eds. *The Global Art World Audiences, Markets, and Museums*. Ostfildern: Hatje Cantz Verlag, 2009.

Berman, Esmé. *The South African Art Market 1971/72*. Johannesburg: Art Institute South Africa, 1972.

Berman, Esmé. *Art and Artists of South Africa* (classic edition). Cape Town: G3 Publishers, 2010.

Beumers, Erna, ed. *Africa meets Africa: the African collection of the Museum of Ethnology Rotterdam*. Rotterdam: Museum of Ethnology, 1996.

Bigalke, E. H., ed. *Southern African Museums Association Bulletin* 16, no. 8 (1985): 353-381.

Bodkin, Thomas. *Hugh Lane and his Pictures*. Dublin: Browne and Nolan, 1952.

Bouman, Arie Cornelis. *Kuns in Suid-Afrika*. Cape Town: HAUM, 1935.

Brokensha, David. Review, "Musuku: Golden Links with Our Past." *African Arts* 34, no. 1 (2001): 87.

Brown, Carol, ed. "South Africa After the Ball." *African Arts* 44, no. 2 (2011).

Bull, Marjorie. *Abraham de Smidt 1829-1908. Artist and Surveyor-General of the Cape Colony*. Cape Town: Self-published, 1981.

Burnett, Ricky. *Tributaries A view of contemporary South African art/Quellen und Strömungen Eine Ausstellung zeitgenössischer südafrikanischer Kunst*. Johannesburg: BMW South Africa, 1985.

Burroughs, Elizabeth, and Karel Nel. *Re/discovery and Memory: The works of Kumalo, Legae, Nitegeka & Villa*. Cape Town: Norval Foundation and the Claire & Edoardo Villa Will Trust, 2018.

Carman, Jillian. "Acquisition policy of the Johannesburg Art Gallery with regard to the South African collection, 1909-1987." *South African Journal of Cultural and Art History* 2, no. 3 (1988): 211, note 40.

Carman, Jillian. *Seventeenth-century Dutch and Flemish paintings in South Africa*. Johannesburg: Johannesburg Art Gallery, 1994.

Carman, Jillian. *Uplifting the colonial philistine*. Johannesburg: Wits University Press, 2006.

Carman, Jillian, ed. *Visual Century South African Art in Context*, vol. 1, 1907-1948. Johannesburg: Wits University Press, 2011.

Catalogue of Exhibition, South African National Gallery, Opening of the New Gallery. Cape Town: Bon Accord Press, 1930.

Container 96 Art Across Oceans. Copenhagen: Kulturby 96, 1996.

Coombes, Annie. *History after Apartheid: Visual Culture and Public Memory in a Democratic South Africa*. Durham and London: Duke University Press, 2003.

Cormack, Malcolm. *Country Pursuits British, American, and French Sporting Art from the Mellon Collections in the Virginia Museum of Fine Arts*. Richmond: University of Virginia Press, 2007.

Cruise, Wilma. Review, "Made in Wood Work from the Western Cape." *De Arte* no. 47 (1993): 39-41.

Crump, Alan, and Raymund van Niekerk (text), and Geoffrey Grundlingh (photographs). *Public Sculpture & Reliefs – Cape Town*. Cape Town: Clifton Publications, 1988.

Davison, Patricia. "Typecast: Representations of the Bushmen at the South African Museum." *Public Archaeology* 1 (2001): 3.

De Jager, E. J. *Contemporary African Art in South Africa*. Cape Town: Struik, 1973.

De Kok, Ingrid, and Karen Press, eds. *Spring is Rebellious*. Cape Town: Buchu Press, 1990.

Dell, Elizabeth, ed. *Evocations of the Child: Fertility Figures of the Southern African Region*. London: Lund Humphries, 1999.

Delmont, Elizabeth. *Maggie Laubser: The Early Works from the Silberberg Collection*. Cape Town: South African National Gallery, 1987.

De Smidt, Abraham. "An Art Gallery for South Africa." *Cape Monthly Magazine*, April 2, 1871, 236-246.

District Six: Image and Representation. Cape Town: South African National Gallery, 1995.

Dolby, Joe. "A short history of the South African National Gallery." *Lantern*, December 1981, 37-50.

Dolby, Joe. *Strat Caldecott: Retrospective*. Cape Town: South African National Gallery, 1986.

Dolby, Joe. *Gerard Sekoto: From the Paris Studio*. Cape Town: Iziko South African National Gallery, 2005.

Donne, J. B. "Guillaume Apollinaire's African Collection." *Newsletter (Museum Ethnographers Group)* 14 (1983): 4-9.

Dubin, Steven C. *Transforming Museums Mounting Queen Victoria in a Democratic South Africa*. New York and Basingstoke: Palgrave MacMillan, 2006.

Dubow, Neville. *Neville Dubow Sequences Series Sites Photographs 1971-1992*. Cape Town: Self-published, 1992.

Dumas, Marlene, and Emma Bedford, eds. *Marlene Dumas: Intimate Relations*. Amsterdam/Johannesburg: Roma Publications/ Jacana Media, 2007.

Du Plessis, Antoinette. "The Cape Town Triennial: a Phenomenon of the Eighties." *De Arte* 45 (1992): 15-24.

Elliot, David. *Art from South Africa/an exhibition organised my MOMA, Oxford, in association with the Zabalaza Festival, London*. Oxford: Museum of Modern Art, 1990.

Enwezor, Okwui, ed. *Trade routes: History and geography: 2nd Johannesburg Biennale 1997*. Johannesburg: Africus Institute of Contemporary Art, 1997.

Enwezor, Okwui, ed. *The Short Century Independence and Liberation Movements in Africa 1945-1994*. Munich, London, New York: Prestel, 2001.

Fairbairn, John. "The South African Art Gallery." *The State* 3, April (1910): 550-560.

Fransen, Hans, comp. *Michaelis Collection. The Old Town House, Cape Town. Catalogue of the Collection of Paintings and Drawings*. Zwolle: Waanders Uitgevers, 1997.

Freschi, Federico. "Other Views: Art History in (South) Africa and the Global South." *Diogenes* 58, no. 3 (2011): 93-101.

Friends' Choice. Cape Town: Friends of the South African National Gallery, 1991.

George Milwa Mnyaluza Pemba: Retrospective. Cape Town: South African National Gallery & Mayibuye Centre, 1996.

Godby, Michael. "Responding to critique." *Art South Africa* 2, no. 2 (2003): 36.

Godby, Michael. *Is there Still Life? Continuity and Change in South African Still Life Painting*. Cape Town: Iziko South African National Gallery, 2007.

Godby, Michael. *The Lie of the Land: Representations of the South African Landscape*. Johannesburg: David Krut Publishing, 2010.

Godby, Michael. *Home Truths: Domestic Interiors in South African Collections*. Cape Town: Primavera Publishing, 2016.

Goldblatt, David. *South Africa The Structure of Things Then*. Cape Town: Oxford University Press, 1998.

Goniwe, Thembinkosi, Mario Pissarra, and Mandisi Majavu, eds. *Visual Century South African Art in Context*, vol. 4, 1907-1948. Johannesburg: Wits University Press, 2011.

Goodnow, Katherine, Jack Lohman, and Jatti Bredekamp. *Challenge and Transformation: Museums in Cape Town and Sydney*. Paris: EdUNESCO-BSI/PUB, 2006.

Gordimer, Nadine. "David Goldblatt: So Far." *Quarterly Bulletin*, no. 13 (1983): unpaginated.

Grigoteit, Ariane. *A Century of Landscapes*. Frankfurt am Main: Deutsche Bank AG, 2002.

Grundlingh, Kathy, ed. *Photosynthesis: Contemporary SA Photography*. Cape Town: South African National Gallery, 1997.

Grundlingh, Kathy ed. *Lines of sight: Perspectives on South African Photography*. Cape Town: South African National Gallery, 2001.

Guillaume, Paul. *Sculptures nègres et Sculptures d'Afrique, d'Amérique, d'Océanie*, catalogue of the exhibition and sale of works from the collections of André Breton and Paul Éluard at Hôtel Drouot, July 2 and 3, 1931. First published 1931; reprinted, New York:

Hacker Art Books, 1973.
Harmsen, Frieda. "The South African Art Library from Bouman to Berman." *De Arte* 18 (1975): 65-68.
Harrison, Ronald. *The Black Christ A journey to freedom*. Claremont: David Philip Publishers, 2006.
Heat-Moon, William Least. *PrairyErth: A Deep Map*. New York: Houghton Mifflin Harcourt, 2014.
Herbert Vladimir Meyerowitz (1900-1945) The Hyman Liberman Memorial Door. Cape Town: South African National Gallery, 1970.
Hillebrand, Melanie. *The Women of Olifantsfontein: South African Studio Ceramics*. Cape Town: South African National Gallery, 1991.
Holscher, Marianne. *Far Far Away: South African Illustrated Children's Books*. Cape Town: South African National Gallery, 1986.
Hope, Christopher. *The Café de Move-on Blues In Search of the New South Africa*. London: Atlantic Books, 2018.
Hulde aan Irma Stern/Homage to Irma Stern 1894-1966. Cape Town: South African National Gallery, 1968.

Jamal, Ashraf. *In the World Essays on South African Contemporary Art*. Milan: Skira editore S.p.A., 2017.
Jameson, Fredric. *A Singular Modernity Essay on the Ontology of the Present*. London and New York: Verso, 2012.
Jansen van Vuuren, Louis. "Preface." *Arts Calendar* 18, 1993, 3.
Jouannais, Jean-Yves. *Un Art Contemporain D'Afrique Du Sud*. Paris: Ed. Plume, 1994.

Kaapstadse Triënnale 1991/Cape Town Triennial 1991. Cape Town: Rembrandt van Rijn Art Foundation/Kunsstigting Rembrandt van Rijn, 1991.
Karp, Ivan, and Steven D. Lavine, eds. *Exhibiting Cultures, The Poetics and Politics of Museum Display*. Washington and London: Smithsonian Institution Press, 1991.
Kauffman, Kyle, D., and David Lindauer, eds. *AIDS and South Africa The Social Expression of A Pandemic*. Houndmills, Basingstoke: Palgrave Macmillan Ltd, 2004.
Kauffman, Kyle D., and Marilyn Martin. *AidsArt / South Africa*. Cape Town: Iziko Museums and Wellesley College, 2003.
Kaufmann, Carol. *Musuku: Golden Links to our Past*. Cape Town: South African National Gallery, 2000.
Kaufmann, Carol. *Iintsimbi: beadwork from South Africa*. Cape Town: Iziko South African National Gallery, 2005.
Kaufmann, Carol. *The 8th Definitive. The luminous beauty of South African beadwork on stamps*. Pretoria: South African Post Office Philatelic Services, 2010.
Kaufmann, Carol, and Andrea Lewis, eds. *Brushing up on Stern, featuring work from the Permanent Collection of the Iziko South African National Gallery*. Cape Town: Iziko South African National Gallery, 2015.
King, Terence. "Tributaries and the Triennial: two South African art exhibitions." *Critical arts* 5, no. 3 (1987): 39-57.

Lamprecht, Andrew. *Bruce Gordon: An Artwork by Ed Young*. Cape Town: South African National Gallery, 2003.
Lamprecht, Andrew, ed. *Tretchikoff The People's Painter*. Jeppestown: Jonathan Ball Publishers , 2011.
Leibhammer, Nessa. "Ezakwantu Beadwork from the Eastern Cape." *African Arts* (UCLA) XXVIII, no. 1 (1995): 81-82.
Lloyd, Angela Read. *The Artist in the Garden The Quest for Moses Tladi*. Noordhoek, Western Cape: Print Matters, 2009.
Lohman Jack, and Katherine Goodnow, eds. *Human Remains & Museum Practice*. Paris: UNESCO, 2006.
Lohman, Jack. *Museums at the Crossroads?*. Victoria, Canada: Royal BC Museum, 2013.
Lundstrom, Jan-Erik, ed. *Head North: Views from the Permanent Collection of the South African National Gallery*. Umeå: Bild Museet, 2001.

Made in Wood Work from the Western Cape. Cape Town: South African National Gallery, 1992.
Madeline, Laurence, and Marilyn Martin, eds. *Picasso and Africa*. Cape Town: Bell Roberts Publishing, 2006.
Marschall, Sabine. "Who is in and who is out? The process of re-writing South African Art History in the 1990s." *Mots Pluriels*, no. 12 (1999): unpaginated. http://motspluriels.arts.uwa.edu.au/MP1299sm.html (accessed March 10, 2016).
Martin, Marilyn. "Uitstalling van Suid-Afrikaanse kuns in Duitsland." *South African Arts Calendar*, June 1985, 5.
Martin, Marilyn. "Is There a Place for Black Abstract Painters in South Africa?." *De Arte* 44 (1991): 25-38.
Martin, Marilyn. "Issues, Reactions and Interpretations." *De Arte* 45 (1992): 35-44.
Martin, Marilyn. "Women, Management and the Arts." Part 1, *South African Arts Calendar* 17, 1992, 14-15 & 18.
Martin, Marilyn. "Women, Management and the Arts." Part 2, *South African Arts Calendar* 18, 1992, 6-7.
Martin, Marilyn. "The Venice Biennale 1993." *Arts Calendar* 18, 1993, 4-5.
Martin, Marilyn. "The Horn of Art's Dilemma." *Leadership* 18, no. 1 (1999): 44-56.
Martin, Marilyn. "Curating HIV/AIDS at the Iziko South African National Gallery." *Kiosk* 1 (2007/08): 57-63 & 73-80.
Martin, Marilyn and Joe Dolby, eds. *Albert Adams: Journey on a Tightrope*. Cape Town: Iziko South African National Gallery, 2008.
Martin, Marilyn. *Thinking, Feeling, Head, Heart*. Cape Town: The New Church Museum, 2014.
Martin, Marilyn, and Paul Weinberg. *The Thinking Eye: Photographs by Neville Dubow*. Cape Town: UCT Libraries, 2015.
Martin, Marilyn. Review, "Home Truths: Domestic Interiors in South African Collections." *De Arte* 51 (2016): 73-76.

McClelland, Lynn, and Lucy Alexander. *Women Artists in South Africa/Vrouekunstenaars in Suid-Afrika*. Cape Town: South African National Gallery, 1985.
Miles, Elza. "Triënnale grense word versit." *De Kat*, November 1991, 84.
Miles, Elza. *Polly Street The Story of an Art Centre*. Johannesburg: The Ampersand Foundation, 2004.
Mofokeng, Santu. *The Black Photo Album, Look at Me: 1890-1950*. Göttingen: Steidl Verlag, 2013.
Monroe, John Warne. Book reviews, "*Paris Primitive: Jacques Chirac's Museum on the Quai Branly* by Sally Price; *Au musée des illusions: Le rendez-vous manqué du quai Branly* by Sally Price." *The Journal of Modern History* 86, no. 1 (2014): 193-196.
Morphet, Anthony. "Miscast review." *Pretexts: Studies in Writing and Culture* 6, no. 1 (1997): 95-99.
Morgan, Jonathan, and Bambanani Women's Group. *Long Life: Positive HIV Stories*. Cape Town: Double
Storey-Juta, 2003.
Murinik, Tracy, ed. *Constructure: 100 years of the JAG building and its evolution of space and meaning*. Johannesburg: David Krut, 2015.

Naidoo, Riason. *The Making of 1910-2010 from Pierneef to Gugulective*. Cape Town: Iziko South African National Gallery, 2010.
National South African Art Collection/Nasionale Suid-Afrikaanse Kunsversameling. Cape Town: South African National Gallery, 1971.
Nettleton, Anitra. "Myth of the transitional: Black art and white markets in South Africa." *South African Journal of Cultural and Art History* 2, no. 4 (1988): 301-310.
Nettleton, Anitra, Fiona Rankin-Smith, and Julia Charlton, eds. *Voice-Overs: Wits Writings Exploring African Artworks*. Johannesburg: University of the Witwatersrand Art Galleries, 2004.
Njami, Simon, ed. *Africa Remix: Contemporary Art of a Continent*. Johannesburg: Jacana, 2007.
Nochlin, Linda. "Learning From "Black Male"." *Art in America* 83, no. 3 (1995): 91.
Nolte, Jacqueline. "Contemporary South African Art." *Third Text* 11, no. 39 (1997): 95-103.
Nuwe Groep/New Group 1938-1954. Cape Town: South African National Gallery, 1988.
Nuttall, Sarah, and Achille Mbembe, eds. *Johannesburg: The Elusive Metropolis (A Public Culture Book)*. Durham: Duke University Press, 2008.

Olivier, Gerrit, ed. *Penny Siopis Time and Again*. Johannesburg: Wits University Press, 2014.

Pancho Guedes Ein Alternativer Modernist/An Alternative Modernist. Basel: Schweizerisches Architekturmuseum, 2007.
Paris, John. *Exhibition of XVII Century Dutch Painting*. Cape Town: South African National Gallery and the Van Riebeeck Festival, 1952.
Payne, Malcolm, ed. *Face Value: old heads in modern masks. A visual, archaeological and historical reading of the Lydenburg Heads*. Cape Town: South African National Gallery, 1993.
Payne, Malcolm, ed. *Face Value: Old Heads in Modern Masks: A Visual, Archaeological and Historical Reading of the Lydenburg Heads*. Cape Town: Axeage Private Press, 1993.
Peffer, John. *Art and the End of Apartheid*. Minneapolis and London: University of Minnesota Press, 2009.
Picturing our World: Contemporary Images of the Western Cape. Cape Town: South African National Gallery and Foundation for the Creative Arts, 1993.
Pissarra, Mario. "Decolonise the mind." *Art South Africa* 2, no. 2 (2003): 37-41.
Pissarra, Mario. "The Luggage is Still Labelled But is it Going to the Right Destination?." *Third Text* 18, no. 2 (2004): 183-191.
Pissarra, Mario, ed. *Visual Century South African Art in Context*, vol. 3, 1907-1948. Johannesburg: Wits University Press, 2011.
Pissarra, Mario. *Against the Grain*. Cape Town: Africa South Art Initiative, 2013.
Pissarra, Mario, ed. *Awakenings: The Art of Lionel Davis*. Cape Town: Africa South Art Institute, 2017.
Pollak, Lloyd. "SA National Gallery's reputation trashed for 2010 show." *South African Art Times*, April 30, 2010, 1& 3.
Pollak, Lloyd, "More Agony than Ecstasy, The Tretchikoff Story – Now showing in vistavision at the SA National Gallery." *South African Art Times*, July 2011, 9-10.
Pollak, Lloyd. " Why Sir Abe Bailey is turning in his grave." *South African Art Times*, March 2012, 8-9.
Pollak, Lloyd. "A Bitter Farewell to Tretchikoff." *South African Art Times*, October 2011, 54.
Powell, Ivor. "Ed Young: Bruce Gordon." *Art South Africa* 1, no. 4 (2003): 62-63.
Powell, Ivor. "A Decade of Democracy: SA Art 1994-2004." *Art South Africa* 2, no. 4 (2004): 62.
Preller, Karin. "The Tretchikoff Conundrum." *Art South Africa* 10, no. 1 (2011): 42-48.
Press, Naomi. *Knots & Nets: Spiritual Connections/Noeuds et Filets: Liens Spirituels*. Washington D.C.: Arts America Program of the United States Information Agency, 1993.
Price, Sally. *Primitive Art in Civilized Places*. Chicago: University of Chicago Press, 2001.
Price, Sally. *Paris Primitive: Jacques Chirac's Museum on the Quai Branly*. Chicago: University of Chicago Press, 2007.

Price, Sally. *Au musée des illusions: Le rendez-vous manqué du quai Branly*, translated by Nelcya Delanoë. Paris: Éditions Denoël, 2011.

Protest on Behalf of the Artists of South Africa against the Slighting, and Belittling Attitude of the authorities on the Occasion of the Inauguration of the South African (National) Gallery on the Third of November, 1930. Cape Town: South African Society of Artists, 1930.

Proud, Hayden, ed. *Hanns Ludwig Katz*. Cape Town: South African National Gallery, 1994.

Proud, Hayden, and Anna Tietze. *The Sir Edmund and Lady Davis Presentation: A Gift of British Art to South Africa*. Cape Town: South African National Gallery, 1999.

Proud, Hayden. *'The Advancement of Art': The South African Society of Artists and its Exhibitions, 1902-1950*. Cape Town: Iziko Museums, 2002.

Proud, Hayden, ed. *Revisions: Expanding the Narrative of South African Art The Campbell Smith Collection*. Pretoria: South African History Online and UNISA Press, 2006.

Proud, Hayden, ed. *Scratches on the Face Antiquity and Contemporaneity in South African works of art from Iziko Museums of Cape Town*. New Delhi and Cape Town: Iziko Museums, 2008.

Proud, Hayden. *Revisions+ expanding the narrative of South African Art*. Stellenbosch: SMAC Gallery, 2008.

Proud, Hayden, ed. *Forty Years of Friendship The Friends of the South African National Gallery 1968-2008*. Cape Town: Friends of the South African National Gallery, 2008.

Proud, Hayden. "Our National Gallery: The 'Book' of our Art?." *Journal of the Helen Suzman Foundation* (2011): 37-44.

Rabbethge-Schiller, Hella. *Memory and Magic: Contemporary Art of the !Xun & Khwe*. Johannesburg: Jacana Media, 2006.

Rankin, Elizabeth. "Recoding the canon: Towards greater representivity in South African art galleries." *Social Dynamics* 21, no. 2 (1995): 56-90.

Rankin-Smith, Fiona, ed. *Halakasha!*. Johannesburg: Wits Art Museum, 2010.

Rassool, Ciraj, and Leslie Witz. "The 1952 Jan Van Riebeeck Tercentenary Festival: Constructing and Contesting Public National History in South Africa." *The Journal of African History* 34, no. 3 (1993): 447-468.

Rubin, William, ed. *"Primitivism" in 20th century art Affinity of the Tribal and the Modern*, vol. II. New York: The Museum of Modern Art, 1984.

Rock Art in Southern Africa. Cape Town: South African National Gallery, 1963.

Sack, Steven. *The Neglected Tradition: Towards a New History of South African Art, 1930-1988*. Johannesburg: Johannesburg Art Gallery, 1988.

Sandell, Richard, ed. *Museums, Society, Inequality*. London and New York: Routledge, 2002.

Sandell, Richard, and Eithne Nightingale. *Museums, Equality and Social Justice*. Abingdon, Oxon: Routledge, 2012.

Sharp, John. "Magic and a mix of cultures." *Democracy in Action* 8, no. 5 (1994): 12.

Skotnes, Pippa, ed. *Miscast: Negotiating the Presence of the Bushmen*. Athens: Ohio University Press, 1998.

Skotnes, Pippa. "Civilised off the Face of the Earth: Museum Display and the Silencing of the /Xam." *Poetics Today* 22, no. 2 (2001): 314.

"South African Art Gallery." *The South African Builder*, February 1933, 11 & 18.

South African National Gallery 1971-197/ Suid-Afrikaanse Nasionale Kunsmuseum. Cape Town: South African National Gallery, 1971.

"Special Feature: The 1991 Triennial." *De Arte* 45 (1992): 24-48.

Spiro, Leslie. *Gerard Sekoto: Unsevered Ties*. Johannesburg: Johannesburg Art Gallery, 1989.

Stevenson, Michael. *Art & Aspirations The Randlords of South Africa and their Collections*. Vlaeberg: Fernwood Press, 2002.

Subirós, Pep, ed. *Apartheid: The South African Mirror*. Barcelona: Centre de Cultura Contemporània de Barcelona, 2007.

Szalay, Miklos, ed. *The Moon As Shoe/Der Mond als Schuh*. Zurich: Scheidegger & Spiess, 2002.

The State of Art in South Africa Conference July 1979. Cape Town: University of Cape Town, 1979.

Tietze, Anna. *The Alfred de Pass Presentation to the South African National Gallery*. Cape Town: South African National Gallery, 1995.

Tietze, Anna. *The Sir Abe Bailey Bequest: A Reappraisal*. Cape Town: Iziko Museums, 2001.

Tietze, Anna. *The Abe Bailey Collection in the South African National Gallery*. Cape Town: Abe Bailey Trust, 2008.

Tietze, Anna. "The Problem of Originality and Value in the Lady Michaelis Gifts to the South African National Gallery." *South African Journal of Art History* 25, no. 2 (2010): 161-176.

Tietze, Anna. "Artistically or historically important? The reception of the Abe Bailey sporting art collection in South Africa." *Journal of the History of Collections* 23, no. 1 (2010): 165-177.

Tietze, Anna. *A History of the Iziko South African National Gallery Reflections on art and national identity*. Cape Town: UCT Press, an imprint of Juta and Company (Pty) Ltd, 2017.
Timmins, Howard. *Tretchikoff*. Cape Town: Howard Timmins, 1969.
Touch Gallery. Cape Town: South African National Gallery, 1977.
Transpositions: Five Swedish Artists in South Africa, 28 March-10 May, 1998. Cape Town: South African National Gallery, 1998.

Ubuntu: Arts et Cultures d'Afrique du Sud. Paris: Editions de la Réunion des musées nationaux, 2002.

Van der Watt, Liese. "Fresh: Seven artists' monographs." *Art South Africa* 2, no. 1 (2003): 61.
Van Robbroeck, Lize. "The Ideology of Community Arts." *De Arte* 46 (1992): 49-57.
Van Robbroeck, Lize. "Reimagining South African National Heritage Two Ten-Years-of-Democracy Exhibitions." *African Arts* XXXVII, no. 4 (2004): 45.
Van Robbroeck, Lize. "Democracy X." *Art South Africa* 2, no. 4 (2004): 65-67.
Van Robbroeck, Lize, ed. *Visual Century South African Art in Context*, vol. 2, 1907-1948. Johannesburg: Wits University Press, 2011.
Van Wegen, Derk Hendrik. *Kunst uit de Kaap: Hollandse en Vlaamse meesterwerken uit de Michaelis collectie te Kaapstad*. Zwolle: Waanders and Maastricht: Bonnefantenmuseum, 2003.
Vergunst, Nicolaas. *Hoerikwaggo: Images of Table Mountain*. Cape Town: South African National Gallery, 2000.

Wiehager, Renate, ed. *The Nominees*. Pretoria: Daimler-Chrysler South Africa, 2007.
Wiehager, Renate, ed. *Heinrich Wolff*. Cologne: Seippel Verlag for Daimler-Chrysler, 2007.
W.H.K., ed. *The Arts in South Africa*. Durban: Knox, 1933-1934.
Williamson, Sue. *Resistance Art in South Africa*. Cape Town: David Philip, 1989.
Woubshet, Dagmawi. "Staging the rainbow nation." *Art South Africa* 2, no. 2 (2003): 33-36.
Wünsche Isabel, and Wiebke Gronemeyer, eds. *Practices of Abstract Art: Between Anarchism and Appropriation*. Newcastle upon Tyne: Cambridge Scholars Publishing, 2016.

Younge, Gavin. *Art of the South African Townships*. London: Thames and Hudson, 1988.

Zeitgenössische Fotokunst Aus Südafrika. Berlin: Neuer Berliner Kunstverein, 2007.
Zerohour, first issued on April 1, 1933 and produced as a memento of the 1985 Institute of South African Architects Congress. Johannesburg: Wits University, 1985.

Theses and Dissertations

Botma, Gabriël. "Manufacturing cultural capital: Arts journalism at *Die Burger* (1990-1999)." PhD diss., University of Stellenbosch, 2011.
Barben, Marc. "What does it mean to be a 'national' gallery when notions of 'nation' transform radically?" MA diss., University of Cape Town, 2015.
Cook, Sashi. "Redress: debates informing exhibitions and acquisitions in selected South African Public Art Galleries (1990 – 1994)." MA diss., Rhodes University, 2009.
Lilla, Quanita. "'The advancement of art': Policy and practice at the South African National Gallery 1940-1962." MA diss., University of Cape Town, 2004.

Acronyms/Abbreviations

ACT – Arts and Culture Trust
ACTAG – Arts and Culture Task Group
ANC – African National Congress
AFAA – Association française d'Action artistique
ASAI – Art South Africa Initiative
AVA – Association for Visual Arts
AWB – Afrikaner Weerstandsbeweging
BASA – Business Arts South Africa
CAP – Community Arts Project
CAPAB – Cape Performing Arts Board
CCA – Centre for Curating the Archive
CCMA – Commission for Conciliation, Mediation and Arbitration
CFAS – Cape Fine Arts Society
CIMAM – International Committee for Museums and Collections of Modern Art
CODESA – Convention for a Democratic South Africa
CTCC – Cape Town City Council
CTF – Cape Tercentenary Foundation
CTT – Cape Town Triennial
DAC – Department of Arts and Culture
DACST – Department of Arts, Culture, Science and Technology
DALRO – Dramatic, Artistic and Literary Rights Organisation
DNE – Department of National Education
DPW – Department of Public works
DAG – Durban Art Gallery
EFF – Economic Freedom Fighters
FCA – Foundation for the Creative Arts
FONG – Friends of the South African National Gallery
FOSACO – Federation of South African Cultural Organisations
FUBA – Federated Union of Black Artists
GEAR – Growth Employment and Redistribution
GEM – Global Electronic Messaging
GRAP – Generally Recognised Accounting Practice
HSRC – Human Sciences Research Council
IA – Institutional Advancement department at Iziko Museums
ICCROM – International Centre for the Study of Preservation and Restoration of Cultural Property
ICOM – International Council of Museums
IFAS – Institut français d'Afrique du Sud
IFP – Inkatha Freedom Party
ISANG – Iziko South African National Gallery
ISM – Irma Stern Museum
Iziko/Iziko Museums – Iziko Museums of South Africa
JAG – Johannesburg Art Gallery
JWG – Joint Working Group
MC – Michaelis Collection
Michaelis/Michaelis School – Michaelis School of Fine Art
MNAAO – Musée national des Arts d'Afrique et d'Océanie
MoMA – Museum of Modern Art, New York
NAC – National Arts Council
NCM – New Church Museum
NDP – National Development Plan
NEHAWU – National Education, Health and Allied Workers' Union
NGO – Non-governmental Organisation
NLB – National Lottery Board
NHC – National Heritage Council
NLM – Natale Labia Museum
NMMAM – Nelson Mandela Metropolitan Art Museum
NP – National Party
NRF – National Research Foundation
OTH – Old Town House
PAC – Pan African Congress
PAM – Pretoria Art Museum
PFMA – Public Finances Management Act
PREMA – PREventive conservation in Museums of Africa
PWD – Public Works Department
RDP – Reconstruction and Development Programme
RIM – Robben Island Museum
RWP – Revised White Paper
SAAA – South African Association of Arts
SAAAH – South African Association of Art Historians
SABC – South African Broadcasting Corporation
SACS – South African College
SAFAA – South African Fine Arts Association
SAHRA – South African Heritage Resources Agency
SANG – South African National Gallery
SAM – South African Museum
SAMA – South African Museums Association
SASA – South African Society of Artists
SAVAH – South African Visual and Art Historians
SFI – Southern Flagship Institution
SYTCC – Sheikh Yusuf Tricentenary Commemoration Committee
TAC – Treatment Action Campaign
TRC – Truth and Reconciliation Commission
UCT – University of Cape Town
UFH – University of Fort Hare
UJ – University of Johannesburg
UN – University of Natal
UNESCO – United Nations Educational, Scientific and Cultural Organisation
UNISA – University of South Africa
UP – United Party
UP – University of Pretoria
US – Stellenbosch University
UWC – University of the Western Cape
VANSA – Visual Arts Network of South Africa
VOC – Dutch East India Company
WAM – Wits Art Museum
WCED – Western Cape Education Department
WHAG – William Humphreys Art Gallery
Wits – University of the Witwatersrand
Zeitz MOCAA – Zeitz Museum of Contemporary Art Africa

Index

C

D

E

L

M

N

O

P

Q

R

S